Communication
Yearbook
19

BRANT R. BURLESON, Editor
ADRIANNE W. KUNKEL, Editorial Assistant

Communication
Yearbook
19

Published Annually for the
International Communication Association

SAGE Publications
International Educational and Professional Publisher
Thousand Oaks   London   New Delhi

Copyright © 1996 by the International Communication Association

For information address:

SAGE Publications, Inc.
2455 Teller Road
Thousand Oaks, California 91320
E-mail: order@sagepub.com

SAGE Publications Ltd.
6 Bonhill Street
London EC2A 4PU
United Kingdom

SAGE Publications India Pvt. Ltd.
M-32 Market
Greater Kailash I
New Delhi 110 048 India

Printed in the United States of America

Library of Congress: 76-45943

ISBN 0-7619-0165-5

ISSN 0147-4642

This book is printed on acid-free paper.

96 97 98 99 10 9 8 7 6 5 4 3 2 1

Sage Production Editor: Astrid Virding
Sage Typesetter: Andrea D. Swanson

CONTENTS

THE INTERNATIONAL COMMUNICATION ASSOCIATION

The International Communication Association (ICA) was formed in 1950, bringing together academicians and other professionals whose interests focus on human communication. The Association maintains an active membership of more than 2,800 individuals, of whom some two-thirds are teaching and conducting research in colleges, universities, and schools around the world. Other members are in government, the media, communication technology, business, law, medicine, and other professions. The wide professional and geographic distribution of the membership provides the basic strength of the ICA. The Association is a meeting ground for sharing research and useful dialogue about communication interests.

Through its Divisions and Interest Groups, publications, annual conferences, and relations with other associations around the world, the ICA promotes the systematic study of communication theories, processes, and skills.

In addition to *Communication Yearbook,* the Association publishes the *Journal of Communication, Human Communication Research, Communication Theory, A Guide to Publishing in Scholarly Communication Journals, ICA Newsletter,* and the *ICA Membership Directory.*

For additional information about the ICA and its activities, contact Robert L. Cox, Executive Director, International Communication Association, P.O. Box 9589, Austin, TX 78766; phone (512) 454-8299; fax (512) 454-4221; e-mail ICAHDQ@UTS.CC.UTEXAS.EDU.

Editors of the *Communication Yearbook* series:

Volumes 1 and 2, Brent D. Ruben
Volumes 3 and 4, Dan Nimmo
Volumes 5 and 6, Michael Burgoon
Volumes 7 and 8, Robert N. Bostrom
Volumes 9 and 10, Margaret L. McLaughlin
Volumes 11, 12, 13, and 14, James A. Anderson
Volumes 15, 16, and 17, Stanley A. Deetz
Volumes 18, 19, and 20, Brant R. Burleson

INTERNATIONAL COMMUNICATION ASSOCIATION
EXECUTIVE COMMITTEE

CONSULTING EDITORS

The following individuals helped make possible this volume of the *Communication Yearbook* by providing insightful reviews of papers and proposals. The editor gratefully acknowledges these scholars for the gifts of their time and wisdom.

EDITOR'S INTRODUCTION

A t its November 1993 meeting, the Board of Directors of the International Communication Association approved a change in the mission and format of the *Communication Yearbook*. The action by the board redefined *CY* as a literature review series that would, henceforth, exclusively publish comprehensive, critical surveys of literature that had appeared on specific, well-defined topics. The current volume, *Communication Yearbook 19*, is the first to be published in accord with the new mission and format.

Why the change in *CY*'s format? What do *Communication Yearbook* and ICA hope to accomplish with the change? What does the new format mean for *CY* readers and contributors? These are important questions, and this is an appropriate forum in which to address them. Let's begin by taking a brief look at the history of the *CY* series.

CY IN PERSPECTIVE

Communication Yearbook had its genesis in a proposal for the publication of a preconvention proceedings volume, which was approved by the ICA Board of Directors in 1975. Brent Ruben was asked to develop that publication concept and to serve as the first editor of the new annual.

The publication Ruben crafted was, from the outset, less a conference proceedings than a review volume. In his overview of *CY1*, Ruben (1977) observed:

> There are a number of publications devoted primarily, if not exclusively, to the publication of specialized studies in communication. There are few, if any, whose primary function is overview and synthesis. It is the pursuit of these generic goals which inspired the development of the *Communication Yearbook* series. (p. 4)

The *Yearbook* developed by Ruben contained three types of articles, each of which aimed to serve particular goals: general reviews and commentaries on theoretical and research matters that cut across specific research areas and specialties, theory and research overviews for each of ICA's (then) eight divisions, and "selected studies" from each of the divisions. The general reviews were commissioned by the editor and sought to "provide substantive input of generic relevance to scholars and researchers in all subdivisions of the field" (Ruben, 1977, p. 6). The annual overviews, authored by ICA divisional chairpersons or their designates, were intended to "examine trends in theory and research in various substantive domains within the field" (p. 6). The "selected studies" were operationally defined as the "top three" papers from each division's annual paper competition for the ICA convention. The first *Communication Yearbook* appeared in 1977, and the next three volumes (with Ruben also editing *CY2* and Dan Nimmo editing *CY3* and *CY4*) followed the format initially developed by Ruben, with only minor variations.

Michael Burgoon, who edited *CY5* and *CY6*, brought about some fundamental changes in the structure and format of the *Yearbook*. Beginning with *CY5*, the top three papers from each division's annual paper competition were no longer automatically guaranteed publication. Rather, papers from the ICA convention underwent a separate review process controlled by the *CY* editor. Burgoon's action served to make the *CY* editor solely responsible for each volume's content and established a policy of peer review for works appearing in *CY*. Even more important changes occurred with *CY6*. Burgoon (1982) dropped the overviews contributed by each division, arguing that "the division overviews were an idea whose time had come and gone" (p. 11). Equally important, Burgoon made an open call for submissions to the general reviews section; previously, the articles appearing in this section had been invited by each editor. Thus, *CY6* published two types of articles: (a) review and commentary chapters that were "general discussions and critiques of substantive matters of generic interest and relevance that transcend the more specialized concerns of scholars working in the highly diversified discipline of communication science," and (b) "edited versions of representative current research that [was] selected competitively for presentation" at annual ICA conferences (Burgoon, 1982, p. 15). The next four volumes of *CY* (with *CY7* and *CY8* edited by Robert Bostrom and *CY9* and *CY10* edited by Margaret McLaughlin) closely followed the format established by Burgoon.

James Anderson, who edited *CY11-CY14*, introduced another round of major changes in the *Yearbook* series. Beginning with *CY11*, the *Yearbook* no longer published any of the papers from the ICA convention. Instead, *CY* exclusively published commissioned overviews and commentaries. For the most part, the overviews constituted extended theoretical essays, an outlet for which was—in the mid-1980s—unavailable elsewhere. *CY* also occasionally continued to publish summaries of specific research programs, as well as some broader literature reviews. This format remained in effect through Anderson's four volumes, the three volumes of *CY* edited by Stan Deetz (*CY15-CY17*), and my first volume (*CY18*).

The evolutionary development exhibited by *CY* from 1977 through 1995 has been a small part of much larger changes taking place in the publication environment for communication scholarship. Certainly, the most important development occurring during this period has been the veritable explosion of the communication literature. For example, of the 56 serials indexed by *ComIndex,* 27 began publication after 1980; another 13 began publication in the 1970s. In addition, both commercial publishers (e.g., Academic Press, Erlbaum, Guilford, Hampton, Sage) and university presses have deepened their lists of communication offerings, especially in edited volumes.

The developments in communication publishing have had profound implications for the *CY* series. Most important, many other outlets have become available for the extended theoretical essays in which *CY* eventually came to specialize. Journals such as *Communication Theory, Critical Studies in Mass Communication,* and *Discourse and Society* now provide publication venues for theoretical essays, with some of these journals (notably *Communication Theory*) regularly publishing commentaries on major essays. The growing numbers of edited volumes published by commercial presses have also provided homes for many of the papers that might otherwise have found a place in *CY*. The increased number of outlets means that authors now have more options available to them when it comes to publishing their works. This has also meant that *CY* has faced ever-tougher competition for readers' dollars. This latter reality has been reflected in progressively declining sales for *CY* from 1986 onward.

Changes in the publication landscape have thus diminished the need for a *CY* specializing in the publication of theoretical essays. But these changes have also created new needs and new opportunities. The rate at which the communication literature is expanding will only continue to increase in the foreseeable future. Moreover, this expansion will add to what is already a huge literature. (For example, *Communication Serials* [Sova & Sova, 1992] lists more than 2,700 communication-related periodicals published at some time between the early 1800s and the present.) Clearly, scholars need ways to digest and integrate those parts of the communication literature they wish to track.

Communication Yearbook has been redesigned with this need in mind. Beginning with the current volume, *CY* will exclusively publish articles providing comprehensive syntheses and critiques of major areas of the communication literature. More specifically, articles in *CY* will review, critique, and integrate bodies of literature that have appeared with respect to specific, relatively narrow topics.

In a sense, then, *CY* has returned to its roots in publishing reviews that seek to synthesize and integrate research literature. However, the literature reviews appearing in *CY19* and subsequent volumes will bear little resemblance to the general reviews and annual overviews that appeared in the early volumes of this series. Twenty years ago, it was possible to review, for example, "the interpersonal communication literature" in a single article-length essay, and such reviews served valuable functions (see Berger, 1977). Today, however, even lengthy handbooks—as useful as they are—cannot provide truly comprehensive reviews of the available literature in an area like interpersonal communication (see Knapp & Miller, 1994). The same is true in virtually every area of communication scholarship. What is needed are reviews of literature on the specific topics on which scholars and students actually conduct research. And that is what the reviews now appearing in *CY* seek to provide.

The communication discipline, to this point, has had no outlet exclusively devoted to the publication of major literature reviews. This contrasts with other social sciences such as psychology and sociology, which have long had multiple outlets dedicated to articles providing reviews and syntheses. For example, psychology has both journals (e.g., *Psychological Bulletin*) and annuals (e.g., *Annual Review of Psychology*) that regularly publish focused literature reviews. These publications have proven to be valuable resources for scholars, important assets for students, and commercial successes for their publishers. The redesigned *Communication Yearbook* has the potential to be known for achieving these functions within the community of communication professionals.

CY AS A LITERATURE REVIEW SERIES

So, what can readers expect from the review articles appearing in the reinvented *Yearbook*? And what kind of articles should prospective contributors to *CY* seek to produce? As the content of *CY19* makes clear, there is no set formula for the good literature review. There are, however, some general features shared by the reviews appearing in *CY19,* and I believe these are characteristics of most good literature reviews. Before discussing these characteristics, I will briefly describe the policies and procedures under which the articles appearing in *CY19* were selected for publication. Potential contributors should take note of this information, as these policies and procedures will remain in effect for future volumes.

Communication Yearbook considers for publication only original, previously unpublished material. All articles appearing in *CY19* were selected competitively through a peer review process. An open call for proposals and manuscripts was published in many of the discipline's newsletters. Leaders of the ICA's divisions and interest groups were also contacted with requests for suggestions concerning topics and potential authors. Submissions were solicited from those nominated by divisional officers, but papers received from these individuals were not privileged in the review process. More than 70 submissions were received in response to the call. All submissions were subjected to blind peer review by at least two referees having special expertise in the relevant subject matter. On the basis of the initial round of reviews, a small subset of the submissions was selected for revision and further development. The revised papers were then subjected to a second round of reviews by external referees. On the basis of this second round of reviews, the 10 articles appearing in *CY19* were selected for publication. A final round of revisions was then undertaken by the authors. This rigorous review-and-revision process is designed to ensure that only high-quality reviews are published in *CY.*

What characteristics do good literature reviews, such as those appearing in *CY19,* share? First, they all make good arguments for their existence. That is, each makes the case that there *is* a distinct body of literature on a particular topic, and that this body of literature merits careful examination and synthesis.

Second, good reviews develop meaningful conceptual frameworks in which different theories, methods, and findings can be arrayed and compared. The well-developed conceptual framework not only serves as a mechanism for helping organize, position, and integrate what are often diverse and scattered bodies of findings, it also helps dissolve anomalies, resolve ambiguities, determine what is actually known, identify areas of confusion that need additional work, and chart directions for future research. The conceptual framework is often the most innovative and important contribution of a review, and it is one of the key features that distinguishes a literature review from an annotated bibliography.

Third, a good review carefully articulates the methodology used in carrying it out. The presentation of method should make it clear how a particular body of literature was constituted or defined, how that literature was searched and collected, and how relevant features of the literature (e.g., research method employed, type of finding) were summarized. The growing use of meta-analytic procedures in conducting literature reviews has helped make more explicit the kinds of methodological considerations that should receive attention in both quantitative and narrative reviews. Obviously, the methods employed should ensure that the resulting review is comprehensive, thorough, and up-to-date.

Fourth, a good literature review contains a critical summary of findings; for most of us, this is the heart of the literature review. Different types of reviews present such summaries in different ways (as the articles in this volume clearly illustrate), but any summary should provide an answer to the question, What do we know about this topic? The central aim of a literature review is not the mere summary of findings. Rather, the good literature review aims to answer questions—questions about what we know, what we do not yet know, and what we need to know. The focus on findings is one of the characteristics that helps distinguish a literature review from a theoretical essay.

Fifth, a good literature review identifies the issues, problems, questions, and concerns that need to be addressed in future research. The understandings acquired through a careful review of a literature should lead somewhere. By addressing the "What next?" questions, reviews can help chart the course for subsequent conceptual, methodological, and empirical efforts. In other words, good literature reviews not only examine avenues previously traveled in a research area, they help locate where new roads need to be built.

These, then, are some general characteristics of good literature reviews. Of course, these abstract characteristics are best illustrated when brought to life in concrete exemplars. Ten such exemplars are included in *CY19.*

OVERVIEW OF *CY19*

The 10 reviews appearing in *CY19* address core concerns of virtually every division and interest group in ICA. This did not come about by design, but rather was a serendipitous outcome of the rigorous review process used to select these reviews.

Chapter 1, by Jon Nussbaum, Mary Lee Hummert, Angie Williams, and Jake Harwood, presents an impressive review of the literature concerning communication by, with, and about older adults. The authors develop a coherent framework for literature concerning communication and aging, specifically addressing issues pertaining to cognition, language, and relationships. Several specific problems are taken up in each of these areas (e.g., the effects of changes in memory on communication; linguistic modifications made when talking with the elderly; relationships characteristic of later life, such as grandparenting). The authors propose a synthetic life-span developmental framework capable of integrating research not only with older adults, but also with children, adolescents, and young adults.

The next three chapters consist of reviews pertaining to different aspects of sexuality and sexual relationships. Sandra Metts and Brian Spitzberg organize the literature concerning sexual communication in interpersonal contexts by forwarding a script-based theory of sexual interactions. This theory maintains that many aspects of sexual interactions, especially during the early phases of a relationship, exhibit a conventional, routinized character. The script theory elaborated by these authors provides a powerful framework for integrating much of the available literature, as evidenced by the authors' detailed reviews of work on flirting, sexual harassment, sexual initiation, token resistance, and the use of condoms, among other topics. This is a fascinating review, and one that should be the foundation for much subsequent work.

Joann Keyton contributes what is almost surely the most comprehensive review on sexual harassment yet to appear in the communication literature. For those interested in this important social problem, her review will provide a firm foundation in what is currently known. Keyton provides a detailed survey of perspectives informing the study of sexual harassment, and then articulates eight core questions around which research on harassment is organized. This review is informed by an impressive blend of legal research, feminist scholarship, survey studies, and laboratory experiments, nicely demonstrating how research from diverse viewpoints can be integrated to serve a common purpose.

Sexual stereotypes depicted in the mass media are often indicted as one factor contributing to sexual harassment and other social problems. But are sexual stereotypes pervasive in the media? And does exposure to these stereotypes really affect the ways people feel, think, and behave? These are the questions taken up by Jennifer Herrett-Skjellum and Mike Allen in their review of sex role stereotyping in television programming. These authors report several meta-analyses of the literature showing that television portrays men and women in highly stereotypical roles. More important (and disturbing), the meta-analyses conducted by these researchers suggest that viewing television programming containing stereotypical images is associated with increased acceptance and endorsement of often pernicious sexual stereotypes. Herrett-Skjellum and Allen conclude their chapter by pointing to several of the policy concerns raised by their analysis of media effects.

The review of research stemming from the "knowledge gap" hypothesis by K. Viswanath and John Finnegan also addresses an important potential effect of mass communication. In essence, the knowledge gap hypothesis maintains that the mass media help the information-rich get richer, while the information-poor get poorer. This controversial hypothesis has been the subject of extensive research over the past 25 years, and the authors develop a framework that helps make sense out of the extensive and sometimes inconsistent findings. Those concerned with the effects of mass communication in general, as well as those with more specialized interests in the effects of particular political, public health, and public information campaigns will find this a valuable review.

The chapters by Herrett-Skjellum and Allen and by Viswanath and Finnegan help us appreciate some of the effects produced by mass communication technology. Michele Jackson charts a somewhat different course in her chapter, reviewing the different ways theorists and researchers have conceptualized the relationship between communication technologies and social context. Rejecting the simple identification of technology as the material artifact, Jackson elaborates a two-dimensional framework centering on the relationship between technology and context. She thus explores different potentials for conceptualizing communication technology, social relations, and human communication. Jackson's framework encourages a dialogue among existing research perspectives and suggests specific directions for future theory building.

Bruce Barry and Mary Watson provide a comprehensive review of the research on compliance gaining within organizational contexts. Compliance gaining has been one of the most active areas of communication scholarship, but comprehensive conceptual models capable of synthesizing the diverse findings have been proposed only rarely. Barry and Watson do a first-rate job of reviewing the issues and findings in contemporary compliance-gaining research. They then develop a powerful integrative model of the dyadic influence process that gives balanced attention to the dynamic perceptual variables that drive both agent and target in influence episodes. Although Barry and Watson focus on issues pertaining to compliance gaining in formal organizations, this chapter will also be of real interest to those concerned with social influence in interpersonal, group, public, and mass contexts.

Not all efforts to gain compliance rely on discursive appeals to reason. The daily headlines are a continual reminder that humans often use coercion and other forms of aggression in efforts to influence and control others. The use of these less-than-desirable forms of influence remains an understudied area in the field of communication. Thus, Infante and Rancer's review of the extensive work on argumentativeness and verbal aggressiveness is especially welcome. Argumentative behaviors are those that advocate and defend positions on controversial issues, whereas aggressive behaviors are those that attack the self-concepts of others in order to inflict psychological pain. Much of the research reviewed in this chapter was carried out by Infante, Rancer, and their colleagues in a variety of interpersonal, educational, and organizational contexts. Infante and Rancer draw 13 major conclusions from the research on argumentativeness and verbal aggressiveness, many of which pertain to the effects of argumentative and aggressive behaviors on social relationships. The authors emphasize the importance of argumentative communication and show how the construct of argumentativeness provides a framework for conceptualizing many of the long-standing concerns of the communication discipline.

The final two chapters contain reviews concerning related aspects of intercultural communication. Guo-Ming Chen and William Starosta present a comprehensive review of the literature on intercultural communication competence. These authors detail why the concept of intercultural competence is increasingly important, develop a conceptual model of intercultural communication competence, and then review research on each of three components of intercultural competence (affective, cognitive, and behavioral). In particular, Chen and Starosta stress a conception of intercultural competence as a means of negotiating cultural identities, a very appropriate conception given that this is a time when people are faced with an ever greater need to move between one identity and another.

An ongoing aim of much of the research on intercultural competence lies in the development of educational and training programs intended to enhance the capabilities of those who interact with members of different cultures. That includes many of us these days, especially those of us living in pluralistic societies and those who travel for pleasure or business. How well are contemporary training programs doing when it comes to enhancing the intercultural competencies of those who travel to other cultures? Aaron Cargile and Howard Giles review the literature evaluating the effectiveness of intercultural training programs, and they come up with some disturbing conclusions. Research on the efficacy of training programs has yielded some supportive, but largely inconclusive, results. Cargile and Giles suggest that one reason training programs have been less than effective is that they have tended to ignore "intergroup" constituents of the training process, such as negative attitudes and stereotypes held about members of different cultures. The authors formulate a new model of intercultural training that promises to address a broader range of factors potentially having impacts on the outcomes of training programs.

The chapters in this volume weave a rich tapestry depicting fragmented pieces of the contemporary landscape in communication research. They obviously do not provide comprehensive coverage of the field as a whole, nor are they intended to. Rather, by brightly illuminating narrow and relatively specific areas of current concern, these reviews should help interested researchers, students, and professionals learn what has been done and what remains to be done in particular research areas. If the reviews in the redesigned *CY* series can achieve this on a regular basis, the series will have accomplished its mission.

ACKNOWLEDGMENTS

The more work like this one does, the more one comes to appreciate all those who make a volume like the *Communication Yearbook* possible. I have been blessed with the help of some very kind, caring, and competent people. First and foremost, I want to thank my editorial assistant, Adrianne Kunkel. Adrianne has kept me organized, on schedule, and on track—and that is no small job. Her efficiency and good humor have made this job much more of a pleasure than it otherwise would have been. Carolyn Parrish and Beverly Robinson provided excellent secretarial services; I thank them for many cheerful acts of speedy help when the need arose. Bob Cox at ICA headquarters supplied continuing support and useful information when called upon. The Department of Communication and School of Liberal Arts at Purdue University continued to provide me with the time and many of the material resources needed to edit this series of volumes. Finally, I want to thank the legion of referees I called upon to review manuscripts. A list of these referees appears elsewhere, but these are the people (along with the contributors, of course) who truly made this volume possible.

Brant R. Burleson
West Lafayette, Indiana

REFERENCES

Berger, C. R. (1977). Interpersonal communication theory and research: An overview. In B. D. Ruben (Ed.), *Communication yearbook 1* (pp. 217-228). New Brunswick, NJ: Transaction.

Burgoon, M. (1982). Preface. In M. Burgoon (Ed.), *Communication yearbook 6* (pp. 11-12). Beverly Hills, CA: Sage.

Knapp, M. L., & Miller, G. R. (Eds.). (1994). *Handbook of interpersonal communication* (2nd ed.). Thousand Oaks, CA: Sage.

Ruben, B. D. (1977). Overview. In B. D. Ruben (Ed.), *Communication yearbook 1* (pp. 3-7). New Brunswick, NJ: Transaction.

Sova, H. W., & Sova, P. L. (Eds.) (1992). *Communication serials: An international guide to periodicals in communication, popular culture, and the performing arts.* Virginia Beach, VA: SovaComm.

CHAPTER CONTENTS

1 Communication and Older Adults

JON F. NUSSBAUM
University of Oklahoma

MARY LEE HUMMERT
University of Kansas

ANGIE WILLIAMS
University of Oklahoma

JAKE HARWOOD
University of Kansas

This chapter reviews research concerning communication and aging, focusing on three central areas. First, the authors look at cognitive developments in normal aging, such as changes in memory and name retrieval, and their implications for communication. This section also addresses research on attitudes toward older adults and the consequences of those attitudes for communication. Second, the authors examine issues relating to language, including research concerning linguistic modifications made by the young when talking to elderly people and changing features of the linguistic production of older adults. Third, the authors discuss relationships—late-life marriages, grandparent-grandchild relationships, and patient-physician relationships, among others—and the central role of communication in facilitating such relationships. Throughout, the authors address limitations in current knowledge and propose avenues for future research. The chapter concludes with a summary that synthesizes the diverse themes presented and offers a coherent life-span framework for future research into communication and aging.

N O single area of research within the general domain of developmental studies has received more attention from social scientists in recent years than has the study of older adults. This intense interest in every aspect of the aging process has occurred in tandem with the fact that the number of older adults in the United States is currently increasing at a rate nearly three times that of the population under age 65. Just as researchers within biology, physiology, and all the medical sciences have produced

Correspondence and requests for reprints: Jon F. Nussbaum, Department of Communication, University of Oklahoma, 610 Elm Avenue, Room 101, Norman, OK 73019-0335.

Communication Yearbook 19, pp. 1-47

volumes of literature attempting to understand and explain the aging process, social scientists from diverse theoretical and methodological perspectives have written extensively in an attempt to reach a richer understanding of the complex interactive world of older adults.

Research on communication and older adults is generally introduced in the context of "pure" demographics. According to the most recent statistics compiled by the American Association of Retired Persons (1991), there are approximately 31.1 million Americans over the age of 65, representing 12.5% of the total U.S. population. The fastest-growing segment of our population are individuals over the age of 85. We are becoming an increasingly older society. Reflecting these numbers is the massive shift in political power toward older adults, which, for researchers interested in the aging process, has led to more than $400 million in congressional appropriations for the National Institute on Aging. We should be cautious, however, about relying solely upon a demographic rationale for researching this area. This could be seen as sending a negative message to demographically weak groups (including, perhaps, older adults in a different era), and does not attend to the theoretical and practical reasons work in this area is of interest independent of demographics.

Beyond demographics and the political budgeting process, scholars in biology, physiology, zoology, psychology, and sociology have documented significant physical and economic changes that occur as we age. Communication scholars, on the other hand, have typically not accounted for life-span developmental changes in their various "mainstream" theories of the communicative process. In this chapter, we will not only review what we consider to be the significant developmental changes within the communicative process that directly affect older people, we will also show how these changes significantly alter the very nature of social life for members of this group. Stated quite simply, we feel that the enormous developmental changes that occur within us and around us as we age have the potential to produce a qualitatively different communication process in later life.

One of the basic principles that guides the writing of this chapter is our belief that communication lies at the core of the aging process. In a very real sense, we do not age alone. As Hummert, Nussbaum, and Wiemann (1994) note: "The abilities to interact and to maintain networks of relationships not only provide us with such affective states as happiness and satisfaction, but also function to meet our basic needs for companionship, success, and, eventually, help us to survive. The interpersonal communication that fuels our social world is as essential to our survival as any biological or physical process that keeps us alive" (p. 3).

During the past 20 years, there has been an explosion of literature concentrating upon numerous aspects of communication and aging. Perhaps the best reflection of this growth may be seen in the recent special issues of journals dedicated solely to communication and aging, such as have appeared in *Communication Research, Language and Communication, Ageing and Society, Journal of Aging Studies, International Journal of Aging and Human Development,* and, soon, *Health Communication.*

In addition, several books have recently been published by communication scholars that have addressed various aspects of the aging process (e.g., Coupland, Coupland, & Giles, 1991; Giles, Coupland, & Wiemann, 1990; Hummert, Wiemann, & Nussbaum, 1994; Nussbaum, Thompson, & Robinson, 1989). To date, however, this literature has not been the subject of critical review and analysis. Our approach toward this synthesis and critical analysis is multidisciplinary, multimethodological, multitheoretical, and life-span oriented. The richness of communication and aging research is the interdisciplinary nature of the topic area, which embraces the diversity found in different methods as well as different theoretical positions. We believe not only that communication research and theory can provide the integrative approach to the study of aging called for by the most prominent members of the gerontological community, but that it is essential for a full understanding of the aging process as it is enacted in individual experience.

Specifically, in this chapter we review, synthesize, and critically analyze three areas of communication and aging research: cognition, language, and relationships. The first major section of the chapter reviews the work of Susan Kemper, Ellen Ryan, Mary Lee Hummert, and many others who have studied the pragmatic effects of working memory, beliefs, and attitudes within the communication process of elderly individuals. A complete understanding of elderly communication cannot occur without knowledge of the cognitive processes influencing, and being influenced by, that communication. The second section of the chapter concentrates upon the work of Nik Coupland and Justine Coupland, Howard Giles, and others who have studied language in aging populations. Naturally, an understanding of the language used by, and to, elderly adults is central to an understanding of their communicative environment. Third, we review the work of Victor Cicirelli, Jon Nussbaum, Ron Adelman, and many others who have investigated older marriages, friendships, sibling relationships, grandparent-grandchild relationships, and physician-elderly patient relationships. Such relationships are built upon communication, and they constitute the social contexts in which most communication takes place. Within each of the three sections described above, we present a critique of current research along with an agenda for future investigations. In the final section of the chapter, we move beyond synthesis and analysis to make a bold statement concerning the future trends, agendas, and possibilities of research concentrating upon communication and older adults. In particular, we reemphasize the themes of interdisciplinary research and a life-span perspective that have been the primary strengths of research in this area since its inception.

COGNITION

The study of communication and aging has addressed the role of cognition on two levels: first, in terms of the effects of physical aging on the cognitive resources employed in the production and processing of oral communication; and second, in terms of the social-cognitive processes that suggest appropriate communication strategies to use with older persons. The former line of research has been pursued primarily by experimental cognitive psychologists, the latter by social psychologists and communication scholars. We consider each of these lines of research in this section, concluding with a critical evaluation of the current approaches and suggestions for future research.

Cognitive Aging and Communication

Cognitive psychologists study many different aspects of the cognitive system, both structural (e.g., sensory registers, working memory, and long-term memory) and processual (e.g., attention, reasoning, rehearsal, processing speed, retrieval) (Howard, 1983). Of particular concern here are those aspects that not only exhibit age differences but also carry implications for the language processing and production capabilities of older persons: working memory (Wingfield, Stine, Lahar, & Aberdeen, 1988), processing speed (Salthouse, 1992), and name retrieval (Cohen & Faulkner, 1986b). Here we consider only those changes in working memory, processing speed, and name retrieval that are associated with normal aging patterns.

Working Memory, Processing Speed, and Language

Declines in working memory capacity and processing speed appear to affect the syntactic and discourse processing abilities of elderly people, even though their semantic knowledge remains intact (Kemper, 1992; Light, 1990; Ryan, 1991). For example, Kemper, Kynette, Rash, O'Brien, and Sprott (1989) collected both oral and written language samples from young adults and three groups of elderly individuals (aged 60-69, 70-79, and 80-92). An age-related loss of syntactic complexity was noted in both oral and written modalities. In particular, the number of clauses per utterance and left-branching clauses declined across the four age groups. Left-branching clauses are those that precede the main predicate in an utterance. These are presumed to be more difficult to process and produce than right-branching clauses because they require an individual to hold information in working memory. Regression analyses showed that working memory capacity, as measured by WAIS backward digit span (Wechsler, 1958), accounted for 82% of the variance in the percentage of left-branching clauses in the samples and 62% of the variance in the number of clauses per utterance. Age, education, health, and forward digit span did not add significantly to the regression equations.

Kemper, Kynette, and Norman (1992) followed the elderly participants in the Kemper et al. (1989) study for 3 years, collecting annual measures of working memory and syntactic complexity. Most of the participants did not experience significant changes in working memory over that period. However, of the 12 who did, 11 also experienced significant declines in syntactic complexity. Kemper et al. noted that these 11 individuals were in their late 70s to early 80s in Year 1, suggesting that this time period may be particularly critical for language development in older adulthood.

Just as working memory is related to elderly adults' production of complex syntactic structures, it also affects their processing of those structures in the discourse of others. Norman, Kemper, Kynette, Cheung, and Anagnopoulos (1991) had college students and elderly adults listen to prose passages that were interrupted by pauses. During the pauses, participants were asked to recall the immediately preceding statements. Analysis showed that elderly participants had much poorer recall than young adults for the syntactically complex statements, but differed only slightly from the young participants in recall of simple statements. Working memory deficits in the elderly participants accounted for the age differences in recall.

Wingfield, Stine, and associates have conducted a number of studies on the language processing capabilities of young and elderly individuals (Stine & Wingfield, 1987; Stine, Wingfield, & Poon, 1986; Wingfield, Lahar, & Stine, 1989; Wingfield, Wayland, & Stine, 1992). Generally, they have used accuracy of recall as the dependent measure of processing capability, with an emphasis on how speaker rate and use of prosody may differentially affect recall of young and elderly persons. Their results show that a fast rate leads to poorer recall from both young and elderly, but that the rate of decline is greater for elderly individuals than for young ones (Stine & Wingfield, 1987; Stine et al., 1986; Wingfield et al., 1992). In terms of prosody, results indicate that elderly individuals, more than young ones, rely on prosodic cues such as pause and inflection to aid their processing of oral discourse (Stine & Wingfield, 1987; Wingfield et al., 1989, 1992).

Like Kemper and her colleagues, these researchers have noted a relationship between working memory measures and the age-related differences in discourse processing observed. For example, Stine and Wingfield (1987) report that listening span, a measure of working memory collected using oral stimuli (Daneman & Carpenter, 1980), accounted for 44% of the variance in recall performance of their subjects when entered into a regression equation prior to age. However, they also note that working memory performance paralleled age differences to such an extent that entering age into the equation removed the significant contribution of working memory.

Name Retrieval and Aging

As noted earlier, research tends to show that although working memory declines in elderly persons, their semantic memory remains intact (Salthouse,

1988). As a result, elderly individuals' word-finding problems are no greater than those of young persons, even though their word search process may show the effects of slower processing speeds (Salthouse, 1988) or speech rates (Light, 1988). However, elderly people are plagued more than young ones by problems in retrieving proper names (see Cohen, 1994, for a review). This problem has been documented through both diary studies (Burke, MacKay, Worthley, & Wade, 1991; Cohen & Faulkner, 1986b) and experimental studies (Burke & Laver, 1990; Crook & West, 1990). To date, this selective deficit for proper names has not been tied definitively to specific changes in the cognitive system (Cohen, 1994). The most promising models (e.g., Burton & Bruce, 1992; Cohen, 1992) posit that the explanation lies in the interaction of lowered cognitive activation levels in older persons with the distinctive nature of the name memory system. As Cohen (1994) suggests, proper names have fewer and more arbitrary attribute links than do common nouns. The attribute links are more arbitrary in the sense that there is no semantic connection between the name *Joe Bradley* and his attribute *works at the bakery* comparable to that between the common noun *baker* and the attribute *bakes bread*. In addition, there are no synonyms for proper names, eliminating another retrieval route available for common nouns.

Cognitive Aging and Communicative Competence

Despite the clear evidence of language production and processing effects of age-related changes in elderly persons' cognitive systems, the implication that these effects equal reduced communicative competence is not supported (Light, 1988; Ryan, 1991). *Communicative competence* refers to the ability to communicate *appropriately* in natural interactions in ways that are *effective* in achieving conversational goals (Canary & Spitzberg, 1989; Wiemann, 1977). Researchers stress that working memory capacity does not decline equally in all older people, and that elderly individuals often develop strategies that mitigate the effects of any decline on interaction (Light, 1990; Ryan, 1991). Older listeners' greater reliance on prosody (Stine & Wingfield, 1987; Stine et al., 1986; Wingfield et al., 1992), for instance, may represent such a strategy. The way in which elderly adults process statements rich in information (i.e., statements with high propositional density; Kintsch & van Dijk, 1978) may constitute another.

Increasing propositional density should place demands on working memory similar to those of increasing syntactic complexity. As a result, the performance of elderly adults might be expected to show more negative effects of high propositional density than that of young adults. In a test of this hypothesis, Wingfield et al. (1992) found instead that the recall of young and elderly participants showed similar rates of decline as propositional density increased, even though young adults had generally better recall than did elderly ones. The researchers suggest that elderly adults may achieve coherence in interpreting informationally rich statements in a way that is qualitatively different from that of young adults. As a result, although elderly persons may have more limited processing resources than do young adults, they may use them more efficiently.

Further, Wingfield et al. (1992) note that despite having generally poorer recall than young adults for prose sentences, elderly adults still have good recall in absolute terms. In their study, accuracy of recall for elderly subjects exceeded 70% even in the most difficult condition (very fast rate combined with anomalous prosody).

Finally, age differences in language performance may sometimes indicate an advantage for elderly persons over young ones. For example, Kemper et al. (1989) found that whereas measures of syntactic complexity favored their young participants over their elderly ones, perceptions of the narratives produced by the subjects favored the elderly participants. Narratives from elderly participants were perceived as both more interesting and clearer than were those of the young.

On the other hand, Cohen (1994) suggests that name retrieval difficulties may interfere with the interpersonal interactions of older adults in a number of ways. These include interruptions of the flow of conversation, the embarrassment of trying to introduce a person whose name is blocked, and the inability to relay new information to a listener (e.g., a recommendation of an author or a listing of good restaurants in another town). Experiencing such name blocks may cause older individuals to question their own communicative (or cognitive) competence and may reinforce negative stereotypes of aging for their communicative partners.

We want to stress that this discussion of cognition and communicative competence is restricted to cognitive changes associated with normal aging. Pathological changes (e.g., stroke-induced aphasia, Alzheimer's disease) are almost inevitably connected with reduced communication competence. The extent of the interference may range from extreme off-target verbosity in conversation stemming from declines in frontal lobe functioning (Arbuckle & Gold, 1993; for a review, see Gold, Arbuckle, & Andres, 1994) to the profound disruption of semantic memory and coherent discourse associated with Alzheimer's disease (see Kemper & Lyons, 1994, for a review).

Social Cognition and Communication With Older Adults

Whereas the role of cognitive aging in communication has been the focus primarily of psychologists, the role of social cognition in communication has received the attention of both psychologists and communication scholars. Given the centrality of social-cognitive processes in the dominant communication theories (e.g., constructivism [Delia, O'Keefe, & O'Keefe, 1982], communication accommodation theory [Giles, Mulac, Bradac, & Johnson, 1987], uncertainty reduction [Berger & Bradac, 1982]), the greater focus of communication researchers on social cognition than on cognitive aging is not surprising. Research interest has centered on how attitudes, stereotypes, and communication-related beliefs influence perceptions of, and communication with, older people (for a more extended review of this literature, see Hummert, Shaner, & Garstka, 1995). Of particular concern have been the ways in which these cognitions may involve low expectations for the communication competence of older persons, leading to the use of "elderspeak" (Cohen & Faulkner, 1986a) or patronizing speech (Ryan, Giles, Bartolucci, & Henwood, 1986; Ryan, Hummert, & Boich, 1995) with older individuals.

Do attitudes, beliefs, and stereotypes of older adults
presume low communication competence?

Several reviews have examined research on attitudes toward, beliefs about, and stereotypes of older adults, including those by Kogan (1979), Lutsky (1980), Green (1981), Palmore (1982), Crockett and Hummert (1987), Kite and Johnson (1988), and Hummert, Shaner, and Garstka (1995). Only Palmore (1982), using historical and economic data, has concluded that perceptions of elderly people are entirely negative. The remainder have reported that the literature includes examples of both positive and negative evaluations of older persons in comparison with younger persons.

To some extent, the nature of these evaluations can be tied to study design and focus: Within-subjects manipulations of target age and a focus on generalized older and younger targets tend to yield more negative evaluations of older targets than younger ones, whereas between-subjects manipulations of age and a focus on specific old versus young targets find either no age effects or evaluations that favor older targets as often as younger ones (Crockett & Hummert, 1987; Kite & Johnson, 1988; Kogan, 1979). However, methodological choices alone cannot account for the mixed positive and negative nature of evaluations of older targets. Even when within-subjects designs or generalized targets are employed, elderly persons are sometimes judged positively in absolute scale values, as no different from young targets, or more positively than young targets on some dimensions (e.g., Braithwaite, 1986; Louis Harris & Associates, 1975; Luszcz & Fitzgerald, 1986; Ryan & Capadano, 1978; Schwalb & Sedlacek, 1990). Likewise, when between-subjects designs have compared perceptions of individualized old and young targets, old targets have sometimes been judged more negatively than young ones on certain dimensions (e.g., O'Connell & Rotter, 1979; Perry & Varney, 1978; Ryan & Laurie, 1990; Stewart & Ryan, 1982).

To illustrate, we consider the speaker perception studies initiated by Ryan and her colleagues (Ryan & Capadano, 1978; Ryan & Johnston, 1987; Ryan & Laurie, 1990; Stewart & Ryan, 1982) and extended by Giles and his colleagues (Giles, Coupland, Henwood, Harriman, & Coupland, 1990; Giles, Henwood, Coupland, Harriman, & Coupland, 1992). Using a within-subjects design, Ryan and Capadano (1978) investigated personality and age perceptions of speakers. Subjects listened to either 32 female or 32 male speakers ranging in age from 12 to 71. Regardless of speakers' sex, participants were able to discriminate their ages with a fair degree of accuracy. Of more importance to our topic, however, is the fact that those who heard female speakers rated the older women as more reserved, passive, "out of it," and inflexible than younger women, but as equally secure and strong. Older men were perceived as different from younger men only in terms of inflexibility.

The remainder of the studies manipulated target age in between-subjects designs, but also found mixed positive and negative evaluations of the old targets. Ryan and Johnston (1987) and Ryan and Laurie (1990) considered the ways in which speaker age and message effectiveness might interact to affect judgments of a speaker. In the former study, competence ratings were affected only by message effectiveness, with the speakers giving effective messages being rated as more competent than those giving ineffective ones. The latter study used less extreme effective and ineffective messages and added messages recorded in white noise to the effectiveness factor. In this case, age interacted with message effectiveness such that an effective message resulted in more positive evaluations for the young speaker but not for the old speaker. Further, the old speaker giving a message in white noise was rated as the least competent target. As Ryan and Laurie point out, this suggests that the old speaker, in comparison with the young one, received more blame for the poor-quality recording and less credit for the effective message.

Stewart and Ryan (1982) asked subjects to evaluate either old or young males speaking at fast, medium, and slow rates. Both age and rate affected competence ratings, with younger and faster speakers seen as more competent than older and slower ones. However, rate played a stronger role than speaker age in causal attributions about the reasons for the speakers' performance.

Giles, Coupland, Henwood, et al. (1990; Giles et al., 1992) extended this line of research by examining the effects of accent (standard or nonstandard British) and rate (fast, medium, slow) on judgments of old and young males describing an automobile accident in which they were involved. In these studies, the voice variables were manipulated using the matched guise technique (Lambert, Hodgson, Gardner, & Fillenbaum, 1960). In this paradigm, judges think that they are listening to two or more different speakers, but in fact they are listening to the same speaker using two or more different guises. Again, the results were equivocal.

In the first study, accent and rate, but not voice age, affected ratings of the speaker on status, benevolence, and integrity (Giles, Coupland, Henwood, et al., 1990). Age effects were found, however, in that the older guises were rated as more frail, old-fashioned, weak, and insecure than younger guises. In the second study, age and accent interacted to affect competence ratings, with accent leading to more extreme judgments of old voices than young voices (Giles et al., 1992). The old-standard voice was rated as most competent and the old-nonstandard voice as least competent. Age also interacted with rate to affect hesitancy and assertiveness ratings. In this case, however, rate differences resulted in more extreme judgments of young-sounding voices than of old-sounding ones, with the young-medium guise rated most positively and the young-slow guise rated most negatively on both dimensions.

Most of these studies assessed perceptions on additional dimensions that also indicate that the views of older persons, in comparison with younger ones, cannot be characterized as either uniformly negative or uniformly positive. Clearly, perceptions of the competence of elderly individuals vary widely, even when study designs are similar. Crockett and Hummert (1987) suggest that multiple stereotypes of the elderly provide the theoretical explanation for this variation. That is, to the extent that the information provided about an older target suggests a positive stereotype, positive evaluations will result. Conversely, older targets who activate negative stereotypes will elicit negative evaluations.

Brewer, Dull, and Lui (1981) first proposed that the category *older adult* functions as a superordinate category that encompasses several more specific stereotypes of elderly persons, just as the superordinate category *bird* includes the subtypes *cardinal* and *crow* (Rosch, 1978). Brewer et al. conceptualized three elderly stereotypes: *grandmother,* a nurturing, family-oriented woman; *elder statesman,* a distinguished, conservative man; and *senior citizen,* an inactive, isolated person of either sex. Using photograph sort, trait inference, and trait recall tasks with college-age subjects, they found support for their conception of these three stereotypes.

Further research on multiple stereotypes has adopted an inductive approach to identifying subcategories (Hummert, 1990; Hummert, Garstka, Shaner, & Strahm, 1994; Schmidt & Boland, 1986). Rather than test subjects' recognition of researcher-defined stereotypes, these studies have used trait generation and trait sorting tasks to ascertain subjects' definitions of the stereotypes. Seven subcategories have emerged across these three studies as stereotypes of elderly people held by young, middle-aged, and elderly subjects—three positive (Perfect Grandparent, Golden Ager, John Wayne Conservative) and four negative (Shrew/Curmudgeon, Despondent, Severely Impaired, Recluse). Table 1.1 presents the traits composing these stereotypes and their category labels.

Support for the idea that these stereotypes of elderly individuals suggest different levels of communication competence comes from a recent study by Hummert, Garstka, and Shaner (in press). These researchers used the Language in Adulthood Questionnaire (LIA) (Ryan, Kwong See, Meneer, & Trovato, 1992) to assess beliefs of young, middle-aged, and elderly participants about their own communication skills and those of four elderly targets. Traits used to characterize the targets corresponded to two positive (Golden Ager, John Wayne Conservative) and two negative (Despondent, Shrew/Curmudgeon) stereotypes (Hummert, Garstka, et al., 1994). Illustrating the per-

TABLE 1.1
Stereotypes of the Elderly Held by
Young, Middle-Aged, and Elderly Adults

Stereotypes	*Traits*
Negative	
Severely Impaired	slow thinking, incompetent, feeble, incoherent, inarticulate, senile
Despondent	depressed, sad, hopeless, afraid, neglected, lonely
Shrew/Curmudgeon	complaining, ill-tempered, bitter, prejudiced, demanding, inflexible, selfish, jealous, stubborn, nosy
Recluse	quiet, timid, naive
Positive	
Golden Ager	lively, adventurous, alert, active, sociable, witty, independent, skilled, productive, successful, capable, volunteer, well traveled, future oriented, fun loving, happy, curious, healthy, sexual, self-accepting, health conscious, courageous, interesting, well-informed
Perfect Grandparent	kind, loving, family oriented, generous, grateful, supportive, understanding, trustworthy, intelligent, wise, knowledgeable
John Wayne Conservative	patriotic, religious, nostalgic, reminiscent, retired, conservative, emotional, mellow, determined, proud

SOURCE: Stereotypes reported in Hummert, Garstka, Shaner, and Strahm (1994).

vasiveness and power of the stereotype-communication belief link, participants of all ages believed that the number of communication problems in
hearing and memory would be lower for the two positive targets than for the
two negative targets. This was true even though the traits of the two negative
targets (see Table 1.1) gave no indication of memory and hearing difficulties.
In addition, perceptions of age-related increases in word recognition and
storytelling skills favored the positive targets over the negative ones. The
Golden Ager was viewed most positively and the Despondent most negatively
in the assessments.

These results support a stereotype-sensitive explanation for positive versus
negative evaluations of elderly persons. Beliefs about the communication
competence of elderly individuals do not derive solely from the persons'
categorization as elderly, but from their categorization as particular types of
elderly individuals.

How do perceptions of elderly adults influence communication?

Beliefs, attitudes, and stereotypes about the communicative competence
(Wiemann, 1977) of people of different ages can influence linguistic and
paralinguistic choices in conversation. Communication accommodation theory (CAT) has been particularly influential in the development of models of
the role of these cognitions in communication with older persons (e.g.,

Coupland, Coupland, Giles, & Henwood, 1988; Hummert, 1994b; Ryan et al., 1986).

The first of these models, developed by Ryan et al. (1986), is termed the *communicative predicament of aging model*. In brief, this model suggests contextual cues to age may activate negative stereotypes of elderly adults in a perceiver. The stereotypes may then lead the perceiver to modify his or her speech to the older target, resulting in patronizing speech. As outlined by Ryan et al. (1995), patronizing speech is characterized by the presence of simplification strategies (e.g., slow speech, low grammatical complexity, a concrete and familiar vocabulary), clarification strategies (e.g., careful articulation and simple sentences), a demeaning emotional tone (e.g., directive, overbearing, or, alternatively, overly familiar), high pitch and variable intonation (Caporael, 1981), and a low quality of talk (i.e., superficial conversation). An extreme form of patronizing speech is the secondary baby talk addressed to institutionalized individuals (Caporael, 1981; Caporael & Culbertson, 1986). According to the model, this modified speech then serves to reinforce age-stereotyped behaviors of older people, constraining their opportunities for communication and contributing to negative psychological events (e.g., loss of personal control and self-esteem) and long-term outcomes in terms of health and societal status. We discuss the research on patronizing speech in detail in the section of this chapter headed "Language."

Coupland et al. (1988) also identify stereotypes of elderly individuals as playing a powerful role in speech accommodations to older persons. As they state, "Younger speakers may regularly overaccommodate . . . their speech to the elderly, producing linguistic behaviours targeted at the often inappropriate, but previously stereotyped, social persona of the 'elderly communicator' " (p. 9).

The communicative predicament of aging (Ryan et al., 1986) and the Coupland et al. (1988) models presume that stereotypes of older adults are uniformly negative, in contrast to research on stereotypes of that group (Brewer et al., 1981; Hummert, 1990; Hummert, Garstka, et al., 1994; Schmidt & Boland, 1986). As a result, Hummert (1994b) developed a model of the role of age-related stereotypes in interaction that extends the earlier models to include the activation cues for and consequences of both positive and negative stereotypes of elderly adults.

Here we consider only the predictions of this model for the communication consequences of positive and negative stereotypes. As the results of the Hummert et al. (in press) study suggest, positive stereotyping of an elderly interactant should lead to beliefs that the individual is a competent communicator who experiences few, if any, age-related communication problems, whereas negative categorizations should be associated with beliefs that the individual has hearing and/or memory difficulties that interfere with communication. Communication directed to this individual should reflect these different assessments of his or her competence, with the negatively stereotyped person, but not the positive one, receiving a high level of age-adapted speech. These adaptations may be either the overaccommodations of patronizing speech (e.g., slow, loud, simple talk) or underaccommodations (e.g., conversational disengagement, dissociative talk), depending upon the nature of the negative stereotype.

Two studies have addressed the predictions of this model regarding the behavior of the perceiver in an interaction with an older adult. Hummert and Shaner (in press) presented college-age subjects with photographs of two elderly women, one described by the traits of the Severely Impaired stereotype and one by the traits of the Perfect Grandparent stereotype. Both subjects' beliefs about how they would address the women and their audiotaped persuasive messages supported the model's prediction that they would use more patronizing speech (overaccommodations) with the Severely Impaired target than with the Perfect Grandparent. In particular, messages to the Severely Impaired person were shorter, less complex, and more demeaning in emotional tone than were those to the Perfect Grandparent. A recently completed study by Hummert, Shaner, Henry, and Garstka (1995) extended this research by collecting messages from young, middle-aged, and elderly subjects and using a less extreme negative stereotype (Despondent). Results showed that the Despondent target, like the Severely Impaired target, was believed to require more age-based overaccommodations than the positive target, as reflected in the messages addressed to the targets.

Critique and Future Directions

The cognition and communication focus of the research reviewed in this section is an important one from our perspective. Understanding the ways in which cognitive aging affects the communication behaviors and preferences of older persons is essential to our ability to determine which, if any, speech accommodations will facilitate communication with older individuals. Clarifying the social-cognitive processes resulting in appropriate or inappropriate accommodations to older persons is an integral step toward reducing the incidence of inappropriate accommodations.

Cognitive Aging and Communication

The processing of language in interaction involves not only the cognitive system, but also the sensory system. An age-related decline in hearing ability, termed presbycusis, has been associated with the degrading of the sensory and neurophysiological systems of hearing in older adults (Corso, 1977, 1987). The ways in which presbycusis may interact with declines in working memory and processing speed to affect language comprehension have been largely neglected in cognitive aging research (Light, 1988; Schneider, Pichora-Fuller, Kowalchuk, & Lamb, 1994). In addition, some aspects of presbycusis are not sensitive to the pure-tone hearing tests used to screen older subjects in cognitive aging studies (Levitt, 1982; Villaume, Brown, & Darling, 1994). As a result, tests of language processing as a function of working memory may have been confounded by the hearing abilities of the participants (Schneider et al., 1994). We see a definite need for research addressing the interrelationship of hearing ability, working memory, and processing speed on the comprehension of language.

As our review of the cognitive aging and language literature illustrates, processing limitations carry specific performance consequences for older communicators. However, the extent to which those performance consequences result in diminished communicative competence for older persons is unclear. As we have pointed out, lower performance measures for older adults than younger adults are not always pragmatically important in absolute terms (e.g., Wingfield et al., 1992) and are sometimes associated with highly positive qualitative judgments of competence (e.g., Kemper et al., 1989). Not surprisingly, the interactional implications of age-related changes in the cognitive system have been largely unexplored by the cognitive psychologists who dominate this area of research. We believe that communication scholars could make a significant contribution to research in this area by addressing the conversational, relational, and competence issues related to changes in the cognitive systems of older persons. As a result, it is our hope that future reviews of the cognitive aging literature will include representative studies from the communication discipline.

Readers may have noticed the apparent links between the declines in working memory, processing speed, and hearing ability discussed and the speech accommodations of patronizing speech (e.g., slow speed, simple sentences, loud speech, exaggerated intonation). It seems that the cognitive aging literature suggests that the speech accommodations of patronizing speech can improve language comprehension for older adults. This issue too must be addressed within our discipline. It is possible that future research will establish that the types of accommodations necessary for effective communication with older adults will be those associated with competent communication in general. Although the cognitive research has established that older adults find fast speech more difficult to comprehend than do younger adults, comprehension at normal speeds does not show extreme age differences (Wingfield et al., 1992). Likewise, although prosodic cues are important comprehension aids for older adults, the prosodic cues needed may be only those associated with normal intonation and stress (Stine & Wingfield, 1987; Wingfield et al., 1989, 1992). The extreme accommodations of patronizing speech derive not from the reality of cognitive aging, but from a distortion of that reality in the more negative stereotypes of impaired older adults. Nevertheless, the documented changes in elderly adults' memory and hearing abilities may require some adaptations beyond those we associate with competent communication in general. Our discipline could contribute significantly to attempts to answer this question.

Social Cognition

The social cognition literature has established that age is a powerful social category, but it has also established that increasing age is not always viewed negatively (Brewer et al., 1981; Giles, Coupland, Henwood, et al., 1990; Heckhausen, Dixon, & Baltes, 1989; Hummert, 1990; Hummert, Garstka, et al., 1994; Ryan & Capadano, 1978; Ryan & Johnston, 1987). It is essential that we understand the conditions under which the social category of age leads to negative evaluations in one instance and positive in another. Thus, we suggest that future research address the activation cues—nonverbal characteristics, behaviors, situations, and so on—that lead to positive versus negative stereotyping of older persons in interaction. Initial research on nonverbal cues indicates that physiognomic and vocal features indicating advanced age (80 years and over) are particularly tied to negative stereotypes (Hummert, 1994a; Hummert, Garstka, & Shaner, 1994; Hummert, Mazloff, & Henry, 1995). Little attention, however, has been paid to individual differences that might make some individuals more prone to categorize elderly people negatively than positively (or vice versa). Potential discriminators suggested include cognitive complexity (Hummert, 1994b; Ryan et al., 1986), perceiver age (Hummert, 1994b), and quality of contact with older people (Fox & Giles, 1993).

A limitation of the attitude and stereotype research is its cultural specificity. Stereotypes of older adults have been assessed primarily within the United States and in other Western cultures (but see Chang, Chang, & Yung, 1984; Ikels et al., 1992). Cross-cultural studies should be incorporated into future research. However, we caution researchers against wholesale transfer of U.S. attitude scales or trait sets to other cultures. Even with accurate translations, there is no guarantee that the traits important to classification of elderly adults in one culture are also important in another. Likewise, the evaluative associations with particular traits in person perception schemata are likely to vary cross-culturally. As a result, we see the inductive approach to the identification of stereotypes (e.g., Hummert, Garstka, et al., 1994; Schmidt & Boland, 1986) as integral to a clear understanding of elderly stereotypes in other cultures.

The models of communication with the elderly described in this section (Coupland et al., 1988; Hummert, 1994b; Ryan et al., 1986) all argue that there is a recursive relationship between cognitions and messages: Just as cognition plays a role in the production of messages directed toward older adults, the messages produced by the two interactants have impacts on cognitions. We see this recursive relationship as an essential focus for future research. Two recent studies exemplify the type of approach we are suggesting. First, Harwood, Giles, Fox, Ryan, and Williams (1993) compared perceptions of old and young persons who responded passively or assertively to patronizing speech. They found some evidence that both old and young passive responders may suggest more negative stereotypes than assertive responders, in that the passive responders were rated as lower in status and control than the assertive ones. Second, Hummert, Mazloff, and Henry (1994) investigated the prediction of the communication models that patronizing speech reinforces negative stereotypes of elderly people. Elderly subjects characterized the recipients of patronizing and nonpatronizing messages and gave their own oral responses to the messages. Results showed that they both selected more negative stereotypes to describe recipients of patronizing than nonpatronizing messages, and themselves responded more passively (i.e., more like negatively stereotyped older persons) to the patronizing messages than the nonpatronizing ones.

Perceptions about the aging process carry emotional overtones, yet current models of communication and aging do not address the role of emotion in the stereotyping of aging populations. Smith (1993) has argued that stereotypes cannot be separated from the situation and motivation or self-interest of the perceiver. These are the factors, Smith suggests, that lead to such different emotional responses—and by extension, communication—as hate, fear, and sympathy to persons from the same stereotyped group. Incorporating motivation and emotion into our social cognition, communication, and aging models and research agenda promises to further our understanding of the complex relationship between stereotypes and communication.

Finally, we have two methodological suggestions for future research. First, we see an experimental approach as necessary to test predictions of the models that have been advanced. These models have been developed to account for behaviors observed in naturalistic studies (e.g., Caporael, 1981). However, we also see the need for methodological triangulation in the investigation of these issues, ideally within the same studies.

Second, we encourage communication and aging researchers to focus more on the models' predictions about subjects' communication *behaviors* than they have in the past. The majority of the studies reviewed in this section have simply asked for subjects' evaluations of messages and speakers. Although those evaluations provide insight into social cognitions, they do not address how those social cognitions affect communicative choices. We would like to see messages—oral, not written—as dependent variables in communication and aging research, not just as independent variables. This move to message analysis is the necessary next step in the study of the interrelationship between social cognition and communication with (and by) older adults.

The following section on language illustrates the key role that messages play in our understanding of life-span communication. Investigations of messages can elaborate and inform the research on cognitive processes just discussed.

LANGUAGE

Language is the purveyor of our attitudes and beliefs, not just explicitly, as when we verbally express our opinions, but also in terms of our style of language, in what is implied by the way we choose to express ourselves. We may place emphasis on certain words and not others to specify particular meanings and intent. In addition, we base our perceptions of others in part on their linguistic performance, using cues to make judgments of them. Often, preconceived notions we have about others' personalities, social standing, group memberships, and so on interact with objective indices in intricate and implicit ways. Language is not as much a medium of transmission of information as it is the very basis of social life. As the literature reviewed in the previous section demonstrates, language is, among other things, a basis for evaluating older adults and a trigger for stereotypical perceptions and interpretations.

As we have noted, communication accommodation theory has predictive and explanatory power for conceptualizing intergenerational communication. It helps us to specify sociopsychological antecedents and consequences of such talk and, more specifically, elderly-to-young as well as young-to-elderly language strategies (Coupland et al., 1988; Hummert, 1994b; Ryan et al., 1986). In this section we describe studies that fall broadly into these two categories. The most extensively investigated elderly-to-young strategy is underaccommodation, whereas the most extensively investigated young-to-elderly strategy is overaccommodation (see Coupland & Coupland, 1990).

Young-to-Old Speech: Overaccommodation

CAT has provided a theoretical frame for many studies of young-to-old talk. Notably, all studies to be reviewed here draw upon one particular young-to-old language strategy, overaccommodation, as outlined and described by Ryan et al. (1986). We are aware that other problematic language strategies exist, many of which are yet to be documented and described. Young-to-old overaccommodation has been variously labeled "patronizing speech" (Ryan et al., 1986, 1995), "elderspeak" (Cohen & Faulkner, 1986a), and "baby talk" (Caporael, 1981).

Although not working within the CAT framework, Caporael and Culbertson (1986; Caporael, 1981) were among the first to document patronizing speech directed from young to elderly interlocutors. They describe an extreme form of patronization to institutionalized elderly people irrespective of their functional ability, which they label "secondary baby talk." Since these initial investigations were conducted, there has been a consistent and lively research interest in this phenomenon, not least because of its potentially serious ramifications for elderly individuals' psychological and physical health (Ryan et al., 1986).

Patronizing speech is perhaps a less extreme form of baby talk and, as we have pointed out above, is distinguished from normal adult speech by being slow, oversimplified (e.g., low grammatical complexity), polite, and overly warm. In addition, clarification strategies such as careful articulation and increased volume may be employed, along with other content and paralinguistic features (Ryan et al., 1986). For the most part, it is assumed that such speech modifications are a response to stereotypical cognitive and physical impairments associated with aging rather than any objective cognitive or functional abilities manifested by the older person.

Originally identified in an institutional context, patronizing speech is by no means confined to such settings, although its prevalence in everyday contexts, and especially in the family, is perhaps still relatively undocumented. However, recently Kemper (1994) confirmed the use of elderspeak by both caregivers (e.g., nurses) and service providers (e.g., craft instructors) when addressing older adults. More important, such talk was not used when younger adults were addressed in comparative contexts and was not sensitive to the functional capabilities of the older adult groups (i.e., demented versus nondemented). In a family context, Montepare, Steinberg, and Rosenberg (1992) have found not only that young adults spontaneously produce patronizing speech when addressing elderly adults within their families, but also that the characteristics of this speech style are readily apparent to naive judges and even sufficient to indicate, in some instances, the identity of the target (e.g., grandmother versus mother).

The motivation for such speech is generally assumed to be an overzealous desire to indicate nurturance and socioemotional support, although in some cases motives may also include a need for dominance and control (Grainger, Atkinson, & Coupland, 1990). To the extent that some extreme forms of patronizing speech convey little respect, the challenge for caregivers, according to Ryan and Cole (1990), is to manage communicatively two competing goals: to indicate nurturance and support while remaining polite and respectful. In support of this contention, Ryan and Cole found that the elderly respondents in their study expressed preferences for speech from young people to be more respectful as well as more nurturant. Differential communication needs according to life circumstances of elders were also evident in Ryan and Cole's results. Elders living in institutions, compared with community-dwelling elders, showed a preference for speech that was simpler and slower, indicating that they may be more tolerant or appreciative of some aspects of patronizing speech.

In recent years, patronizing speech has been studied extensively using an experimental format in which respondents are asked to read and respond to vignettes that vary speech style (patronizing, neutral), participants (e.g., nurses, receptionists, nursing home residents, neighbors), and contexts (institutional and community). A typical example is the work of Ryan, Bourhis, and Knops (1991), who used a written vignette concerning a middle-aged nurse talking with an elderly nursing home resident to elicit evaluative perceptions of the nurse and the resident. Speech style was manipulated by the wording of the vignette to indicate a neutral or patronizing message. The latter contained condescending and simplified speech, for instance, presumption of the resident's inability to understand a television program and the expressions "be a good girl" and "poor dear." The results of this study revealed that patronizing speech was downgraded by observer judges as significantly less respectful and nurturant than the more neutral variant. In addition, both the nurse and the resident were seen as significantly more frustrated in the patronizing condition. Further, inferences elicited from respondents indicated that they could "hear" the patronizing conversation as shrill and having exaggerated intonation. Recently, other nonverbal correlates of patronizing speech such as gaze, facial expressions, postures, and gestures have also been investigated (Edwards & Noller, 1993; Ryan, MacLean, & Orange, 1994).

Giles, Fox, and Smith (1993) have confirmed the general pattern of these findings. However, the Giles et al. study included older as well as young adults as observer judges. Older respondents were particularly sensitive to the characteristics of the individual receiving the patronization. When the nurse spoke patronizingly, older (but not younger) respondents rated the resident as less competent, weaker, and less alert. At one level, this implies that older adults incorporate contextual cues in their evaluations of particular episodes of talk, whereas younger individuals appear less inclined to do so. However, it also suggests that elderly people may be more willing to denigrate their peers on dimensions of competence as a result of the particular kinds of talk directed at them. A follow-up questionnaire investigation with the same elderly respondents indicated that many of them claimed to have been patronized themselves (albeit to a lesser extent than they believe others of their own age to be patronized), and that it made them extremely irritated.

Harwood et al. (1993) extended this research with two main goals: first, to examine patronizing talk from older to younger recipients and vice versa; and second, to examine the comparative worth of various response strategies. Previous work had portrayed the older targets of patronizing talk as relatively passive and hence as possibly colluding with the patronizing behavior (see Edwards & Noller, 1993; Ryan, Meredith, & Shantz, 1994). In order to confront the dilemmas and management problems associated with accommodating to patronization, Harwood et al.'s study design included conditions in which the recipient of patronization was either "accepting" (i.e., neutral) or "assertive." Results showed that both old and young people were evaluated negatively when being patronizing and that intergenerational communication was seen as far more satisfying when patronizing talk was not present. Assertive responses from the patronized person led to evaluations of her as higher status, more controlling, and less nurturing than when she provided a neutral response. Patronizing individuals who were the recipients of this response mode were evaluated as less satisfied and less in control than when they received an accepting response.

Adaptations to older listeners may occur at the topic level as well as at the linguistic and nonverbal levels. For instance, Carver and de la Garza (1984) asked two groups of students in Florida to read the same brief five-line description of an automobile accident involving either an "old" (84-year-old) or a "young" (22-year-old) male driver-protagonist. They were then to rank order questions directed to the driver in terms of the questions' perceived importance for the ability to assign responsibility for the accident. As predicted, respondents endorsed questions concerning the physical, mental, and sensory inadequacies of the older driver and questions concerning speeding and alcohol consumption of the young driver. Thus, both young and old drivers invoked questions concerning their competence, but the types of competence questions varied with target age and were in line with stereotypical age assumptions.

A follow-up study extended the design to include 77-, 66-, and 54-year-olds as well as 84- and 22-year-olds (Franklyn-Stokes, Harriman, Giles, & Coupland, 1988). As age of target increased, the importance of questions about health, physical condition, quickness of reaction, and mental competence also increased in a linear fashion. The reverse pattern occurred for questions more frequently asked of young targets and tailed off linearly as the target's age increased. In a further study conducted in New Zealand (Ng, Moody, & Giles, 1991), the ages of targets were extended to cover the life span from 16 to 91 (in 10-year age bands). Again, health and competence information was more frequently sought from older speakers, and speeding and alcohol information was perceived as more relevant for younger targets. However, rather than a steady linear trend, as in the previous study, the importance of health and competence information seeking was observed to increase most sharply at 31 and 81 years. As in the previous study, information seeking based on speeding and alcohol showed a negative linear trend. In this case, therefore, negative age stereotypes seemed to guide information seeking from both young and older drivers. Specifically, a decrement perception of growing older was evident even in questions for middle-aged targets, increasing dramatically when the target was around 31 years of age, and an irresponsibility perception of young adulthood was apparent in questions to the younger drivers.

Old-to-Young Speech: Underaccommodation

In their typology of old-to-young language strategies, Ryan et al. (1986) identify underaccommodation as a predominant perception of older adults' talk. This perception has been supported by studies of intergenerational communication utilizing both self-report and interactional discourse data (Coupland, Henwood, Coupland, & Giles, 1990; Giles, Coupland, & Wiemann, 1991; Williams & Giles, 1995). The research to be discussed below describes and explores various dimensions of old underaccommodation, its realization in talk, as well as young people's attempts to negotiate this when interacting with older partners.

A study of intergenerational discourse conducted in Wales paired young (30- to 40-year-old) women with older (70- to 87-year-old) women and videotaped their interactions (Coupland et al., 1991). The women were strangers and were told by way of instruction "to get to know one another." The elderly women were members of adult day centers, were mostly from upper-working-class backgrounds, lived alone, and were widowed. The younger women were recruited through newspaper ads and could be characterized as lower-middle-class and working-class. Of the interaction pairs, 20 were intergenerational and 10 each were peer-old and peer-young.

Coupland et al. found that the elderly women in this study spent approximately one-sixth of their time disclosing personally painful information (e.g., accidents, illness, bereavement, social deprivation), whereas the younger women spent less than 2% of the time doing so. This phenomenon was termed painful self-disclosure (PSD) by the authors. Of the 20 intergenerational dyads, 16 manifested instances of older PSD, with only 1 young person reciprocating. In the 10 peer-elderly dyads, there were 9 instances of reciprocation, whereas in the 10 peer-young dyads, there were only 4 instances of the phenomenon. Even more interesting than the facts and figures documenting the quantity of PSD are the processes by which PSDs were introduced into discourse, responded to, and curtailed.

The majority of disclosures could be characterized as introduced by the older people themselves, although a substantial portion were elicited by the younger persons. An initial PSD often led to others, a phenomenon the researchers refer to as "chaining." Such patterns of disclosure are typically thought unusual and rather inappropriate for first-acquaintance interactions (Berger & Bradac, 1982). Thus, the young interactional partners could be characterized as faced with a number of interactional dilemmas in responding to such revelations. For example, they could switch topics and discourage further disclosure, or they could express interest and risk encouraging more disclosure. The first strategy may seem rather rude and dismissive, whereas the second may lead to an escalation of disclosure and further interactional dilemmas. A third option is to express sympathy, but this may seem rather overaccommodative or even patronizing. Often, the young partners seemed to settle for minimal responses, such as "mmm," "good heavens," or "oh dear."

Among other things, this pattern suggests that the older people (in this context) were not utilizing the full range of topics potentially available to them. Thus, the possibility arises that in some cases, self-disclosures initiated in order to share feelings and tell who one is (see Boden & Bielby, 1983) may become ritualized into prolonged negative exchanges, which may enhance and lend salience to negative feelings, possibly reinforcing and re-creating them by their very enactment (see Rotenberg & Hamel, 1988).

In a follow-up study, a complementary sample of young women listened to and commented upon audiotaped extracts of PSD from the interaction study (Coupland et al., 1990). In group discussions, a few of the young women denied that the use of PSDs was a problem, some found it "sad," and others said it was strategic (as, for example, an attempt to gain sympathy). But most felt that it was underaccommodative—the elderly women were egocentric, focusing on their own problems, and were underattentive to the younger women and their conversational needs.

We must be cautious about stretching the findings regarding PSD in the Welsh community too far beyond their context (adult day-care centers), cohort (working-class 70- to 80-year-olds), culture (Wales, U.K.), and life circumstances of the interactants. However, evidence of PSDs has also been found in conversations of well-educated, middle-class, community-dwelling older individuals from the midwestern United States. Shaner, Hummert, Kemper, and Vandeputte (1994) collected intergenerational and peer conversations in a manner similar to that used by Coupland et al. (1991). Conversations were coded for both painful and painless self-disclosures. Although elderly participants made fewer self-disclosures than did young ones, a higher proportion of their self-disclosures were PSDs. In addition, the older participants tended to introduce these PSDs into the conversations on their own initiative, without any prompting from the other conversant through questions or the like. In contrast, the disclosures of young participants were primarily painless and occurred in response to direct inquiries on the part of their partners.

The general notion that young people may characterize elders as rather underaccommodative has received support from other studies as well. In one such study, Williams (1992) asked a large sample of California students to describe and rate satisfying and dissatisfying intergenerational encounters. One of the four factors found to differentiate significantly between such encounters was one labeled "underaccommodative negativity." Items loading high on this factor included "The older person talked excessively and exclusively about his/her own problems" and "I didn't know what to say in return to the older person's complaints," the latter item reflecting much of the notion of accommodative dilemmas mentioned above. Furthermore, those respondents who viewed their dissatisfying encounters more in terms of an awareness of themselves as young and the older person as old (i.e., those people for whom age was salient) claimed to have endured more of this negative underaccommodation than those for whom age was not so salient.

These findings have been further endorsed in a recent study by Williams and Giles (1995). Respondents in this case, however, were Americans in their 20s commenting upon dissatisfying conversations with older partners (aged about 70). Among the underaccommodative features of the elders' conversation commented upon by more than three-fourths of the sample were their not listening, their interrupting, and their talking off-target (being out of touch and forcing unwanted topics).

Although underaccommodation from elderly to young speakers may predominate, overaccommodations to the negative aspects of young stereotypes (immaturity, lack of respect, experience, and so on) may produce old-to-young patronizing speech. Giles and Williams (1994) conducted a series of studies that examined young people's reactions to patronizing talk from older to younger adults. In the first stage of this research, undergraduates reported that they were the recipients of patronizing speech from older individuals. They were asked to describe how older people patronized them, and a content analysis of these data revealed eight main categories of old-to-young patronizing speech. The second stage of this research presented undergraduates with two examples of each of these categories and asked them to make similarity judgments of each paired combination. Multidimensional scaling analysis was then used to reveal three main clusters underlying cognitive representations of these categories. The clusters were labeled as follows: nonlistening (e.g., "The elderly don't listen to what I have to say"), disapproving (e.g., "You're all party animals!"), and overparenting (e.g., "When you get older you will see this was best").

In a third and final study in this set, a vignette was written employing these three different kinds of patronization for social evaluation by young respondents. Compared with a nonpatronizing (neutral) control, these three forms of patronization were seen very negatively by young people whether used by a 40-year-old or a 70-year-old. However, a hierarchy emerged depending on the question posed. Stereotypical disapproving was considered by young judges to convey the most negative intent, but nonlistening was considered the most difficult to manage communicatively. Overparenting was considered the least offensive of the three. Different attributions were assigned to the older targets depending on whether they were characterized as 40 or 70 years old. In short, "age envy" (characterized by comments such as "She is jealous of the young woman's youth") was more often attributed to the 40-year-old than to the 70-year-old target.

Critique and Future Directions

Relatively speaking, the study of language and aging is in its infancy, and there is much to be done. The above review demonstrates the utility of methodological diversity. Experimental methods, discourse analysis, and self-reports and surveys have all been used with considerable success.

As illustrated, most vignette studies have concentrated on patronizing speech and, arguably, one dimension of patronizing speech—a misguided attempt to nurture. Although there is no doubt that this is a crucial area of study, there is more to intergenerational language than patronizing speech per se, and perhaps there is more to patronizing speech than misguided nurturing. For example, certain features of patronizing speech may serve as a conversational "one-up" move (e.g., the use of diminutives such as "dearie"). Such insincere pseudoendearments might be used as a divergent power move in intergenerational as well as other conversations.

Although very important in its own right, the research attention given to young persons' overaccommodation to older people and the concurrent emphasis on the vignette methodology leads to both methodological and theoretical lacunae. It has been demonstrated that in some contexts, older individuals overaccommodate the young (Giles & Williams, 1994). Future research might investigate this more closely to find out its contextual range, motivations, and consequences. On the flip side, when, if ever, and why do young people underaccommodate to older people? How do patterns of intergenerational over- and underaccommodation function together to reinforce intergenerational relations in our society?

Relatedly, as we have discussed above in our review of the social cognition literature, a number of *different* positive and negative stereotypes of older people could be triggered by experimental stimuli such as voices on tapes or vignettes (Brewer et al., 1981; Hummert, Garstka, & Shaner, 1994). As yet, except for generalized person perception questions, language studies have not attempted to measure the more specific stereotypes conjured up by stimulus materials. Thus, the magnitude of results from some language studies has perhaps been confounded by the existence of multiple positive and negative stereotypes of elderly persons. This is particularly the case where stimulus materials are not designed to invoke a particular image of the older person, although some, such as Ryan's (1991) description of an elderly resident as "confused," do seem to invoke specific stereotypes. Future studies should invoke multiple stereotypes of older people and describe the variable effects on language strategies (see Hummert & Shaner, in press).

Older people are still notoriously underrepresented as respondents in language studies. In many cases, the reason for this may be a combination of the convenience of having younger populations available along with the fact that younger people are perhaps more socialized into completing lengthy questionnaires, whereas older people are more reluctant to devote time to completing such instruments, which, for many of them, may seem meaningless. We need to confront these issues and actively recruit older people to take part in our studies.

Finally, there is a pressing need to begin to bring relational variables into language studies. Almost all the language studies cited above assumed, often at an implicit level, that the conversations are taking place between strangers. Even when the conversation has been characterized in vignettes as taking place between a nurse and an institutional resident who may have some level of personal relationship, the level of intimacy in the intergenerational relationship has never been considered as an independent variable. Yet the majority of intergenerational contact occurs within the family or between younger and older individuals who know each other well. We need to address issues such as the ways in which patronizing speech functions within a family and how it may be used to negotiate changing roles across the life span.

RELATIONSHIPS

The relationships to be discussed in this section are accomplished through a complex communicative process that incorporates both cognition and language. As we age and adapt to the developmental changes in cognition and language, our relationships also change. The nature of these familial, friendship, and professional relationships and the pragmatic functions they serve have been studied by numerous social gerontologists. As will become quite evident, compared with scholars in sister disciplines, communication scholars have not invested as much research effort into unlocking the uniqueness of elderly relationships. Yet some of the most intriguing findings about marriage in later life, older adult-elderly parent relationships, older adult sibling relationships, grandparent-grandchild relationships, and elderly patient-physician relationships have emerged from our discipline. In this section we briefly review the major research findings in each of these relationship types and critically analyze the significance of these findings for scholars interested in developmental communication.

Marriage in Later Life

Perhaps no familial relationship has received more attention from social scientists than the marital relationship. Whether we like it or not, the institution of marriage is as popular today as it has ever been. However, until the past 20 years or so, most empirical studies of marriage have not included individuals past the age of 65. For whatever reason, our objective knowledge of marriage in later life is new and limited.

Three general themes of research have dominated the literature concerned with marriage in later life. The first of these centers on marital satisfaction. Two recent reviews of marital satisfaction within later-life marriages point to somewhat inconsistent findings (Mares & Fitzpatrick, 1995; Nussbaum et al., 1989). However, the authors of these reviews agree that marriages that have lasted through the honeymoon, child rearing, and middle adulthood and into later adulthood tend to be higher in satisfaction than marriages that are engaged in child rearing. It may be an oversimplification, but the research does suggest that the two highest periods of marital satisfaction are during the "honeymoon" phase and during the later-life phase. Perhaps the best explanation for this resurgence of satisfaction in an elderly marriage is the fact that the children have left home and both individuals can concentrate on the marriage once again. The research upon which these findings are based, however, is quite limited, not only in the measurement of marital satisfaction, but also in the focus on first marriages that have lasted for 40 or 50 years. The satisfaction measurement issue is not unique to elderly individuals and is a constant topic of discussion for family researchers (Mares & Fitzpatrick, 1995). The lack of studies investigating second and third marriages or new marriages past the age of 65 is indeed a serious omission within the elderly marriage literature. For instance, we know very little about why divorce rates increase for people in their 60s, what factors are associated with marital satisfaction for individuals who marry after age 60 for a second or third time, whether age of the spouse matters for elderly marital satisfaction, or whether the entire concept of marital satisfaction among those who are over age 65 is different from that for younger people.

An area of research related to the marital satisfaction literature is that concerned with the possible effects of marriage on general satisfaction with life for elderly individuals. Citing numerous studies, Nussbaum et al. (1989) report that married elderly individuals are better off than nonmarried elderly individuals because the married elderly typically have higher incomes, more emotional support, better health, lower suicide rates, and more social integration in the local community. All of these factors lead to higher levels of life satisfaction among the married elderly. The great majority of data available within this domain, however, have been collected from individuals who are not only healthy but also live above the poverty level. Once again, not much is known about elderly marriages among poor, nonhealthy individuals. A final note of some importance is the point Nussbaum et al. (1989) make concerning marital as well as life satisfaction for men versus women among this cohort of individuals. Elderly men are much more satisfied with life when they are married than are elderly women because of the amount of nurturing, care, and support provided by their spouses. This cohort of individuals formed ideas about marriage before the notion of marital equality became widespread. Although it may be true that many members of this cohort have now internalized marital equality, the fact still remains that much more care and support flows from the female toward the male than vice versa, which makes for a very comfortable situation on the part of the husband.

A second general theme of elderly marriages that dominates the research literature is a focus on the life events that occur as we age and enter later life. Events such as children completely leaving the home, retirement, physiological changes that affect sexual activity, and poor health leading to caretaking are not as common at any other stage of life. Such changes have the power to affect the marital relationship significantly (Mares & Fitzpatrick, 1995). On the positive side, as the children leave home, a couple can spend more time concentrating on the marriage. However, once retirement occurs, the retired individual has lost his or her work role and often spends a great deal of time in the home, which can result in a disruption of normal daily activities. The research is quite clear that major life events such as retirement have differential impacts upon husbands and wives. Keating and Cole (1980) found significant gender differences in perceived satisfaction with marriage after retirement, with husbands being the more satisfied partners. Just because a retired man is now at home a great deal, does not mean that he will share household duties or "permit" his wife to spend time away from him with her friends.

Perhaps the one life event that has the greatest impact on marriage is failing health. Although individuals of all ages can and do get sick, older people are most susceptible to prolonged illnesses that demand heroic caregiving. From rather simple and common viruses that may affect sexual functioning to Alzheimer's disease, the longer a marriage lasts, the more likely it is there will be a significant period of caregiving by one spouse. In their review of late-life marriages, Mares and Fitzpatrick (1995) conclude that both husbands and wives provide considerable care for their ailing spouses and seem to adjust to the caregiving role quite well. At the same time, however, the stress and physical exhaustion related to caregiving greatly affects the marriage. Communication researchers have provided no systematic information as to how prolonged caregiving affects the marital relationship. We know very little about what occurs between two individuals in their most intimate relationship as one spouse becomes ill. The effects of the illness on the communicative behavior within that relationship surely must be consequential. Short of death, there are few more significant life events than the onset of Alzheimer's disease, yet no data have emerged from the communication literature on the effects of this disease on a marriage. During the later stages of Alzheimer's, a spouse will forget he or she is married. What are the consequences of no knowledge of marriage upon the marriage?

A final theme of elderly marriages that has emerged from the literature concerns the actual communication behaviors within the marriage. In three separate reviews of elderly marriages, Sillars and Wilmot (1989), Sillars and Zietlow (1993), and Mares and Fitzpatrick (1995) lament the paucity of research that has directly investigated communicative activity within late-life marriages. Sillars and Wilmot (1989) conclude their review of literature with the speculation that older couples are likely to be more passive and congenial in their marital interactions, compared with younger couples, and that younger couples are likely to appear to be more intense and expressive. In a partial test of this hypothesis, Sillars and Zietlow (1993) studied 77 couples, including 30 couples who were retired and living at home. The results of their investigation reveal rather strong differences in communication patterns across the life span. Young couples felt that a primary function of their communication was explicit negotiation of conflict. The youngest couples had the highest percentage of "irrelevant," "analytic," and "confrontive" remarks in a conflict situation. The older couples had the highest percentage of noncommittal remarks. When salience of the discussion topic was controlled, older couples were found to be more affected than younger couples. Specifically, older couples were more confrontive when issues were salient and extremely congenial when topics were nonsalient. A final finding of this investigation was that older couples had a much stronger tendency to reciprocate confrontive remarks by a partner than did couples from other age groups. The older couples were more likely to escalate their conflicts when confrontive remarks entered the discussion. Sillars and Zietlow conclude their article by reshaping their earlier assumption that older couples would be more passive and congenial with the statement that no evidence exists that as our marriages age we become less communicatively active. Indeed, explicit conversation retains a vital function in late-life marriages.

Adult Child-Elderly Parent Relationship

A common myth about the aging process is that elderly individuals eventually become alienated from their families. Essentially, this suggests that close family members begin ignoring their elderly relatives once they become a burden. The family members who have been most demeaned by this alienation myth are adult children. An additional myth, which at times surfaces in popular media outlets, centers on elderly parents' becoming an economic burden whose sole purpose is to spend the money of younger generations. On the one hand, adult children are supposedly ignoring their parents; on the other, parents are spending their children into poverty. These myths are not only destructive, they are very far from the truth (Nussbaum et al., 1989). The great majority of adult child-elderly parent relationships remain strong and vital until they can no longer function as a result of death. Cicirelli (1981) reports that nearly 90% of the 78%-90% of the elderly population who have adult children report close or very close relationships with them. Numerous studies indicate that more than 90% of elderly parents visit or speak to each of their adult children at least once a week (Cicirelli, 1983a, 1983b; Shanas, 1979; Troll, 1971). Indeed, the myth of alienation between adult children and their elderly parents is simply not supported by the facts.

The parent-child relationship can last 70 years or even longer. Two theories have been advanced to explain the dynamic characteristics of this lifelong relationship. Bengtson, Olander, and Haddad (1976) originally proposed a model of family solidarity based upon sociological work within small group dynamics. The theory of intergenerational solidarity places emphasis upon close contact, affection, and agreement on values, beliefs, and opinions. The adult child-elderly parent relationship remains strong because the participants constantly contact one another, show affection toward each other, and reach some consensus on values, beliefs, and opinions.

A second theory advanced to explain the lifelong nature of this relationship has a much more psychological flavor. Cicirelli (1991) has extended attachment theory (Bowlby, 1979, 1980) through the life span. Life-span attachment is an internal feeling that parents and children feel toward one another that leads to various attachment behaviors. In an excellent review of attachment theory in old age, Cicirelli discusses numerous studies that document attachment behavior well into old age. After the first few years of life, attachment behaviors begin to include communication, and this communicative behavior gains significance throughout the life span. As crying, clinging, and proximity-seeking behaviors wane in childhood, these behaviors are replaced by writing, telephoning, and frequent visits in adulthood. Cicirelli (1981) posits that symbolic attachment emerges in adulthood: "In symbolic attachment, the adult child is able to use covert thoughts to symbolize or represent the attachment figure and thereby experience closeness and imagined communication on a psychological level" (p. 30). When adults find it impossible to communicate with their parents, symbolic attachment serves to maintain the close child-parent bond.

The majority of investigations attempting to describe the adult child-elderly parent relationship have concentrated upon the caregiving function of the adult child. Although it is true that parents care for their children much more than children care for their parents, the time often comes when the responsibility of giving aid shifts from the parents to the children. The literature is rich with solid investigations showing that when parents have physical or emotional needs, adult children are there to provide for those needs (Cicirelli, 1981; Troll, 1986). Factors such as residential proximity, attachment, filial obligation, economic well-being, number of children, parental attitudes toward receiving help, sex of the child, and type of aid needed all affect the aid given to parents, but, for the most part, adult children do a remarkable job of caring for their parents. Troll (1986) notes simply that adult children "provide more care and more difficult care over a much longer time than such children did in the 'good old days' " (p. 83).

Social gerontologists have conducted a great deal of research investigating numerous aspects of the adult child-elderly parent relationship. Several of these scholars have explicitly called for more research into the communicative behaviors shared within this relationship. Cicirelli (1981) has gone so far as to predict that shared communication may be the primary predictor of whether adult children know their parents are in need and whether aid will be provided. In addition, both intergenerational solidarity theory and life-span attachment theory consider communication to be a central component in the life-span nature of the child-parent relationship. Communication researchers, however, have not responded to this call for action. At this point in time, our knowledge of the communicative behaviors shared by elderly parents and their adult children is limited.

Henwood (1995) has written an exceptional article outlining the significant contribution a communication scholar can make to our understanding of the older adult-elderly parent relationship. From a feminist, discursive perspective, she discusses the older daughter-mother relationship as the participants attempt to construct family order and relational identity. The very nature of the mother-daughter relationship changes as those involved in the relationship age. Through communication, these changes are negotiated and a reconstructed relationship emerges. In the most simple sense, as adults age into later life, the relational power within their child-parent relationships shifts. Each daughter and each son must come to grips with this power shift through interaction with her or his parents. This relationship provides the perfect context for studying the reconstruction of relational identities through the shifting power dynamics of the relationship across the life span.

Grandparent-Grandchild Relationship

As our average life span has steadily increased throughout this century, several relationships have become more common and taken on additional meaning. One such relationship is the grandparent-grandchild relationship. Nussbaum et al. (1989) report that 75% of all individuals over the age of 65 are grandparents. Individuals may become grandparents when they are as young as 30 years of age, thus, grandparenting is not a role only for those who are considered elderly. Several excellent reviews of the grandparent-grandchild literature exist (Bengtson & Robertson, 1985; Cherlin & Furstenberg, 1986; Downs, 1989; McKay, 1995); each highlights not only the complexity of the relationship but also the major function it plays in the modern family.

A recurring theme in the grandparenthood literature centers on the diverse and heterogeneous nature of the grandparent role. Troll (1983) portrays the grandparent as the "family watchdog" who is called upon when a family crisis or emergency arises. In effect, grandparents relinquish control and assistance in the rearing of their grandchildren during normal family functioning, but take an active role in times of family crisis. Troll (1983), Kivinck (1981), Cherlin and Furstenberg (1986), and others have attempted to uncover distinct styles of grandparenting, to point toward the different ways grandparents functions within families. Styles such as the "fun seeker," the "surrogate parent," and the "distant figure" have emerged in the literature. Although attempts have been made to link these styles to successful aging and to successful grandparenting, no research has been able to establish any such links.

In a rather controversial article, Kornhaber (1985) argues that "a great many grandparents have given up emotional attachments to their grandchildren. They have ceded the power to determine their grandparenting relationship to the grandchild's parents and, in effect, have turned their back on an entire generation" (p. 159). The research evidence, however, does not support this notion of grandparents "giving up" on an active role within the family. The reviews listed above document that the grandparent-grandchild relationship is strong and that the attachment formed when the grandchild is born remains strong throughout the life of the grandparent.

Two factors that do have some impact upon the grandparent-grandchild relationship are sex of the grandparent and age of the grandparent. Nussbaum et al. (1989) report that the grandmothers in their study were more likely to have warm, close relationships with their grandchildren, whereas grandfathers tended to be more concerned with financial matters and played more often with their grandchildren once the children reached a mature age. There also appears to be an age factor in how grandparents perceive their grandchildren. Grandparents in their 40s or 80s were more critical when describing their grandchildren, whereas grandparents in their 50s, 60s, and 70s were more likely to say good things.

To test one possible communicative result of the sex difference, Nussbaum and Bettini (1994) asked grandparents and their young adult grandchildren to share stories that captured the meaning of life for them. Grandfathers for the most part told stories of war or work experiences to both granddaughters and grandsons. Grandmothers told stories of the joys of family life and of simply interacting with grandchildren. The grandparents did not change their stories in any meaningful way depending on the sex of the grandchildren. Inasmuch as these life stories functioned to educate and inform grandchildren as well as to define the nature of this relationship, this investigation represents one exploratory step toward uncovering the communicative implications that the grandparent-grandchild relationship has for the participants. An interesting side note that emerged from this study was the lack of storytelling on the part of the grandchildren. The grandchildren reported extreme anxiety when attempting to share their stories, and none of the 120 grandchild subjects completed the assignment.

Elderly Sibling Relationships

Of the four major family relationships, the elderly sibling relationship has produced the least amount of scholarly research. For excellent reviews of this literature, see Cicirelli and Nussbaum (1989) and Cicirelli (1991). The sibling relationship has been described as one of the most intriguing, dynamic relationships that individuals maintain throughout their lives. Nussbaum et al. (1989) write that the sibling relationship is the very best example of a life-span developmental relationship; it can be viewed as the most enduring familial bond, with the potential to last longer than any other relationship. Cicirelli (1982) reports that more than 90% of individuals living beyond age 65 have at least one living sibling. Cicirelli and Nussbaum (1989) point to the uniqueness of this relationship in that siblings share a complex, yet similar, history spanning every phase of life. The great majority of siblings share a common biology as well as a common environment.

Several dimensions of the elderly sibling relationship have been explored in the literature. Sibling closeness has been linked to gender composition of the dyad, marital status, and contact. Elderly siblings in relationships with a female composition report closer relationships than sibling dyads with a purely male composition. In addition, elderly siblings who are widowed or single report closer sibling relationships than do married siblings. Finally, closeness is related to shared contact. Closer elderly siblings report spending more time with one another (Cicirelli, 1991).

This concept of shared contact has produced numerous investigations into elderly sibling relationships. The findings indicate that as siblings age past 65, their contact increases. Several authors have speculated that once their children have left home, individuals seek out their own siblings for a more intense feeling of family. The siblings who have the most contact in old age are those who live close to one another; are single, widowed, or divorced; have no children at home; and are sisters. As noted above, this contact is then related to feelings of closeness.

A third dimension of the elderly sibling relationship that has received research attention centers on social support. Connidis (1989) reports that siblings are called upon to offer various forms of social support. A minority of elderly siblings actually report receiving help, but the great majority report being available to give help if needed. Individuals with more than one sibling report receiving more help from a sibling than do individuals with only one sibling. Finally, there is some evidence to suggest that the sibling relationship in old age provides for psychological needs in the areas of intimacy and self-esteem more than any other familial or friendship relationship (Simons, 1984).

Older Adult Friendships

Within the past several years, a number of books have been published that report upon the latest findings and original research into older adult friendships (Adams & Blieszner, 1989; Blieszner & Adams, 1992; Matthews, 1986; Rawlins, 1992). These books reflect the interdisciplinary nature of study into friendships across the life span; only one was written by a scholar within the communication discipline (Rawlins, 1992). The older adult friendship literature reflects several different streams of research. Throughout the 1970s and 1980s, the friendship relationship emerged as a critical predictor of life satisfaction for elderly individuals. The fact that close friendships are more strongly associated with well-being than are family relationships was rather shocking. Nussbaum et al. (1989) conclude that the literature is quite clear that close friendships play an important role in the psychological adjustment and morale of our elderly population.

Kahn and Antonucci (1980) and Crohan and Antonucci (1989) have developed a "convoy" theory of social support to help explain the positive relationship between older adult friendship and well-being. As we progress through the life span, those of us who are surrounded by a convoy of significant relational partners with whom we can exchange support will be better suited to adapt to life's various crises. The friendship relationship serves older individuals better than certain familial relationships because of its nonobligatory as well as egalitarian nature. Social support is given freely by friends, with very few of the strings often attached to familial support. When support is part of a friendship relationship, it is given or received in a manner that positively affects daily life.

Social support within a friendship relationship serves several important functions in later life. First, friends help to maintain an individual's contact with the larger society; often, an individual's first visit to a senior center is friendship related. Second, friendship in later life is an excellent buffer against overwhelming feelings of loneliness and depression that result from significant loss as we age. Third, friendship can provide a very secure context in which declining health can be managed. Finally, friendships can provide emotional support that may no longer be available from family members (Nussbaum et al., 1989).

A second area of older adult friendship research has involved the attempt to describe the structural components of friendship. Research that has investigated the internal structure of older adult friendships is quite contradictory. No clear patterns have emerged as to whether the size of an elderly individual's friendship network or the homogeneity, density, or feelings of solidarity within that network affect the overall well-being of the individual. One solid, close friend appears to serve as well as an entire network of friends. Nussbaum et al. (1989) discuss the enormous effect that external structural factors have upon the formation and maintenance of close friendship bonds. Factors such as failing health, loss of mobility, moving out of town, institutionalization, and family interference often have negative impacts on the friendship relationship. The external factors are reasoned to affect older adult friendships more than younger friendships because of the unique effects of age upon an individual's freedom to interact.

The work of Rawlins (1992) has had significant impact on social gerontologists who study older adult friendships. Rawlins views friendship as an ongoing communicative achievement, a relationship that is constantly negotiated in the face of incompatible requirements. Results from his extensive study of friendship across the life span indicate that managing the inherent contradictions of friendship remains a major feature of friendship into old age. The dialectics that appear to be most salient for older adult friendships include the dialectic of the freedom to be independent versus dependent, the dialectic of judgment and acceptance, and the dialectic of expressiveness and protectiveness (Rawlins, 1992). This study is an impressive example of communication scholarship within the general domain of elderly friendships because it is methodologically sound as well as theoretically rich.

Additional research conducted by scholars within the discipline of communication has attempted to uncover the changing nature of friendship as we age (Nussbaum, 1994; Patterson, Bettini, & Nussbaum, 1993). In-depth interviews with both young and old adults concerning what friendship means to them have produced several interesting findings. Older adults who were interviewed discussed friendship as having many more levels of closeness than did younger adults. In other words, younger adults make a clear distinction between best friends and all other friends. Older adults report many different levels of closeness for best friends that serve different functions. A second finding helps to explain how older adults can remain separated from their friends for long periods and still report them as being close friends. In old age, consistent and frequent communicative contact with friends may not be as important as that contact is for young adults. Older adults are able to maintain their close friendships without a regular pattern of interaction. Young adult friendships are much more dependent upon frequent conversation.

The Elderly Patient-Physician Relationship

A professional relationship that has received an impressive amount of attention from social scientists because of its important role in the lives of older adults is the elderly patient-physician relationship. As with all of the other relationships discussed in this section, several excellent reviews of the pertinent literature exist (e.g., Beisecker & Thompson, 1995; Haug & Ory, 1987). It is wrong to assume that all elderly individuals are unhealthy and so must interact constantly with physicians. However, as individuals age beyond 75, the probability that they will interact with physicians begins to increase significantly. Data indicate that individuals beyond the age of 65 visit physicians an average of eight times per year, whereas younger individuals visit five times a year (U.S. Senate Special Committee on Aging, 1991).

The research literature focusing upon elderly patient-physician interaction indicates that this relationship may be qualitatively different from younger patient-physician interaction. There are two factors that make this proposition plausible. First, the physiological factors that bring the patient to the physician in the first place are quite different as we age. Second, the older patient experiences health care in ways very different from those of younger patients. Perhaps the most devastating difference between younger and older patients' physiological difficulties is the probability of cure. Younger patients simply recover at higher rates than do elderly patients, who are more likely to suffer chronic as opposed to acute disease (Adelman, Greene, & Charon, 1991). Within the actual experience of health care, younger patients ask questions more frequently, talk about their problems more, give information in more detail, and are more assertive than elderly patients (Beisecker & Thompson, 1995). In addition, research has pointed to possible ageism on the part of some physicians; some not only have negative attitudes toward their elderly patients, but have been found to be more condescending, abrupt, and indifferent to older patients than to younger ones (Adelman et al., 1991).

Elderly patient outcome variables have received considerable attention from health care researchers. In general, elderly patients are satisfied both with their care and their relationships with their physicians (Beisecker & Thompson, 1995). A second outcome variable of extreme importance is patient compliance. Elderly patients' compliance with their physicians' wishes has been discussed as a major problem within the health care literature (Thompson, 1994). In general, a relationship has been found between elderly patient compliance and physician communication behavior. Physicians who take the time to explain treatment or medication regimens and who adapt their language to the level of understanding of their patients have higher rates of compliance.

Beisecker (1989) investigated the health care consequences of having a third person involved in the health care encounter between elderly patient and physician. It is not uncommon for an elderly individual to bring a companion along to the physician's office. Research is rather new in this regard, but the evidence does seem to indicate that a companion can aid the patient-physician interaction. Companions have been found to ask important questions during the examination and can be utilized by the physician to gain compliance from the patient once the examination is over. That said, there are also dangers of the patient becoming depersonalized, as the physician and companion may discuss the patient as if he or she were not present.

Critique and Future Directions

The research reviewed within this section is quite extensive and often quite sound. However, we wish to make some critical comments about that research as well as point to specific directions for future research.

The research literature concerning marriages of all lengths and ages suffers from several weaknesses. Two of the major problems in this literature are overly simple operationalizations of "marital satisfaction" and the reliance upon couples in stress as research participants. The literature that focuses on marriage among elderly couples has the additional problem of not investigating issues such as second or third marriages, new marriages after the age of 65, and the unique nature of the marital relationship as we age into later life.

Direct observation of the communicative behaviors of older couples is very sparse. There are considerable design difficulties for researchers interested in capturing ongoing communication within a late-life marriage, however, the interesting findings of Sillars and Zietlow (1993) give some insight into the richness of such investigations. It is obvious that numerous questions need to be addressed. After 30 or 40 years of marriage, just what do couples talk about? Are there communicative differences in newly married 20-year-olds versus newly married 70-year-olds? How do individuals who have spent the majority of their lives together negotiate conflict? Can we uncover cohort differences in the communicative behavior of couples married in the 1930s versus those married in the 1950s? And perhaps the most important question of all: Do couples manage their marriages differently as they age, and, if so, how does communication function in this process?

The literature examining the grandparent-grandchild relationship has focused mainly on the role of the grandparent within the extended family. The various functions grandparenthood serves and the possibilities of positive feelings this role produces for the grandparent have received considerable attention. There is considerable room, however, for communication scholars to utilize their unique perspectives and methodologies to enhance our understanding of the grandparent-grandchild relationship. In contrast to the social circumstances at the turn of the century, this relationship now has the potential to last 50 years or more. Thus, numerous redefinitions of the relationship will occur. No scholars have attempted to track these relational redefinitions, as evidenced in the changing communicative behavior of the relationship. Simple descriptive research documenting how different grandparents talk to different grandchildren in various types of family situations has not received any research attention. The way different styles of grandparenting are communicatively acted out has not received any research attention. Perhaps most important, research has not concentrated on the grandchild as an active participant within this relationship. Though many social scientists, government officials, and commentators on modern life have discussed the importance of values within the family, the individuals most responsible for passing on those values within the modern family, the grandparents, and those who can be most influenced by this continuity of value exchange, the grandchildren, have been neglected as active partners in the creation of family values. Finally, the unique position of the grandparent-grandchild relationship within the family creates several interesting communication dilemmas. For instance, how do parents discipline their children when grandparents are offering advice? How is power negotiated among grandparent, parent, and grandchild? What happens to all of these relationships when a great-grandchild arrives?

As we have mentioned, social scientists have produced scant research on the elderly sibling relationship. In addition, that research has been neither theoretically rich nor methodologically sophisticated. The great majority of studies have used simple frequency counts of contact or one-item measures of relational closeness. The research does not capture the rich feelings and emotions that exist within this lifelong bond. In addition, although solidarity theories and attachment theories have been borrowed to explain the closeness shared within the sibling pair, these theories have not been extended to fit the unique qualities of this relationship. Much like several other life-span relationships, the sibling relationship functions quite differently at various points in the life span. The negotiation that takes place within the sibling pair to redefine the relationship throughout the life span has been virtually ignored. As families change and more step-siblings grow up together, it is reasonable to expect blended families to produce relationships unlike those that are now studied within our literature. To this point, researchers investigating elderly siblings are not in tune with future generations of sibling relationships.

The older adult friendship literature is methodologically sophisticated and diverse. Experimental studies, survey research, and qualitative work that utilizes discourse as well as ethnographic methods can be found within this literature. Good progress has been made during the past 20 years in attempts to explain the positive relationship between friendship and psychological well-being. In addition, solid work has been performed in describing how elderly individuals negotiate their friendships and manage to keep them vital. Communication researchers have made significant contributions to the older adult friendship literature and have laid a solid foundation for future contributions.

The major strength of research investigating the elderly patient-physician relationship is its methodological diversity. Experimental methods, survey research, discourse analysis, and various conversation-analytic techniques have all been utilized in appropriate ways to answer the research questions posed. In addition, many of these studies have been conducted by scholars within the communication discipline, who tend to ask questions beyond mere frequency counts of interaction or simple measures of satisfaction. A weakness that can be found in this literature is a result of the applied demands of those who are involved in the interactions. Physicians desperately need advice about and examples of competent communication. Therefore, many studies have attempted to produce checklists of behaviors that physicians can simply enact to improve their performance. These studies have tended to create a very simple, linear interactive world for physicians and patients, ignoring the dynamic, interactive nature of their relationships. Checklists of appropriate behaviors tend to stifle the dynamism of the physician-patient relationship and do more harm than good. Communication researchers are in the perfect position to point out the complexity of the relationship and to design sound investigations to capture this complexity.

FUTURE TRENDS, AGENDAS, AND POSSIBILITIES

In the previous sections of this chapter we have reviewed, synthesized, and critically analyzed the communication and aging literature in the areas of cognition, language, and relationships. Within each section, we have highlighted the strengths and weaknesses of the literature and have made suggestions for possible future research. In this final section, we wish to go beyond the various programmatic research efforts within each general area to broaden the scope and range of our attempts to understand the communication and aging process.

As may be obvious from the review above, a major strength of this literature is its interdisciplinary nature. For the most part, psychologists and sociologists dominate the cognition and relationship literatures, whereas sociolinguists and communication scholars play a much more active role in the study of language. The interdisciplinary nature of the research, nevertheless, has played, and can continue to play, a very positive role in our attempts to understand how elderly people produce, and are affected by, communication in later life. Scholars trained in different methodological and theoretical traditions bring with them a healthy diversity of ideas that, when shared, produce a higher level of inquiry. All scholars who wish to make substantial contributions to the literature concerning communication and aging must read outside the artificial walls built around their particular disciplines.

The separation of the three areas of research reviewed in this chapter is artificial. The clever reader has not only observed the inherent overlap within the research, but quite possibly has already made note that all of these scholars need to meet and work on a more unifying perspective. After all, language cannot be produced in any meaningful way without cognitions, relationships are not possible without language that reshapes our cognitions, and so on. On top of all of this interplay among cognition, language, and relationship is the fact that the particular human beings having the cognitions, producing the language, and pursuing the relationships have fascinating life histories that may affect the entire process of communication. Indeed, the one indisputable fact that emerges from the literature is that as we age and experience life, our lives change. The explanations that help us understand the links among cognition, language, and relationships in college-age subjects may have little meaning for individuals past the age of 65. Each of us can observe and experience the physiological and biological changes that occur throughout our life span. It is more difficult to observe or understand the psychosocial and communicative changes that also occur. By this we do not mean to imply that our communicative lives must decline just as our bodies appear to decline. Among the most interesting aspects of communication within elderly populations are the constant adaptations occurring that make life better. As we age, our thoughts, beliefs, and values can be refined, our language can better express our thoughts and can be produced in a much more competent manner, and our relationships can mature.

A perspective that incorporates not only multiple methodologies but also multiple theories into the study of communication is the life-span developmental perspective (Coupland & Nussbaum, 1993; Nussbaum, 1989). Several assumptions of this perspective can help to reframe common notions of communication that appear in our literature and, at the same time, help to emphasize the importance of research concerned with elderly communication. An important assumption of life-span development is that no one period in life is more important than any other period of life. Developmental scholars, including those in communication, have long discussed the importance of infancy and childhood development. Life-span developmentalists do not believe that early development is more important than development at any other point in life. Our parents may be as important to our well-being when we are 40 as they were when we were infants. The concept of well-being will change as we age, and we may need further investigation to uncover the importance of the role any relationship plays in that well-being. A second assumption of life-span development is that change occurs throughout life. Early theories of human development postulated that development, or at least the interesting components of development, occurs entirely by the time an individual is 13 years old. The research reported in this chapter shows quite clearly that phenomenal changes in cognition, language, and relationships occur in later life. The cognitive changes in an older adult's brain are as important for us to attend to as similar changes in an infant's brain. Our task is to document all such changes and aim for understandings that transcend age boundaries to achieve theories of life-span cognitive development. From such theories, our understandings of life-span communication will broaden and deepen.

As mentioned above, the most enticing component of the life-span developmental perspective is its acceptance of multiple methods and diverse theoretical perspectives that can be utilized to help us understand communication and older adulthood. The research synthesized and critically analyzed in this chapter has made use of experimental methods, survey methods, clinical case methods, discourse analysis, ethnomethodology, and conversation analysis. No method is viewed as the only method useful for capturing communication and aging. In addition, numerous theories have been incorporated to explain the communication process for elderly individuals. Communication accommodation theory, the communication predicament of aging model, life-span attachment theory, and intergenerational solidarity theory have all been helpful in our attempts to understand elderly communicative behavior. This acceptance of diversity creates a research climate of inclusion rather than exclusion. All valid research is considered in serious, scholarly discussions, rather than being dismissed because of methodological or theoretical biases.

Perhaps the most significant point that we wish to make in this review is the central role of *communication* in the aging process. To reach a reasonable understanding of human aging, one must be aware of the *social* nature of development. Research evidence strongly indicates that as we age, our communicative behaviors change, as do the types of communication directed toward us. Our physical as well as psychological well-being is often dependent upon our ability to adapt to these changes and to produce language and maintain relationships that accomplish those goals necessary to our survival. Communication scholars are in a rather unique position to join with other scholars to provide a much richer explanation of the aging process.

A final possibility for communication scholars exists within the larger community of scientists who at this moment are attempting to explain longevity in the human species. The simplest explanations, as well as the explanations that make most sense to a technologically sophisticated society, center on biology: If an individual has "good genes," he or she will live a long time. Social scientists have shown that longevity may have as much to do with changes in public health and lifelong patterns of behavior as it does with good genes (Friedman et al., 1995). Most important, these are elements that are within our power to change— maintaining a positive outlook on life and nurturing positive relationships are goals we can all actively pursue. We can think of no more important task than to tie our research into predicting and promoting successful living.

REFERENCES

Adams, R. G., & Blieszner, R. (Eds.). (1989). *Older adult friendship: Structure and process.* Newbury Park, CA: Sage.

Adelman, R. D., Greene, M. G., & Charon, R. (1991). Issues in physician-elderly patient interaction. *Ageing and Society, 11,* 127-148.

American Association of Retired Persons. (1991). *A profile of older Americans: 1990.* Washington, DC: Author.

Arbuckle, T., & Gold, D. P. (1993). Aging, inhibition, and verbosity. *Journal of Gerontology: Psychological Sciences, 48,* 225-232.

Beisecker, A. E. (1989). The influence of a companion on the doctor-elderly patient interaction. *Health Communication, 1,* 55-70.

Beisecker, A. E., & Thompson, T. L. (1995). The elderly patient-physician interaction. In J. F. Nussbaum & J. Coupland (Eds.), *Handbook of communication and aging research.* Hillsdale, NJ: Lawrence Erlbaum.

Bengtson, V. L., Olander, G., & Haddad, A. A. (1976). The generation gap and aging family members: Toward a conceptual model. In J. J. Gubrium (Ed.), *Time, roles, and self in old age* (pp. 237-263). New York: Human Sciences Press.

Bengtson, V. L., & Robertson, J. F. (Eds.). (1985). *Grandparenthood.* Beverly Hills, CA: Sage.

Berger, C. R., & Bradac, J. J. (1982). *Language and social knowledge.* London: Edward Arnold.

Blieszner, R., & Adams, R. G. (1992). *Adult friendship.* Newbury Park, CA: Sage.

Boden, D., & Bielby, D. (1983). The past as resource: A conversational analysis of elderly talk. *Human Development, 26,* 308-319.

Bowlby, J. (1979). *The making and breaking of affectual bonds.* London: Tavistock.

Bowlby, J. (1980). *Attachment and loss: Loss, stress, and depression.* New York: Basic Books.

Braithwaite, V. A. (1986). Old age stereotypes: Reconciling contradictions. *Journal of Gerontology, 41,* 353-360.

Brewer, M. B., Dull, V., & Lui, L. (1981). Perceptions of the elderly: Stereotypes as prototypes. *Journal of Personality and Social Psychology, 41,* 656-670.

Burke, D. M., & Laver, G. D. (1990). Aging and word retrieval: Selective age deficits in language. In E. A. Lovelace (Ed.), *Aging and cognition: Mental processes, self-awareness, and interventions* (pp. 281-300). New York: Elsevier North-Holland.

Burke, D. M., MacKay, D. G., Worthley, J. S., & Wade, E. (1991). On the tip of the tongue: What causes word finding failures in young and older adults? *Journal of Memory and Language, 30,* 542-579.

Burton, A. M., & Bruce, V. (1992). I recognize your face but I can't remember your name: A simple explanation? *British Journal of Psychology, 83,* 45-60.

Canary, D., & Spitzberg, B. (1989). A model of the perceived competence of conflict strategies. *Human Communication Research, 15,* 630-649.

Caporael, L. R. (1981). The paralanguage of caregiving: Baby talk to the institutionalized aged. *Journal of Personality and Social Psychology, 40,* 876-884.

Caporael, L. R., & Culbertson, G. H. (1986). Verbal response modes of baby talk and other speech at institutions for the aged. *Language and Communication, 6,* 99-112.

Carver, C. S., & de la Garza, N. H. (1984). Schema guided information search in stereotyping of the elderly. *Journal of Applied Social Psychology, 14,* 69-81.

Chang, B. L., Chang, A. F., & Yung, A. S. (1984). Attitudes toward aging in the United States and Taiwan. *Journal of Comparative Family Studies, 15,* 109-130.

Cherlin, A., & Furstenberg, F. F. (1986). *The new American grandparent: A place in the family, a life apart.* New York: Basic Books.

Cicirelli, V. G. (1981). *Helping elderly parents: The role of adult children.* Boston: Auburn House.

Cicirelli, V. G. (1982). Sibling influence throughout the lifespan. In M. E. Lamb & B. Sutton Smith (Eds.), *Sibling relationships: Their nature and significance across the lifespan* (pp. 267-284). Hillsdale, NJ: Lawrence Erlbaum.

Cicirelli, V. G. (1983a). Adult children and their elderly parents. In T. H. Brubaker (Ed.), *Family relationships in later life* (pp. 47-62). Beverly Hills, CA: Sage.

Cicirelli, V. G. (1983b). Adult children's attachment and helping behavior to elderly parents: A path model. *Journal of Marriage and the Family, 45,* 815-823.

Cicirelli, V. G. (1991). Sibling relationships in adulthood. *Marriage and Family Review, 16,* 291-310.

Cicirelli, V. G., & Nussbaum, J. F. (1989). Relationships with siblings in later life. In J. F. Nussbaum (Ed.), *Lifespan communication: Normative processes* (pp. 283-297). Hillsdale, NJ: Lawrence Erlbaum.

Cohen, G. (1992). Why is it difficult to put names to faces? *British Journal of Psychology, 81,* 287-297.

Cohen, G. (1994). Age-related problems in the use of proper names in communication. In M. L. Hummert, J. M. Wiemann, & J. F. Nussbaum (Eds.), *Interpersonal communication in older adulthood: Interdisciplinary theory and research* (pp. 40-57). Thousand Oaks, CA: Sage.

Cohen, G., & Faulkner, D. (1986a). Does "elderspeak" work? The effect of intonation and stress on comprehension and recall of spoken discourse in old age. *Language and Communication, 6,* 91-98.

Cohen, G., & Faulkner, D. (1986b). Memory for proper names: Age differences in retrieval. *British Journal of Developmental Psychology, 4,* 187-197.

Connidis, I. A. (1989). Contact between siblings in later life. *Canadian Journal of Sociology, 14,* 429-442.

Corso, J. F. (1977). Auditory perception and communication. In J. E. Birren & K. W. Schaie (Eds.), *Handbook of the psychology of aging* (pp. 535-553). New York: Van Nostrand Reinhold.

Corso, J. F. (1987). Sensory-perceptual processes and aging. In K. W. Schaie (Ed.), *Annual review of gerontology and geriatrics* (Vol. 7, pp. 29-56). New York: Springer.

Coupland, N., & Coupland, J. (1990). Language and later life. In H. Giles & W. P. Robinson (Eds.), *Handbook of language and social psychology* (pp. 451-468). London: John Wiley.

Coupland, N., Coupland, J., & Giles, H. (1991). *Language, society and the elderly.* Oxford: Basil Blackwell.

Coupland, N., Coupland, J., Giles, H., & Henwood, K. (1988). Accommodating the elderly: Invoking and extending a theory. *Language and Society, 17,* 1-41.

Coupland, N., Henwood, K., Coupland, J., & Giles, H. (1990). Accommodating troubles talk: The young's management of elderly self-disclosure. In G. M. McGregor & R. White (Eds.), *Reception and response: Hearer creativity and analysis of spoken and written texts* (pp. 112-144). London: Croom Helm.

Coupland, N., & Nussbaum, J. F. (Eds.). (1993). *Discourse and lifespan identity.* Newbury Park, CA: Sage.

Crockett, W. H., & Hummert, M. L. (1987). Perceptions of aging and the elderly. In K. W. Schaie (Ed.), *Annual review of gerontology and geriatrics* (Vol. 7, pp. 217-241). New York: Springer.

Crohan, S. E., & Antonucci, T. C. (1989). Friends as a source of social support in old age. In R. G. Adams & R. Blieszner (Eds.), *Older adult friendship: Structure and process* (pp. 129-146). Newbury Park, CA: Sage.

Crook, T. H., & West, R. L. (1990). Name-recall performance across the adult lifespan. *British Journal of Psychology, 81,* 335-349.

Daneman, M., & Carpenter, P. A. (1980). Individual differences in working memory and reading. *Journal of Verbal Learning and Verbal Behavior, 19,* 450-466.

Delia, J. G., O'Keefe, B. J., & O'Keefe, D. J. (1982). The constructivist approach to communication. In F. E. X. Dance (Ed.), *Human communication theory* (pp. 147-191). New York: Harper & Row.

Downs, V. C. (1989). The grandparent-grandchild relationship. In J. F. Nussbaum (Ed.), *Lifespan communication: Normative processes* (pp. 257-281). Hillsdale, NJ: Lawrence Erlbaum.

Edwards, H., & Noller, P. (1993). Perceptions of over-accommodation used by nurses in communication with the elderly. *Journal of Language and Social Psychology, 12,* 207-223.

Fox, S., & Giles, H. (1993). Accommodating intergenerational contact: A critique and theoretical model. *Journal of Aging Studies, 7,* 423-451.

Franklyn-Stokes, A., Harriman, J., Giles, H., & Coupland, N. (1988). Information-seeking across the lifespan. *Journal of Social Psychology, 128,* 419-421.

Friedman, H. S., Tucker, J. S., Schwartz, J. E., Tomlinson-Keasey, C., Martin, L. R., Wingard, D. L., & Criqui, M. H. (1995). Psychosocial and behavioral predictors of longevity. *American Psychologist, 50,* 69-78.

Giles, H., Coupland, N., Henwood, K., Harriman, J., & Coupland, J. (1990). The social meaning of R.P.: An intergenerational perspective. In S. Ramsaran (Ed.), *Studies in the pronunciation of English: A commemorative volume in honor of A. C. Gimson* (pp. 191-221). London: Routledge.

Giles, H., Coupland, N., & Wiemann, J. M. (Eds.). (1990). *Communication, health and the elderly.* Manchester: Manchester University Press.

Giles, H., Coupland, N., & Wiemann, J. M. (1991). "Talk is cheap" but "my word is my bond": Beliefs about talk. In K. Bolton & H. Kwock (Eds.), *Sociolinguistics today: Eastern and Western perspectives* (pp. 218-243). London: Routledge.

Giles, H., Fox, S., & Smith, E. (1993). Patronizing the elderly: Intergenerational evaluations. *Research in Language and Social Interaction, 26,* 129-149.

Giles, H., Henwood, K., Coupland, N., Harriman, J., & Coupland, J. (1992). Language attitudes and cognitive mediation. *Human Communication Research, 18,* 500-527.

Giles, H., Mulac, A., Bradac, J. J., & Johnson, P. (1987). Speech accommodation theory: The first decade and beyond. In M. L. McLaughlin (Ed.), *Communication yearbook 10* (pp. 13-48). Newbury Park, CA: Sage.

Giles, H., & Williams, A. (1994). Patronizing the young: Forms and evaluations. *International Journal of Aging and Human Development, 39,* 33-53.

Gold, D. P., Arbuckle, T. Y., & Andres, D. (1994). Verbosity in older adults. In M. L. Hummert, J. M. Wiemann, & J. F. Nussbaum (Eds.), *Interpersonal communication in older adulthood: Interdisciplinary theory and research* (pp. 107-129). Thousand Oaks, CA: Sage.

Grainger, K., Atkinson, K., & Coupland, N. (1990). Responding to the elderly: Troubles-talk in the caring context. In H. Giles, N. Coupland, & J. M. Wiemann (Eds.), *Communication, health and the elderly* (pp. 192-212). Manchester: Manchester University Press.

Green, S. K. (1981). Attitudes and perceptions about the elderly: Current and future perspectives. *International Journal of Aging and Human Development, 13,* 99-119.

Louis Harris & Associates. (1975). *The myth and reality of aging in America.* Washington, DC: National Council on Aging.

Harwood, J., Giles, H., Fox, S., Ryan, E. B., & Williams, A. (1993). Patronizing young and elderly adults: Response strategies in a community setting. *Journal of Applied Communication Research, 21,* 211-226.

Haug, M. R., & Ory, M. G. (1987). Issues in elderly patient-provider interactions. *Research on Aging, 9,* 3-44.

Heckhausen, J., Dixon, R. A., & Baltes, P. B. (1989). Gains and losses in development throughout adulthood as perceived by different adult age groups. *Developmental Psychology, 25,* 109-121.

Henwood, K. L. (1995). Adult parent-child relationships: A view from feminist and discoursive social psychology. In J. F. Nussbaum & J. Coupland (Eds.), *Handbook of communication and aging research.* Hillsdale, NJ: Lawrence Erlbaum.

Howard, D. V. (1983). *Cognitive psychology: Memory, language, and thought.* New York: Macmillan.

Hummert, M. L. (1990). Multiple stereotypes of elderly and young adults: A comparison of structure and evaluations. *Psychology and Aging, 5,* 182-193.

Hummert, M. L. (1994a). Physiognomic cues to age and the activation of stereotypes of the elderly in interaction. *International Journal of Aging and Human Development, 39,* 5-20.

Hummert, M. L. (1994b). Stereotypes of the elderly and patronizing speech. In M. L. Hummert, J. M. Wiemann, & J. F. Nussbaum (Eds.), *Interpersonal communication in older adulthood: Interdisciplinary theory and research* (pp. 162-184). Thousand Oaks, CA: Sage.

Hummert, M. L., Garstka, T. A., & Shaner, J. L. (1994, November). *Stereotype judgments of older adults: Effects of perceived age, sex, and facial expression.* Paper presented at the annual meeting of the Gerontological Society of America, Atlanta, GA.

Hummert, M. L., Garstka, T. A., & Shaner, J. L. (in press). Beliefs about language performance: Adults' perceptions about self and elderly targets. *Journal of Language and Social Psychology.*

Hummert, M. L., Garstka, T. A., Shaner, J. L., & Strahm, S. (1994). Stereotypes of the elderly held by young, middle-aged, and elderly adults. *Journal of Gerontology: Psychological Sciences, 49,* 240-249.

Hummert, M. L., Mazloff, D., & Henry, C. (1994, May). *Older adults' responses to patronizing vs. affirming messages.* Paper presented at the Second International Conference on Communication, Aging and Health, Hamilton, Ontario, Canada.

Hummert, M. L., Mazloff, D., & Henry, C. (1995, November). *Vocal characteristics of older adults and stereotyping.* Paper presented at the annual meeting of the Speech Communication Association, San Antonio, TX.

Hummert, M. L., Nussbaum, J. F., & Wiemann, J. M. (1994). Interpersonal communication and older adulthood: An introduction. In M. L. Hummert, J. M. Wiemann, & J. F. Nussbaum (Eds.), *Interpersonal communication in older adulthood: Interdisciplinary theory and research* (pp. 1-14). Thousand Oaks, CA: Sage.

Hummert, M. L., & Shaner, J. L. (in press). Patronizing speech to the elderly: Relationship to stereotyping. *Communication Studies.*

Hummert, M. L., Shaner, J. L., & Garstka, T. A. (1995). Cognitive processes affecting communication with older adults: The case for stereotypes, attitudes, and beliefs about communication. In J. F. Nussbaum & J. Coupland (Eds.), *Handbook of communication and aging research.* Hillsdale, NJ: Lawrence Erlbaum.

Hummert, M. L., Shaner, J. L., Henry, C., & Garstka, T. A. (1995). *Patronizing speech to the elderly: Relationship to subject age and stereotypes.* Manuscript in preparation.

Hummert, M. L., Wiemann, J. M., & Nussbaum, J. F. (Eds.). (1994). *Interpersonal communication in older adulthood: Interdisciplinary theory and research.* Thousand Oaks, CA: Sage.

Ikels, C., Keith, J., Dickerson-Putman, J., Draper, P., Fry, C., Glascock, A., & Harpending, H. (1992). Perceptions of the adult life-course: A cross-cultural analysis. *Ageing and Society, 12,* 49-84.

Kahn, R. L., & Antonucci, T. C. (1980). Convoys over the life course: Attachment, roles, and social support. In P. B. Baltes & O. Brim (Eds.), *Life span development and behavior* (Vol. 3, pp. 253-286). New York: Academic Press.

Keating, N. C., & Cole, P. (1980). What do I do with him 24 hours a day? Changes in the housewife role after retirement. *The Gerontologist, 20,* 84-89.

Kemper, S. (1992). Language and aging. In F. I. M. Craik & T. Salthouse (Eds.), *Handbook of aging and cognition* (pp. 213-270). Hillsdale, NJ: Lawrence Erlbaum.

Kemper, S. (1994). "Elderspeak": Speech accommodation to older adults. *Aging and Cognition, 1,* 17-28.

Kemper, S., Kynette, D., & Norman, S. (1992). Age differences in spoken language. In R. West & J. Sinnot (Eds.), *Everyday memory and aging* (pp. 138-154). New York: Springer-Verlag.

Kemper, S., Kynette, D., Rash, S., O'Brien, K., & Sprott, R. (1989). Lifespan changes to adults' language: Effects of memory and genre. *Applied Psycholinguistics, 10,* 49-66.

Kemper, S., & Lyons, K. (1994). The effects of Alzheimer's dementia on language and communication. In M. L. Hummert, J. M. Wiemann, & J. F. Nussbaum (Eds.), *Interpersonal communication in older adulthood: Interdisciplinary theory and research* (pp. 58-82). Thousand Oaks, CA: Sage.

Kintsch, W., & van Dijk, T. A. (1978). Toward a model of text comprehension and production. *Psychological Bulletin, 85,* 363-394.

Kite, M. E., & Johnson, B. T. (1988). Attitudes toward older and younger adults: A meta-analysis. *Psychology and Aging, 3,* 233-244.

Kivinck, H. (1981). Grandparenthood and the mental health of grandparents. *Ageing and Society, 1,* 365-381.

Kogan, N. (1979). Beliefs, attitudes, and stereotypes about old people: A new look at some old issues. *Research on Aging, 2,* 11- 36.

Kornhaber, A. (1985). Grandparenthood and the "new social contract." In V. L. Bengtson & J. F. Robertson (Eds.), *Grandparenthood* (pp. 159-172). Beverly Hills, CA: Sage.

Lambert, W. E., Hodgson, R., Gardner, R. C., & Fillenbaum, S. (1960). Evaluational reactions to spoken language. *Journal of Abnormal and Social Psychology, 60,* 44-51.

Levitt, H. (1982). Speech discrimination ability in the hearing impaired: Spectrum considerations. In G. A. Studebaker & F. H. Bess (Eds.), *The Vanderbilt hearing-aid report: State of the art research needs* (pp. 32-43). Upper Darby, PA: Monographs in Contemporary Audiology.

Light, L. L. (1988). Language and aging: Competence vs. performance. In J. E. Birren & V. L. Bengtson (Eds.), *Emergent theories of aging* (pp. 177-213). New York: Springer.

Light, L. L. (1990). Interactions between memory and language in old age. In J. E. Birren & K. W. Schaie (Eds.), *The handbook of the psychology of aging* (pp. 275-290). San Diego, CA: Academic Press.

Luszcz, M. A., & Fitzgerald, K. M. (1986). Understanding cohort differences in cross-generational, self, and peer perceptions. *Journal of Gerontology, 41,* 234-240.

Lutsky, N. S. (1980). Attitudes toward old age and elderly persons. In C. Eisdorfer (Ed.), *Annual review of gerontology and geriatrics* (Vol. 1, pp. 287-336). New York: Springer.

Mares, M.-L., & Fitzpatrick, M. A. (1995). The aging couple. In J. F. Nussbaum & J. Coupland (Eds.), *Handbook of communication and aging research.* Hillsdale, NJ: Lawrence Erlbaum.

Matthews, S. H. (1986). *Friendship through the life course: Oral biographies of old age.* Beverly Hills, CA: Sage.

McKay, V. C. (1995). Relationships in later life: The nature of inter- and intra-generational ties between grandparents, grandchildren, and adult siblings. In J. F. Nussbaum & J. Coupland (Eds.), *Handbook of communication and aging research.* Hillsdale, NJ: Lawrence Erlbaum.

Montepare, J. M., Steinberg, J., & Rosenberg, B. (1992). Characteristics of vocal communication between young adults and their parents and grandparents. *Communication Research, 19,* 479-492.

Ng, S. H., Moody, J., & Giles, H. (1991). Information-seeking triggered by age. *International Journal of Aging and Human Development, 33,* 269-277.

Norman, S., Kemper, S., Kynette, D., Cheung, H., & Anagnopoulos, C. (1991). Syntactic complexity and adults' running memory span. *Journal of Gerontology: Psychological Sciences, 46,* 346-351.

Nussbaum, J. F. (1989). *Lifespan communication: Normative processes.* Hillsdale NJ: Lawrence Erlbaum.

Nussbaum, J. F. (1994). Friendship in older adulthood. In M. L. Hummert, J. M. Wiemann, & J. F. Nussbaum (Eds.), *Interpersonal communication in older adulthood: Interdisciplinary theory and research* (pp. 209-225). Thousand Oaks, CA: Sage.

Nussbaum, J. F., & Bettini, L. M. (1994). Shared stories of the grandparent-grandchild relationship. *International Journal of Aging and Human Development, 39,* 67-80.

Nussbaum, J. F., Thompson, T., & Robinson, J. D. (1989). *Communication and aging.* New York: Harper & Row.

O'Connell, A. N., & Rotter, N. G. (1979). The influence of stimulus age and sex on person perception. *Journal of Gerontology, 34,* 220-228.

Palmore, E. B. (1982). Attitudes toward the aged: What we know and need to know. *Research on Aging, 4,* 333-348.

Patterson, B. R., Bettini, L., & Nussbaum, J. F. (1993). The meaning of friendship across the lifespan: Two studies. *Communication Quarterly, 41,* 145-160.

Perry, J. S., & Varney, T. L. (1978). College students' attitudes toward workers' competence and age. *Psychological Reports, 42,* 1319-1322.

Rawlins, W. K. (1992). *Friendship matters: Communication, dialectics, and the life course.* New York: Aldine de Gruyter.

Rosch, E. (1978). Principles of categorization. In E. Rosch & B. Lloyd (Eds.), *Cognition and organization* (pp. 27-48). Hillsdale, NJ: Lawrence Erlbaum.

Rotenberg, K. J., & Hamel, J. (1988). Social interaction and depression in elderly individuals. *International Journal of Aging and Human Development, 27,* 307-320.

Ryan, E. B. (1991). Normal aging and language. In R. Lubinski (Ed.), *Dementia and communication: Clinical and research issues* (pp. 84-97). Toronto: B. C. Decker.

Ryan, E. B., Bourhis, R. Y., & Knops, U. (1991). Evaluative perceptions of patronizing speech addressed to elders. *Psychology and Aging, 6,* 442-450.

Ryan, E. B., & Capadano, H. L. (1978). Age perceptions and evaluative reactions toward adult speakers. *Journal of Gerontology, 33,* 98-102.

Ryan, E. B., & Cole, R. (1990). Evaluative perceptions of interpersonal communication with elders. In H. Giles, N. Coupland, & J. M. Wiemann (Eds.), *Communication, health and the elderly* (pp. 172-191). Manchester: Manchester University Press.

Ryan, E. B., Giles, H., Bartolucci, G., & Henwood, K. (1986). Psycholinguistic and social psychological components of communication by and with the elderly. *Language and Communication, 6,* 1-24.

Ryan, E. B., Hummert, M. L., & Boich, L. L. (1995). Communication predicaments of aging: Patronizing behavior toward older adults. *Journal of Language and Social Psychology, 14,* 144-166.

Ryan, E. B., & Johnston, D. G. (1987). The influence of communication effectiveness on evaluations of younger and older adult speakers. *Journal of Gerontology: Psychological Sciences, 42,* 163-164.

Ryan, E. B., Kwong See, S., Meneer, W. B., & Trovato, D. (1992). Age-based perceptions of language performance among younger and older adults. *Communication Research, 19,* 423-443.

Ryan, E. B., & Laurie, S. (1990). Evaluations of older and younger adult speakers: The influence of communication effectiveness and noise. *Psychology and Aging, 5,* 513-518.

Ryan, E. B., MacLean, M., & Orange, J. B. (1994). Inappropriate accommodation in communication to elders: Inferences about nonverbal correlates. *International Journal of Aging and Human Development, 39,* 273-291.

Ryan, E. B., Meredith, S. D., & Shantz, G. B. (1994). Evaluative perceptions of patronizing speech addressed to institutionalized elders in contrasting conversational contexts. *Canadian Journal on Aging, 13,* 236-248.

Salthouse, T. A. (1988). Effects of aging on verbal abilities: Examination of the psychometric literature. In L. L. Light & D. Burke (Eds.), *Language, memory, and aging* (pp. 17-35). New York: Cambridge University Press.

Salthouse, T. A. (1992). *Mechanisms of age-cognition relations in adulthood.* Hillsdale, NJ: Lawrence Erlbaum.

Schmidt, D. F., & Boland, S. M. (1986). The structure of impressions of older adults: Evidence for multiple stereotypes. *Psychology and Aging, 1,* 255-260.

Schneider, B. A., Pichora-Fuller, M. K., Kowalchuk, D., & Lamb, M. (1994). Gap detection and the precedence effect in young and old adults. *Journal of the Acoustical Society of America, 95,* 980-991.

Schwalb, S. J., & Sedlacek, W. E. (1990). Have college students' attitudes toward older people changed? *Journal of College Student Development, 31,* 127-132.

Shanas E. (1979). The family as a social support system in old age. *The Gerontologist, 19,* 169-174.

Shaner, J. L., Hummert, M. L., Kemper, S., & Vandeputte, D. D. (1994, November). *Elderly self-disclosure: A replication with a new coding scheme.* Paper presented at the annual meeting of the Gerontological Society of America, Atlanta, GA.

Sillars, A. L., & Wilmot, W. W. (1989). Marital communication across the lifespan. In J. F. Nussbaum (Ed.), *Lifespan communication: Normative processes* (pp. 225-253). Hillsdale, NJ: Lawrence Erlbaum.

Sillars, A. L., & Zietlow, P. H. (1993). Investigations of marital communication and lifespan development. In N. Coupland & J. F. Nussbaum (Eds.), *Discourse and lifespan identity* (pp. 237-261). Newbury Park, CA: Sage.

Simons, R. L. (1984). Specificity and substitution in the social networks of the elderly. *International Journal of Aging and Human Development, 18,* 121-139.

Smith, E. R. (1993). Social identity and social emotions: Toward new conceptualizations of prejudice. In D. Mackie & D. L. Hamilton (Eds.), *Affect, cognition, and stereotyping: Interactive processes in group perception* (pp. 297-315). New York: Academic Press.

Stewart, M. A., & Ryan, E. B. (1982). Attitudes toward younger and older adult speakers: Effect of varying speech rates. *Journal of Language and Social Psychology, 1,* 91-109.

Stine, E. L., & Wingfield, A. (1987). Process and strategy in memory for speech among younger and older adults. *Psychology and Aging, 2,* 272-279.

Stine, E. L., Wingfield, A., & Poon, L. W. (1986). How much and how fast: Rapid processing of spoken language in later adulthood. *Psychology and Aging, 1,* 303-311.

Thompson, T. L. (1994). Interpersonal communication and health care. In M. L. Knapp & G. R. Miller (Eds.), *Handbook of interpersonal communication* (2nd ed., pp. 696-725). Thousand Oaks, CA: Sage.

Troll, L. E. (1971). The family of later life: A decade review. *Journal of Marriage and the Family, 33,* 263-290.

Troll, L. E. (1983). Grandparents: The family watchdogs. In T. H. Brubaker (Ed.), *Family relationships in later life* (pp. 63-74). Beverly Hills, CA: Sage.

Troll, L. E. (1986). Parents and children in later life. *Generations, 10,* 23-25.

U.S. Senate Special Committee on Aging. (1991). *Aging America: Trends and projections* (DHHS Publication No. FCOA 91-28001). Washington, DC: Government Printing Office.

Villaume, W. A., Brown, M. H., & Darling, R. (1994). Presbycusis, communication, and older adults. In M. L. Hummert, J. M. Wiemann, & J. F. Nussbaum (Eds.), *Interpersonal communication in older adulthood: Interdisciplinary theory and research* (pp. 83-106). Thousand Oaks, CA: Sage.

Wechsler, D. (1958). *The measurement and appraisal of adult intelligence.* Baltimore, MD: Williams & Wilkins.

Wiemann, J. M. (1977). Explication and test of a model of communicative competence. *Human Communication Research, 3,* 195-213.

Williams, A. (1992). *Intergenerational communication satisfaction: An intergroup analysis.* Unpublished master's thesis, University of California, Santa Barbara, Communication Department.

Williams, A., & Giles, H. (1995). *Satisfying-dissatisfying intergenerational conversations: An intergroup perspective.* Unpublished manuscript.

Wingfield, A., Lahar, C. J., & Stine, E. L. (1989). Age and decision strategies in running memory for speech: Effects of prosody and linguistic structure. *Journal of Gerontology: Psychological Sciences, 44,* 106-113.

Wingfield, A., Stine, E. L., Lahar, C. J., & Aberdeen, J. S. (1988). Does the capacity of working memory change with age? *Experimental Aging Research, 14,* 103-107.

Wingfield, A., Wayland, S. C., & Stine, E. L. (1992). Adult age differences in the use of prosody for syntactic parsing and recall of spoken sentences. *Journal of Gerontology: Psychological Sciences, 47,* 350-356.

CHAPTER CONTENTS

2 Sexual Communication in Interpersonal Contexts: A Script-Based Approach

SANDRA METTS
Illinois State University

BRIAN H. SPITZBERG
San Diego State University

Sexual communication is the means by which individuals come to select potential partners for sexual relations, and through which the meanings, functions, and effects of sexual relations are negotiated. Most cultures, relationships, and individuals develop standard expectancies and practices through which sexual relations are initiated and completed. These standard expectancies and practices can be viewed as scripts that identify some degree of the content, sequence, and boundaries of appropriate behavior for pursuing, negotiating, and enacting the sexual act. This chapter reviews the research relevant to sexual scripts as well as their descriptive and explanatory value in depicting communication and sexual relations. Scripts are shown to reveal both competent and incompetent influences in the unfolding of sexual interactions.

EX may be one of life's greatest pleasures, but it is also a source of some of our thorniest interpersonal and social problems. Some of these problems are as old as the species itself (e.g., conveying sexual interest); others are very contemporary (e.g., modifying sexual behavior in the face of the AIDS epidemic). Unfortunately, the most appealing media influences, such as television, film, and popular magazines, tend to emphasize the pleasures of sexual encounters and de-emphasize the challenges. Young people in the United States grow to sexual maturity amid visions of physically beautiful couples who progress rapidly but gracefully toward sexual encounters that culminate in sexual gratification. The reality of managing personal inhibitions and vulnerability, and of anticipating and coping with relational, social, and physical consequences, is portrayed less often. Thus, the achievement

Correspondence and requests for reprints: Sandra Metts, Department of Communication, Illinois State University, 434 Fell Hall, Normal, IL 61790-4480.

Communication Yearbook 19, pp. 49-91

of mutually endorsed goals and expectations, the enactment of coordinated sexual actions, and the realization of mutually satisfying sexual experiences are not likely to be accomplished without some degree of effort on the part of the individuals involved in actual sexual encounters.

In this chapter we examine the role of communication in accomplishing sexual involvement and managing potential sex-related interpersonal and social problems. More specifically, we illustrate the ways in which communicative patterns reflect and adapt sexual scripts. Sexual scripts are cognitive structures specifying appropriate goals in sexually relevant contexts and specifying sequences of behavior, or plans, that are appropriate and efficacious for achieving those goals. Scripts thereby function as both interpretive filters and guides for behavior.

Although the nuances of individual scripts vary, they are strongly influenced by the prevailing cultural-level sexual script, particularly early in relationships, when actions and interpretations are based on sociological rather than personal knowledge. Ironically, the influence of the prevailing cultural script both facilitates and hinders initial sexual interactions. On the one hand, cognitive representations of prototypical sexual interactions, ranging from flirting to sexual intercourse, provide potential partners with shared expectations and a repertoire of coordinated behavioral options. On the other hand, blind adherence to a sexual script when it is inappropriate or dysfunctional in a given circumstance or with a particular partner precludes the possibility of negotiation and mutuality. Thus, communication is essential not only for the skillful enactment of sexual scripts, but also for clarifying meaning and for negotiating changes in scripts that are responsive to individual, relational, and situational features.

This chapter focuses on three areas of theoretical and pragmatic importance. The first is the signaling of sexual interest, commonly called flirting. Research on the types of behaviors perceived to be flirtatious indicates that a relatively limited and commonly recognized set of behaviors function to express sexual interest and to show appreciation for this interest. The strategic ambiguity characteristic of flirtatious behavior allows maximum flexibility in assessing mutual interest, while minimizing face loss. Research also indicates, however, that similar behaviors can be used to coerce, rather than assess, sexual interest. Thus, we include in the section on communication of sexual interest a brief discussion of sexual harassment.

The second area of sexual interaction addressed in this chapter is the negotiation of sexual involvement, commonly known as sexual compliance gaining. Even when potential partners both desire sexual gratification, traditional sex role expectations prescribe somewhat different scripts for males and females. Couples negotiating sexual involvement in early stages of relationships are in essence negotiating the extent to which they will enact the traditional sexual script and the extent to which they expect their partners to do the same. Research indicates that this process is complicated and occasionally problematic. This section explores the process of sexual initiation and refusal, both as mutually choreographed and as unilaterally imposed, particularly when the result is sexual coercion and date rape.

The third area of concern in this chapter is the role of communication in sexual health. Although college student samples acknowledge the importance of safer sex practices, they do not consistently practice them. This suggests that media campaigns to educate sexually active persons about HIV transmission and the advisability of using condoms have been more successful at the level of attitude change than at the level of behavioral change. Thus, the goal of safer sex is beginning to enter the interpersonal sexual scripts of dating individuals, but a coherent behavioral plan to incorporate those practices is not uniformly available. We examine the literature on communicating about potential risk with a sexual partner and communication about condom use in this section.

Our selection of script theory as an organizing framework and our focus on three contexts of sexual communication (signaling sexual interest, negotiating sexual involvement, and maintaining sexual health) necessarily exclude consideration of many other issues falling within the rubric of sexual communication (see McKinney & Sprecher, 1989). We do not, for example, address the important domain of sexual communication within marriage. However, we believe that an understanding of normative patterns in early sexual involvement is a useful window through which to view the emergent and idiosyncratic practices created by couples over time. Because couples' scripts evolve from their early experiences with other sexual partners and with each other, knowledge about normative patterns is essential to our understanding of the content and process of adaptation.

The use of script theory also implies a sense of order and predictability to sexual episodes, which some would argue are largely improvisational (e.g., Adelman, 1992; Ruelfi, 1985). However, improvisation can be understood only in terms of normative patterns. Sexual partners enter sexual relationships with some sense of how to get from point A to point B and some sense of appropriate messages that might be uttered along the way. What partners improvise are the specific behaviors and specific messages used to facilitate this general progression. Thus, a full understanding of cultural scripts is prerequisite to an understanding of episode-specific improvisation.

Finally, initial sexual interactions are not only theoretically interesting for what they reveal about sex role expectations and behavior, and about compliance gaining, negotiation, and other communicative functions, they are pragmatically important as well. Persistent reports of unsatisfying and even violent sexual interactions, date rape, sexual harassment, and the continued spread of AIDS and other sexually transmitted diseases underscore the importance of our learning more about communication in the sexually relevant contexts that form the focus of this review.

We begin with a definition of *sexual scripts* to provide a foundation for the interpretation of the research in the three sexual contexts identified above:

signaling sexual interest, negotiating sexual involvement, and maintaining sexual health.

SEXUAL SCRIPTS

Interpersonal sexual scripts, like other social schemata, are cognitive structures or plans that specify goals, organize the interpretation of events, and guide the performance of actions in situated episodes (Abelson, 1981; Ginsburg, 1988; Schank & Abelson, 1977). In the case of sexual scripts, the elements that make up the "domain of application are those sequences which arise from, explain, and accomplish sexual activity" (Metts & Cupach, 1989). They specify a "who," a "what," and "a circumstance" for sexual actions (i.e., what kind of person does what under what circumstances) (Gagnon, 1990; Gagnon & Simon, 1973; Laumann, Gagnon, Michael, & Michaels, 1994).

Interpersonal sexual scripts are strongly influenced by broader cultural-level scripts and by individual intrapsychic-level scripts (Simon & Gagnon, 1986, 1987). *Cultural-level scripts* are those scenarios presented in the media, folklore, and mythology that "instruct" cultural members in appropriate goals, desirable qualities, and typical behaviors for sexual and potentially sexual experiences. *Intrapsychic-level scripts* are unique representations of the sexual "I," including individual desires, motives, and actions that create and sustain sexual arousal. It is important to note that *interpersonal-level sexual* scripts vary in the extent to which they incorporate prescriptions from cultural sexual scripts, including rights and obligations attending sex roles and strategies for acting in accord with these prescriptions. Also, interpersonal sexual scripts vary in their number and diversity of strategies for expressing personal desires and needs as well as for responding to those expressions from partners (see Metts & Cupach, 1989).

Interpersonal sexual scripts also vary on those dimensions that characterize any type of social script, including strength, specificity, distinctiveness, and internal coherence (Ginsburg, 1988). They may also be more or less efficient. For example, a script may be coherent, but if it lacks distinctiveness (i.e., fails to distinguish among superficially similar situations) and fails to accommodate unexpected events in a sequence, it is not efficient. Finally, like other scripts, sexual scripts are "contingent" patterns of action, activated by certain conditions that lead persons to enter and commit to participating in the scripts. For example, flirtation is a familiar and routinized "activating" sequence that often prompts commitment to a more fully developed sexual script. However, the mere presence of a script, including an interpersonal sexual script, is neither a necessary nor a sufficient condition for action, although a script should be more likely to be employed as a situation becomes more familiar and routinized.

The enactment of interpersonal sexual scripts is a communication process. During sexual encounters, communication is the means by which individuals express their sexual needs and desires and enact behavioral strategies for satisfying these needs. Communication is also the means by which differences or incompatibilities in the interpersonal scripts of partners are negotiated. Finally, communication is the means by which the meaning of sexual activity is understood and negotiated. We turn now to a discussion of research that has investigated these forms of communication.

COMMUNICATION OF SEXUAL INTEREST

Flirtation is the prototypical example of messages that signal sexual interest. Such messages, when enacted skillfully and mutually choreographed, provide potential sexual partners with a system for expressing, accepting, and refusing sexual interest in subtle and face-preserving ways. However, when sexual interest is not welcome or appropriate, cannot be stopped, and/or is associated with more powerful others, it becomes coercive. Such messages, known as sexual harassment, form the focus of the second topic in this section.

Flirtation

Flirtation is a form of nascent sexual communication. It often exists in a netherworld of subtlety and innuendo, typically integrated within the stream of normal, "innocent" interaction (e.g., smiling, complimenting, glancing during laughter). Although not inherently sexual, flirtation is commonly associated with sex in several senses. First, flirtation often is sexually suggestive or even sexually explicit (Abrahams, 1995). Second, flirtation is frequently viewed as preliminary to and preparatory for eventual sexual relations as a normative sequence in the dating script (Rose & Frieze, 1993). Third, flirtation is a source of both arousal and attraction that sustains and maintains relationships in which sex is probable or possible (e.g., cross-sex friendships; O'Meara, 1989; Sapadin, 1988), or even common (i.e., marriage). Fourth, flirtation is frequently a testing ground for the ascertainment of sexual intentions (Sabini & Silver, 1982), including in relationships normatively considered platonic (Egland, Zormeier, & Spitzberg, 1995). Finally, flirtation may serve numerous manipulative ends aside from sex, but nevertheless uses sex as the attributed "bait" underlying the influence process (Buss, 1994). So, even if sex is not the proximal outcome, the socially ascribed meaning of flirtation is generally sexual in nature.

The flirtation script consists of a common and recognizable routine. In some cases, it activates participation in a sexual script that leads to sexual involvement; in some cases, it does not. Either way, flirtation functions to signal interest and to allow individuals to ascertain, indirectly, whether sexual interest is (or may be) reciprocated. Indeed, ambiguity, as an integral feature of flirtation (Sabini & Silver, 1982; Silver, 1994), provides participants with several advantages, including (a) infusing sexuality into interaction without violating norms against explicit sex talk among relative strangers, (b) the option of deniability of intent, and (c) safe "testing" of receivers' intentions. Once sex is clearly and unambiguously understood as the objective, the communication is no longer flirtation, but sexual pursuit.

The empirical research on flirtation tends to be of two types: research concerned with identifying the behaviors that constitute flirting and research concerned with factors influencing the interpretation of these behaviors, particularly the sex of the actor and observer. Both types of research provide evidence that flirtation is strongly influenced by the cultural sexual script.

Flirting Behaviors

Research on flirting behaviors suggests that a relatively limited number of verbal and nonverbal communication strategies constitute the system by which people signal their sexual interest (Fichten, Tagalakis, Judd, Wright, & Amsel, 1992). For example, Muehlenhard, Koralewski, Andrews, and Burdick (1986) developed a series of brief videotaped vignettes of women displaying a behavior "indicating interest in dating" (as determined by pilot studies). Men rated the probability the woman would accept a date request by the male and how attractive her personality was. Women rated the probability of acceptance and the likelihood they would use the same behaviors as the actor. The researchers identified 17 verbal cues (e.g., she compliments him, she keeps talking rather than ending the conversation, she asks him questions about himself) and 14 nonverbal cues (e.g., eye contact, smiling, forward leaning, touching while laughing) that were fairly consistently viewed as indicative of both female interest and potential use.

Moreover, if these behaviors are part of a relatively coherent script, we would expect them to be contingent and sequential in much the same structure as dates themselves (Rose & Frieze, 1993). That is, we should expect a repertoire of possible options that range from subtle to more direct, with more direct behaviors showing greater distinctiveness from ordinary conversational maintenance behaviors. In a sense, increasing directness is contingent upon the effectiveness of less-direct actions (LaPlante, McCormick, & Brannigan, 1980). We should also expect that these behaviors function to advance sequential goals, for example, gaining attention, continuing the interaction, ascertaining other's interest in sexual activity, and so forth. The research indicates that both of these conditions are true.

Behaviors associated with flirtation vary in degree of perceived "flirtatiousness" based primarily on explicitness of the tactics and the degree to which they can be distinguished from ordinary conversational behavior. For example, Silver and Spitzberg (1992) analyzed four categories of flirting behaviors that they label *recognition* (e.g., waves, mouths "hello" from a distance), *conversation* (e.g., asks you about yourself), *stereotyped* (e.g., buys you a drink, asks for your phone number), and *nonverbal involvement* (e.g., rubs your neck, puts arm around you). They found that stereotypical "pickup lines" (e.g., asks for a date with you, asks for your phone number) and physically direct behaviors (e.g., nibbles on your ear, grabs and kisses you) were seen as most flirtatious. Similarly, Abrahams (1994, 1995) found that tactics associated with a category of behavior he labels *small talk* (e.g., "I made small talk with a guy I met the previous night in the cafeteria. I was friendly and smiled.") were perceived to be less flirtatious than tactics associated with a category he terms *responsiveness* (e.g., "At a party, I looked directly into this guy's eyes, leaned forward, and stood closer than usual."). But both of these categories were perceived to be less flirtatious than a category Abrahams labels *proposition* (e.g., "I didn't say much—I just tried to look at him coy-like, giving him a great big smile. I then gave him a sexy 'I-want-you' look with my eyes.") and one he labels *contact* (e.g., "I kept making eye contact with him and asked him about his activities. Then, I gave him a really good back rub."). It seems that the prototypical flirtation script involves (a) recognition, (b) conversation and small talk, (c) immediacy and responsiveness, (d) physical contact, and (e) declaration of intentions.

In a series of qualitative and ethnoexperimental studies, Moore (1985) and Moore and Butler (1989) identified an extensive catalog of flirtation behaviors from an observational study of 200 women in natural social contexts. These researchers also tested the assumption that these behaviors are designed to signal availability for a male's approach. Moore (1985) hypothesized that if these behaviors function as solicitation moves, they should be manifested in the presence of potential mates but be absent in nonsexual contexts, and should be associated with a male's approach. Observations of female nonverbal behavior in various settings (e.g., a library, a women's reading room, a snack bar, and a singles bar) confirmed these expectations.

Finally, if flirtation is scripted, plans should include not only behavioral options, but sequences of moves situated in ongoing interaction. This is evidenced in the work of Givens (1978), who identifies five general stages in the flirtation sequence: *attention* (noticing and indication of noticing target), *recognition* (signaling interest in being noticed), *positioning* (orienting to permit interaction), *invitations* (appeals for sexually oriented interaction), and *resolution* (sexual intentions are confirmed or complied with). The sequential structure of flirtation is also suggested in the qualitative research of Snow, Robinson, and McCall (1991), who identify the basic moves of male advance, female "cooling out," and male "cooperative management of rejection" in preserving the interaction order.

Based on the literature reviewed to this point, we can assume that the interactional characteristics of flirting are recognizable and evocative. They may not always lead to sexual encounters, as the research on rejection moves indicates (Trost & Engstrom, 1994), but they are viewed by research participants as directed toward that end. Although this suggests a highly coordinated "quasi-sexual ritual," flirtation is in practice often marked by miscommunication (Abbey, 1987). This is due in part to the highly ambiguous nature of the signals and in part to variations in the communicative competence of actors who send and interpret the signals. But it is also in part a result of the sex role expectations inherent in the traditional cultural script. To the extent that men are cast in the role of sexual initiator, we should expect them to orient toward ambiguous situations as potentially sexual, at least to a greater degree than women. We turn now to a more detailed discussion of this research.

Sex Differences in Display and Interpretation of Flirtatious Behavior

Research indicates that the sex of the person who displays flirtatious behaviors and the sex of the person observing the behavior influence the interpretation of the behaviors. For example, Abbey (1982) concludes from subject ratings of observed male-female interactions that, compared with females, males have a perceptual bias toward seeing friendly behavior as more sexual (promiscuous and flirtatious). Shotland and Craig (1988) asked college students to rate videotaped interactions varying in displays of "interested" versus "friendly" behavior. A significant interaction effect between actor intent (interested or friendly) and sex of actor suggested that raters could differentiate friendly behaviors from interested behaviors. However, there was also a significant sex-of-rater effect, such that males perceived all interactions as more interested.

Koeppel, Montaigne-Miller, O'Hair, and Cody (1993) hypothesized distinctions in the nonverbal behavior of "friendly" (e.g., small amounts of smiling, relaxed body, no touch), "flirtatious" (e.g., moderate to large amounts of smiling, open mouth, childlike expressions, moderate touch), and "seductive" (e.g., constant smiling, relaxed body, touching on hand/leg) episodes. They manipulated these behaviors in four conditions (including a control condition lacking these behaviors) displaying a male and a female college student presumably waiting to see a professor, which were rated by both males and females. When the female initiated, the episode was viewed as more seductive, "regardless of the level of intimacy of the display" (p. 30). Moreover, although both males and females could distinguish flirting, seductive, and friendly episodes based on the behaviors displayed, males were found to "characterize encounters as sexual merely on the basis of who initiates the conversation" (p. 30; see also Shotland & Craig, 1988). Downey and Vitulli (1987) similarly found that in response to a variety of flirtation-relevant scenario descriptions, men, compared with women, indicated more interest in returning a flirtatious move, were more sexually motivated in response to flirtation, and believed they were more able to seduce married people of the opposite sex.

Clearly, individuals differ in the extent to which their interpersonal scripts are influenced by sex role prescriptions inherent in the cultural-level script. Shy men may never initiate sexually suggestive interactions, and assertive women may do so routinely. The popular appeal of movies such as *Disclosure* suggests that in this society, the possibility of role reversals is at least interesting, if not commonplace. We move now to a brief discussion of situations in which flirtation episodes are not merely occasions of miscommunication, but instances of power exerted within the structure of flirtation.

Sexual Harassment

When rejection is not accepted and implicit or explicit sexual communication continues, and when the target is constrained by the social or professional setting to remain in the field, expression of sexual interest can be construed as sexual harassment. We offer here a brief discussion of sexual harassment as it might be explained by script theory (see Keyton, Chapter 3, this volume, for a more thorough treatment of the topic of sexual harassment).

Although definitions of sexual harassment vary, "most include one or more of the following characteristics: the behavior is unwanted (as perceived by the victim) and/or repeated and/or deliberate, there is some harm or negative outcome for the victim, a wide range of behaviors is included, and the offender has more power than the victim" (McKinney & Maroules, 1991, p. 29). In general, sexual harassment is presumed to be a coercive message form or pattern of action in which a person of higher recognized power exploits the sexual dimension of a relationship with a coworker or subordinate. This exploitation may or may not imply contingent sexual performance on the part of the victim, but either way, the harassment constructs a unilaterally defined sexual dimension that is unwanted by the victim (Schneider, 1991; Sheffield, 1987). Such a relationship may be negotiated very subtly and with messages that reinforce doubt and fear associated with exposure, so that the victim feels further entrapped by the relationship (Bingham, 1991).

Sexual harassment occurs for a number of reasons, including belief in any of several patriarchal myths (e.g., sexual harassment is fun or trivial; it affects only women in low-status jobs; women use claims of sexual harassment to get ahead; see Evans, 1978). Other causes include sex role socialization that implies greater male power or status relative to women and organizational cultures that relegate women to lower status (regardless of organizational position). Finally, sexual harassment occurs because it is difficult to identify and eliminate, in part because in its early stages it bears a superficial resemblance to the flirtation episode. Indeed, many of the behaviors included in surveys about sexual harassment are virtually identical to the items employed in the study of flirtation (e.g., eyes me up and down, stares at me, kisses me on the cheek, touches me on arm/back; Popovich, Licata, Nokovich, Martelli, & Zoloty, 1986). Moreover, the ambiguity characteristic of sexually harassing messages (as well as flirtation) makes them easy to reframe and difficult to challenge (Fairhurst, 1986). This is compounded by the tendency for men to view ambiguous, but potentially harassing, behaviors as less inappropriate and less offensive than do women (Gutek, Morasch, & Cohen, 1983; Gutek, Nakumura, Gahart, & Handschumacher, 1980; Hemphill & Pfeiffer, 1986).

Gutek (1985) operationalized sexual harassment in terms of eight behaviors: "sexual comments meant to be complimentary, sexual comments meant to be insulting, looks and gestures meant to be complimentary, looks and gestures meant to be insulting, nonsexual touching, sexual touching, socializing or dating as a requirement of the job, and sex as a requirement of the job" (p. 43). In Gutek's sample, women were more likely than men to label each one of these behaviors as harassment. In addition, although men reported experiencing these behaviors from women, they did not tend to view them as unidirectional or detrimental. Indeed, a number of studies have found a perceptual bias among men to view ambiguous behaviors as more flirtatious and sexy than harassing (e.g., Booth-Butterfield, 1991; Johnson, Stockdale, & Saal, 1991; Keyton, 1993; Mongeau & Blalock, 1992).

One of the largest surveys conducted to date on sexual harassment indicates that although sexual harassment has become more salient to most adults since 1980, gender biases do not reflect significant change. In 1987 the U.S. Merit Systems Protection Board (1988) conducted a survey of 8,523 federal employees to replicate a similar study performed in 1980. Results indicated that (a) employees were generally more likely to label a variety of behaviors as harassing in 1987 than in 1980; (b) well over a majority viewed pressure for sexual favors, deliberate touching, uninvited sexual letters and calls, and pressure for dates as forms of sexual harassment; and (c) in general, men still labeled fewer behaviors as harassing than did females.

Research on the nature of responses directed to harassing behaviors has been more limited than that directed toward the behaviors themselves. In general, survey research tends to view responses to harassment as varying from passive to assertive (Clair, McGown, & Spirek, 1993; Gruber, 1989). This continuum includes *avoidance* (e.g., ignoring, quitting), *diffusion* (e.g., trivializing, joking), *negotiation* (e.g., direct request, threats to expose, and seeking outside help), and *confrontation* (e.g., direct complaint to the organization). In the Merit Board study cited above, for example, the most common responses were avoidance ("I ignored the behavior or did nothing," females = 52%, males = 42%; "I avoided the person," females = 43%, males = 31%), followed by negotiation ("I asked/told the person to stop," females = 44%, males = 25%) and diffusion ("I made a joke of the behavior," females = 20%, males = 20%) (U.S. Merit Systems Protection Board, 1988).

Laboratory research has taken a somewhat more theoretical approach to the responses to sexual harassment. For example, Bingham and Burleson (1989) developed an alternative message response typology derived from O'Keefe's (1988) analysis of message design logics. *Expressive* messages represent the inner thoughts and feelings of the interactant in an unedited and forthright manner. *Conventional* messages attempt to conform to, and instrumentally capitalize upon, the rules of the game, or the context within which the communicator is interacting. *Rhetorical* messages reflect the recognition that social contexts are constructed, defined, and redefined communicatively. Bingham and Burleson designed harassment response messages to represent each design logic at one of three levels of "multifunctionality" (the extent to which each message pursued multiple goals) in two sexual harassment situations (quid pro quo and condition of work). In general, the more multifunctional the message, the more competent the victim response was perceived to be (e.g., it maintained relational rapport, diffused anger, avoided retaliation). In addition, rhetorical responses were perceived to be more competent than conventional messages, which were in turn perceived to be more competent than expressive messages. From a script perspective, in which ambiguity is employed to protect face options and/or multiple identities, it follows that rhetorically complex and sensitive responses would be the most competent at preserving a harasser's face in the event of rejection.

Additional research on responses to harassment is necessary in two areas. First, it is important to determine the effectiveness of types of responses. If avoidance and directness are effective in most cases, then more sophisticated strategies may not often be necessary. If more sophisticated strategies such as those represented by rhetorical design logic are necessary, do their effects correspond with subject ratings of competence? Second, and more germane to the discussion of sexual scripts, research is necessary to determine the extent to which ambiguous harassment behaviors activate a response pattern similar to that found in flirtation episodes. In both cases, the typical goal is to reject signals of sexual interest and simultaneously invoke familiar patterns of behavior (e.g., ignoring, avoiding, joking). Comparison of rejection plans when harassment behavior is ambiguous, infrequent, or from a peer, with rejection plans when harassment behavior is clearly perceived as such by the target would point to areas of overlap and differentiation in the two scripts.

Summary

The movement toward sexual involvement typically begins with an expression of sexual attraction and interest. When this interest is reciprocated, interpersonal sexual scripts facilitate progression to more advanced levels of involvement by providing shared interpretations of ambiguous messages. When interest is not reciprocated, the episode usually ends and the flirtation episode is exited. In some cases, however, one person may continue to enact a quasi-sexual script and the target will be forced to use increasingly more direct and face-threatening closure moves. When such episodes occur in professional, academic, and occupational settings, when hints become coercive, and when the target is not able to withdraw from the scene, ostensibly flirtatious behaviors become sexual harassment.

A similar pattern is evident in the negotiation of sexual involvement. Reliance on culturally shared scripts facilitates the coordination of behavior and meanings necessary to move a couple through the intricate and subtle web of desire, apprehension, and vulnerability characteristic of initial sexual intercourse. Generally, decisions to exit the script by either partner at any point terminate the episode. However, persistence and coercion can be used to force compliance when expressions of refusal are not accepted. We turn now to a summary of the literature on collaborative and noncollaborative sexual episodes.

COMMUNICATION AND SEXUAL INVOLVEMENT

Sexual involvement is a highly salient relational event. It distinguishes romantic from nonromantic relationships (Davis & Todd, 1985) and signals an important turning point in developing relationships (Baxter & Bullis, 1986; Huston, Surra, Fitzgerald, & Cate, 1981). However, it also occurs in relationships that last no longer than the sexual episode itself (e.g., "one-night stands" and some "date rapes"). Clearly, the circumstances in which sexual episodes occur are important aspects of their meanings and consequences.

In this section we review two domains of literature that investigate sexual involvement. The first is concerned with communicative practices apparent in sexual episodes where the extent of involvement is negotiated more or less collaboratively. Such negotiations might be smooth or awkward, accomplished in a single encounter or extended over a series of interactions. They are nevertheless accomplished in such a way that level of sexual involvement is established without the use of coercive practices. The second domain of literature is concerned with sexual episodes in which the extent of sexual involvement is unilaterally determined through coercive means. We label the first domain of interest *negotiated sexual involvement* and the second *coercive sexual involvement*. From a script perspective, negotiated sexual involvement would ordinarily involve persons operating with similar scripts, or at least clear understandings of each other's scripts. Coercive involvement would entail incompatible and/or misunderstood scripts, resulting in the imposition of one person's goal to have sex on an unwilling partner.

Negotiated Sexual Involvement

Even in cases where potential sexual partners share the goal of sexual gratification and have highly compatible interpersonal sexual scripts, communication is a key feature in the unfolding of a sexual episode. If for no other reason than to reveal similarity in scripts (i.e., goals, expectations, values, and expected behavioral sequences), communication is important. In those cases where interpersonal scripts are not synchronized in terms of goals and/or the plans to achieve those goals, even greater demands are placed on the communicative skills of partners to negotiate the extent and meaning of sexual involvement (Cupach & Metts, 1991).

Although sexual negotiation is often routinely accomplished, it is perhaps more difficult than might be immediately apparent. Part of the difficulty that confronts potential sexual partners is the fact that sexual involvement is embedded in complicated ways within contemporary dating scripts (Laws & Schwartz, 1977; Reed & Weinberg, 1984). Historically, the dating stage called courtship has been a publicly recognized transition into marriage. At this stage, sexual relations were framed by relationship commitment and understood in this light. Currently, however, the greater incidence of sexual activity prior to marriage and in early stages of dating (Walsh, 1989) places enormous demands on interpersonal interaction, both in setting limits for sexual involvement and in interpreting the meaning of sexual involvement (Reed & Weinberg, 1984). In the absence of a coherent and dominant cultural-level relationship script to frame sexual involvement, the burden of interpretation falls to the couple and, in many cases, to the social networks around them.

One option available to sexually active individuals is to separate sexual behavior from the relationship frame. In such cases, one or both partners mark it explicitly as "recreational sex," with no expectation of future commitments. Although this is reasonable in the abstract, in actual practice, women tend to be downgraded by such contact in those instances where traditional sex role expectations are still operative. Evidence of traditional sex role differences is seen in the research on self-disclosure of first coitus. Patterns of how quickly and how widely this information is shared within the network indicate that it is viewed as a "rite of passage" for males, but as a relationally significant and carefully screened revelation for females (Carns, 1973; Muehlenhard & Cook, 1988).

A second option is to tie sexual involvement directly to a relationship frame (e.g., "seriously dating"), and thereby neutralize the force of traditional sex role expectations. The cultural-level sexual script specifying the "who," "what," and "under what circumstances" legitimates a male prerogative to seek sex under almost all circumstances, but prescribes for the female the role of resisting sex except under certain circumstances—circumstances that tend to be relational and emotional (LaPlante et al., 1980). Hence, the exemptions afforded by the emotional abandon of romantic love or the security of greater relationship commitment (e.g., going steady) recast women's roles to accommodate the duality of being a "nice girl" and being sexual. Under these circumstances, norms for sexual behavior and evaluation of those behaviors move into alignment. This is illustrated in research such as that conducted by Roche (1986), who has reported men to be more permissive than women in their attitudes as to what is proper sexual behavior in the early stages of dating, but to be similar to women at the stage of "dating one person only and being in love." McCabe and Collins (1984) found that men between the ages of 16 and 25 desired significantly higher levels of sexual activity on a first date than women in the same age group, but both desired similar levels of sexual activity after several dates or when going steady. It is no surprise that the practice of "serial monogamy" has become an increasingly popular trend in contemporary Western society (Laws & Schwartz, 1977). It minimizes accusations of sexual promiscuity while permitting sexual experimentation within the courtship script.

The difficulty, of course, is that the two options of recreational sex and relational sex are prototypical "solutions" to the management of sexual experience and sexual meaning. The reality lies in infinite and emergent levels of adaptation and redefinition across this spectrum of scripts. At any given moment, partners may not understand their own sexual and relational goals, may not be able to communicate these goals, and may not have any efficient or coherent plan to accomplish these goals. Moreover, couples may not share the same goals and may find that accommodation is necessary. Clearly, sexual communication becomes the mechanism for expressing and coordinating sexual actions and their meaning. We turn now to the sequences of moves and countermoves involved in the early stages of sexual involvement.

Sexual Initiation

The phrase *sexual compliance gaining* is unfortunately overly static, intentional, linear, and noninteractional. It implies that people formulate plans to get sex from unwilling (but persuadable) partners and implement these strategies in the form of unilateral and unidirectional packages of behavior. Sexual negotiation in developing relationships is more complex than this. Nevertheless, research has focused on relatively "molar" strategies (e.g., reward) or on fairly unidirectional tactics (e.g., compliments) (e.g., Christopher, 1988, 1993; Christopher & Frandsen, 1990). According to the sexual script in North American culture, males are expected to initiate sex more often and females are expected to refuse it more often, and, viewed merely at this level, the script generally appears to be in full force (e.g., LaPlante et al., 1980; O'Sullivan & Byers, 1992, 1993; Perper & Weis, 1987).

Characteristic behaviors of the initiator role associated with men are greater directness and greater variability in initiating sexual involvement, although Buss (1994) notes that extremely direct tactics are less effective than more subtle tactics. Characteristic behaviors of the limit-setting role associated with women are greater variability and greater directness in refusing sexual initiatives. The prevalence of these sex role scripts is evidenced in descriptions of sexual episodes and in ratings of how comfortable men and women are with employing various tactics. For example, McCormick (1979; see also Edgar & Fitzpatrick, 1990; LaPlante et al., 1980) coded 229 student essays on the topic of how the student might influence someone to have sex or avoid having sex with someone he or she had been dating. Analysis revealed 10 "come-on" and "put-off" strategies. Men were more likely to report using seduction (i.e., a step-by-step plan to achieve intercourse), whereas women were more likely to use the more indirect tactics of manipulation (e.g., hinting) and body language (e.g., facial expressions) to have sex. Women were more likely to use coercion and relationship conceptualizing to avoid having sex, whereas men were more likely to use logic and manipulation. When asked to stereotype the strategies in terms of whether males or females were more likely to use them, the subjects viewed all the strategies to have sex as male-typed and all the strategies for avoiding sex as female-typed. In addition, research by Grauerholz and Serpe (1985) in which college students assessed the reported use of proactive power (e.g., initiate sex with someone you don't know well) and reactive power (say no to a lover) indicates that "despite similarity in men and women's casual sexual experience and activity, women generally do not feel as comfortable initiating sex and are much more comfortable refusing sexual intercourse than are men" (p. 1055).

This is not to suggest that the role of women is entirely passive, however. Consistent with Moore's (1985) interpretation of female nonverbal solicitation cues described previously, Perper and Weis (1987) suggest that women signal availability and then men respond with more overt behaviors. Based on descriptions of "proceptive strategies" in the essays of college women, Perper and Weis conclude that contrary to traditional expectations, the data "flatly contradict the belief that women invariably defer to, or rely on, men to initiate sexual encounters" (p. 474). Similarly, O'Sullivan and Byers (1993) found that in recalled episodes in which a woman wanted more sex than the man wanted to provide, more than 95% of women were described as employing "at least one sexual influence strategy" (p. 280). Women apparently are able to tap a rich repertoire of proceptive strategies. However, O'Sullivan and Byers note, once these strategies are initiated the pattern is for the woman to expect the man to "get the hint" and take over, or to give up if the man does not get the hint. Thus, although women may initiate, their directness is still limited to the initial signaling of sexual interest in early phases of the sexual episode. Indeed, whether women need to do much of anything to signal proceptivity is open to debate. Though perhaps overstating the point, Greer and Buss (1994) summarize their findings with the claim that "women often need to do nothing to promote a sexual encounter. Simply existing in time and space and being naked under their clothes is often enough to trigger approach attempts by men" (p. 197).

Finally, evidence of a prevailing sexual script for men and women, and evidence of the embeddedness of this script in larger social roles, can be found in the content of influence tactics. Greer and Buss (1994) used a sociobiological perspective (Buss, 1994; Buss & Schmitt, 1993) to study tactics for "promoting sexual encounters" in small samples of college students. Consistent with the script that males generally pursue sex and females generally pursue relationships, males perceived that tactics signaling sexual availability (e.g., She asked him if he wanted to sleep with her) were most effective, whereas females perceived that tactics signaling commitment and emotional involvement (e.g., He told her that he really loved her) were most effective. All tactics were perceived to be more effective when used by women.

When Greer and Buss had men and women rate the frequency with which they used and received these same tactics, they found several similarities. Indeed, 17 of the 122 acts rated were also on the lists of the 20 most frequently used tactics for both males and females, indicating that although there is a broad range of possible script elements, only a few are viewed as normative. Women reported using tactics that enhance their physical attractiveness more than men, and men reported using a larger variety of tactics and using several of them more often than women (including "get target drunk," "go to private or secluded area," "indicate sexual attractiveness of target," "directly request sex," and "create a romantic atmosphere"). In general, it appears that the males engage in more proceptive strategies than do females. Yet, according to subject ratings of effectiveness, "the more overt the sexual advances by men, the less attractive women find them" (Buss, 1994, p. 117).

In summary, the predominant script for sexual initiation in North American young adult courtship relations appears to contain a number of features:

1. Despite an extensive potential repertoire of sexual pursuit tactics, only a relatively small subset of tactics are considered highly normative.
2. Men are inclined to engage in the more direct forms of these tactics, and may have a larger repertoire of such direct tactics.
3. When women do employ such tactics, they are inclined to use the more indirect forms.
4. Direct tactics by men are not perceived to be as effective as more indirect tactics.
5. Any tactics employed by women are perceived to be effective, given men's proclivities to pursue sex.
6. For better or worse, men are cast in the role of proactive initiator and pursuer of sex, and women are cast in the role of reactive regulator and sexual gatekeeper.

Token Resistance

Given the script described above, it is little surprise that women are assumed to resist sexual initiation, and that such resistance is occasionally "token" in nature. This assumption is held not only by men in general (Muehlenhard, 1988) and rapists in particular (Scully & Morolla, 1984), but by college student females and males as well. When asked about perceived use of token resistance in others, more than 90% of males and females in one study indicated that they believe females sometimes use token resistance

(Muehlenhard, Giusti, & Rodgers, 1993). Indeed, sanctions against promiscuity, the importance of emotional involvement as a frame for sexual relations, and the prospect of pregnancy contribute to the script that token resistance is something of a ritualistic obligation of women. Further features of this script are suggested by Byers's (1988) finding that most men became compliant in role plays after the female's second refusal, but that about a third of the males claimed they would try again that same evening. Similarly, Mills and Granoff (1992) found that for those who believe women engage in token resistance, a woman needs to say no an average of 2.6 times to be believed. Shotland and Goodstein (1992) found evidence of a precedence effect, in which the more prior sexual experience a woman has had with a sexual initiator, the less serious or legitimate he assumes her refusals to be. In sum, because token resistance is so closely tied to the traditional female script, written large, legitimate refusals are often presumed to be part of the role, and not necessarily a true reflection of actor's intent.

Token resistance (TR) is typically defined as a person's indication of "unwillingness to engage in the sexual activity, although he or she had every intention to and [was] willing to engage in the sexual activity with that partner at that time" (O'Sullivan & Allgeier, 1994, p. 1036). Scholars investigating TR have claimed that it must involve the feigning of intent. It is thus considered distinct from instances in which a person desires but knowingly chooses not to engage in sex and instances in which the person is indicating maybe by saying no.

In all, it appears that from 18% to 40% of college students report having experienced TR (Mills & Granoff, 1992; Muehlenhard et al., 1993; Muehlenhard & Hollabough, 1988; Muehlenhard & McCoy, 1991; O'Sullivan & Allgeier, 1994; Sprecher, Hatfield, Cortese, Potapova, & Levitskaya, 1994). Estimates vary by method of data collection (e.g., checklist versus open-ended essay) and culture. When the question is rephrased to include "saying no when meaning maybe," the estimates tend to be much higher. In addition, there is some evidence that men engage in token resistance as often as females do. Given the unexpected nature of this finding, the motives and effects of TR merit examination.

Research on the effects of TR indicates that it has both positive and negative outcomes. In some relationships it functions as play and increases arousal. This is consistent with findings that much token resistance occurs in established relationships in which sex has already occurred (Muehlenhard et al., 1993, O'Sullivan & Allgeier, 1994; Shotland & Hunter, 1995). In O'Sullivan and Allgeier's (1994) study, more than half of the subjects reported that the TR episode was extremely pleasant, more than one-third claimed that their romantic interest did not change as a result of the TR, and 44% experienced improvement in their romantic interest as a result.

However, two types of negative outcomes are also possible. A seldom-examined outcome of TR is the prospect that the scripted refusal is occasionally offered and accepted as "real." In such instances, people may miss a desired opportunity for sex. In Muehlenhard and Hollabaugh's (1988) study, almost 12% of women experienced this outcome; the actual percentage may be much higher (Muehlenhard & McCoy, 1991).

Another negative outcome that may be associated indirectly with TR is verbal coercion. For example, Muehlenhard and Cook (1988) constructed a "token no" scale to assess "the belief that women often pretend not to want sex when they really do in order not to appear promiscuous" (p. 62). Across a sample of 959 college students, belief that token resistance occurs revealed a small but significant correlation to partner's verbal coercion as a reason for submitting to unwanted sex (scores were uncorrelated to physical coercion).

Scripts have the advantage of providing efficient cognitive and social structures by which action can be learned, recalled, and implemented. But they can be followed too literally, discounted as not "real," and misread (or miscast?). Consequently, token resistance is often used unproblematically, but it also presents numerous possibilities for unwanted interpretations and outcomes.

Legitimate Resistance

Certainly, not all resistance to sexual initiation moves is token (Emmers & Allen, 1994). Below, we examine legitimate resistance and the two types of episodes that might unfold. We look first at the research studying noncoercive episodes, where the extent of sexual involvement is negotiated by partners. If the resistance to "normal" sexual initiations is offered legitimately and accepted, then the script is essentially cooperative even though involving disagreement. Second, we review research that investigates coercive situations, where resistance is not accepted and sexual involvement is imposed on an unwilling partner through verbal or physical force. In such instances, it is possible that stereotyped scripts are being enacted (e.g., the romance novel prototype of the male pushing on despite the female's obligatory resistance until the female swoons into submission), although there may be more psychologically disturbing reasons unrelated to such script notions.

Noncoercive Episodes

O'Sullivan and Byers (1992) report that, among their respondents, the vast majority of males (90.9%) and females (82.9%) claimed to have complied with recalled sexual initiations on recent dates, typically with no verbal response (males = 41.8%, females = 46.1%) or verbal acceptance (males = 34.5%, females = 28.9%). Verbal refusals were offered only between 2% and 4% of the time, and negative nonverbal responses were offered only between 4% and 5% of the time. In a sample of married and cohabiting individuals (22 men and 55 women), employing a one-week self-monitoring procedure, Byers and Heinlein (1989) found that 73% of initiations were responded to positively. In both Byers and Heinlein's (1989) and O'Sullivan and Byers's (1992) studies, men and women were equally likely to refuse sexual initiation. This finding indicates the adaptation of the traditional sexual script (i.e., men as initiators and women as gatekeepers) in developed relationships. It seems that, in general, people operate with a coordinated script such that on-record refusals, which would be highly face-threatening, are unnecessary.

When disagreements do occur in established relationships, evidence suggests that they are resolved fairly easily. Byers and Lewis' (1988) survey of college daters indicates that over a 4-week period, the average student had slightly more than 10 dates, 73% of which involved some form of sexual activity. "Disagreements in which the man desired to engage in a more intimate sexual activity than did the woman constituted 7% of the total dates, or 10% of the dates on which there was some sexual activity" (p. 19). Only about 14% of the disagreements occurred on the first date, with almost 40% occurring in the context of "long-term relationships." The majority of men (60.7%) "unquestionably stopped their advances, many also apologizing" (p. 22); 7% continued with verbally coercive tactics, and almost 11% physically continued with their advances. Overall, only 10%-16% of subjects reported a decrease in romantic interest after the disagreement. Quinn, Sanchez-Hucles, Coates, and Gillen (1991) also found that the vast majority of men complied when women said no, regardless of how assertively the refusals were offered.

Elements of the traditional sexual script sometimes lead women to believe that men will become angry when sex is refused (Lewin, 1985; Motley & Reeder, 1995). However, it appears that most men do not resent, and may actually expect, refusal. Motley and Reeder (1994, 1995), using both quantitative and qualitative methods, found that females are more concerned about potentially negative relational consequences to their sexual refusals, whereas men seem to take refusals very much in stride. It may be that females, aware of the script of males pursing sex, perceive rejection as highly frustrating and face-threatening, whereas men, aware of the script of women refusing, simply expect refusal as a normative possibility.

In general, studies suggest that most of the times when women offer refusals, (a) the refusals tend to be verbal and (b) relatively direct; (c) when their refusals are not complied with, stronger, more direct, and more nonverbal refusals are offered, but that (d) most refusals are respected by males (Byers, 1988; Murnen, Perot, & Byrne, 1989).

The script may call for females to offer refusal (at least early on in relationships), but it does not narrowly specify the tactics of refusal. McCormick (1979) developed a taxonomy of 10 strategies that could be used for either seeking compliance or resisting compliance. In general, indirect strategies were preferred for seeking sex, whereas direct strategies were preferred for refusing sex (see Jesser, 1978). Perper and Weis (1987) content analyzed women's essays on sexual influence. Rejection themes included such techniques as simple rejection, avoiding proceptivity, avoiding intimate situations, creating distractions, making excuses, physical resistance, departure, hinting, expressing disapproval of the man, and making arguments to delay.

In an investigation of sexual disagreements in script reversals, O'Sullivan and Byers (1993) studied recalled episodes in which females were in the situation of influencing reluctant males to have sex. More than half of the college students in the sample could recall such episodes. The disagreements occurred, on average, after the tenth date, and close to 60% had already engaged in the disputed sexual activity previously in the relationship. About a third of the men's refusals were described as fairly direct nonverbal rejection (i.e., move away), whereas almost 70% provided some form of verbal refusal. Men's refusals were rated as slightly unclear, even though almost 70% of the refusals were respected. It appears that the traditional script can be reversed in more established dating relationships.

The most detailed examination conducted thus far of the communication of resistance is found in a series of studies by Motley and Reeder (1994, 1995). These researchers found that, for all resistance messages, females claimed to intend greater resistance than men attributed to the messages. When males selected interpretations for each resistance message, only the direct rejection messages were interpreted as strictly indicating no desire to go further. In instances of indirect resistance, a nonresistance interpretation was the modal interpretation offered by males. Finally, focus group discussions held separately with male and female subjects indicated that females tend to anticipate negative relational implications when refusing directly, whereas males tend to perceive nothing more negative than general disappointment.

In short, men overattribute sexual possibility in messages that women intend as restricting sexual possibility. Only the most direct resistance messages are interpreted literally by men, yet these are precisely the messages that women are reluctant to use for fear of negative relationship implications—implications that males do not perceive as likely. In contrast, males apparently anticipate refusals—which they often interpret as token in nature—as normative, but generally comply nonetheless, at least initially. Some evidence suggests that direct and open communication of intentions by the female can be both appropriate and effective (Muehlenhard & Andrews, 1985).

Coercive Episodes

Sexual resistance takes many forms. In more collaborative encounters, no generally means no, and often, no does not even have to be said. However, as sexual compliance gaining becomes more unidirectional and coercive, the effectiveness of resistance becomes more important. Sexual coercion occurs when a person is pressured or manipulated into having sex against his or her will. Rape, an extreme form of sexual coercion, typically requires three conditions: (a) Sexual acts are performed (most typically intercourse, but reform statutes often include oral and anal forms of penetration) (b) against the person's will and without the person's consent, (c) with force, or threat of force. In this review, we focus almost entirely upon sexual coercion in the date and acquaintance context, given the interest in understanding coercion as a communicative phenomenon rather than a psychopathological phenomenon.

Research suggests that sexual coercion and violence are scripted (Gagnon, 1990), and that there are several sources of *mis*communication involved in the occurrence of sexual coercion. None of this research should be taken to imply that the victim is responsible for the coercion. Rather, it should be taken to imply that communication plays a complex and integral role in facilitating a script in which coercion occurs. Such a script appears to have the actors read parts that facilitate individual goals, without much shared understanding or congruence. There are at least four ways in which miscommunication is likely to occur in sexual episodes: through perceptual biases, through indirectness and misinterpreted ambiguity, through liberal interpretation of verbal "no" messages, and through intentional miscommunication (see also Grauerholz & Crew Solomon, 1989).

Perceptual biases. One of the most consistent findings in the sexual communication literature is that males live in a more sexualized world than do females (Bradley, Prentice, & Briggs, 1990; Bruschi & Raymond, 1990; Knoth, Boyd, & Singer, 1988). Males desire higher levels of sexual activity, especially in earlier stages of relationships (McCabe & Collins, 1984). Baier, Rosenzweig, and Whipple (1991) found that among their subjects almost 52% of males and more than 73% of females had "ever had another person misinterpret the level of sexual intimacy you desired." This percentage was not affected by sexual orientation (heterosexual versus gay/bisexual).

Several studies have indicated that males read more sexual interest and intent into women's behavior than women interpret or intend (Abbey, 1991b; Bostwick & DeLucia, 1992; Saal, Johnson, & Weber, 1989). This perceptual disparity is no doubt linked to a number of widely shared cultural scripts (e.g., a man deserves sex if he spends a lot of money on a woman, or if she is wearing revealing clothing; Margolin, Miller, & Moran, 1989) and the double standard (i.e., men are supposed to pursue sex and enjoy sex *qua* sex, whereas women initially are supposed to resist sex and view it as sex *qua* relationship; Muehlenhard, 1988). Consistent with traditional courtship scripts, meta-analysis (Emmers & Allen, 1995) has found that in evaluating sexual aggression situations, both men and women perceive females as more willing to have sex when the date is in an apartment, when the man pays for the date, and when the female has initiated the date. Further, men in general perceive forced sex as more acceptable, and women as more interested in sex, than women do.

Malamuth and Brown (1994), who tested three theoretical accounts of sexual aggression and communication, conclude that, in general, the pattern of results favors the suspicion schema model, in which men simply discount the truthfulness of women's rejection. In particular, more sexually aggressive attitudes among male raters in their study were associated with the perception of less hostility and negativity in the hostile rejection scenario. This is also consistent with the male presumption and discounting of the scripted female refusal. Thus, although all three models anticipate communication problems as integral to sexual disagreement situations, the data tend to suggest that male courtship scripts lead some men to misperceive female messages.

Indirectness and misinterpreted ambiguity. The studies reviewed thus far indicate that female behavior is generally overinterpreted with sexual intent, regardless of message type. Here we are concerned with the types of messages that contribute to that misperception. Indirect or ambiguous restraint messages that are intended to signal "stop" are interpreted by men as "token resistance" moves (Muehlenhard & Hollabaugh, 1988). Perper and Weis (1987) note that some men may not perceive the cluster of restraint moves they call "incomplete rejection" as rejection at all, "but as an opportunity to enact the role of ardent male who 'does not take no for an answer' " (p. 476).

Despite considerable evidence that men overattribute sexual intent to women's messages, two studies qualify this finding. Abbey and Melby (1986) found that the males in their sample viewed female behavior as more sexy, seductive, promiscuous, and flirtatious than did their female subjects. However, the ambiguity of the message did not have a main effect on interpretations. Kowalski (1993) specified the possibility of message effects further by investigating mundane dating behaviors (e.g., smiles), romantic behaviors (e.g., leans head on shoulder), and sexual behaviors (e.g., removes clothing). The results indicate that the men and women in the study differed in their perceptions of sexual connotativeness only in reference to the mundane behaviors, which the men viewed as more sexual in intent. There were also effects for stereotypical sex role beliefs, suggesting that the stronger the adherence to traditional scripts, the more pronounced the attribution of sexual connotations to mundane behavior.

Liberal interpretation of verbal "no" messages. The previous discussion of possibilities for miscommunication concerned the inclination of males to overattribute sexual intent (and/or females to underinterpret sexual intent). Studies also indicate that regardless of the underlying intentions (e.g., impression management or lack of sexual interest), males often do not take sexual refusals seriously. In a survey of 800 college males and females, Holcomb, Holcomb, Sondag, and Williams (1991) found that 78.1% of males and 89.8% of females agreed with the statement, "If a woman says 'no' to having sex, she means 'no.' " However, when the question was rephrased to read, "If a woman says 'no' to having sex, she means 'maybe' or even 'yes,' " the percentages were still notable for both men (36.9%) and women (21.1%). Byers and Wilson (1985) found that women who provided an excuse with a no (someone was expected to come over) were interpreted (by both men and women) as meaning that the man should try again later that evening. As we noted earlier, in our review of the token resistance literature, people not only often presume that no does not mean no, they also presume that others frequently do not mean no, and sizable minorities of people admit to saying no occasionally and not meaning it.

Intentional miscommunication. Finally, although not extensively studied, deception and deliberate miscommunication appear to be employed frequently as sexual compliance-gaining tactics. The way that token resistance has been operationalized classifies it as a form of deception in resisting sex. However, there are forms of deception involved in sexual compliance gaining as well (Tooke & Camire, 1991). Mills and Granoff (1992) included a cryptic item on their survey of college students: "Have you ever been tricked into a sexual act?" Almost 10% of their sample said they had experienced this at least once. Lane and Gwartney-Gibbs (1985) found that 22% of the males, but only 2.5% of the females, "said things you didn't mean in order to have sexual intercourse." Similarly, Anderson and Cummings (1993) found that 25% of college females surveyed claimed to have "found out that a man had obtained sexual intercourse with you by saying things he didn't really mean." Kanin's (1985) study specified what some of these "things" might be: falsely professing love or falsely promising "pinning," engagement, or marriage. Also, although not necessarily deceptive, threatening to terminate the relationship or to leave the woman stranded were exploitative techniques employed. Poppen and Segal (1988) found that 37% of males and 8% of females claimed to have told lies in order to get sex, and 14% of males and 28% of females claimed to have been lied to in attempts to gain sexual compliance. Cochran and Mays (1990) found that 34% of men and 10% of women claimed to have lied in order to have sex, and 47% of men and 60% of women believed they had been lied to for sex. In essence, in sexual relations, what is said is not always what is meant.

Miller and Marshall (1987) surveyed 795 college students with a question on "sexual teasing." Self-reports indicated that 65% of women "engaged in sexually teasing behavior when they really did not want to go as far as sexual intercourse." In a figure remarkably similar to the female estimate of teasing, 66% of the males reported that they had experienced a female's "engaging in sexually teasing behavior when she did not want sexual intercourse to occur" (p. 44).

Collectively, the research that displays miscommunication in the sexual compliance episode suggests a script in which ambiguity plays a key role in permitting exploitation, misdirection, and equivocation. Apparently, direct metacommunication is rare, and what direct communication exists is often not taken seriously. This script may work well for saving face in a relational sense, but it apparently often includes miscues for considering other personal objectives. One of the most damaging consequences occurs when a person falls victim to date rape.

Date Rape

The extensive research on date rape (for reviews, see Benson, Charlton, & Goodhart, 1992; Berkowitz, 1992; Craig, 1990; Hall, 1990; Shotland, 1989, 1992) suggests two general approaches to the subject that appear to have parallels in people's script conceptions of rape (Kahn, Mathie, & Torgler, 1994; Ryan, 1988). The first approach views date rape, like other forms of rape (e.g., stranger, acquaintance, incest), as a product of a predatory personality. This model, based upon the actual and stereotyped script of the stranger with a weapon waiting in the bushes, presumes that rape, regardless of the context, is a crime in which sex is used to obtain power. This need for power is associated with a variety of attitude complexes, including acceptance of rape myths (Burt, 1980; Lonsway & Fitzgerald, 1994; Lottes, 1988), adversarial sex beliefs (i.e., sexual relationships are basically gamelike, competitive, and the point is to win), acceptance of interpersonal violence (viewing violence and force as acceptable modes of conflict resolution), and belief in traditional sex role scripts. Although many studies have included these attitudes (e.g., Christopher, Owens, & Stecker, 1993; Craig, Kalichman, & Follingstad, 1989; Koralewski & Conger, 1992; Malamuth, Sockloskie, Koss, & Tanaka, 1991; Muehlenhard & Falcon, 1990; Murphy, Coleman, & Haynes, 1986; Overholser & Beck, 1986; Rapaport & Burkhart, 1984; Walker, Rowe, & Quinsey, 1993), collectively their zero-order effect on sexual coercion tends to range from .00 to .40 (see Spitzberg, 1995).

An alternative model is that date rape largely tends to be an interactional concern. This model presumes that date rape is a crime in which power is used to obtain sex (Bechhofer & Parrot, 1991). Date rape generally does not involve physical violence such as beating or use of weapons (Koralewski & Conger, 1992; Koss, 1988; Yegidis, 1986); rather, it tends to involve "mismatched wrestling contests" (Kanin, 1984, p. 101) in which the male typically employs his greater size and strength to hold the woman down (Koss, 1988) or employs threats of harm (Koss, Dinero, Seibel, & Cox, 1988). The efficacy of these techniques is reinforced by the debilitating and distorting effects of alcohol consumption (Abbey, 1991a; Koss et al., 1988; Norris & Cubbins, 1992), the arousal of foreplay (Kanin, 1984; Kanin & Parcell, 1977), reliance on the often ambiguous interpretation of nonverbal cues (Goodchilds & Zellman, 1984; Perper & Weis, 1987), and overreliance on scripts (Kahn et al., 1994; Muehlenhard & MacNaughton, 1988; O'Sullivan & Byers, 1993; Remer & Witten, 1988; Ryan, 1988). One of the script elements that contributes to miscommunication is the double standard by which men are encouraged to pursue sex whereas women are encouraged to provide resistance, which may or may not be token in nature (Goodchilds, Zellman, Johnson, & Giarrusso, 1988; Muehlenhard, 1988; Muehlenhard & McCoy, 1991).

Given this litany of factors, date rapes, especially compared with nonromantic and family rapes, are commonly viewed by the victims as a form of "miscommunication" rather than a form of rape (Koss et al., 1988). This tendency to avoid labeling the experience as rape appears to be directly proportional to the romantic intimacy level of the dating relationship (Bell, Kuriloff, & Lottes, 1994; Kanekar, Shaherwalla, Franco, Kunju, & Pinto, 1991; Klemmack & Klemmack, 1976).

Even when aggression is attempted, it is not always successful. As many as 40%-60% of attempts at sexual aggression in courtship are unsuccessful (Kanin & Parcell, 1977; Murnen et al., 1989). Resistance takes many forms, but most commonly seems to reflect reasoning, pleading, turning cold, physical struggle, or crying (Koss et al., 1988). Some research indicates that the more active strategies are more effective in avoiding the aggression (Levine-MacCombie & Koss, 1986), although integrative strategies (Burgoyne & Spitzberg, 1992; Metts, Cupach, & Imahori, 1992), and even persistence (Kanin, 1984), may also have some potential. As indicated previously, even though many refusals are presumed to be token and scripted in nature, they are also generally respected.

Summary

The traditional sexual script is one in which males play the role of initiator and females play the role of regulator. Although females often initiate proceptive cues of sexual interest, these cues tend to be suggestive and vague, selecting and inviting more overtly seductive activities on the part of the male. Explicit or elaborate sexual communication appears to be relatively unlikely in early stages of courtship, and instead, ambiguity seems to be extensive. This is indicated in the strong reliance upon nonverbal behavior for interpreting sexual intent and the opportunities for overinterpreting sexual intentions underlying general immediacy cues. Even when direct communication does occur, as in refusal messages, it is generally accepted, but apparently as much out of politeness as from attribution of legitimate intent. Given the considerable ambiguity involved in the traditional sexual communication courtship script, the possibilities for exploitation, deception, and coercion, with the most extreme form being date rape, are substantial. These possibilities are made more likely to the extent that people adhere to traditional scripts of male "rights" to sex and female "obligations" to provide sex, particularly when sex has previously occurred in the relationship.

Unwanted sexual activity and rape are examples of the pragmatic concerns associated with research on sexual communication. Another concern that has recently become important is the role of sexual communication in health, particularly control of the spread of AIDS and other sexually transmitted diseases. We turn now to a discussion of that literature.

COMMUNICATION AND SEXUAL HEALTH

The advent of the AIDS epidemic has prompted a concerted effort on the part of researchers to understand communication practices in two relevant areas of sexual health: assessing partner risk of being HIV positive and implementing the use of condoms during sexual intercourse. The research reveals a persistent disparity between what sexually active people believe is necessary and what they actually do. For example, in their study of college student ratings of the "necessity" and "typicality" of various behaviors in a hypothetical one-night stand script, Edgar and Fitzpatrick (1993) found that the actions "discuss whether or not they need to use protection" and "used a condom" both received very high necessity ratings but very low typicality ratings. In a survey of college students in California, Baldwin and Baldwin (1988) found that less than 20% of those who were sexually active (both women and men) reported using condoms 75% of the time or more. Those respondents who had had three or more sexual partners in the past three months were more worried about AIDS than were their less active counterparts, but were no more likely to use condoms. Similarly, in a survey of 479 sexually active college students, Cline and McKenzie (1994) found that condoms were not used consistently despite the fact that respondents, especially women, indicated positive attitudes toward condoms on several items (e.g., associating condoms with responsible sex, but not with embarrassment or damage to the relationship).

The gap between knowledge/attitudes and behavior suggests that interpersonal sexual scripts do not typically contain coherent plans organized around the specific goal of sexual health. The study of the descriptions of hypothetical "one-night stands" by Edgar and Fitzpatrick (1993) noted previously illustrates this point. When asked to describe a hypothetical one-night stand date, respondents produced scripted (and gender-similar) descriptions of moves that would occur both in the public setting of the date (at a bar or dance) and subsequently in the private setting (an apartment). However, "communication about birth control or condoms" was mentioned by only 28% of the men (as the final step in the private seduction script) and 26% of the women (as the next-to-last step in the private seduction scripts). These actions as described by respondents tended to be vague and diverse, ranging from reference to the use of condoms to guard against the spread of sexually transmitted diseases such as AIDS, to references to birth control, to references to "protection with no obvious referent." However, when respondents were asked later in the survey whether a condom had been used in the scenario they described, 80% of the men and 70% of the women said yes. It appears that respondents recognize the advisability of condom use, but do not spontaneously include this as a characteristic in their cognitive representations of seduction sequences.

The lack of such a step is problematic, but in many ways it is not surprising. Few models for seeking risk information or using condoms are available in media depictions of sexual activity (Adelman, 1992; Metts & Fitzpatrick, 1992). Moreover, direct questioning about the potential risk of a person as a sexual partner is essentially an "interruption" in the normative actions of dating scripts (e.g., Rose & Frieze, 1993), even those that have sexual involvement as their defining characteristic (i.e., one-night stands). Explicit questions about sexual history and the advisability of using condoms violate the cultural norm for indirectness during sexual intimacy and the cultural prescription for women to be sexually inexperienced. And for males and females who believe that condoms reduce physical pleasure, condom use is likely to inhibit full expression of their intrapsychic scripts. We turn now to a more detailed discussion of the role of scripts—or, perhaps more accurately, the absence of scripts—in the assessment of partner risk and initiation of the use of condoms during sexual episodes.

Assessment of Partner Risk

Since the U.S. surgeon general's admonition to "know your partner," questions that prospective sexual partners should ask of one another have been widely publicized. People are encouraged to ask any potential partner about IV drug use, blood transfusions, homosexual encounters or encounters with prostitutes, previous sexual partners (number, recency, drug use), and whether or not the person has been tested for HIV. Although the intent of such questions is to gather enough information to determine the possibility of HIV infection in a potential sexual partner, their utility is compromised by several factors. People do not always know the sexual histories of their previous partners. People sometimes manage impressions and lie about their own sexual histories (Cochran & Mays, 1990). In order to avoid the embarrassment and awkwardness of explicit strategies, people often "guess" about whether a potential partner may have been exposed to AIDS rather than ask directly (Gray & Saracino, 1991). People also tend to gather information that is only tangentially related to potential risk (e.g., they ask questions about family and social background or make observations about cleanliness and clothing) and then, using implicit personality theory, infer safety (American Social Health Association, 1994).

From a script perspective, this would suggest that although media campaigns may have made the goal of assessing risk salient to sexually active people, many do not seek or provide the most useful information because to do so violates norms of indirectness and romantic abandon. In short, risk assessment runs contrary to the traditional sexual-romantic script and is thus avoided or done inferentially. This trend is evident in the research on frequency and explicitness of risk assessment communication.

Frequency

Specific information about the frequency and patterning of risk assessment talk is limited. Data from national random samples are not yet available as to how often individuals explicitly discuss risk factors with current (or potential) sexual partners relative to the number of times they do not, and the impact on sexual involvement in both cases.

Some insights as to normative patterns can be gained, however, from research dealing with AIDS discussions between sexual or potentially sexual partners. Not surprisingly, this research indicates that most college students are able to recall one instance of discussing AIDS with a partner or potential sexual partner. For example, Bowen and Michal-Johnson (1989) found that at least one episode where AIDS was discussed with a "partner" could be recalled by slightly more than 50% of college student respondents (64.6% of females, 52.4% of males; N = 243). Cline, Freeman, and Johnson (1990; Cline, Johnson, and Freeman, 1992) found that at least one episode where AIDS was discussed with a "sexual partner or a potential sexual partner" could be recalled by approximately two-thirds (63.6%) of sexually active college students who responded to a mailed survey (N = 497), with women being more likely to report such episodes than were men (72.5% of females, 53.7% of males). Whether these respondents "typically" or "consistently" discuss AIDS with their sexual partners is not known, nor is the extent of AIDS talk among the 712 students who chose not to return the survey.

Only 63 students (13.4%) answered yes to the question, "Have you ever wanted to talk with a sexual partner (or a potential sexual partner) about AIDS but did not do so?" Of these respondents, 42 also described an episode where they *had* talked about AIDS. Thus, the occurrence of "inhibited" AIDS discussions seems to be relatively small. Another 23% of the respondents had not discussed AIDS, but had not wanted to.

The reasons given for not talking about AIDS underscore its incompatibility with the traditional romantic dating script. They include embarrassment, lack of self-confidence, not knowing partner, fear of hurting or offending partner, fear of ruining the mood, belief that the relationship was too casual or brief, and feeling that "things were happening too fast" (Bowen & Michal-Johnson, 1989; Cline et al., 1992).

Although it might be tempting to assume that students who could recall at least one episode of discussing AIDS have adapted the traditional romantic script to the task of assessing partner risk, this assumption is not fully supported when the explicitness of the interactions is analyzed.

Explicitness

The question of whether sexual partners engage in explicit discussion of risk behaviors related to potential HIV infection is answered somewhat differently depending upon the research design used for the research. When respondents are given a checklist of information-seeking strategies, they tend to report a preference for directness. In developing and validating the AIDS Discussion Strategy Scale, Snell and Finney (1990) identified six strategies that college students might use *if* they "wanted to discuss the topic of AIDS with a sexual partner (either a current sexual partner or a future sexual partner)" (p. 449). These strategies included *rational* (e.g., I would explain the reason why I wanted to discuss AIDS), *manipulative* (I would use deception to get my partner to talk about AIDS), *withdrawal* (I would refrain from sexual contact until we discussed AIDS), *charm* (e.g., I would be especially sweet, charming, and pleasant before bringing up the subject of AIDS), *subtle* (e.g., I would drop subtle hints that I wanted to talk about AIDS), and *persistence* (e.g., I would continually attempt to discuss the issue of AIDS). Based on ratings of likelihood of use, Snell and Finney conclude that direct approaches to the discussion of AIDS are most common. They found that although females reported greater likelihood of using rational strategies and less likelihood of using manipulation and charm strategies compared with males, both females and males reported high likelihood of use for rational strategies and low likelihood of use for manipulation, withdrawal, and charm.

Other research, however, that distinguishes among specific topics that might be included in a discussion about AIDS, has found a preference for directness *only* when information is salient. And to most college student samples, relationship assessment seems to be more salient information than health risk information. Edgar, Freimuth, Hammond, McDonald, and Fink (1992) asked 204 college students who had sex with a new partner over the past 12 months to select from a list of options the strategy they used for gathering information about issues that concerned them. Slightly more than a third of the respondents chose the option "I asked him or her directly." Another 17% indicated that asking was not even necessary because their partners "volunteered the information without an effort on my part." Thus, more than half of the respondents (56%) indicated that risk assessment discussions were straightforward. However, this pattern reflects only topics that were salient enough to merit attention. A number of issues were not salient to respondents contemplating sexual involvement. For example, few respondents expressed concern about their partners' homosexual activity (11.3%), AIDS symptoms (11.8%), experience with anal sex (18%), or IV drug use (12.7%), although 52.6% reported that the question of whether or not the other person was infected with the AIDS virus had occurred to them. Of greater concern to these respondents, perhaps because of their relevance to the development of the *relationship,* were the number of previous sexual partners (76%), recency of the last new sex partner (63.2%), and feelings about using condoms (65%). Thus, the nature of the information sought (relational versus health) and its degree of threat to the sexual privacy of the partner seem to influence how directly it is discussed. It appears that risk assessment strategies are still constrained by the prevailing romantic script, although this may be more pronounced for those who adhere more strongly to the traditional script.

Research that has asked respondents to describe actual talk episodes has produced findings consistent with this view. Bowen and Michal-Johnson (1989) content analyzed open-ended responses to the request for college students ($N = 243$) to describe an episode in which they discussed AIDS with "a partner." In general, the talk about AIDS tended to be indirect and casual, often triggered by a television program or commercial, and sometimes performed in a joking manner. The authors summarize their impressions of the episode descriptions as a manifestation of relational rather than sexual health concerns:

> While individuals may not be able to articulate the function of talk in relationships, it is clear that they are both aware of talk and afraid of its consequences. . . . Implicitly, they were aware that once they discussed the risks of their past or present behaviors, the risk of AIDS would be a real entity that had to be faced. (p. 17)

Similarly, Cline et al. (1992) found that in their sample most AIDS discussions were about AIDS in general (e.g., generalized risks in sleeping around, AIDS prevention) and less often included topics specifically focused on personal safety in a respondent's own relationship (e.g., using a condom or partner's sexual history). Of particular interest was the association between the circumstances that prompted these discussions and the directness of the content of the discussion. Contingency tables indicated that general AIDS discussions were likely to be prompted by a television program on AIDS or by a topic that arose during casual conversation, whereas relationship-specific discussions were more likely to be associated with imminent sexual encounters. Paradoxically, as a couple moves more completely into the sexual involvement script, explicit discussion of risk factors becomes increasingly discordant with such relational elements as trust, specialness, and romantic abandon. Certainly, risk assessment strategies can include statements framing the questions as important because this particular relationship is important. Unfortunately, the limited data we have suggest that most college students who serve as subjects do not have very sophisticated assessment routines in their general sexual scripts. Even more disturbing is the possibility that having discussed AIDS with a partner, no matter how general the discussion, might create a sense of trust and security that actually reduces the likelihood of using a condom during sexual intercourse with a new partner (Cline et al., 1992; but also see Shoop & Davidson, 1994). We turn now to a more detailed discussion of communication and condom use.

Condom Use

Evidence suggests that plans for using condoms are not a common aspect of individual sexual scripts (Edgar & Fitzpatrick, 1993) or a common feature in media portrayals. As Adelman (1992) notes about television, "Portrayals of sex scenes usually dissolve into commercial breaks, trains going into tunnels, or waves breaking onto the shore" (p. 85). However, studies indicate that plans can be developed (Metts & Cupach, 1991), can be used to overcome resistance to condom usage (Baffi, Schroeder, Redican, & McCluskey, 1989), and can reconcile the incongruity between erotic abandon and pragmatic concerns through playful transformations (Adelman, 1991). Moreover, women with less-traditional attitudes toward the double standard are more likely to suggest using condoms and to provide condoms, compared with women who hold traditional attitudes (traditional attitudes have not been found to influence men's behavior) (Caron, Davis, Halteman, & Stickle, 1993).

Nonetheless, condom use during sexual intercourse among teenagers and young adults tends to be moderate at best and used primarily as a method of birth control rather than disease control. As with risk assessment discussions, people are reluctant to imply that they or their partners are unsafe. The need to use protection and the desire to avoid unpleasant topics poses a communicative challenge for sexually active people. As Edgar, Hammond, and Freimuth (1989) note, condom use may be affected by any one of three interpersonal communication factors: self-presentation (the need to maintain a positive image for self and partner), conflict management (if disagreements arise over use of condoms and threaten the relationship), and persuasion (skills employed to persuade a reluctant partner to use a condom). Various aspects of these concerns are evident in the empirical literature on condom use, although some scholars suggest that "simply asking" that a condom be used is the most common and effective plan.

One line of research that assumes an implicit compliance-gaining model of condom use is characterized by having respondents rate strategies on dimensions of effectiveness, comfortableness, and likelihood of use. This research, much like the assessment findings, suggests that direct (face-threatening) strategies are perceived as effective but not necessarily comfortable, although men and women display somewhat different preferences.

The work by De Bro, Campbell, and Peplau (1994) typifies this approach. College students ($N = 393$) were asked to rate six power strategies on perceived effectiveness and comfortableness for convincing a partner to use a condom and convincing a partner not to use a condom when it had been requested. The strategies included *reward* (e.g., "I would emphasize that _____'s respect for my feelings about using a condom would really enhance our relationship"), *emotional coercion* (e.g., "I would say that if _____ pressured me about using a condom, then _____ must not care about me very much"), *risk information* (e.g., "I would inform _____ that there have been very few cases of AIDS among heterosexual college students, so there is no need to use a condom"), *deception* (e.g., "Even though I want to use a condom because I'm worried about sexually transmitted diseases, I'd make up a different reason to tell _____"), *seduction* (e.g., "Before _____ had a chance to object to the use of a condom, I would get _____ so 'turned on' that _____ would forget about the condom") and *withhold sex* (single item, "I would just tell _____ that I will make love only if we use [do not use] a condom").

Results indicated that when the goal was to gain compliance in using a condom, strategies were rated as more likely to be used by a woman, whereas when the goal was to avoid the use of a condom, strategies were rated as more likely to be used by a man. Ratings of effectiveness and comfort revealed that all strategies, regardless of goal, were rated as more effective than comfortable. Interaction effects, however, were also found. When the goal was getting the partner to use a condom, women rated reward, risk information, and withhold sex as significantly more effective than did men, whereas men rated seduction as more effective than did women. Women also rated reward, emotional coercion, risk information, and withhold sex as significantly more comfortable than did men, whereas men rated seduction as more comfortable than did women.

In essence, then, these results indicate that women feel generally more positive than men toward all strategies to gain compliance in condom use except seduction. Interestingly, gender differences in actual practice disappear for all strategies except seduction. For those respondents who were sexually experienced (had engaged in sexual intercourse at least once), men and women were equally likely to have used all of the power strategies to convince a partner to use a condom except seduction. Men reported that they had used seduction more than any other strategy and were, in fact, three times more likely than women respondents to report its use.

Gender differences were also found for strategies to avoid using a condom. Men rated the risk information strategy as more effective for avoiding condom use compared with women. Women rated the withhold sex strategy as more effective compared with men. Men reported that the use of seduction and risk information was more comfortable compared with women. For measures of actual use, seduction was the most commonly used strategy by both sexes for resisting condom use, but men were more likely than women to have used it. De Bro et al. (1994) conclude that, overall, their findings confirm the presence of the traditional sexual script even in negotiating the use of condoms.

The important question, however, is whether condom use has to be "negotiated." Some research suggests that the compliance-gaining perspective and accompanying checklist taps into scripts for problematic situations where resistance is expected. As we noted previously in the discussion of sexual involvement, shared goals and synchronized behavior characterize most sexual episodes. This seems to be true for requesting condom use as well.

Research that has compared sexual encounters in which condoms were used and those in which they were not indicates that any form of request to use a condom is likely to be met with agreement. For example, Edgar et al. (1992) analyzed the experiences of 204 students who had sex with a new partner during the previous year. The respondents who had used a condom (43%) were asked to describe "the interaction, focusing on the messages about condom use that were exchanged." Analysis of the open-ended responses revealed that women were more likely to have used a "power" strategy (no condom, no sex) or a direct request. Men were more likely to describe preemptive nonverbal moves (e.g., used it without asking) or to have allowed the woman to choose (I asked her preference). Of note is the fact that in 83% of the interactions, the partner complied immediately. In another 5% of the cases, the partner agreed reluctantly, and in only 4% of the cases was continued resistance reported.

This finding is supported indirectly by a two-part study conducted by Reel and Thompson (1994), who asked 70 heterosexual respondents (adults and college students) to list messages they had sent to or received from actual or potential sex partners regarding condom use. This procedure produced 30 different message categories. In the second phase of the study, undergraduate students rated their likelihood of use for each message type, their likelihood of using a condom if they received each message from a sexual partner, and their likely verbal response to each message (open-ended). Results indicated that although "we"-focused strategies and more direct request strategies had particularly high ratings for likely condom use, all messages received generally high ratings. Reel and Thompson conclude that, "with few exceptions, all one needs to do is 'bring up' the topic of AIDS or condoms in order to get a partner to use a condom" (p. 137).

This finding is consistent with a study of sexually active females aged 12 to 18 conducted by Catania et al. (1989). These authors found, as might be expected, that greater enjoyment of condoms was associated with greater condom use. Somewhat more surprising was the fact that only one of three measures of sexual communication was associated with frequency of condom use: willingness to request that partners use condoms. Neither perceived quality of sexual communication with partner nor health-related communication (i.e., ability to discuss sexual history and condom use) was predictive of condom use. Also not predictive of condom use were egocentrism, susceptibility and self-efficacy beliefs, AIDS anxiety, and condom norms.

Taken together, these findings are both encouraging and frustrating. They suggest that many sexually active people have incorporated a condom use contingency into their larger sexual scripts. The association between condoms and responsible sex in public discourse seems to have provided a frame of legitimacy for the use of condoms. The fortunate consequence is that a simple request to use a condom typically results in compliance. On the other hand, few studies have found that more than 40%-50% of respondents had used condoms in their recent sexual experiences, and fewer yet reported that they always use condoms. Clearly, some sexually active individuals have not internalized the goal of safer sex, or have not incorporated a plan for condom use as a way to meet that goal. In some cases, the overriding limitations of sex role expectations (e.g., women should be naive and sexually inexperienced, hence unfamiliar with condoms; men should be sexual "performers" and, to the extent that condoms interfere with natural pleasure, they should be avoided) minimize the likelihood that condoms will be used. For those who fear that condoms will "spoil the mood," positive experiences with eroticizing condom use should dispel such fears.

CONCLUSION

Because sexual behavior is intimate and private, we tend to think of it as personal and idiosyncratic. In fact, there is a structure and pattern that is remarkably consistent across sexual episodes in the early phases of relationships. It would be strange if this were not the case, given the proclivity for human beings to absorb and enact cultural values and behavioral patterns. In this chapter we have explored the nature of such patterns in the form and function of sexual communication. We have presented the notion of sexual scripts as guides for sexual partners, particularly during initial sexual involvement, when normative expectations are most salient. We have discussed flirtation as a prototypical example of ritualized expression of sexual interest in which ambiguity facilitates assessment of sexual interest with minimal face threat. We have also discussed sexual harassment as a prototypical example of coercive expression of sexual interest built onto the scaffold of flirtation sequences. We have presented sexual involvement as consisting of more or less collaborative endeavors in which partners respond in expectable (scripted) ways to such moves as being proceptive (typically women), making sexual advances (typically men), and limiting the rate and extent of involvement (typically women). We have used script theory to explain some cases of noncollaborative sexual episodes as well—cases in which blind adherence to the assumption that all resistance is merely token and that, once entered, a sexual script must culminate in sexual intercourse leads to sexual coercion. Finally, we have examined the relatively new area of research on communication and sexual health. It appears that this is a good news/bad news story. Findings indicate that sexually active college students believe they should learn about the risk factors of their potential sexual partners and should, regardless of what they learn, use condoms during sexual intercourse. They also report that if they need to gain compliance, they have strategies to do so. These strategies are based on stereotypical sex roles: Women are more comfortable in the role of limit setter (no condom, no sex) and men are more comfortable in the role of resisting condoms. Even more heartening is the fact that a simple request generally leads to condom use. The bad news is that condoms are not routinely used; this indicates that some individuals have not incorporated this sequence into their sexual scripts.

Despite the increasingly rich literature available on sexual communication in the areas we have selected for this review, we note several limitations that merit systematic attention. First, we propose a more concentrated study of special populations for whom the traditional "dating" script may hold little relevance. Most of what we know about sexual communication is provided to us by college sophomores and heterosexual married couples in their early years of marriage. In these populations, media and peer messages provide relevant and thereby easily adapted sexual scripts. This is not the case for many other populations. For example, despite the fact that sexual interest continues throughout the life span (Riportella-Muller, 1989), communication scholars have made little effort to understand how sexual episodes among widowed and divorced adults compare with those of young dating singles. We strongly encourage researchers to seek more diverse samples for future studies.

Second, we propose investigation of how communication creates, defines, and evaluates sexual activity. Much of the research reviewed here approaches sexual activity as an event or occurrence that is largely unevaluated by a couple. Script theory tends to foreground structural patterns that are for the most part divorced from the emotional fabric that accompanies this structure. We suspect that two couples might follow very similar scripts, but one might experience a much higher level of quality than the other. We encourage researchers to examine the interface between scripts and the relationships in which they are enacted and transformed. From this perspective, sexual activity would be examined as a "construal" that is re-created and understood through subsequent episodes and in subsequent talk, both with partners and with others (Plummer, 1995). For example, under what circumstances and through what types of messages does a first sexual activity for a couple become a relational turning point versus a one-night stand? Or to what extent and under what circumstances does the use of certain types of accounts for sexual involvement define the meaning of that event ("I was in love" versus "I was drunk")? Finally, to what extent and under what circumstances does sexual activity become itself a form of communication, expressing power, control, trust, or intimacy?

We have no easy answers for these questions, but we believe that research undertaken to answer them could provide a more complete view of sexual experience than is currently available. The notion of sexual scripts as a guide for accomplishing sexual involvement is a useful grounding for understanding variation and adaptation. We encourage future researchers to explore the process of adaptation. This information may serve to provide early indications of couples who will adapt the cultural script in productive ways and those who will not.

REFERENCES

Abbey, A. (1982). Sex differences in attributions for friendly behavior: Do males misperceive females' friendliness? *Journal of Personality and Social Psychology, 42,* 830-838.

Abbey, A. (1987). Misperceptions of friendly behavior as sexual interest: A survey of naturally occurring incidents. *Psychology of Women Quarterly, 11,* 173-194.

Abbey, A. (1991a). Acquaintance rape and alcohol consumption on college campuses: How are they linked? *Journal of American College Health, 39,* 165-169.

Abbey, A. (1991b). Misperceptions as an antecedent of acquaintance rape: A consequence of ambiguity in communication between men and women. In A. Parrot & L. Bechhofer (Eds.), *Acquaintance rape: The hidden crime* (pp. 96-112). New York: John Wiley.

Abbey, A., & Melby, C. (1986). The effects of nonverbal cues on gender differences in perceptions of sexual intent. *Sex Roles, 15,* 283-298.

Abelson, R. (1981). Psychological status of the script concept. *American Psychologist, 36,* 715-729.

Abrahams, M. F. (1994, July). *Perceiving flirtatious communication: An exploration of the perceptual dimensions underlying judgments of flirtatiousness.* Paper presented at the annual meeting of the International Communication Association, Sydney.

Abrahams, M. F. (1995, February). *Perceiving flirtatious communication II: Distinguishing among types of flirtatious communication.* Paper presented at the annual meeting of the Western States Communication Association, Portland, OR.

Adelman, M. B. (1991). Play and incongruity: Framing safe-sex talk. *Health Communication, 3,* 139-155.

Adelman, M. B. (1992). Healthy passions: Safer sex as play. In T. Edgar, M. A. Fitzpatrick, & V. S. Freimuth (Eds.), *AIDS: A communication perspective* (pp. 69-89). Hillsdale, NJ: Lawrence Erlbaum.

American Social Health Association. (1994). *Finding the words: How to communicate about sexual health.* Research Triangle Park, NC: Author.

Anderson, W. P., & Cummings, K. (1993). Women's acceptance of rape myths and their sexual experiences. *Journal of College Student Development, 34,* 53-57.

Baffi, C. A., Schroeder, K. K., Redican, K. J., & McCluskey, L. (1989). Factors influencing selected heterosexual male college students' condom use. *Journal of American College Health, 38,* 137-141.

Baier, J. L., Rosenzweig, M. G., & Whipple, E. G. (1991). Patterns of sexual behavior, coercion, and victimization of university students. *Journal of College Student Development, 32,* 310-322.

Baldwin, J. D., & Baldwin, J. I. (1988). Factors affecting AIDS-related sexual risk-taking behavior among college students. *Journal of Sex Research, 25,* 181-196.

Baxter, L. A., & Bullis, C. (1986). Turning points in developing romantic relationships. *Human Communication Research, 12,* 469-493.

Bechhofer, L., & Parrot, A. (1991). What is acquaintance rape? In A. Parrot & L. Bechhofer (Eds.), *Acquaintance rape: The hidden crime* (pp. 9-25). New York: John Wiley.

Bell, S. T., Kuriloff, P. J., & Lottes, I. (1994). Understanding attributions of blame in stranger rape and date rape situations: An examination of gender, race, identification, and students' social perceptions of rape victims. *Journal of Applied Social Psychology, 24,* 1719-1734.

Benson, D., Charlton, C., & Goodhart, F. (1992). Acquaintance rape on campus: A literature review. *Journal of American College Health, 40,* 157-165.

Berkowitz, A. (1992). College men as perpetrators of acquaintance rape and sexual assault: A review of recent research. *Journal of American College Health, 40,* 175-181.

Bingham, S. G. (1991). Communication strategies for managing sexual harassment in organizations: Understanding message options and their effects. *Journal of Applied Communication Research, 19,* 88-115.

Bingham, S. G., & Burleson, B. R. (1989). Multiple effects of messages with multiple goals: Some perceived outcomes of responses to sexual harassment. *Human Communication Research, 16,* 184-216.

Booth-Butterfield, M. (1991, February). *Sexual harassment or immediacy attempts: Can receivers differentiate?* Paper presented at the annual meeting of the Western Speech Communication Association, Phoenix, AZ.

Bostwick, T. D., & DeLucia, J. L. (1992). Effects of gender and specific dating behaviors on perceptions of sex willingness and date rape. *Journal of Social and Clinical Psychology, 11,* 14-25.

Bowen, S. P., & Michal-Johnson, P. (1989). The crisis of communication relationships: Confronting the threat of AIDS. *AIDS and Public Policy Journal, 4,* 10-19.

Bradley, D. W., Prentice, D. S., & Briggs, N. E. (1990). Assessing two domains for communicating romance: Behavioral context and mode of interaction. *Communication Research Reports, 7,* 94-99.

Bruschi, I. G., & Raymond, B. (1990). What women think and what men think women think: Perceptions of abuse and kindness in dating relationships. *Psychological Reports, 67,* 115-128.

Burgoyne, S. G., & Spitzberg, B. (1992, July). *An examination of communication strategies and tactics used in potential date rape episodes.* Paper presented at the annual meeting of the International Society for the Study of Personal Relationships, Orono, ME.

Burt, M. R. (1980). Cultural myths and supports for rape. *Journal of Personality and Social Psychology, 38,* 217-230.

Buss, D. M. (1994). *The evolution of desire: Strategies in dating relationships.* New York: Basic Books.

Buss, D. M., & Schmitt, D. P. (1993). Sexual strategies theory: An evolutionary perspective on human mating. *Psychological Bulletin, 100,* 204-232.

Byers, E. S. (1988). Effects of sexual arousal on men's and women's behavior in sexual disagreement situations. *Journal of Sex Research, 25,* 235-254.

Byers, E. S., & Heinlein, L. (1989). Predicting initiations and refusals of sexual activities in married and cohabiting heterosexual couples. *Journal of Sex Research, 26,* 210-231.

Byers, E. S., & Lewis, K. (1988). Dating couples' disagreements over the desired level of sexual intimacy. *Journal of Sex Research, 24,* 15-29.

Byers, E. S., & Wilson, P. (1985). Accuracy of women's expectations regarding men's responses to refusals of sexual advances in dating situations. *International Journal of Women's Studies, 4,* 376-387.

Carns, D. (1973). Talking about sex: Notes on first coitus and the double standard. *Journal of Marriage and the Family, 35,* 677-687.

Caron, S. L., Davis, C. M., Halteman, W. A., & Stickle, M. (1993). Predictors of condom-related behaviors among first-year college students. *Journal of Sex Research, 30,* 252-259.

Catania, J. A., Coates, T. J., Greenblatt, R. M., Dolcini, M. M., Kegeles, S. M., Puckett, S., Corman, M., & Miller, J. (1989). Predictors of condom use and multiple partnered sex among sexually active adolescent women: Implications for AIDS-related health interventions. *Journal of Sex Research, 4,* 514-524.

Christopher, F. S. (1988). An initial investigation into a continuum of premarital sexual pressure. *Journal of Sex Research, 25,* 255-266.

Christopher, F. S. (1993, July). *Sexual involvement in dating: The role of relationship and individual variables.* Paper presented at the meeting of the International Network on Personal Relationships, Milwaukee, WI.

Christopher, F. S., & Frandsen, M. M. (1990). Strategies of influence in sex and dating. *Journal of Social and Personal Relationships, 7,* 89-105.

Christopher, F. S., Owens, L. A., & Stecker, H. L. (1993). Exploring the dark side of courtship: A test of a model of male premarital sexual aggressiveness. *Journal of Marriage and the Family, 55,* 469-479.

Clair, R. P., McGown, M. J., & Spirek, M. M. (1993). Sexual harassment responses of working women: An assessment of current communication-oriented typologies and perceived effectiveness of the response. In G. L. Kreps (Ed.), *Sexual harassment in the workplace* (pp. 200-224). Creskill, NJ: Hampton.

Cline, R. J. W., Freeman, K. E., & Johnson, S. J. (1990). Talk among sexual partners about AIDS: Factors differentiating those who talk from those who do not. *Communication Research, 17,* 792-808.

Cline, R. J. W., Johnson, S. J., & Freeman, K. E. (1992). Talk among sexual partners about AIDS: Interpersonal communication for risk reduction or risk enhancement? *Health Communication, 4,* 39-56.

Cline, R. J. W., & McKenzie, N. J. (1994). Sex differences in communication and the construction of HIV/AIDS. *Journal of Applied Communication Research, 22,* 322-337.

Cochran, S. D., & Mays, V. M. (1990). Sex, lies, and HIV. *New England Journal of Medicine, 322,* 774-775.

Craig, M. E. (1990). Coercive sexuality in dating relationships: A situational model. *Clinical Psychology Review, 10,* 395-423.

Craig, M. E., Kalichman, S. C., & Follingstad, D. R. (1989). Verbal coercive sexual behavior among college students. *Archives of Sexual Behavior, 18,* 421-434.

Cupach, W. R., & Metts, S. (1991). Sexuality and communication in close relationships. In K. McKinney & S. Sprecher (Eds.), *Sexuality in close relationships* (pp. 93-107). Hillsdale, NJ: Lawrence Erlbaum.

Davis, K. E., & Todd, M. J. (1985). Assessing friendship: Prototypes, paradigm cases and relationship description. In S. Duck & D. Perlman (Eds.), *Understanding personal relationships: An interdisciplinary approach* (pp. 17-38). London: Sage.

De Bro, S. C., Campbell, S. M., & Peplau, L. A. (1994). Influencing a partner to use a condom: A college student perspective. *Psychology of Women Quarterly, 18,* 165-182.

Downey, J. L., & Vitulli, W. F. (1987). Self-report measures of behavioral attributions related to interpersonal flirtation situations. *Psychological Reports, 61,* 899-904.

Edgar, T., & Fitzpatrick, M. A. (1990). Communicating sexual desire: Message tactics for having and avoiding intercourse. In J. P. Dillard (Ed.), *Seeking compliance: The production of interpersonal influence messages* (pp. 107-122). Scottsdale, AZ: Gorsuch Scarisbrick.

Edgar, T., & Fitzpatrick, M. A. (1993). Expectations for sexual interaction: A cognitive test of the sequencing of sexual communication behaviors. *Health Communication, 5,* 239-261.

Edgar, T., Freimuth, V. S., Hammond, S. L., McDonald, D. A., & Fink, E. L. (1992). Strategic sexual communication: Condom use resistance and response. *Health Communication, 4,* 105-120.

Edgar, T., Hammond, S. L., & Freimuth, V. S. (1989). The role of the mass media and interpersonal communication in promoting AIDS-related behavioral change. *AIDS and Public Policy Journal, 4,* 3-9.

Egland, K. L., Zormeier, M. M., & Spitzberg, B. H. (1995, November). *Flirtation in platonic and romantic relationships.* Paper presented at the annual meeting of the Speech Communication Association, San Antonio, TX.

Emmers, T. M., & Allen, M. (1994, November). *Factors contributing to sexually coercive behaviors: A meta-analysis.* Paper presented at the annual meeting of the Speech Communication Association, San Antonio, TX.

Emmers, T. M., & Allen, M. (1995, February). *Resistance to sexual coercion behaviors: A meta-analysis.* Paper presented at the annual meeting of the Western States Communication Association, Portland, OR.

Evans, L. J. (1978). Sexual harassment: Women's hidden occupational hazard. In J. R. Chapman & M. Gates (Eds.), *The victimization of women* (pp. 203-224). Beverly Hills, CA: Sage.

Fairhurst, G. T. (1986). Male-female communication on the job: Literature review and commentary. In M. L. McLaughlin (Ed.), *Communication yearbook 9* (pp. 83-116). Beverly Hills, CA: Sage.

Fichten, C. S., Tagalakis, V., Judd, D., Wright, J., & Amsel, R. (1992). Verbal and nonverbal communication cues in daily conversations and dating. *Journal of Social Psychology, 132,* 751-769.

Gagnon, J. H. (1990). The explicit and implicit use of the scripting perspective in sex research. In J. Bancroft (Ed.), *Annual review of sex research* (Vol. 1, pp. 1-44). Lake Mills, IA: Society for the Scientific Study of Sex.

Gagnon, J. H., & Simon, W. (1973). *Sexual conduct: The social sources of human sexuality.* Chicago: Aldine.

Ginsburg, G. P. (1988). Rules, scripts and prototypes in personal relationships. In S. W. Duck (Ed.), *Handbook of personal relationships* (pp. 23-39). London: John Wiley.

Givens, D. B. (1978). The nonverbal basis of attraction: Flirtation, courtship, and seduction. *Psychiatry, 41,* 346-359.

Goodchilds, J. D., & Zellman, G. L. (1984). Sexual signaling and sexual aggression in adolescent relationships. In N. M. Malamuth & E. Donnerstein (Eds.), *Pornography and sexual aggression* (pp. 233-243). New York: Academic Press.

Goodchilds, J. D., Zellman, G. L., Johnson, P. B., & Giarrusso, R. (1988). Adolescents and their perceptions of sexual interactions. In A. W. Burgess (Ed.), *Rape and sexual assault II* (pp. 245-270). New York: Garland.

Grauerholz, E., & Crew Solomon, J. (1989). Sexual coercion: Power and violence. In K. McKinney & S. Sprecher (Eds.), *Human sexuality: The societal and interpersonal context* (pp. 350-369). Norwood, NJ: Ablex.

Grauerholz, E., & Serpe, R. T. (1985). Initiation and response: The dynamics of sexual interaction. *Sex Roles, 12,* 1041-1059.

Gray, L. A., & Saracino, M. (1991). College students' attitudes, beliefs, and behaviors about AIDS: Implications for family life educators. *Family Relations, 40, 258-263.*

Greer, A. E., & Buss, D. M. (1994). Tactics for promoting sexual encounters. *Journal of Sex Research, 31,* 185-201.

Gruber, J. E. (1989). How women handle sexual harassment: A literature review. *Sociology and Social Research, 74,* 3-7.

Gutek, B. A. (1985). *Sex and the workplace.* San Francisco: Jossey-Bass.

Gutek, B. A., Morasch, B., & Cohen, A. (1983). Interpreting social-sexual harassment of women at work. *Journal of Social Issues, 38,* 55-74.

Gutek, B. A., Nakumura, C. Y., Gahart, M., & Handschumacher, I. (1980). Sexuality and the workplace. *Basic and Applied Social Psychology, 1,* 255-265.

Hall, G. C. N. (1990). Prediction of sexual aggression. *Clinical Psychology Review, 10,* 229-245.

Hemphill, M. R., & Pfeiffer, A. L. (1986). Sexual spillover in the workplace: Testing the appropriateness of male-female interaction. *Women's Studies in Communication, 9,* 52-66.

Holcomb, D. R., Holcomb, L. C., Sondag, K. A., & Williams, N. (1991). Attitudes about date rape: Gender differences among college students. *College Student Journal, 25,* 434-439.

Huston, T. L., Surra, C., Fitzgerald, N., & Cate, R. (1981). From courtship to marriage: Mate selection as an interpersonal process. In S. W. Duck & R. Gilmour (Eds.), *Personal relationships 2: Developing personal relationships* (pp. 53-88). New York: Academic Press.

Jesser, C. J. (1978). Male responses to direct verbal sexual initiatives of females. *Journal of Sex Research, 14,* 118-128.

Johnson, C. B., Stockdale, M. S., & Saal, F. E. (1991). Persistence of men's misperceptions of friendly cues across a variety of interpersonal encounters. *Psychology of Women Quarterly, 15,* 463-475.

Kahn, A. S., Mathie, V. A., & Torgler, C. (1994). Rape scripts and rape acknowledgement. *Psychology of Women Quarterly, 18,* 53-66.

Kanekar, S., Shaherwalla, A., Franco, B., Kunju, T., & Pinto, A. J. (1991). The acquaintance predicament of a rape victim. *Journal of Applied Social Psychology, 21,* 1524-1544.

Kanin, E. J. (1984). Date rape: Unofficial criminals and victims. *Victimology: An International Journal, 9,* 95-108.

Kanin, E. J. (1985). Date rapists: Differential sexual socialization and relative deprivation. *Archives of Sexual Behavior, 14,* 219-231.

Kanin, E. J., & Parcell, S. R. (1977). Sexual aggression: A second look at the offended female. *Archives of Sexual Behavior, 6,* 67-76.

Keyton, J. (1993, November). *Examining flirting in social and work contexts: Are there implications for harassment?* Paper presented at the annual meeting of the Speech Communication Association, Miami, FL.

Klemmack, S. H., & Klemmack, D. L. (1976). The social definition of rape. In M. J. Walker & S. L. Brodsky (Eds.), *Sexual assault: The victim and the rapist* (pp. 135-147). Lexington, MA: Lexington.

Knoth, R., Boyd, K., & Singer, B. (1988). Empirical tests of sexual selection theory: Predictions of sex differences in onset, intensity, and time course of sexual arousal. *Journal of Sex Research, 24,* 73-89.

Koeppel, L. B., Montaigne-Miller, Y., O'Hair, D., & Cody, M. J. (1993). Friendly? Flirting? Wrong? In P. J. Kalbfleisch (Ed.), *Interpersonal communication: Evolving interpersonal relationships* (pp. 13-32). Hillsdale, NJ: Lawrence Erlbaum.

Koralewski, M. A., & Conger, J. C. (1992). The assessment of social skills among sexually coercive college males. *Journal of Sex Research, 29,* 169-188.

Koss, M. P. (1988). Hidden rape: Sexual aggression and victimization in a national sample of students in higher education. In A. W. Burgess (Ed.), *Rape and sexual assault II* (pp. 3-25). New York: Garland.

Koss, M. P., Dinero, T. E., Seibel, C. A., & Cox, S. L. (1988). Stranger and acquaintance rape: Are there differences in the victim's experience? *Psychology of Women Quarterly, 12,* 1-24.

Kowalski, R. M. (1993). Inferring sexual interest from behavioral cues: Effects of gender and sexually relevant attitudes. *Sex Roles, 29,* 13-36.

Lane, K. E., & Gwartney-Gibbs, P. A. (1985). Violence in the context of dating and sex. *Journal of Family Issues, 6,* 45-59.

LaPlante, M. N., McCormick, N., & Brannigan, G. G. (1980). Living the sexual script: College students' views of influence in sexual encounters. *Journal of Sex Research, 16,* 338-355.

Laumann, E. O., Gagnon, J. H., Michael, R. T., & Michaels, S. (1994). *The social organizaiton of sexuality: Sexual practices in the United States.* Chicago: University of Chicago Press.

Laws, J. L., & Schwartz, P. (1977). *Sexual scripts: The social construction of female sexuality.* Hinsdale, IL: Dryden.

Levine-MacCombie, J., & Koss, M. P. (1986). Acquaintance rape: Effective avoidance strategies. *Psychology of Women Quarterly, 10,* 311-320.

Lewin, M. (1985). Unwanted intercourse: The difficulty of saying no. *Psychology of Women Quarterly, 9,* 184-192.

Lonsway, K. A., & Fitzgerald, L. F. (1994). Rape myths. *Psychology of Women Quarterly, 18,* 133-164.

Lottes, I. L. (1988). Sexual socialization and attitudes toward rape. In A. W. Burgess (Ed.), *Rape and sexual assault II* (pp. 193-220). New York: Garland.

Malamuth, N. M., & Brown, L. M. (1994). Sexually aggressive men's perceptions of women's communications: Testing three explanations. *Journal of Personality and Social Psychology, 67,* 699-712.

Malamuth, N. M., Sockloskie, R. J., Koss, M. P., & Tanaka, J. S. (1991). Characteristics of aggressors against women: Testing a model using a national sample of college students. *Journal of Consulting and Clinical Psychology, 59,* 670-681.

Margolin, L., Miller, M., & Moran, P. B. (1989). When a kiss is not just a kiss: Relating violations of consent in kissing to rape myth acceptance. *Sex Roles, 20,* 231-243.

McCabe, M. P., & Collins, J. K. (1984). Measurement of depth of desired and experienced sexual involvement at different stages of dating. *Journal of Sex Research, 20,* 377-390.

McCormick, N. B. (1979). Come-ons and put-offs: Unmarried students' strategies for having and avoiding sexual intercourse. *Psychology of Women Quarterly, 4,* 194-211.

McKinney, K., & Maroules, N. (1991). Sexual harassment. In E. Grauerholz & M. A. Koralewski (Eds.), *Sexual coercion: A sourcebook on its nature, causes, and prevention* (pp. 29-44). Lexington, MA: Lexington.

McKinney, K., & Sprecher, S. (Eds.). (1989). *Human sexuality: The societal and interpersonal context.* Norwood, NJ: Ablex.

Metts, S., & Cupach, W. R. (1989). The role of communication in human sexuality. In K. McKinney & S. Sprecher (Eds.), *Human sexuality: The societal and interpersonal context* (pp. 139-161). Norwood, NJ: Ablex.

Metts, S., & Cupach, W. R. (1991, May). *Plans for seeking and resisting the use of condoms.* Paper presented at the annual meeting of the International Communication Association, Chicago.

Metts, S., Cupach, W. R., & Imahori, T. T. (1992). Perceptions of sexual compliance-resisting messages in three types of cross-sex relationships. *Western Journal of Communication, 56,* 1-17.

Metts, S., & Fitzpatrick, M. A. (1992). Thinking about safer sex: The risky business of "know your partner" advice. In T. Edgar, M. A. Fitzpatrick, & V. Freimuth (Eds.), *AIDS: A communication perspective* (pp. 1-20). Hillsdale, NJ: Lawrence Erlbaum.

Miller, B., & Marshall, J. C. (1987). Coercive sex on the university campus. *Journal of College Student Personnel, 28,* 38-47.

Mills, C. S., & Granoff, B. J. (1992). Date and acquaintance rape among a sample of college students. *Social Work, 37,* 504-509.

Mongeau, P. A., & Blalock, J. (1992, February). *Differentiating sexual harassment from immediacy attempts: A replication and extension.* Paper presented at the annual meeting of the Western States Communication Association, Albuquerque, NM.

Moore, M. M. (1985). Nonverbal courtship patterns in women: Context and consequences. *Ethology and Sociobiology, 6,* 237-247.

Moore, M. M., & Butler, D. L. (1989). Predictive aspects of nonverbal courtship behavior in women. *Semiotica, 76,* 205-215.

Motley, M. T., & Reeder, H. M. (1994, November). *Messages used by women to thwart male escalation of sexual intimacy: One more instance of male/female misunderstandings.* Paper presented at the annual meeting of the Speech Communication Association, New Orleans.

Motley, M. T., & Reeder, H. M. (1995, February). *Unwanted escalation of sexual intimacy: Male/female perceptions regarding connotations and relational consequences of resistance messages.* Paper presented at the annual meeting of the Western States Communication Association, Portland, OR.

Muehlenhard, C. L. (1988). "Nice women" don't say yes and "real men" don't say no: How miscommunication and the double standard can cause sexual problems. *Women and Therapy, 7,* 95-108.

Muehlenhard, C. L., & Andrews, S. L. (1985, November). *Open communication about sex: Will it reduce risk factors related to date rape?* Paper presented at the annual meeting of the Association for Advancement of Behavior Therapy, Houston, TX.

Muehlenhard, C. L., & Cook, S. W. (1988). Men's self-reports of unwanted sexual activity. *Journal of Sex Research, 24,* 58-72.

Muehlenhard, C. L., & Falcon, P. L. (1990). Men's heterosocial skill and attitudes toward women as predictors of verbal sexual coercion and forceful rape. *Sex Roles, 23,* 241-259.

Muehlenhard, C. L., Giusti, L. M., & Rodgers, C. S. (1993, October). *The social construction of "token resistance to sex": The nature and function of the myth.* Paper presented at the annual meeting of the Scientific Study of Sex, Chicago.

Muehlenhard, C. L., & Hollabaugh, L. C. (1988). Do women sometimes say no when they mean yes? The prevalence and correlates of women's token resistance to sex. *Journal of Personality and Social Psychology, 54,* 872-879.

Muehlenhard, C. L., Koralewski, M. A., Andrews, S. L., & Burdick, C. A. (1986). Verbal and nonverbal cues that convey interest in dating: Two studies. *Behavior Therapy, 17,* 404-419.

Muehlenhard, C. L., & MacNaughton, J. S. (1988). Women's beliefs about women who "lead men on." *Journal of Social and Clinical Psychology, 7,* 65-79.

Muehlenhard, C. L., & McCoy, M. L. (1991). Double standard/double bind: The sexual double standard and women's communication about sex. *Psychology of Women Quarterly, 15,* 447-461.

Murnen, S. K., Perot, A., & Byrne, D. (1989). Coping with unwanted sexual activity: Normative responses, situational determinants, and individual differences. *Journal of Sex Research, 26,* 85-106.

Murphy, W. D., Coleman, E. M., & Haynes, M. R. (1986). Factors related to coercive sexual behavior in a nonclinical sample of males. *Violence and Victims, 1,* 255-278.

Norris, J., & Cubbins, L. A. (1992). Dating, drinking, and rape: Effects of victim's and assailant's alcohol consumption on judgments of their behavior and traits. *Psychology of Women Quarterly, 16,* 179-191.

90 COMMUNICATION YEARBOOK 19

O'Keefe, B. J. (1988). The logic of message design: Individual differences in reasoning about communication. *Communication Monographs, 55,* 80-103.

O'Meara, J. D. (1989). Cross-sex friendship: Four basic challenges of an ignored relationship. *Sex Roles, 21,* 525-543.

O'Sullivan, L. F., & Allgeier, E. R. (1994). Disassembling a stereotype: Gender differences in the use of token resistance. *Journal of Applied Social Psychology, 24,* 1035-1055.

O'Sullivan, L. F., & Byers, E. S. (1992). College students' incorporation of initiator and restrictor roles in sexual dating interactions. *Journal of Sex Research, 29,* 435-446.

O'Sullivan, L. F., & Byers, E. S. (1993). Eroding stereotypes: College women's attempts to influence reluctant male sexual partners. *Journal of Sex Research, 30,* 270-282.

Overholser, J. C., & Beck, S. (1986). Multimethod assessment of rapists, child molesters, and three control groups on behavioral and psychological measures. *Journal of Consulting and Clinical Psychology, 54,* 682-687.

Perper, T., & Weis, D. L. (1987). Proceptive and rejective strategies of U.S. and Canadian college women. *Journal of Sex Research, 23,* 455-480.

Plummer, K. (1995). *Telling sexual stories: Power, change and social worlds.* London: Routledge.

Popovich, P. M., Licata, B. J., Nokovich, D., Martelli, T., & Zoloty, S. (1986). Assessing the incidence and perceptions of sexual harassment behaviors among American undergraduates. *Journal of Psychology, 120,* 387-396.

Poppen, P. J., & Segal, N. J. (1988). The influence of sex and sex role orientation on sexual coercion. *Sex Roles, 19,* 689-701.

Quinn, K., Sanchez-Hucles, J., Coates, G., & Gillen, B. (1991). Men's compliance with a woman's resistance to unwanted sexual advances. *Journal of Offender Rehabilitation, 17,* 13-31.

Rapaport, K., & Burkhart, B. R. (1984). Personality and attitudinal characteristics of sexually coercive college males. *Journal of Abnormal Psychology, 93,* 216-221.

Reed, D., & Weinberg, M. S. (1984). Premarital coitus: Developing and established sexual scripts. *Social Psychology Quarterly, 47,* 129-138.

Reel, B. W., & Thompson, T. L. (1994). A test of the effectiveness of strategies for talking about AIDS and condom use. *Journal of Applied Communication Research, 22,* 127-140.

Remer, R., & Witten, B. J. (1988). Conceptions of rape. *Violence and Victims, 3,* 217-232.

Riportella-Muller, R. (1989). Sexuality in the elderly: A review. In K. McKinney & S. Sprecher (Eds.), *Human sexuality: The societal and interpersonal context* (pp. 210-236). Norwood, NJ: Ablex.

Roche, J. P. (1986). Premarital sex: Attitudes and behavior by dating stage. *Adolescence, 21,* 107-121.

Rose, S., & Frieze, I. H. (1993). Young singles' contemporary dating scripts. *Sex Roles, 28,* 499-509.

Ruelfi, T. (1985). Explorations of the improvisational side of sex: Charting the future of the sociology of sex. *Archives of Sexual Behavior, 14,* 189-199.

Ryan, K. M. (1988). Rape and seduction scripts. *Psychology of Women Quarterly, 12,* 237-245.

Saal, F. E., Johnson, C. B., & Weber, N. (1989). Friendly or sexy? It may depend on whom you ask. *Psychology of Women Quarterly, 13,* 263-276.

Sabini, J., & Silver, M. (1982). *Moralities of everyday life.* Oxford: Oxford University Press.

Sapadin, L. A. (1988). Friendship and gender: Perspectives of professional men and women. *Journal of Social and Personal Relationships, 5,* 387-404.

Schank, R. C., & Abelson, R. (1977). *Scripts, goals, plans, and understanding.* Hillsdale, NJ: Lawrence Erlbaum.

Schneider, B. E. (1991). Put up and shut up: Workplace sexual assaults. *Gender & Society, 5,* 533-548.

Scully, D., & Morolla, J. (1984). Convicted rapists' vocabulary of motive: Excuses and justifications. *Social Problems, 31,* 530-544.

Sheffield, C. J. (1987). Sexual terrorism: The social control of women. In B. B. Hess & M. M. Ferree (Eds.), *Analyzing gender: A handbook of social science research* (pp. 171-189). Newbury Park, CA: Sage.

Shoop, D. M., & Davidson, P. M. (1994). AIDS and adolescents: The relation of parent and partner communication to adolescent condom use. *Journal of Adolescence, 17,* 137-148.

Shotland, R. L. (1989). A model of the causes of date rape in developing and close relationships. In C. Hendrick (Ed.), *Close relationships* (pp. 247-270). Newbury Park, CA: Sage.

Shotland, R. L. (1992). A theory of the causes of courtship rape: Part 2. *Journal of Social Issues, 48,* 127-143.

Shotland, R. L., & Craig, J. M. (1988). Can men and women differentiate between friendly and sexually interested behavior? *Social Psychology Quarterly, 51,* 66-73.

Shotland, R. L., & Goodstein, L. (1992). Sexual precedence reduces the perceived legitimacy of sexual refusal: An examination of attributions concerning date rape and consensual sex. *Personality and Social Psychology Bulletin, 18,* 756-764.

Shotland, R. L., & Hunter, B. A. (1995). Women's "token resistant" and compliant sexual behaviors are related to uncertain sexual intentions and rape. *Personality and Social Psychology Bulletin, 21,* 226-236.

Silver, C. A. (1994, February). *Observations of heterosexual flirtatious communication in local drinking establishments.* Paper presented at the annual meeting of the Western States Communication Association, San Jose, CA.

Silver, C. A., & Spitzberg, B. H. (1992, July). *Flirtation as social intercourse: Developing a measure of flirtatious behavior.* Paper presented at the annual meeting of the International Society for the Study of Personal Relationships, Orono, ME.

Simon, W., & Gagnon, J. H. (1986). Sexual scripts: Permanence and change. *Archives of Sexual Behavior, 15,* 97-120.

Simon, W., & Gagnon, J. H. (1987). A sexual scripts approach. In J. H. Geer & W. O'Donohue (Eds.), *Theories of human sexuality* (pp. 363-383). New York: Plenum.

Snell, W. E., & Finney, P. D. (1990). Interpersonal strategies associated with the discussion of AIDS. *Annals of Sex Research, 3,* 425-451.

Snow, D. A., Robinson, C., & McCall, P. L. (1991). "Cooling out" men in singles bars and nightclubs: Observations on the interpersonal survival strategies of women in public places. *Journal of Contemporary Ethnography, 19,* 423-449.

Spitzberg, B. H. (1995, November). *Communication predictors of sexual coercion.* Paper presented at the annual meeting of the Speech Communication Association, San Antonio, TX.

Sprecher, S., Hatfield, E., Cortese, A., Potapova, E., & Levitskaya, A. (1994). Token resistance to sexual intercourse and consent to unwanted sexual intercourse: College students' dating experiences in three countries. *Journal of Sex Research, 31,* 125-132.

Tooke, W., & Camire, L. (1991). Patterns of deception in intersexual and intrasexual mating strategies. *Ethology and Sociobiology, 12,* 345-364.

Trost, M. R., & Engstrom, C. (1994, February). *"Hit the road, Jack": Strategies for rejecting flirtatious advances.* Paper presented at the annual meeting of the Western Speech Communication Association, San Jose, CA.

U.S. Merit Systems Protection Board. (1988). *Sexual harassment in the federal government: An update.* Washington, DC: Author.

Walker, W. D., Rowe, R. C., & Quinsey, V. L. (1993). Authoritarianism and sexual aggression. *Journal of Personality and Social Psychology, 65,* 1036-1045.

Walsh, R. H. (1989). Premarital sex among teenagers and young adults. In K. McKinney & S. Sprecher (Eds.), *Human sexuality: The societal and interpersonal context* (pp. 162-186). Norwood, NJ: Ablex.

Yegidis, B. L. (1986). Date rape and other forced sexual encounters among college students. *Journal of Sex Education and Therapy, 12,* 51-54.

CHAPTER CONTENTS

3 Sexual Harassment: A Multidisciplinary Synthesis and Critique

JOANN KEYTON
University of Memphis

The two seemingly incompatible concepts of sex and work have created serious implications for employees and organizations. Sexual harassment is a pervasive organizational phenomenon that continues to plague individual employees, organizations, and society. The dynamic and pervasive qualities of sexual harassment have captured the attention of researchers from a variety of disciplines, who have approached the task of identifying, describing, explaining, and predicting from competing explanations or research perspectives. This essay reviews the findings and positions of researchers in communication, counseling, law, management, psychology, sociology, and women's studies. Five types of works emerged in the literature selected for this review: reports of the results of surveys documenting the phenomenon of sexual harassment in the workplace; traditional social science examinations—quasi-experimental, laboratory, and field studies—of sexual harassment issues; research reports using discursive methods of narrative and textual analyses to explore sexual harassment; legal summaries and analyses of court decisions; and analyses of certain aspects of sexual harassment that offer positions for reflection or research. This chapter presents the findings and conclusions drawn from the literature in response to eight key questions about sexual harassment.

S EX and work—these two seemingly incompatible areas have created serious implications for employees and organizations. Sexual feelings can be stimulated in settings characterized by close physical and psychological proximity (Bradford, Sargent, & Sprague, 1980) in sexually integrated workplaces (Dillard, 1987). Workplace power can be an aphrodisiac and a component of attraction, or, if manifested in sexually negative ways,

AUTHOR'S NOTE: I would like to thank Steven C. Rhodes, Western Michigan University, for his thoughtful comments and encouragement along the way, Jim Schafer for his help with the literature search, and two anonymous reviewers for their detailed comments on an earlier draft.

Correspondence and requests for reprints: Joann Keyton, Department of Communication, University of Memphis, TCA 143, Memphis, TN 38152.

Communication Yearbook 19, pp. 93-155

can result in sexual harassment—unwelcome sexual advances or requests for sexual favors from a superior, subordinate, or peer at work or the existence of a sexually intimidating, hostile, or offensive work environment. Sexual harassment in the workplace has only recently been identified as a legal phenomenon, but it has always been a part of organizational life. The issue was for some time partially obscured because the concept of sexuality at work did not mesh with rational models of organizational behavior (Gutek, 1985), and society was unable to accept the negative sexual experiences of women. "One inescapable conclusion . . . is that sexual behavior in various forms is present in the workplace, despite the fact that work organizations do nothing officially to encourage sexual overtures among employees" (Gutek, 1989, p. 66).

The act of naming the phenomenon *sexual harassment* brought these negative experiences forward into legal, organizational, and public consciousness and conscience. Clearly, sexual harassment persists. In 1991, sexual harassment ranked fourth among unlawful employment practices reported by the U.S. Equal Employment Opportunity Commission (EEOC), and there are clear indications that the numbers of complaints are rising (Apruzzese, 1992). Reports indicate that "between 1990 and 1993, the number of EEOC sexual harassment claims more than doubled, from 6,100 to 12,500" ("Sex, Laws," 1994, p. 14), with a 50% increase occurring after Clarence Thomas's Supreme Court nomination confirmation hearings (Machson & Monteleone, 1994).

The dynamic and pervasive qualities of sexual harassment have captured the attention of researchers from a variety of disciplines, who have approached the task of identifying, describing, explaining, and predicting this phenomenon from competing philosophical perspectives. In this essay, I will review the findings and positions of researchers in communication, counseling, law, management, psychology, sociology, and women's studies. The inclusion of the work of researchers in disciplines other than communication is necessary to a thorough review of this topic, given the far-reaching effects of sexual harassment on individuals, organizations, and society.

The communication discipline is appropriately situated for a review of sexual harassment because sexual harassment is one type of message sending and message receiving (Gilsdorf, 1990). Moreover, the communication discipline spans the dynamics of intrapersonal, interpersonal, organizational, and societal contexts that shape this phenomenon. As Kreps (1993a) notes, "Communication is the primary medium through which sexual harassment is expressed; it is the means by which those who are harassed respond to harassment, and it is also the primary means by which policies for eliminating sexual harassment in the workplace can be implemented" (p. 1). Wood (1993) explains the relationship between communication and sexual harassment:

> Whatever else sexual harassment may entail—power issues, psychological motives and dysfunctions, cultural constructions including gender roles—it is unde-

TABLE 3.1
Sexual Harassment Citations by Database

Database	1990	1991	1992	1993	1994
PsycLIT		33	42	48	10[a]
ABI/INFORM			102	203	59[a]
Infotrac			222	183	270
ERIC	45	50	76	93	46[a]

a. Full calendar year 1994 not represented

niably a communication phenomenon. It is so in at least two ways. First, the existence and meaning of sexual harassment are constructed symbolically both through culturally formed and legitimated definitions and through the processes whereby individuals interpret experiences. Second, sexual harassment and the responses to it are enacted through communication. (p. 10)

Kreps (1993a) proposes that communication can be used to (a) raise public consciousness, (b) legitimate the plight of harassment victims, (c) denigrate perpetrators of harassment, and (d) help develop cultural norms that inhibit and condemn sexual harassment in addition to educating organizational members.

Because this literature includes a variety of methodologies and perspectives, I do not limit my review in this chapter to empirical studies. Although I cannot review all of the research published on sexual harassment, I made every effort to present the topic as it has been approached by varying researchers with differing perspectives and using different methodologies. The literature search was restricted to works published in the United States, with the exception of a few articles published in Canada and England; convention papers were not included. This review focuses on sexual harassment as it relates to the organizational context and excludes general societal harassment (Kramarae, 1992), gender orientation harassment, and intragender sexual harassment.[1] Because the research literature is broad and expansive, I have excluded articles and books published by the popular press, as well as commercial training materials.

The scope of this literature is vast, but I found that five general types of works emerged in the literature selected for review: (a) reports of the results of surveys documenting the phenomenon of sexual harassment in the workplace; (b) traditional social science examinations—quasi-experimental, laboratory, and field studies—of harassment issues; (c) reports of research using discursive practices of narrative and textual analyses to explore sexual harassment; (d) legal summaries and analyses of court decisions; and (c) analyses of particular aspects of sexual harassment in which the authors present positions for reflection or research. Tables 3.1 and 3.2 illustrate the diversity of the sexual harassment literature. Table 3.1 displays the number of citations

TABLE 3.2
Sexual Harassment Citations Presented in This Review

| | Discipline of Journal | | | | | | | | | Women's | |
	Anthropology	Communication	Counseling	Education	Government	Law	Management	Psychology	Sociology	Studies	Interdisciplinary
1972								1			
1978										1	
1979										1	
1980							1	1			
1981					1		3	1			
1982						1		6			
1983				1		1	1	2			
1984							1				
1985	2		1				1	1			1
1986	1		1	1			1	2		1	5
1987	1		1	1	1		1	2			2
1988	2						2	2			1
1989	2						4	2			1
1990	2		1			2	1				2
1991	2					1		2			1
1992	6ᵃ					7	1	1			5
1993	15ᵇ	1				6	5	9			2
1994	15ᶜ					5	3	2			2
1995		2					1				

NOTE: Items shown for 1995 include works currently in press.
a. Primarily from a special issue of the *Journal of Applied Communication Research*.
b. Primarily from Kreps (1993b).
c. Primarily from Bingham (1994a).

available on sexual harassment from several electronic databases. Table 3.2 shows the distribution of the works reviewed in this chapter by year and by discipline.

To position understanding of the sexual harassment phenomenon, I will examine the term *sexual harassment* as it has been named, defined, explained theoretically, and approached by researchers. I will then turn to a presentation of the findings and conclusions drawn from the literature in response to eight key questions about sexual harassment. I conclude the essay with a summary and suggested directions for future research. This organizing scheme encourages cross-referencing of perspective, methodology, and discipline, and can help the reader to ascertain how well research, as a whole, has answered critical questions about sexual harassment.

IDENTIFYING AND NAMING SEXUAL HARASSMENT

Gutek (1985) reports that the issue of sexuality at work and the identification of behaviors known as sexual harassment appeared first as journalistic accounts in women's magazines; MacKinnon (1979) attributes the first use of the term *sexual harassment* to the Working Women United Institute and the Alliance Against Sexual Coercion. One of the first extensive surveys regarding sexual harassment was conducted by *Harvard Business Review* for *Redbook* magazine (Collins & Blodgett, 1981). But it was analyses by Farley (1978) and MacKinnon (1979) that brought sexual harassment from obscurity into legal, organizational, and public reality and provided a feminist framework with which to conceptualize the phenomenon.

Public Awareness of Sexual Harassment

Farley's (1978) journalistic account argues that "the end result of male sexual harassment of women on the job is the extortion of female subservience at work" (p. 11). Farley defines sexual harassment as unsolicited and nonreciprocal behavior of men toward women in which female sex roles overshadow female work roles. She examines capitalism and patriarchy as foundations for sexual harassment, noting that patriarchy has "perpetuated itself through insuring the subordination of female labor by endlessly maintaining and adapting its systems of hierarchical control" (p. 28). Farley's book, which was triggered by a women's consciousness-raising session at which participants told of quitting or having been fired from jobs because they were uncomfortable with the behavior of men at their workplaces, explores sexual harassment in both traditional and nontraditional jobs.

MacKinnon's (1979) work has provided the legal foundation for sexual harassment. MacKinnon defines sexual harassment as "the unwanted imposition of sexual requirements in the context of a relationship of unequal power" (p. 1). This power dynamic consists of two inequalities—sexual and material—that legitimate "male sexual dominance of women and employers' control of workers" (p. 1). MacKinnon argues that because workplace sexual harassment is primarily a problem for women, it should be regarded as sex discrimination, and that victims of sexual harassment should be provided the same legal protection as those who suffer other forms of discrimination. From the feminist perspective, MacKinnon notes that sexual harassment derives its meaning not from personality or biology, but from social context: "The defining dimensions of this social context are employer-employee relations (given women's position in the labor force) and the relationship between the sexes in American society as a whole, of which sexual relations are one expression" (p. 2). MacKinnon's work has contributed to the advancement of public policy with regard to sexual harassment, and the EEOC has adopted many of her positions.

EEOC Guidelines and Judicial Interpretations

As a result of the attention directed to the phenomenon of sexual harassment, the EEOC developed guidelines to define sexual harassment and ruled that sexual harassment is considered an unlawful employment practice under Title VII of the 1964 Civil Rights Act. Prior to the issuance of the EEOC's guidelines in 1980, however, courts were not receptive to claims of sexual harassment. Rather, they viewed these types of complaints as characteristic of ineffective relationships or as the result of natural attraction, or found that sexual harassment was not claimable under Title VII (Koen, 1989). This is in direct contrast to the EEOC guidelines, which identify sexual harassment as

> unwelcome sexual advances, requests for sexual favors, and other verbal or physical conduct of a sexual nature when (1) submission to such conduct is made either explicitly or implicitly a term or condition of an individual's employment, (2) submission to or rejection of such conduct by an individual is used as the basis for employment decisions affecting such individual, or (3) such conduct has the purpose or effect of unreasonably interfering with an individual's work performance or creating an intimidating, hostile, or offensive work environment.

The EEOC's statements and subsequent judiciary findings have proven to be a powerful cultural force in advancing victims' rights and social awareness (Wood, 1994).

It is important to note that although "the EEOC Guidelines are merely an administrative interpretation of Title VII and do not have the force of law, federal courts have relied heavily upon them" (Hetherington & Wallace, 1992, p. 50). The U.S. Supreme Court has given its approval to the guidelines, indicating that they are based upon a body of judicial decision and EEOC precedent representing a body of experience and informed judgment that can provide direction for courts and litigants (Hetherington & Wallace, 1992).

Although intended to provide direction, the guidelines are admittedly vague. "To be sure, the EEOC very intentionally wrote a broad, general definition so all possible forms of sexual harassment would be covered" (Linenberger, 1983, p. 243). As a result, the definition leaves executives, managers, and individual employees with the responsibility of recognizing sexual harassment on a day-to-day basis as it occurs (Linenberger, 1983). Woerner and Oswald (1990) note that the lack of court agreement about what constitutes sexual harassment only serves "to add new terms and provide new angles, without defining the term itself. The decisions seem to overturn so regularly that the entire issue seems to be in a state of chaos. Sometimes it seems that future litigation may only be limited by the imagination of the litigant" (pp. 792-793). What has resulted is case-by-case determination of sexual harassment, because it cannot be determined solely by an a priori EEOC definition (McCaslin, 1994).

The EEOC guidelines distinguish between two types of sexual harassment: quid pro quo and hostile work environment. *Quid pro quo harassment* is intentional harassment in which the victim is required by the harasser to provide sexual favors to avoid threatened loss of economic opportunity. This form of harassment is easiest to recognize as a form of illegal sex discrimination. Endorsed by the U.S. Supreme Court as a form of illegal sex discrimination in the 1986 *Meritor Savings Bank v. Vinson* decision, a hostile work environment is described as one that interferes with an employee's work performance or creates an intimidating, hostile, or offensive work environment. In deciding *Meritor Savings Bank v. Vinson,* the Court indicated that unwelcomeness is a defining criterion. Koen (1989) and Paetzold and O'Leary-Kelly (1993) provide legal and historical explorations of *hostile work environment harassment.* Although economic loss is key to quid pro quo harassment, the Supreme Court has indicated that economic loss is not needed to support a claim of hostile work environment harassment. George (1993) notes that courts have generally found quid pro quo claims of sexual harassment to be more acceptable than hostile environment claims because "the harm is far less concrete and identifiable [in hostile environment claims] than lost promotion or pay raise at issue in the quid pro quo cases" (p. 11).

Research Definitions of Sexual Harassment

Social scientists eager to operationalize the sexual harassment phenomenon have developed several typologies for defining harassment. Adams, Kottke, and Padgitt (1983) first developed broad behavioral categories of sexual harassment based upon case law and other research. Later, Fitzgerald et al. (1988) identified the five general categories of gender harassment, seductive behavior, sexual bribery, sexual coercion, and sexual assault in their Sexual Experiences Questionnaire. Validity studies have revealed that the two most severe forms of harassment cluster together, leaving gender harassment as a separate entity.

Gruber (1992) examined 17 studies representing a broad spectrum of survey research on women's experiences with sexual harassment and created a typology of 11 forms of sexual harassment arranged in three general types of sexual harassment—verbal requests, verbal comments, and nonverbal displays. Gruber argues that this typology can help researchers to capture contextual variation as well as environmental forms of harassment.

Wood (1992, 1993, 1994) has played a pivotal role in describing the social and historical processes through which sexual harassment has been identified, named, and interpreted. She asserts that "the history of sexual harassment dramatically illustrates how discourse constructs experience. While sexual harassment has always occurred, until recently, it was not named and, thus, had no social existence" (1994, p. 18). Wood has been prominent in promoting narrative discourse as a primary methodology because it is open to multiple enactments, meanings, and identities.

> Naming sexual harassment entails more than simply coining new terms. Because meanings arise out of the principles that order culture, we must also heed how names are justified, with what other terms they are associated, whose interests they serve, what frameworks are invoked to explain them, into what contexts it is insinuated, and with what motives and consequences they are linked. All of these contribute to what a name comes to represent and to sustaining the discursive conditions that legitimate it, so all become issues that call for attention from both researchers and participants in the world of work. (Wood, 1992, p. 355)

For women, the naming of sexual harassment provided a socially legitimate label that made it possible for them to discuss their experiences. For men, however, "sexual harassment was neither salient nor a problem. Unhampered by sexual harassment, men had no compelling reason to distinguish it from the flux of ordinary life by naming it" (Wood, 1994, p. 19).

RESEARCH PERSPECTIVES FOR AND
THEORETICAL EXPLANATIONS OF SEXUAL HARASSMENT

As with any complex social phenomenon, scholars have provided various explanations for sexual harassment from many research perspectives. Traditionally, research perspectives guide the methodological choices that result in theoretical explanations. The academic sexual harassment literature did not develop in such a fashion. After Farley's and MacKinnon's books were published in the late 1970s, social scientists immediately started to investigate sexual harassment through survey techniques (e.g., Powell, 1983b; Reilly, Carpenter, Dull, & Bartlett, 1982). Following the lead established by the U.S. Merit Systems Protection Board (USMSPB), researchers in several disciplines sought to substantiate the claim that sexual harassment is indeed pervasive and negative. Unfortunately, many of these surveys lacked theoretical focus; moreover, the research was largely nonprogrammatic. Later, social scientists began to use more sophisticated methodologies, including experimental designs, which helped to establish some programmatic research lines and provide theory-based explanations for sexual harassment phenomena. Although both Farley and MacKinnon approached sexual harassment from a feminist perspective, for the most part the work of feminist scholars (including critical and postmodern scholars) did not reappear in academic publications on this topic until the early 1990s.

Retrospectively, Bingham (1994b) identified sexual harassment research as grounded in a functionalist or discursive perspective. The functionalist perspective generally encompasses research conducted through traditional social scientific methods. The discursive perspective generally encompasses the work of critical, feminist, and postmodern scholars who analyze the discourse or narratives of sexual harassment experiences. Whereas functionalist research is found across many disciplines, research from the discursive perspective in largely centered in the communication discipline. The gap between the early feminist work of Farley and MacKinnon and later research, however, was not ignored by functionalists; Bingham (1994b) concludes that this "research has reflected feminist insights, albeit it has frequently not partaken of feminist modes of inquiry" (p. 4).

Because sexual harassment is a social and cultural phenomenon, the chronological order of the sexual harassment literature is important to its understanding and interpretation. Below, I will first describe the early competing models for sexual harassment and then describe the work of Gutek and her colleagues, who developed the first programmatic line of research on harassment. Following that, I will present expanded discussions of both the functionalist and discursive research perspectives. I will also describe the moral perspective, a relatively untested perspective from which to understand sexual harassment. I conclude this section with an exploration of some of the problems related to the methodological practices of sexual harassment research.

Models for Explaining Sexual Harassment

Early on, Tangri, Burt, and Johnson (1982) developed and tested three competing models as explanations for sexual harassment. The first, the natural/biological model, explains sexual harassment as a result of biological urges or natural attraction between two employees. As such, this type of explanation denies that sexual harassment behavior is discriminatory. The second model, the organizational model, argues that sexual harassment occurs as a result of organizational characteristics. Factors such as hierarchical structure, authority to reward and punish, job assignments that include overtime or business trips, and the sex ratios of the organization, job, occupation, and work unit combine to create an organizational culture that provides opportunities for sexual harassment to occur. The third model, the sociocultural model, explains sexual harassment as an expression of power and hostility maintained by social patterns of male-female interaction. Because of their position within society, females are most likely to be harassed, as patriarchal society rewards males for aggressiveness and domineering behavior. In this model, sexual harassment has little to do with sexuality. Using data from federal workers, Tangri et al. did not find clear support for any of the three models. They conclude, however, that "sexual harassment is not a unitary phenomenon" across or within the sexes (pp. 51-52).

Gutek and her colleagues have also offered three models—a feminist perspective, a legal perspective, and an organizational or managerial perspective—to explain sexual harassment (Gutek, 1985; Gutek & Morasch, 1982). In a recent publication, Gutek (1993) explains that "these points of view are neither independent nor mutually exclusive" (p. 329). From a feminist perspective, social changes will be needed to eliminate sexual harassment, because it stems from the existence of sexism in our society, which results in power imbalances of male employees over female employees in the workplace. For feminists, Gutek (1985) explains, sexual harassment "has relatively little to say about the workplace itself. The workplace is just another sphere of male domination and another arena—like marriage—where men can exert their power over women" (p. 11). A similar imbalance exists within the legal perspective, but the perspective is expanded to include terms of employment as well as work environment characteristics. Within this perspective, the focus is on the effects of harassing behavior. From an organizational or managerial perspective, sexual harassment occurs because of (a) misunderstandings or (b) improper use of power in interpersonal relationships at work. The former trivializes harassing interaction and minimizes the victim's experiences; the latter encourages organizations to treat harassment as an interpersonal issue with which the organization must be involved. As with the Tangri, Burt, and Johnson model, Gutek (1985) argues that these models are "also unlikely to explain the broader concept of sexuality" in the workplace (p. 15). Characteristics of each, however, are present in Gutek and Morasch's (1982) sex role spillover model.

Sex role spillover is the carryover of gender-based roles from society to work (Nieva & Gutek, 1981) and from imbalanced sex ratios in occupations, jobs, and within work groups (Gutek, 1985). As such, sex roles based upon traditional characteristics promote the role of women as subservient to the aggressive leadership role of men. This model recognizes the confluence of work roles and sex roles because "if people at work behaved within the narrow confines of work roles, then sexual jokes, flirtatious behavior, sexual overtures, and sexual coercion would not exist" (Gutek, 1985, p. 17). Gutek (1985) explains that the sex role spillover model contains some aspects of Tangri et al.'s (1982) organizational and sociocultural models, but also takes into account Nieva and Gutek's (1981) explanations of structural institutional, sex roles, and intergroup relationships.

Later, Gutek, Cohen, and Konrad (1990) integrated sex role spillover with the natural/biological and organizational explanations of sexual harassment into two hypotheses. The gender hypothesis suggests, as does the natural/biological model, that men initiate more and women report more social-sexual behavior at work, independent of intergender contact. The contact hypothesis, like the organization model, suggests that sexualization of the work environment results from contact with employees of the other gender. In other words, structural characteristics of the work—including organizational, job, and work unit sex ratios—provide contact opportunity that increases harassment opportunity. This research culminated in the "sexualization of the workplace" explanation for sexual harassment.

Gutek (1985) and her colleagues have explored in detail the level of sexualization in the workplace and its likelihood of affecting employees' and management's recognition of harassing behaviors. Social-sexual behaviors contribute to the sexualization of the work environment, which is described as "any non-work-related behavior having a sexual component; it includes sexual harassment, initiating dating, flirting, and the like" (Gutek et al., 1990, p. 560). Konrad and Gutek (1986) argue that a sexualized workplace may depress the number of behaviors labeled as sexual harassment because workers become habituated to sexual behavior through constant exposure. Thus, sexualization of the workplace becomes a reasonable explanation for sexual harassment, particularly given that men and women report nonharassing sexual behavior equally (Gutek et al., 1990). Examining sexual harassment as one aspect of sexualization in the workplace situates harassment within an organizational context with mechanisms for change.

This explanation is guided by Gutek, Nakamura, Gahart, Handschumacher, and Russell's (1980) assumptions about the shifting nature of the social-sexual continuum:

> Some of the behaviors, particularly complimentary comments or remarks of a sexual nature, are probably ego-enhancing at least some of the time to both males and females. As the degree of imposition increases and is coupled with the loss of control over the situation or detraction from attention to work-related behavior, the social-sexual encounter is probably more likely to be viewed as sexual harassment rather than sexual interest. (p. 265)

Acknowledging the breadth of sexual contact and activity in the workplace allows us to conceptualize sexual harassment as one form of workplace sexuality and to interpret and manage it in relationship to other workplace intergender relationships and sexual activities.

Other explanations of sexual harassment are provided by two sociological theories: conflict theory and role theory (Gill, 1993). Emphasizing power differences and competition between groups, conflict theory examines the effects of these differences on behavior definition, involvement in behaviors, and reactions to behaviors. A conflict model assumes that males are the harassers and that they have influence over what behaviors are identified as harassment. Role theory examines the positions, responsibilities, and privileges associated with roles that affect views of harassment. This theoretical model assumes that supervisors view sexual harassment differently than do subordinates. Although many researchers use superior/subordinate identifications of perpetrators and victims as well as gender identifications in their research, most do not explicitly examine these assumptions.

The common element among these early competing explanations is their reliance upon traditional social science methods. The ideologies and values that guide this type of research have been identified as belonging to the functionalist perspective.

The Functionalist Research Perspective

As the courts have adjudicated cases, the definition of sexual harassment has been modified, often in expansive ways. At the same time, researchers studying sexual harassment have used alternative operationalizations in lieu of the vague EEOC guidelines. Thus, researchers attempting to legitimate the existence of sexual harassment have documented its occurrence as a wide variety of behaviors. This approach, which Bingham (1994b) identifies as functionalism, conceptualizes "sexual harassment as consisting of behavioral, psychological, and structural elements envisioning (1) verbal and nonverbal behaviors or interaction that have negative effects on victims and that (2) are coercive, discriminatory, or perceived as inappropriate and hostile, and that (3) are inspired or enabled by organizational and social structures and processes" (p. 4).

Bingham (1994b) describes the behavioral aspects of this research as emphasizing the "behavioral elements of sexual harassment . . . as something harassers do" (p. 5). From this approach (e.g., Fitzgerald et al., 1988; Gruber, 1992; Terpstra & Baker, 1987), research serves to identify the extent, nature, and effects of sexual harassment as well as its antecedents and consequences. Such an approach, Bingham (1994b) argues, "transforms sexual harassment into a linear, chain-like process involving a series of causes and effects" (p. 5), reflecting a mechanistic view. A second aspect of functionalism, the psychological aspect, emphasizes perceptions and evaluations of social-sexual behaviors (Bingham, 1994b). As might be expected, researchers using this framework examine cognitive processes as individuals provide their perceptions of real and hypothetical sexual harassment incidents (e.g., Gutek, Morasch, & Cohen, 1983; York, 1989). Many researchers have attempted to understand what individuals perceive to be sexual harassment by asking study participants to identify which of a range of social-sexual behaviors they consider to be sexual harassment. Frequently these pen-and-paper studies remove harassment from the context in which it occurs and use broad definitional categories (e.g., gestures, proposition, staring, direct sexual request, touches me on arm/back). The third aspect of functionalist research captures the social or organizational structures that facilitate sexual harassment. This research perspective is illustrated by Tangri et al.'s organizational model, Gutek's organizational/managerial sex role spillover model, and sexualization of the workplace explanations of sexual harassment.

Criticism of the functionalist research perspective. A functionalist perspective envisions sexual harassment as something that exists and, because it does, is worthy of research attention. "Functionalist researchers tend to view social reality and social structures" independent of the processes that create them (Bingham, 1994b, p. 4). As such, communication is only one aspect of harassing interaction (and the reason this literature review reaches beyond the communication discipline). From a functionalist perspective, researchers have examined biological characteristics, attitudes and perceptions, psychological characteristics, demographic characteristics, and organizational characteristics. "While this research is useful to lawyers and policy analysts who are trying to establish and enforce laws and policies" (Gutek, 1989, p. 57), it does little to explain sexuality at work as an organizational phenomenon. Missing from these examinations is the role of society and culture in the occurrence of and response to sexual harassment. Bingham (1994b) concludes that "research that relies entirely upon psychological and behavioral conceptualizations of sexual harassment ignores the organizational contexts, cultural practices, material conditions, and individual experiences that shape identities and interpretations" (p. 8).

An additional criticism of functionalist research is that it reflects management's interest or bias in the topic, as some research highlights the legal risks or threats to productivity and profit or attempts to identify "normative" perceptions (Bingham, 1994b). I would argue, however, that this conclusion cannot be applied to all social scientific research; clearly, not all functionalist research represents such a bias. However, this criticism is validated by many commercial publications and journalistic reports of researchers' findings. Bingham (1994b) criticizes the behavioral aspect of functionalist research for making the problem of sexual harassment seem orderly and thus manageable, and argues that although the structural aspect of functionalist research moves the conceptualization of sexual harassment closer to the view of feminist scholars, such research often views as static the structures that empower sexual harassment. Clearly, a line is drawn between researchers who choose to conduct research through traditional social science methodologies and those who choose methods more aligned with a discursive perspective. Although some social science research is informed by feminist thinking and some feminist scholars favor traditional social science methodologies, feminist scholarship is more frequently aligned with discursive analyses. Encompassing critical, feminist, and postmodern approaches, the discursive approach to sexual harassment research may be described as recognizing communication as central, as viewing social structures as "produced and reproduced," and as "offering more promising avenues for bringing about changes" (Bingham, 1994b, p. 9).

The Discursive Research Perspective

The discursive perspective for understanding sexual harassment has been centrally supported by Bingham's (1994a) edited collection as well as by the work of other feminist, critical, and postmodern communication scholars. Bingham (1994b) describes the discursive framework as "pluralistic in its embracing of diverse perspectives" (p. 9). The discursive perspective is central to understanding sexual harassment in that "discourse names, orders, and defines experience, it shapes what and how societies and individuals know" (Wood, 1994, p. 17). Wood (1994) argues that a discursive understanding (a) situates interaction within material and social practices, (b) allows examination of the production and reproduction of ideologies and social organizations, (c) constitutes subject(ivitie)s and provides standpoints that are epistemologically significant, (d) governs both self-control and social control, and (e) provides an understanding that is neither neutral nor universal, as discourses always emanate from particular positions. Within the discursive framework, communication has a more central place in the study of sexual harassment, as the scholar's task "is to locate such narratives within the horizons of their cultural, political, institutional, social and personal locations. . . . This approach reveals how both meanings of experiences such as sexual harassment and the subjective identities of individuals arise and are sustained in communicative interactions" (Wood, 1992, p. 357).

Critical theorists believe that imbalances of power result from social structures and social processes that lead to the alienation and oppression of certain groups. The role of the critical theorist in sexual harassment research is to reveal the imbalance so that oppressed voices can be heard by those in power. As a component of the critical perspective, hegemonic theory provides a clear description of sexual harassment as a discursive practice, as both dominant and subjugated groups and individuals participate actively in the socially constructed environment. An exemplar of such an approach to sexual harassment is Clair's (1993b) study of framing devices discovered through women's stories about harassment. Using a critical feminist approach, Clair investigated how stories of sexual harassment are kept from becoming public knowledge, thereby reinforcing sexual harassment. Clair explored six framing devices: accepting the dominant interests, simple misunderstanding, reification, trivialization, denotative hesitancy, and public/private expression. Predominantly, women used three framing techniques—trivialization, denotative hesitancy, and invoking private domain or private expression—in describing their harassment experiences, thus participating in their oppression by members of the dominant group. Clair's analysis highlights how women use communication to resist sexual harassment as well as how women participate in hegemonic practices.

Grauerholz (1994) argues that feminist theory is the "most powerful theory used to explain gender differences in sexual harassment" (p. 33). Wood (1995) describes its contributions as (a) a focus on inequalities and how inequalities are normalized in social structures and practices, (b) identification and alteration of oppressive processes that mute and marginalize women, and (c) analysis of the embedded nature of the relationship to its context. Although initial research focused on attitudes and behaviors, it "produced informative profiles of harassers and victims but shed little light on processes that normalize harassment and discourage resistance" (p. 115). The primary contribution, then, of feminist inquiry is that it critically analyzes gender differences that exist in the incidence, labeling, and identification of, and responses to, sexual harassment within its cultural, social, and work context. Research from this perspective allows one to answer the question, "How does men's institutional power give rise to women's personal experiences of powerlessness?" (Grauerholz, 1994, p. 33). Such powerlessness is reported by Taylor and Conrad (1992), who analyze the irony of harassment victims who continue to maintain friendly relationships with their harassers as defined by organizational requirements. Taylor and Conrad's narrative analyses further demonstrate that harassment is enabled when others fail to support victims largely because of organizational constraints.

Although the experiences of women are often the primary emphasis of feminist research, Clair (1994a) claims that men are also sexually harassed and that this aspect of the phenomenon "does not in any way undermine a feminist explanation of sexual harassment" (p. 59). Both men and women can suffer from patriarchal systems, as "sexual harassment is a political tool of oppression that privileges the dominant ideology and marginalizes other views" (p. 59). Such an approach provides explanations for harassment incidents by viewing accounts with respect to gender relationships constructed within organizations. Using a case study approach, Clair (1994b) examined a male nurse's experiences with sexual harassment and found the

> complex nature of oppression and resistance. . . . Oppression becomes resistance when the female nurses oppress Michael through sexual harassment in order to resist being infiltrated by a male. Resistance becomes oppression when the nurses accept sexual harassment from the patients in order to dominate them. Furthermore, the female nurses contribute to their own oppression through their reliance on and use of sexual orientation to taunt Michael. (p. 252)

Postmodern theorists find scientific reasoning and rational critical inquiry insufficient for recognizing the changing nature of our lives. Rather, they view knowledge as situated and look to the outside level of culture that pervades organizations. Strine (1992) describes poststructural research as that in which "meaning and the processes(es) of differentiation in and through which they arise are understood as socially embedded constructions, an interpretive function of historically variable and changing social interactions rather than their starting point" (p. 392). One example of this approach is Clair's (1993a) deconstruction of sexual harassment policies at the Big Ten universities, in which she examines the relationship between individual and organizational responses to sexual harassment.

Criticism of the discursive research perspective. All research perspectives have their advantages, and all have limitations. Scholars working from a discursive perspective must rely on the subjective experiences and recall of research participants. The advantage is that the study of sexual harassment is then "perceived and constructed by those who have endured it" (Wood, 1993, p. 23). The disadvantage is that "those involved often lack the distance from personal history and appreciation of systemic processes underlying individual experience that enable reflection and insight" (Wood, 1992, p. 356). Exposing narratives are powerful and emotional reminders of the harms of harassment, yet discursive research practices provide embedded pictures of harassment, making it difficult to establish consensus or to generalize beyond specific cases. Pringle (1989) argues that although feminists have drawn attention to sexuality at work, attention has been generally restricted to its coercive dimension, perhaps obscuring other forms of male power.

The Moral Perspective

Recently, Feary (1994) has advanced the moral perspective, which places blame for sexual harassment at both individual and organizational levels. Feary argues that sexual harassment should be considered from a moral perspective for seven reasons. Most basic of these is that "sexual harassment is morally wrong because it physically and psychologically harms victims, and because environments which permit sexual harassment seem to encourage such harms" (pp. 658-659). Further, it "demonstrates the kind of disrespect for persons which is incompatible with Kantian conceptions of the moral point of view" (p. 660). Sexual harassment also violates privacy rights, liberty rights, and rights of equality of opportunity. Included in the argument is the relationship between sexual harassment and employment discrimination. Finally, sexual harassment is a moral issue "because it undermines utilitarian justifications for the very free enterprise system upon which the business community depends" (pp. 660-661). Feary concludes that "sexual harassment is not merely an abuse of power . . . not merely a legal problem, a cultural problem, a gender problem or a communication problem. . . . Sexual harassment is a serious moral problem" (p. 661).

Examining morality as an aspect of business ethics, Wells and Kracher (1993) argue that "morality is a relevant source of standards for business since, other than legal precedent, it is the only other criterion for determining what is just or fair" (p. 425). Because moral theory requires the mutual respect of persons and the natural duty not to harm the innocent, Wells and Kracher assert that organizational policies and procedures should be enacted from the perspective of the reasonable victim (in cases of hostile environment), which is usually from the woman's perspective. Some would argue, however, that morality has not been sufficient in stemming sexual harassment. Wood (1992) has noted that organizations did not initially respond to moral arguments in addressing sexual harassment, but "became suddenly attentive when court rulings established their legal and financial liability" (p. 351). Gutek (1993) also questions the ability of moral arguments to stop harassment, pointing out that "organizations do not rely exclusively on people's consciences to keep them from stealing from the organization, nor do they rely completely on an employee's word to be sure that he/she is honest" (p. 337).

This stream of research is not as developed as research from functionalist and discursive perspectives. Although the moral position appears both socially and politically situated, the application of this perspective in empirical research is limited so far to one study of employee ethical ideology and its relationship to employees' perceptions of sexual harassment (Keyton & Rhodes, in press).

Methodological Problems in the Study of Sexual Harassment

Focusing on traditional social science survey methodologies, Gruber (1990, 1992) has analyzed the methodological practices of sexual harassment research. He claims that substantial differences in "sample size, survey response rate, sample diversity, harassment frame of reference, number of harassment categories, and types of words/phrases used to elicit responses" (1990, p. 237) have made comparisons among research studies difficult, inhibiting generalization of results. He identifies three methodological problems that contribute to the overreporting or underreporting of sexual harassment: (a) use of different terms to describe similar phenomena, (b) use of harassment categories that are not exhaustive or mutually exclusive, and (c) lack of attention to variation in the severity of harassment captured.

Another problem in measuring sexual harassment involves retaining context. Written vignettes provide some contextualization of harassing behavior, but they are frequently limited in their description (e.g., an item from the Harassment Sensitivity Index reads, "Lynn is a typist for an insurance company where Rob is a salesman. Last week Rob came up behind Lynn at her desk and began rubbing her shoulders. He has done things like this frequently in the past"; Lee & Heppner, 1991). Booth-Butterfield's (1989) Perceptions of Sexual Harassment instrument describes harassing incidents in one sentence. Other instruments are completely devoid of context (e.g., this item from the Incident Characteristics Questionnaire: "Person A experiences unwelcome sexual advances or other physical conduct of a sexual nature from

Person B. Such conduct involves an expressed or implied condition of employment or is the basis for any employment decision affecting Person A"; Popovich, Gehlauf, Jolton, Somers, & Godinho, 1992). If sexual harassment is socially and organizationally embedded, lack of contextual clues is likely to affect responses.

Another methodological flaw in sexual harassment research has been the use of student samples to generalize to worker populations (e.g., Bursik, 1992; Powell, 1986; Tata, 1993). Although many college students work, asking them to take the perspective of workers invested in their organizations and careers may stretch the relevance and importance of their limited work experiences. Students working at part-time jobs may perceive their experiences as transient and may not respond to organizational hierarchical pressures in the same way as more invested workers.

Because many sexual harassment studies have exclusively used college-age populations, it is important to note the differences found when both student and employee populations have been used. Terpstra and Baker (1987) found that, compared with female college students, working women identified more behaviors as sexual harassment. They conclude that "working women may have experienced more instances of sexual harassment than had female students and, as a result, become more sensitized and less tolerant of such behavior" (p. 604). Alternatively, "college is viewed by some men and women as an opportunity for increased socialization and interaction with the opposite sex, and therefore, the attitudes and norms regarding social-sexual behaviors held by college students may be somewhat different than those held by working women" (p. 604). Booth-Butterfield (1989) found that the workforce participants in her study labeled more behaviors as sexual harassment than did the college student participants, indicating that "studies based on undergraduate samples may actually underestimate a working population's sensitivity and concern over sexually harassing cues" (p. 272). Moreover, her data suggest that work experience and gender interact: "As people gain work experience the gap between what women label as harassing behavior and what men label as harassing behavior narrows" (p. 271).

Yet another flaw of some research is the a priori assumption that sexual harassment is enacted by men toward women. Some studies assume that only men are harassers (e.g., Pryor & Day, 1988). This assumption may unnecessarily skew policy and procedural implications toward a bias that marks male superiors as harassers and female subordinates as victims, further perpetuating role and gender stereotypes. Males as well as females have been harassed (Allen & Okawa, 1987; Bartling & Eisenman, 1993; Grieco, 1987; Keyton & Rhodes, in press; Waks & Starr, 1982), and peers, not managers, are more typically harassers (Mazer & Percival, 1989).

Some of the problems encountered in quantitative methodologies are overcome by research from the discursive perspective. Foss and Rogers (1994) affirm the use of discursive practice in sexual harassment research because it seeks to identify broad discursive structures and because it highlights which social structures are constructed and which are counted as real. "It illuminates how sexual harassment is enacted, interpreted, and especially how it is normalized and challenged through discursive practices" (Bingham, 1994b, p. 9). Bingham (1994b) recommends discursive methodologies because they challenge "researchers to locate intersections between theoretical understanding and lived experience" (p. 173). Strine's (1992) examination of narrative accounts of harassed women demonstrates how analyses of discourse provide new understanding of sexual harassment. The discursive constitution of subject(ivity) illustrates how women occupying subject positions of the dominant patriarchal order may feel a need to keep that order intact. (Re)presenting sexual harassment experiences "apart from the systemic gender-based power relations normalized within the academy" (Strine, 1992, p. 397) can be illuminating. Such methodologies uncover the critical intervention and the psychodynamics of cultural (re)production, which emphasizes male harassers' need to control and stabilize the "order threatened by the rise of women" (p. 399).

Yet these methodological practices are not without their limitations. Although admittedly powerful, textual/narrative interpretations should be considered as partial as other analyses (Foss & Rogers, 1994). Narrative accounts frequently represent the stories of women (primarily students) in the university setting (e.g., "Our Stories," 1992), but two examples of studies that have considered women in other settings are Clair's (1993b) exploration of the narratives of working women and Yount's (1991) research with women coal miners.

Summary

Within the varied explanations and research perspectives, many core questions about sexual harassment exist, and researchers have attempted to answer them by using sometimes opposing methods. Working from issues initially identified by Tangri et al. (1982) and Terpstra and Baker (1986), I have created an organizing framework for the research reviewed in the following sections of this chapter based on questions central to our understanding of the sexual harassment phenomenon: What constitutes sexual harassment? Who are the victims and perpetrators of sexual harassment? What characteristics and structures enable sexual harassment? How do victims respond to sexual harassment? What are the effects of sexual harassment on individuals? How do organizations respond to sexual harassment? What are the effects of sexual harassment on organizations? What are the effects of sexual harassment on society?

WHAT CONSTITUTES SEXUAL HARASSMENT?

Earlier in this essay, I provided the EEOC guidelines for both quid pro quo and hostile environment sexual harassment. But how victims, perpetrators, organizational officials, and researchers define sexual harassment depends largely upon the perspectives they adopt. Differing definitions of sexual harassment are a salient issue, given the intended vagueness of the EEOC guidelines. The question of what constitutes sexual harassment can be answered by legal interpretations or legal precedents as claims are adjudicated by the courts, by asking people who believe they have been harassed to describe those actions, and by asking research participants to evaluate categories of behaviors for their intrinsic qualities in evoking harassment judgments. Using these three strategies to answer this question provides the broadest possible responses and does not privilege one methodology over another.

Legal Interpretations of Harassment

The legal literature is replete with summaries and interpretations of court decisions (Costello, 1992; Davis & Wetherfield, 1992; Larson, 1992; Petersen & Massengill, 1992-1993; Woerner & Oswald, 1990). These summaries provide the most definitive sources for an understanding of what constitutes sexual harassment from a legal perspective, especially given that, as McCaslin (1994) notes, "sexual harassment, the experience, has become sexual harassment, the legal claim" (p. 761). Several are especially helpful on specific issues. Radford (1994) examines the proof of welcomeness in quid pro quo cases, and Lebacqz (1993) explores sexual harassment claims based on a criterion of justice. Robinson, Fink, and Allen (1994) conclude that although the courts have "clearly told us what 'severity' is not (it is not, exclusively, psychological harm), [they have] failed to tell us what it is" with regard to hostile environment (p. 114). Browne (1991) provides an excellent summary of hostile environment harassment and its relationship to free speech, and Strauss (1990) examines sexist speech in relation to the First Amendment and sexual harassment. Hetherington and Wallace (1992) provided an especially complete description and analysis of Title VII, its relationship to sexual harassment, and employer liabilities.

Linenberger (1983) explains why the EEOC chose purposely to furnish only a broad guideline for identifying sexual harassment. From the broadness of court decisions, law summaries, and legal analyses, one could conclude that there is no specific behavioral definition for sexual harassment. However, certain characteristics have been used to evaluate the validity of sexual harassment complaints. Robinson, Allen, Franklin, and Duhon (1993) summarize the characteristics for identifying quid pro quo sexual harassment as follows: (a) The victim belongs to a protected class (his or her gender), (b) the act is unwelcome—neither solicited nor invited, (c) the unwelcomed harassment is based upon sex, and (d) the victim's reaction to the unwelcomed harassment affects some tangible employment benefit.

Likewise, a number of characteristics have been used to determine whether or not certain work environments are hostile. These have been enumerated as follows: "1) whether the conduct was verbal, physical or both; 2) how frequently it was repeated; 3) whether the harasser was a coworker or supervisor; 4) whether the conduct was hostile or patently offensive; 5) whether others joined in perpetrating the harassment; and 6) whether the harassment was directed at more than one individual" ("EEOC Speaks," 1994, p. 19). Of these characteristics, no single factor drives the determination process. The employer assumes liability for hostile work environment harassment if "1) the employer had knowledge of the unwelcomed conduct; 2) the employer is in a position to control the offending conduct; and 3) the employer fails to take immediate and appropriate corrective action" (Robinson et al., 1993, p. 129).

Acknowledging the occurrence of other sexual interaction within the workplace, George (1993) explains the courts' difficulty in distinguishing between flirtatious behavior and sexual harassment. He notes that "the courts' underlying assumption in hostile environment cases remains unchallenged: when men and women work in the same environment, some 'flirting' or other comparable behavior is inevitable and appropriate" (pp. 22-23). George argues that our assumption should be quite the opposite—that sexually oriented conduct of any type in the workplace is demeaning to women and therefore improper. Thus, it appears that the debate continues about what constitutes sexual harassment and why it is wrong.

Also ongoing is the debate over the reasonable woman/reasonable victim distinction in claims of hostile environment sexual harassment (Schultz, 1993); Title VII does not identify who decides what is reasonable (Martell & Sullivan, 1994). Paetzold and Shaw (1994) debate contrasting viewpoints. Paetzold argues that " 'reasonableness' preserves male privilege in law in a manner parallel to the way sexual harassment preserves male privilege in the workplace" (p. 681). She continues that the reasonableness standard stems from a need to protect defendants from the claims of particularly sensitive individuals, which means that courts must determine if the harm is idiosyncratic to a given person or systemic, which would indicate that "not all individuals are worthy of protection" (p. 683). The reasonableness standard serves to screen out some plaintiffs; as a result, their worth is devalued. Paetzold concludes, "Reasonableness operates so as to treat sexual harassment as misunderstood communication (i.e., 'natural' interpersonal encounters between sexual beings that go wrong) or the relatively innocent introduction of traditional sex/gender-based stereotypes into the workplace" (p. 684). She refutes this standard of reasonableness, arguing that organizations should focus on creating organizational cultures that foster equal opportunity for all employees, regardless of sex. Shaw responds to Paetzold's arguments, defending the inclusion of the reasonableness standard by saying that excising it would move sexual harassment into a broader classification of absolute liability.

In an analysis of federal court cases involving sexual harassment from 1974 to 1989 and analyses of EEOC cases filed in Illinois, Terpstra and Baker

(1988, 1992) found that five characteristics predicted the likelihood of a judgment for the complainant: severity of the harassment, witnesses and documents to support the claim, the claimant's having given notice to management prior to filing charges, and lack of organizational action. Thus, these researchers conclude that the 1986 *Meritor v. Vinson* case had no significant effect on subsequent court cases. Rather, the Supreme Court decision merely affirmed what earlier appellate courts had decided. Using Terpstra and Baker's findings, one can conclude that the judicial system puts greater emphasis on the conditions of the harassing interaction and the reporting of such behavior than on behaviors enacted in the harassment.

In a similar analysis of harassment cases filed with the Illinois Department of Human Rights from 1981 to 1983, Terpstra and Cook (1985) found that filed claims did not "support the hypothesis that only the most serious forms of sexual harassment [sexual assault and threats of negatives changes in employment conditions] are associated with the filing of formal charges" (p. 569). Rather, unwanted physical contact, offensive language, sexual propositions unlinked to employment conditions, and socialization or date requests were more frequently the causes of complaints. In a similar analysis of sexual harassment cases from a California county, alleged sexual harassment occupied both ends of the severity continuum. "Verbal and slight physical contact seem to be at one end of the scale, while persistent sexual advances, assault, and attempted rape seem to be at the other" (Coles, 1986, p. 88).

Sexual harassment also pervades college campuses. Sexual harassment between academic colleagues is similar to that found in other types of organizations, but sexual harassment between professors and students has unique consequences (Hickson, Grierson, & Linder, 1990). Title IX of the Education Amendments of 1972 prohibits sex discrimination in educational institutions receiving federal funds. More recent legislation broadens this impact by forcing universities receiving any federal funds for any type of program to respond to all complaints of sexual harassment.

Frequently, we turn to courts and legal experts to provide objective definitions of social concerns. As the above discussion has shown, however, the EEOC guidelines on sexual harassment are provisional and open to alternative interpretations and change.

Interpreting Occurrences as Sexual Harassment

Another strategy for identifying what constitutes sexual harassment is to ask participants how they have been harassed. Some of the most powerful descriptions of harassment are found in research from the critical perspective. Narrative analyses by Strine (1992) and Taylor and Conrad (1992) focus on victims' identifications of sexual harassment as being of process and in process rather than on identifying sexual harassment in more traditional behavioral and incidental accounts. For example, Strine (1992) notes that one narrative recalls the "prolonged series of remarks, incidents, and so forth which 'seemed designed to remind me that I was trespassing in the boys' locker room' " (p. 394). Strine's analyses point to identifying sexual harassment as "personally alienating, disempowering, and lingering" (p. 394), focusing on the emotional and psychological consequences rather than the specific behaviors that caused those feelings. Power imbalances between professors and students defined harassment in some of the narratives (e.g., being friendly, allowing uninvited touching, embracing and kissing, use of sexist and embarrassing examples). These victims' experiences illustrate powerfully that harassment is contextualized by both gender and hierarchical structures.

Content analyses of surveys, accounts of harassment, court decisions, and the EEOC guidelines led Gruber (1992) to identify 11 distinct forms of remarks, requests, and nonverbal displays that victims experience as sexual harassment. He arranges these distinct types according to severity by adapting findings of Fitzgerald and Hesson-McInnis (1989) and Baker, Terpstra, and Larntz (1990). Verbal sexual harassment (from more to less severe) includes sexual bribery, sexual advances, relational advances, and subtle pressures/advances. Sexually harassing verbal comments (from more to less severe) are personal remarks, subjective objectification, and sexual categorical remarks. Finally, nonverbal sexual harassment displays (from more to less severe) are sexual assault, sexual touching, sexual posturing, and sexual materials. Gruber concludes that the actual amount of sexual harassment has been underestimated because researchers frequently do not include environmental and nonpersonal forms of harassment in their research designs.

Typical of survey reports, Powell (1983a) found that "although staring and flirting were two of the three most prevalent forms of attention, they were generally not seen as sexual harassment" (p. 115). The definition of sexual harassment that emerged from Powell's respondents was that it consists of sexual propositions and touching/grabbing/brushing. Some of the participants described sexual remarks, suggestive gestures, and sexual relations as sexual harassment, but others did not. Such surveys have documented that severe harassment is typically initiated by superiors, whereas milder forms of harassment generally are at the hands of peers (Loy & Stewart, 1984). Leonard et al. (1993) surveyed female students, professors, and college staff and found that almost 40% had experienced unwanted sexist comments—the most often reported of harassment types across the groups of women in the study. Garlick (1994) found that in "situations where harassing behavior is not explicit or direct, how a person subjectively experiences that behavior is often the most important determinant of how the behavior is interpreted and frequently serves as the basis for attributions about the perpetrator's intentions" (p. 154). A limitation to the use of surveys that ask participants to identify the harassment they have experienced is noted by Popovich, Licata, Nokovich, Martelli, and Zoloty (1986): If the participants do not perceive themselves to have been harassed, researchers may underestimate the nature or severity of the problem. Although sexual harassment is believed to be widespread in our society, it is minimally recognized in some organizations. A more expansive method for capturing definitions of harassment is described below.

Judgments and Perceptions About Sexual Harassment

Another strategy used by researchers to identify sexual harassment is to present subjects with behavior or interaction descriptors, written vignettes, or audio- or videotaped interactions and ask them to identify the behaviors they believe to be sexual harassment. Powell (1986) asked both males and females to identify which among 10 behaviors they perceived to be sexual harassment. The majority agreed that the following could be classified as sexual harassment: sexual activity, socializing, or dating as a requirement of the job; sexual touching/grabbing/brushing; sexual remarks, looks, and gestures meant to be insulting; and sexual propositions. Terpstra and Baker (1987) asked participants to judge situational incidents and found a marked distinction between sexual harassment and nonharassment identifications across working women, female students, and male students. Yet participants generally agreed that job propositions, touching a female's breast, rape, direct gestures, sexual propositions, superior putting arms around a subordinate, sexual remarks, and graffiti directed at a subordinate were sexual harassment.

Using written vignettes to describe male superior-female subordinate interaction in performance appraisal interviews, Remland and Jones (1985) found that participants were unlikely to identify behaviors as sexually harassing when "the evidence is quite clear that the target is 'going along' with the perpetrator's offer" (p. 171). They conclude that "sexual initiatives viewed as unwelcome are considered more harassing and inappropriate than sexual initiatives that are clearly accepted. Judges seem to be willing to accept verbal or nonverbal signs of rejection by the target as evidence that the sexual advance of a superior is harassing, even when those signs are inconsistent" (p. 173). This study demonstrates the impact of contextual factors on participants' determinations of harassment. The most exhaustive use of vignettes was undertaken in a study by Reilly et al. (1982), who used computer generation to create a unique set of vignettes about a college instructor and a student for each participant based upon the following: instructor's status, age, and marital status; class standing of the female student; setting of the interaction; nature of the student-instructor relationship; behavior of the student; verbal behavior of the instructor; physical acts by the instructor; and presence/absence of threat or coercion. The motivation behind this extensive stimulus creation "was to determine which features of an interaction had the most impact on judgments of harassment when averaged across many different contexts" (p. 103). Reilly et al. found that "the most extreme cases of harassment, and cases that were clearly not harassment, were recognized with high consensus across respondents" (p. 107). Actions of the female student, age of the male instructor, the nature of their past relationship, the instructor's verbal behavior and physical actions, and presence of threat or coercion significantly contributed to ratings of harassment.

Examples of research using videotaped interaction between superiors and subordinates is reported by Keyton and Rhodes (1994, in press), who found that student participants used relatively few cues to make the distinction between flirting and sexual harassment. The most frequently identified cues were verbal; of the nonverbal cues, tone of voice was most often used to make a sexual harassment identification. Keyton and Rhodes (in press) also found ethical ideology to have an effect on employees' identifications of verbal cues as sexual harassment; the same effect was not demonstrated for nonverbal sexually harassing cues. Employees describing their ethical ideology as reflecting a high interest in universal ideals and a high interest in the situational nature of ethical dilemmas identified significantly fewer sexually harassing cues than did other ideological types. Keyton and Rhodes's findings imply that individual characteristics affect sexual harassment identifications. Other characteristics may also produce differences in definitions.

From the third-party perspective, York (1989) found consistency in the harassment identifications made by academic equal employment opportunity officers and university students. Both groups relied upon evidence of coercion, the victim's reaction, and job consequences as the primary criteria for identifying quid pro quo sexual harassment and for making recommendations to the victim about filing formal charges. The perceptions of EEO/AA officers would likely be an important element in believing the alleged victim or the alleged perpetrator about the occurrence of harassment.

Few studies have moved beyond interpersonal harassment to examine hostile environment forms of sexual harassment. Hemmasi, Graf, and Russ (1994) focused their efforts on the use of humor in the workplace, as "gender has always been an important variable in the analysis of humor" (p. 1115) and as sex-related humor is frequently found in work environments. They found that employees were more likely to perceive both sexist and sexual gender-related jokes as sexual harassment when told by a superior than when told by a coworker. Both sexes reported sexual humor as funny, but employees sensitive to sexist issues found this type of humor to be sexual harassment when it occurred in the workplace. Thus, it appears that employees use perceptual filters from nonwork situations to make sexual harassment identifications in the workplace.

Perceptual studies are important to the study of sexual harassment because they provide clues as to how and why individuals decide what is sexual harassment. Given the number of constructs that could affect perceptual judgments about sexual harassment (e.g., Terpstra & Baker, 1986), much research remains to be completed. Researchers have a great deal to accomplish with respect to investigating sexual harassment in various types of organizations, but one constant element across most sexual harassment research is the distinction between how men define it and how women define it. This is the focus of the next subsection.

Gender Differences in Defining Sexual Harassment

Many studies have found gender differences in the identification of sexual harassment (Gutek et al., 1980, 1983; Konrad & Gutek, 1986; Padgitt & Padgitt, 1986; Popovich et al., 1992; Powell, 1986), but other studies have not (Barr, 1993; Gutek, 1985; Keyton & Rhodes, in press; Lee & Heppner, 1991; McKinney, 1990; Terpstra & Baker, 1987). When gender differences are discovered, females appear to be more sensitive to sexual cues. Fitzgerald and Ormerod (1991) found that when harassment was severe, both males and females agreed that harassment had occurred. However, when the behavior was less explicit, women were more likely to identify it as harassment. Female students were more sensitive to offensive and suggestive jokes and more likely to view romantic or sexual attention as harassment. Likewise, female students identified subtle forms of harassment more frequently than did male students.

Yet gender differences reverse with respect to flirtatious, seductive, and promiscuous behavior. Males tend to misinterpret friendly behaviors as sexual behaviors, implying that they view the world in sexual terms (Abbey, 1982; Abbey & Melby, 1986; Saal, Johnson, & Weber, 1989). Williams and Cyr (1992) found that "males and females differ in their perceptions of sexual harassment, particularly when a female target makes prior commitments to having a friendly relationship" (p. 66). Padgitt and Padgitt (1986) found that "women clearly distinguished between offensive and harassing behavior," whereas men did not (p. 37); Shotland and Craig (1988) found that both male and female subjects differentiated between sexually interested behavior and friendly behavior.

Grauerholz (1994), who examined gender differences in socialized roles, notes that such "differences result in distinct communication styles for men and women," and that sexual harassment can result "as an outcome of these different communication styles" (p. 42). Extending the focus on gender differences to participants' masculinity and femininity, Powell (1986) found that "the sex effect remained strong despite the inclusion of sex role identity" (p. 17). In Powell's research, the most compelling effect of sex role identity existed in an interaction between sex and masculinity. In Bursik's (1992) study, "masculinity and femininity scores were not significantly associated with any of the harassment measures" (p. 409).

Moving to the gender identification of the stimulus perpetrator and victim, Gutek et al. (1983) found that harassment incidents initiated by women were less likely to be viewed as harassment, as participants viewed the relationship between the female initiator and male victim as more favorable and more in line with the woman's work role. Bursik (1992) found gender differences only in subjects' evaluation of male perpetrators. Gender distinctions disappear when severe forms (sexual bribery, sexual coercion, and sexual assault) are investigated in comparison with milder forms of harassment (Keyton & Rhodes, in press; Tata, 1993).

Summary

Booth-Butterfield (1989) cautions researchers about placing too much importance on gender differences. She argues that "when people respond to potentially harassing communication situations, they are not simply seeing the action through the eyes of their gender" (p. 272); both trait and contextual cues are responsible for study participants' harassment interpretations. However, researchers should not forget that both "sexes simply do not have 'equal opportunity' to experience sexual harassment" (Mazer & Percival, 1989, p. 17).

In asking what constitutes sexual harassment, researchers "must explicitly acknowledge the impact of different operational definitions of harassment on reported rates of harassment. . . . A smaller percentage of harassment will be 'found' if respondents are allowed to define the term sexual harassment themselves . . . than when they respond to a list of behaviors the researchers provide" (McKinney, 1990, p. 436). Employees' hesitancy or willingness to view or name some behavior as sexual harassment is at the core of the debate. The effect of this hesitancy is powerful "because it is not sexual harassment until it is so interpreted. Sexual harassment is not the physical act; it is the interpretation of that physical act" (Bowker, 1993, p. 200).

WHO ARE THE VICTIMS AND PERPETRATORS
OF SEXUAL HARASSMENT?

Although seemingly simple, Who are the victims and perpetrators of sexual harassment? is a question with multiple answers, depending upon which definition of sexual harassment is used. Legally, sexual harassment victims are identified when an actionable complaint is confirmed by the EEOC. Yet many sexual harassment complaints do not reach that stage of deliberation; lawyers estimate that 95% of cases settle before trial (Apruzzese, 1992). Of those that go to trial, formal complaint data document that women are far more likely than men to be sexual harassment victims, and men are more likely than women to be their alleged harassers. Estimates suggest that male-to-female harassment accounts for 90% of EEOC claims, female-to-male harassment accounts for 9%, and same-gender harassment accounts for 1%. These figures are estimates because the EEOC documents only the gender of the victim and not that of the alleged harasser. Using closed files from a county office of the California Fair Employment and Housing Department between 1979 and 1983, Coles (1986) found that complainants were predominantly Caucasian and distributed among age groups. Earlier, MacKinnon (1979) reported that victimization crosses lines of age, marital status, physical appearance, race, class, occupation, and pay range. The broadness of victim characteristics is an especially potent argument that sexual harassment is a sexual as well as a power issue, given that the most "common denominator is that the perpetrators tend to be men, the victims women" (p. 28).

Although most sexual harassment reports document information about victims, these reports often overlook the fact that plaintiffs are not necessarily the harassed ("Identifying Sexual Harassment," 1993). Even when employment opportunities or benefits are offered or incurred because one employee submits to an employer's or supervisor's request for sexual favors, other employees denied those opportunities or benefits can also claim sexual harassment. Thus, in quid pro quo claims, third persons to the actual incidents of harassment may also be victims.

Surveys have been useful for establishing victim status. Using six forms of behavior (uninvited pressure for sexual favors, deliberate touching, suggestive looks, letters and calls, uninvited pressure for dates, and sexual remarks), the U.S. Merit Systems Protection Board (1981) found that 42% of females and 15% of males in a sample of 20,000 federal employees had been harassed in the previous 24 months. Surprisingly, peer harassment was found to be more common than superior harassment of subordinates. The USMSPB's (1988) follow-up survey indicated almost identical results with respect to both the occurrence of sexual harassment and the presence of peer harassment. In Keyton and Rhodes's (in press) study of municipal employees, about 30% of female and 12% of male participants identified themselves as victims of sexual harassment. In a survey of working adults in Connecticut, half of the female respondents indicated that they had experienced sexual harassment (Loy & Stewart, 1984).

Some studies have attempted to identify victims within specific professions. Maypole (1986) found that more than one-third of female and one-seventh of male social workers had been harassed by coworkers, clients, or agency administrators, with women under 44 years old appearing to be particularly vulnerable. In a study of nurses, Grieco (1987) found that 82% of female and 67% of male nurses in one Missouri county had been sexually harassed. Hansen (1992) asked attorneys and judges in the federal courts in nine western states to identify sexual harassment in their work environments. Ironically, one-third of the women surveyed said they had been sexually harassed by another lawyer; 6% attributed harassment to a judge.

Turning to the task of identifying perpetrators, Quinn and Lees (1984) note that all of the early landmark cases involved supervisors as harassers. In Coles's (1986) examination of claims filed in one California county, business owners and supervisors were predominantly identified as perpetrators; however, data regarding perpetrators' sex were not captured. In the 1981 *Bundy v. Jackson* case, courts acknowledged, however, that coworkers had power over the workplace environment in lieu of hierarchical power and could also take on the harasser role. "Although those lower in the hierarchy will always be more vulnerable, the sheer number of co-workers suggests that horizontal harassment may be more common than hierarchical harassment" (Quinn & Lees, 1984, p. 42).

Stereotypically, the public in general, and frequently researchers, assume that perpetrators of sexual harassment are male (Lee & Heppner, 1991; Pryor, 1987; Pryor & Day, 1988). Although most of the attention has been focused on male superiors as harassers, female supervisors and colleagues have taken on the role of the perpetrator as well. This element should not be overlooked, particularly because, as Gutek (1985) has found, the majority of sexual advances at work are directed toward peers, not subordinates. Interestingly, "the general public is more forgiving of questionable behavior when the boss is a woman, the offender is not the boss, or the offense happens only occasionally" ("Sex, Laws," 1994, p. 14). In contrast, sexual behaviors at work are frequently seen as more severe when they are initiated by men, particularly supervisors. In Maypole's (1986) survey of social workers, harassment was reported by both men and women.

Other attempts to identify perpetrators have taken the form of personality measurements. Pryor (1987) developed the Likelihood to Sexually Harass (LSH) scale to measure the propensity of males to inflict severe forms of sexual harassment. In three studies using male undergraduates, Pryor found that men who scored high on the LSH were adversarial in their sexual beliefs, had higher rape proclivities than did lower scorers, had more negative feelings about sexuality than did lower scorers, had difficulty assuming others' perspectives, and were high in authoritarianism and low in Machiavellianism. They also described themselves in socially undesirable masculine terms and took the opportunity to behave in sexual ways when their motives could be disguised by the interaction situation. In a later study, Pryor and Stoller (1994) found that men who score high on the LSH may perceive ambiguous social situations as sexually charged. Research has not demonstrated, however, that participants with high LSH scores are more likely to be involved in harassing incidents. Gutek (1985) found that male harassers are virtually indistinguishable from other male workers with respect to personal characteristics. The one distinguishing quality of harassers is that they tend to approach more than one victim.

Reilly, Lott, and Gallogly (1986) surveyed students about their personal experiences with harassment in the classroom and in university work settings. Female students in the sample reported being subjected to harassing interactions by male professors and male graduate students more often than male students reported being harassed. Data from a survey of university students at Central Michigan University (Roscoe, Goodwin, Repp, & Rose, 1987) indicate that male course instructors were primarily the harassers of female students. However, males also reported being harassed by males. McKinney (1990) found that although female faculty members were more likely to be harassed by colleagues, some male faculty reported potentially harassing behaviors by students. Leonard et al. (1993) also investigated sexual harassment among female undergraduates, graduate students, staff, and faculty. Surprisingly, female participants named both males and females as the initiators of sexually harassing comments. In the professor-student relationship, 87% of students reported being harassed by a professor, instructor, or teaching/research assistant, with a majority of the harassment reported in public classroom settings rather than in private settings.

Summary

Who are the victims of sexual harassment? Conventional wisdom would say that women are, and legal documentation and surveys confirm this. However, although most research attention has been directed to the victim-as-female, some reports have documented that males also experience harassment (Allen & Okawa, 1987; Bartling & Eisenman, 1993; Grieco, 1987; Keyton & Rhodes, in press; Murrell & Dietz-Uhler, 1993; Roscoe et al., 1987; Waks & Starr, 1982).

Who are the perpetrators of sexual harassment? They are overwhelmingly reported to be males. Unfortunately, limited reporting mechanisms and research participants' fears of retribution and desires to provide socially and politically correct responses restrict our knowledge about these individuals. Researchers are likely to avoid asking research participants to self-report activities that amount to illegal interactions involving other persons. Overall, our presumptions about victims and perpetrators are confirmed, but there is evidence that sometimes females do harass males, and that same-gender harassment occurs as well (Leonard et al., 1993; Mazer & Percival, 1989; Vaux, 1993; Waks & Starr, 1982).

Are increases in the reporting of sexual harassment a result of heightened sensitivity about what "counts" as sexual harassment? Or are they due to changes in the characteristics and structures that enable sexual harassment? The next section explores these issues.

WHAT CHARACTERISTICS AND STRUCTURES ENABLE SEXUAL HARASSMENT?

Given the frequency with which sexual harassment occurs and the broadness of its definitional boundaries, an obvious next question concerns why harassment occurs. Because this literature review focuses on organizational sexual harassment, I will address this question in two subsections concerning individual characteristics and organizational structures.

Individual Characteristics

Research that attempts to explain why some individuals harass has been quite deficient. Researchers who may want to approach this question meet obvious ethical dilemmas; it would be very difficult, for instance, to ask respondents, Have you harassed someone in your organization? Because the behavior of interest is illegal, such a question would most likely prompt the socially desirable response: No, I haven't harassed anyone! Tracking harassers through organizational procedures has been difficult, given the "code of silence" suggested or required by most organizational sexual harassment policies. Tracking harassers through EEOC claims is difficult because the reporting mechanisms focus on the victims and because many claims are "resolved" before they can be publicly scrutinized.

Some researchers have content analyzed adjudicated claims, but such analyses miss the many hostile work environment claims against coworkers believed to be the most prevalent type of harassment. Unlike perpetrators of rape, who often serve jail time in which counseling is mandated (and data collected), perpetrators of harassment are not saddled with such penalties or punishments. Once again, researchers' abilities to track this group are hampered.

The natural/biological explanation for sexual harassment implies that the sex drive of males is stronger than that of females, making males more frequent harassers. Many studies have documented that men are more frequently identified as harassers, but it is unlikely that this can be attributed to sex drive, as females possess equally strong sex drives and are less frequently harassers (MacKinnon, 1979). A deviant personality explanation has also been advanced (Pryor, 1987; Pryor & Day, 1988; Pryor & Stoller, 1994). Extending this type of research to both males and females, Bartling and Eisenman (1993) found that "the personality profiles for those likely to initiate sexually harassing behaviors appear to be similar for men and women. Adversarial sexual beliefs and weak empathy skills may predispose both men and women to initiate sexually harassing behaviors" (p. 192).

Research is equally deficient in the area of identifying characteristics that make individuals likely victims of sexual harassment. It does not appear that personality characteristics enable the victim role. Feminist critiques of women's stories do not reveal victims as weak. Rather, victims become disabled by contexts that disempower them. The abuse of power is a frequently cited cause of harassment, but it is the linkage of power to organizational hierarchies, relationships, and norms that allows it to be used in abusive ways. The next subsection examines the organizational structures that promote sexual harassment.

Organizational Structures

Frequently, formal hierarchical power over others in organizations is a prime factor in sexual harassment. The relationship of men to power can be viewed in two ways. First, men have power in organizations and choose to use it sexually. An alternative view is that some men have little power in their organizations or other areas of their lives and so choose to use sex as power at work because the organizational culture supports this norm. However, because harassment occurs between coworkers, we must examine the concept of power in other terms. Power of one coworker over another may be evidence of a carryover of societal power of men over women into the organization. Organizational cultures, therefore, should be examined for evidence of this phenomenon.

Kenig and Ryan (1986) found consistent sex differences in the identification of sexual harassment when behaviors were ambiguous (resulting in the mildest forms of harassing behavior). Women had lower levels of tolerance and tended to maximize the range of behaviors they defined as harassment, whereas men tended to minimize the range of behaviors they saw as harassment. These differences, the researchers argue, result from normative organizational structures. Kenig and Ryan hypothesized at the beginning of their study that "the level of tolerance of harassment within an organization would reflect the relative strength of these two normative structures, male vs. female" (pp. 544). As a result, an organizational culture can be simultaneously viewed as a structure of opportunity, a structure of power, and a structure that positions women relative to men.

Conrad and Taylor (1994) examined organizational hierarchical structures, norms, and responses to support their argument that "organizations are sites in which cultural assumptions are instantiated inaction" (p. 45). These authors identify vertical stratification of bureaucracy, individual employees in highly autonomous positions, the extent to which women are isolated from one another, the effectiveness of grievance procedures, and organizational power imbalances between men and women as organizational characteristics that increase the potential for harassment to occur. Sexual harassment is a social phenomenon, but it cannot be fully explained in this manner—or most organizations would equally embrace harassment. "Organizations differ in the extent to which they allow and sanction harassing behavior, and patterns of action within organizations reproduce the conditions that foster, suppress, or repress harassment" (Conrad & Taylor, 1994, p. 55).

Organizational romances have been linked to sexual harassment. Apruzzese (1992) notes that because hostile work environment claims center on welcomeness, "a significant problem exists when previously welcomed conduct becomes unwelcomed" (p. 334). When a voluntary office relationship ceases, repeated attempts to continue the relationship by one party (on or off the work site) can constitute harassment. Further, attempts by one employee to initiate a relationship with another employee who does not want a personal relationship with the solicitor also constitute harassment. Dillard and Witteman (1985) found that highly formalized organizations suppress organizational romance, which serves to prohibit interaction that is not work related and thereby decreases the likelihood that intimate relationships will develop. Likewise, highly formal organizations are likely to exhibit low levels of workplace sexualization (Gutek, 1985), making it more difficult for potential harassers to take advantage of the interaction environment.

Booth-Butterfield (1986) provides an analysis of harassment-prone organizational climates by juxtaposing individual and organizational sensitivity to harassment. Just as there are individual differences in the tolerance and perceptions of harassment, there are also differing levels of organizational awareness, tolerance, and response to sexual harassment. At low levels of tolerance, organizations "do not tolerate harassment or discrimination and act decisively on alleged violations. At the upper end of the continuum are organizations that tolerate higher levels of sexually objectionable communication. They may be considered harassment-prone cultures in that harassment may go unnoticed or unpunished in such climates" (p. 43). Booth-Butterfield (1986) identifies several characteristics of harassment-prone organizations. First, organizations in which managers believe they have fulfilled EEOC guidelines by posting notices tend to pay little attention to the harassment opportunities that exist within the organizations. Second, imbalanced distribution of males and females within an organizational hierarchy promotes male managerial structures that provide opportunities for harassment to occur. Third, "if harassment is conspicuously absent as a discussion topic (unless it is a subject of humor), this may indicate lack of awareness or insensitivity to sexual harassment" (p. 44). Likewise, jokes about sex or sexual issues, or jokes that denigrate women, promote general insensitivity to the potential of harassment. Fifth, the use of politeness within an organization signals the sex role spillover of gender-based expectations into the organization. "Overly polite behavior accorded to women in organizations may be a sign that coworkers view them first as females and only secondarily, and less seriously, as responsible employees" (p. 45).

Gutek's (1985) investigation of sex role spillover suggests organizational characteristics that may promote the incidence or tolerance of sexual harassment. These include the following: (a) men working in a more gender homogeneous environment than women; (b) men occupying higher-status work positions than women, women working in more pleasant working conditions, and women being subjected to criteria of personableness and physical attractiveness whereas men are not; (c) the appearance of social-sexual behaviors that are accepted and reciprocated, and a high incidence of sexual behaviors at work (caring, intimacy, flattery, and physical attraction); (d) men and women having different perceptions about the appropriateness of social-sexual behavior at work; and (e) the existence of an unprofessional work environment. Gutek's findings illuminate the effects of imbalanced sex ratios and sexualization of work environments. Sex role spillover is clearly evident in organizations that promote a "hyper-masculine culture where men are Select Men, not to be held to ordinary standards" (Vaux, 1993, p. 129). This type of cultural influence may explain the occurrence and cover-up of harassment found in the Tailhook incident. As Konrad and Gutek (1986) have found, men and women differ in their attitudes toward sex in the workplace, which may partially explain their tendency to differ in labeling sexual harassment. Also of note, Konrad and Gutek argue that the effect of a sexualized workplace extends beyond those currently engaged in the interaction climate. "The sexualization of the work environment is likely to affect selection and placement, turnover, and job satisfaction" (p. 435).

Summary

There is little evidence to suggest that a particular type of employee will be a harasser. Whereas some may point to characteristics that may enable individuals to use their positions or relational power in sexually negative ways, others with similar power bases do not harass. Although the most frequent victims of sexual harassment are women, there does not appear to be any other common denominator among them.

Clearly, many of the organizational structural characteristics that facilitate sexual harassment exist because society at large endorses them (MacKinnon, 1979). Sexual harassment is not limited to the workplace, but the courts have legal recourse to punish organizations that allow it to occur. Given that organizations have the legal responsibility to allow employees to pursue their economic livelihood in the absence of sexual harassment, the impact of societal effects becomes magnified (and contested) in organizational contexts. Simply, organizational structure factors are easier to capture than the multitude of individual characteristics that might affect the incidence of sexual harassment; the research to date reflects this methodological logistic.

HOW DO VICTIMS RESPOND TO SEXUAL HARASSMENT?

Individual employees respond to harassment based upon their identification and labeling of interactions as sexual harassment and based upon the effects such interactions have on them. Some employees do not respond immediately when they are sexually harassed because they feel paralyzed. Not all harassment effects are immediate; some are long-term. Thus, this section and the next cannot be linearly derived. Effects determine responses. In turn, new effects are manifested as responses are deemed effective or ineffective. We will begin with responses, as more research exists in this area.

Few studies have reported the actions of victims in response to sexual harassment. The 1988 USMSPB report cited previously indicates that victims use informal remedies even when they are aware that formal remedies are available; less than 5% of the sexual harassment victims surveyed reported using formal procedures. Subjects indicated that informal responses were generally effective. Asked to explain why they did not initiate formal procedures, they indicated there was no need to report the behaviors, suggesting perhaps that informal responses are indeed effective. Other interpretations include that "victims simply resigned themselves to tolerating behavior that they may have viewed as bothersome" (p. 27). Others reported that taking formal action would make the work environment unpleasant or that nothing would be done as a result of their action anyway.

As in the data reported by the USMSPB, Gutek (1985) found that females were angered by harassment but assumed personal responsibility for handling it, and wanted to do so without hurting their harassers. More recently, Jones and Remland (1992) have reported that 24% of the respondents in their study said they would either verbally confront the harasser or report the harasser. Avoiding the harasser was the strategy of 19% of the respondents. Fewer victims would comply with a perpetrator's sexual advances (7%), show nonverbal discomfort (7%), refocus the discussion (4.5%), or use verbal or physical violence (3.5%). Jones and Remland's respondents were also more likely to report the perpetrator when harassment was severe, and females were more likely than males to say they would report the harasser.

Because the response process is frequently fraught with problems—psychological and financial—and formal actions are perceived to achieve relatively meager gains (Livingston, 1982), many victims choose informal or interpersonal means by which to confront sexual harassment. Gruber (1989) provides a summary of the four major types of individual response—avoidance, defusion, negotiation, and confrontation. He argues that

> a particular response to harassment is shaped by, among other things, the success of previous responses to the harasser; a woman's knowledge of the response that other women in the workplace have given to harassment; the degree to which harassment, discrimination, and/or unprofessional behavior are tolerated in the workplace; and the perceived likelihood that a more assertive response will escalate the tension or antagonism. (p. 6)

Clair, McGoun, and Spirek (1993) found that harassed women used response messages that were brief yet capable of sustaining multiple interpretations as well as multiple goals. Frequently, women report the use of embedded covert threats. In an experimental study of harassment responses, Bingham and Burleson (1989) found that messages with more sophisticated design logics or goal structures were not perceived as more effective at stopping harassment. Later, Bingham (1991) combined the theoretical message frameworks of assertiveness, intraorganizational influences, and message design logic to construct both a typology of responses to sexual harassment and an approach for managing the phenomenon within organizations. She notes that the multiple-goal orientation of instrumental, relational, and identity objectives creates difficulty in the face-to-face presentation of management strategies. That difficulty may be exacerbated as victims "are forced to use rhetorical process that by its very nature omits their own ontological integrity, as they are members of a group that is not the dominant power in the culture" (Bowker, 1993, p. 196).

Bingham and Scherer (1993) evaluated selection of response strategies to harassment and levels of satisfaction with outcomes, and found that "employees who perceived the perpetrator's behavior as sexual harassment were more likely to file a formal complaint, to make an informal complaint to an authority person outside their department, and to discuss the incident with coworkers" (p. 262). Yet the use of formal and informal complaint procedures did not result in high levels of satisfaction with the outcomes of the sexual harassment situation. Employees were more satisfied when they personally confronted their harassers, indicating that interpersonal response strategies may be personally empowering for victims (Bingham, 1991).

Kaland and Geist (1994) used narratives describing women's responses to incidents of sexual harassment to develop an ideological model based upon the degree of empowerment and severity of the harassment. These authors identify four types of victim responses. The *peacemaker* perceives mild sexual harassment to be part of organizational life and often takes the path of least resistance, assuming part of the responsibility for the harassment. The *hostage* experiences moderate to severe sexual harassment and responds in a way "that will alleviate the situation without aggravating the harasser" (p. 148). The *rebel* is defined by her intolerance of any level of sexual harassment and her willingness to confront the harasser directly and pursue organizational remedies. The *activist* faces severe sexual harassment and seeks individual and organizational remedies, because "living with abusive or disturbing conduct is not acceptable" (p. 151).

Such research establishes a rule orientation for responding to sexual harassment. Other researchers have also adopted a rule orientation by suggesting strategically developed responses. For example, Payne (1993) explored responses to campus sexual harassment by viewing harassment incidents as a game with rules for play. She argues that social rules on campus promote harassment, and that these rules develop from and are maintained by myths. By viewing harassment as a game that can be played, victims can maintain the myth and promote harassment or change the game by playing in such a way that it becomes uncomfortable for the perpetrator to harass. One way to play and change the game rules would be to use humor. Brown (1993) identifies effective coping strategies that "employ ingenuity and some humor in turning the tables on the offender" (p. 127). Her research demonstrates that some women prefer such approaches over more formal mechanisms.

One of the most dramatic examinations of individual responses to sexual harassment is reported by Yount (1991), whose field study indicates that women working within the traditionally male-oriented culture of underground coal mines respond to sexual harassment with three distinctive gender role adaptations, which she calls "ladies," "flirts," and "tomboys." "These approaches involved efforts to establish social identities with respect to both the labor process and sociosexual relations with men" (p. 397). Ladies evidenced a low tolerance for sexual harassment, but were highly reluctant to object or to file sexual harassment complaints. Their reluctance was fueled by the concern that "pursuing charges would bring their sexual reputation to the fore as a public issue"; they "also feared retaliation in the form of intensified hostilities from colleagues and assignments to difficult, uncomfortable, and isolated work" (p. 404). In light of these anticipated consequences, ladies used response strategies based on nonconfrontation. They believed that if they acted "like ladies," "men would honor this status and treat them courteously" (p. 404). Unable to distance themselves from their harassers physically, ladies distanced themselves mentally and emotionally.

Flirts were characterized by their youth, status of marital availability, and physical attractiveness. Flirts engaged in the sexual attention of the male coal miners as "defensive maneuvers to curb unwanted advances" (p. 408). Flirts used their femininity to "sexually manipulate men into doing their work and to solicit easy tasks" (p. 409). Tomboys, who ranged in age from mid-20s to mid-30s, attempted to "center their social identities on their status as coal miners and to conscientiously dissociate themselves from the female stereotype" (p. 412). Tomboys thwarted men's sexual attention by avoiding cues symbolizing their female identity and by taking indifferent attitudes toward compliments. Tomboys evidenced the highest tolerance of sexual harassment.

Taylor and Conrad's (1992) analyses of harassment accounts point to the systematic distortion of sexual harassment responses. Some victims feel trauma over an extended period of time, sometimes creating a time lag in understanding and acting upon what has happened to them. Others vacillate between silence and speech as they gain strength and lose it relative to their organizational position and their use of or isolation from support structures. Finally, victims' views of harassment incidents can become distorted when they are confronted by perpetrators who deny such actions.

Thus, victims of sexual harassment respond in a variety of ways—some reactive, some strategic, some not at all. Some responses provide psychological relief, some behavioral relief. As public awareness of sexual harassment increases, victims are likely to be encouraged to talk about their experiences, allowing researchers to analyze their responses for effectiveness at individual, relational, and organizational levels.

WHAT ARE THE EFFECTS OF
SEXUAL HARASSMENT ON INDIVIDUALS?

Hickson, Grierson, and Linder (1991) identify two consequences of sexual harassment: psychological and economic. Gilsdorf (1990) notes that "the human cost can rarely be put in monetary terms. The human damage is potentially very grave, to the victim and the victim's family, to the harasser and the harasser's family, and to all others affected by the incident, both inside and outside the organization" (p. 74). Examining effects in relation to individuals' organizational roles, Taylor and Conrad (1992) conclude that harassment keeps organizational members from "informed, consenting, ethical, reflective, and empowered participation in their evolving community" (p. 413), which in turn limits their individual growth.

Effects on Victims

It is clear that noncompliance with sexual pressures can lead to negative consequences. Alternatively, there is no guarantee that submitting to sexual demands will result in promised consequences. Job-related consequences can take the form of losing one's job, being denied a promotion, being demoted, being denied access to normal communication channels, and even being physically assaulted (Quinn & Lees, 1984). In addition, acquiescing to sexual demands undermines an employee's credibility and effectiveness. Such employment-related consequences are critical variables in victims' decisions about filing formal sexual harassment complaints. In examining formal cases filed in Illinois, Terpstra and Cook (1985) found that being discharged from the job was the most frequent consequence, accounting for 66% of the cases. Less frequently, victims had quit (16%) or were demoted (11%) as a result of their harassment.

Beyond job consequences, victims are likely to lose self-esteem and self-respect (Hetherington & Wallace, 1992; Quinn & Lees, 1984; Reilly et al., 1986). Samoluk and Pretty (1994) found that victims of interpersonal sexual harassment (compared with environmental harassment) reported more dysphoria, other-person blame, and anticipated assertiveness. These effects increased as the harassment continued. As women received unwanted sexual interaction, they reported self-blame, embarrassment, and humiliation up until the point where they perceived themselves as being sexually harassed.

Workplace stress has been linked to sexual harassment. Harassed women have reported psychological stress (nervousness or depression) and physical stress symptoms (headaches, stomachaches, or changes in weight or blood pressure) (Offermann & Armitage, 1993). For female students, Reilly et al. (1986) report, stress can be manifested as discouragement from entering particular fields of study and decreased interest in personal growth.

Littler-Bishop, Seidler-Feller, and Opaluch (1982) found that female flight attendants evaluated harassment interaction more favorably when it was initiated by pilots than when it came from other crew and staff, indicating that more habitual harassing interaction from pilots to flight attendants causes flight attendants to be more tolerant of such interaction. Thus, sexual harassment in this occupation serves to desensitize women. Murrell and Dietz-Uhler

(1993) also found a desensitizing effect. They found that male students who had been victims of sexual harassment had more tolerant sexual attitudes, suggesting another type of desensitization effect.

The combined impact of physical, emotional, and job-related consequences of sexual harassment has been referred to as "sexual harassment syndrome" (Hetherington & Wallace, 1992). Gilsdorf (1990) summarizes: "The victim who initiates a complaint, then, puts a career and a life at hazard. If the accusation is true but the plaintiff is unable to make a strong enough case, that individual is generally victimized even further—through job loss, a reputation as a troublemaker, diminished economic status and self-esteem, and untold emotional erosion" (pp. 74-75). Given these negative effects, "it does not seem as though women want to be sexually harassed at work. Nor do they, as a rule, find it flattering" (MacKinnon, 1979, p. 47).

It is unclear how male victims are affected by harassment, as little research has examined this role. Clair's (1994b) case study of one man's experience demonstrates that he was affected in many of the same ways women are. Additionally, he was subjected to questioning about his sexual orientation when he refused to submit to female sexual oppression. Although this victim filed an EEOC complaint, most male harassment victims may be inhibited by social norms from filing reports, as "both machismo and homophobia work against a man's likelihood to file a complaint about harassment" (Quinn & Lees, 1984, p. 43).

Effects on Harassers

One concern of organizations and male supervisors is that charges of sexual harassment may be used by subordinates as a means of getting even for other employment-related complaints. "The belief is that, for instance, a woman who receives a poor performance evaluation from her supervisor will charge that the evaluation is a result of her rejection of his sexual advances, rather than of poor work performance" (Quinn & Lees, 1984, p. 43). It is likely that this "anticipation" effect may cause some men to reevaluate their workplace behaviors.

For the accused who "had no intention to harass but is treated like a harasser anyway, that individual endures unjustified suffering and humiliation" (Gilsdorf, 1990, p. 75). Shedletsky (1993) tells his story of being accused of sexual harassment in relation to an employment decision he made. He says that his immediate concerns were "What does one do who is falsely accused? How do I redress this attack against me?" (p. 85). He reports that he had feelings of helplessness because organizational support structures did not exist for an alleged harasser. Further, "I never got my day in court. The accusation against me was, therefore, never erased. Somewhere the document accusing me still exists" (p. 86). Shedletsky's story reveals the anguish of a man who believes he did the right thing and was unjustly punished for following his conscience.

He says also that the effects of the accusation continue, in his sense of being undermined for taking responsibility for his own decisions and his fearfulness that unjust accusations might be made again.

Witteman (1993) suggests that harassers may have interpersonal problems if they remain in their organizations after they have been identified as harassers. First, if a victim has confronted the harasser and the harassment has stopped, the perpetrator may want or be required to maintain a work relationship with the victim (due to job function) within a negative communication climate. Second, if a victim has confronted the harasser it is likely that other organizational members know about it, and this can negatively affect the perpetrator's ability to perform in the organization. Witteman suggests that some of these problems may occur because of the perpetrator's lack of communication competence, both in terms of sending repairing messages and in terms of sensing what is wrong.

Because harassment occurs within an organizational context, public attention may be focused on the organization, so that the identity of the harasser is displaced and shielded. Other harassers suffer financial liability; some lose their jobs. Many times, however, claims are resolved out of court and the accused are allowed to leave their jobs with few negative implications. As alternatives to being fired, the accused can resign or retire and still find employment elsewhere.

Summary

The effects of sexual harassment prompt responses that, in turn, prompt a second level of effects. For example, Loy and Stewart (1984) note that women who pursue aggressive strategies for stopping harassment suffer the most personal and organizational consequences: "Almost half of the women who directly confronted their harassers received some type of negative organizational sanction" (p. 42). Another type of effects-response link is seen when individuals want to pursue legal claims against their harassers. "Although state and federal agencies may take the case to court acting as plaintiff in the victim's behalf, most often the victim must bring action on her own after the agency has issued a 'right to suit' " (Livingston, 1982, p. 14). Cases can drag on for years through various hearings and appeals, all the while costing the victim considerable legal fees and psychological distress.

HOW DO ORGANIZATIONS RESPOND
TO SEXUAL HARASSMENT?

"Just as most people didn't buckle up until seatbelt laws went into effect, most companies started paying attention to sexual harassment only after the courts began taking it seriously in the mid-1980s" ("Sex, Laws," 1994, p. 14).

And, like the effects on and responses of individual employees, the effects on and responses of organizations are also inextricably intertwined.

Using Weick's model of organizing and the principle of requisite variety to examine the influences of communication on sexual harassment, Kreps (1994) identifies sexual harassment as an equivocal phenomenon that is relatively complex, unpredictable, and ambiguous. As such, an organization's most effective response is also likely to be complex. However, many organizations fail to take such an approach when sexual harassment is trivialized. Complex responses would include an integrated approach of holding seminars and workshops to educate employees about the seriousness and complexity of sexual harassment, direct communication with employees to increase awareness, establishment of support groups for victims, and the appointment of ombudsmen to help both victims and perpetrators. Organizational rules for dealing with harassment need to emanate from organizational leaders to establish priority and importance. The formalization and institutionalization of organizational responses to sexual harassment can preserve organizational intelligence for handling future sexual harassment incidents. Kreps argues that such steps "can effectively combat sexual harassment only to the extent that they reduce equivocality, help actors identify effective response strategies, and preserve these strategies as organizational intelligence" (p. 135).

Legal authors advise that "an effective sexual harassment policy should define behavior which constitutes sexual harassment" (Pechman, 1993, p. 59). As noted earlier, legal interpretations and court decisions provide little consensus on definitional issues. Kronenberger and Bourke (1981) suggest using both judicial cases and in-house cases in sexual harassment training to provide employees with adequate definitions and to avoid confusion. "Employees may be confused when company officials cannot adequately answer the many questions that arise or explain the concept properly" (p. 880). Organizational training, policies, and procedures that rely on the EEOC guidelines as a foundation are woefully shortsighted, and perhaps misdirected. Rather, managers should assess how harassment occurs or has the potential to occur in their own organizations, and then use this knowledge to amplify the EEOC guidelines.

As is common in many organizations, the USMSPB (1988) reports that training efforts are often directed at managers, human resources/personnel employees, and EEO/AA officials rather than nonsupervisory employees. Some companies may fear that educating their workforces about sexual harassment will increase the number of sexual harassment complaints. Brooks and Perot (1991) conclude that organizations could facilitate more reporting of sexual harassment if potential victims were encouraged through education and policy to identify inappropriate sexual behaviors. They argue that the "silent reaction" to harassment helps maintain its existence. In Beauvais's (1986) study, sexual harassment training was found to help participants form and reevaluate their attitudes and opinions about sexual harassment.

Recommendations for sexual harassment training are broad. Wells and Kracher (1993) promote consciousness-raising, specifically with attention to the differing workplace perspectives and expectations of men and women. They also recommend assertiveness training to help potential victims respond forcefully "so that harassers clearly understand there is a perspective other than their own" (p. 428). Berryman-Fink (1993) suggests training that explores differences in male and female communication styles. Bingham (1991) argues that employee communication training should help employees to (a) analyze sexually harassing incidents in terms of both multiple goals and obstacles, (b) determine whether interpersonal communication strategies are viable options, (c) choose appropriate message strategies, (d) initiate their selection, and (e) anticipate the effectiveness of the selected strategies. Role-playing may be a viable training technique for helping employees to achieve these objectives.

Licata and Popovich (1987) suggest role negotiation techniques to help employees resolve their own work/sex role conflicts as well as state their role expectations of others. The ultimate objective is to open communication channels so that issues of offensive and harassing behaviors and work expectations can be discussed. Another type of sexual harassment training is suggested by Blaxall, Parsonson, and Robertson (1993), who reason that sexual harassment policies and procedures are underutilized, in part, because organizational personnel responsible for leading victims through the process lack the necessary knowledge. To that end, they suggest training for the person in the organization who is responsible for taking sexual harassment complaints. Their evaluation of such a program provides evidence that when trained, these persons "knew more of the information necessary to provide effective service and had more confidence in their ability to provide such service" (pp. 158-159).

Training, however, is not an adequate organizational response because its effects are limited and reach only those who have been trained. Organizations should also develop, distribute, promote, and enforce organizational sexual harassment policies and procedures. Example policies and procedures are described in detail by the New York State Bar Association Committee on Women in the Law (1993). This group recommends that sexual harassment policies include a statement of the organizational philosophy to keep the workplace free of discrimination and harassment; a definition of sexual harassment, with examples of inappropriate, offensive, hostile, and intimidating behaviors; a description of who is covered by the policy; procedures on how to report complaints, both informally and formally; information about how complaints will be treated and processed; information about how complaints will be resolved; and identification of the records to be developed and kept with regard to the complaints. Robinson et al. (1993) also detail what should be included in sexual harassment policies and procedures. Finally, Witteman (1993) suggests that policies should treat the larger social-sexual continuum by including rules about organizational romances.

Before formulating policies and procedures to establish the severity and prevalence of sexual harassment, Griffin-Shelley (1985) suggests, organizations should perform some type of organizational analysis. By doing so, rather than employing boilerplate policies and procedures that do not reflect the particular organizational culture, they can create policies and procedures that will meet their own specific needs and objectives. Wholesale adoption of EEOC guidelines or the policies of others may weaken their effects. For example, Livingston (1982) notes that the "strength and detail of the statement may tell employees how seriously the employer is committed to providing a work environment free of sexual harassment" (p. 10). A statement such as "Company X strongly disapproves of sexual harassment in any form" is clearly stronger than "Although there has been no evidence of widespread sexual harassment within Company X . . . ."

Organizational response to sexual harassment is not limited to the downward flow of communication via policies, procedures, and training. Paetzold and O'Leary-Kelly (1993) identify communication relationships among the harasser, the victim, and the organization as needing to be addressed for the prevention and management of sexual harassment. These authors argue that the strength and content of the communication linkages among these three elements affect court judgments. In terms of prevention, organizations bear the responsibility for communicating the standard of a desexualized work environment. Facilitating a culture and climate in which women are encouraged to report harassment is also a responsibility of the organization. Moreover, managers must endorse company policy and refrain from personally practicing harassing behaviors. Managers who do not "walk what they talk" create the "expectation that sexual harassment is a behavior that is done by those who can get away with it" (p. 80). Using a rights and responsibilities framework, Koen (1989) views employees' legal rights (e.g., a workplace free from discriminatory sexual harassment) as a mandate for organizational responsibility. He argues that employees must assume the responsibility of using organizational complaint procedures for reporting and resolving sexual harassment, and he extends employee responsibilities to keeping allegations confidential and managing their own behavior so as not to invite harassment.

Lach and Gwartney-Gibbs (1993) call for organizations to respond to sexual harassment as one type of "gendered" workplace dispute. Placing sexual harassment charges within a larger dispute context may encourage organizations to move from resolution of incidents to systematic reform. Organizational responses may be tied to what Feary (1994) describes as one organizational myth: "The only time moral problems are business problems is when they become legal problems" (p. 651). This is a fallacy, she explains, as only the most immoral conduct is illegal. Guidelines that stem immoral practices should emerge from the business community itself rather than be imposed by organizational objectives to avoid legal financial liability.

WHAT ARE THE EFFECTS OF
SEXUAL HARASSMENT ON ORGANIZATIONS?

When harassment occurs, organizations suffer "diminished productivity, increased absenteeism, and higher employee turnover . . . according to a 1988 survey of 160 'Fortune 500' companies, an average business lost $6.7 million every year because of sexual harassment" (Hetherington & Wallace, 1992, p. 42), in addition to the tremendous costs of litigation and settling claims. Robinson et al. (1993) note that the legal and resulting financial consequences for organization are enormous, as the 1980 EEOC guidelines impose broad burdens on employers for harassing conduct on the job premises or under circumstances subject to the employer's control. Moreover, the EEOC guidelines impose strict liability on employers when the harasser is a supervisor. Organizations are liable for coworker harassment, but only if it can be shown that the employer knew, or should have known, about the conduct.

The consequence to the organization of sexual harassment is most frequently focused on economic concerns, in terms of litigation expenses and judgments for victims. Monetary damages soar (Feary, 1994), as successful claimants can file through state and federal antidiscrimination laws in addition to common law. Apruzzese (1992) notes that the concomitant indirect costs to organizations as time devoted to litigation instead of the workplace have economic ramifications: "Energies devoted to pretrial preparation with counsel, depositions, and testimony at trial, can be and usually are significant. In addition, the tremendous amount of adverse publicity that may be generated by such cases can have a severe adverse impact on a corporation" (p. 336). Other consequences include loss of organizational credibility, which can result in lost income as a result of lost opportunities. For universities and other organizations dependent upon federal funds, repeal or denial of funding can occur (Hickson et al., 1991).

Relational effects in the organization extend beyond victims and perpetrators. The resulting impact on coworker and superior-subordinate relationships essential to the completion of superordinate organizational goals should not be overlooked. Heightened attention to sexual harassment may also cause a general uneasiness in male-female interaction as employees try to establish new interaction patterns when established values and morals come under fire. Often a major portion of an organization is in an uproar while an incident is being investigated. Even if the case is settled and justice appears to have been done, the incident can still leave lingering ill will. A negative consequence of imposing regulations on male-female interaction in the workplace is that some men may steer away from warm, friendly contact with female subordinates or coworkers for fear of being charged with sexual harassment. George (1993) argues, however, that "we should be willing to sacrifice warmth toward some working women if we can eliminate or diminish the harassment of others" (p. 24).

Kronenberger and Bourke (1981) note that credibility issues are at stake for employees and their organizations' personnel departments. Personnel department employees "may encounter a general disbelief among many male employees who cannot believe that their language, attitudes and jokes can now be construed as sexual harassment" (p. 880). Victims may no longer trust personnel department members, or EEO/AA officers, if they fail to act or to uphold organizational policy and procedure.

Even when organizations develop sexual harassment policies, male and female employees may respond differently and have differing expectations from their employers. Using attribution theory, Kenig and Ryan (1986) explain that "males seek to avoid blame by shifting responsibility to the victim" (p. 546); thus, they would want organizational responsibility and its policies and procedures to be minimized. Women also shift blame to the victim, but to a lesser extent, and "therefore assign a more central policy role to the organization than would men" (p. 546), expecting the organization to control every type of potentially harassing behavior.

Some positive organizational effects can result from sexual harassment complaints. For example, information about "latent employee dissatisfaction and performance discrepancies" may be uncovered (Kronenberger & Bourke, 1981). Additionally, such complaints might also expose reasons for problems of absenteeism, negative attitudes, and social problems. If organizations use this evidence of organizational ineffectiveness, serious training efforts can become real attempts to change the communication climate of the organization and can result in more effective workplace interaction (Licata & Popovich, 1987).

A broader, more philosophical effect that can surface in educational institutions is described by Sharpe and Mascia-Lees (1993), who argue that the application of sexual harassment law to academic settings is in conflict with "some of the central humanist assumptions on which the academy is based" (p. 91), and thus power in "the academy may not be completely analogous to economic power in the workplace or male physical force in rape" (p. 91).

> Sexual harassment law designed to prevent intimidating, hostile, or offensive environments, already problematic to interpret and apply in work settings, becomes even more so in an educational setting where the goal of challenging students' assumptions and introducing them to unfamiliar perspectives may well produce an environment that they find unsettling and perceive as hostile. (p. 91)

Summary

Most organizations take a reactive, partial, and cyclical approach to the issue of sexual harassment. For example, an incident occurs. While that incident is being investigated or dismissed, organizational policies and procedures (to keep this same type of incident from occurring) are formulated and organizational rules are initiated. As effects of the initial incident widen or as other incidents occur, yet other policies, rules, and procedures proliferate. As a result, the organization may end up with a nonintegrated approach to sexual harassment and/or policies and procedures that conflict.[2] Researchers may find ethnographic methods effective for investigating the link between organizational effects and responses.

WHAT ARE THE EFFECTS OF
SEXUAL HARASSMENT ON SOCIETY?

"As a result of this attention [to sexual harassment], most people now recognize that a line needs to be drawn between acceptable and unacceptable sexually oriented behavior in the workplace . . . where should the line be drawn?" (Powell, 1988, p. 116). Those in the training industry have recognized an opportunity, and "sexual harassment has now become a thriving business" (Feary, 1994, p. 653). Sexual harassment experts are numerous, and training packages are well distributed. Such attention places the boundaries of male-female interaction in a public forum. Although most training programs appear to supply "the" answers to sexual harassment, a great deal of ambiguity is still present. George (1993) argues that the ambiguity surrounding sexual harassment is fueled when courts impose "evidentiary burdens not required for other kinds of sex discrimination claims" (p. 1). Such legal procedures convey ambiguous messages about the seriousness and viability of claims. For women, sexual harassment happens regularly, "yet the attendant legal claim continues to be of questionable status. Accounts of sexual harassment are routinely denied, if not scorned. The few victims of harassment courageous enough to challenge the offensive behavior often themselves becomes targets of inquiry" (George, 1993, p. 2). This was clearly the case when Anita Hill came forward.

The highly publicized claims of Anita Hill against then Supreme Court nominee Clarence Thomas had a significant impact on how individuals think and feel about sexual harassment. Darwin (in press) asks, "How is it truth can be derived when there is no evidence of such sexually charged imposition?" Not only did different rhetorics develop to account for and rationalize the alleged events, these mediated rhetorics became familiar beyond the Senate chambers, spilling over into conversations "between friends, colleagues, and family members in living rooms, bars, kitchens, and offices across the country" (Kreps, 1993a, p. 314). Hale, Cooks, and DeWine (1994) have analyzed the hearing transcripts for efforts at truth seeking. Focusing on the questions and comments directed toward Hill and Thomas, these authors found evidence of a dialectic of rationality versus irrationality. Rationality was "determined through male experience, leaving little room for the validation of female memory and female ways of going through the world" (p. 76).

They found a second dialectical tension of fairness versus unfairness in Senator Joseph Biden's opening comments at the hearings. For Judge Thomas, fairness was the opportunity to confront the charges against him. Alternatively, fairness for Professor Hill was dismissed in favor of the preeminence of Thomas. Finally, Hale et al. discovered the dialectical tension of choice versus circumstance. The Senate committee had choices in its handling of Professor Hill's allegations. Other choices existed in how Hill brought her complaints forward. Yet the committee responded as if it had no choices: "The claim was made that the committee had no options other than to (1) ignore the allegation and, now, (2) conduct a formal, public investigation" (p. 83). Thus, the committee perceived lack of choice. However, committee members demonstrated considerably less understanding in how the circumstances of Hill's experiences affected her choices—when the harassment occurred and in the hearing. As such, "the testimony of Anita Hill before the Senate Judiciary Committee will long be remembered as an important turning point for women concerning the issue of sexual harassment" (Muir & Mangus, 1994, p. 91).

This profound mediated experience brought sexual harassment to the public forefront, but the hearings did little to create societal consensus about what defines harassment, its effects, or how it should be managed. Gill (1993) warns that "with strong opinion and sentiment supporting both Hill and Thomas, subjects [in her campus survey] may have been more confused by what really constitutes harassment and how harassment is viewed" (p. 165). Although the hearings brought sexual harassment into the public forum, they may have served to confuse rather than illuminate the problem.

Such effects are aptly illustrated in Linda Bloodworth-Thomason's script for an episode of *Designing Women* in which the television program's main characters take sides on the Thomas hearings, re-creating the public debate in dramatic form. Other evidence of the societal effects of harassment appears in Axelrod's (1993) analysis of sexual harassment incidents in movies. Typically, portrayals of mediated sexual harassment reinforce and glamorize its existence; doing so condones this type of behavior. Recently, *Disclosure*, Michael Crichton's successful novel and the film based on it, brought sexual harassment into living rooms and movies theaters, but this time harassment was reversed—a female superior is portrayed as the harasser of her male subordinate. Although the movie and book appear to be less about harassment than about other organizational strategies and politics, the popularity of both forced viewers and readers (and those who had to listen to those viewers and readers, and the critics) to deal with this issue.

More typically, females are portrayed as the victims of sexual harassment. As Axelrod (1993) explains, synthetic experiences such as those provided by movies allow those who have not experienced sexual harassment to do so indirectly. She warns that viewers continually bombarded by such images (especially by portrayals of sexual harassment as humorous) may trivialize sexual harassment or accept it as normal and commonplace. The importance of these mediated images should not be overlooked, as "discourse names, orders, and defines experiences; it shapes what and how societies and individuals know" (Wood, 1994, p. 17).

Talk radio and television call-in shows have also been a prevalent force for examining the effects of sexual harassment on society. Muir and Mangus (1994) analyzed viewer calls about the Thomas hearings to call-in programs on C-SPAN and found that many callers assessed Hill as a scorned woman and were critical of the time frame in which the events unfolded. Some were suspicious of Hill's allegations because she had followed Thomas when he went to work at the EEOC. Most important, however, callers judged the truthfulness of Hill's story by comparison with their own reality of sexual harassment. Those who believed sexual harassment to be a fact of life and that women should just learn to deal with it referred to Hill's time lag to rationalize their own avoidance behavior. Victims who had used formal reporting mechanisms described their experiences as unsuccessful, reflecting the inability of the Senate committee to believe Hill.

The mass media also drew our attention to the Tailhook incident, again challenging societal views of cultural institutions and the workplace behavior of men and women. As complainants use the legal system to seek redress, the media draw our attention to the judges and juries who award settlements to successful plaintiffs to send clear messages to other offenders (Larson, 1992). Such cases typically involve quid pro quo sexual harassment, and this in effect reduces our understanding and awareness of the more subtle and pervasive effects of the kinds of harassment imposed by hostile work environments.

Other societal effects have occurred. As Muir and Mangus (1994) report, after the Thomas hearings, "more women began to tell their stories and express outrage over the callous nature of the Senate Judiciary Committee. Some women decided to run for political office, others acted through the voting process" (p. 101). Newspapers and magazines printed editorials and letters to the editors reflecting the "changing nature of the workplace" (p. 101). The effects of increased societal attention to sexual harassment are also evident in the fact that sexual harassment has become the topic of college courses, classroom discussion, and homework assignments. Pollock (1994) describes the tremendous emotional impact of this awareness on students' views about and responses to sexual harassment as evidenced in classroom behavior and assignments. Obviously, societal effects upon scholars' activities are not limited to the classroom. Writing in Bingham's (1994a) edited collection, Foss and Rogers (1994) note that "this book is part of the discourse on sexual harassment, and as such, is equally constitutive of its objects" (p. 160). Other academic texts exist, as do thousands of academic and popular press articles that describe, explain, and predict certain aspects of sexual harassment phenomena.

As a result of increased numbers of sexual harassment complaints, the Civil Rights Act of 1991 created the Glass Ceiling Commission, which is charged with studying and making recommendations concerning artificial barriers to the advancement of women and increasing opportunities for women to move into management and decision-making positions (Costello, 1992). Although sexual harassment has been largely viewed as an organizational issue (because organizations are often the sites of legal redress), it may reflect the decline of broader societal values, morals, and ethics. The ability to distinguish right from wrong, the belief that harming others is wrong, and the belief that it is wrong to take unfair advantage of others are all moral issues that simply surface at the organizational level. They may be symptomatic of larger ethical issues and may require a redefinition of civil conduct (Vaux, 1993).

CONCLUSIONS AND SUMMARY

How well have we responded to the issue of sexual harassment as researchers? Overwhelmingly, the research focus has been on identifying or naming sexual harassment and documenting its occurrence. Beyond the naming of sexual coercion and rape as harassment, there is a lack of consensus on what behaviors constitute less severe forms of sexual harassment. Documenting the occurrence of sexual harassment has taken on multiple interpretations, depending on the nature of the research. An examination of the legal research indicates that sexual harassment occurs frequently to women, most often by male supervisors, and takes a quid pro quo form. Using behavioral definitions, researchers have found that sexual harassment is initiated more frequently by coworkers than by superiors and that it consists of milder and environmental forms. Definitional issues are key; the point at which an employee decides harassment occurs is critical—particularly from a legal standpoint (Martell & Sullivan, 1994). This decision then leads the victim to deal with the public/private dichotomy of harassment. One study has demonstrated that "female workers define sexual harassment in general as a public issue, but their own harassment as a personal problem" (Loy & Stewart, 1984, p. 42).

As a body of literature, the research to date provides relatively little information about the individual effects of sexual harassment and their relationship to individual responses. Although we have better documentation (e.g., media reports) than in the past about the economic effects of sexual harassment on organizations, we know very little about the internal effects of harassment within organizations. Organizational responses to sexual harassment in the form of policies, procedures, and training are familiar; however, the effectiveness of such practices has seldom been studied.

One important element in the understanding of sexual harassment is the link between individual responses and organizational responses. Clair's (1993a) deconstruction of the sexual harassment policies of the Big Ten universities reveals that the strategic ambiguity, exclusionary positioning, and taken-for-granted nature of the policies "privilege the interests of the dominant group by encouraging the bureaucratization, commodification, and privatization of sexual harassment" (p. 147). The most frequently recommended individual responses—"Say no," "Keep a record," and "Report it"—serve to place responsibility on the victim for incurring the harassment and to discredit the victim's position while the organization appears to be taking some action. Clair's study does "not support earlier contentions that policies and procedures are in effect and are offering satisfactory solutions to the problem of sexual harassment" (p. 148).

Unfortunately, filing a formal suit against an alleged harasser and/or the organization may serve to make the organization aware of the threat of lawsuits rather than make it view sexual harassment as a threat to productivity or look for a way to resolve the underlying problems (Gutek, 1985). In response to sexual harassment claims, organizations might purchase additional liability insurance, hire additional legal counsel, or take some other legalistic route rather than address the incidents themselves.

Livingston (1982) argues that "the effectiveness of any remedial action depends on the extent to which it adequately deals with the problem's causal factors" (p. 19). Although the rights of employees and the responsibilities of organizations with regard to harassment have been better delineated, "these actions in themselves do not change the structural causes" (p. 19) of sexual harassment.

> These actions still focus on case-by-case resolution, becoming, in effect, individual remedies. Courts have ruled that harassment is illegal, but they have not required an increase in women's access to power. Policies also focus on individual action, requiring individuals to refrain from harassing and victims to take responsibility for enforcing the policy . . . but they have not provided a remedy that changes basic causal factors. (pp. 20-21)

Livingston's conclusion is strikingly underscored by the fact that more than 14,000 sexual harassment cases were filed with or accepted by the EEOC in 1994, in comparison with slightly fewer than 7,000 cases in 1991. This tremendous increase has heightened attention to sexual harassment, but certainly has not stopped it. Bingham (1991) argues that "individual action is the ultimate basis of societal change. Social systems are changed ultimately through the actions of individuals" (p. 91). Unfortunately, many victims view formal actions against their harassers as unacceptable because of their financial, temporal, and psychological costs. As a result, many victims prefer to respond interpersonally to sexual harassment.

One notable feature revealed in this literature review is the apparent lag time between identification of a social problem and its academic examination. Sexual harassment continues to exist in spite of legislation designed to eliminate it. Claims of sexual harassment continue to rise. Definitions of sexual harassment continue to broaden. But publishing delays, coupled with the dynamics discussed above, are among the reasons that academic research on sexual harassment has limited effects on policy reformulation at societal as well as organizational levels. Since Farley's (1978) and MacKinnon's (1979) initial exposure of sexual harassment, policies have been enacted at the federal level. More recently, society (with help from the insurance industry) has moved ahead with respect to managing sexual harassment by offering liability insurance against sexual harassment claims for both individuals and organizations. If the adoption of such insurance becomes widespread, will committing sexual harassment come to be viewed casually, as though it were as innocuous as being involved in an automobile fender bender? If individuals and organizations place faith in such remedies, this is likely to happen. An interesting analysis would be to evaluate and compare the talk of managers about sexual harassment in organizations with such protection and in those without.

The broad approaches—both theoretical and methodological—brought to the study of sexual harassment have created varied interpretations of sexual harassment in published research. These are evident in nearly every published academic work on sexual harassment in the form of extensive literature reviews offered to situate sexual harassment as a pervasive and severe problem. After reading several of these, one senses a suitable level of redundancy. An alternative approach would be to provide the reader with the assumptions of the theory and methodology used in the investigation. This would serve a more useful purpose for the interpretation and application of results than once again affirming that sexual harassment is a problem. Although researchers may not agree on theoretical or methodological positions, most positions could be more informed if researchers would broaden their nets for previously published conflicting/contrasting results.

Many researchers situate sexual harassment as a type of intergender communication that exists along a continuum of social-sexual behavior in organizations. Although all sexual harassment does not begin with flirting or organizational romance, and all flirting interactions and organizational romances do not develop into sexual harassment, there does appear to be a point on the social-sexual continuum that blurs their identifications. The positioning of sexual harassment within a larger social-sexual environment prompts attention to organizational romances (Mainiero, 1993) and flirting in the workplace. As Driscoll (1981) notes, "Both sexual attraction and harassment must be dealt with if men and women are to develop truly productive working relationships. Each issue is separate, yet each affects and complicates the other" (p. 34).

Clearly, flirtation in the workplace is part of the social-sexual continuum. Alberts (1992) argues that teasing, one type of flirtation, "possesses this dual nature, [and] its interpretation is important—and often in doubt. Consequently, when a man offers a sexual tease to a woman, the meaning of the tease as well as its intent is highly uncertain. The woman may feel harassed, whereas the man believes he is engaging in play" (p. 186). Several studies have explored flirting and social-sexual behaviors at work (e.g., Dillard, 1987; Dillard & Witteman, 1985), and Koeppel, Montagne-Miller, O'Hair, and Cody (1993) have explored flirting between students in a university setting. Their results are of particular interest to sexual harassment researchers, as they conclude, "It may well be that men and women misinterpret initiation as interest and respond based on that misinterpretation" (p. 30). Cozby and Rosenblatt (1972) provide a broader overview of flirtatious behavior, particularly noting the strategic aspect of this type of interaction, a similarity flirting shares with sexual harassment.

The difficulty some employees may have in distinguishing harassing behavior from other sexual behavior has been studied by Abbey (1982) and Abbey and Melby (1986). These authors found that their male subjects tended to see more sexuality in females than vice versa, and few nonverbal cues were needed for these assessments (Abbey & Melby, 1986). Abbey (1982) found that sometimes men do mistake women's friendliness for seduction, as men have a greater tendency to make sexual judgments. Stockdale (1993) outlines how such misperceptions and differing sexual interpretations create explanations for sexual harassment. Focusing on the relationship between sexual harassment and organizational romance, Witteman (1993) found that "it is unclear where harassing communication begins and communication reflecting the natural development of cross-gender friendships and ORs [organizational romances] end" (p. 35). Witteman provides three arguments for continuing the exploration of the complete social-sexual interaction dimension. First, women's roles in organizations are not likely to diminish; rather, they are likely to continue to increase. Second, society has an inherent interest in sexual relationships. Third, organizational characteristics that foster intergender interaction are also not likely to change, but may even replace "the family as the context in which a person's social needs are met" (p. 54). Other arguments advanced by Gutek (1989) include the propositions that "people tend to think positively about sex" and that "people tend to evaluate social-sexual encounters as interpersonal rather than as organizational," failing to see "sexual overtures as a product of the organization's culture or norms" (p. 58).

This literature review makes it clear that sexual harassment is not a phenomenon isolated from other workplace or sociocultural factors. As Taylor and Conrad (1992) observe, where organizations have "correctly recognized [sexual harassment] as a disorderly force, sexuality has . . . been regulated by organizational authorities (e.g., through policies forbidding office romances), marginalized as a private and personal issue, and 'evacuated' from theory. Despite this official pretense," organizations must deal with sexuality (p. 403). Legal scholars Waks and Starr (1982) argue that it must be clear "that not all conduct with sexual overtones constitutes sexual harassment. Consequently, a boundary line must be drawn between conduct that consti-

tutes sexual harassment and conduct that is an acceptable—or at least toler-
able—aspect of the work environment" (p. 573). Making such a distinction
is likely to be quite difficult. As Lobel (1993) argues, "Even if people were
to agree upon what constitutes sexuality, there would still be differences in
opinion as to what kinds of sexuality are appropriate at work" (p. 147).

Whereas many authors posit that sexual harassment is about power and not
about sex, MacKinnon (1979) acknowledges that the

> analysis of sexuality must not be severed and abstracted from analysis of gender.
> What the current interpretations of rape fail to grasp (indeed, seem to avoid most
> strenuously as they approach) is the argument most conducive to conceiving
> sexual harassment as sex discrimination: a crime of sex is a crime of power.
> Sexual harassment (and rape) have everything to do with sexuality. Gender *is* a
> power division and sexuality is one sphere of its expression. (pp. 220-221)

Given this argument, it would seem appropriate for researchers to consider
the spectrum of sexual interaction in the workplace. Gutek et al. (1990) argue
that sexual harassment has caught the public attention "because it creates
legal liability whereas other social-sexual behavior does not. Nonharassing
sexual behavior has been assumed to be more benign in its effects . . . [and]
it has therefore received little attention. Since nonharassing sexual behavior
is more common, however, it maybe more important for understanding men's
and women's behavior at work" (p. 561). Pringle (1989) argues that "it makes
no sense to banish sexuality from the workplace. What needs to be challenged
is the way it is treated as an intruder . . . by making it visible, exposing the
masculinity that lurks behind gender-neutrality" (p. 177).

Future Research Directions

A social phenomenon such as sexual harassment, which has intrapersonal,
interpersonal, work unit, organizational, and societal implications, challenges
the skills of researchers. Our ability to answer research questions about sexual
harassment is hampered somewhat by the fact that it is an illegal activity, one
with serious consequences for victims, perpetrators, and employing organizations. As a result, many organizations and professional associations are
hesitant to allow researchers to inquire about or document such activity. Many
organizational executives claim, "We have no harassment; no EEO claims
have been filed." Such claims are justified by the belief of executives that "if
we don't know about it, it's not happening." As a result, many questions
remain to be answered—and should be answered with data from both functionalist and discursive research perspectives. Researchers from the discursive perspective seek societal change and seek to unlock individual and
marginalized voices to bring about such change. Frequently dismissed for
their focus on organizational or management prerogatives, researchers from

the functionalist perspective are motivated by change that can occur in organizational settings—sites of female economic and cultural oppression. Researchers from these two perspectives are likely to be working toward the same goal of making sexuality visible in organizations (Gutek, 1989), with researchers from each perspective recognizing the opportunities (and limitations) of their position.

Much of the research on sexual harassment has been conducted in university settings or has relied on easily available student populations. Although harassment is evident in educational settings, faculty-student relationships differ from superior-subordinate and coworker relationships. Students represent a relatively transient population, occupy the university environment for shorter periods than employees occupy their workplaces, and have more opportunities to avoid harassers or harassing situations. Unless the researcher's interest specifically concerns sexual harassment in educational institutions, inquiry should take place in more appropriate locations and with more appropriate populations. Thus, researchers who are interested in organizational sexual harassment must be innovative in their use of methodologies and research perspectives in order to accomplish all that is left to be done.

Most of the research on sexual harassment has focused on victims. Because researchers have ignored perpetrators as individuals also situated within relational, societal, and organizational contexts, we know very little about perpetrators' motivations, intentions, competencies, attitudes, and goals. Specifically, we need to understand how men's attitudes toward sexual harassment are "discursively produced, reproduced, and altered" (Wood, 1994, p. 28).

Wood (1993) suggests that "theory and practice would benefit by more in-depth knowledge of conditions and personal qualities—both between and within the genders—that tend to give rise to alternative ways of conceiving harassing situations" (p. 17). Many researchers echo Wood's call for knowing more about why employees initiate, tolerate, and/or resist sexual harassment and the payoffs and consequences for doing so. To expose sexual harassment at its causal level, researchers should explore the "conditions in individuals, relationships, organizations, and culture" that "legitimate, perpetuate, and sometimes promote" sexual harassment (Wood, 1993, p. 17). Bingham (1994c) urges researchers "to bridge the apparent rift between individual tactics for surviving sexual harassment within the current system and strategies that contribute to changing the system itself" (p. 175). Foss and Rogers (1994) suggest that researchers should explore the "subversive forms of resistance" (p. 169) that empower perpetrators.

Finally, research would benefit from the development of a theoretical explanation that would tie together, or at least account for, the individual, relational, organizational, and societal factors that enable harassment. Acknowledgment of the factors that both facilitate and constrain the occurrence of sexual harassment would strengthen our understanding of the embedded processes and power dynamics that shape it.

I began this literature review with a definitional focus; it seems to appropriate to end with one also. Foss and Rogers (1994) suggest that

> a monolithic definition of sexual harassment needs to exist for legal purposes and that the creation of such a definition proves empowering to many women who would not have previously defined certain behaviors as harassing . . . [but as] discourses vary across the social formation, we need to take into account all of the reactions and definitions women have about sexual harassment. Often these individual views are invalidated in the quest for agreement about the legal definition. (p. 167)

Likewise, Sheffey and Tindale (1992) conclude:

> Reaching a consensus as to what constitutes sexual harassment (in a practical rather than legal sense) may be a nearly impossible task. Although certain behaviors may be easily defined as sexual harassment (e.g., coercion, discrimination in terms of hiring, promotion, etc.), the more subtle and ambiguous forms of harassment, which may make women and men feel uncomfortable at work, may be extremely difficult to classify consistently. . . . Such classification difficulties make eliminating sexual harassment a complex, but not necessarily unsolvable, problem. (pp. 1515-1516)

In their efforts to provide answers about sexual harassment, researchers should be careful not to privilege one definitional approach over others or to dismiss other research perspectives; legal interpretations, employee perceptions, and victims' experiences all add to our understanding of this complex phenomenon.

NOTES

1. To date, the courts have not agreed on identifying same-sex harassment as covered under the federal 1991 Civil Rights Act ("Same-Sex Harassment," 1994), although early EEOC promotional documentation indicated that victims did not have to be of the opposite sex. Employment attorneys estimate that 5% of all sexual harassment cases are filed against persons of the same gender as the victims, but other experts believe that figure to be low. One survey conducted for the Society for Human Resource Management found 14% of reported harassment incidents to involve intragender harassment ("Close Encounters," 1994). Early on, MacKinnon (1979) acknowledged gay and bisexual harassment as having a "far larger place in the conceptual life of sex discrimination law than it does in its practice" (p. 200).

2. Although not documented in any research literature, evidence of such a piecemeal approach to resolving sexual harassment has arisen in my own consulting experiences.

REFERENCES

Abbey, A. (1982). Sex differences in attributions for friendly behavior: Do males misperceive females' friendliness? *Journal of Personality and Social Psychology, 42,* 830-838.

Abbey, A., & Melby, C. (1986). The effects of nonverbal cues on gender differences in perceptions of sexual intent. *Sex Roles, 15,* 283-298.

Adams, J. W., Kottke, J. L., & Padgitt, J. S. (1983). Sexual harassment of university students.
Journal of College Student Personnel, 24, 484-490.

Alberts, J. K. (1992). Teasing and sexual harassment: Double-bind communication in the
workplace. In L. A. M. Perry, L. H. Turner, & H. M. Sterk (Eds.), *Constructing and
reconstructing gender: The links among communication, language, and gender* (pp. 185-196).
Albany: State University of New York Press.

Allen, D., & Okawa, J. B. (1987, Fall). A counseling center looks at sexual harassment. *Journal
of NAWDAC,* pp. 9-16.

Apruzzese, V. J. (1992). Selected recent developments in EEO law: The Civil Rights Act of 1991,
sexual harassment, and the emerging role of ADR. *Labor Law Journal, 43,* 325-337.

Axelrod, J. (1993). Sexual harassment in the movies and its effect on the audience. In G. L. Kreps
(Ed.), *Sexual harassment: Communication implications* (pp. 107-117). Cresskill, NJ: Hampton.

Baker, D., Terpstra, D., & Larntz, K. (1990). The influence of individual characteristics and
severity of harassing behavior on reactions to sexual harassment. *Sex Roles, 22,* 304-325.

Barr, P. A. (1993). Perceptions of sexual harassment. *Sociological Inquiry, 63,* 460-470.

Bartling, C. A., & Eisenman, R. (1993). Sexual harassment proclivities in men and women.
Bulletin of the Psychonomic Society, 31, 189-192.

Beauvais, K. (1986). Workshops to combat sexual harassment: A case study of changing attitudes.
Signs, 12, 130-145.

Berryman-Fink, C. (1993). Preventing sexual harassment through male-female communication
training. In G. L. Kreps (Ed.), *Sexual harassment: Communication implications* (pp. 267-
280). Cresskill, NJ: Hampton.

Bingham, S. G. (1991). Communication strategies for managing sexual harassment in organizations: Understanding message options and their effects. *Journal of Applied Communication
Research, 19,* 88-115.

Bingham, S. G. (Ed.). (1994a). *Conceptualizing sexual harassment as discursive practice.*
Westport, CT: Praeger.

Bingham, S. G. (1994b). Introduction: Framing sexual harassment—defining a discursive focus
of study. In S. G. Bingham (Ed.), *Conceptualizing sexual harassment as discursive practice*
(pp. 1-14). Westport, CT: Praeger.

Bingham, S. G. (1994c). Epilogue: Research on sexual harassment—continuing the conversation. In S. G. Bingham (Ed.), *Conceptualizing sexual harassment as discursive practice*
(pp. 173-178). Westport, CT: Praeger.

Bingham, S. G., & Burleson, B. R. (1989). Multiple effects of messages with multiple goals:
Some perceived outcomes of responses to sexual harassment. *Human Communication Research, 16,* 184-215.

Bingham, S. G., & Scherer, L. L. (1993). Factors associated with responses to sexual harassment
and satisfaction with outcome. *Sex Roles, 29,* 239-269.

Blaxall, M. C. D., Parsonson, B. S., & Robertson, N. R. (1993). The development and evaluation
of a sexual harassment contact person training package. *Behavior Modification, 17,* 148-163.

Booth-Butterfield, M. (1986). Recognizing and communicating in harassment-prone organizational climates. *Women's Studies in Communication, 9,* 42-51.

Booth-Butterfield, M. (1989). Perception of harassing communication as a function of locus of
control, work force participation, and gender. *Communication Quarterly, 37,* 262-275.

Bowker, J. K. (1993). Reporting sexual harassment: Reconciling power, knowledge, and perspective. In G. L. Kreps (Ed.), *Sexual harassment: Communication implications* (pp. 195-205).
Cresskill, NJ: Hampton.

Bradford, D. L., Sargent, A. G., & Sprague, M. S. (1980). The executive man and woman: The
issue of sexuality. In D. A. Neugarten & J. M. Shafritz (Eds.), *Sexuality in organizations*
(pp. 17-28). Oak Park, IL: Moore.

Brooks, L., & Perot, A. R. (1991). Reporting sexual harassment: Exploring a predictive model. *Psychology of Women Quarterly, 15,* 31-47.

Brown, M. H. (1993). Sex and the workplace: Watch your behind, or they'll watch it for you. In G. L. Kreps (Ed.), *Sexual harassment: Communication implications* (pp. 118-130). Cresskill, NJ: Hampton.

Browne, K. R. (1991). Title VII as censorship: Hostile-environment harassment and the First Amendment. *Ohio State Law Journal, 52,* 481-550.

Bursik, K. (1992). Perceptions of sexual harassment in an academic context. *Sex Roles, 27,* 401-412.

Clair, R. P. (1993a). The bureaucratization, commodification, and privatization of sexual harassment through institutional discourse: A study of the Big Ten universities. *Management Communication Quarterly, 7,* 123-157.

Clair, R. P. (1993b). The use of framing devices to sequester organizational narratives: Hegemony and harassment. *Communication Monographs, 60,* 113-136.

Clair, R. P. (1994a). Hegemony and harassment: A discursive practice. In S. G. Bingham (Ed.), *Conceptualizing sexual harassment as discursive practice* (pp. 59-70). Westport, CT: Praeger.

Clair, R. P. (1994b). Resistance and oppression as a self-contained opposite: An organizational communication analysis of one man's story of sexual harassment. *Western Journal of Communication, 58,* 235-262.

Clair, R. P., McGoun, M. J., & Spirek, M. M. (1993). Sexual harassment response of working women: An assessment of current communication-oriented typologies and perceived effectiveness of the response. In G. L. Kreps (Ed.), *Sexual harassment: Communication implications* (pp. 209-233). Cresskill, NJ: Hampton.

Close encounters of a new kind. (1994, December). *Working Woman,* p. 11.

Coles, F. S. (1986). Forced to quit: Sexual harassment complaints and agency response. *Sex Roles, 14,* 81-95.

Collins, E., & Blodgett, T. (1981). Sexual harassment: Some see it, some won't. *Harvard Business Review, 59,* 76-96.

Conrad, C., & Taylor, B. (1994). The context(s) of sexual harassment: Power, silences, and academe. In S. G. Bingham (Ed.), *Conceptualizing sexual harassment as discursive practice* (pp. 45-58). Westport, CT: Praeger.

Costello, E. J., Jr. (1992). Sexual harassment after the Civil Rights Act of 1991. *UWLA Law Review, 23,* 21-38.

Cozby, P. C., & Rosenblatt, P. C. (1972). Flirting. *Sexual Behavior, 2*(10), 10-16.

Darwin, T. (in press). Telling the truth: The rhetoric of consistency and credibility in the Thomas-Hill hearings. In S. Ragan, D. Bystrom, L. L. Kaid, & C. Beck (Eds.), *The lynching of language: Gender, politics, and power in the Hill-Thomas hearings.* Urbana: University of Illinois Press.

Davis, M. F., & Wetherfield, A. (1992). A primer on sexual harassment law. *Clearinghouse Review, 26,* 306-311.

Dillard, J. P. (1987). Close relationships at work: Perceptions of the motive and performance of relational participants. *Journal of Social and Personal Relationships, 4,* 179-193.

Dillard, J. P., & Witteman, H. (1985). Romantic relationships at work: Organizational and personal influences. *Human Communication Research, 12,* 99-116.

Driscoll, J. B. (1981, January). Sexual attraction and harassment: Management's new problems. *Personnel Journal,* pp. 33-38.

EEOC speaks plainly about sexual harassment. (1994, May). *HRFocus,* p. 19.

Equal Employment Opportunity Commission. (1980, November). Guidelines on discrimination because of sex (Sect. 1604.11). *Federal Register, 45,* 74676-74677.

Farley, L. (1978). *Sexual shakedown: The sexual harassment of women on the job.* New York: McGraw-Hill.

Feary, V. M. (1994). Sexual harassment: Why the corporate world still doesn't "get it." *Journal of Business Ethics, 13,* 649-662.

Fitzgerald, L. F., & Hesson-McInnis, M. (1989). The dimensions of sexual harassment: A structural analysis. *Journal of Vocational Behavior, 35,* 309-326.

Fitzgerald, L. F., & Ormerod, A. J. (1991). Perceptions of sexual harassment: The influence of gender and academic context. *Psychology of Women Quarterly, 15,* 281-294.

Fitzgerald, L. F., Shullman, S. L., Bailey, N., Richards, M., Swecker, J., Gold, Y., Ormerod, M., & Weitzman, L. (1988). The incidence and dimensions of sexual harassment in academia and the workplace. *Journal of Vocational Behavior, 32,* 152-175.

Foss, K. A., & Rogers, R. A. (1994). Particularities and possibilities: Reconceptualizing knowledge and power in sexual harassment research. In S. G. Bingham (Ed.), *Conceptualizing sexual harassment as discursive practice* (pp. 159-172). Westport, CT: Praeger.

Garlick, R. (1994). Male and female responses to ambiguous instructor behaviors. *Sex Roles, 30,* 135-158.

George, B. G. (1993). The back door: Legitimizing sexual harassment claims. *Boston University Law Review, 73,* 1-38.

Gill, M. M. (1993). Academic sexual harassment: Perceptions of behaviors. In G. L. Kreps (Ed.), *Sexual harassment: Communication implications* (pp. 149-169). Cresskill, NJ: Hampton.

Gilsdorf, J. W. (1990). Sexual harassment as a liability issue in communication. *Bulletin of the Association for Business Communication, 53*(3), 68-75.

Grauerholz, E. (1994). Gender socialization and communication: The inscription of sexual harassment in social life. In S. G. Bingham (Ed.), *Conceptualizing sexual harassment as discursive practice* (pp. 33-44). Westport, CT: Praeger.

Grieco, A. (1987). Scope and nature of sexual harassment in nursing. *Journal of Sex Research, 23,* 261-266.

Griffin-Shelley, E. (1985). Sexual harassment: One organization's response. *Journal of Counseling and Development, 64,* 72-73.

Gruber, J. E. (1989). How women handle sexual harassment: A literature review. *Sociology and Social Research, 74,* 3-7.

Gruber, J. E. (1990). Methodological problems and policy implications in sexual harassment research. *Population Research and Policy Review, 9,* 235-254.

Gruber, J. E. (1992). A typology of personal and environmental sexual harassment: Research and policy implications for the 1990s. *Sex Roles, 26,* 447-464.

Gutek, B. (1985). *Sex and the workplace: The impact of sexual behavior and harassment on women, men, and organizations.* San Francisco: Jossey-Bass.

Gutek, B. A. (1989). Sexuality in the workplace: Key issues in social research and organizational practice. In J. Hearn, D. L. Sheppard, P. Tancred-Sheriff, & G. Burrell (Eds.), *The sexuality of organizations* (pp. 56-70). London: Sage.

Gutek, B. A. (1993). Sexual harassment: Rights and responsibilities. *Employee Responsibilities and Rights Journal, 6,* 325-340.

Gutek, B. A., Cohen, A. G., & Konrad, A. M. (1990). Predicting social-sexual behavior at work: A contact hypothesis. *Academy of Management Journal, 33,* 560-577.

Gutek, B. A., & Morasch, B. (1982). Sex-ratios, sex-role spillover, and sexual harassment of women at work. *Journal of Social Issues, 38,* 55-74.

Gutek, B. A., Morasch, B., & Cohen, A. G. (1983). Interpreting social-sexual behavior in a work setting. *Journal of Vocational Behavior, 22,* 30-48.

Gutek, B. A., Nakamura, C. Y., Gahart, M., Handschumacher, I., & Russell, D. (1980). Sexuality and the workplace. *Basic and Applied Social Psychology, 1,* 255-265.

Hale, C. L., Cooks, L. M., & DeWine, S. (1994). Anita Hill on trial: A dialectical analysis of a persuasive interrogation. In S. G. Bingham (Ed.), *Conceptualizing sexual harassment as discursive practice* (pp. 71-87). Westport, CT: Praeger.

Hansen, M. (1992, November). 9th Circuit studies gender bias. *ABA Journal,* p. 30.

Hemmasi, M., Graf, L. A., & Russ, G. S. (1994). Gender-related jokes in the workplace: Sexual humor or sexual harassment? *Journal of Applied Social Psychology, 24,* 1114-1128.

Hetherington, R. A., & Wallace, B. C. (1992). Recent developments in sexual harassment law. *Mississippi College Law Review, 13,* 37-90.

Hickson, M., Grierson, R. D., & Linder, B. C. (1990, October). A communication model of sexual harassment. *ACA Bulletin,* pp. 22-33.

Hickson, M., Grierson, R. D., & Linder, B. C. (1991). A communication perspective on sexual harassment: Affiliative nonverbal behaviors in asynchronous relationship. *Communication Quarterly, 39,* 111-118.

Identifying sexual harassment in the legal profession: What is it and why is it a problem? (1993). *New York State Bar Journal, 65,* 28-31.

Jones, T. S., & Remland, M. S. (1992). Sources of variability in perceptions of and responses to sexual harassment. *Sex Roles, 27,* 121-142.

Kaland, D. M., & Geist, P. (1994). Secrets of the corporation: A model of ideological positioning of sexual harassment victims. In S. G. Bingham (Ed.), *Conceptualizing sexual harassment as discursive practice* (pp. 139-155). Westport, CT: Praeger.

Kenig, S., & Ryan, J. (1986). Sex differences in levels of tolerance and attribution of blame for sexual harassment on a university campus. *Sex Roles, 15,* 535-549.

Keyton, J., & Rhodes, S. (1994). The effect of listener preference style on identification of sexual harassment. *Journal of the International Listening Association, 8,* 50-79.

Keyton, J., & Rhodes, S. (in press). Sexual harassment: A matter of individual ethics, legal definitions, or organizational policy? *Journal of Business Ethics.*

Koen, C. M., Jr. (1989). Sexual harassment: Defining hostile environment. *Employee Responsibilities and Rights Journal, 2,* 289-301.

Koeppel, L. B., Montagne-Miller, Y., O'Hair, D., & Cody, M. J. (1993). Friendly? Flirting? Wrong? In P. J. Kalbfleisch (Ed.), *Interpersonal communication: Evolving interpersonal relationships* (pp. 13-32). Hillsdale, NJ: Lawrence Erlbaum.

Konrad, A. M., & Gutek, B. A. (1986). Impact of work experiences on attitudes toward sexual harassment. *Administrative Science Quarterly, 31,* 422-438.

Kramarae, C. (1992). Harassment and everyday life. In L. F. Rakow (Ed.), *Women making meaning: New feminist directions in communication* (pp. 100-120). New York: Routledge.

Kreps, G. L. (1993a). Promoting a sociocultural evolutionary approach to preventing sexual harassment: Metacommunication and cultural approach. In G. L. Kreps (Ed.), *Sexual harassment: Communication implications* (pp. 310-318). Cresskill, NJ: Hampton.

Kreps, G. L. (Ed.). (1993b). *Sexual harassment: Communication implications.* Cresskill, NJ: Hampton.

Kreps, G. L. (1994). Sexual harassment as information equivocality: Communication and requisite variety. In S. G. Bingham (Ed.), *Conceptualizing sexual harassment as discursive practice* (pp. 127-137). Westport, CT: Praeger.

Kronenberger, G. K., & Bourke, D. L. (1981, November). Effective training and the elimination of sexual harassment. *Personnel Journal,* pp. 879-883.

Lach, D. H., & Gwartney-Gibbs, P. A. (1993). Sociological perspectives on sexual harassment and workplace dispute resolution. *Journal of Vocational Behavior, 42,* 102-115.

Larson, D. A. (1992). What can you say, where can you say it, and to whom? A guide to understanding and preventing unlawful sexual harassment. *Creighton Law Review, 25,* 827-854.

Lebacqz, K. (1993). Justice and sexual harassment. *Capital University Law Review, 22,* 605-622.

Lee, L. A., & Heppner, P. P. (1991). The development and evaluation of a sexual harassment inventory. *Journal of Counseling and Development, 69,* 512-517.

Leonard, R., Ling, L. C., Hankins, G. A., Maidon, C. H., Potorti, P. F., & Rogers, J. M. (1993). Sexual harassment at North Carolina State University. In G. L. Kreps (Ed.), *Sexual harassment: Communication implications* (pp. 170-194). Cresskill, NJ: Hampton.

Licata, B. J., & Popovich, P. M. (1987, May). Preventing sexual harassment: A proactive approach. *Training and Development Journal*, pp. 34-38.

Linenberger, P. (1983). What behavior constitutes sexual harassment? *Labor Law Journal, 34*, 238-247.

Littler-Bishop, S., Seidler-Feller, D., & Opaluch, R. E. (1982). Sexual harassment in the workplace as a function of initiator's status: The case of airline personnel. *Journal of Social Issues, 38*, 137-148.

Livingston, J. A. (1982). Responses to sexual harassment on the job: Legal, organizational, and individual actions. *Journal of Social Issues, 38*(4), 5-22.

Lobel, S. A. (1993). Sexuality at work: Where do we go from here? *Journal of Vocational Behavior, 42*, 136-152.

Loy, P. H., & Stewart, L. P. (1984). The extent and effects of sexual harassment of working women. *Sociological Focus, 17*, 31-43.

Machson, R. A., & Monteleone, J. P. (1994). Insurance coverage for wrongful employment practices claims under various liability policies. *Business Lawyer, 49*, 689-714.

MacKinnon, C. (1979). *Sexual harassment of working women*. New Haven, CT: Yale University Press.

Mainiero, L. A. (1993). Dangerous liaisons? A review of current issues concerning male and female romantic relationships in the workplace. In E. A. Fagenson (Ed.), *Women in management: Trends, issues, and challenges in managerial diversity* (pp. 162-185). Newbury Park, CA: Sage.

Martell, K., & Sullivan, G. (1994). Sexual harassment: The continuing workplace crisis. *Labor Law Journal, 45*, 195-207.

Maypole, D. (1986). Sexual harassment of social workers at work: Injustice within? *Social Work, 31*, 29-34.

Mazer, D. B., & Percival, E. F. (1989). Students' experiences of sexual harassment at a small university. *Sex Roles, 20*, 1-22.

McCaslin, L. R. (1994). *Harris v. Forklift Systems, Inc.*: Defining the plaintiff's burden in hostile environment sexual harassment claims. *Tulsa Law Journal, 29*, 761-779.

McKinney, K. (1990). Sexual harassment of university faculty by colleagues and students. *Sex Roles, 23*, 421-438.

Muir, J. K., & Mangus, K. (1994). Talk about sexual harassment: Women's stories on a woman's story. In S. G. Bingham (Ed.), *Conceptualizing sexual harassment as discursive practice* (pp. 92-105). Westport, CT: Praeger.

Murrell, A. J., & Dietz-Uhler, B. L. (1993). Gender identity and adversarial sexual beliefs as predictors of attitudes toward sexual harassment. *Psychology of Women Quarterly, 17*, 169-175.

New York State Bar Association Committee on Women in the Law. (1993). Sexual harassment: A report and model policy for law firms. *New York State Bar Journal, 65*, 33-36.

Nieva, V. F., & Gutek, B. A. (1981). *Women and work: A psychological perspective*. New York: Praeger.

Offermann, L. R., & Armitage, M. A. (1993). Stress and the woman manager: Sources, health outcomes, and interventions. In E. A. Fagenson (Ed.), *Women in management: Trends, issues, and challenges in managerial diversity* (pp. 131-161). Newbury Park, CA: Sage.

"Our stories": Communication professionals' narratives of sexual harassment. (1992). *Journal of Applied Communication Research, 20*, 363-390.

Padgitt, S. C., & Padgitt, J. S. (1986). Cognitive structure of sexual harassment: Implications for university policy. *Journal of College Student Personnel, 27*, 34-39.

Paetzold, R. L., & O'Leary-Kelly, A. M. (1993). Organizational communication and the legal dimensions of hostile work environment sexual harassment. In G. L. Kreps (Ed.), *Sexual harassment: Communication implications* (pp. 63-77). Cresskill, NJ: Hampton.

Paetzold, R. L., & Shaw, B. (1994). A postmodern feminist view of "reasonableness" in hostile environment sexual harassment. *Journal of Business Ethics, 13*, 681-691.

Payne, K. E. (1993). The power game: Sexual harassment on the college campus. In G. L. Kreps (Ed.), *Sexual harassment: Communication implications* (pp. 133-148). Cresskill, NJ: Hampton.

Pechman, L. (1993). Emerging issues in hostile work environment sexual harassment. *New York State Bar Journal, 65,* 38-41, 59.

Petersen, D. J., & Massengill, D. P. (1992-93). Sexual harassment cases five years after *Meritor Savings Bank v. Vinson. Employee Relations Law Journal, 18,* 489-515.

Pollock, D. (1994). (Un)becoming "voices": Representing sexual harassment in performance. In S. G. Bingham (Ed.), *Conceptualizing sexual harassment as discursive practice* (pp. 107-125). Westport, CT: Praeger.

Popovich, P. M., Gehlauf, D. N., Jolton, J. A., Somers, J. M., & Godinho, R. M. (1992). Perceptions of sexual harassment as a function of sex of rater and incident form and consequence. *Sex Roles, 27,* 609-625.

Popovich, P. M., Licata, B. J., Nokovich, D., Martelli, T., & Zoloty, S. (1986). Assessing the incidence and perceptions of sexual harassment behaviors among American undergraduates. *Journal of Psychology, 120,* 387-396.

Powell, G. N. (1983a). Definition of sexual harassment and sexual attention experienced. *Journal of Psychology, 113,* 113-117.

Powell, G. N. (1983b, July-August). Sexual harassment: Confronting the issue of definition. *Business Horizons,* pp. 24-28.

Powell, G. N. (1986). Effects of sex role identity and sex on definitions of sexual harassment. *Sex Roles, 14,* 9-19.

Powell, G. N. (1988). *Women and men in management.* Newbury Park, CA: Sage.

Pringle, R. (1989). Bureaucracy, rationality and sexuality: The case of secretaries. In J. Hearn, D. L. Sheppard, P. Tancred-Sheriff, & G. Burrell (Eds.), *The sexuality of organization* (pp. 158-177). London: Sage.

Pryor, J. B. (1987). Sexual harassment proclivities in men. *Sex Roles, 17,* 269-290.

Pryor, J. B., & Day, J. D. (1988). Interpretations of sexual harassment: An attributional analysis. *Sex Roles, 18,* 405-417.

Pryor, J. B., & Stoller, L. M. (1994). Sexual cognition processes in men high in the likelihood to sexually harass. *Personality and Social Psychology Bulletin, 20,* 163-169.

Quinn, R. E., & Lees, P. L. (1984). Attraction and harassment: Dynamics of sexual politics in the workplace. *Organizational Dynamics, 13*(2), 35-46.

Radford, M. F. (1994). By invitation only: The proof of welcomeness in sexual harassment cases. *North Carolina Law Review, 72,* 499-548.

Reilly, M. E., Lott, B., & Gallogly, S. M. (1986). Sexual harassment of university students. *Sex Roles, 15,* 333-358.

Reilly, T., Carpenter, S., Dull, V., & Bartlett, K. (1982). The factorial survey: An approach to defining sexual harassment on campus. *Journal of Social Issues, 38*(4), 99-110.

Remland, M. S., & Jones, T. S. (1985). Sex differences, communication consistency, and judgments of sexual harassment in a performance appraisal interview. *Southern Speech Communication Journal, 50,* 156-176.

Robinson, R. K., Allen, B. M., Franklin, G. M., & Duhon, D. L. (1993). Sexual harassment in the workplace: A review of the legal rights and responsibilities of all parties. *Public Personnel Management, 22,* 123-135.

Robinson, R. K., Fink, R. L., & Allen, B. M. (1994). Unresolved issues in hostile environment claims of sexual harassment. *Labor Law Journal, 45,* 110-114.

Roscoe, B., Goodwin, M. P., Repp, S. E., & Rose, M. (1987). Sexual harassment of university students and student-employees: Findings and implications. *College Student Journal, 21,* 254-273.

Saal, F. E., Johnson, C. B., & Weber, N. (1989). Friendly or sexy? It may depend on whom you ask. *Psychology of Women Quarterly, 13,* 263-276.

Same-sex harassment is not illegal, judge rules. (1994, December 31). *New York Times National*, p. 7.

Samoluk, S. B., & Pretty, G. M. H. (1994). The impact of sexual harassment simulations on women's thoughts and feelings. *Sex Roles, 30,* 679-699.

Schultz, D. (1993). From reasonable man to unreasonable victim? Assessing *Harris v. Forklift Systems* and shifting standards of proof and perspective in Title VII sexual harassment law. *Suffolk University Law Review, 27,* 717-748.

Sex, laws, and video training. (1994, April). *American Demographics*, p. 14.

Sharpe, P., & Mascia-Lees, F. E. (1993). "Always believe the victim," "innocent until proven guilty," "there is no truth": The competing claims of feminism, humanism, and postmodernism in interpreting charges of harassment in the academy. *Anthropological Quarterly, 66,* 87-98.

Shedletsky, L. J. (1993). Accused of sexual harassment. In G. L. Kreps (Ed.), *Sexual harassment: Communication implications* (pp. 81-89). Cresskill, NJ: Hampton.

Sheffey, S., & Tindale, R. S. (1992). Perceptions of sexual harassment in the workplace. *Journal of Applied Social Psychology, 22,* 1502-1520.

Shotland, R. L., & Craig, J. M. (1988). Can men and women differentiate between friendly and sexually interested behavior? *Social Psychology Quarterly, 51,* 66-73.

Stockdale, M. S. (1993). The role of sexual misperceptions of women's friendliness in an emerging theory of sexual harassment. *Journal of Vocational Behavior, 42,* 84-101.

Strauss, M. (1990). Sexist speech in the workplace. *Harvard Civil Rights-Civil Liberties Law Review, 25,* 1-51.

Strine, M. S. (1992). Understanding "how things work": Sexual harassment and academic culture. *Journal of Applied Communication Research, 20,* 391-400.

Tangri, S. S., Burt, M. R., & Johnson, L. B. (1982). Sexual harassment at work: Three explanatory models. *Journal of Social Issues, 38*(4), 33-54.

Tata, J. (1993). The structure and phenomenon of sexual harassment: Impact of category of sexually harassing behavior, gender, and hierarchical level. *Journal of Applied Social Psychology, 23,* 199-211.

Taylor, B., & Conrad, C. (1992). Narratives of sexual harassment: Organizational dimensions. *Journal of Applied Communication Research, 20,* 401-418.

Terpstra, D. E., & Baker, D. D. (1986). Psychological and demographic correlates of perception of sexual harassment. *Genetic, Social, and General Psychology Monographs, 112,* 459-478.

Terpstra, D. E., & Baker, D. D. (1987). A hierarchy of sexual harassment. *Journal of Psychology, 121,* 599-605.

Terpstra, D. E., & Baker, D. D. (1988). Outcomes of sexual harassment charges. *Academy of Management Journal, 31,* 185-194.

Terpstra, D. E., & Baker, D. D. (1992). Outcomes of federal court decisions on sexual harassment. *Academy of Management Journal, 35,* 181-190.

Terpstra, D. E., & Cook, S. E. (1985). Complainant characteristics and reported behaviors and consequences associated with formal sexual harassment charges. *Personnel Psychology, 38,* 559-574.

U.S. Merit Systems Protection Board. (1981). *Sexual harassment in the federal workforce: Is it a problem?* Washington, DC: Government Printing Office.

U.S. Merit Systems Protection Board. (1988). *Sexual harassment in the federal workforce: An update.* Washington, DC: Government Printing Office.

Vaux, A. (1993). Paradigmatic assumptions in sexual harassment research: Being guided without being misled. *Journal of Vocational Behavior, 42,* 116-135.

Waks, J. W., & Starr, M. G. (1982). The "sexual shakedown" in perspective: Sexual harassment in its social and legal contexts. *Employee Relations Law Journal, 7,* 567-593.

Wells, D. L., & Kracher, B. J. (1993). Justice, sexual harassment, and the reasonable victim standard. *Journal of Business Ethics, 12,* 423-431.

Williams, K. B., & Cyr, R. R. (1992). Escalating commitment to a relationship: The sexual harassment trap. *Sex Roles, 27,* 47-72.

Witteman, H. (1993). The interface between sexual harassment and organizational romance. In G. L. Kreps (Ed.), *Sexual harassment: Communication implications* (pp. 27-62). Cresskill, NJ: Hampton.

Woerner, W. L., & Oswald, S. L. (1990). Sexual harassment in the workplace: A view through the eyes of the courts. *Labor Law Journal, 41,* 786-793.

Wood, J. T. (1992). Telling our stories: Narratives as a basis for theorizing sexual harassment. *Journal of Applied Communication Research, 20,* 349-362.

Wood, J. T. (1993). Naming and interpreting sexual harassment: A conceptual framework for scholarship. In G. L. Kreps (Ed.), *Sexual harassment: Communication implications* (pp. 9-26). Cresskill, NJ: Hampton.

Wood, J. T. (1994). Saying it makes it so: The discursive construction of sexual harassment. In S. G. Bingham (Ed.), *Conceptualizing sexual harassment as discursive practice* (pp. 17-30). Westport, CT: Praeger.

Wood, J. T. (1995). Feminist scholarship and the study of relationships. *Journal of Social and Personal Relationships, 12,* 103-120.

York, K. M. (1989). Defining sexual harassment in workplaces: A policy-capturing approach. *Academy of Management Journal, 32,* 830-850.

Yount, K. R. (1991). Ladies, flirts, and tomboys: Strategies for managing sexual harassment in an underground coal mine. *Journal of Contemporary Ethnography, 19,* 396-422.

CHAPTER CONTENTS

4 Television Programming and Sex Stereotyping: A Meta-Analysis

JENNIFER HERRETT-SKJELLUM
East Mississippi Community College

MIKE ALLEN
University of Wisconsin—Milwaukee

This chapter reports the results of three meta-analyses of studies considering the relationship between television programming and sexual stereotypes. The first statistical summary indicates that television content contains numerous sexual stereotypes. The results of the meta-analytic summaries of experimental and nonexperimental investigations demonstrate that exposure to televised material increases the acceptance of sexual stereotypes.

ONE major concern regarding the possible impact of television content is the issue of whether or not television promotes the development and promulgation of sex role stereotypes. The earliest research examining this media effect can be traced back to the 1970s (see Wartella & Reeves, 1985). Although research conducted between 1900 and 1960 included children, the impact of media exposure on sex role formation was not examined systematically until the 1970s. Durkin (1985c) defines a sex role as a "collection of behaviors or activities that a given society deems more appropriate to members of one sex than to members of the other sex" (p. 9). The current debate centers on television's role in shaping children's sex role repertoires. Few researchers, if any, argue that television has no influence on children's attitudes about "proper" sex roles. Rather, the debated issue is: How does exposure to television programming interact with children's experiences to shape or reinforce sex role stereotypes? Researchers have examined the amount of total television exposure (using nonexperimental methodologies) and have manipulated that exposure (using

Correspondence and requests for reprints: Jennifer Herrett-Skjellum, 1155 Southgate Drive, Starkville, MS 39759.

Communication Yearbook 19, pp. 157-185

experimental procedures) to understand how it is related to the endorsement of sexual stereotypes.

In this chapter we treat the terms *sex role* and *sexual stereotype* as interchangeable. Generally, sex roles are made up of the actions, events, attitudes, and objects that are associated with masculine and feminine roles. A person of either biological gender can be associated with either or both sex roles, or can adopt one sex role in response to some situation and use a different sex role in another situation. Sexual stereotypes are assumptions that all males or all females possess specific characteristics. For example, two common sexual stereotypes are that all men are aggressive and that all women are nurturers. Within this domain of research, the conceptual argument is that televised images portray men and women in types of sex role situations that reinforce or create sexual stereotypes.

Numerous content analyses of media content provide a basis for the claim that the content of televised material serves to reinforce traditional sex roles (Courtney & Whipple, 1974; Dohrmann, 1975; Dominick & Rauch, 1972; Levinson, 1975; Lovdal, 1989; Seggar & Wheeler, 1973; Sternglanz & Serbin, 1974; Stout & Mouritsen, 1988; Welch, Huston-Stein, Wright, & Plehal, 1977). The conclusion seems clear: Television programming generally portrays men and women in traditional gender stereotypical roles. Data supporting this conclusion are summarized in the first part of this literature summary. Establishing this conclusion is a necessary prerequisite to the argument that television contributes to the development of sexually stereotyped attitudes.

Researchers have conducted numerous studies to examine the impact of television on sex role stereotypes (e.g., Durkin, 1985c; Lipinski & Calvert, 1985). Lipinski and Calvert (1985) conclude, in a review of three correlational studies (Beuf, 1974; Frueh & McGhee, 1975; McGhee & Frueh, 1980) and four experimental studies (Cobbs, Stevens-Long, & Goldstein, 1982; Davidson, Yasuna, & Tower, 1979; Liebert, Sprafkin, & Davidson, 1982; McArthur & Eisen, 1976), that the research demonstrates a link between television viewing and sex-stereotyped attitudes. Lipinski and Calvert's conclusion assumes that individual research results support a more substantial inductive argument. The seven studies in their review represent only a portion of the data, and other reviewers might not accept the causal connection, let alone any consistent connection, based on that data pool. One problem of narrative reviews is that they are often unable to provide the objectivity necessary to convince other scholars to accept the conclusions.

Durkin (1985b, 1985c) presents an in-depth analysis of many studies published between 1974 and 1983, both correlational and experimental, examining television's effects on sex role stereotyping in children. Durkin provides not only a comprehensive review of the literature, but a critique of the findings based on the methods used in the individual studies. He is more cautious than Lipinski and Calvert (1985), arguing that "while correlational findings are interesting they do not demonstrate causality" (p. 68). He goes on to assert that no interpretation of the evidence suggests a linear relationship between sexual stereotypical content of the televised material and/or the amount of exposure to that material and the level of acceptance or endorsement of sexual stereotypes. Durkin (1985c) does not dispute the possibility of a relationship between television viewing and sex role formation, but he cautions the reader about the possible existence of complex relationships. People are not socialized by television alone; many other sources of information and inspiration provide the bases for individuals' decisions and beliefs. Television is one source of information, a source competing with and compared with other information sources that help socialize and develop individuals.

Both Durkin's (1985c) and Lipinski and Calvert's (1985) literature reviews provide a starting place for the present investigation. Rather than repeat past narrative reviews, we will determine, using meta-analysis, whether or not the research in this area indicates a positive correlation between amount of television exposure and sex role stereotyping among children. Before presenting a detailed discussion of our approach, we will first review the studies included in this analysis that were completed after Durkin's (1985c) review.

TYPES OF RESEARCH DESIGNS USED TO ASSESS MEDIA EFFECTS ON SEX ROLE ATTITUDES

The data that have been collected that are relevant to an assessment of the relationship between media exposure and the development of sexual stereotypes come in two forms: correlational (nonexperimental) and experimental. Nonexperimental designs take a naturally occurring phenomenon (the watching of television programming) and measure that feature. The correlation calculates an association between some measure of television viewing (amount of viewing or the viewing of specific programs) and some measure of sex role stereotyping. The argument is that if the data indicate a positive correlation between the amount of television viewed and acceptance of sexual stereotypes, then the conditions exist for a causal claim. It should be noted that the existence of a correlation constitutes a *necessary* rather than a *sufficient* condition for causality. The choice of nonexperimental empirical design is subject to criticism because it lacks control over other possible factors that may contribute to the existence of a relationship.

In experimental designs, researchers control the stimuli that participants view. In a typical independent groups design, different persons view different stimuli. Any difference in a dependent measure between the two groups is attributed to the difference in the stimuli. For example, an experimental design might provide two different groups of children with television programs having different content. One set of content might demonstrate male and female characters performing traditional roles, whereas another set of content could show male and female characters performing a mixture of traditional and nontraditional roles. After watching the respective programs, the children would then be given choices of toys to play with (toys typed as "male," "female," or "neutral"). If differences exist between the groups along the lines of the programs viewed, then the argument could be made that the difference in content "caused" the outcomes and therefore a causal relationship exists between program content and the development of sexual stereotypes.

Experimental designs are vulnerable to criticism for reasons of both internal and external validity. Several arguments exist about the susceptibility of experimental designs to possible alternative interpretations and to design limitations and flaws (Campbell & Stanley, 1963; Cook & Campbell, 1979). Although some of the issues with regard to design can be assessed and corrected for mathematically (attenuated measurement, regression to the mean, restriction in range; see Hunter & Schmidt, 1990, for a discussion), many must be evaluated on the basis of argument. Experimental results provide some evidence for the existence of potential effects but fail to provide proof of causality. In the following two subsections, we consider evidence provided by both types of design and several of the issues that both types of empirical investigations must deal with in order to provide evidence.

Correlational Nonexperimental Studies

Correlational nonexperimental studies generally use survey methodology to collect information on the relationship between television viewing and sex role attitudes. The majority of the correlational studies that have examined the relationship between television viewing and sex role formation were conducted in the late 1970s and early 1980s. For example, Signorelli's (1989) study used data from National Opinion Research Center surveys conducted during this period. Signorelli performed a secondary analysis of the data after dividing the responses into two time periods: (a) 1975, 1977, 1978; and (b) 1983, 1985, 1986. Respondents originally answered numerous questions, including an index of sexism. Signorelli claims mixed support for the hypothesis that television viewing and sexist attitudes are positively related, arguing that "essentially men, women, whites, liberals, those with some college education, middle-class, and middle-aged respondents are more likely, when heavy viewers, to give the sexist response to these questions" (p. 353). In addition, Morgan (1987) found that television cultivates agreement with sexist attitudes among viewers.

The detailed meta-analytic summary provided here incorporates and expands on these findings to assess the consistency of the relationship between amount of television viewing and the acceptance of sex role stereotypes. A problem lies in generating a consistent quantitative estimate of the relationship between the phenomena. Reviews by Durkin (1985a, 1985b, 1985c) indicate a lack of consensus about the research findings. A need exists to examine the evidence in a systematic manner to determine the character and consistency of the findings.

Experimental Studies

In a study of three Canadian communities ("Notel," "Unitel," and "Multitel"), Kimball (1986) examined perceptions of sex roles among children. She surveyed children before and after television was introduced in Notel. Although she found that children's attitudes were more strongly stereotyped after television was introduced, after 2 years their attitudes did not differ from those of children in the other two communities with television. This study provides evidence for a direct impact of television on the formation of sex roles among children. Another study, by Silverman-Watkins, Levi, and Klein (1986), looked at children's comprehension of different news stories based on the sex of the reporters. The results indicate that sex-stereotyped content in news could constitute an important variable in children's comprehension and recall of the information. These two experiments can be contrasted with other experiments that have not generated significant findings between independent groups viewing different materials.

Further, the outcomes of experimental and nonexperimental studies need to be compared. Are the two methodological approaches generating different relationships between television content and sex role attitudes? The goal is to provide a basis for comparing the outcomes of different techniques of research. The need for methodological triangulation should stimulate the search for a method that permits a synthesis and accumulation of results. Only on that basis can a full picture of the literature emerge.

CONSIDERING DURKIN'S APPROACHES

Durkin (1985c) identifies four basic approaches to the consideration of the relationship between television content and sex role attitudes or sexual stereotypes: (a) the cultural ratification model, (b) the effects model, (c) the uses and gratifications model, and (d) script theory. Although statistical analysis alone cannot determine which of these four models represents the most accurate account of the relationship between media exposure and sex role attitudes, this meta-analysis contributes to an understanding of various features of each model.

Durkin argues that children grow up in an environment of televised material. Television functions as a source of entertainment and information on just about every aspect of human existence. Televised content is not some "hypodermic" stuck into the minds of children, injecting them with stereotyped images for consumption and emulation. Instead, television interacts with the social images, family values, and everyday life experiences of the individual, serving multiple functions. We do not address in this review the complex web of social interaction and individual differences that interact with any effect television produces on the development of sexual stereotypes. Instead, we consider whether a consistent body of evidence points to the probable existence of an effect.

We briefly examine below each of the models Durkin identifies. The current meta-analysis cannot touch on all aspects of each of the models; rather, our aim is to examine those parts of the models relevant to the meta-analysis. In the conclusion of the material on each model, we express our expectations about the relationships the model predicts a meta-analysis should find.

Cultural Ratification Model

Proponents of the cultural ratification model assert that the content of television serves to promote or endorse existing dominant social themes. Basically, media images reflect the agenda of the dominant group in society and repress or undermine all other competing images. Because the dominant group finds the existence of sexual stereotypes beneficial, the media reflect those values and therefore promote the adoption of sexual stereotypes.

Schwichtenberg (1989) notes that feminist scholarship often addresses this theme by arguing that media content expresses a patriarchal voice or attitude. The results are programs, such as *Charlie's Angels,* that provide examples of how "the complementary systems of capitalism and patriarchy construct, merchandise, and exchange the female image" (p. 293). The goal is the construction of a message that endorses and exaggerates the existing traditional message.

Turow (1989) provides a case study of how the medical establishment interfered with the 1950s television series *Medic.* A panel of doctors insisted on reviewing every script and required revisions on technical medical issues as well as grammatical phrasing. The media reacted to the possibility of offending an existing powerful group in the society and worked to protect that image. The net result of such cases is the creation of images that reflect an existing social order the media serve to confirm. The contrary line suggests that if the media provide alternative views or critiques of existing norms, then viewers should consider change because of the media endorsement of the new image. This analysis argues that because women constitute a group that is less powerful than others, they become the objects of oppression (patriarchy). Although the examples provided include only case studies, and thus are of little scientific value, they point to the possibility of real intrusions into the content of the medium. The impact of powerful groups serving to promulgate the existence of stereotypes within programming constitutes a serious consideration.

For the cultural ratification model, it is irrelevant whether persons self-select images of sexual stereotypes or television causes such images per se. The argument here is that the actual content of the medium reflects dominant images. Because, within this meta-analysis, there is no link to existing attitudes on sexism by those in control, there can be no evaluation. Only if and when the attitudes of those in control change should that change cause shifts in the content of televised programs. Proponents of the cultural ratification model hypothesize a positive relationship between amount of television viewing and the acceptance of sexual stereotypes.

Experimental research should demonstrate a positive correlation between exposure to television content and attitudes. The material is accepted simply by virtue of the experimenter's providing it. The attitude that material on TV should be accepted as true indicates that the content of the material is accepted because the material is acceptable. In a sense, the impact comes from the creation of an experimental demand effect relating to the legitimacy that a televised image provides for the implicit or explicit belief.

Durkin (1985c) points out that the cultural ratification model remains limited because of its "inability to specify causal dimensions" (p. 16). The problem is that the model really argues that the media simply reflect existing power relationships within society. From this viewpoint, television serves only to reinforce what already exists within the complex web of social relationships.

Effects Model

The effects model covers a variety of models concerned with the idea that television generates an impact on the viewers through mere exposure. The terms *hypodermic, learning,* and *conditioning* are often associated with this approach as well (Durkin, 1985c, p. 16). Proponents of this model argue that the televised image provides individuals with a basis for comparing their lives to the lives of others. The adage "Monkey see, monkey do" represents an oversimplification of this premise. Television provides a vicarious sense of experiences about the real world. If television content demonstrates that male and female characters lead good lives, get great rewards, or are punished for violating sexual stereotypes, those messages have impacts. The viewer simply watches and learns from the images provided by the appliance. As Lipinski and Calvert (1985) note, "Children can learn modelled behavior without physically performing the behavior" (p. 3). If a person on a television program is rewarded for behaving in ways consistent with stereotypes, then children learn, vicariously, to imitate that behavior.

The effects model usually assumes a linear effect for the impact of the medium. That is, the more a person watches the material, the greater the impact of that material on his or her behaviors and values. For this model to receive support, nonexperimental investigations must demonstrate a correlation between the amount of television viewing and the attitudes of viewers.

The effects model fails to specify the mechanisms, either cognitive or behavioral, through which exposure to media content is translated to the actions or attitudes of media viewers. That kind of analysis would require some intervening (mediating) processes that remain unspecified as well as tests vis-à-vis the model to examine the nature of the processes occurring within the individual. A meta-analytic summary can test assumptions concerning whether or not a connection exists, but it cannot test the assumed underlying mechanisms. As a test of this model, the meta-analysis would be incomplete, partly because the model fails to provide the necessary details for testing.

Uses and Gratifications Model

Proponents of the uses and gratifications model argue that the media serve certain functions for media consumers. Consumers use the media as a source of gratifications for particular desires, such as for information, personal identity, integration, social interaction, and entertainment (Durkin, 1985c). The media, unlike in the effects models, are not understood simply to act on the consumer; rather, they provide stimuli that are used by the consumer. The consumer uses the media to fulfill some type of need.

The uses and gratifications model provides a sense that the media are not simply providing unidirectional influence. In a real sense, the media are acted upon by the consumer, who makes a series of decisions: what to consume, how to consume, how to interpret, and what to remember. In addition, a single media program can serve a variety of purposes for one individual or completely different (and opposite) purposes for different individuals. There are a variety of social/psychological antecedents to the existence of any effect. People come with both emotional and historical baggage and experiences that serve as filters to the content of television. Uses and gratifications researchers examine the effects of television viewing by considering the psychological/social issues of consumers prior to exposure that contribute to or reinforce the impacts of exposure.

Proponents of the uses and gratifications model state no clear hypotheses about the impacts of the medium of television. Such hypothesis would require some prior knowledge or claim about how the individuals consuming the material use television to gratify desires. The issues within an experimental setting require some attention. It is understandable that surveys may find that persons with higher degrees of sexually stereotyped behavior watch more televised content. If televised content is saturated with sexual stereotypes, then a person would choose to watch those programs for some reason. However, in an experimental setting subjects do not choose the content of the programs they watch. In fact, the use of random assignments to groups would indicate that the content of the medium is not chosen by the subjects. Whereas nonexperimental research should show an effect for program choices, perhaps to confirm previously held images, it is unclear what the impacts of an experimental setting should be.

In an experimental condition, the fundamental ability of a person to use televised material to gain gratifications might be lost. One could reasonably expect that within the confines of an experiment the material should show little impact, if any. One possible test of this expectation might be the homogeneity assumptions of meta-analysis. Experiments use a variety of stimuli. If the findings are heterogeneous, then the argument could be made that the subjects reacted by reinterpreting the variety of material. Because the only constant variable or controlled variable is the level of sexual stereotyping in the material, the demonstration of homogeneous impacts could indicate that despite the nature of the material, its functions and uses remained constant.

The fundamental problem in this line of theoretical thinking is the identification of the kinds of gratifications persons seek from televised content. Without a complete understanding of how these gratifications work within the framework of program selection and individuals' values, it is unclear whether one could reach conclusions about a generalizable effect for such a model.

Script Model

Script theory provides an approach that examines how persons organize information. "A script is a generalized and hierarchically ordered event representation, typically organized towards a goal or sets of goals" (Durkin, 1985c, p. 19). The idea is that a person develops a script as a form of routinized sequence of behaviors to handle or analyze social interaction. The key is that a script constitutes a move toward regulating the conduct of social behavior. Essentially, script theory comes from schemata approaches and the study of memory relating to artificial intelligence (Schank, 1982).

Television, it is argued, functions to provide individuals with examples of scripts about human behavior. The media work to embellish and elaborate on existing beliefs about behavior. If television characters exhibit patterns of sexually stereotypical behavior, then the viewers are encouraged to emulate those successful scripts. To the degree that any text provides a consistent body of such material, it may contribute to viewers' development of such scripts (Bower, Black, & Turner, 1979). C. Hansen has examined the scripts of rock music videos (Hansen & Hansen, 1988, 1990) and argues that the level of arousal within the form contributes to priming the audience (Hansen & Krygowski, 1994). The impact of priming is to make the information recorded in memory more accessible and probably more likely to be repeated at a later date in another situation.

The media might make certain types of scripts more universal by providing millions of persons access to common sets of assumptions about social interaction. Individuals make inferences from these messages, and this in turn contributes to the impacts the message have (Kellermann & Lim, 1989). Thus, there exists the potential for the development of scripts that would accentuate or reinforce stereotypical behaviors and attitudes.

The predictions of this model are less clear. Although one would expect the existence of a positive relationship between exposure to media content and the development of sexual stereotypical attitudes, the real issue is behavioral. Script theory is less concerned with attitudes than with how individuals learn patterned sequences of behavior. The contribution of this learning to information stored in memory from mass media sources is important (Kellermann, 1985).

Within the confines of this meta-analysis, the script approach is not directly testable. The dependent measures are not behavioral, nor do they directly test knowledge about such behavior. The only indirect tests are studies that ask participants to evaluate the appropriateness of occupations, attitudes, or chores by individuals (male versus female). The information provides a sense about how a person would probably use the values in the future. What is informative is the existence of a large correlation between attitudes and behaviors ($r = .80$) as demonstrated through meta-analysis (Kim & Hunter, 1993a, 1993b). The generation of behavioral scripts or intentions to undertake behavior is probably related to prior attitudes.

The current project provides some evidence, not of scripts, but of the attitudinal endorsement necessary for scripts to exist. The problem is that the current studies only indirectly access information about the existence of scripts. The studies do not access behavioral information to find out whether the scripts exist or what the relationship is between scripts and media content.

Theoretical Summary

The problem in assessing the available models stems from the lack of commitment to a specified set of conditions or expectations about the nature of effects for the televised material. The failure to specify empirically testable assumptions suggests that any finding of this or any other meta-analysis provides little evidence for evaluating the sufficiency of any model. Instead, ambiguity and lack of specific commitments permit the models to handle any existing empirical data.

ARGUMENT FOR THE USE OF META-ANALYSIS

Many empirical investigations have been conducted to examine various issues surrounding the effects of sex roles on television. The availability of the findings of these investigations suggests the value of synthesizing such studies. Meta-analysis provides a more accurate assessment of large bodies of literature than do narrative or box-score reviews (Allen & Preiss, 1993; Preiss & Allen, 1994).

Meta-analysis represents the technique of quantitative literature synthesis. The procedure requires that investigators gather relevant literature on a topic and then combine individual study estimates to generate an average effect across the literature. The advantages of meta-analysis as a technique for summarizing quantitative literature are well established (Allen & Preiss, 1993; Hunter & Schmidt, 1990; Preiss & Allen, 1994). In particular, meta-analysis, when used in a series of summaries, creates a complete picture of effects for theoretical inspection.

The problem with any area of the social sciences is that studies on a given subject often accumulate rapidly. When few studies exist, the ability to review the literature systematically remains easy. However, as the number of studies begins to expand, the ability to represent the available quantitative literature easily and accurately diminishes. One problem stems from the existence of both Type I and Type II errors. Type I error is normatively set at 5%. Type II error is the result of a combination of factors (size of the effect, level of Type I error, and size of the sample). The only one of these factors within the control of the investigator is usually the sample size: The larger the sample size, the more accurate the estimation of any parameter. The net effect of increasing sample size becomes reflected in what Cohen (1987) calls increased statistical power, or the ability of a statistic to define as significant a particular effect size with a particular sample size.

The problem is that the accuracy of the estimation of any parameter is based on the size of the sample. Sampling error is random, not systematic, so the impact of the error could diminish or increase the observed sample parameter relative to the actual population parameter. The normal Type II error for an average sample size ($N = 80$) with an average correlation ($r = .20$) is about 50%. That means that randomly 50% of investigations would demonstrate a significant effect and another 50% would find a nonsignificant relationship. The difference between the nonsignificant and significant findings represents the result of random sampling error, because in this example a real effect is presumed to exist ($r = .20$).

The impact of this random error becomes demonstrated in the synthesizing of existing empirical literature. It should be virtually impossible for a scholar to summarize literature with a host of random errors without some type of mechanism to assess the impact of the random error of the significance test (sampling error). The person conducting the literature summary is at the mercy of sampling error when trying to assess the existence of any given effect.

Meta-analysis solves this problem by correcting for sampling error by averaging effects across studies. The net impact of averaging across studies is to increase the available sample for the estimation of the parameter. Combining across investigations permits the estimated parameter to have the power of the combined samples, rather than the power of the individual samples. However, the averaging process is justified if the differences in effects observed among the outcomes of individual studies reflect random sampling error. The moderator test constitutes a test of the normality or the sampling distribution of the observed set of effects. If the effects are homogeneous (all variation in effects can be explained by sampling error), then the average comes from a set of correlations that differ only as a function of random chance (due to sampling error).

Consideration of the issues within media effects and the impact of television on the development of sexual stereotypes demonstrates the possibility of this confusion. In her review of research, Busby (1975) goes through the existing literature and tries to point out effects and the consistent body of findings. Her conclusions seem to indicate a rather uniform set of conclusions across a variety of types of investigations. This contrasts with the review conducted by Collins (1975), who argues that the empirical investigations demonstrate that television's effect is mediated by age and issues relating to comprehension and evaluation. Durkin (1985b) points out that "the evidence of modest associations between amount of viewing and degree of sex typing claimed in some studies must be interpreted with caution, and it is pointed out that correlations have not always been found" (p. 191). This conclusion is common across the social sciences (the difficulty of finding consistent significant effects across a domain of research). Such an outcome unfortunately retards the progress of science and, without some basis for resolving such disputes using agreed-upon procedures, leaves the dispute unresolved. The key thing to remember about sampling error is that the error is random and uncertain (especially with small samples). The only solution is some method of getting rid of that error (or reducing it significantly) so that the consistency of the empirical investigations can then be assessed.

Meta-analysis represents an "uncritical" method, compared with narrative reviews. Narrative reviews of the literature often spend a great deal of time discussing the methodology of investigations and offering methodological differences as explanations for divergent findings. The reviewers comment on and compare the "quality" of studies as a basis for differences in findings, or "weak" studies are eliminated. The problem with such a procedure is that almost all studies contain some form of "weakness," and the results of such comparisons sometimes are more wishful thinking than systematic analysis. Meta-analysis, as a procedure, does not ignore the issue of methodological quality. Instead, it explicitly codes for these features and uses the methodological artifacts as a basis for a moderator test. In other words, *any* methodological artifact capable of articulation can be coded and tested as an explicit part of the analysis. It is not that meta-analysis lacks a "critical" framework; instead, meta-analysis operates using an explicit critical framework. The ability of a group of studies to generate a homogeneous finding operates to disprove the claim that methodological divergence creates inconsistency in findings. A homogeneous solution indicates that the studies differ only on the basis of sampling error. When such a finding comes from a large and methodologically heterogeneous set of studies, the possibility of generalization becomes greater because an argument can be made that despite methodological differences, there exists an overall homogeneous effect for the investigations.

The problem of inconsistent findings and use of statistical remedies is not unique to the social sciences. Hedges (1987) points out that a comparison of the results of investigations in particle physics with results in various areas in psychology shows that the diversity in findings is about the same for both fields. The solution for physics has been some form of meta-analysis or statistical aggregation of findings. The title of Hedges's article—"How Hard Is Hard Science, and How Soft Is Soft Science? The Empirical Cumulativeness of Research"—emphasizes that ironic twist. What Hedges points out is that physicists handle the same issue that quantitative social scientists must address—variability in research findings. Meta-analysis represents the method of handling that variability.

CONDUCT OF THE META-ANALYSIS

The Literature Search

To generate the original bibliography for this investigation, we undertook a computer search of *PsycLIT* and *ComIndex* using the keyword combination "television" and "sex roles." We also searched all reference sections of available articles, particularly reviews of the literature, for additional sources of information (Busby, 1975; Chaffee & Tims, 1976; Comstock, 1975; Durkin, 1985a, 1985b, 1985c; Eisenstock, 1984; Hearold, 1979, 1986; Janus, 1977; Kear, 1985; Lipinski & Calvert, 1985; Potter, 1993; Rakow, 1986; Rubinstein, 1983; Signorelli, 1993; Steeves, 1987; Wartella & Reeves, 1985). We obtained and subjected to scrutiny more than 200 published works.

We included a study in the analysis if it met the following conditions: (a) The published results contained an estimate of the amount of television the participants watched associated with some measure of sex role stereotype acceptance (nonexperimental), or some type of exposure that the participants consumed associated with some type of measurement of sexual stereotypes (experimental), or a method of assessing the degree to which the characterization of individuals within the media indicated a sexual stereotype (content analysis);[1] and (b) it permitted the calculation of an effect size between the two measures.[2]

If a study reported information from other reports (Courtney & Whipple, 1974; Seggar, 1977; Seggar & Wheeler, 1973), we excluded the portion of data from those other reports. The unit of analysis required that even if data had been published multiple times, they were used only once in any primary analysis.

The content analyses included constitute investigations in which the researchers took some televised content and then compared the male and female characters on the basis of some coded dimensions. The analyses might simply have counted the number of total characters or assessed the occupations, roles, or importance of the various characters. The goal of these studies was to provide some basis for comparing the representations of men and women within some aspect of televised material (advertisements, cartoon, or other genres of content).

Nonexperimental investigations included addressed the issue of a connection between television and sex role attitudes through survey methodology. The studies asked respondents to provide estimates of the time spent watching television during some period (day, week, month) and then to complete some self-report measure of sexual stereotypes. These investigations provide simple correlations between amount of television viewed and sex stereotyping attitudes.

The experimental investigations included used a design in which participants viewed some version of television content (high or low in sexual stereotyping) and then completed some self-report measure of sexual stereotyping. These investigations provide an experimental demonstration of how televised content affects the attitudes of the receivers.

Coding for Moderator Variables

Moderator variables reflect possible additional theoretical or methodological features that may change the nature of the effect. A moderating variable should be distinguished from a mediating variable. A mediating variable acts to affect the process that relates the underlying variables. A moderator, for example, could be that the date of data collection has an impact on the observed association. If television content, social attitudes, or other features change with time, then the impact of televised material could change over time as well. A mediating variable might be some type of cognitive processing variable that creates an explanation for the relationship between the two variables.

One potential moderator variable coded was the age of participants within the investigation. The argument would be that as the age of the participants increases, the impact of televised content should change. The analysis would consider the trend between the size of the effect and the age of the participants. The analysis would produce a correlation between age and the size of the effect.[3]

Statistical Analysis

The statistical analysis used here relies on Hunter and Schmidt's (1990) variance-centered method of meta-analysis. This technique is standard and is accepted as a reasonable and accurate method of conducting this analysis. There is some disagreement over the use of confidence intervals versus significance tests for issues surrounding the analysis of moderator variables (Johnson, Mullen, & Salas, 1995). Other methods of meta-analysis (Hedges & Olkin, 1985; Rosenthal, 1984) use a general model of the significance test for all estimates provided. Although Hunter and Schmidt's model permits the use of significance tests, it argues against total reliance on those because of the possibility of Type I and Type II errors. The use of significance tests within meta-analysis reintroduces the errors (often with the same problems of false positives and false negatives).

The analysis provides for a weighted averaging model of effects and then a test for homogeneity of the observed average effect. The chi-square test for moderators tests whether the amount of variability in the actual sample of correlations may be due to sampling error. If the chi-square is larger than would be expected due to chance, then the amount of error is larger than expected by sampling error. A significant result indicates that a moderator variable is present. The calculation of the chi-square using the Hunter and Schmidt (1990) procedures has greater power (Spector & Levine, 1987) than comparative procedures (Hedges & Olkin, 1985; Rosenthal, 1984).

Effects reported within original reports can be corrected for various statistical artifacts. Measurement error caused by attenuated measurement, dichotomization of continuous variables, and the like works to diminish the size of the observed correlation and can be corrected for (Hunter & Schmidt, 1990). Whenever possible and appropriate, the reports were corrected for artifacts.[4]

RESULTS

Content Analysis

The content analysis compares the issues surrounding representation of women and men in programs. The nature of the comparison involves the number of characters (and types of characters) on television, the behavior of those individuals, and the representations of various individuals. The normal comparison is that of the percentages of males and females in particular categories. The use of percentage data comparisons permits the conversion to a correlation coefficient (Glass, McGaw, & Smith, 1980), or the data can be treated in some cases as a binomial distribution and data converted using that logic.

The representation of the data and descriptions of the content studies appear in Table 4.1. The eight investigations represent an overall average effect indicating sexual stereotyping ($r = .457$, $N = 3,670$) that is heterogeneous ($\chi^2_{(7)} = 58.65$, $p < .05$). It should be noted that all effects are positive. A positive correlation indicates that males are seen more often on television, appear more often in major roles, exhibit dominant behaviors and attitudes, and are represented outside the home in jobs of authority. All content analyses illustrate the consistent finding that men are more often on TV, in higher-status roles as characters, and are represented as having greater power than women.

TABLE 4.1
Content Analysis Data

Study	Year(s) Data Collected	Summary of Study Subject
Courtney & Whipple, 1974	1971-1973	data from three studies: women use products as housewives, less authority figures than men ($r = .517$, $N = 260$)
Dohrmann, 1975	1974	educational television examined—*Sesame Street, Electric Company, Mister Rogers' Neighborhood, Captain Kangaroo*; active vs. passive behaviors of characters by gender ($r = .370$, $N = 613$)
Dominick & Rauch, 1972	1971	women in network TV commercials compared with male occupations ($r = .540$, $N = 385$)
Levinson, 1975	1973	numbers of males and females in Saturday-morning cartoons ($r = .500$, $N = 745$)
Lovdal, 1989	1988	sex associated with product and role of person in advertisements ($r = .430$, $N = 720$)
Miller & Reeves, 1976	1974	genders of TV characters in prime time by occupation, importance, favorability of portrayal ($r = .590$, $N = 449$)
Seggar et al., 1981	1971-1980	numbers of major characters by genders, prime time ($r = .360$, $N = 645$)
Sternglanz & Serbin, 1974	1971-1972	children's programming, behavior rated and compared, male and female characters ($r = .114$, $N = 137$)
Welch et al., 1977	1977	60 toy advertisements from Saturday-morning cartoons, compared male, neutral, and female cartoons on basis of action ($r = .260$, $N = 60$)

We conducted an analysis to determine what kinds of potential moderator influences might be at work. We analyzed the nature of the dependent measure. There were four studies that used occupational representation of the dependent variable. The average positive heterogeneous correlation ($r = .495$, $N = 2,115$, $\chi^2_{(3)} = 16.25$, $p < .05$) was higher than in the three studies examining some aspect of dominant behaviors ($r = .319$, $N = 810$, $\chi^2_{(2)} = 9.37$, $p < .05$). One study examined the number of characters ($r = .500$, $N = 745$).

The existence of only eight data sets prevents a more detailed consideration of other potential moderating variables. The data, however, clearly point to a consistency in the findings in terms of direction—television represents males more frequently than females, and as more dominant characters. The existence of a moderator indicates that there are potentially some features that separate larger from smaller positive influences. The moderator analysis undertaken in this investigation indicates that the choice of roles (doctor versus nurse, or housewife versus businessman) is probably subject to more sexual stereotyping than are actual behaviors. Behaviors (nurturing [female], autonomy [male], dominance [male], deference [female]) are associated with the genders of characters, but the impact appears smaller in magnitude than that of role choice. The results of this analysis demonstrate that we may conclude that the content of the media incorporates a large number of sexual stereotypes. This finding is necessary for the arguments about interpreting nonexperimental and experimental findings. If nonexperimental findings demonstrate an association between the amount of television viewing and acceptance of sexual stereotypes, the current analysis helps interpret those finding by demonstrating that televised content contains stereotypical images. If experimental investigations demonstrate a positive correlation, the current analysis demonstrates that the programs generating that effect do exist in the environment.

Nonexperimental Analysis

Information on the individual nonexperimental studies is presented in Table 4.2. The data demonstrate an average positive correlation between self-reported amount of television viewing and acceptance of sexual stereotypes ($r = .101$, $k = 20$, $N = 11,940$). However, the average correlation was heterogeneous ($\chi^2_{(19)} = 161.09$, $p < .05$). Heterogeneity indicates that the average correlation should be interpreted cautiously, because of the probable existence of a moderator variable. However, examination of the effects depicted in Table 4.1 reveals no negative effects. The lack of negative correlations indicates that the average effect will be positive and the moderator analysis will be discriminating between small and larger positive correlations. The next step was to consider the problems of outliers and estimation issues. Two studies had correlations so large (Frueh & McGhee, 1975, $r = .867$; McGhee & Frueh, 1980, $r = .818$) that we deleted them from the analysis. In addition, some studies reporting nonsignificant correlations (Meyer, 1980, I and II; Reep & Dambrot, 1990) were assigned correlations of .000; as these estimations might be in error (underestimations), we deleted these studies from the next analysis. The danger of deleting these zero correlations is that the resulting average may be an overestimation, because the correlations deleted are all smaller than those retained (an even larger threat to the estimation of the parameter exists if the correlations, although nonsignificant, are less than zero).

The new average correlation remained heterogeneous and identical to the correlation from the previous analysis ($r = .101$, $k = 15$, $N = 10,735$, $\chi^2_{(14)} = 71.52$, $p < .05$). The results of the analysis demonstrate that as television viewing increased, so did the acceptance of sexual stereotypes. The existence of heterogeneous findings indicates the probable existence of moderator variables. The next steps involved a search for possible moderating variables by considering the age of the persons within the studies and the type of dependent measure used to assess sexual stereotyping.

The studies that could be coded for age (as shown in Table 4.2) were used in this analysis (some studies—Kimball, 1986; Signorelli, 1989, I and II—did not

TABLE 4.2
Effect Size Estimates for Nonexperimental Data

Study	r	N	Age of Subjects	Stereotype Measure
Beuf, 1974	.330	63	4.5 years	occupation
Frueh & McGhee, 1975	.867	75	8.0 years (avg.)	sex roles
Kimball, 1986	.071	536	unknown	sex roles
McGhee & Frueh, 1980	.818	64	11.0 years (avg.)	sex stereotype
Meyer, 1980, I	.000	79	6.5 years	activities, occupation
Meyer, 1980, II	.000	71	10.5 years	same as I
Miller & Reeves, 1976	.125	200	10.0 years (avg.)	occupation
Morgan, 1982	.221	349	14.0 years (avg.)	role stereotypes
Morgan & Rothschild, 1983	.190	287	13.0 years	activities
Perloff, 1977	.082	95	11.0 years	sex roles
Pingree, 1978	.066	227	10.0 years	traditional attitudes
Reep & Dambrot, 1990	.000	916	22.0 years	sex role
Repetti, 1984	.041	40	6.0 years	toy choice, occupation
Ross et al., 1982	.350	78	21.0 years	sex role
	.430	18	55.0 years	sex role
Signorelli, 1989, I	.070	3,743	unknown	sex role
Signorelli, 1989, II	.046	3,306	unknown	sex role
Signorelli & Lears, 1992	.100	526	9.5 years	attitudes toward chores
Wroblewski & Huston, 1987	.444	65	11.0 years	occupation
Zemach & Cohen, 1986	.260	1,202	adults	roles, occupation

provide enough information for coding by age of the participant and are not included in this analysis). The studies were divided into the following groups: (a) under 5 years of age, (b) 6-10 years of age, (c) 11-15 years of age, (d) adult (probably college age), and (e) over 55 years of age. The results of this analysis are displayed in Table 4.3. The data demonstrate no pattern associated with age; there is no trend of increase or decrease based on the age of the participants.

The analysis by type of dependent measure revealed heterogeneous findings for each group. All the findings are significant and positive, indicating that, regardless of the dependent measure used, the net impact was to increase the acceptance of sexual stereotypes. The only interesting finding was that the effect for occupation ($r = .221$) was larger than that associated with sex roles ($r = .075$) or behavior ($r = .105$). This parallels the finding for the content analysis, in which the largest correlation was found for occupation and smaller correlations were found for sex roles and behaviors. This supports the idea that the content of television programming is reflected in the attitudes of viewers.

Experimental Analysis

A total of 11 studies were averaged for this analysis, and the relevant information appears in Table 4.4. The average positive correlation ($r = .207$,

TABLE 4.3
Testing for Moderator Variables in Nonexperimental Data Sets

	Age Analysis				
	Under 5	6-10	11-15	Adult	Over 55
k	1	6	7	3	1
N	63	1,034	1,044	2,196	55
Average r	.330	.159	.211	.155	.430
Chi-square		44.44*	40.59*	40.12*	
df		5	6	2	

	Stereotype Measure		
	Occupation	Sex Roles	Behavior
k	7	11	2
N	1,720	9,207	1,013
Average r	.221	.075	.105
Chi-square	18.98*	107.24*	
df	6	10	

*Significant at .05 level.

TABLE 4.4
Experimental Analyses of Media Impact on Sexual Stereotype Development

Study	Age	Effect	Sample Size	Program Content	Stereotype Measure
Drabman et al., 1981, I	9	.329	88	doctor/nurse	job/gender
Drabman et al., 1981, II	9	.386	130	doctor/nurse	job/gender
Drabman et al., 1981, III	4	.566	23	doctor/nurse	job/gender
Grusec & Brinker, 1972	6	.082	144	nurturing/ aggressive	recall of sex with behavior
McArthur & Eisen, 1976	4	.305	40	activities	behaviors
O'Bryant & Corder-Bolz, 1978	7	.323	67	occupation commercials	occupation preferences
Pingree, 1978	10	.173	227	commercials	traditional sex roles
Ruble et al., 1981	5	.100	100	commercials	toy choice
Silverman-Watkins et al., 1986	11	.100	96	newscasts	retention, liking
Tan, 1979	17	.082	56	beauty ads	sex roles
Tan et al., 1980	9	.207	120	newscasts	retention, believability

$k = 11$, $N = 1,091$) comes from a homogeneous set of estimates ($\chi^2_{(10)} = 16.79$, $p < .05$). The existence of a homogeneous set of results indicates that there probably are not any moderator variables present. Thus, we conducted no analysis of moderating conditions.

The failure to find a moderating variable may not be surprising, because these investigations used experimental methods. Experimental investigations permit researchers to assign subjects to conditions randomly and to control subjects' exposure to stimuli. This differs from survey (nonexperimental) or content analysis research, where the existence of materials in the environment is not within the control of the investigator. The positive correlation indicates that the viewing of material demonstrating traditional sexual stereotypes increased the endorsement of those attitudes.

CONCLUSIONS

The data analysis offers some systematic summarization of the quantitative literature gathered to date. The ability to assess the connection between televised content and the acceptance of sex role stereotypes is an important issue that deserves consideration. The results of the content analysis point to some strong evidence for the promulgation of sex-stereotyped images within the media. Television content provides a great deal of material that is consistent with traditional images. The findings demonstrate that stereotypes are more commonly found in occupational depictions than in characters' behaviors. The results indicate that as the amount of television watched increases, so does the acceptance of stereotypical images of women. The nonexperimental (survey) data demonstrate the largest impact on occupation and less on attitudes toward behavior and sex roles. The experimental data demonstrate that, in comparisons of random samples of individuals, television material depicting traditional sexual stereotypes has some impact.

The data do not point to some type of clear resolution to the various issues raised by Durkin (1985c). It is not possible to take the results of the current analysis and translate them into a convincing argument for or against any specific theoretical perspective. However, the results do point to some consistency in the effects of television on sexual stereotyping.

The cultural ratification model receives support only to the extent that the content of the media reflects stereotypical values. Further conclusions would require a test of societal elites and a correlation between their values and the values exhibited in the media. The findings of the experimental and nonexperimental studies support the notion that television is an important element for elites to control. Within experimental settings, television was found to contribute to the adoption of values by viewers.

The effects model articulated by Durkin (1985c) receives rather strong support from the current findings. Not only do the nonexperimental findings demonstrate a relationship between quantity of viewing and attitude, they also show that type of media content is aligned with the size of the effect. The content of television is most sex stereotypical in regard to occupations; it is less so in the area of the actions of male versus female characters. The effects of media consumption have been shown to be largest on occupational choice and weaker on attitudes toward behaviors and sex roles. The model does not provide a mechanism to isolate media as a cause independent of other causes, so a complete test of the model cannot be conducted.

The uses and gratifications model receives some level of disconfirmation from the experimental studies that demonstrate consistent effects. However, the inconsistency in the nonexperimental studies suggests that the consistency in experimental results is an artifact of laboratory experimental settings, where researchers might standardize gratifications or perhaps change or eliminate them altogether. It is clear that large numbers of viewers are selecting television programs that contain sexual stereotypes, and the uses and gratifications perspective would indicate the probability of this continuing. The uses and gratifications inconsistencies might stem from the lack of consideration that the antecedents of exposure have received in this analysis. There is a need for further meta-analyses considering individual differences as an explanation for the relationships observed in this analysis. Thus, it remains premature to assume that the uses and gratifications model lacks the ability to account for the results of this summary.

We did not directly test the script model in this analysis, but indirect results indicate that the attitudinal prerequisites necessary to the formation of stereotypical scripts exist within the content of the media and that persons indicate endorsement of those. If the attitude-behavior/intention-behavior model is accurate (as previous meta-analyses indicate), then the formation and activation of scripted behavior consistent with stereotypes cannot be far behind.

The current theoretical paradigms fail to provide a basis for interpretation or analysis of the current set of findings. Future theoretical and/or methodological arguments should consider the lack of homogeneity when conducting explorations of issues. Theorists should articulate the assumptions about the causal processes at work within the framework of the theories. The commitment to testable propositions would improve researchers' ability to evaluate the current findings. The development of sophisticated individual-difference models would improve the thinking and possible application of the theoretical tenets. Uses and gratifications theory contains elements that translate into possible individual-difference models. The results of this investigation do not consider or address those issues.

One problem exhibited in this report is a consistency across experimental investigations that was absent within the nonexperimental investigations. The ability of consumers to engage in selective viewing offers a possible explanation for the difference between the experimental and nonexperimental findings, with regard to homogeneity. Clearly, experimental investigations assume a lack of choice of material; the control of the material forms the basis of what constitutes an experiment. Nonexperimental designs assume that persons choose material for themselves and define how that material fits within their own life experiences.

TABLE 4.5
Interpreting the Impact of the Observed Nonexperimental Effect Size

Score in Sexist Attitudes	Watches More Than Average Amount of TV (%)	Watches Less Than Average Amount of TV (%)	Ratio	Chance Person Past Point Watches More TV (%)
Above average	55.00	45.00	1.22:1	55
Fairly sexist (greater than 1 standard deviation)	18.41	13.57	1.36:1	58
Very sexist (greater than 2 standard deviations)	2.87	1.79	1.60:1	62
Extremely sexist (greater than 3 standard deviations)	0.19	0.10	1.90:1	66

The data in Table 4.5 indicate how important the magnitude of the correlation ($r = .101$) is when one is considering relevant issues. Many persons would argue that 1% of the variance (taking the r and squaring it) is trivial and should not be considered important. Although it may be true that comparing the impacts on the "average" person is not important, that is not the only basis of comparison. Another technique for illustrating the impact of different effects is based on the binomial effect size display (BESD) method of illustrating the impact of various effect sizes (Allen, in press; Rosenthal, 1984). BESD shows how correlations of different sizes affect the ability to discriminate among two or more groups.

If one considers tails of the distribution, the impact of television watching on the ability to identify sexist attitudes becomes more extreme. Although the difference is small at the "average" level, only about a 20% increase, that level goes to a full 2:1 ratio at the extreme edge of the tail. What this indicates is that very sexist persons are twice as likely also to be heavy viewers of television (because simple correlations are symmetric, it also means that heavy television viewers are twice as likely as other viewers to profess sexually stereotypical attitudes).

The concern of those addressing the image of women in televised content receives some support in this analysis. The results indicate that the amount of televised content consumed is associated with the acceptance of sexual stereotypes. The deficiency in the analysis is the inability to isolate the effect and suggest clear evidence of causality. The analysis suggests reason for social concerns, as well as the need for additional research and meta-analyses.

One consideration is whether television program content in the future will maintain the portrayal of women and men in stereotypic roles. There could be a trend toward more nontraditional or varied programming. Whether programming with "nontraditional" depictions exists in sufficient variety and with enough diversity to develop a trend remains unclear. Whether such programming would represent a temporary aberration and would eventually be replaced with more traditional programming in the future remains unknown. Nontraditional programming may always exist but constitute only a small percentage of programming. This programming may or may not eventually be watched by greater numbers of persons. With the development of cable television channels and the growing numbers of opportunities viewers have to consume diverse content, it is possible that nontraditional programming will exist, but it may still maintain a limited viewership.

The issue of an effect is always relative to other important associations or potential causes of a relationship. The factors leading to the acceptance of sex role stereotypes probably include television as one source among many. Factors such as school, family, and religion might serve (and one would reasonably expect to serve) as more important sources of influence on the development of sex role attitudes. The results of our meta-analysis indicate that there is only a small association between television programming and acceptance of sexual stereotypes. The myriad other influences that contribute to the moral and social development of children's attitudes probably represent far greater influences.

The importance of sex roles in at least one area has been established by a meta-analysis of mental health outcomes conducted by Bassoff and Glass (1983). Their findings indicate that persons (both males and females) with high masculinity orientation operate at a healthier level than do persons with high feminine orientation. This may be an indication that our society places a positive value on masculine characteristics, whereas "feminine individuals, on the other hand, may be unrecognized in a society that emphasizes ambition and achievement, and they may come to devalue themselves" (p. 110). If this is true, then the consumption of televised material with a high degree of stereotyping may promote unhealthy self-images in women. The content analysis summary presented in this investigation provides evidence that the content of television may contribute to such self-images. Television portrays success as the outcome of persons' having powerful masculine characteristics, whereas feminine characteristics are associated with powerlessness and less success. This may help to create the conditions that Bassoff and Glass conclude may be mentally unhealthy for those with feminine orientation.

Our results do not provide the basis for a causal claim; they constitute a *necessary*, but not a *sufficient*, condition for causality. The combination of results provides the basis for various theoretical claims about television. The problem is that the inability to account for the existence of heterogeneity across the various results means that the explanations remain incomplete and alternative explanations remain not only possible, but inevitable. The next step in the research requires an examination of the possible reasons for heterogeneous results. This should permit the construction and testing of various theoretical models that would make it possible for researchers to explore the implications of the results.

If the relationship between media depictions and sex role stereotypes were causal, one would expect to see a lot more males growing up to become cowboys, police officers, and athletes. Obviously, viewing images does not necessarily translate into long-term permanent changes. Rather, images may have more subtle influences on values and belief systems. For example, males may not become cowboys or policemen, but may adopt the rugged values of the characters they have seen in such roles. Women may not become models, housewives, or lawyers, but they might adopt the fashion, style, and personal values exhibited by television characters.

A feminist analysis would point to the fact that television is dominated by traditional power elites, largely white males. The devaluation of the feminine on television hardly appears surprising. Rakow (1988) argues that technology is essentially gendered, and that the practices of technology reaffirm the existing elites. Her argument about gender differences as biological or even sociological perhaps becomes misplaced, because the terms relating to gender are not defined (Rakow, 1986). Meta-analytic studies of communication behaviors have found only small gender differences, pointing to the need for researchers to rethink the use of gender as a variable (Canary & Hause, 1993). Steeves (1987) enlarges this picture by arguing for the inclusion of sexual orientation, race, and class as issues deserving of consideration.

The problem with including these issues is that most feminist positions assume the need for social transformation (Harding, 1991; Rakow, 1989). Traditional scientific positions, of which this chapter is a part, put forth knowledge claims with a sense of objectivity rather than as part of any political agenda. Although it may be permissible, and perhaps even desirable, to call for and participate in social transformations, the conclusions drawn from our data sets do not inherently mandate such actions. The data provide an important contribution to such discussions and may be helpful for finding resolutions to problems or for determining whether there is a need for political action.

There is a growing body of findings about the impacts of the mass media on the social lives of individuals. Every meta-analysis to date has demonstrated the media's impacts on both the attitudes and the behaviors of individuals (Allen, D'Alessio, & Brezgel, in press; Allen, Emmers, Gebhardt, & Giery, 1995; Hearold, 1979, 1986; Paik & Comstock, 1994). These findings are the beginnings of a web of information indicating the magnitude of the media's influence on people's attitudes and behaviors. The theoretical and/or practical implications of the various findings still await exploration. The data point to some small associations that are worthy of consideration. If the subsequent data provide evidence for causal connections, then some kind of political action may be warranted. Feminist theorists talk about the impact of social institutions on people's development of various attitudes; the current analysis demonstrates the reality of that concern. The next step for scientists is to provide a complete, clear, comprehensive, and convincing explanation for the small effects we have reported.

NOTES

1. Some studies did not fit a design that could be included within this analysis. We considered the Dambrot, Reep, and Bell (1988) study inappropriate for this summary because the research design had individuals rate the masculinity/femininity of various television characters and compare the perceptions of television characters to the attitudes of the viewers. The study made use of persons who had experience watching a particular program (nonviewers were eliminated), but took no overall measurement of television viewing. The design was not a content analysis because the measure asked individuals for their perceptions of particular characters rather than for some objective measure of content. We also considered Eisenstock's (1984) experiment, an attempt to change subjects' identification with counterstereotypical televised portrayals, to be inappropriate for inclusion here. We did not include studies that had no recognizable measure of sexual stereotyping (Buerkel-Rothfuss, Greenberg, Atkin, & Neuendorf, 1982; Stout & Mouritsen, 1988) or measure of the amount of television viewed (Katz & Walsh, 1991; Lewin & Tragos, 1987; Reeves & Miller, 1978), and we eliminated one study that used a medium other than television (Pingree, Hawkins, Butler, & Paisley, 1976). Finally, we did not use Hansen and Krygowski's (1994) examination of rock music videos; although the study addressed issues relating to gender, the authors' use of MANOVA made the data nonrecoverable and the design did not measure sex roles as a dependent measure.

2. Some works lacked sufficient statistical information to permit the calculation of an effect (Cordua, McGraw, & Drabman, 1979; Fisher, 1989; Yussen, 1974; Zuckerman, Singer, & Singer, 1980).

3. One reviewer suggested that the cultures or nationalities of subjects might have some impact on the results, and we considered and coded for this feature. However, virtually all the studies were conducted in English-speaking countries, with few foreign nations or alternatives. This lack of cultural diversity indicates that the data pool is restricted culturally, and results may not generalize to other cultures.

4. A complete set of the data, literature search procedures, coding, and various corrections is available upon request.

REFERENCES

Allen, M. (in press). Research productivity and positive teaching evaluations: Examining the relationship using meta-analysis. *Journal of the Association of Communication Administrators.*

Allen, M., D'Alessio, D., & Brezgel, K. (in press). Summarizing the effects of pornography using meta-analysis: Aggression after exposure. *Human Communication Research.*

Allen, M., Emmers, T., Gebhardt, L., & Giery, M. (1995). Pornography and rape myth acceptance. *Journal of Communication, 45*(1), 5-26.

Allen, M., & Preiss, R. (1993). Replication and meta-analysis: A necessary connection. *Journal of Social Behavior and Personality, 8,* 9-20.

Bassoff, E., & Glass, E. (1983). The relationship between sex roles and mental health: A meta-analysis of twenty-six studies. *Counseling Psychologist, 10,* 105-112.

Beuf, A. (1974). Doctor, lawyer, household drudge. *Journal of Communication, 24*(2), 142-145.

Bower, G., Black, J., & Turner, J. (1979). Scripts in text comprehension and memory. *Cognitive Psychology, 11,* 177-220.

Buerkel-Rothfuss, N., Greenberg, B., Atkin, C., & Neuendorf, K. (1982). Learning about the family from television. *Journal of Communication, 32*(3), 191-201.

Busby, L. (1975). Sex-role research on the mass media. *Journal of Communication, 25*(4), 107-131.

Campbell, D. T., & Stanley, J. C. (1963). *Experimental and quasi-experimental designs for research.* Chicago: Rand McNally.

Canary, D., & Hause, K. (1993). Is there any reason to research sex differences in communication? *Communication Quarterly, 41,* 129-144.

Chaffee, S., & Tims, A. (1976). Interpersonal factors in adolescent television use. *Journal of Social Issues, 32,* 98-115.

Cobbs, N., Stevens-Long, J., & Goldstein, S. (1982). The influence of televised models on toy preferences in children. *Sex Roles, 8,* 1075-1080.

Cohen, J. (1987). *Statistical power analysis for the behavioral sciences* (rev. ed.). Hillsdale, NJ: Lawrence Erlbaum.

Collins, W. (1975). The developing child as viewer. *Journal of Communication, 25*(4), 35-44.

Comstock, G. (1975). The evidence so far. *Journal of Communication, 25*(4), 25-34.

Cook, T., & Campbell, D. T. (1979). *Quasi-experimentation: Design and analysis issues for field settings.* Chicago: Rand McNally.

Cordua, G., McGraw, K., & Drabman, R. (1979). Doctor or nurse: Children's perception of sex typed occupations. *Child Development, 50,* 590-593.

Courtney, A., & Whipple, T. (1974). Women in TV commercials. *Journal of Communication, 24*(2), 110-118.

Dambrot, F., Reep, D., & Bell, D. (1988). Television sex roles in the 1980s: Do viewers' sex and sex role orientation change the picture? *Sex Roles, 19,* 387-401.

Davidson, E., Yasuna, A., & Tower, A. (1979). The effects of television cartoons on sex-role stereotyping in young girls. *Child Development, 50,* 596-600.

Dohrmann, R. (1975). A gender profile of children's educational TV. *Journal of Communication, 25*(4), 56-65.

Dominick J., & Rauch, G. (1972). The image of women in network TV commercials. *Journal of Broadcasting, 16,* 259-265.

Drabman, R., Robertson, S., Patterson, J., Jarvie, G., Hammer, D., & Cordua, G. (1981). Children's perception of media-portrayed sex roles. *Sex Roles, 7,* 379-389.

Durkin, K. (1985a). Television and sex-role acquisition 1: Content. *British Journal of Social Psychology, 24,* 101-113.

Durkin, K. (1985b). Television and sex-role acquisition 2: Effects. *British Journal of Social Psychology, 24,* 191-210.

Durkin, K. (1985c). *Television, sex roles, and children: A developmental social psychological account.* Philadelphia: Open University Press.

Eisenstock, B. (1984). Sex-role differences in children's identification with counterstereotypical televised portrayals. *Sex Roles, 10,* 417-430.

Fisher, G. (1989). Mass media effects on sex role attitudes of incarcerated men. *Sex Roles, 20,* 191-203.

Frueh, T., & McGhee, P. (1975). Traditional sex role development and amount of time spent watching television. *Developmental Psychology, 11,* 109.

Glass, G., McGaw, B., & Smith, M. (1980). *Meta-analysis in social research.* Beverly Hills, CA: Sage.

Grusec, J., & Brinker, D. (1972). Reinforcement for imitation as a social learning determinant with implications for sex-role development. *Journal of Personality and Social Psychology, 21,* 149-158.

Hansen, C., & Hansen, R. (1988). Priming stereotypical appraisal of social interactions: How rock music videos can change what's seen when boy meets girl. *Sex Roles, 19,* 287-319.

Hansen, C., & Hansen, R. (1990). Rock music videos and antisocial behavior. *Basic and Applied Social Psychology, 11,* 357-370.

Hansen, C., & Krygowski, W. (1994). Arousal-augmented priming effects: Rock music videos and sex object schemas. *Communication Research, 21,* 24-47.

Harding, S. (1991). *Whose science? Whose knowledge?* Ithaca, NY: Cornell University Press.

Hearold, S. (1979). *Meta-analysis of the effects of television on social behavior.* Unpublished doctoral dissertation, University of Colorado, Boulder.

Hearold, S. (1986). A synthesis of 1043 effects of television on social behavior. In G. Comstock (Ed.), *Public communication and behavior* (Vol. 1, pp. 65-133). Orlando, FL: Academic Press.

Hedges, L. (1987). How hard is hard science, and how soft is soft science? The empirical cumulativeness of research. *American Psychologist, 42*, 443-455.

Hedges, L., & Olkin, I. (1985). *Statistical methods for meta-analysis.* Orlando, FL: Academic Press.

Hunter, J. E., & Schmidt, F. L. (1990). *Methods of meta-analysis: Correcting for error and bias in research findings.* Newbury Park, CA: Sage.

Janus, N. (1977). Research on sex-roles in the mass media: Toward a critical approach. *Insurgent Sociology, 7*, 19-32.

Johnson, B., Mullen, B., & Salas, E. (1995). Comparison of three major meta-analytic approaches. *Journal of Applied Psychology, 80*, 94-106.

Katz, P., & Walsh, P. (1991). Modification of children's gender-stereotyped behavior. *Child Development, 62*, 338-351.

Kear, L. (1985). *Television and sex roles: A selected annotated bibliography.* Unpublished manuscript, Georgia State University. (ERIC Document Reproduction Service No. ED 262 444)

Kellermann, K. (1985). Memory processes in media effects. *Communication Research, 12*, 83-131.

Kellermann, K., & Lim, T. (1989). Inference-generating knowledge structures in message processing. In J. Bradac (Ed.), *Message effects in communication science* (pp. 102-128). Newbury Park, CA: Sage.

Kim, M., & Hunter, J. (1993a). Attitude-behavior relations: A meta-analysis of attitudinal relevance and topic. *Journal of Communication, 43*, 101-142.

Kim, M., & Hunter, J. (1993b). Relationships among attitudes, behavioral intentions, and behavior. *Communication Research, 20*, 331-364.

Kimball, M. (1986). Television and sex-attitudes. In T. M. Williams (Ed.), *The impact of television: A natural experiment in three communities* (pp. 265-301). Orlando, FL: Academic Press.

Levinson, R. (1975). From Olive Oyl to Sweet Polly Purebread: Sex role stereotypes and televised cartoons. *Journal of Popular Culture, 9*, 561-572.

Lewin, M., & Tragos, L. (1987). Has the feminist movement influenced adolescent sex role attitudes? A reassessment after a quarter century. *Sex Roles, 16*, 125-135.

Liebert, R., Sprafkin, J., & Davidson, E. (1982). *The early window* (2nd ed.). Elmsford, NY: Pergamon.

Lipinski, J., & Calvert, S. (1985). *The influence of television on children's sex typing.* Paper presented at the Tenth Annual Southeastern Child and Family Symposium, Knoxville, TN. (ERIC Document Reproduction Service No. ED 016 419)

Lovdal, L. (1989). Sex role messages in television commercials: An update. *Sex Roles, 21*, 715-724.

McArthur, L., & Eisen, S. (1976). Television and sex-role stereotyping. *Journal of Applied Social Psychology, 6*, 329-351.

McGhee, P., & Frueh, T. (1980). Television viewing and the learning of sex-role stereotypes. *Sex Roles, 6*, 179-188.

Meyer, B. (1980). The development of girls' sex-role attitudes. *Child Development, 51*, 508-514.

Miller, M., & Reeves, B. (1976). Dramatic TV content and children's sex-role stereotypes. *Journal of Broadcasting, 20*, 35-50.

Morgan, M. (1982). Television and adolescents' sex role stereotypes: A longitudinal study. *Journal of Personality and Social Psychology, 43*, 947-955.

Morgan, M. (1987). Television, sex-role attitudes, and sex-role behavior. *Journal of Early Adolescence, 7*, 269-282.

Morgan, M., & Rothschild, N. (1983). Impact of the new television technology: Cable TV, peers, and sex-role cultivation in the electronic environment. *Youth & Society, 15*, 33-50.

O'Bryant, S., & Corder-Bolz, C. (1978). The effects of television on children's stereotyping of women's work roles *Journal of Vocational Behavior, 12,* 233-244.

Paik, H., & Comstock, G. (1994). The effects of television violence on antisocial behavior: A meta-analysis. *Communication Research, 21,* 516-546.

Perloff, R. (1977). Some antecedents of children's sex-role stereotypes. *Psychological Reports, 40,* 463-466.

Pingree, S. (1978). The effects of nonsexist television commercials and perceptions of reality on children's attitudes about women. *Psychology of Women Quarterly, 2,* 262-277.

Pingree, S., Hawkins, R., Butler, M., & Paisley, W. (1976). A scale for sexism. *Journal of Communication, 26*(4), 193-200.

Potter, J. (1993). Cultivation theory and research: A conceptual analysis. *Human Communication Research, 19,* 564-601.

Preiss, R., & Allen, M. (1994). Prospects and precautions in the use of meta-analysis. In M. Allen & R. Preiss (Eds.), *Prospects and precautions in the use of meta-analysis* (pp. 1-33). Dubuque, IA: Brown & Benchmark.

Rakow, L. (1986). Rethinking gender research in communication. *Journal of Communication, 36*(4), 11-26.

Rakow, L. (1988). Gendered technology, gendered practice. *Critical Studies in Mass Communication, 5,* 57-70.

Rakow, L. (1989). Feminist studies: The next stage. *Critical Studies in Mass Communication, 6,* 209-215.

Reep, D., & Dambrot, F. (1990). Effects of frequent television viewing on stereotypes: "Drip, drip" or "drench." *Journalism Quarterly, 55,* 542-550.

Reeves, B., & Miller, M. (1978). A multidimensional measure of children's identification with television characters. *Journal of Broadcasting, 22,* 71-86.

Repetti, R. (1984). Determinants of children's sex stereotyping: Parental sex-role traits and television viewing. *Personality and Social Psychology Bulletin, 10,* 457-468.

Rosenthal, R. (1984). *Meta-analysis for social research.* Beverly Hills, CA: Sage.

Ross, L., Anderson, D., & Wisocki, P. (1982). Television viewing and adult sex-role attitudes. *Sex Roles, 8,* 589-592.

Rubinstein, E. (1983). Television and behavior: Research conclusions of the 1982 NIMH report and their policy implications. *American Psychologist, 38,* 820-825.

Ruble, D., Balaban, T., & Cooper, J. (1981). Gender consumer and the effects of sex-typed televised toy commercials. *Child Development, 52,* 667-673.

Schank, R. (1982). *Dynamic memory: A theory of reminding and learning in computers and people.* Cambridge: Cambridge University Press.

Schwichtenberg, C. (1989). The "mother lode" of feminist research: Congruent paradigms in the analysis of beauty culture. In B. Dervin, L. Grossberg, B. O'Keefe, & E. Wartella (Eds.), *Rethinking communication* (Vol. 2, pp. 291-306). Newbury Park, CA: Sage.

Seggar, J. (1977). Television's portrayal of minorities and women, 1971-75. *Journal of Broadcasting, 21,* 435-446.

Seggar, J., Hafen, J., & Hannonen-Gladden, H. (1981). Television's portrayals of minorities and women in drama and comedy drama 1971-1980. *Journal of Broadcasting, 25,* 277-288.

Seggar, J., & Wheeler, P. (1973). World of work on TV: Ethnic and sex representation in TV drama. *Journal of Broadcasting, 17,* 201-214.

Signorelli, N. (1989). Television and conceptions about sex roles: Maintaining conventionality and the status quo. *Sex Roles, 21,* 341-361.

Signorelli, N. (1993). Television, the portrayal of women, and children's attitudes. In G. Berry & J. Asamen (Eds.), *Children and television: Images in a changing sociocultural world* (pp. 229-243). Newbury Park, CA: Sage.

Signorelli, N., & Lears, M. (1992). Children, television, and conceptions about chores: Attitudes and behaviors. *Sex Roles, 27,* 157-170.

Silverman-Watkins, L., Levi, S., & Klein, M. (1986). Sex-stereotyping as a factor in children's comprehension of television news. *Journalism Quarterly, 63,* 3-11.

Spector, P., & Levine, E. (1987). Meta-analysis for integrating study outcomes: A Monte Carlo study of its susceptibility to Type I and Type II errors. *Journal of Applied Psychology, 72,* 3-9.

Steeves, H. (1987). Feminist theories and media studies. *Critical Studies in Mass Communication, 4,* 95-135.

Sternglanz, S., & Serbin, L. (1974). Sex role stereotyping in children's television programs. *Developmental Psychology, 10,* 710-715.

Stout, D., & Mouritsen, R. (1988). Prosocial behavior in advertising aimed at children: A content analysis. *Southern Speech Communication Journal, 53,* 159-174.

Tan, A. (1979). TV beauty ads and role expectations of adolescent female viewers. *Journalism Quarterly, 56,* 283-288.

Tan, A., Raudy, J., Huff, C., & Miles, J. (1980). Children's reactions to male and female newscasters: Effectiveness and believability. *Quarterly Journal of Speech, 66,* 201-205.

Turow, J. (1989). Television and institutional power: The case of medicine. In B. Dervin, L. Grossberg, B. O'Keefe, & E. Wartella (Eds.), *Rethinking communication* (Vol. 2, pp. 454-473). Newbury Park, CA: Sage.

Wartella, E., & Reeves, B. (1985). Historical trends in research on children and the media: 1900-1960. *Journal of Communication, 35*(2), 118-133.

Welch, R., Huston-Stein, A., Wright, J., & Plehal, R. (1977). Subtle sex-role cues in children's commercials. *Journal of Communication, 27*(2), 202-211.

Wroblewski, R., & Huston, A. (1987). Televised occupational stereotypes and their effects on early adolescents: Are they changing? *Journal of Early Adolescence, 7,* 283-297.

Yussen, S. (1974). Determinants of visual attention and recall in observational learning by preschoolers and second graders. *Developmental Psychology, 10,* 93-100.

Zemach, T., & Cohen, A. (1986). Perception of gender equality on television and in social reality. *Journal of Broadcasting and Electronic Media, 30,* 427-444.

Zuckerman, D., Singer, D., & Singer, J. (1980). Children's television viewing, racial, and sex-role attitudes. *Journal of Applied Social Psychology, 10,* 281-294.

CHAPTER CONTENTS

5 The Knowledge Gap Hypothesis: Twenty-Five Years Later

K. VISWANATH
The Ohio State University

JOHN R. FINNEGAN, JR.
University of Minnesota

Citizens' acquisition of mass media information has long been a concern of social scientists and policy makers. The conventional wisdom that increasing the flow of information will ensure its widespread acquisition has been criticized based on studies showing inequitable information acquisition between groups of higher and lower socioeconomic status. The knowledge gap hypothesis, formalized in 1970, posits increasing differences in knowledge due to social structure-based inequities. Because of its important theoretical and policy implications, this hypothesis has generated considerable research and continues to concern social scientists and policy makers worldwide. This chapter reviews and critiques the development of the knowledge gap hypothesis over the past 25 years. Based on a comprehensive examination of studies, critiques, and dissertations, the authors identify the variables that potentially influence the gap phenomenon, the conditions under which gaps expand and contract, and areas that require further research. Finally, the authors evaluate the knowledge gap hypothesis as a scientific research program, using a sophisticated falsificationist perspective.

POLITICAL theorists have long contended that power is based in the spread and possession of knowledge and information. They have argued that the republican form of government is about making conscious choices and therefore have asserted the indispensability of an informed citizenry. In modern times, the mass media have developed as powerful

AUTHORS' NOTE: We are profoundly grateful to Professor Phillip Tichenor for his comments on earlier drafts of this chapter. We also acknowledge the generous advice of Dr. Cecilie Gaziano and the very thorough critiques of Professors Lee Becker and Eric Fredin of the Ohio State University. The first author would also like to thank his research assistants, Misha Tsiroulnikov and Lisa Chiu.

Correspondence and requests for reprints: K. Viswanath, School of Journalism, Ohio State University, 242 West 18th Avenue, Columbus, OH 43210-1107.

Communication Yearbook 19, pp. 187-227

instruments of information and knowledge propelling social and political influence. In the second half of the twentieth century, their pivotal role has continued to unfold, especially in light of national preferences for strategies of planned, rational change to manage political, social, and economic issues and problems.

Following the emergence of empirical social science, however, researchers have frequently observed that information and knowledge seldom spread equitably to all groups within social systems. "Gaps" in knowledge or information have been consistently found between social groups, whether involving information of a general nature or communication campaigns seeking some intended effect. Early such evidence was found by Hyman and Sheatsley (1947), who first observed the difficulty of reaching some groups—which they labeled "chronic know-nothings"—with any information. A few years later, Star and Hughes (1950) reported that a campaign to inform Cincinnati citizens about the United Nations resulted in the inequitable distribution of information. People with more formal education gained information from the campaign, but their less educated counterparts benefited little. Many subsequent studies, such as the "Coleman report" on the equality of educational opportunity (Coleman et al., 1966; Mosteller & Moynihan, 1972) and evaluations of public television's *Sesame Street* (Ball & Bogatz, 1970; Cook et al., 1975; Katzman, 1974) and other purposive communication projects (Hornik, 1989; Rogers, 1976; Roling, Ascroft, & Wa Chege, 1976), have found similar unintended outcomes favoring information "haves" over "have-nots." These studies have raised serious questions about the nature of such gaps, whether and how they might be bridged, and whether and how the phenomenon constrains the capacity of democratic social systems to manage change and conflict and to make informed decisions.

Tichenor, Donohue, and Olien in 1970 formalized this research finding as the *knowledge gap hypothesis*: "As the infusion of mass media information into a social system increases, segments of the population with higher socioeconomic status tend to acquire the information at a faster rate than the lower status segments, so that the gap between these segments tends to increase rather than decrease" (pp. 159-160). This was an important formalization and expansion of previous findings because it proposed that media-generated publicity flowing into a community potentially increased knowledge disparities between social groups rather than reduced them. It ran counter to the general expectation of information campaign effects by proposing that purposive communication would most often benefit the "information rich" and disadvantage the "information poor" (Price & Zaller, 1993).

Since its formal articulation 25 years ago, the knowledge gap hypothesis has generated strong interest among social scientists and policy makers in the United States and worldwide. This interest in knowledge gap research has been steadily increasing in the past quarter century. For example, our data show that there have been *at least* 70 pieces published on the knowledge gap hypothesis over the past 25 years, and the number of studies has increased recently. In fact, in the first decade, 1970-1979, there were 13 studies; in the second decade, 1980-1989, there were 32 studies; and in the last half decade, 1990-1994, there have already been 26 studies, including dissertations.[1] The continuing concern of this line of research is about knowledge and its control as the basis of social power and social action. As theorists have long suggested, knowledge inequities are a profound concern in democratic social systems. They may lead to serious power differentials and reflect on the capacity of such systems to serve the needs of all their members equitably (Donohue, Olien, & Tichenor, 1987; Olien, Donohue, & Tichenor, 1983).

Dozens of studies have examined the knowledge gap phenomenon, seeking to test the hypothesis at least implicitly and to refine, modify, and even expand it.[2] In this chapter, we review the important issues raised by knowledge gap research. Specifically, we review empirical studies, commentaries, and critiques of this research generated since 1970. Finally, we evaluate the scientific integrity of the research program, using the "sophisticated falsificationist" perspective described by Lakatos (1968). Issues reviewed here include the following:

1. contingent conditions that affect knowledge gaps, including differences in topics and content domains, their functionality and geographic scope, complexity of knowledge, channel influence differences, and the role of media publicity in campaign and noncampaign communication;
2. macrosocial contrasted with individual-level explanations for knowledge gaps;
3. conceptual and methodological issues in study design, operational definitions, and measurement;
4. ideological considerations, including the meaning of gaps and how they occur; and
5. the development of the knowledge gap hypothesis as a formal research program in mass communication studies.

METHODS

In reviewing each study, we took the following key characteristics (Gaziano, 1983) into account: (a) the author(s), (b) date or year of the study, (c) topic or content domain (local, national, or international; science, health, or public affairs), (d) whether the study dealt with a campaign or a secular topic, (e) study design, (f) measurement of knowledge, (g) type of knowledge measured, (h) type of the community, (i) place or location of the study, and (j) medium. For this review we located as much of the published work as possible through *Social Science Citations Index, Sociological Abstracts, Psychological Abstracts,* and the Education Resources Information Clearinghouse. We also used the reference lists in the articles we found to locate fugitive materials. Gaziano's (1983) review was especially helpful in this regard. We located three kinds of articles: (a) those that examined knowledge gap explicitly; (b) those that looked at correlations between education and knowledge, and social class and knowledge; and (c) critical reviews of and commentaries on the hypothesis itself.

EARLY REFINEMENTS AND REVISIONS

Using formal schooling as a socioeconomic status (SES) indicator, early studies supported the knowledge gap hypothesis in certain topical areas, including public affairs, science, space research, and health. Some studies examining news diffusion also showed that education was related to current-events knowledge (DeFleur, 1987). Soon, however, studies emerged that did not appear to support the hypothesis as originally formulated. Some studies in the United States and in India did not find widening gaps (Ettema & Kline, 1977; Shinghi & Mody, 1976), and a rare few even found reverse gaps, in which those with less formal education demonstrated greater knowledge than those with more education (Douglas, Westley, & Chaffee, 1970; Fathi, 1973). These developments led researchers to consider contingent conditions constraining the intractability of knowledge gaps. This work raised new issues with somewhat more optimistic implications, especially for communication campaigns (Clarke & Kline, 1974; Dervin, 1980; Ettema & Kline, 1977; Friemuth, 1989).

Revising the original hypothesis, Donohue, Tichenor, and Olien (1975) drew attention to several relevant conditions affecting knowledge gaps: the geographic scope of a topic or issue, its local community impact, the conflict level surrounding a topic or issue, social structure, and information flow (amount and repetition of topical information in a social system). Ettema and Kline (1977) sought further refinements in individual-level conditions. They proposed that knowledge gaps are due to social group differences in motivation to acquire information and the lack of relevance and utility of much media-generated information for individuals in lower-SES groups. They also argued that "ceiling effects" on knowledge among higher-SES groups could produce conditions permitting lower-SES groups to catch up and thereby close gaps in social group differences in knowledge.

In an extensive review, Gaziano (1983) examined the role of variables such as topic type and geographic scope, operational definitions of knowledge, types of communication channels studied, and research design and data collection methods.

CONTENT DOMAIN AND INFORMATION UTILITY

Supporting Ettema and Kline (1977), a number of studies have reported gaps in public affairs knowledge between less and more educated groups and among those differing in topical interest (Delli-Carpini, Keeter, & Kennamer, 1994; Fredin, Monnett, & Kosicki, 1994; Fry, 1979; Gaziano, 1983; Genova & Greenberg, 1979; Horstmann, 1991; Kanervo, 1979; Kleinnijenhuis, 1991; McLeod & Perse, 1994; Moore, 1987; Pan, 1990; Robinson, 1972; Robinson & Levy, 1986; Rucinski & Ryu, 1991; Simmons & Garda, 1982; Tichenor, Donohue, & Olien, 1980; Wade & Schramm, 1969). Some studies also have shown differences in learning from news between those reporting previous knowledge of a topic and those reporting little or no previous knowledge (Price & Zaller, 1993; Robinson & Levy, 1986).

Donohue et al. (1975) studied knowledge about the environment and found gaps between different education groups. At least two other studies also found large gaps on environmental topic knowledge (Griffin, 1990; Lovrich & Pierce, 1984). In these three studies (Donohue et al., 1975; Griffin, 1990; Lovrich & Pierce, 1984), the researchers also found that knowledge gaps narrowed over time. These studies suggest that narrowing gaps may be due to heightened salience caused by increased community conflict over the issues examined. Such conflict may activate public discussion, leading to a more equitable distribution of information (Donohue et al., 1975; Lovrich & Pierce, 1984). In the study by Griffin (1990), declining media publicity may also have resulted in narrowing gaps.

Health knowledge, a topic of nearly universal interest, has received considerable study. The very first article on the knowledge gap reported SES-based knowledge differences about the link between smoking and cancer (Tichenor et al., 1970). Other studies have also reported SES- or motivation-based knowledge differences (Butler, 1990; Chew & Palmer, 1994; Douglas & Stacey, 1972; Erskine, 1963; Gallup Omnibus, 1977; Horowitz, 1992; Nazzaro, 1989; Snyder, 1990; Yows, Salmon, Hawkins, & Love, 1991; Zandpour & Fellow, 1992), although gaps have narrowed in some cases as a result of community campaigns in both developed (Ettema, Brown, & Luepker, 1983) and developing nations (Galloway, 1977).

Longitudinal studies of health knowledge have reported that gaps usually expand initially but close over time. These studies suggest that gaps are less likely if a topic involves communities, if an issue is defined by powerful groups as a significant problem, if communities are sufficiently pluralistic to provide specialized information (Donohue, Olien, & Tichenor, 1990; Finnegan, Viswanath, Kahn, & Hannan, 1993; Viswanath, 1990; Viswanath, Finnegan, Hertog, Pirie, & Murray, 1994; Viswanath, Finnegan, & Kahn, 1993), or if special promotional efforts have encouraged widespread exposure (Chew & Palmer, 1994). One study found that over time there were no SES-based differences in the acquisition of information, but also found differences in information retention (Snyder, 1990).

Studies have also examined other topical areas. In a study of knowledge gaps in a developing country, Galloway (1977) found narrowing gaps in knowledge of 10 agricultural innovations. Genova and Greenberg (1979) found SES-based knowledge differences on a sports-related topic (an NFL players' strike).

In summary, the evidence suggests that knowledge gaps may be found in both public affairs and non-public affairs topics (Table 5.1). Although content domain is important, research suggests there are other factors that influence knowledge gaps, including social conflict, media access, knowledge complexity, and community social structure.

COMMUNITY BOUNDEDNESS

Researchers have observed that the more an issue or topic is defined as important to a local community, the fewer knowledge gaps will exist between SES groups in that community. This idea of *community boundedness* may also affect knowledge gaps in communities not defined geographically but by some other common characteristic, such as ethnicity or association—"communities without propinquity" (Webber, 1963). Delli-Carpini et al. (1994), for example, found that although residents of northern Virginia knew less about their state than did residents of Richmond, the state capital, they were better informed about national issues. These results undoubtedly were due to the influence of Washington, D.C., media in northern Virginia and the fact that many residents of that part of the state work in Washington.

Several studies of issues important to local communities have reported a "slight tendency" for fewer SES-based knowledge gaps (Becker & Whitney, 1980; Donohue et al., 1975; Palmgreen, 1979; Viswanath, Kosicki, Park, & Fredin, 1993). On the other hand, Gaziano (1984) found knowledge of local interest topics to vary between groups of differing education. A Swedish study by Brantgarde (1983) reports more modest gaps on local issues.

On the other hand, several studies of nonlocal issues have reported enduring SES-based gaps (Clarke & Kline, 1974; Donohue et al, 1975; Genova & Greenberg, 1979; Gunaratne, 1976; Moore, 1987; Robinson, 1972). Gandy and El Waylly (1985) and other investigators have reported SES-based gaps in knowledge on international topics both in the United States and abroad (Gunaratne, 1976; McNelly & Molina, 1972; McNelly, Rush, & Bishop, 1968; Robinson, 1967, 1972; Star & Hughes, 1950). Along these lines, Brantgarde (1983) found that better-educated persons reporting greater exposure to national issues were also likely to demonstrate greater knowledge of local issues.

A recent study examined knowledge gaps between African Americans and the majority population on an issue involving civil rights and crime. The authors report that gaps were less likely among African Americans, compared with the majority population, because the issue was of greater immediate relevance to their community (Viswanath, Kosicki, et al., 1993).

(text continues on p. 197)

TABLE 5.1
Summary of Studies Reporting Impact
of Major Explanatory Variables on Knowledge Gaps

Contingent Variable	Studies Demonstrating Presence or Enduring Gaps	Studies Demonstrating Absence or Narrowing Gaps
Nature of the topic		
Content domain		
public affairs	Fredin et al., 1994; Price & Zaller, 1993; Robinson & Levy, 1986; see also diffusion studies cited in DeFleur (1987)	
environment[a]	Donohue at al., 1975; Griffin, 1990; Lovrich & Pierce, 1984	Donohue at al., 1975; Griffin, 1990; Lovrich & Pierce, 1984
health	Butler, 1990; Chew & Palmer, 1994; Douglas & Stacey, 1972; Erskine, 1963; Gallup Omnibus, 1977; Horowitz, 1992; McDivitt, 1985; Nazzaro, 1989; Snyder, 1990; Tichenor et al., 1970; Yows et al., 1991; Zandpour & Fellow, 1992	Chew & Palmer, 1994; Donohue et al., 1975; Ettema et al., 1983; Galloway, 1977; Snyder, 1990; Viswanath, 1990; Viswanath, Finnegan, & Kahn, 1993
agriculture	Hornik, 1989	Galloway, 1977
sports	Genova & Greenberg, 1979	
Community boundedness		
local issues	Brantgarde, 1983; Gaziano, 1984	Becker & Whitney, 1980; Donohue et al., 1975; Palmgreen, 1979; Viswanath, Kosicki, et al., 1993b
nonlocal or statewide issues	Delli-Carpini et al., 1994; Donohue et al., 1975; Moore, 1987	
international issues	Brantgarde, 1983; Gandy & El Waylly, 1985	
Complexity of knowledge		
Awareness or simple knowledge		Galloway, 1977; Viswanath et al., 1994
Complex knowledge	Gaziano, 1984; Genova & Greenberg, 1979; Moore, 1987; Price & Zaller, 1993; Snyder, 1990; Spitzer & Denzin, 1965; Viswanath et al., 1994	

(continued)

TABLE 5.1
Continued

Contingent Variable	Studies Demonstrating Presence or Enduring Gaps	Studies Demonstrating Absence or Narrowing Gaps
Role of publicity		
Increasing flow of information into a system, either because of campaigns or for "secular" (noncampaign) reasons	Cook et al., 1975; Donohue et al., 1990; Hornik, 1988; Moore, 1987; Mosteller & Moynihan, 1972; Nazzaro, 1989; Rogers, 1983; Snyder, 1990; Star & Hughes, 1950; Viswanath, Finnegan, & Kahn, 1993[b]	Chew & Palmer, 1994; Donohue et al., 1975; Ettema et al., 1983; Greenberg, 1964; Griffin, 1990; Spitzer & Denzin, 1965; Viswanath, 1990; Viswanath et al., 1994; Viswanath, Finnegan, & Kahn, 1993
Channel influence		
Print media (exposure)[c]	Gaziano, 1984;[d] Griffin, 1990; Kleinnijenhuis, 1991; McLeod & Perse, 1994; Price & Zaller, 1993;[e] Robinson, 1972; Simmons & Garda, 1982	Gandy & El Waylly, 1985; Gaziano, 1984
Television	Gandy & El Waylly, 1985; Griffin, 1990; Gunter, 1987; Horstmann, 1991; McLeod & Perse, 1994; Shinghi et al., 1982; Simmons & Garda, 1982	Brantgarde, 1983; Chew & Palmer, 1994; Galloway, 1977; Gantz, 1978; Kleinnijenhuis, 1991; Miller & MacKeun, 1979; Mulugetta, 1986; Neuman, 1976; Sharp, 1984; Shinghi et al., 1982; Shinghi & Mody, 1976; Tomita, 1989; Torsvik, 1972
Newspapers versus television[f]	Clarke & Fredin, 1978; Lang & Lang, 1984; McLeod & Perse, 1994; Price & Zaller, 1993; Simmons & Garda, 1982	
Interpersonal discussion[g]		Donohue et al., 1975; Galloway, 1977; Genova & Greenberg, 1979; Griffin, 1990; Hornik, 1989; Horstmann, 1991; Price & Zaller, 1993; Robinson & Levy, 1986; Roy et al., 1969
Individual-level variables[h]		
Interest	Genova & Greenberg, 1979; Horstmann, 1991; McLeod & Perse, 1994; Neuman, 1976; Pan, 1990	
Importance and threat	Ettema et al., 1983	
Involvement	Salmon, 1985	

(continued)

TABLE 5.1
Continued

Contingent Variable	Studies Demonstrating Presence or Enduring Gaps	Studies Demonstrating Absence or Narrowing Gaps
Concern and salience	Chew & Palmer, 1994; Ettema et al., 1983; Nazzaro, 1989; Zandpour & Fellow, 1992	
Cognitive schemata	Fredin et al., 1994	
Individual participation	Horstmann, 1991; Lovrich & Pierce, 1984	
Individual-level variables versus SES with greater association between knowledge and SES compared with interest and knowledge	Gandy & El Waylly, 1985; Gaziano, 1984; Griffin, 1990; McLeod & Perse, 1994; Price & Zaller, 1993; Rucinski & Ryu, 1991; Simmons & Garda, 1982; Snyder, 1990; Viswanath, Kahn, et al., 1993; Yows et al., 1991	
Macro-level variables		
Homogeneous communities	Pearson, 1990; Viswanath et al., 1994; Viswanath, Finnegan, & Kahn, 1994	Donohue et al., 1975; Douglas et al., 1970; Ettema at al., 1983; Galloway, 1977; Olien et al., 1983; Shinghi & Mody, 1976; Tichenor, Donohue, & Olien, 1973, 1980
Heterogeneous communities	Donohue et al., 1975; Gandy & El Waylly, 1985; Olien et al., 1983; Tichenor et al., 1973, 1980	Melwani et al., 1994; Viswanath et al., 1994; Viswanath, Finnegan, & Kahn, 1993
Social conflict and mobilization	Frazier, 1986; Gaziano, 1984; Lovrich & Pierce, 1984	Donohue at al., 1975; Frazier, 1986; Genova & Greenberg, 1979; Tichenor et al., 1980
Participation and involvement with groups		Brantgarde, 1983; Galloway, 1977; Gaziano, 1984
Degree of control[i]		Ettema et al., 1983; Galloway, 1977; Olien at al., 1983; Shinghi at al., 1982; Shinghi & Mody, 1976
Conceptual and methodological influences		
Ceiling effects simple measures		Donohue et al., 1990; Ettema & Kline, 1977; Galloway, 1977; Greenberg, 1964; Spitzer & Denzin, 1965; Viswanath et al., 1994

(continued)

TABLE 5.1
Continued

Contingent Variable	Studies Demonstrating Presence or Enduring Gaps	Studies Demonstrating Absence or Narrowing Gaps
complex measures	Donohue et al., 1990; Moore, 1987	
Operational measure of knowledge[j]		
closed-ended	gaps usually reported; e.g., Chew & Palmer, 1994; Ettema at al., 1983; Galloway, 1977; Genova & Greenberg, 1979	
open-ended	Benton & Frazier, 1976; Clarke & Kline, 1974; Donohue et al., 1975; Edelstein, 1973; Finnegan et al., 1990; Gandy & El Waylly, 1985; Gaziano, 1983, 1984; Lovrich & Pierce, 1984; McLeod at al., 1988; Viswanath, Finnegan, & Kahn, 1993	Palmgreen, 1979;[k] Viswanath, Finnegan, & Kahn, 1993
Study design		
one-shot studies	most diffusion studies; see also Donohue at al., 1975; Finnegan et al., 1988, 1990; Gandy & El Waylly, 1985; Gaziano, 1984; Tichenor et al., 1980	
longitudinal	Cook et al., 1975; Moore, 1987; Pan, 1990; Price & Zaller, 1993; Snyder, 1990; Viswanath, 1990;[l] Viswanath et al., 1994; Viswanath, Finnegan, & Kahn, 1993	Abbott, 1978; Bailey, 1971; Bogart, 1957-1958; Chew & Palmer, 1994; Donohue et al., 1975; Douglas at al., 1970; Ettema et al., 1983; Galloway, 1977; Gaziano, 1983, 1984; Genova & Greenberg, 1979; Griffin, 1990; Horstmann, 1991; Mulugetta, 1986; Shinghi & Mody, 1976; Star & Hughes, 1950; Viswanath, 1990; Viswanath et al., 1994; Viswanath, Finnegan, & Kahn, 1993

NOTE: Caution is advised in interpreting this table. The findings in the studies cited have been simplified for ease of reporting and are intended only to indicate and summarize findings in the broadest sense. The complexity of the findings is discussed in greater detail in the text. Although most of the relevant studies are cited here, the entries are not exhaustive.
a. Gaps were found initially, but they narrowed over time, as reported in the third column.
b. Gaps narrowed on campaign-emphasized knowledge initially, whereas they widened in the topics not emphasized in the campaigns.
c. These studies found positive association between knowledge and print media exposure and reported knowledge gaps between readers and nonreaders.
d. Gaziano (1984) also reports gaps between high and low educational groups among the readers.

TABLE 5.1
Continued

---

e. Reduced to nonsignificance in a multivariate model.

f. These studies reported stronger association between newspaper exposure and knowledge and widening gaps between those exposed to newspapers compared with those exposed to television.

g. Few studies in knowledge gap actually used interpersonal communication as a variable. Among those that did examine the variable, a narrowing of gaps as a result of interpersonal discussion was reported.

h. Most studies reported greater gaps between those who were interested or motivated and those who were not interested or not motivated. Some compared the predictive power of a micro-level variable, such as interest or salience, with education, as shown below.

i. This variable was not the explicit focus in any study. It has been offered as an ex post facto explanation by some for the success of campaigns that reduced knowledge gaps (Viswanath et al., 1991).

j. In general, whether it is an open-ended or closed-ended measure of knowledge does not appear to matter.

k. For local affairs knowledge only.

l. Viswanath and his colleagues reported the effects of campaigns on knowledge gaps in three community pairs over time and, in general, reported that gaps closed initially on most issues, whereas they widened on certain other issues.

To summarize, the research clarifies that knowledge gaps are less likely to be found on issues defined as important to communities whether communities are defined geographically or by some other nongeographic common characteristic (see Table 5.1). On community ties and knowledge gaps, Pearson (1993) found that length of residence and political activity were related to knowledge among rural Alaskans, whereas organizational membership was related to knowledge among urban Alaskans. Local political activity was related to knowledge in all three samples: rural Alaskans, urban Alaskans, and Anchorage residents. Although Viswanath, Kosicki, et al. (1993) did not find support for the proposition that community ties are related to knowledge gaps, they note that community boundedness of the issue, which is related to community orientation, may provide a basis for understanding differences on certain issues. The relationship between community ties and orientation to media use is, of course, well documented in the literature (Stamm, 1985; Stamm & Fortini-Campbell, 1983; Stamm & Weiss, 1983; Viswanath, Finnegan, Rooney, & Potter, 1990).

DEPTH OF KNOWLEDGE

Knowledge gaps frequently differ based on type of knowledge measured. SES-based gaps are usually observed when knowledge is measured as more than simple familiarity with an issue. Research suggests that gaps rarely narrow due to increased publicity. However, research also suggests that serious SES-based differences are less likely to be found when knowledge is defined simply, for instance as awareness of an event or program (Galloway, 1977; Viswanath et al., 1994).

Evidence from many studies points to gaps based on education and interest for in-depth knowledge, that is, respondents' deeper understanding of an event's relationships, causes, or larger context. The study by Genova and

Greenberg (1979) on knowledge of the National Football League strike and the charges against President Richard Nixon and Gaziano's (1984) study of in-depth knowledge of crime, housing, economic development, and schools report both education-based and interest-based gaps. Sustained media attention because of information campaigns or an event's inherently high news value has been found to lead to narrowing gaps, but wider education-based differences in depth knowledge have also been observed (Snyder, 1990; Spitzer & Denzin, 1965; Viswanath et al., 1994). Some studies have also reported larger education-based gaps on more complex topics, including taxation policies, nuclear power plant user fees, and health insurance, whereas smaller gaps were apparent on less complex issues, such as "broad-based taxes" and an airline disaster (Moore, 1987; Price & Zaller, 1993).

Knowledge complexity thus appears to influence SES-based gaps. Although increasing conflict and salience may equalize general knowledge of an issue or topic, gaps appear to continue or even to widen for in-depth issue knowledge. The research suggests some reasons for this. Higher formal education provides a "trained capacity" to follow certain issues, to relate these to other similar events and causes, and to comprehend their significance. In addition, members of higher-SES groups are more likely to have extensive contact networks and access to information through organizational memberships and other sources (Gaziano, 1984; Hyman, Wright, & Reed, 1975; Price & Zaller, 1993), which may reinforce their interest and knowledge (Donohue et al., 1975). They are thus in a better position to supplement mass media information with organizational and interpersonal sources to gain more in-depth understanding of issues. In short, the advantage of the "information rich" would seem to derive from greater resources, both personal (as a function of the capacity-building effect of education) and external (as a function of greater access to information sources).

THE ROLE OF PUBLICITY

The role of publicity is a key concept in knowledge gap research. A widely shared proposition is that increased publicity, and the consequent information repetition, is sufficient stimulus for people to develop knowledge and to use it purposively. A central issue, therefore, is whether planned efforts such as campaigns are capable of equalizing the distribution of information throughout populations. Some propose that traditional knowledge gaps may abate if publicity or campaigns are intense enough or long enough (Moore, 1987).

The evidence supporting this proposition is mixed (see Table 5.1). Lending support to the proposition, heart disease prevention campaigns have reduced education-based knowledge gaps and resulted in respondents' learning about a heart health program (Ettema et al., 1983; Viswanath et al., 1994). Earlier studies also found that concentrated media attention tended to equalize knowledge of a news event (Greenberg, 1964; Spitzer & Denzin, 1965). A study of a campaign that encouraged participation in a program aimed at changes in diet and cancer prevention found that initial SES-based gaps narrowed modestly over time (Chew & Palmer, 1994). Paradoxically, declines in media publicity may also sometimes be associated with reductions in knowledge gaps (Donohue et al., 1975; Griffin, 1990).

In contrast, the literature is also replete with studies that echo early evidence that media publicity often has few such effects on knowledge (Moore, 1987). Some studies from the perspectives of innovation diffusion, social interventions, and campaign research have shown limited effects (Cook et al., 1975; Hornik, 1988; Mosteller & Moynihan, 1972; Nazzaro, 1989; Rogers, 1976, 1983; Snyder, 1990; Star & Hughes, 1950; Viswanath, Finnegan, & Kahn, 1993).

To help clarify these mixed results, a couple of tentative generalizations may be drawn from these and other studies. First, media publicity, when accompanied by increased salience, is usually at least partially successful in equalizing knowledge levels. Salience often increases due to conflict or controversy surrounding an issue, especially involving struggles over power of some kind. This kind of increased salience may activate interpersonal and community group contacts to intensify discussion of an issue.

Second, media publicity may also at least partially contribute to equalizing knowledge on topics that are generally accepted as important national issues and are therefore covered continuously by the media. These issues have enjoyed long, widespread acceptance as meriting public attention even though they may pose conditions of little immediate conflict or struggle to communities or to the nation as a whole. Some broad health issues, such as heart disease and cancer prevention, appear to fall into this category (Viswanath, Finnegan, Hannan, & Luepker, 1991). These issues attract attention initially from social elites, including scientists, policy makers, and other opinion leaders. For example, although there were SES-based knowledge differences on the health effects of smoking beginning with the U.S. surgeon general's report in 1964, decades of increased research, activism, policy making, and media coverage have resulted in broad awareness of the issue (Donohue et al., 1990). Although this has not in itself eliminated class-based behavioral differences (members of lower-SES groups are more likely to smoke today than are members of higher-SES groups), differences in knowledge and behavior have narrowed substantially over 30 years. The implication for the knowledge gap hypothesis is that when issues transform from particular to general and communal interest, the tendency is for SES-based knowledge gaps to decrease (see Hilgartner & Bosk, 1988).

These generalizations add a couple of refinements to our understanding of knowledge gaps. First, the transformation of issues in their acceptance by the population as of constant and general import may occur over long periods. Therefore, the equalization of knowledge among SES groups may often be a long-term rather than a short-term phenomenon. Second, knowledge is not static. New knowledge is created and disseminated perpetually, especially through science, and SES-based knowledge gaps will continue to be observed even on issues long accepted as important.

CHANNEL INFLUENCE AND KNOWLEDGE GAPS

Research has also suggested that media reliance or dependence and the characteristics of individual media and other communication channels can affect knowledge gaps. Evidence about channel influence has emphasized mainly the role of print media, the comparative effectiveness of print and broadcast media, and the potential of television as a knowledge equalizer (see Table 5.1).

Some have argued that print mass media (newspapers, magazines, books) can significantly increase knowledge gaps. Reasons include their middle-class orientation (Robinson, 1972; Tichenor et al., 1970) and the fact that higher-SES groups are more dependent on them, whereas lower-SES groups depend more on television (Bogart, 1981; Robinson, 1972; Tichenor et al., 1970). Further, print media permit much more in-depth coverage than do electronic media, and those who depend on print spend more time with print media than do others (Kleinnijenhuis, 1991). Support for the association between knowledge and print media exposure comes from many studies (Gandy & El Waylly, 1985; Gaziano, 1984; Griffin, 1990; Kleinnijenhuis, 1991; McLeod & Perse, 1994; Mulugetta, 1986; Pan, 1990; Price & Zaller, 1993; Robinson, 1972; Simmons & Garda, 1982). Gaziano (1984) found that education-based knowledge gaps were greater among newspaper nonreaders than among readers.

In contrast, some studies have focused on the role of television in reducing knowledge gaps. Two issues are important in this research. First, does television reduce gaps? Second, if so, are the effects the same for simple and in-depth information (Miyo, 1983; Mulugetta, 1986)? Neuman (1976) offers several reasons television may bridge knowledge gaps. First, television viewing—unlike other media use—is not well correlated with education. Second, members of lower-SES groups tend to prefer to get their news from television rather than from other sources. Third, the motivations people have for viewing television are different from their motivations for using other media. Fourth, the nature of viewing television is analogic rather than random access. That is, television viewers are less able than other media users to be selective about viewing some news stories and not others.[3]

In a study of story recall of network news, Neuman (1976) found no significant education-based differences either in content or story type recall. The only difference he found was related to interest in news. Those seeking to stay informed recalled more stories than did casual viewers. However, this study was limited by some important omissions. It did not analyze knowledge of specific subjects, whether respondents supplemented their television viewing with other sources, or differences between those who watched and those who did not. This last point is key, because people who did not view network news on the day of the interview were excluded from the sample. However, this study still makes an insightful point: When television viewing occurs, education-based gaps are less likely. Other studies in the United States and in developing nations have supported this finding (Brantgarde, 1983; Chew & Palmer, 1994; Galloway, 1977; Gantz, 1978; Kleinnijenhuis, 1991; Miller & MacKeun, 1979; Miyo, 1983; Sharp, 1984; Shinghi & Mody, 1976; Tomita, 1989; Torsvik, 1972).[4]

In contrast, some studies have found television use to be negatively related to knowledge (Gandy & El Waylly, 1985; Griffin, 1990; Gunter, 1987; Horstmann, 1991; McLeod & Perse, 1994; Simmons & Garda, 1982). Gandy and El Waylly (1985) report that African Americans in their study reported watching more TV yet scored lower on knowledge. One study from India reports mixed results: Although television viewing was associated with narrowing gaps in a "backward" village, it was associated with larger gaps in a "progressive" village (Shinghi, Kaur, & Rai, 1982).

Studies that have compared newspaper use with television use usually have shown that print is more strongly associated with both simple and in-depth knowledge (Clarke & Fredin, 1978; Lang & Lang, 1984; McLeod & Perse, 1994; Price & Zaller, 1993; Simmons & Garda, 1982). In an election study, less educated people who preferred newspapers appeared to gain more than did more highly educated respondents (Mulugetta, 1986). The caveat here is that education level is generally associated with newspaper reading. The few studies that have not found an association between education and local newspaper use have reported that metro or regional newspaper use is associated with education (Donohue, Tichenor, & Olien, 1986). This implies that gaps may open on certain issues between "cosmopolites" who read regional papers and those who do not (Merton, 1968).

The more common finding in the literature, however, is that although television has the potential to increase knowledge among lower-SES groups, its record as an information provider has been poor because it has emphasized entertainment rather than learning (Gunter, 1987; Robinson & Levy, 1986), especially compared with other media (see also Becker & Whitney, 1980; Clarke & Fredin, 1978; and Kennamer, 1983, and Robinson, 1976, both cited in Robinson & Levy, 1986).

Research has also suggested the importance of interpersonal discussion in affecting knowledge gaps, although its precise impact is unclear despite calls for research in this area (Chaffee, 1972). The general proposition is that interpersonal discussion may be activated as a function of increased issue salience caused by social conflict and/or heavy media publicity. The result is that information about the issue will diffuse more rapidly among all social groups, helping to equalize knowledge. Interpersonal discussion thus plays a role in propelling, if not accelerating, this process through reinforcement of media-generated information (Childers, 1975; Donohue et al., 1975; Hornik, 1989). It appears that media exposure supplemented by interpersonal discussion is highly effective in equalizing knowledge in both developed and developing nations (Galloway, 1977; Genova & Greenberg, 1979; Griffin, 1990; Horstmann, 1991; Price & Zaller, 1993; Robinson & Levy, 1986; Roy, Waisanen, & Rogers, 1969). Participation in organizations (Brantgarde, 1983; Gaziano, 1984) and other community attachments (Finnegan et al., 1990) are also perhaps associated with increased knowledge. Considerable evidence from research on the diffusion of innovations also points to the importance of interpersonal communication (Rogers, 1983).

The evidence about interpersonal communication thus far suggests the need for more systematic study. Two directions offer promising avenues for refining the hypothesis. First, how are knowledge gaps affected by interpersonal communication between similar and dissimilar audiences? Second, does the role played by interpersonal communication differ between heterogeneous and homogeneous communities? A recent study provides some initial groundwork to address these questions. Melwani, Viswanath, Becker, and Kosicki (1994) argue that weaker social ties in heterogeneous communities may be advantageous because they allow interaction among people with "diverse interests and knowledge enabling learning on specialized topics." This is the idea of the strength of "weak ties" (Granovetter, 1973). On the other hand, closer ties and homogeneity of interests in less pluralistic systems could be disadvantageous to learning new information.[5] If investigators find empirical evidence for these ideas, it will certainly help to refine major axioms of the knowledge gap hypothesis.

In summary, findings on channel influence and the knowledge gap are inconclusive and suggest needed areas of study. It is possible that when exposure is equal, information gains are comparable (Robinson, 1972). But exposure itself is usually related to other factors, including SES and arousal as a function of social conflict or organized activity. More important, however, are reasons for use of specific media in the first place. If media use is purposive and equal across social groups, knowledge differences are much less evident (Chaffee, Ward, & Tipton, 1970; see also Pearson, 1993). However, there are differences in media attention, use, and information processing, especially in the case of print media. Loges and Ball-Rokeach (1993) found that in their sample, the affluent and the less affluent read newspapers for different reasons. Subjects in the higher-income group were more likely to read newspapers for status-related reasons, such as "staying on top of the community," making voting decisions, and understanding community events. Similarly, Griffin (1990) found that more educated respondents were more likely to pay attention to print media public affairs content and that the relationship between newspaper use and knowledge was significant for the more educated but not for the less educated. Kleinnijenhuis's (1991) study in the Netherlands also indicates that newspaper exposure is more advantageous to those with more formal education.

This suggests that gaps in knowledge are likely as the result of differences in media attention, processing, and dependency relations between the lower- and higher-SES groups (Gunter, 1987; Robinson & Levy, 1986). SES will likely remain a dominant factor in knowledge gaps unless some major structural adjustments improve media access for the less educated (Donohue et al., 1987). Some have argued that new technologies such as cable television, videotext, and computers could alleviate gaps (Compaine, 1986; Parker & Dunn, 1972), but this is questionable, because higher-SES groups are more likely to adopt and to benefit from such innovations (Berg, 1984; Ettema, 1984; Finnegan, Viswanath, & Loken, 1988; Rogers, 1976; Scherer, 1989; Tomita, 1989).

THE KNOWLEDGE GAP AS A MULTILEVEL PHENOMENON

Mass communication research, like many other social and behavioral sciences, has experienced a continuing debate about the levels at which phenomena should be measured (Berger & Chaffee, 1987; Huber, 1991; Paisley, 1984; Pan & McLeod, 1991). This is certainly true of the knowledge gap hypothesis. The original hypothesis was proposed as a social structural phenomenon (Donohue et al., 1975; Olien et al., 1983; Tichenor et al., 1970; Tichenor, Donohue, & Olien, 1973; Tichenor, Rodenkirchen, Olien, & Donohue, 1973), though some of the reasons given for gaps were social psychological. As research expanded, however, individual-level explanations such as motivation and information functionality have been offered (Ettema & Kline, 1977; Gaziano & Gaziano, 1994; Tichenor et al., 1970). The measurement of gaps at both levels sometimes leads to a lack of explanatory clarity, but the debate over which level is better is less fruitful and often less informative. The social structural and individual-difference approaches examine the gap phenomenon at distinctly different levels of reality. The emphasis ought to be on finding distinctive links between the two levels (Alexander, Giesen, Munch, & Smelser, 1987; Pan & McLeod, 1991). In this sense, the knowledge gap offers a chance for the development of such a multilevel perspective and the identification and illumination of "cross-level linkages" (Pan & McLeod, 1991).

Individual-Level Explanations

Ettema and his colleagues (Ettema & Kline, 1977; Ettema et al., 1983) have proposed an alternative hypothesis, suggesting that motivational and situational variables may be more important than SES:

As infusion of mass media information into a social system increases, segments of the population motivated to acquire that information and/or for which the information is functional tend to acquire the information at a faster rate than those not motivated or for which it is not functional, so that the gap in knowledge between these segments tends to increase rather than decrease. (Ettema & Kline, 1977, p. 188)

The assumption behind this argument is that the effect of SES can be overridden by individual-level factors (Clarke & Kline, 1974, Dervin, 1980; Robinson, 1972; Sears & Freedman, 1967). A number of such variables have been studied, including interest (Genova & Greenberg, 1979; Horstmann, 1991; Neuman, 1976; Pan, 1990), importance and threat (Ettema et al., 1983), involvement (Salmon, 1985), concern and salience (Chew & Palmer, 1994; Ettema et al., 1983; Nazzaro, 1989; Zandpour & Fellow, 1992), cognitive schemata (i.e., "packets" of facts and beliefs; Fredin et al., 1994), and individual participation (Horstmann, 1991; Lovrich & Pierce, 1984). Each has been found to be associated with knowledge, and some more strongly than SES and its surrogate, education (see Table 5.1).

However, other studies have raised doubts about the strength of such factors of individual difference in overriding SES as a knowledge gap determinant (Gandy & El Waylly, 1985; Gaziano, 1984; Griffin, 1990; McLeod & Perse, 1994; Price & Zaller, 1993; Rucinski & Ryu, 1991; Simmons & Garda, 1982; Snyder, 1990; Viswanath, 1990; Yows et al., 1991), even gender and age (Butler, 1990). Lovrich and Pierce (1984) found that motivational variables were stronger predictors of knowledge than SES, but that education was a stronger predictor of "problem articulation" (a measure of information-processing skills) than were motivational variables. Income was also a predictor, although participation in the issue was a stronger predictor of familiarity with technical terms. Only in self-assessed knowledge were motivation variables (use and participation) significant predictors compared with SES variables. Recent research has compared knowledge between groups more and less motivated and found education-based gaps in both groups, although the size of the gap was smaller in the motivated group (Viswanath, Kahn, Finnegan, Hertog, & Potter, 1993).

Several generalizations emerge from this work. First, a number of individual motivational factors are surely related to knowledge and may occasionally mitigate the impact of SES and its surrogate, education. Second, it is conceivable that motivational factors themselves could gain strength as a result of gains in knowledge. This suggests that the causal link between knowledge and motivation is not so clear in the research that directionality may be assumed. It may require reassessment (Horstmann, 1991). A third issue has to do with who is more motivated to acquire information and why they are motivated. Some studies have noted that motivation to acquire information is itself associated with greater education (Viswanath, Kahn, et al., 1993), although there have also been contrary findings (Chew & Palmer, 1994).[6] In any case, the suggestion is that motivation to acquire information may itself have an underlying social structural cause. For example, community leaders and people deeply involved in their communities may be motivated to acquire information on a broad variety of subjects that have little individual concern or immediate personal interest attached (Price & Zaller, 1993; Viswanath, 1988). Keeping up with national and international news may be perceived by these individuals as critical for their performance of their elite roles. The diversity of interests held by those with more formal education and their ability to capitalize on their prior knowledge are well documented (McLeod & Perse, 1994; Price & Zaller, 1993). That is, a structural factor such as SES (education) could account for greater attention, interest, motivation, and knowledge (Fredin et al., 1994).

Structural Explanations

The knowledge gap hypothesis was originally formulated in the context of the sociology of development and has therefore focused on the important role of the social environments of communities in mediating communication effects. Thus, factors playing a crucial role in knowledge gaps include social conflict, community social structure, and information control, such as mobilization functions exercised by campaign planners, policy makers, and other advocates and actors.

Community Structure and Environment

Complex and pluralistic community environments affect knowledge gaps through their structural diversity, specialized expertise, and multiple sources of power (Aiken & Mott, 1970; Tichenor et al., 1980; Vidich & Bensman, 1958; Vidich, Bensman, & Stein, 1964; Warren, 1973, 1978; Williams, Herman, Liebman, & Dye, 1965). Because of these factors, decisions affecting the community are necessarily discussed more broadly in the public arena, of which the news media constitute a key gatekeeper. In pluralistic communities there is competition among groups and other actors for power and influence, and thus the likelihood of overt conflict is greater than in more homogeneous communities (Coleman, 1957).

In such a heterogeneous system, members rely on the mass media and other secondary communication channels to keep track of various groups' actions and other relevant information. Mass media may be further supplemented by other formal and informal information sources. Exposure patterns are selective and may vary by interests. Because of the relatively specialized environment, much information about specific issues may appeal only narrowly to those segments with well-defined interests who have access to it and who already may have some information about it.

In relatively small, homogeneous communities, the primary mode of communication is interpersonal. Single individuals may fulfill multiple power and leadership roles. One leader in such a setting may be simultaneously a member of the city council, an officer of a local club, and a member of the planning board. Power is therefore relatively narrowly distributed, and decisions are likely to be made by fewer individuals than in heterogeneous communities, and often with less public scrutiny (Vidich & Bensman, 1958). News media (especially newspapers) may be accountable to the local power base, which often includes the local editor or publisher (Edelstein & Schulz, 1963). News media are more likely to avoid reporting conflict than they would be in larger communities, and therefore are more likely to reflect the consensus style of small towns (Tichenor et al., 1980). Because of the informal nature of the information environment and interpersonal interaction, it is possible that some kinds of information may flow faster and perhaps more equally to all social groups than in other environments.

A majority of studies using this perspective have found that knowledge gaps were greater in large, heterogeneous communities compared with smaller, homogeneous communities (see discussion by Gaziano, 1988; Tichenor et al., 1980) (Table 5.1). Gandy and El Waylly (1985), for instance, found education-based knowledge gaps based in a study of a foreign affairs issue in Washington, D.C. As a corollary to these findings, gaps were not found as a result of a heart disease prevention campaign in a small, homogeneous community (Ettema et al., 1983). Other campaign studies in homogeneous communities in India have reported no gaps or narrowing gaps (Galloway, 1977; Shinghi & Mody, 1976), and, in the case of a study in the United States, even reverse gaps have been found, in which less educated groups learned more than their more educated counterparts (Douglas et al., 1970).

Nevertheless, some recent studies have identified conditions under which this proposition may not hold. Expected SES-based gaps in heart disease prevention knowledge did not appear in more complex compared to less complex communities. There has also been the suggestion that temporarily appearing SES-based gaps may have closed more rapidly in pluralistic communities, in contrast to the findings reviewed above (Viswanath et al., 1994; Viswanath, Finnegan, & Kahn, 1993). And in a study of one community, the magnitude of expected SES-based gaps actually decreased over 16 years as the community became more pluralistic (Melwani et al., 1994).

There are several possible ways to account for these rare but contrasting findings about pluralism and its effects on knowledge. First, specialization may actually work to the advantage of information flow on certain topics. That is, urban communities are likely to have more diverse channels, and specialized information on such topics as science and health may be more readily available. In fact, Finnegan et al. (1993) studied exposure to sources of information on heart disease prevention in different community types and concluded that respondents in the most complex community reported exposure to a greater number as well as a greater variety of sources, compared with less complex communities (though this exposure difference narrowed over 10 years). Pearson (1990, 1993), in a study comparing rural and urban

Alaskan media environments, found larger gaps in rural areas. This suggests the limiting effect of media-poor environments on "information redundancy," that is, the repetition of the same information in multiple media channels. McDivitt (1985) and Hornik (1989) also found that knowledge gaps narrowed in a prodevelopment community in Gambia, Africa.

Second, an analysis of metropolitan daily newspaper circulation "pullback" in Minnesota by Donohue et al. (1986) showed decreasing penetration of metro dailies in nonmetropolitan areas, increasing association between education and metro daily reading in regional cities, and an association between metro daily reading and education in rural areas. These changes, the authors warn, may potentially increase knowledge gaps between metropolitan communities and regional and outlying areas, because metro daily news coverage is more comprehensive. In further analyses, Tichenor, Olien, and Donohue (1987) confirmed that metro daily newspaper use in small towns is also related to education, suggesting further potential of widening knowledge gaps. Among readers of a metro paper, however, the usual association between knowledge and education disappeared (Horstmann, 1991). These three studies suggest important limitations on the capacity of rural communities to compensate for a lack of channels, including specialized ones prevalent in urban areas (Donohue et al., 1986; Pearson, 1990; Tichenor et al., 1987).

Third, the potential for conflict is greater in heterogeneous communities compared with homogeneous communities (as discussed further below) (Donohue, Olien, & Tichenor, 1985).

The foregoing discussion raises some important theoretical and policy issues about the knowledge gap hypothesis. It appears that when information is of a specialized nature, pluralistic communities may have an advantage due to the information-rich diverse environment. Under such conditions, knowledge gaps may be more likely in less pluralistic communities (Abrahamsson, 1982). If information is of a more general, less specialized nature, smaller, homogeneous communities may have the advantage and experience fewer knowledge gaps due to structural considerations. The problem, however, is an increasing sense among researchers and policy makers that full participation in public decision making involves access to specialized information sources, thus, rural communities are at a decided disadvantage. It is these differences in access to information channels between rural and urban areas and their consequences that warrant further study.

Social Conflict and Mobilization

Conflict is a crucial process influencing social change. As Coser (1956, 1967) has argued, conflict may be both functional and dysfunctional in a social system. Conflict within a social system may increase concern and salience and thus increase media coverage on specific conflictual issues. Donohue et al. (1975) argue that community tensions "stimulate communicative activity," including the flow of information via interpersonal channels. As discussed earlier, research has suggested an inverse relationship between the level of community conflict over an issue and SES-based knowledge gaps. Because overt conflict is more likely in more pluralistic communities, the potential for narrowing gaps may be higher in such communities. The association between decreased knowledge gaps and conflict has been supported in some studies in the United States and India (Donohue et al., 1975; Frazier, 1986; Galloway, 1977; Genova & Greenberg, 1979), although Frazier (1986) also reports gaps in inaccurate knowledge. However, in at least one study education-based knowledge differentials were evident despite increased social conflict (Lovrich & Pierce, 1984).

Social conflict, however, is often accompanied by and sometimes propelled by community groups, organizations, and institutions that seek to mobilize their members and the general public to affect public issues. This activity may take the form of efforts to redress a perceived injustice or to take purposive action to ameliorate a social problem. Such activity also has the potential to equalize knowledge across population subgroups (Viswanath, 1990).

Mobilized community groups may help further propel information diffusion to population subgroups, because they are dependable and early sources of information and provide opportunities for informal discussion. Such a tendency toward equalization has been confirmed in some studies in the United States and abroad (Brantgarde, 1983; Galloway, 1977; Gaziano, 1984).

Like social conflict, mobilization may also be dysfunctional to communities. Organizations may stratify their activities between more and less influential members and constituencies. Because less educated groups are less likely to be active, organizations may contribute to knowledge inequities between active and less active members (Galloway, 1977; Gaziano, 1984; Lovrich & Pierce, 1984). Gaziano (1984) found, for example, that even on issues involving high levels of visible organizational action, better-educated readers of a neighborhood newspaper learned more about the issues than did readers with less education.

Information Control

Lazarsfeld and Merton (1948/1960) identify three conditions under which mass media may be effective in influencing social change: monopolization, canalization, and supplementation. *Monopolization* is the extent to which one can control information about a topic or issue in a communication channel with a dominant message. *Canalization* refers to the use of mass media to promote and direct preexisting attitudes and behavior patterns. *Source supplementation* refers to interpersonal interaction as an addition to mass media exposure.

Research suggests that effective social change campaigns have succeeded in narrowing or eliminating knowledge gaps because they have been able to achieve some level of monopolization and supplementation (e.g., following media campaigns with face-to-face interaction and community mobilization). However, an important question is whether guided social change through research and demonstration projects may achieve such results in highly pluralistic communities in which resources may be insufficient to achieve the level of control necessary. The evidence here is thin but suggests a positive direction. For example, demonstration projects such as the "green revolution" in developing countries have had qualified success. This has likely been due to interventions mounted at multiple social levels over a sustained period and with consensus that a particular issue is a national priority. This may provide a plausible explanation why some directed social change programs in developing and developed countries have not experienced SES-based knowledge differences (Ettema et al., 1983; Galloway, 1977; Olien et al., 1983; Shinghi et al., 1982; Shinghi & Mody, 1976).

In summary, the degree of control over information exercised by communicators over the message environment appears to be an important variable affecting knowledge gaps.[7]

Levels of Analysis: A Summary

The foregoing review of individual- and structural-level explanations for the knowledge gap suggests that variables at each level interact to affect knowledge outcomes. Less is understood about their precise relationship, however. The knowledge gap hypothesis offers a fruitful avenue for linking these levels of analysis (Pan & McLeod, 1991). The problem is to identify relationships that link levels of analysis—the so-called situational and trans-situational variables. Studies drawing these links do succeed in improving our understanding of the role of individual-level variables under varying structural conditions (Gaziano, 1984; Viswanath et al., 1991; Viswanath, Kahn, et al., 1993). Such studies can also identify and explicate the mediating factors between structure and knowledge (Fredin et al., 1994).[8]

The implications of these different levels of explanation applied to social change are profound. The unintended consequence of explaining gaps due to a lack of motivation shifts the focus from social structure to individuals, perhaps unintentionally engaging in "victim blaming." This kind of interpretation is unlikely to encourage powerful community groups to consider systemic adjustments to reduce inequities. Nevertheless, the debate over individual difference and social structure as the source of knowledge gaps has been productive in advancing development of the hypothesis.

CONCEPTUAL AND METHODOLOGICAL CONSIDERATIONS

The conceptual meaning of the knowledge gap has varied somewhat in the literature. As originally conceptualized, the knowledge gap was the difference in knowledge between members of higher and lower SES, with education often used as an SES indicator. Many studies and textbooks have used the term in this sense but have been careful to elaborate on the empirical evidence (Severin & Tankard, 1992; Tan, 1985). Other terms have also been used: "information gaps" (Brantgarde, 1983; Compaine, 1986; Nowak, 1977), "communication gaps" (Dervin, 1980), information or communication "inequities" (Dervin, 1980, 1989), "information redistribution" (McNelly, 1973), "information differentials" (Tan, 1985), and "information holding" (Clarke & Kline, 1974). Rogers (1976, 1983) has proposed the terms "communication effects gap" and "socioeconomic benefits gap" to indicate whether innovations have increased gaps in socioeconomic status and/or knowledge of information (Galloway, 1977; Shinghi & Mody, 1976).

One group of researchers has sought to widen the concept to include political participation—"equivalence in informed political participation," with knowledge equivalence as one part of participation (McLeod, Bybee, & Durall, 1981). Others have studied "influence gaps" as the ability of higher-SES groups to influence decision making (Brantgarde, 1983; Severin & Tankard, 1992). Although knowledge gap research has conventionally emphasized SES differences as the distinguishing effect, some critiques have sought to distinguish "education-based" from "interest-based" gaps, that is, gaps due to differences in education and gaps due to differences in motivation or interest (Chew & Palmer, 1994; Ettema et al., 1983; Viswanath, Kahn, et al., 1993). Others have used sociodemographic rather than SES comparisons per se. These have included differences between the young and the old (McLeod et al., 1981), men compared with women (Finnegan et al., 1988), and those more and less involved in their communities (Viswanath, Kosicki, et al., 1993).

We next turn to some important methodology issues, including ceiling effects, operational measures, and study design.

Ceiling Effects

Ettema and Kline (1977) have offered ceiling effects as a possible explanation for narrowing knowledge gaps among SES groups. The idea of a ceiling effect is that knowledge diffuses rapidly among higher-SES groups but completes its diffusion at an asymptote signifying that most members of the group know the information—little further diffusion can therefore take place. Because lower-SES groups experience slower information diffusion, they will be in a position of perpetually "catching up" to higher-SES groups, where diffusion has plateaued. The ceiling effect thus may lead to a conclusion that knowledge gaps narrow over time between groups. This has often been shown to be the case with less complex information (Galloway, 1977; Greenberg, 1964; Spitzer & Denzin, 1965; Viswanath et al., 1994), but other studies have shown that gaps remain on more complex knowledge measures (Moore, 1987).

Ceiling effects, however, raise some important conceptual issues. The assumption here is that once higher-SES groups learn a particular bit of information, they do not continue to learn it, and lower-SES groups eventually "catch up." This idea of catching up has a corollary version widely shared in the literature: the "trickle-down effect." That is, information, like innovations, technology, and wealth, is often expected to trickle down to lower-SES groups (Compaine, 1986).[9]

This assumption that knowledge on specific issues will remain stationary among higher-SES groups while lower-SES groups catch up is questionable for three reasons. First, there is evidence that although simple familiarity may increase over time with publicity, gaps in complex information may endure (Moore, 1987; Viswanath et al., 1994). For example, although knowledge about the link between smoking and lung disease is widespread, other ill effects of smoking are not as well known (Donohue et al., 1990; U.S. Department of Health and Human Services, 1989). This suggests that ceiling effects may be a measurement artifact of the kind of knowledge studied.

Second, knowledge and information are seldom stationary. New information born of science, politics, health, and other fields is discovered and reported every day. Learning new information—particularly specialized information—often requires some prior knowledge base from which to interpret and convert it to some use. Higher-SES group members are more likely to possess prior knowledge in a variety of areas and are therefore more likely to acquire new information than are lower-SES group members (Price & Zaller, 1993; Scherer, 1989). This has serious determinist implications, as proposed recently by Donohue et al. (1990). That is, gaps may close in certain knowledge domains, but they will continue and even expand in other domains. As Tichenor et al. (1970) argue, media have limited resources, suggesting the possibility that although some information is widely distributed, most other information may not be, and gaps may continue.

Third, as Price and Zaller (1993) report, those who know more will continue to know more. Prior knowledge in many cases is the strongest predictor of subsequent knowledge. Ceiling effects, however, merit further study; perhaps they can be best approached through longitudinal research designs.

Operational Measures of Knowledge

Clarke and Kline (1974) assert that operationalizing knowledge through structured, closed-ended items may disadvantage lower-SES respondents. They argue that such measures reflect researchers' biases about what information people ought to know, irrespective of the information's relevance or utility to respondents. They propose that a "respondent-centered and open-ended" measure would tap information holding by including the dimension of salience or value to respondents. An open-ended measure, Clarke and Kline argue, should give respondents a chance to articulate knowledge in their own terms and to elaborate on topics of personal concern.[10]

However, use of open-ended knowledge measures has not demonstrated that SES-based gaps disappear (Benton & Frazier, 1976; Clarke & Kline, 1974; Donohue et al., 1975; Edelstein, 1973; Finnegan et al., 1990; Gandy & El Waylly, 1985; Gaziano, 1984; Lovrich & Pierce, 1984; Viswanath, 1990), although gaps have been reported to be lower in magnitude (Gaziano, 1983). Other studies in the United States and India that have used closed-ended measures have found significant associations between knowledge and education or knowledge and interest (Chew & Palmer, 1994; Ettema et al., 1983; Galloway, 1977; Genova & Greenberg, 1979). Thus, the operationalizing of knowledge through open or closed approaches does not seem to affect gaps as much as other variables, but it is possible that their magnitude is somewhat reduced (see Table 5.1).

Two studies evaluating the open-ended approach are germane here. Finnegan, Viswanath, Hannan, Weisbrod, and Jacobs (1989) found that message discrimination (an open-ended measure of information holding) did not necessarily work to the advantage of less educated respondents. Their data showed that younger respondents with more formal education were likely to discriminate more messages than were less educated, older respondents. McLeod, Pan, Rucinski, and Kosicki (1988) found knowledge differentials in both open-ended and closed-ended measures. They also reported that open and closed items did not necessarily measure the same dimensions of knowledge, suggesting one cannot substitute for the other.

Study Design as a Factor

The knowledge gap hypothesis would seem to require longitudinal study designs, but substantial evidence for the hypothesis has been developed from cross-sectional studies (Donohue et al., 1975; Finnegan et al., 1988, 1990; Gandy & El Waylly, 1985; Tichenor et al., 1980). Reviews by Gaziano (1983) as well as our own work indicate mixed findings in both types of designs. Some longitudinal studies in both developing and developed countries have shown declining gaps (Bailey, 1971; Chew & Palmer, 1994; Donohue et al., 1975; Douglas et al., 1970; Ettema et al., 1983; Galloway, 1977; Gaziano, 1983, 1984; Genova & Greenberg, 1979; Griffin, 1990; Miyo, 1983; Viswanath, Finnegan, & Kahn, 1993), whereas others have shown no change (Abbott, 1978; Bogart, 1957-1958; Horstmann, 1991; Shinghi & Mody, 1976; Star & Hughes, 1950) or increasing gaps (Cook et al., 1975; Moore, 1987; Pan, 1990; Price & Zaller, 1993; Snyder, 1990; Viswanath, Finnegan, & Kahn, 1993).

Longitudinal studies suggest considerable promise for helping us to understand the role of contingent conditions affecting gaps. More such studies will provide useful information on long-term trends as well as changes in knowledge over time as a result of changes in community conditions.

THE FUTURE OF KNOWLEDGE GAP RESEARCH: TENTATIVE DIRECTIONS

In light of the values underlying knowledge gap research and its extensive development as a research program, what is our current understanding of the hypothesis? Optimistic scenarios lead to the conclusion that knowledge gaps are not inevitable or intractable, but may be bridged with careful planning and structural adjustments. On the other hand, the potential for gaps is an ever-present danger in future guided social change efforts and in efforts to influence social problems using media publicity. There are at least three areas that could prove fruitful for future research: the role of community structure, the role of interpersonal communication, and media dependency and orientations.

The Role of Community Structure

Although early studies led to the conclusion that knowledge gaps are most likely to be found in relatively pluralistic systems, recent evidence suggests that this proposition may be wrong. Phenomena that deserve further study in this connection include the continued development in cities of diverse media channels; the reduction of information and channel availability in rural areas, and the consequent marginalization of rural residents as participants in the flow of information; the increasing complexity of information surrounding public policy and decision making, and how rural communities compensate in light of their having less access to information; and finally, how these changes may affect community conflict.

The Role of Interpersonal Communication

Despite calls for research into the role of interpersonal communication, few studies have examined its role explicitly in studying knowledge gaps. The literature suggests at least two avenues of research. First, what role does interpersonal communication between similar and dissimilar groups play in knowledge gaps? Second, does the role of interpersonal communication vary by community structure? Answers to both questions could also help to build linkages between structural- and individual-level explanations for the knowledge gap.

Media Dependency, Orientations, and Knowledge Gaps

Many studies have examined the roles that different media play in knowledge gaps. Some have argued that gaps are likely because of the middle- and upper-class orientation of print media. Others have suggested that television could be a knowledge leveler. Studies suggest that audiences' reasons for media use vary, and that these have a differential impact on knowledge acquisition. More research on variable media attention, processing, and dependency relationships could add considerably to our understanding of the knowledge gap. In fact, studies in this area could provide fruitful connections with studies in the uses and gratifications and media dependency traditions.

IDEOLOGICAL CONSIDERATIONS:
WHAT DO GAPS MEAN?

As we suggested at the outset of this chapter, the knowledge gap hypothesis arises out of a particular understanding of the role of information and control in social systems (Donohue, Tichenor, & Olien, 1973). As such, knowledge gap research is driven by values and insights related to power and its growth and distribution in society. For example, in a seminal 1949 article, Moore and Tumin identified the consequences of ignorance (the "counterpoint of knowledge") for different SES groups. They examined the consequences of the increasing division of labor and suggested that differential access to knowledge tends to perpetuate the power of the privileged few. Ignorance among lower-SES groups tends to hide preferential treatment and to mask unjust reward structures in a social system. This is particularly relevant to public policy making, in which higher-SES groups often take advantage of their superior access to knowledge. Moore and Tumin also suggest that a class system is open only to the extent that the capacity to move up the social ladder is based on equal access to knowledge. SES-based knowledge differentials constrain the social mobility of lower-SES groups. The idea that knowledge is an essential element of citizens' full participation in a republican democracy and mobility into higher social classes has long been a concern of U.S. society (Watkinson, 1990), and knowledge gap research continues this tradition.

We next turn to a discussion of the evolution of the hypothesis and how it relates to other hypotheses in media studies.

Ideological Critique of the Knowledge Gap

Some scholars have raised paradigmatic and ideological considerations about knowledge gap research (e.g., Dervin, 1980; Friemuth, 1989). Dervin (1980), for example, has used the knowledge gap to critique logical positivism and the "source-receiver" communication model. She reaches the following conclusions:

- Knowledge gap research, like other "traditional" models of communication, adopts the source-receiver model, where a source is "seen" to be sending a message to the audience and then evaluating whether the audience received the message or not.
- The idea of the knowledge gap was introduced as an explanation of "why limited effects were available" at a time when researchers were disenchanted with the concepts of the "obstinate audience" and "limited media effects."

- One of the challenges to the knowledge gap hypothesis comes from the literature that points to the social system as the problem, rather than the individual.

- The knowledge gap approach, along with diffusion of innovations research, "blames the victims"—that is, the audience—for a lack of media-generated outcomes, especially through campaigns.

The bases of Dervin's criticisms are in part ideological and in part theoretical. First, although there are some commonalities, there are also crucial differences among the assumptions of the limited effects and diffusion of innovations models and knowledge gap research. Second, the differences in implications derived from these different assumptions are masked and unfairly group the knowledge gap approach with diffusion of innovations research in Dervin's critique. Third, her view that proponents of the knowledge gap "hang on" to the hypothesis in the face of contradictory evidence is certainly arguable if one looks at the knowledge gap as a coherent scientific research program from a philosophy of science point of view (Lakatos, 1968).

It is important to put knowledge gap research in perspective while addressing this critique. We will do this by looking at the intellectual roots of the knowledge gap and of the so-called traditional model of communication, and by addressing whether the knowledge gap is really a "scientific research program" (Lakatos, 1968, 1970).

THE KNOWLEDGE GAP AND LIMITED EFFECTS

Dervin's critique of the knowledge gap places the hypothesis in the same category as the "limited effects" model of mass communication research. We argue that the differences between these approaches outweigh their similarities. Much of the limited effects model evolved from two sets of studies: political communication research by the Columbia group, including Lazarsfeld and his colleagues (Katz & Lazarsfeld, 1955; Lazarsfeld, Berelson, & Gaudet, 1944; Lazarsfeld & Stanton, 1941, 1944, 1949), and attitude change studies by the Yale group represented in the work of Hovland and his colleagues (Hovland, 1954; Hovland, Janis, & Kelley, 1953; Hovland & Rosenberg, 1960; Sherif & Hovland, 1960). Neither group, nor researchers such as Klapper (1960), suggested that media have limited effects; rather, they argued that media effects are "limited" by certain contingent conditions.[11] This is a careful assessment by careful researchers. However, for a variety of reasons this careful interpretation has often been overinterpreted by researchers and policy makers who assumed that these early communication researchers were urging that the mass media be viewed as of negligible power and influence. Recent reevaluations of their work have raised four points. First, media effects were actually larger in their studies than stated in their published work (Becker, McCombs, & McLeod, 1975; Chaffee & Hocheimer, 1985; Delia, 1987; Gitlin, 1978). Second, media effects may be even more pronounced if research were to emphasize cognitive rather than affective changes resulting from media exposure (Becker et al., 1975; Clarke & Kline, 1974; Noelle-Neumann, 1993; Roberts & Bachen, 1985). Third, media effects are not uniform, but vary for different population subgroups (Tichenor et al., 1970). Fourth, new media technologies have emerged since the completion of this early work.[12]

Unlike the limited effects model, knowledge gap studies have dealt with the impact of mass media on cognitive rather than affective variables. Additionally, unlike the Columbia studies, knowledge gap research has hypothesized differential impacts on population subgroups.

Another major difference is that the limited effects model implied a trickle-down impact of mass media through which there could be eventual equalization of benefits. Knowledge gap research, however, posits the potential of enduring gaps between information "haves" and "have-nots."

Similarly, the intellectual assumptions of knowledge gap research, although sharing some commonalities, also differ from the assumptions of diffusion of innovations research. The latter is largely informed by the "modernization" paradigm, in which communication has been viewed as the "magic multiplier" of modern qualities among "traditionals." Modernization scholars have assumed that if the people of a nation develop certain psychological attributes, such as "empathy" or "psychological mobility," there could be an aggregate movement toward development. As Portes (1976) and Lee (1980) have pointed out, this research is flawed in the sense that it has applied a uniquely European experience to nation making, development, and social change in the developing world. It has also been criticized for using the social psychological variables of empathy, need achievement, fatalism, and modernity, among others, to explain macrosocial transformations. Both have their roots in the classical functionalism of Parsons and others.

In contrast, knowledge gap research draws its intellectual inspiration from functional conflict theories that raise the issue of resource and power inequities in social systems (Coser, 1956, 1967; Dahrendorf, 1959). This brings us to Dervin's (1980) point about "blaming the victim."[13] Dervin argues that the knowledge gap approach passes moral judgment on individuals for not knowing about a topic. We argue that because of the concern with resource and power inequities, the knowledge gap actually focuses on social structure and its constraints rather than on individuals. In fact, this was one of the first approaches in mass communication research to draw attention to structural and institutional factors regarding mass media effects. For many scholars from the developing world, the knowledge gap approach has offered a useful framework for addressing the weaknesses of the diffusion research paradigm by providing an explanatory framework for campaign effects.

Dervin's final point—that knowledge gap researchers "hang on" to the hypothesis despite contradictory evidence—can be addressed only from a philosophy of science point of view.

IS THE KNOWLEDGE GAP HYPOTHESIS
A PROGRAM OF RESEARCH?

Sir Karl Popper, in his work *The Logic of Scientific Discovery* (1968) and his other writings (e.g., Popper, 1970), argues that scientific enterprise is essentially "critical," consisting of "bold conjectures, controlled by criticism," where the theory is logically deduced. To Popper, scientific enterprise is the systematic testing of theories and statements to solve problems. Experiments and observation attempt to validate prior theories and hypotheses. The failure to validate is the failure of the theory itself. Therefore, for Popper, a theory is acceptable only when it can specify in advance the conditions under which it could be falsified.

In a debate with Popper, Kuhn (1970) has argued that Popper's description of scientific enterprise as a systematic testing of theories is not an accurate description of most scientific enterprise. In fact, according to Kuhn, it applies only to "extraordinary science"—it usually occurs in moments of crisis. In contrast, Kuhn focuses on the psychology of science and on individual scientists, rather than on science itself.[14]

Kuhn (1970) argues that scientists are interested in solving puzzles. For Kuhn, falsification is not enough, nor should it be the criterion for scientific progress. He asserts that it is not always possible to identify in advance all the conditions under which a theory could be rejected. Kuhn argues that science can move forward only on the basis of knowledge existing at the moment. As Tichenor and McLeod (1989) suggest, investigators seek partial explanations and provide only partial knowledge. According to Kuhn, scientists accept a new theory only when it solves all numerical puzzles that have been treated by the predecessor theory, and this occurs only during periods of "extraordinary science." Kuhn's point is that scientists work under one dominant set of assumptions, "a paradigm." Popper posits that Kuhn's description of scientific progress from normal science under one dominant framework interrupted by periods of revolution may not fit all types of science. Both Popper (1970) and Watkins (1970) take exception to Kuhn's suggestion and argue that any given time there can be more than one dominant theoretical framework. Popper's (1970) preferred term is "research program"—"a mode of explanation which is considered so satisfactory by some scientists that they demand its general acceptance" (p. 55).

In comparison with Popper and Kuhn, Lakatos (1970) has proposed an even bolder approach to understanding the scientific enterprise. Lakatos agrees with Popper that "descriptive units of science are not isolated hypotheses but a coherent program of research." [15] Such a program is characterized by a solid theoretical core with a "vast protective belt of auxiliary hypotheses," unexplained anomalies, and unsolved problems. Differing from Popper, Lakatos offers a "sophisticated methodological falsificationist" approach outlining a set of rules of acceptance and demarcation of science from pseudoscience and progressive science from degenerative science.

Lakatos (1970) suggests that a sophisticated falsificationist view would look at a series of theories (a research program) and not at one hypothesis. Such a series can be falsified only when a new theory can "corroborate excess empirical content over the previous theories." This occurs in the form of discovery of novel facts that the "rival" theory could not predict or might even "forbid" prediction. The newer theory should also be able to explain all of the success of the older theory, as well as whatever the older theory could not explain.

In this view, science is not a series of "refutations and conjectures," which is more suited to Kuhn's description of paradigmatic crisis, but is a program of research leading to the discovery of new facts, explanations of anomalies, and improvements on previous theory. Only when we have a better one can the original theory be "falsified." Lakatos terms this a "progressive problem-shift." For a sophisticated falsificationist, then, a proliferation of theories is vital and essential. A sophisticated falsificationist is also a theoretical pluralist.

The evolution of knowledge gap research can be evaluated in such sophisticated falsificationist terms. The original hypothesis (Tichenor et al., 1970) was an improvement over previous explanations and comes close to meeting the Lakatosian criteria in these aspects:

- It explains the lack of "success" of information campaigns in social systems. Previous theorists argued that certain population segments were unreachable through any public communication efforts. In contrast, knowledge gap research explains that a lack of success in information campaigns occurs as the result of structural limitations rather than individual faults, and that such campaigns often have the unintended consequence of widening gaps between SES groups.
- The knowledge gap hypothesis predicts the impact of information flow on knowledge equalization. Based on its structural understanding, it predicts in advance the consequences of information flow into social systems: Effects are differential, with some segments gaining more than others.
- Over time, as a result of continuing research and inconsistent results, the knowledge gap hypothesis has been refined and has identified the conditions under which gaps may or may not occur. That is, the hypothesis meets the Popperian and Lakatosian criteria that require the conditions under which hypothesis could be falsified. However, according to the sophisticated falsificationist approach, offering refinements and alternative hypotheses does not necessarily refute the original knowledge gap hypothesis (if we accept the Lakatosian criteria instead of "naive" falsificationism), but evolves into a series of hypotheses identifying conditions and limitations of the original.

Thus, in Lakatosian terms, this continuity "welds" knowledge gap work into a "methodology of research programs" instead of "pseudoscientific" explanations. The hallmark of any such program, then, is a contribution to the understanding and explanation of society, which ought to be the basis of any social action.

NOTES

1. These numbers include only those studies, critiques, and dissertations in which the explicit focus is the knowledge gap hypothesis or knowledge gap and other communication hypotheses. The numbers would be much higher if we were to include all the studies that have constituted implicit tests of the knowledge gap hypothesis. It is possible that we might have missed some conference papers and some other publications, despite our best efforts to secure all of them.

2. Although the "gap" phenomenon has engaged the attention of many scholars since the 1970 publication, not all use the term *knowledge gap* or cite the original article by Tichenor et al. (1970).

3. Neuman's article was written before the advent of large cable television systems and widespread diffusion of VCRs. Both technologies may facilitate greater viewing selectivity through "channel surfing" and "time shifting."

4. Sharp (1984) presents only indirect evidence for the knowledge gap hypothesis, as her measure of knowledge is the respondent's ability to name an "important problem in the community."

5. This could also apply to different SES groups. As Childers (1975) argues, the "poor" are often locked into an "information ghetto" that cuts them off from the information flow in the larger society.

6. Chew and Palmer (1994) evaluated the impact of a television program on nutrition and compared the roles played by interest and education in affecting knowledge gaps. The difference between education-based and interest-based knowledge gaps, however, were too small to generalize and in any case measurements were difficult because viewers were invited to watch the program.

7. A clear question for future research concerns how to operationalize and measure "degree of control."

8. Fredin et al. (1994) used a somewhat different measure of knowledge: a summary of respondents' opinions on issues, approval or disapproval of local officials, and suggestions to resolve the problem under discussion. These authors argue that even though these are not strictly knowledge items, answering them required "some basis in knowledge."

9. This was accepted in some early political communication studies by the Columbia group in their formulation of the "two-step" flow hypothesis (Katz & Lazarsfeld, 1955).

10. Of course, even an open-ended knowledge measure may impose an artificial ceiling if the number of responses to be recorded is limited. Given an opportunity, more educated respondents are likely to give more responses to open-ended questions. However, researchers usually decide to record no more than a certain number (Finnegan et al., 1989).

11. This is a subtle but important difference and was their response to the widely held idea of powerful mass media. They did not say that media effects do not occur, but rather that effects were not all-encompassing, as many believed. It is also important to note that what they saw as "limited effects"—that is, "mere reinforcement"—were in fact quite powerful insofar as media supported the status quo (Gitlin, 1978).

12. TV was in its early stages of growth, and social control through media was not yet a major factor in the research perspectives of the 1940s through the 1960s when the "limited effects" model emerged. As Galbraith (1983) implies, "conditioning power," before the advent of major changes in media technologies, was perhaps more strongly exercised by other institutions: the church, family, and school.

13. This phrase was first used by Ryan (1971), who examined the social conditions of African Americans.

14. See also Watkins (1970) on this point.

15. See the version of Lakatos's Open University lecture published in 1968 and his 1970 article, which was part of the continuing debate with Popper and Kuhn and was published as part of a collection of papers from a conference on Kuhn.

REFERENCES

Abbott, E. A. (1978, August). *Effects of year-long newspaper energy series on reader knowledge and action.* Paper presented at the annual meeting of the Association for Education in Journalism and Mass Communication, Seattle.

Abrahamsson, K. (1982). Knowledge gaps, bureaucracy, and citizen participation: Towards alternative communication models. *Communication, 7,* 75-102.

Aiken, M., & Mott, P. E. (Eds.). (1970). *The structure of community power.* New York: Random House.

Alexander, J. C., Giesen, B., Munch, R., & Smelser, N. J. (Eds.). (1987). *The micro-macro link.* Berkeley: University of California Press.

Bailey, G. A. (1971). The public, the media, and the knowledge gap. *Journal of Environmental Education, 2*(4), 3-8.

Ball, S., & Bogatz, G. A. (1970). *The first year of Sesame Street: An evaluation.* Princeton, NJ: Educational Testing Service.

Becker, L. B., McCombs, M. E., & McLeod, J. M. (1975). The development of political cognitions. In S. H. Chaffee (Ed.), *Political communication* (pp. 21-63). Beverly Hills, CA: Sage.

Becker, L. B., & Whitney, D. C. (1980). Effects of media dependencies. *Communication Research, 7,* 95-120.

Benton, M., & Frazier, P. J. (1976). The agenda setting function of the mass media at three levels of "information holding." *Communication Research, 3,* 261-274.

Berg, L. C. (1984). *Use of an extension computer decision-aid program by home vegetable gardeners.* Unpublished doctoral dissertation, University of Wisconsin—Madison.

Berger, C. R., & Chaffee, S. H. (1987). The study of communication as a science. In C. R. Berger & S. H. Chaffee (Eds.), *Handbook of communication science* (pp. 15-19). Newbury Park, CA: Sage.

Bogart, L. (1957-1958). Measuring the effectiveness of an overseas information campaign: A case history. *Public Opinion Quarterly, 21,* 475-498.

Bogart, L. (1981). *Press and the public: Who reads what, when, where, and why in American newspapers.* Hillsdale, NJ: Lawrence Erlbaum.

Brantgarde, L. (1983). The information gap and municipal politics in Sweden. *Communication Research, 10,* 357-373.

Butler, N. C. (1990). *An investigation of direct-to-consumer prescription drug advertising in terms of the knowledge gap hypothesis.* Unpublished doctoral dissertation, University of Minnesota, Minneapolis.

Chaffee, S. H. (1972). The interpersonal context of mass communication. In F. G. Kline & P. J. Tichenor (Eds.), *Current perspectives in mass communication research* (pp. 95-120). Beverly Hills, CA: Sage.

Chaffee, S. H., & Hocheimer, J. (1985). The beginnings of political communication research in the United States: Origins of the limited effects model. In E. M. Rogers & F. Balle (Eds.), *The media revolution in America and Western Europe* (pp. 259-296). Norwood, NJ: Ablex.

Chaffee, S. H., Ward, S., & Tipton, L. (1970). Mass communication and political socialization in the 1968 campaign. *Journalism Quarterly, 47,* 647-659.

Chew, F., & Palmer, S. (1994). Interest, the knowledge gap, and television programming. *Journal of Broadcasting and Electronic Media, 38,* 271-287.

Childers, T., with Post, J. A. (1975). *The information poor in America.* Metuchen, NJ: Scarecrow.

Clarke, P., & Fredin, E. (1978). Newspapers, television, and political reasoning. *Public Opinion Quarterly, 42,* 143-160.

Clarke, P., & Kline, F. G. (1974). Media effects reconsidered: Some new strategies for communication research. *Communication Research, 1,* 224-240.

Coleman, J. S. (1957). *Community conflict.* New York: Macmillan.

Coleman, J. S., Campbell, E. Q., Hobson, C. J., McPartland, J., Mood, A. M., Weinfeld, F. D., & York, R. L. (1966). *Equality of educational opportunity* (Vols. 1-2). Washington, DC: U.S. Department of Health, Education and Welfare, Office of Education.

Compaine, B. M. (1986). Information gaps: Myth or reality. *Telecommunications Policy, 10,* 5-12.

Cook, T. D., Appleton, H., Conner, R. F., Shaffer, A., Tamkin, G. A., & Weber, S. J. (1975). *Sesame Street revisited.* New York: Russell Sage.

Coser, L. A. (1956). *Functions of social conflict.* New York: Free Press.

Coser, L. A. (1967). *Continuities in the study of social conflict.* New York: Free Press.

Dahrendorf, R. (1959). *Class and conflict in industrial society.* Stanford, CA: Stanford University Press.

DeFleur, M. (1987). The growth and decline of research on the diffusion of the news, 1945-85. *Communication Research, 14,* 109-130.

Delia, J. N. (1987). Communication research: A history. C. R. Berger & S. H. Chaffee (Eds.), *Handbook of communication science* (pp. 20-98). Newbury Park, CA: Sage.

Delli-Carpini, M. X., Keeter, S., & Kennamer, J. D. (1994). Effects of the news media environment on citizen knowledge of state politics and government. *Journalism Quarterly, 71,* 443-456.

Dervin, B. (1980). Communication gaps and inequities: Moving toward a re-conceptualization. In B. Dervin & M. J. Voigt (Eds.), *Progress in communication sciences* (Vol. 2, pp. 73-112). Norwood, NJ: Ablex.

Dervin, B. (1989). Users as research inventions: How research categories perpetuate inequities. *Journal of Communication, 39,* 216-232.

Donohue, G. A., Olien, C. N., & Tichenor, P. J. (1985). Reporting conflict by pluralism, newspaper type and ownership. *Journalism Quarterly, 62,* 489-499, 507.

Donohue, G. A., Olien, C. N., & Tichenor, P. J. (1987). Media access and knowledge gaps. *Critical Studies in Mass Communication, 4,* 87-92.

Donohue, G. A., Olien, C. N., & Tichenor, P. J. (1990, May). *Knowledge gaps and smoking behavior.* Paper presented at the annual meeting of the American Association for Public Opinion Research, Lancaster, PA.

Donohue, G. A., Tichenor, P. J., & Olien, C. N. (1973). Mass media functions, knowledge and social control. *Journalism Quarterly, 50,* 652-659.

Donohue, G. A., Tichenor, P. J., & Olien, C. N. (1975). Mass media and the knowledge gap: A hypothesis reconsidered. *Communication Research, 2,* 3-23.

Donohue, G. A., Tichenor, P. J., & Olien, C. N. (1986). Metro daily pull-back and knowledge gaps within and between communities. *Communication Research, 13,* 453-471.

Douglas, C. W., & Stacey, D. C. (1972). Demographic characteristics and social factors related to public opinion on fluoridation. *Journal of Public Health Dentistry, 32,* 128-134.

Douglas, D. F., Westley, B. W., & Chaffee, S. H. (1970). An information campaign that changed community attitudes. *Journalism Quarterly, 47,* 479-487, 492.

Edelstein, A. S. (1973). Decision-making and mass communication: A conceptual and methodological approach to public opinion. In P. Clarke (Ed.), *New models for mass communication research* (pp. 81-118). Beverly Hills, CA: Sage.

Edelstein, A. S., & Schulz, J. B. (1963). The weekly newspaper's leadership role as seen by community leaders. *Journalism Quarterly, 40,* 565-574.

Erskine, H. G. (1963). The polls: Exposure to domestic information. *Public Opinion Quarterly, 27,* 491-500.

Ettema, J. S. (1984). Three phases in the creation of information inequities: An empirical assessment of a prototype videotex system. *Journal of Broadcasting, 28,* 383-395.

Ettema, J. S., Brown, J., & Luepker, R. V. (1983). Knowledge gap effects in a health information campaign. *Public Opinion Quarterly, 47,* 516-527.

Ettema, J. S., & Kline, F. G. (1977). Deficits, differences, and ceilings: Contingent conditions for understanding the knowledge gap. *Communication Research, 4,* 179-202.

Fathi, A. (1973). Diffusion of a "happy" news event. *Journalism Quarterly, 50,* 271-277.

Finnegan, J. R., Viswanath, K., Hannan, P. J., Weisbrod, R., & Jacobs, D. (1989). Message discrimination: A study of its use in a campaign research project. *Communication Research, 16,* 770-792.

Finnegan, J. R., Viswanath, K., Kahn, E., & Hannan, P. (1993). Exposure to the sources of heart disease prevention information: Community type and social group differences. *Journalism Quarterly, 70,* 569-584.

Finnegan, J. R., Viswanath, K., & Loken, B. (1988). Predictors of cardiovascular health knowledge among suburban cable TV subscribers and non-subscribers. *Health Education Research: Theory & Practice, 3,* 141-151.

Finnegan, J. R., Viswanath, K., Rooney, B., McGovern, P., Baxter, J., Elmer, P., Graves, K., Hertog, J., Mullis, R., Pirie, P., Trenkner, L., & Potter, J. (1990). Predictors of healthy eating in a rural midwestern U.S. city. *Health Education Research: Theory & Practice, 5,* 421-431.

Frazier, P. J. (1986). *Community conflict and the structure and social distribution of opinion.* Unpublished doctoral dissertation, University of Minnesota, Minneapolis.

Fredin, E., Monnett, T. H., Kosicki, G. M. (1994). Knowledge gaps, social locators, and media schemata: Gaps, reverse gaps, and gaps of disaffection. *Journalism Quarterly, 71,* 176-190.

Friemuth, V. S. (1989). The chronically uninformed: Closing the knowledge gap in health. In E. B. Ray & L. Donohew (Eds.), *Communication and health: Systems and applications* (pp. 171-186). Hillsdale, NJ: Lawrence Erlbaum.

Fry, D. L. (1979, August). *The knowledge gap hypothesis and media dependence: An initial study.* Paper presented at the annual meeting of the Association for Education in Journalism and Mass Communication, Houston.

Galbraith, J. K. (1983). *The anatomy of power.* Boston: Houghton Mifflin.

Galloway, J. J. (1977). The analysis and significance of communication effects gaps. *Communication Research, 4,* 363-386.

Gallup Omnibus. (1977). *A survey concerning water fluoridation.* Princeton, NJ: Gallup Organization.

Gandy, O., Jr., & El Waylly, M. (1985). The knowledge gap and foreign affairs: The Palestinian-Israeli conflict. *Journalism Quarterly, 62,* 777-783.

Gantz, W. (1978). How uses and gratifications affect recall of television news. *Journalism Quarterly, 55,* 664-672, 681.

Gaziano, C. (1983). Knowledge gap: An analytical review of media effects. *Communication Research, 10,* 447-486.

Gaziano, C. (1984). Neighborhood newspapers, citizen groups and public affairs knowledge gaps. *Journalism Quarterly, 16,* 556-566, 599.

Gaziano, C. (1988). Community knowledge gaps. *Critical Studies in Mass Communication, 5,* 351-357.

Gaziano, E., & Gaziano, C. (1994, November). *Collective volunteerism and public affairs knowledge: A typology for knowledge gap theory development.* Paper presented at the annual meeting of the Midwest Association for Public Opinion Research, Chicago.

Genova, B. K. L., & Greenberg, B. S. (1979). Interests in news and the knowledge gap. *Public Opinion Quarterly, 43,* 79-91.

Gitlin, T. (1978). Media sociology: The dominant paradigm. *Theory and Society, 6,* 205-253.

Granovetter, M. (1973). The strength of weak ties. *American Journal of Sociology, 78,* 1360-1380.

Greenberg, B. S. (1964). Diffusion of the Kennedy assassination. *Public Opinion Quarterly, 28,* 225-232.

Griffin, R. (1990). Energy in the eighties: Education, communication and the knowledge gap. *Journalism Quarterly, 67,* 554-566.

Gunaratne, S. A. (1976). *Modernization and knowledge: A study of four Ceylonese villages.* Singapore: Asian Mass Communication Research and Information Center.

Gunter, B. (1987). *Poor reception: Misunderstanding and forgetting broadcast news*. Hillsdale, NJ: Lawrence Erlbaum.

Hilgartner, S., & Bosk, C. L. (1988). The rise and fall of social problems: A public arenas model. *American Journal of Sociology, 94,* 53-77.

Hornik, R. C. (1988). *Development communication*. New York: Longman.

Hornik, R. C. (1989). The knowledge-behavior gap. In C. T. Salmon (Ed.), *Information campaigns: Balancing social values with social change* (pp. 113-138). Newbury Park, CA: Sage.

Horowitz, A. M. (1992). *Gaps in knowledge among women about gynecologic and colorectal cancer screening procedures*. Unpublished doctoral dissertation, University of Maryland, College Park.

Horstmann, R. (1991). Knowledge gaps revisited: Secondary analyses from Germany. *European Journal of Communication, 6,* 77-93.

Hovland, C. I. (1954). The effects of the mass media on communication. In G. Lindzey (Ed.), *Handbook of social psychology* (Vol. 2). Reading, MA: Addison-Wesley.

Hovland, C. I., Janis, I. L., & Kelley, H. H. (1953). *Communication and persuasion*. New Haven, CT: Yale University Press.

Hovland, C. I., & Rosenberg, M. J. (Eds.). (1960). *Attitude organization and change*. New Haven, CT: Yale University Press.

Huber, J. (Ed.). (1991). *Macro-micro links in sociology*. Newbury Park, CA: Sage.

Hyman, H. H., & Sheatsley, P. B. (1947). Some reasons why information campaigns fail. *Public Opinion Quarterly, 11,* 412-423.

Hyman, H. H., Wright, C. R., & Reed, J. S. (1975). *The enduring effects of education*. Chicago: University of Chicago Press.

Kanervo, E. W. (1979, August). *How people acquire information: A model for public affairs information attainment process*. Paper presented at the annual meeting of the Association for Education in Journalism and Mass Communication, Houston.

Katz, E., & Lazarsfeld, P. F. (1955). *Personal influence*. New York: Free Press.

Katzman, N. (1974). The impact of communication technology: Promises and prospects. *Journal of Communication, 24*(4), 47-58.

Kennamer, D. J. (1983, May). *A comparison of media use measures: The relationship of four measures of media use to economic knowledge and discussion*. Paper presented at the annual meeting of the American Association for Public Opinion Research, Buck Hill Falls, PA.

Klapper, J. T. (1960). *The effects of mass communication*. New York: Free Press.

Kleinnijenhuis, J. (1991). Newspaper complexity and the knowledge gap. *European Journal of Communication, 6,* 499-522.

Kuhn, T. S. (1970). Logic of discovery or psychology of research. In I. Lakatos & A. Musgrave (Eds.), *Criticism and the growth of knowledge* (pp. 1-23). Cambridge: Cambridge University Press.

Lakatos, I. (1968). Criticism and the methodology of scientific research programmes. *Proceedings of the Aristotelian Society, 69,* 149-186.

Lakatos, I. (1970). Falsification and the methodology of scientific research programmes. In I. Lakatos & A. Musgrave (Eds.), *Criticism and the growth of knowledge* (pp. 91-196). Cambridge: Cambridge University Press.

Lang, G. E., & Lang, K. (1984). *Politics and television revisited*. Beverly Hills, CA: Sage.

Lazarsfeld, P. F., Berelson, B., & Gaudet, H. (1944). *The people's choice*. New York: Duell, Sloan, & Pearce.

Lazarsfeld, P. F., & Merton, R. K. (1960). Mass communication, popular taste and organized social action. In W. L. Schramm (Ed.), *Mass communications* (pp. 492-512). Urbana: University of Illinois Press. (Original work published 1948)

Lazarsfeld, P. F., & Stanton, F. N. (Eds.). (1941). *Radio research, 1941*. New York: Duell, Sloan, & Pearce.

Lazarsfeld, P. F., & Stanton, F. N. (Eds.). (1944). *Radio research, 1942-43*. New York: Duell, Sloan, & Pearce.

Lazarsfeld, P. F., & Stanton, F. N. (Eds.). (1949). *Communications research, 1948-49*. New York: Harper & Row.

Lee, C. C. (1980). *Media imperialism reconsidered*. Beverly Hills, CA: Sage.

Loges, W. E., & Ball-Rokeach, S. J. (1993). Dependency relations and newspaper readership. *Journalism Quarterly, 70*, 602-614.

Lovrich, N. P., Jr., & Pierce, J. C. (1984). Knowledge gap phenomena: Effects of situation-specific and trans-situational factors. *Communication Research, 11*, 415-434.

McDivitt, J. A. (1985). *Constraints to knowledge gain and behavior change in response to a multi-media health education project in the Gambia, West Africa*. Unpublished doctoral dissertation, University of Pennsylvania.

McLeod, J. M., Bybee, C. R., & Durall, J. A. (1981). Equivalence of informed political participation: The 1976 debates as a source of influence. In G. C. Wilhoit & H. de Bock (Eds.), *Mass communication review yearbook 2* (pp. 469-493). Beverly Hills, CA: Sage.

McLeod, J. M., Pan, Z., Rucinski, D. M., & Kosicki, G. (1988, November). *Using open-ended questions to measure audience cognitive structures in a survey setting*. Paper presented at the annual meeting of the Midwest Association of Public Opinion Research, Chicago.

McLeod, D. M., & Perse, E. M. (1994). Direct and indirect effects of socioeconomic status on public affairs knowledge. *Journalism Quarterly, 71*, 433-442.

McNelly, J. T. (1973). Mass media and information redistribution. *Environmental Education, 5*, 31-64.

McNelly, J. T., & Molina, J. R. (1972). Communication, stratification and international affairs information in a developing urban society. *Journalism Quarterly, 49*, 316-326, 339.

McNelly, J. T., Rush, R. R., & Bishop M. E. (1968). Cosmopolitan media usage in the diffusion of international news. *Journalism Quarterly, 45*, 329-332.

Melwani, G., Viswanath, K., Becker, L. B., & Kosicki, G. M. (1994, November). *Community complexity and knowledge gaps: A longitudinal study of one community*. Paper presented at the annual meeting of the Midwest Association for Public Opinion Research, Chicago.

Merton, R. K. (1968). *Social theory and social structure*. New York: Free Press.

Miller, A. H., & MacKeun, M. (1979). Learning about the candidates: The 1976 presidential debates. *Public Opinion Quarterly, 43*, 326-346.

Miyo, Y. (1983). The knowledge gap hypothesis and media dependency. In R. N. Bostrom (Ed.), *Communication yearbook 7* (pp. 626-650). Beverly Hills, CA: Sage.

Moore, D. W. (1987). Political campaigns and the knowledge gap hypothesis. *Public Opinion Quarterly, 51*, 186-200.

Moore, W. E., & Tumin, M. M. (1949). Some social functions of ignorance. *American Sociological Review, 14*, 787-795.

Mosteller, F., & Moynihan, D. P. (1972). *On equality of educational opportunity*. New York: Random House.

Mulugetta, Y. M. (1986). *Knowledge gap hypothesis and media preference*. Unpublished doctoral dissertation, University of Wisconsin—Madison.

Nazzaro, A. (1989). *The knowledge gap hypothesis and salience in the context of health maintenance organizations and the elderly (information campaigns)*. Unpublished doctoral dissertation, University of Pennsylvania.

Neuman, R. (1976). Patterns of recall among television news viewers. *Public Opinion Quarterly, 40*, 115-123.

Noelle-Neumann, E. (1993). *The spiral of silence—public opinion: Our social skin* (2nd ed.). Chicago: University of Chicago Press.

Nowak, K. (1977). From information gaps to communication potential. In M. Berg, P. Hemanus, J. Ekecrantz, F. Mortensen, & P. Sepstrup (Eds.), *Current theories in Scandinavian communication research* (pp. 231-258). Grenaa, Denmark: GMT.

Olien, C. N., Donohue, G. A., & Tichenor, P. J. (1983). Structure, communication, and social power: Evolution of the knowledge gap hypothesis. In E. Wartella & D. C. Whitney (Eds.), *Mass communication review yearbook 4* (pp. 455-462). Beverly Hills, CA: Sage.

Paisley, W. (1984). Communication in the communication sciences. In B. Dervin & M. Voigt (Eds.), *Progress in communication sciences* (Vol. 5, pp. 1-43). Norwood, NJ: Ablex.

Palmgreen, P. (1979). Mass media use and political knowledge. *Journalism Monographs, 61.*

Pan, Z. (1990). *Inequalities in knowledge acquisition from mass media: Cross generational changes and maintenance.* Unpublished doctoral dissertation, University of Wisconsin—Madison.

Pan, Z., & McLeod, J. M. (1991). Multilevel analysis in mass communication research. *Communication Research, 18,* 140-173.

Parker, E. B., & Dunn, D. A. (1972). Information technology: Its social potential. *Science, 176,* 1392-1398.

Pearson, L. L. (1990). *Media-rich, media-poor: Knowledge gaps and communication policy in Alaska (media deprivation).* Unpublished doctoral dissertation, University of Minnesota, Minneapolis.

Pearson, L. L. (1993). Desert Storm and Tundra Telegraph: Information diffusion in a media poor environment. In B. S. Greenberg & W. Gantz (Eds.), *Desert Storm and the mass media* (pp. 182-196). Cresskill, NJ: Hampton.

Popper, K. R. (1968). *The logic of scientific discovery.* London: Hutchinson.

Popper, K. R. (1970). Normal science and its dangers. In I. Lakatos & A. Musgrave (Eds.), *Criticism and the growth of knowledge* (pp. 51-58). Cambridge: Cambridge University Press.

Portes, A. (1976). On the sociology of national development: Theories and issues. *American Journal of Sociology, 82,* 55-85.

Price, V., & Zaller J. (1993). Who gets the news? Alternative measures of news perceptions and their implications for research. *Public Opinion Quarterly, 57,* 133-164.

Roberts, D. F., & Bachen, C. (1985). Mass communication effects. In D. C. Whitney & E. Wartella (Eds.), *Mass communication review yearbook 6* (pp. 29-78). Beverly Hills, CA: Sage.

Robinson, J. P. (1967). World affairs information and mass media exposure. *Journalism Quarterly, 44,* 23-31.

Robinson, J. P. (1972). Mass communication and information diffusion. In F. G. Kline & P. J. Tichenor (Eds.), *Current perspectives in mass communication research* (pp. 71-93). Beverly Hills, CA: Sage.

Robinson, J. P., & Levy, M. R. (1986). *The main source: Learning from television news.* Beverly Hills, CA: Sage.

Robinson, M. (1976). Public affairs television and the growth of political malaise: The case of "The selling of the Pentagon." *American Political Science Review, 70,* 409-432.

Rogers, E. M. (1976). Communication and national development: The passing of the dominant paradigm. *Communication Research, 3,* 213-240.

Rogers, E. M. (1983). *Diffusion of innovations* (3rd ed.). New York: Free Press.

Roling, N. G., Ascroft, J., & Wa Chege, F. (1976). The diffusion of innovations and the issue of equity in rural development. *Communication Research, 3,* 155-170.

Roy, P., Waisanen, F. B., & Rogers, E. M. (1969). *The impact of communication on rural development.* Paris: UNESCO and the National Institute of Community Development.

Rucinski, D., & Ryu, C. (1991, May). *Social comparisons and the knowledge gap.* Paper presented at the annual meeting of the International Communication Association, Chicago.

Ryan, W. (1971). *Blaming the victim.* New York: Pantheon.

Salmon, C. T. (1985). *The role of involvement in health information acquisition and processing.* Unpublished doctoral dissertation, University of Minnesota, Minneapolis.

Scherer, C. W. (1989). The videocassette recorder and the information inequity. *Journal of Communication, 39*(3), 94-109.

Sears, D., & Freedman, J. (1967). Selective exposure to information: A critical review. *Public Opinion Quarterly, 31,* 194-213.

Severin, W. J., & Tankard, J. W. (1992). *Communication theories: Origins, methods, and uses in the mass media.* New York: Longman.

Sharp, E. B. (1984). Consequences of local government under the klieg lights. *Communication Research, 11,* 497-517.

Sherif, M., & Hovland, C. I. (1960). *Social judgement.* New Haven, CT: Yale University Press.

Shinghi, P., Kaur, G., & Rai, R. P. (1982). *Television and knowledge gap hypothesis.* Ahmedabad: Indian Institute of Management.

Shinghi, P., & Mody, B. (1976). The communication effects gap: A field experiment on television and agricultural ignorance in India. *Communication Research, 3,* 171-190.

Simmons, R. E., & Garda, E. C. (1982). Dogmatism and the "knowledge gap" among Brazilian mass media users. *Gazette, 30,* 121-133.

Snyder, L. B. (1990). Channel effectiveness over time and knowledge and behavior gaps. *Journalism Quarterly, 67,* 875-886.

Spitzer, S. P., & Denzin, N. K. (1965). Levels of knowledge in an emergent crisis. *Social Forces, 44,* 234-237.

Stamm, K. (1985). *Newspaper use and community ties: Towards a dynamic theory.* Norwood, NJ: Ablex.

Stamm, K., & Fortini-Campbell, L. (1983). The relationship of community ties to newspaper use. *Journalism Monographs, 84.*

Stamm, K., & Weiss, R. (1983, August). *Newspaper subscribing and community integration: Separating facts from artifacts.* Paper presented at the annual meeting of the Association for Education in Journalism and Mass Communication, Corvallis, OR.

Star, S. A., & Hughes, H. M. (1950). Report on an educational campaign: The Cincinnati Plan for the United Nations. *American Journal of Sociology, 55,* 389-400.

Tan, A. (1985). *Mass communication theories and research.* New York: John Wiley.

Tichenor, P. J., Donohue, G. A., & Olien, C. N. (1970). Mass media flow and differential growth in knowledge. *Public Opinion Quarterly, 34,* 159-170.

Tichenor, P. J., Donohue, G. A., & Olien, C. N. (1973). Mass communication research: Evolution of a structural model. *Journalism Quarterly, 50,* 419-425.

Tichenor, P. J., Donohue, G. A., & Olien, C. N. (1980). *Community conflict and the press.* Beverly Hills, CA: Sage.

Tichenor, P. J., & McLeod, D. M. (1989). The logic of social and behavioral science. In G. H. Stempel & B. H. Westley (Eds.), *Research methods in mass communication* (pp. 10-29). Englewood Cliffs, NJ: Prentice Hall.

Tichenor, P. J., Olien, C. N., & Donohue, G. A. (1987). Effect of use of metro dailies on the knowledge gap in small towns. *Journalism Quarterly, 64,* 329-336.

Tichenor, P. J., Rodenkirchen, J. M., Olien, C. N., & Donohue, G. A. (1973). Community issues, conflict, and public affairs knowledge. In P. Clarke (Ed.), *New models for mass communications research* (pp. 45-79). Beverly Hills, CA: Sage.

Tomita, M. R. (1989). *The role of cable television in providing information on world news: A test of the knowledge gap hypothesis.* Unpublished doctoral dissertation, University of Minnesota, Minneapolis.

Torsvik, P. (1972). Television and information. *Scandinavian Political Studies, 7,* 215-234.

U.S. Department of Health and Human Services. (1989). *Reducing the health consequences of smoking: 25 years of progress* (A report of the surgeon general, DHHS Publication No. CDC 89-8411). Washington, DC: Government Printing Office.

Vidich, A. J., & Bensman, J. (1958). *Small town in mass society.* Princeton, NJ: Princeton University Press.

Vidich, A. J., Bensman, J., & Stein, M. (1964). *Reflections on community studies.* New York: Harper Torchbooks.

Viswanath, K. (1988). International news in the U.S. media: Perceptions of foreign students. *Journalism Quarterly, 65,* 952-959.

Viswanath, K. (1990). *Knowledge gap effects in a cardiovascular disease prevention campaign: A longitudinal study of two community pairs.* Unpublished doctoral dissertation, University of Minnesota, Minneapolis.

Viswanath, K., Finnegan, J. R., Hannan, P. J., & Luepker, R. V. (1991). Health and knowledge gaps: Some lessons from the Minnesota Heart Health Program. *American Behavioral Scientist, 34,* 712-726.

Viswanath, K., Finnegan, J. R., Hertog, J., Pirie, P., & Murray, D. (1994). Community type and the diffusion of campaign information. *Gazette, 54,* 39-59.

Viswanath, K., Finnegan, J. R., & Kahn, E. (1993, May). *Community pluralism and knowledge gaps: A longitudinal study of campaign effects in three community pairs.* Paper presented at the annual meeting of the International Communication Association, Washington, DC.

Viswanath, K., Finnegan, J. R., Rooney B., & Potter, J. (1990). Community ties and use of newspapers and cable TV in a rural midwestern community. *Journalism Quarterly, 67,* 899-911.

Viswanath, K., Kahn, E., Finnegan, J. R., Hertog, J., & Potter, J. (1993). Motivation and the "knowledge gap": Effects of a campaign to reduce diet-related cancer risk. *Communication Research, 20,* 546-563.

Viswanath, K., Kosicki, G. M., Park, E., & Fredin, E. (1993, November). *Community ties and knowledge gaps.* Paper presented at the annual meeting of the Midwest Association for Public Opinion Research, Chicago.

Wade, S., & Schramm, W. L. (1969). The mass media as sources of public affairs, science and health knowledge. *Public Opinion Quarterly, 33,* 197-209.

Warren, R. L. (1973). *Perspectives on the American community.* Chicago: Rand McNally.

Warren, R. L. (1978). *The community in America.* Chicago: Rand McNally.

Watkins, J. W. N. (1970). Against "normal science." In I. Lakatos & A. Musgrave (Eds.), *Criticism and the growth of knowledge* (pp. 25-37). Cambridge: Cambridge University Press.

Watkinson, J. D. (1990). Useful knowledge? Concepts, values, and access in American education, 1776-1840. *History of Education Quarterly, 30,* 351-370.

Webber, M. (1963). Order in diversity: Community without propinquity. In L. Wingo, Jr. (Ed.), *Cities and space: The future use of urban land* (pp. 23-54). Baltimore, MD: Johns Hopkins University Press.

Williams, O. P., Herman, H., Liebman, C. S., & Dye, T. R. (1965). *Suburban differences and metropolitan policies: A Philadelphia story.* Philadelphia: University of Pennsylvania Press.

Yows, S., Salmon, C. T., Hawkins, R., & Love, R. (1991). Motivational and structural factors in predicting different kinds of cancer knowledge. *American Behavioral Scientist, 34,* 727-741.

Zandpour, F., & Fellow, A. R. (1992). Knowledge gap effects: Audience and media factors in alcohol-related health communication. *Mass Communication Review, 19*(3), 34-41.

CHAPTER CONTENTS

6 The Meaning of "Communication Technology": The Technology-Context Scheme

MICHELE H. JACKSON
Florida State University

This chapter examines *communication technology* as a construct for theory building in communication. The simple identification of technology as the material artifact is rejected in favor of a two-dimensional framework centering on the relationship between technology and context. The implications of this framework are discussed for both current and future theory building. Special attention is given to implications for more recent constructionist theories, and an alternate definition of communication technology is presented.

FUNDAMENTAL to the study of computer-based communication technology is the question, Do computers make a difference? This is not simply a question for empirical investigation; it is also a test to determine if computers are worthy of the attention of communication scholars. The expectation is that the use of computer technology will create some new communication phenomenon, something that sets computer-assisted communication apart from other modes of interaction. The study of computer-based communication technology has become both the search for this difference and the search for ways to explain and predict this difference.

No claims are made in this chapter one way or the other on this question of difference. The comparison of computer-assisted communication with non-computer-assisted communication is not at issue. Rather, the aim in this work is to critique the nature of the search itself. I argue for a new starting place for theory building. Communication scholars have directed increasing attention

AUTHOR'S NOTE: I wish to thank Marshall Scott Poole for his comments and guidance on previous drafts of this chapter. Research for this chapter was supported by the Adelle and Erwin Tomash Fellowship, awarded by the Charles Babbage Institute for the History of Information Processing.

Correspondence and requests for reprints: Michele H. Jackson, Department of Communication, Florida State University, 356 Diffenbaugh Building, Tallahassee, FL 32306-2064.

Communication Yearbook 19, pp. 229-267

toward understanding and explaining the consequences of communication technology use, yet little attention has been given to communication technology as a theoretical construct. One result of this inattention is that the assumptions behind the construct have gone unexamined. My central project in this review is to examine communication technology critically as a construct for theory building in the discipline of communication.

Steinfield and Fulk (1990) noted at the start of this decade that the field of communication technology was in "the midst of a data glut" (p. 13). They argued that the field had by that time produced a large body of empirical work, but had as yet developed few theoretical structures from which to explain and analyze empirical findings. A similar claim can be made today concerning the state of reviews of communication technology. A number of careful and thorough reviews of empirical research in communication technology have been undertaken (Hiemstra, 1982; Johansen, 1977; Johansen, Vallee, & Spangler, 1979; Kerr & Hiltz, 1982; Kiesler, Siegel, & McGuire, 1984; Kraemer & Pinsonneault, 1990; Short, Williams, & Christie, 1976; Williams, 1977), yet there remains little infrastructure to support the analysis and understanding of the relationships among theoretical approaches to the study of communication technology.

The objective of this review is to help build such an infrastructure. Several distinct theoretical perspectives have emerged in communication technology research. A scheme is proposed for classifying these perspectives based on two assumptions concerning the relationship between technology and context. I will then analyze examples of existing research in communication in terms of this new classification. In the last section of the chapter I present a reconceptualization of the technological artifact that I propose to be more useful and powerful for theory building in communication.

THE MOMENT OF INTRODUCTION:
TECHNOLOGY AS THE MATERIAL ARTIFACT

The development of computer-based technologies that may be used for human communication has presented an exciting opportunity for communication researchers. The use of computer technology for communication now extends to every social context, from business to government to the home. The opportunities for communication—and for potential change in communication—are significant. Not surprisingly, some theorists have predicted that the effects of computers on human thought and interaction may be equally significant (Heim, 1987; Poster, 1990; Sproull & Kiesler, 1991; Turkle, 1984; Zuboff, 1988). Computer-based communication technologies (CBCTs) are increasing rapidly, both in number of products available and in distribution of those products throughout society.[1]

Given this context, it is easy to understand why communication research in this area has focused, to a great extent, on identifying and predicting the effects that CBCT use has on the nature of communication.[2] The typical research study compares, within similar contexts, communication that uses CBCT to communication that does not. Technology use, in other words, is an independent variable. Further, most research in this area uses one of three methods to study CBCT effects. The first of these is the case study, where the researcher studies the effect of a CBCT introduced into a specific, preexisting context. Communication occurring before the introduction of the technology is then compared with communication occurring after introduction. Steinfield (1986), for example, examined factors surrounding the introduction of an electronic mail system into an organizational context. Hiemstra (1983) conducted an ethnographic analysis of the phrase *information technology* and the meanings associated with it among members of four organizations. Research has also considered the effects of technology on specific organizational contexts. Danowski and Edison-Swift (1985) examined electronic mail messages occurring within an organization over a year and observed changes in the number and structure of messages sent during times of crisis.

The second type of method often used to study CBCT effects is the controlled laboratory experiment. Subjects, assigned to a condition in which a CBCT is either present or absent, are asked to complete a standard task. Communication and interaction are then compared across the technology conditions. For example, Kiesler et al. (1984) used laboratory experiments to investigate how the use of a computerized messaging system might influence patterns of nonverbal and socioemotional cues. Poole and DeSanctis (1987, 1992) examined the effects of a group decision support system on user satisfaction and perceived quality of decision making. Hiltz and her colleagues studied the use of a computerized conferencing system and its effects on decision making, participation, and expressiveness (Hiltz, 1978, 1982; Hiltz, Johnson & Turoff, 1986; Hiltz & Turoff, 1978, 1981, 1992; Hiltz, Turoff, & Johnson, 1989).

A third type of method increasingly is being used to study the effects of CBCTs: the analysis of computerized or electronic messages themselves. This method is not new. More than a decade ago, Rice (1982; see also Rice & Barnett, 1986) studied the communication networks of users of a computer conferencing system. Danowski (1982) has performed content analyses of messages sent on a computer bulletin board. However, the use of this method is well suited to textual analysis, content analysis, or rhetorical criticism. For example, the relational aspects of communication that uses a computer conferencing system have been examined by Walther (1992), Walther and Burgoon (1992), and Rice and Love (1987). Rafaeli and LaRose (1993) examined the content and diversity of bulletin board systems. A number of essays published in a collection edited by Jones (1995) explore the dynamics, norms, and relationships that develop in communities created and sustained solely by electronic communication.

Regardless of the method used, the common element in this research is an emphasis on the presence of the technology in the form of a material artifact.

Material is meant here as the tangible, physical element of technology, or what Winner (1977) terms "apparatus":

> The class of objects we normally refer to as technological—tools, instruments, machines, appliances, weapons, gadgets—which are used in accomplishing a wide variety of tasks. . . . For many persons, "technology" actually means apparatus, that is, the physical devices of technical performance. (p. 11)

Material artifacts are the devices that perform the work of the technology, the "things" with which we come in contact. Computer technology introduces certain complexities to Winner's definition. The tasks of computer technology are accomplished by both physical devices in the traditional sense—the so-called *hardware* of computer systems—and devices that consist of sequences of numbers or words—the *software* that enables the computer to perform tasks. Both of these types of devices, hardware and software, constitute the material artifact of computer technology.[3] Material artifacts associated with computer technology include objects we can touch or manipulate—such as computer consoles, keyboards and other input devices, terminals, monitors, and printers—as well as seemingly intangible objects necessary to allow those devices to accomplish desired tasks—such as computer programs. Generally, CBCT researchers make little distinction between these two; rather, the material artifact is defined by what task is accomplished. In other words, hardware and software are components that make it possible for a user to do something or to communicate in some way. So, for example, the point at which researchers begin comparison is with the introduction of the electronic mail system, the direct connection to a main data processing system, or the first contact with group decision support software. Research in CBCTs is research of a situation that is created when the material artifact is introduced to a context and that remains in existence as long as the material artifact is present.[4]

In many ways, this emphasis on the material artifact is reasonable. Identifying the presence of artifacts is straightforward, as they can be observed and identified easily. Their features can be specified and standardized for study. Further, as users of technologies ourselves, we can identify when we have been introduced to a technology and, conversely, when it is no longer available to us. However, we should challenge this reasonableness. To emphasize the material artifact is to adopt a perspective, with the attendant assumptions, biases, and limitations of that perspective. At least three assumptions behind this perspective have important implications for research.

The first assumption is that technology and context are separable. On one level, this means that the two may be separated physically. In this case, the presence of "technology" is defined as the presence of the material artifact. The technology may be introduced or removed from the context of interest simply by introducing or removing the material artifact. A further implication of this physical separability is the relative mobility of technology and context. Context anchors the comparison. In other words, research seeks to understand how context changes as a result of the presence of technology. Thus, context is immobile: it may be dynamic and changing, but it is specifically located. The organization, for example, exists before technology is introduced and after it is removed. The general context of group communication will continue with or without the presence of technology. Technology, in contrast, is mobile. It is introduced to the context in the form of the material artifact. It may be moved around within that context, at times made available to more individuals and at other times to fewer individuals, or it may be removed entirely.

On a deeper level, technology and context are assumed to be separable ontologically: They do not constitute each other. The observation that technology is introduced into a context is also a claim that the technology exists before that introduction. It does not become a particular technology as a result of its introduction. A corollary is also true: The particular technology still exists once it is removed from a context. The definition or constitution of "technology," therefore, does not depend upon context. Instead, technology is constituted by what moves among contexts: that is, the material artifact. For example, we do not say that an electronic mail system actually becomes 20 different technologies when it is implemented in 20 different organizations. Nor do we say that it ceases being an electronic mail system when those organizations no longer use it.

The other side of this separability is the implication that a particular context exists independent of a technological artifact. In other words, context does not come into existence as a result of technology; it does not depend upon technology for its definition. Context is merely the location of technology. The presence or use of technology may alter the nature of the context and, similarly, the conditions of a context may result in changes to a technological artifact, but this is always a causal connection between two separate, distinct entities. Technology and context do not join in meaning; one does not constitute the other; one does not become the other.

The second assumption is the conceptualization of a "moment of introduction." By emphasizing the presence of technology in the form of a material artifact, it becomes theoretically possible to identify the point at which technology enters a context. Empirical research translates this moment as t_1, or the time of initial contact between users or subjects and the technological artifact. More important, the moment of introduction signals the point at which technological artifacts become important to communication research. The moment of introduction acknowledges that a technology must be developed, but discounts that period of development as something left behind once the technology enters the context of use. Technology enters a context of use as a clean slate, without meaning or context and possessing only function.

The final assumption is a derivation of the first two: Technology is wholly represented by the material artifact. As Winner (1977) points out, several definitions of "technology" exist. However, the predominant meaning used by communication researchers studying CBCTs is *apparatus*. Because the presence of a definite apparatus or artifact is central to a study, a description of the material artifact becomes a sufficient description of "technology." Factors that might have been important to the development of the artifact, such as the intentions of designers or constraints on resources, become irrelevant to defining and representing the technology. Within the current dominant perspective, there is no principled reason for considering factors of the development context. Artifacts are acontextual, ahistorical, and without meaning, because materiality does not rely on context, history, or meaning for its existence. These things are social, and materiality is not social. Materiality is physical. In essence, the artifact becomes a black box. Yet the box does not hide how the artifact functions, for that can be described clearly in technical terms. Rather, the box hides how and why the artifact came to function that way. The artifact, as a black box, simply exists. Further, the box hides the information that challenges the separability of material artifact and context.

These three assumptions have had a pervasive influence on communication research in CBCTs. Despite the range of theories that have been developed to explain and predict the effects of computer-based communication technology, at base each shares a reliance on a traditional perspective of technology, one that defines technology as the artifact and defines the artifact as the material. This perspective has not been a matter of controversy; there is no obvious reason it should. The material artifact is a clear and identifiable focus for investigation. Its presence or absence can be observed clearly and its use measured. The moment of introduction is a definite and context-neutral starting point for research. Further, it seems intuitive to claim that at some point an object enters a context where before it was not present. Finally, the separation of artifact from context parallels the separation of material from social. The base characteristic of the social is change, and of the material, stability. Consequently, answering the question, Do computers make a difference? becomes the straightforward task of mapping various technical qualities of technology along with various social qualities of context onto the changes that are observed in communication.

For many years, this traditional definition of technology—what I will call the *material definition of the artifact*—guided the classification of new communication technology. Defining the parameters of study was simply a matter of identifying the central features of the material artifact.[5] An early move was to devise parameters centering on technological properties that created new channels of communication. Williams's (1977) classic review of the literature positioned computers with other telecommunications media such as audio conferencing, emphasizing the contrast of mediated interaction with face-to-face interaction. Rice et al. (1984) echo this mediated versus face-to-face contrast, although they aim to make a further distinction between traditional and "new" media. New media are "those communication technologies, typically involving computer capabilities (microprocessor or mainframe) that allow or facilitate interactivity among users or between users and information" (p. 35), where *interactivity* is defined as the opportunity for choice on the individual level. Interactivity, these authors acknowledge, may be interpreted broadly, and hence may include a wide range of technologies, including, in addition to computer-based technologies, cable and satellite television, videotex, teletex, videodisc, office automation, and audio and video conferencing.

A more prominent approach has been to argue—or, more accurately, to start from the assumption—that computer technology is itself a distinct and separate medium for communication. In this approach, computer-based communication technologies use computers in support of human symbolic activity. CBCTs include technologies that facilitate the manipulation of symbols, such as word processing (Heim, 1987) or information retrieval systems (Culnan, 1985), as well as those that mediate or aid human-human interaction. Typically, studies using this approach see the features of CBCTs as altering the "traditional" nature of communication. For example, Kiesler et al. (1984), operating from a social psychological perspective, argue that electronic messaging will produce changes in communication due to the particular nature of the medium, such as its lack of nonverbal cues, feedback, and established norms. Similarly, Kerr and Hiltz (1982) suggest that computer-mediated communication systems are a "new form of enhanced human communication" (p. 3); all such systems share certain characteristics, the most fundamental (in terms of their effects) being that all communication takes place through typing and reading, and the communication may be asynchronous.[6]

Despite these efforts to provide clear descriptive boundaries, there is today no consensus as to what features define CBCTs. The struggle in defining CBCTs concerns generalizing or abstracting from concrete experience a set of essential or definitive elements. In other words, definitions of CBCTs are based on the features and capabilities of artifacts that come into the foreground in our experiences as users of those artifacts. Yet our experiences deceive us—no experience reflects features or capabilities inherent to technology. A technology is not a static entity; it has no necessary end state. Many technological artifacts are modifications of previous artifacts, as incremental developments add features or eliminate previous problems. Technological artifacts often change, and as they change, so do our experiences. The response of users then may motivate even further technological change. Elements that once were considered "definitive" or "essential" prove not to be so at all. Electronic mail systems, for example, may be changed to allow a user to call back messages that have been sent but not yet read; shared or collaborative editing systems may be changed so that the markings of individual editors appear in different colors; a video display of each participant may be added to text-based computer conferencing. Definitions based on our experiences as users will be transient—or quickly outdated—as the technologies we are defining change in shape, form, and capabilities.

This struggle suggests an important weakness in how researchers in the discipline of communication have studied computer technology. The need to define the object of study is basic to any field of study. Yet it is clear that defining "technology" by the material artifact is inadequate. An alternative definition, one that incorporates but does not center on materiality, requires abandoning the assumption of the moment of introduction and considering technology as inseparable from context.

We should be wary altogether of assuming a moment of introduction, for two reasons. First, little historical or empirical evidence supports this moment. Technology development does not proceed in a systematic and determined manner toward a point at which an artifact emerges in a predestined, singular form. At the very minimum, there is no standard for defining which "contact" should count as the moment of introduction. Is a technology introduced when a decision is made in an organization to buy an artifact? Or when the artifact is delivered to the organization? Or when it is installed? Or when it is made accessible to potential users? Or when it is used? Even these points are too gross, assuming that a single coherent artifact can be tracked through a single and linear process.[7] Often, communication technologies are complex, offering many levels of features. Which of these counts as the technological artifact?

Further, studies of technology design and development show it to be a messy, indeterminate process. Turner (1987) has pointed out that "design is ad-hoc and associative, the process is individual and experimental based, the solutions produced by different designers are usually different, much of the design proceeds bottom up, and solutions and problem definition are intertwined" (p. 102). Examples suggest that artifacts have no natural gestation periods after which they emerge whole and complete to be introduced into a context of use. Consider the example of electronic mail or messaging, a standard example of communication technology. The use of computers to support human-human communication was made possible by technology designed to support computer-computer data transmission between specific sites (Norberg & O'Neill, 1992). The fact that such features could also support communication between people was seen as an irrelevant by-product that violated the intended use of new networking technologies (Roberts, 1969). Those who did communicate electronically had no standard protocol for data transmission and, therefore, needed technical expertise for the task. Standard protocols were not adopted widely until the late 1970s, well after the volume of use suggested such protocols would be important (Palme, 1985; Panko, 1977). The line between development and use, and that between developers and users, has been a convenience for researchers, assumed rather than investigated. There is no singular, unproblematic starting place for communication technology studies. Thus, a methodological convenience has been reified into an assumed characteristic of technology.

The second reason we should be wary of the assumption of the moment of introduction is that it contradicts the position that context plays an important role in our understanding and evaluation of technology. The assumption separates the contexts of design and use, allowing the technological artifact to pass between them in a form independent of either context. The existence of this ahistorical, acontextual artifact denies context any fundamental importance: Because a technology can be removed from context, context is not an essential element of technology. In order to operate from the position that context is fundamental to the study of technology, we must deny the possibility of an acontextual artifact. We should not be able to conceptualize a technology that can exist without history and without context. There can be no force intrinsic to technology or extrinsic to it that separates technology from its context at a particular moment. Similarly, as a technology passes through contexts, there is no force that separates technology from one context and places it in another. Thus, again, the line between design and use is a convenience.

REJECTING THE MOMENT OF INTRODUCTION: IMPLICATIONS FOR RESEARCH IN COMMUNICATION TECHNOLOGY

The conceptualization of communication technology as the material artifact has been central in framing how scholars have tried to understand the effects of technology. Indeed, the separation of technology and context frames two decades of CBCT research. A central dichotomy in communication research is related to this separation. Current reviews identify this dichotomy as "technology-centered" versus "social-centered" research perspectives; technology-centered research perspectives emphasize characteristics of the artifact as causing changes in communication, whereas social-centered perspectives emphasize characteristics of the social surroundings.

Before going on, it is important to distinguish this technology-social dichotomy from the idea laid out thus far of the separation of technology and context. In both of these pairs, "technology" is equivalent to "artifact" or, more specifically, the material artifact. However, the temptation to define "social" and "context" also as equivalent should be avoided. The two terms arise from different circumstances and possess differing relationships to "technology." Social-centered research perspectives emerged, generally, in response to the technology-centered perspectives that dominated early research in CBCTs. Technology-centered perspectives, for the most part, assume the artifact to be a sufficient determinant of change, possessing an inherent and unvarying logic of use. Social-centered perspectives, to varying extents, challenge this technological determinism, holding instead that the artifact is only one variable in the social milieu—albeit the one that particular researchers might be most interested in—and that any changes in communication are a result of the dynamics in this complex of factors. Most social-centered perspectives challenge technological determinism by endowing human subjects with the ability to act, to choose, and to influence the way technology is used. This is reflected in the terminology chosen to represent the social-centered perspective. For example, Nass and Mason (1990) refer to the "social-actor-centered perspective," and Fulk (1993) refers to "social constructivist theories." [8]

Thus, the technology-social dichotomy is a product of the historical circumstances of communication research. Social-centered perspectives in practice have not challenged the conception of technology as a material artifact; they have proposed theories and frameworks that accord more emphasis to social elements than to material elements. Social-centered perspectives, in essence, reclaim from technology-centered approaches the explanatory power that had been bestowed on the artifact at the expense of traditional social and communicative elements such as relationships, networks, and the conscious choice of actors. As argued below, extending the emphasis on social elements and the interdependence of situational factors challenges, in principle, the material definition of technology. The implications of this challenge, however, have not yet been explored.

In contrast, the distinction between "context" and "technology" proposed in this chapter arises by necessity from a material definition of the artifact. In other words, the distinction follows logically from the common assumptions of communication technology research discussed above: Technology and context are separable, technology enters context in a moment of introduction, and technology is wholly represented by the material artifact. Context is what the technology—that is, the material artifact—is introduced into; it is what is left behind when the technology leaves. Thus, the importance of context is as the necessary backdrop for technology. It is what technology is not.

Thus understood, "context" is much broader than "social." Context includes social elements, and also material elements that are not associated with the artifact. However, the temptation to identify context as a set of elements must be avoided. So should the urge to delineate that set of elements. The constitution of context is unimportant. Yet, given the history of communication research in CBCTs, this is a powerful temptation. Both technology-centered and social-centered perspectives have attempted to identify the elements that play a role in effecting change, with the difference between the two being mainly the elements that are emphasized. In contrast, in the technology-context distinction, the importance of "context" is not in its use as an empirical tool, but as a conceptual tool. Focusing on this distinction as opposed to the technology-social distinction reveals that communication research—whether technology-centered or social-centered—conceptualizes context as separate from technology. From this separation emerges the material definition of the artifact. Alternative definitions of the artifact lie in denying this separation. One such alternative is suggested below.

The distinction between technology-centered perspectives and social-centered perspectives has been the primary heuristic for locating or classifying specific theories or research approaches in CBCT research (Rice, 1993).[9] The limitation of the technology-social distinction is that it is one-dimensional; specific approaches are categorized as more or less technology-centered or social-centered. Occasionally, the two general perspectives are subdivided (e.g., Kling, 1980), but, typically, the subdivision is a listing of types of approaches that fall within each perspective, with no way to compare the lists across the two general perspectives. More often, the distinction is used simply to introduce and position a particular theory of interest within the general CBCT research literature. Though originally a useful device, the technology-social distinction has little generative power remaining to contribute to the building of new communication technology theory.

The separation of context and technology offers a similar, but more powerful, scheme for comparing existing theories and for furthering theory building. The foundation of the classification scheme is the context-technology separation itself. As stated in the first assumption of the material definition of the artifact discussed above, context and technology are separable from each other in that they are independently constituted. The line between technology and context is drawn clearly and is easily identified by the black box of the material artifact—the physical devices and apparatus used in performing or accomplishing a task. What counts as technology does not depend upon context—rather, technology is acontextual. What counts as context does not depend upon the technology—context is atechnological. Communication research has considered this separation as actual, a reflection of reality. An alternative is to regard the separation as conceptual, a reflection of a perspective of reality. Once this move is made, other perspectives are generated easily by varying the combinations of the technology-context separation.

The proposed technology-context (T-C) scheme performs two functions. First, it locates existing communication technology theories in relation to each other. The advantage of this scheme over the traditional social-technology distinction is that here theories are located according to their fundamental assumptions of how technology and context relate to one another. In other words, the T-C scheme does not catalog existing theories. Rather, the scheme is principle based and, thus, is prior to any particular theory. This new starting place enables comparison that does more than articulate how classes of theories emphasize either technological or social elements; instead, different classes of theories exist because of varying foundational assumptions. It is these assumptions that then give rise to different emphases on technology or social interaction.

The second function performed by the T-C scheme is to contribute to theory building in the general area of communication technology.[10] By articulating assumptions behind various perspectives, the T-C scheme identifies tensions

TABLE 6.1
Technology-Context Separation:
Classification of Communication Technology Theories

| | | *Q1: Is the constitution of technology separable from context?* | |
		Yes	*No*
Q2: Is the constitution of context separable from technology?	Yes	1. Determinism	2. Context as filter
	No	3. Technology as change agent	4. Integration

that need to be resolved in existing theories. Specifically, the scheme challenges the singularity of the material definition of the artifact. The common assumption in communication research is that technology—that is, the artifact itself—is wholly represented by the material artifact, even when this representation contradicts central elements or assumptions of the theory. The T-C scheme makes explicit any contradiction and provides justification for building alternative definitions of the technological artifact.[11]

The T-C scheme classifies theoretical perspectives according to how they relate technology and context to each other (see Table 6.1). The scheme is composed of four cells, generated from answers to two questions. The first of these questions is, Is the constitution of technology separable from context? To determine an answer to this question, these related questions can be asked:

- Is technology essentially acontextual?
- Can technology be removed from context, with no residue of context left over in the artifact?
- Or, stated in reverse, is the definition of technology dependent on the context in which the material artifact is located?
- Is it meaningful to talk of technology apart from context?

The second question is, Is the constitution of context separable from technology? To determine an answer to this question, these related questions can be asked:

- Is context essentially atechnological?
- Can technology be removed from context, with no residue of the technology left over in the context?
- Or, stated in reverse, is the definition of context dependent on the material artifact located within it?
- Does a technological artifact become an inherent part of context?

Note that these questions focus specifically on the constitution of technology and context vis-à-vis each other. They do not ask if context and technology are related to each other such that changes in one will result in changes in the other, nor do they ask if one or the other has power to predict technology use. A perspective may hold that the constitution of technology and context are separable from each other, yet still hold that a relationship exists between the two. The key is that this perspective would still hold the two elements as constitutively or definitionally independent.

Crossing these questions produces four cells representing four categories of perspectives. Each of these categories will be discussed below in terms of the following questions:

- What is the relationship between context and technology?
- What does this relationship mean for
    attributions of changes observed in communication?
    central research approaches?
    considering technological development in studying technology use?
    defining or conceptualizing the artifact?

Cell 1: Determinism

- Is the constitution of technology separable from context? *Yes*
- Is the constitution of context separable from technology? *Yes*

Within this cell, technology and context are independent entities that remain constant and stable. The separation of technology and context enables the technological artifact to be a consistent and predictable cause of change in that it is an artifact's set of physical, tangible features—such as allowing asynchronous communication or a graphically based user interface—that determines what effect the technology will have on communication. Thus, technological determinism is the central characteristic of the Cell 1 perspective.

Research from this perspective consists of mapping the effects of technology as a function of the characteristics of the material artifact. Central research programs have been devoted to generating extensive lists of the effects expected from the use of communication technologies (e.g., Johansen et al., 1979; Kerr & Hiltz, 1982). Theories in this perspective vary, however, in how complex they expect this map to be. A useful way to characterize this variation is the distinction between hard-line and soft-line determinism (Gutek, Bikson, & Mankin, 1984).

For hard-line determinists, the particulars of context are irrelevant to an artifact's effects on communication. Changes in communication may be attributed to the use of technology because (a) technology possesses an inherent logic that causes consistency in use, and (b) communication characteristics are sufficiently consistent across contexts such that the particulars of context are insignificant. In contrast, soft-line determinists acknowledge that effects of an artifact's use may vary across contexts. Context is a multifaceted background for technological effects. Context may be considered a factor in variation of effects for at least two reasons. First, elements in the context— such as task, organizational culture, group size—change. Second, context may interact with the technology. These changes can be observed and measured, however, and therefore accounted for in predictions of change. For example, media richness theory explains media choice as an outcome based on the combination of communication goals and characteristics of the artifact (Daft & Lengel, 1986; Trevino, Daft, & Lengel, 1990; Valacich, Paranka, George, & Nunamaker, 1993). Likewise, social identity theory (Spears & Lea, 1994) challenges that line of analysis that looks only to technology as the cause of changes in influence and power in social relationships. This theory suggests, instead, that internal psychological forces must also be considered when explaining or predicting behavioral outcomes. The determinist equation may become more complex with a soft-line approach, but not dynamic or indeterminate.

The determinist perspective ushered in the study of technology as an area for communication research. Reviews of research (e.g., Short et al., 1976; Sproull & Kiesler, 1991) demonstrate the historical dominance of deterministic approaches in communication technology studies. Generally, however, hard-line determinism is loosening its hold. Approaches falling within the pure technological form increasingly acknowledge the complexity of prediction and assume soft-line rather than hard-line determinism. Yet for either position, elements of context and technology behave rationally; thus, the task of research is to identify configurations of technology and context that have more or less predictable and consistent effects.

In determinism, technology is defined, clearly, as the material artifact. Definite boundaries exist between technology and context. Of the four perspectives proposed by the T-C scheme, determinism is the only one in which the assumptions are perfectly consistent with the traditional material definition of the artifact. Thus, there are no tensions within the perspective that require redefinition of the material artifact. However, the rejection of the moment of introduction as a valid concept requires that determinism address new questions. The place in the research where this will have an effect is in identifying exactly which technological artifact is present at various stages of research. Typically, artifacts are classified according to some property. Examples include the following:

- Listing of material elements (Williams, 1977).[12]
- Level of a central characteristic. An example is interactivity, or the ability of an individual user to influence the behavior of the technology (Heeter, 1989; Rice et al., 1984).
- Dimensions of effects (Katzman, 1974; Williams, Rice, & Dordick, 1985).

- Comparison with a baseline of a non-computer-mediated mode of communication. This mode may be specific, often face-to-face communication (e.g., Chesebro, 1985; Sproull & Kiesler, 1991), or more general, encompassing all noncomputer modes (e.g., Bannon, 1986; Culnan & Bair, 1983).

Each of these approaches assumes that an artifact's properties remain constant throughout use. Rejecting the moment of introduction denies the grounds for this assumption. Developers may promise features that are not immediately available; the material artifact may be altered after a period of use to meet the needs of the users; users may be given different versions of the same artifact or different artifact components (e.g., different display terminals). Research conducted from a Cell 1 perspective must be responsible for monitoring more closely the exact nature of the artifact throughout the course of the study. More detailed descriptions of the artifact must be provided, as well as accounts of any changes made to the artifact.

Cell 2: Technology as Change Agent

- Is the constitution of technology separable from context? *Yes*
- Is the constitution of context separable from technology? *No*

Within this cell, technology remains constant, separate from context. The definition of technology does not depend on context; context is not part of technology. The definition of context, in contrast, does depend on technology; technology is a constitutive part of context. The presence of technology alters the constitution of context such that the definition of context becomes dependent upon that technology. Theories and approaches classified in Cell 2 will grant that (a) technology may be identified and defined independent of contextual elements, and (b) changes in context will not change the constitution of technology. Technology is integrated into context; context cannot be conceived of independent of technology. Technology, as an autonomous agent, changes the intrinsic nature of its surroundings. Thus, technology as change agent is the central characteristic of the Cell 2 perspective.

In this perspective, specifications of the technological artifact are insufficient for generalizing to the use or effects of that technology. Research, instead, focuses on how technology will change the context in which it is located. In contrast to Cell 1, context is more than a backdrop against which change is observed: Context itself substantively changes. It is these changes to context that are then considered for their impact on communication processes.

This change agent perspective is marked by a wide range of theories, perhaps due to the uncertainty in predicting how technology will change fundamental social processes. For example, pronouncements have appeared consistently for decades concerning the potential of computers to change the essential nature of human beings; a now classic example is Weizenbaum's

(1976) warning of dehumanization. More recently, Turkle's (1984) influential study of children and computers suggests that humans are incorporating technology into fundamental worldviews. According to Chesebro and Bonsall (1989), technology is becoming established as an archetypal metaphor for communication, changing at a fundamental level the way we talk. Heim (1987) analyzes the effect of word processing on our understanding of space and time. A number of theorists have argued, through analysis of historical trends, that new communication technologies will usher in a "second orality" or a "new literacy," changing entirely the ways we communicate with each other (Compaine, 1988; Innis, 1972; Ong, 1982).

Adding to the complexity of these predictions is the determination of the inevitability of change. Gronbeck (1990) suggests that change is not inevitable and that, instead of trying to predict change from elements of the technological artifact, we should focus on alignments among technology, the cultural arena, and the mind-sets of people within that arena to find "laws of resonance" that may be postulated and tested. A similar call has been made by Rogers and Rafaeli (1985), who criticize the reliance of previous research on linear models for studying technology and communication. More appropriate, they argue, are convergence models that emphasize interactivity and the process of achieving mutual understanding and agreement.

Another approach within the perspective of technology as change agent focuses less on predicting change and instead aims to construct models based on contingencies resulting from the interaction of technology and context. This approach emphasizes how the technological artifact becomes part of context. Kling (1987), for example, postulates the "web model of computing," emphasizing the integration of social and technological factors in the process of "computerization":

> Computerization refers to the social practices through which computer-based systems and services are made available to various groups, arrangements for training people in the skills they need to use systems effectively, practices that alter accountability, changes in patterns of control, etc. Computerization is a combination of technical, social and political processes. (p. 337)

In this model, context is reconstituted through computerization.[13] Another example is the "social impacts of technology" theory (e.g., Danziger & Kraemer, 1986), which explains variation in end-user adoption and behavior by examining several factors, including organizational context, the "computer package" (hardware, software, provided technical and administrative support), and the characteristics of the user. Similarly, Zmud's (1990) information-processing approach emphasizes the interactions of factors—intentions of actors, attributes of technology, and organizational processes—to understand and explain technology use.

The soft-line determinism possible in Cell 1 may seem to be similar to the approaches of Cell 2, because soft-line determinism also emphasizes the importance of context to change. The distinction between the two lies in how context is constituted. In soft-line determinism, the potential variation in contexts is independent of technology. For example, the communication networks in organizations may vary, individuals may vary in their communication styles, or groups may have varying histories working together, regardless of technology. In contingency approaches of Cell 2, the variation in contexts is dependent upon, or created by (not simply affected by), technology. For Cell 2 contingency theorists, context and technology interact such that context constitutively changes. The emphasis in Cell 2 approaches is not on identifying all relevant contingencies. Rather, the emphasis is on the dynamic and changing nature of context, and on the role technology plays in increasing the number of possible contingencies by increasing the complexity of the context. Thus, it is possible for a theory to hold that some contingencies may never be foreseen (Sproull & Kiesler, 1991).

The perspective of technology as change agent begins to challenge the material definition of the artifact because context is dependent on, rather than independent of, technology. There is an inherent tension in this perspective, however, because technology is separable from context, but context is not separable from technology. From a viewpoint anchored to technology, technology may move from one context to another by moving the material artifact. Yet from a viewpoint anchored to context, technology becomes incorporated into its surroundings; context must be redefined to include technology as represented by changes in thought and interaction.

This tension is not recognized explicitly in current research, nor is it resolved. Studies assume the material definition of the artifact by examining technology as it is introduced into a context of use from a context of development. Though they do not resolve it, various strategies diffuse this tension. For example, technology is used as a metaphor for context, as in the "computerization" of the mind or of society. Such metaphors are derived theoretically or philosophically, extrapolated from general characteristics of technologies or from a small number of observations or experiences. They are then projected on a wide scale, as Weizenbaum (1976) projects changes in society or Zuboff (1988) projects changes in work. This strategy allows context and technology to be connected in a manner that does not depend upon the presence of the material artifact.

Another strategy for diffusing the tension is to accentuate the interactions between technology and contextual factors rather than to focus on the material artifact. This is the strategy common among contingency theories. In other words, most important to understanding change is the study of the links between elements in the context and between context and technology. There is less need to provide details of a particular material artifact as long as the relationships in the overall context can be articulated and defined.

These strategies, in effect, render the moment of introduction unimportant for studying effects of use. Although the artifact is the underlying change agent, the perspective emphasizes the role of context in change. In fact, when the locus of change is societal, the introduction of technology to a specific context is, essentially, a meaningless concept. Thus, Weizenbaum (1976) argues against the computer less in terms of specific applications than for its embodiment of "scientific rationality."

Cell 3: Context as Filter

- Is the constitution of technology separable from context? *No*
- Is the constitution of context separable from technology? *Yes*

Within this cell, context remains constant, separate from technology. Changes in the technology will not change the constitution of context. Changes in context, however, will change technology. The constitution of technology cannot be separated from context. In a direct challenge to the material definition of the artifact, technology is constituted by how it is perceived, and perceptions arise from and are filtered through context: Technology is never acontextual. As Contractor and Eisenberg (1990) state, "There is no such thing as pure technology. To understand technology, one must first understand social relationships" (p. 143). Thus, context as filter is the central characteristic of the Cell 3 perspective.

Central to the context-as-filter perspective is the assumption that meaning is socially created. Meanings—or definitions—do not reside within objects, independent of people. Determining how and when and why to use an object is a function of the meanings that are ascribed to that object. Technology, then, comes into and remains in existence as long as it is perceived to exist; it is used according to the shared meanings concerning how it should be used. The most powerful computer is a doorstop if that is the function it is perceived to have. "Sneakerware" is collaborative editing if people define it that way.[14] Context is the filter between the material artifact and the constitution of technology. In order to determine the effects of technology in a particular context, researchers must first determine how technology is defined by the social actors within that context.

This perspective directly challenges the material definition of the artifact. Material elements of the artifact become irrelevant to the goal of understanding how technology effects changes in communication (although they may be relevant to the prior question of how artifacts come to have meaning). In effect, a social definition of the artifact replaces the material definition. One advantage of this approach is that the researchers' prior descriptions or articulations of the particular details of the material artifact are of little importance to understanding the effects of technology. Descriptions of the material artifact need to be sufficient for distinguishing general classes of technology from one another, rather than for distinguishing artifacts within the same class. Important details are those that surface as important to user perceptions and definitions. Social factors, the traditional arena of communication research, displace technological/material factors as key elements in studying the effects of CBCTs.

A central example of this perspective is the social influence model (Fulk, Schmitz, & Steinfield, 1990; Schmitz & Fulk, 1991), which criticizes previous theories, such as media-use theories, because they are rationalist and adhere to technological determinism. In contrast, the social influence model holds that the key influence on change is not technology, but rather the social world. Whatever fixed or inherent properties a technology may have are largely irrelevant to how the technology is used. People are not black boxes capable of making independent and rational choices concerning which media to use to communicate; rather, these choices rely more on contextual elements. Using the social influence model, Fulk (1993) studied the use of electronic mail among scientists and engineers. She found that social influence indicators were able to explain the variance in individual attitudes and behaviors. The social influence model proposes that although technical factors play some role in determining how technology is perceived, these perceptions are in large part subjective and socially created.

Paradoxically, studies in the context-as-filter perspective start from the same place as deterministic studies, despite their reliance on a social definition of the artifact. That is, they start with the introduction of a material artifact into a context. They assume a moment of introduction. The contradiction of this starting place with the Cell 3 perspective should be obvious. If we accept that there is no such thing as "pure technology," that technology is always filtered by context, then there exists no independent, acontextual standpoint from which researchers can identify a moment of introduction. Even if we could identify when a material artifact was introduced, we could not define the introduction of that artifact as the introduction of technology, which is determined by the perception of users in the particular context. Thus, theoretically, technology is not at all dependent upon any particular material artifact.[15]

This paradox plagues both Cell 3 and, as discussed below, Cell 4 perspectives. The source of this paradox is the "problem of materiality." The problem is simple: How do we account for the material artifact? Materiality is not a problem for perspectives that grant technology independence from its surroundings (Cells 1 and 2). On the contrary, the materiality of the artifact is a basic assumption. The problem of materiality arises only when we start from the opposing assumption that the constitution of technology depends on its surroundings. The difficulty inherent in this assumption is the ordinary, material existence of the artifact. Artifacts are not wholly constituted by our perceptions; they exist and can be sensed. Perceptions cannot account for a host of ordinary events—a computer crash, a "buggy" program, a faulty interface device, a delayed delivery. Such events clearly involve material elements of the artifact; yet material elements are denied explanatory status within the context-as-filter perspective. Consequently, in order to avoid the problem of materiality, research from this perspective must study technology that is unassuming, stable, and predictable.

Avoiding the problem, of course, does not resolve it. One path for resolution is to eliminate from our research the opportunities for the material artifact to come into sharp focus. One such opportunity is the moment of introduction. Introduction, as currently conceived, is a material-centered event: When does the technological artifact enter the context of use? As an alternative, research could begin with the introduction of meanings and definitions of the artifact. Artifacts do not appear out of thin air into a context; they are preceded by marketing, advertising, and training, and when they are delivered, more training and instruction may be offered. All of these efforts are aimed at creating in the context of use a shared meaning—a meaning created by developers, managers, and trainers. For example, disagreements in the context of use concerning how technology is perceived might reflect disagreements of meaning in development rather than some characteristic of the material artifact.[16] This starting place would eliminate the focus on the artifact at some "moment" and, instead, would create a consistent focus on perceptions. The artifact would be always social, it would not "become" social through use.

Cell 4: Integration

- Is the constitution of technology separable from context? *No*
- Is the constitution of context separable from technology? *No*

Within this cell, technology and context are inseparable and interdependent. From this perspective, the technology-context distinction itself is meaningless and senseless. Neither exists prior to the other; the two, in fact, are integrated as one entity. The implication of this integration is the denial of any separate, objective ground or standpoint that can provide an anchor to define communication technology. Technology is captured neither by a description of material elements nor by an account of how it is perceived by others. Rather, technology and context are constructed continually. Thus, integration is the central characteristic of the Cell 4 perspective.

The integration perspective poses a great challenge to the communication researcher. If neither context nor technology is consistent and stable, models and theories of change must be capable of tracking and explaining effects as dynamic processes. In other words, if we introduce an electronic mail product into 20 different organizations, then, according to the assumptions of the integration perspective, we would say there now could exist at least 20 different electronic mail technologies. Of course, even this example is too simple, because the technology could not be represented simply by the material artifact; instead, technology would be the integration of social and material elements.

Few examples exist of theories adopting an integration perspective. Those that do exist emphasize social processes, particularly processes by which technology and technological effects are created. One example is Contractor and Eisenberg's (1990) theory of emergent technology, which draws on systems and network theory. Contractor and Eisenberg suggest that technologies in organizations should be studied from a perspective holding that the uses and consequences of information technology emerge unpredictably from complex social interactions. They use as illustrations a number of technologies: computer conferencing, electronic mail, teleconferencing, and voice mail. Contractor and Eisenberg do not discuss any of these technologies as part of existing social systems at their times of introduction; the introduction of each is represented wholly by the introduction of the material artifact. Let me be clear: These authors are sensitive to social elements surrounding the circumstances of introduction, but the introduction of the technology itself is accomplished by the introduction of the material artifact.

Several researchers have advanced theoretical positions based on Giddens's (1984) theory of structuration (see also, e.g., Banks & Riley, 1993; Barley, 1986; Cohen, 1989). This set of positions also is referred to as the emergent perspective.

Essential to structuration theory is the relationship between structure and action. Human action is constrained or made predictable by structure; yet that same action produces, maintains, and reproduces those structures. The enactment of this relationship is the process of structuration. Poole and DeSanctis (1992) define structuration as "the production and reproduction of a social system through members' application of generative rules and resources, or structures" (p. 10). The inherent recursiveness of action to structure means that structures are inherent dualities, having no force apart from the social systems they constitute and that constitute them. Thus, the structures that constitute any given social system are unique, what Poole and DeSanctis call the specific configuration of "structures-in-use."

For any given context, there are a number of potential structures that may serve to pattern action. Further, the configuration of that same context is a function of the particular structures that are appropriated by human action from the set of potential structures. Within this perspective, the ability to name a context or a social system is technically the recognition of predictable and stable patterns of appropriation. These become "sedimented" structures, or social institutions. For example, Poole, Seibold, and McPhee (1985) redefine "group":

Defining a "group" by such properties [objective characteristics] tacitly separates structure and process, placing the structure of the group prior to (and therefore outside) its interaction; first the set of people are a group, then they interact. To avoid reversing the order of group constitution like this, a structurational definition of a group will be cast in terms of action: a group is that which acts like a group. Only a group can validate an internal role structure or make a social decision, so when a set of people take, or prepare to take such actions, they are a group. (p. 83)

A group is not defined by objective characteristics of either the context or the interaction, but by the patterns of appropriation. In other words, the configuration of the relationship between structure and action allows us to recognize a "group."

The concerns expressed by Poole et al. (1985) for defining "group" are the same as those expressed here for defining "technology." The material definition of the artifact separates structure and process, placing the structure—the physical, material elements—prior to its interaction. To rephrase parallel to the rejected definition of "group" given above: First the set of elements constitutes a technological artifact, then the elements are used in interaction. This cannot be a structurational definition, for it does not cast the artifact in terms of action.

The focus of the emergent perspective is the relationship between information technology and organizational change. Markus and Robey (1988) identify the emergent perspective as one perspective on the nature of causality, what they call "causal agency." The emergent perspective is contrasted to the technological imperative and the organizational imperative, which correspond in essence to the familiar technology-social distinction discussed above. In the technological imperative, forces external to people cause change; in the organizational imperative, change results from people acting purposefully. The emergent perspective combines these two, holding that "change emerges from the interaction of people and events" (Markus & Robey, 1988, p. 584). Considering the process of interaction introduces an element of indeterminacy to organizational change, such that the nature of change cannot be predicted by a simple combination of technological and contextual elements.

Indeterminacy poses a particular problem for the emergent perspective. Posed as an alternative theory of causal agency, the emergent perspective model must aid the processes of explanation and prediction. Indeterminacy makes this a difficult task:

By refusing to acknowledge a dominant cause of change, emergent models differ qualitatively from the deterministic causal arguments of the two imperatives. Prediction in the emergent perspective requires detailed understanding of dynamic organizational processes in addition to knowledge about the intentions of actors and features of information technology. This added complexity makes emergent models difficult to construct. (Markus & Robey, 1988, p. 589)

The primary difficulty is modeling interaction. A common solution is to string out a list of analytic categories or elements that might play a role in change. This list, essentially a large contingency model, guides the focus of research, but does not provide mechanisms for explaining how the elements interact. These models, in other words, assume process or interaction, but do not explain it.

In an example of the emergent perspective, Orlikowski and Robey (1991) turn to Giddens's theory of structuration. They argue that two perspectives of information technology are present in research. These also correspond to the technology-social distinction discussed above. The objectivist—or technological—approach regards the technological artifact as an independent variable capable of causing organizational change. The subjectivist—or social— approach privileges human interpretation and meaning in explaining change. Structuration integrates these positions by assuming a duality of structure, which is the notion that "the structure or institutional properties of social systems are created by human action, and then serve to shape future action" (Orlikowski & Robey, 1991, p. 145). Social structure, then, is both the medium and the outcome of interaction.

Structuration shifts the focus of theory and research from both material elements or interpretations toward the abstract structures that constrain and enable human action. Emphasis is placed instead on understanding the interaction between technology and organizations. Orlikowski and Robey (1991) posit a model of this interaction consisting of three elements: information technology, institutional properties, and human actors. The relationship between these elements is represented by four "key influences" (pp. 153-155). First, information technology is the product of human action; it is created by humans and must be used by humans to have an effect. Second, information technology is the medium of human action; the conditions of technology use simultaneously enable and constrain possibilities for action. Third, conditions of human action are influenced by institutional properties. Fourth, consequences of information technology interaction sustain or change institutional properties. Note here that the conceptualization of technology leaves intact the independence of the technological artifact. The material definition of the artifact still is used, though the role and function of the artifact are expanded such that it has properties of both structure and agency.

The central perspective to have extended Giddens's theory of structuration to explain and predict the effects of communication technology is adaptive structuration theory (AST) (DeSanctis & Poole, 1991, 1994; Poole & DeSanctis, 1987, 1990, 1992). The need to reconceptualize the traditional perspective of technology from a structurational perspective was recognized by Poole and DeSanctis as early as 1987. In proposing the use of group decision support systems (GDSSs) as an adaptive process, Poole and DeSanctis (1987) emphasize that researchers must examine "deeper, less obvious [communication] processes through which technology is incorporated into the group's work processes, subtly structuring group thought and action, and in turn being restructured by the group" (p. 7). Further, they argue that we cannot expect people to use technology in predefined ways, "rather, we can expect that users will alter a system as they use it" (p. 9). Consistent with the premises of the integration perspective, technology and context constitute each other. The task of the researcher is to articulate and explain this relationship.

This task increases the complexity of communication technology research, yet it is through the rejection of the material artifact that construction theories have the greatest opportunity to contribute to understanding and predicting technology use. Suggestions of this complexity are represented currently in AST in the concept of "spirit." In a recent and extensive articulation of this concept, Poole and DeSanctis (1992; DeSanctis & Poole, 1994) construe spirit as the general intent of a technology reflected in its design and how it is implemented. Spirit is neither the intentions of the designers nor the interpretations or perceptions of the users. Rather, it is a "reading" of the material artifact as a "text."

"Spirit" contributes to the redefinition of the technological artifact in two ways. First, in providing a number of sources of "evidence" to consider when constructing the spirit of a technology, Poole and DeSanctis (1992, pp. 12-13) outline as well the beginnings of a methodology for constructing a valid depiction of an alternative definition of the artifact. Second, spirit (as a structurational construct) suggests a way in which the technological artifact may be expected to be relatively stable across contexts. Spirit provides a mechanism for explaining why the constitution of a technology appears to remain stable across new and unrelated contexts: The elements of the artifact are sufficiently coherent such that the process of structuration can be predicted.

Further relationships between the integrated definition of the artifact and the theory of structuration should be explored in future research. It is clear at this point, however, that the adoption of the integration definition offers an opportunity to resolve existing tensions in current AST research. However, an important demand is also made: that all assumptions of an objective or independent technology and the underlying "intervention" model be abandoned.

The actual approach taken by AST, however, has retreated from this position. Rather than being located inextricably in a material-social matrix, technology is portrayed as the interface between social institutions and the independent reality of the material/physical world. AST considers technology as a container—a metaphor of materiality—presenting a group with an array of potential structures, carried by "material software and hardware" that "give incorporated structures more immediacy, body, and salience" and make those structures less diffuse and more easily defined (Poole & DeSanctis, 1992, p. 11). The technology is an "intervention" into the group process to which the group must adapt or adjust (DeSanctis & Poole, 1991; Poole & DeSanctis, 1987). The models for the study of GDSS appropriation are nonrecursive, using the traditional linear input-process-output form (e.g., Poole & DeSanctis,

1987, Fig. 1; Poole, Holmes, & DeSanctis, 1991, p. 928; Poole, Holmes, Watson, & DeSanctis, 1993, p. 180).[17] Further, the models separate structures outside of interaction or group process. In other words, structures themselves are "given" rather than "appropriated" or defined through use.

In a critical review and extension of AST, Contractor and Seibold (1993) advance several arguments similar to those made here. They suggest that, as currently formulated, AST cannot explain change, for it contains no generative mechanism suitable for the explanation of dynamic processes; hypotheses currently deduced from AST "make predictions on the basis of stable, intended consequences" (p. 535). In an effort to redress this limitation, Contractor and Seibold use self-organizing systems theory (SOST) as a mechanism to increase AST's explanatory power. Yet the SOST model they advance (p. 538) does not address the GDSS technology itself. Rather, the model concerns only the nature of the "GDSS-based discussion" (pp. 537-538). The artifact itself is not problematized: for example, the moment of introduction is assumed to exist (p. 539).

The obstacle preventing current theories in the integrated perspective from moving beyond how it has been used, from moving beyond the confines of the material artifact, is the problem of materiality. How do we account for the material artifact? How do we represent spirit, or any other concept of context, when technology is so clearly seen and sensed by the physical object? Unlike the context-as-filter perspective, a social definition of the artifact is not an acceptable alternative, because theories in the integration perspective hold context as inseparable from technology.

Resolving—rather than circumventing—the problem of materiality must be a priority for the integration perspective for this reason: The material definition of the artifact disproves the fundamental assumption of the inseparability of technology and context. The task of defining the artifact is a small, efficient test of the integration perspective. Theory building and empirical research in the integration perspective are complex and time-consuming. If technology can be wholly represented by the material artifact, there is little justification for expending effort pursuing the Cell 4 approach. Such effort would be put to better use in one of the other perspectives.

The potential of the integration perspective to communication theory in general makes the pursuit of a redefinition worthwhile. The integration of the social and the material into a definition of the technological artifact may contribute to scholarship in the communication discipline beyond increasing our understanding of communication technology. If context is an inextricable component of material, communication acts not only toward the creation and coordination of meaning in our social environment, but toward the creation of our material environment as well. The exciting consequence is that artifacts join discourse as a communication activity. Artifacts represent and produce intentions, motives, and interests. They are players in the social creation and sharing of beliefs and meanings.

AN INTEGRATED DEFINITION OF THE ARTIFACT

My final objective in this review is to develop an alternative definition of the artifact built on a set of assumptions consistent with the integrated perspective of Cell 4. In this alternative definition, the artifact is constituted by both material and social elements continuously and simultaneously; the alternative offers an example of an integrated definition of the artifact.

The integrated definition begins with the following requirements:

Technology and context are inseparable. It cannot be possible to conceive of an acontextual, ahistorical artifact. Technology is always located in time and place. Similarly, there is no borderline that sets context apart from technology; there is no independent vantage point from which to assess and observe technology. The meaning of technology is always mediated through context.

The definitional or essential feature of the artifact cannot lie in either material or social elements alone. The material definition, for example, holds the material artifact as wholly representing the technological artifact. The social definition holds perceptions or meanings given to the (material) artifact as sufficiently representing the technological artifact for purposes of theory and research. Neither of these is acceptable, for both contradict the first requirement. Neither material nor social can be sufficient; both must be necessary and inseparable—that is, they must be integrated.

The definition must be capable of explaining the dominance of the material definition of the artifact. In other words, it must explain why it has seemed reasonable to equate technology with the material artifact. This final requirement is, in some ways, the most important, for it is a test of the validity of the definition. The material definition has dominated technology studies because it seems objective, natural, and an accurate portrayal of reality. Unlike the choice of whether technological factors or social factors should be emphasized in theory or research, with regard to defining the artifact, there has been no perception of a choice at all. The integrated definition must explain this transparency. Thus, though the integrated definition challenges fundamental assumptions of the material definition, it does not in itself challenge the body of theory and research that has been built on that definition. Instead, the integrated definition encompasses and extends this existing work while providing a base for new theoretical development.

The task of an integrated definition is to represent the technological artifact as simultaneously material and social. The integrated definition builds from a starting place that is different from that of either the material definition or the social definition. The material definition is grounded in what the artifact "is." The social definition is grounded in what the artifact is "perceived to be." The integrated definition proposed here is grounded in what the artifact "does." Technological artifacts, as distinguished from other objects or entities in the world, are tools; they serve instrumental purposes. We use technology. As Winner (1986) notes, this is a commonplace assumption:

According to conventional views, the human relationship to technical things is too obvious to merit serious reflection. . . . Once things have been made, we interact with them on occasion to achieve specific purposes. One picks up a tool, uses it, and puts it down. One picks up a telephone, talks on it, and then does not use it for a time. A person gets on an airplane, flies from point A to point B, and then gets off. The proper interpretation of the meaning of technology in the mode of use seems to be nothing more complicated than an occasional, limited, and nonproblematic interaction. (pp. 5-6)

Functionality—the ability of an artifact to be used to accomplish a social task—is the primary requirement of technology, prior to the material and social definitions of the artifact.[18] If an artifact is not functional, it will not come into the purview of the material or social definitions. The artifact will not be recognized as technology and, therefore, will not be even a candidate for attention. Achieving functionality, however, is not a certain feat. To be functional, an artifact must meet two requirements: First, someone must perceive that it can be used to accomplish a particular task, and, second, it must be capable of performing that task.

To understand these requirements, consider how a material object comes to be a technology. Take a simple example of a wedge of wood, a scrap left over from some carpentry project. The piece of wood can be sensed, described, measured, and so forth. We might say the wedge is cut from a 2 × 4-inch cedar board, and is 2 inches high and 3 inches long. Yet these descriptions and measurements give only more information about the material object. By themselves, they do not make the wedge a technological artifact because they do not make the wedge instrumental to serving a purpose. Similarly, the wood is perceived or given meaning. When it was created, it was perceived as unneeded scrap. Perceptions or meanings, by themselves, also do not make the wood a technological artifact. Yet, in principle, there is no reason the material or social definitions of the artifact cannot be applied at this point. Neither definition has a mechanism to explain why this wedge of wood is not an artifact.

The integrated definition, on the other hand, provides a clear explanation. Because neither of the requirements set out above has been met, the wood has no functionality. Someone, however, might come across this wedge of wood and decide that it could be used as a doorstop. That person—or someone else—might envision further uses for the wedge, as a hammer, or a bookend, or a lever. Thus, the artifact would be interpreted as being capable of serving some purpose. The wedge would be expected to perform a particular task. Thus, the first requirement would be fulfilled. However, the artifact is not yet functional. There is no guarantee, of course, that expectations will be fulfilled. The material elements of the artifact must be capable of fulfilling the task to at least the minimum extent of what is expected. The wedge must adequately prop open a door, drive a nail, hold up books, and so forth. If successful, the wedge of wood is functional. Only then is it a tool, a technological artifact.[19]

The wedge of wood in this example could be replaced easily with more complex artifacts. A computer program, for example, could be purchased by a manager in an organization because it is expected to help individuals produce more effective materials for presentations. The program may or may not be capable of meeting these expectations adequately. If it cannot, and if no other purposes are served by the program, it is ignored or discarded. It is not functional. In this example, the computer program already exists, but that need not be the case. A computer programmer may wish to build a program that will be useful to those who must prepare presentation materials. Design and development efforts, then, are directed toward producing an artifact that will be capable of sufficiently achieving this expectation. The technology is "finished" when the capabilities of the program match the expectations. A single material artifact also may be subjected to different expectations simultaneously. A second computer programmer, working with the first, may wish to build a program that has an efficient and elegant set of program code for graphic drawing. For this second programmer, the technology is "finished" when these alternative expectations are met, not when the first programmer's objectives are met.

The purpose of these examples is to illustrate the requirements for functionality. These requirements may also be translated into a basic representation of the artifact, as appears in Figure 6.1. This representation is the model for an integrated definition of the artifact. The model consists of two sets of elements: social and material. Taken together, they constitute the technological artifact. The social elements are the expectations of what the artifact will or can do. They act to conscribe or enlist the artifact in the accomplishment of some particular purpose or task. The material elements are the components of the artifact that do not depend upon our perception or interpretation of them for their existence. They are the matter of an artifact: the wedge of wood, for example, or the computer program. If all social elements were removed, these are the elements that would remain as separate entities, though they would no longer be elements of technology.

The third component of the model is the positioning of these two sets of elements in relation to each other: Expectations buffer our perceptions of the material elements. In other words, although the matter of material components may be perceived directly, these components may not be perceived directly as technology; they may be perceived directly only as matter. The prior requirement for the perception of technology is that some set of material components is interpreted as being a tool that can be used (or has the potential to be used). Only then do the capabilities (as opposed to the properties) of the material components become a matter of consideration. Capabilities, functions, and potentials are all social entities. They arise from and are sustained by a context. Thus, they cannot be inherent properties of the material components, which, by definition, are independent of context.

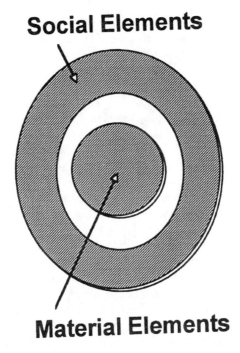

Social Elements

Material Elements

Figure 6.1. Integrated Definition of the Artifact: Basic Representation

It might be argued that the order of priority should be reversed, that the material components must first be capable of performing a task before they can be perceived as having that capability. Thus, functionality is inherent in the material components, only waiting to be perceived. One problem with this argument is that it can never be tested. A researcher would be unable to document the functions of a material artifact without first perceiving or interpreting what those functions might be. In other words, functions are not self-evident in the material artifact. They are perceptible only after the artifact is placed in a context. Even if the functions could be documented, they could not be tested without recourse to using the material artifact in a context. A second problem with this argument is that it presumes that functions exist outside of time or place. Thus, functions may lie dormant in material components, waiting to be discovered. Yet the terms themselves are meaningless outside of a context. A function is an activity or task performed to fulfill a specific need or want. Needs and wants do not exist outside of human experience or interpretation. Thus, even conceiving of functions presumes a social ground. Functions cannot be inherent in material components, which are timeless and placeless. To be explicit, whether or not the material components existed before the social components is irrelevant, for a technological artifact can exist only after a function or a purpose is perceived to exist.

In this basic form, the model comprises the integrated definition of the artifact used in this study. The definition is grounded in what an artifact does, rather than in what an artifact is or is perceived to be. Thus, the foundational requirement for a technological artifact is functionality.

A functionality-based model fulfills the three requirements of an integrated definition of the artifact set out above. First, technology and context are inseparable. In a functionality-based model, the definitional element of technology is its instrumentality, its ability to serve a purpose. Because purposes are contextual, technology is constituted only in context.[20] Context cannot be removed from the constitution of technology. Similarly, technology cannot be removed from the constitution of context. There is no independent vantage point from which to view technology, because the very act of identifying or perceiving a technology is part of that technology. The two cannot be separated into independent entities.

The second requirement of an integrated definition is that the definitional or essential feature of the artifact cannot lie in either material or social elements alone. The functionality-based model clearly meets this requirement. Material elements alone cannot be perceived as technology; they are simply objects. Social elements alone cannot perform functions or accomplish tasks. If material elements are not capable of meeting expectations adequately, the artifact is not functional. Thus, both material and social elements are necessary.

The final requirement of an integrated definition is that it must explain the dominance of the material definition of the artifact and not merely offer an alternative. A functional-based definition offers an ironic explanation: The material definition of the artifact is made possible by the achievement of functionality. In other words, when material components of the artifact match social expectations of how that artifact should function, those expectations are no longer perceived as existing. Technology—the device—is simply there, ready to be used in "nonproblematic interaction."

Telephones, for example, are a common technology in U.S. society. We use them regularly and, mostly, without incident to converse with people in many different locations. The functionality of the telephone has been achieved so well that we normally do not notice our expectations that telephones have devices for speaking and listening, or that they reliably connect us to each other. If, however, we cannot connect with the people we want to reach, or if we experience problems speaking to or hearing each other, these expectations become clear; they are the reasons we use for why the telephone "is not working," for why it is not functional.[21]

In other words, when we say that a technological artifact "works," what we are really saying is that the artifact is performing just as we expect. But expectations are the first to be dropped off this definition. We do not identify a telephone by saying, "This object matches my expectations of what a telephone should be able to do." Instead, we say, "This object is a telephone because I can use it to talk with other people." When functionality is achieved, the definitional elements of the artifact are transferred, without reflection, to the material components. We do not perceive our expectations because they have merged seamlessly with the material components of the artifact and become transparent. Thus, the technology seems wholly constituted by the material artifact and the material definition of the artifact seems objective and natural.

CONCLUSION

Lying unstated, unrecognized, and unchallenged at the base of the growing body of research in computer-based communication technologies has been a single conception of technology as the material artifact. Although recent years have seen the development of truly innovative approaches to understanding communication technology, the assumptions of the material definition of the artifact have guided and shaped the possibilities for building theory.

Making this definition and its assumptions explicit provides a frame for classifying possible perspectives for communication technology research. Examining the examples of theories and research that correspond to each perspective makes apparent that the material definition of the artifact poses a fundamental contradiction to two of the perspectives: context as filter and integration. Although the context-as-filter perspective may substitute a social center for the material center of the present definition, integration does not have this option. Material and social both must be integrated into a definition of the artifact.

The contribution of this chapter is to offer a new foundation for understanding, comparing, and evaluating theories that seek to understand and explain the relationship between communication and computer-based communication technologies. Beyond its use as a classification device, the technology-context scheme fulfills an immediate need for a genuine common ground for exchange among a rapidly increasing number of perspectives on the question of whether or not computers make a difference.

NOTES

1. There are nearly as many terms and acronyms for computer-based communication technologies as there are research programs developing or studying these new technologies. Several terms center on the communication rather than the technology: for example, *computer-based communication* (CBC), *computer-mediated communication* (CMC), and *computer-assisted communication*. Each of the "middle" terms—*based, mediated, assisted*—ascribes a role to computer technology in relation to communication. Several other terms center on the type of task or function the technology performs: for example, *electronic mail* (e-mail), *computer conferencing* (CC), *group decision support systems* (GDSS), *electronic meeting systems* (EMS),

groupware. The most general term in use is *new communication technology* (e.g., Rice et al., 1984), which encompasses a wide range of technologies, including noncomputer technologies across the telecommunications area. I use *computer-based communication technologies* here because it is a descriptive term. No particular relation between communication and computer technology is assumed. The term encompasses all computer technologies that may be used by individuals to communicate with each other. Generally excluded are computer technologies that assist a single user. There is a significant body of research addressing theories of the human-computer interface (Carroll, 1989; Carroll & Kellogg, 1989; Cathcart & Gumpert, 1985; Downes, 1987; Ehrlich, 1987; Elam & Mea, 1987; Fields, 1987; Mohrman & Lawler, 1984).

2. An exception to this is the body of work on technology adoption and diffusion (e.g., Markus, 1983; Rogers, 1983). Generally, however, this research also shares the assumptions discussed below.

3. The position that software is material or physical stems directly from the historical development of computer systems. Early computer systems had operating instructions built in, or "hardwired." Changing the operation of these systems required changing the physical configuration of various components. Programmed computers removed the command structure or operating system one level beyond the actual physical configuration of the components, so that changes in the operation of the system could be accomplished simply by changing the written or encoded programmed instructions (Sammet, 1969).

4. Recently, researchers have recognized that technology might be understood better as a complex of factors. Definitions of group decision support systems, for example, include nonartifactual elements such as people and procedures as central to the technology (DeSanctis & Gallupe, 1987; Huber, 1984). These definitions do succeed in reducing the focus on the material artifact, but, whatever other elements might be included in the definition, the assumption of a material artifact still exists. Even within these definitions, the presence of the material artifact is necessary for the technology—such as the GDSS—to exist. Without the material artifact, the remaining elements are simply a procedure or a method. Further, the inclusion of other elements such as "procedures" can be regarded as simply a further extension of the move begun with software and explained in note 3: These additional elements are still standard, easily identified, and easily described. People might be included as important elements in the working of the technology (such as serving as a facilitator), but technology is still separable from context. The importance of this distinction is made clear below.

5. Rather by default, *communication technology* or *new communication technology* has been used to refer to computer-based technologies that act as a channel for communication or that provide support structures for communication in various contexts. The primary technologies that appear in communication research are computer based: electronic mail, electronic messaging, computer conferencing, bulletin boards, and group decision support systems. Technologies not based centrally on computer technology, such as satellite and cable television, videotex, and teleconferencing, are generally referenced as separate, placed in the areas of telecommunication, mass media, or journalism (see, e.g., the *Index to Periodicals in Communication*; Matlon & Facciola, 1993). Whether or not there is any principled reason for this divining of technologies across areas, limiting the meaning of *communication technology* to computer-based technologies is a useful convenience, consistent with existing research, and will be used in this study.

6. Even within this approach, partitioning of technologies is not uncommon. As noted by Poole, Holmes, Watson, and DeSanctis (1993), genres of CBCTs, such as computer conferencing, GDSS, and collaborative writing, are studied apart from one another.

7. Arguments against this assumption have been well developed in the field of the social study of technology (Callon & Law, 1982; Hughes, 1983; Pinch & Bijker, 1987; Vergragt, 1988).

8. "Social" elements should not be confused with "software" or procedures for using technology to accomplish a task. Social elements may interface with the material elements (in other words, the technology), but they are not part of the physical makeup or constitution of the technology. It is precisely their separability from the artifact and their ability to act in response

to the artifact that distinguish social elements from the elements of the technology itself. For a more detailed discussion of the distinction between these two perspectives, see Nass and Mason (1990).

9. Other heuristics that have appeared recently echo the tension between technology and social elements. Walther, Anderson, and Park (1994) review the "cues-filtered-out" approach and set against it "social information processing." DeSanctis and Poole (1994) suggest that theoretical approaches may be organized by three major perspectives to technology and organizational change: the decision-making school, the social technology school, and the institutional school.

10. The importance of theory building in communication technology research has been emphasized in a recent collection edited by Fulk and Steinfield (1990).

11. It should be noted that the T-C scheme does not perform a normative function. Because the dimensions of the scheme are conceptual and not descriptive, the scheme is inappropriate for use as a means of choosing what theory or perspective to use in a particular study. Further, a particular theory may fall into more than one category, depending on its assumptions. However, it is likely that such a theory may have internal inconsistencies on the assumptive level that need to be resolved.

12. Paradoxically, this is also the approach recently advocated by Poole et al. (1993): "We suggest the following approach: . . . (b) spell out the ensemble of features in the specific GDSS under study and use these to identify which impacts from the general set should result in the specific study" (p. 178). The paradox arises because Poole and DeSanctis are the authors of a constructionist approach, adaptive structuration theory, which is discussed in detail below.

13. Despite the acknowledgment of uncertainty due to contextual factors, Kling's (1987) perspective still holds the technological artifact as separate from context: "Computer-based systems which can be perfectible under static laboratory conditions and when supported by a rich array of resources may be very problematic when introduced into dynamic social settings. . . . the simple development of 'good technologies' is not sufficient to insure that social life will be improved for many participants" (p. 337).

14. *Sneakerware* refers to copying a program or a document to a disk and carrying it to another person.

15. One might argue that the material artifact is the minimally necessary element for technology, and further research explores and traces the various meanings that are given to it. This move grants an independence to technology as well as to context, thus returning to an essentially deterministic approach.

16. This is essentially a position taken by some developers of technology, as in, for example, Personick's (1993) emphasis on user feedback in the philosophy of iterative development at Bellcore.

17. It should be pointed out that even this linearity is not consistent. DeSanctis and Poole (1991), for example, suggest a recursive loop. However, this model also begins with the introduction of the artifact into a group context.

18. This holds true as well for definitions of technology as processes. See, for example, Thompson (1967) and Perrow (1972).

19. This example is simplified for purposes of illustration. Making a judgment as to whether a particular object is or is not a particular artifact may be a much longer process. The wedge of wood, for example, may fail in propping open a particular door, yet we may not want to say it is not a doorstop. Instead, because it resembles strongly other doorstops from our past experience, we may extend faith that there is some door, somewhere, that the wedge of wood can prop open. Of course, even this expectation could, theoretically, be tested empirically. If it failed this test, we would reject it as a doorstop, as that particular tool. Thus, my point still holds: The definition of an artifact is dependent on the ability of the artifact to serve a particular purpose in a concrete situation. Presumably, there is some way to represent the number of failures we would allow before judging that the particular object is not an example of that artifact. However, finding that number is not a concern here.

20. *Context* is meant here in a general sense as a contrast to *acontextual* or *context independent*. The details of context may change—indeed, they can be expected to. Similarly, the claim here is not that purposes are bound to any particular context, only that they have meaning only within some context.

21. Expectations, then, form a kind of tacit understanding about the technology (Polanyi, 1967).

REFERENCES

Banks, S. P., & Riley, P. (1993). Structuration theory as an ontology for communication research. In S. A. Deetz (Ed.), *Communication yearbook 16* (pp. 167-196). Newbury Park, CA: Sage.

Bannon, L. J. (1986). Computer-mediated communication. In D. A. Norman & S. W. H. Draper (Eds.), *User centered system design: New perspectives on human-computer interaction* (pp. 433-452). Hillsdale, NJ: Lawrence Erlbaum.

Barley, S. R. (1986). Technology as an occasion for structuring: Evidence from observations of CT scanners and the social order of radiology departments. *Administrative Science Quarterly, 31,* 78-108.

Callon, M., & Law, J. (1982). On interests and their transformation: Enrollment and counter-enrollment. *Social Studies of Science, 12,* 612-625.

Carroll, J. M. (1989). Evaluation, description, and invention: Paradigms for human-computer interaction. *Advances in Computers, 29,* 47-77.

Carroll, J. M., & Kellogg, W. A. (1989). Artifact as theory-nexus: Hermeneutics meets theory-based design. In *CHI '89 Proceedings: Wings for the mind* (pp. 7-14). New York: ACM.

Cathcart, R., & Gumpert, G. (1985). The person-computer interaction: A unique source. *Information and Behavior, 1,* 113-124.

Chesebro, J. W. (1985). Computer-mediated interpersonal communication. *Information and Behavior, 1,* 202-222.

Chesebro, J. W., & Bonsall, D. G. (1989). *Computer-mediated communication: Human relationships in a computerized world.* Tuscaloosa: University of Alabama Press.

Cohen, I. J. (1989). *Structuration theory: Anthony Giddens and the constitution of social life.* London: Macmillan.

Compaine, B. M. (1988). Information technology and cultural change: Toward a new literacy. In B. M. Compaine (Ed.), *Issues in new information technology* (pp. 145-178). Norwood, NJ: Ablex.

Contractor, N. S., & Eisenberg, E. M. (1990). Communication networks and new media in organizations. In J. Fulk & C. W. Steinfield (Eds.), *Organizations and communication technologies* (pp. 143-172). Newbury Park, CA: Sage.

Contractor, N. S., & Seibold, D. R. (1993). Theoretical frameworks for the study of structuring processes in group decision support systems: Adaptive structuration theory and self-organizing systems theory. *Human Communication Research, 19,* 528-563.

Culnan, M. J. (1985). The dimensions of perceived accessibility to information: Implications for the delivery of information systems and services. *Journal of the American Society for Information Science, 36,* 302-308.

Culnan, M. J., & Bair, J. H. (1983). Human communication needs and organizational productivity: The potential impact of office automation. *Journal of the American Society for Information Science, 34,* 215-221.

Daft, R. L., & Lengel, R. (1986). Organizational information requirements, media richness, and structural design. *Management Science, 32,* 554-571.

Danowski, J. A. (1982). Computer-mediated communication: A network-based content analysis using a CBBS conference. In M. Burgoon (Ed.), *Communication yearbook 6* (pp. 905-924). Beverly Hills, CA: Sage.

Danowski, J. A., & Edison-Swift, P. (1985). Crisis effects on intraorganizational computer-based communication. *Communication Research, 12,* 251-270.

Danziger, J. N., & Kraemer, K. L. (1986). *People and computers: The impacts of computing on end users in organizations.* New York: Columbia University Press.

DeSanctis, G., & Poole, M. S. (1991, July). *The hidden complexity in advanced technology use: Adaptive structuration theory.* Unpublished manuscript, University of Minnesota, Minneapolis.

DeSanctis, G., & Poole, M. S. (1994). Capturing the complexity in advanced technology use: Adaptive structuration theory. *Organization Science, 5,* 121-147.

DeSanctis, G., & Gallupe, R. B. (1987). A foundation for the study of group decision support systems. *Management Science, 33,* 589-609.

Downes, S. (1987). Human-computer interaction: A critical synthesis. *Social Epistemology, 1,* 27-36.

Ehrlich, S. F. (1987). Social and psychological factors influencing the design of office communication systems. In J. M. Carroll & P. T. Tanner (Eds.), *Human factors in computing systems and graphical interface: Proceedings of CHI&GI 1987* (pp. 323-329). New York: ACM.

Elam, J. J., & Mea, M. (1987). Designing for creativity: Considerations for DSS development. *Information and Management, 13,* 215-222.

Fields, C. (1987). Human-computer interaction: A critical synthesis. *Social Epistemology, 1,* 5-25.

Fulk, J. (1993). Social construction of communication technology. *Academy of Management Journal, 36,* 921-950.

Fulk, J., Schmitz, J., & Steinfield, C. W. (1990). A social influence model of technology use. In J. Fulk & C. W. Steinfield (Eds.), *Organizations and communication technologies* (pp. 117-140). Newbury Park, CA: Sage.

Fulk, J., & Steinfield, C. W. (Eds.). (1990). *Organizations and communication technologies.* Newbury Park, CA: Sage.

Giddens, A. (1984). *The constitution of society: Outline of the theory of structuration.* Berkeley: University of California Press.

Gronbeck, B. E. (1990). Communication technology, consciousness, and culture: Supplementing FM-2030's view of transhumanity. In M. J. Medhurst, A. Gonzalez, & T. R. Peterson (Eds.), *Communication and the culture of technology* (pp. 3-18). Pullman: Washington State University Press.

Gutek, B. A., Bikson, T. K., & Mankin, D. (1984). Individual and organizational consequences of computer-based office information technology. *Applied Social Psychology Annual: Applications in Organizational Settings, 5,* 231-254.

Heeter, C. (1989). Implications of new interactive technologies for conceptualizing communication. In J. L. Salvaggio & J. Bryant (Eds.), *Media use in the information age* (pp. 217-235). Hillsdale, NJ: Lawrence Erlbaum.

Heim, M. (1987). *Electric language: A philosophical study of word processing.* New Haven, CT: Yale University Press.

Hiemstra, G. (1982). Teleconferencing, concern for face, and organizational culture. In M. Burgoon (Ed.), *Communication yearbook 6* (pp. 874-904). Beverly Hills, CA: Sage.

Hiemstra, G. (1983). You say you want a revolution? "Information technology" in organizations. In R. N. Bostrom (Ed.), *Communication yearbook 7* (pp. 802-827). Beverly Hills, CA: Sage.

Hiltz, S. R. (1978). Controlled experiments with computerized conferencing: Results of a pilot study. *Bulletin of the American Society for Information Science, 4,* 11-12.

Hiltz, S. R. (1982). Experiments and experiences with computerized conferencing. In R. M. Landau, J. H. Bair, & J. H. Siegman (Eds.), *Emerging office systems: Based on proceedings of the Stanford University International Symposium on Office Automation* (pp. 187-204). Norwood, NJ: Ablex.

Hiltz, S. R., Johnson, K., & Turoff, M. (1986). Experiments in group decision making: Communication processes and outcome in face-to-face versus computerized conferences. *Human Communication Research, 13,* 225-252.

Hiltz, S. R., & Turoff, M. (1978). *The network nation: Human communication via computer.* Reading, MA: Addison-Wesley.

Hiltz, S. R., & Turoff, M. (1981). The evolution of user behavior in a computerized conferencing system. *Communications of the ACM, 24,* 739-751.

Hiltz, S. R., & Turoff, M. (1992). *The network nation: Human communication via computer* (rev. ed.). Reading, MA: Addison-Wesley.

Hiltz, S. R., Turoff, M., & Johnson, K. (1989). Experiments in group decision making, 3: Disinhibition, deindividuation, and group process in pen name and real name computer conferences. *Decision Support Systems, 5,* 217-232.

Huber, G. P. (1984). The nature and design of post-industrial organizations. *Management Science, 30,* 928-951.

Hughes, T. P. (1983). *Networks of power: Electrification in Western society, 1880-1930.* Baltimore, MD: Johns Hopkins University Press.

Innis, H. (1972). *Empire and communications.* Toronto: University of Toronto Press.

Johansen, R. (1977). Social evaluations of teleconferencing. *Telecommunications Policy, 1,* 395-419.

Johansen, R., Vallee, J., & Spangler, K. (1979). *Electronic meetings: Technical alternatives and social choices.* Reading, MA: Addison-Wesley.

Jones, S. J. (Ed.). (1995). *CyberSociety: Computer-mediated communication and community.* Thousand Oaks, CA: Sage.

Katzman, N. (1974). The impact of communication technology: Promises and prospects. *Journal of Communication, 24,* 47- 58.

Kerr, E. B., & Hiltz, S. R. (1982). *Computer-mediated communication systems: Status and evaluation.* New York: Academic Press.

Kiesler, S., Siegel, J., & McGuire, T. W. (1984). Social psychological aspects of computer-mediated communication. *American Psychologist, 39,* 1123- 1134.

Kling, R. (1980). Social analyses of computing: Theoretical perspectives in recent empirical research. *Computing Surveys, 12,* 61-110.

Kling, R. (1987). The social dimensions of computerization. In J. M. Carroll & P. P. Tanner (Eds.), *Human factors in computing systems and graphics interfaces: Proceedings of CHI&GI 1987* (pp. 337-339). New York: ACM.

Kraemer, K. L., & Pinsonneault, A. (1990). Technology and groups: Assessments of the empirical research. In J. Galegher, R. Kraut, & C. Egido (Eds.), *Intellectual teamwork: Social and technological foundations of cooperative work* (pp. 373-405). Hillsdale, NJ: Lawrence Erlbaum.

Markus, M. L. (1983). Power, politics, and MIS implementation. *Communications of the ACM, 26,* 430-444.

Markus, M. L., & Robey, D. (1988). Information technology and organizational change: Causal structure in theory and research. *Management Science, 34,* 583-598.

Matlon, R. J., & Facciola, P. C. (Eds.). (1993). *Index to periodicals in communication* (rev. ed.). Annandale, VA: Speech Communication Association.

Mohrman, A. M., Jr., & Lawler, E. E. (1984). A review of theory and research. In F. W. McFarlan (Ed.), *The information systems research challenge: Proceedings of the Harvard Business School Colloquium* (pp. 135-164). Boston: Harvard Business School Press.

Nass, C., & Mason, L. (1990). On the study of technology and task: A variable-based approach. In J. Fulk & C. W. Steinfield (Eds.), *Organizations and communication technologies* (pp. 46-68). Newbury Park, CA: Sage.

Norberg, A. L., & O'Neill, J. E. (1992). *A history of the Information Processing Techniques Office of the Defense Advanced Research Projects Agency.* Minneapolis: Charles Babbage Institute.

Ong, W. (1982). *Orality and literacy: The technologizing of the word.* London: Methuen.

Orlikowski, W. J., & Robey, D. (1991). Information technology and the structuring of organizations. *Information Systems Research, 2,* 143-169.

Palme, J. (1985). Survey of computer-based messaging systems. In B. Shackel (Ed.), *Human-computer interaction: INTERACT '84* (pp. 923-928). Amsterdam: Elsevier North-Holland.

Panko, R. R. (1977). The outlook for computer mail. *Telecommunications Policy, 1,* 242-253.

Perrow, C. (1972). *Complex organizations: A critical essay.* Glenview, IL: Scott, Foresman.

Personick, S. (1993, May). *Iteration in designing new technology.* Paper presented at the annual meeting of the International Communication Association, Washington, DC.

Pinch, T. J., & Bijker, W. E. (1987). The social construction of facts and artifacts: Or how the sociology of science and the sociology of technology might benefit each other. In W. E. Bijker, T. P. Hughes, & T. Pinch (Eds.), *The social construction of technological systems: New directions in the sociology and history of technology* (pp. 17-50). Cambridge: MIT Press.

Polanyi, M. (1967). *The tacit dimension.* Garden City, NY: Anchor.

Poole, M. S., & DeSanctis, G. (1987). *Group decision making and group decision support systems* (MISRC Working Paper Series 88-02). Minneapolis: University of Minnesota, MIS Research Center.

Poole, M. S., & DeSanctis, G. (1990). Understanding the use of group decision support systems: The theory of adaptive structuration. In J. Fulk & C. W. Steinfield (Eds.), *Organizations and communication technologies* (pp. 173-193). Newbury Park, CA: Sage.

Poole, M. S., & DeSanctis, G. (1992). Microlevel structuration in computer-supported group decision making. *Human Communication Research, 19,* 5-49.

Poole, M. S., Holmes, M., & DeSanctis, G. (1991). Conflict management in a computer-supported meeting environment. *Management Science, 37,* 926-953.

Poole, M. S., Holmes, M., Watson, R., & DeSanctis, G. (1993). Group decision support systems and group communication: A comparison of decision making in computer-supported and nonsupported groups. *Communication Research, 20,* 176-213.

Poole, M. S., Seibold, D. R., & McPhee, R. D. (1985). Group decision-making as a structurational process. *Quarterly Journal of Speech, 71,* 74-102.

Poster, M. (1990). *The mode of information: Poststructuralism and social context.* Chicago: University of Chicago Press.

Rafaeli, S., & LaRose, R. J. (1993). Electronic bulletin boards and "public goods" explanations of collaborative mass media. *Communication Research, 20,* 277-297.

Rice, R. E. (1982). Communication networking in computer-conferencing systems: A longitudinal study of group roles and system structure. In M. Burgoon (Ed.), *Communication yearbook 6* (pp. 925-944). Beverly Hills, CA: Sage.

Rice, R. E. (1993). Media appropriateness: Using social presence theory to compare traditional and new organizational media. *Human Communication Research, 19,* 451-484.

Rice, R. E., & Barnett, G. A. (1986). Group communication networking in an information environment: Applying metric multidimensional scaling. In M. L. McLaughlin (Ed.), *Communication yearbook 9* (pp. 315-338). Beverly Hills, CA: Sage.

Rice, R. E., & Love, G. (1987). Electronic emotion: Socioemotional content in a computer-mediated communication network. *Communication Research, 14,* 85-108.

Rice, R. E., Bair, J. H., Chen, M., Dimmick, J., Dozier, D. M., Jacob, M. E., Johnson, B. M., Penniman, W. D., Svenning, L. L., Rogers, E. M., Rothenbuhler, E. W., Ruchinskas, J. E., &

Williams, F. (1984). *The new media: Communication, research, and technology.* Beverly Hills, CA: Sage.

Roberts, L. G. (1969). ARPA/Information processing techniques computer network concept. In W. D. Gerhard (Ed.), *Proceedings of invitational workshop on network of computers* (Publication No. NOC-68) (p. 115). Fort George G. Meade, MD: National Security Agency.

Rogers, E. M. (1983). *Diffusion of innovations* (3rd ed.). New York: Free Press.

Rogers, E. M., & Rafaeli, S. (1985). Computers and communication. *Information and Behavior, 1,* 95-112.

Sammet, J. E. (1969). *Programming languages: History and fundamentals.* Englewood Cliffs, NJ: Prentice Hall.

Schmitz, J., & Fulk, J. (1991). Organizational colleagues, media richness, and e-mail: A test of the social influence model of technology use. *Communication Research, 18,* 487-523.

Short, J., Williams, E., & Christie, B. (1976). *The social psychology of telecommunications.* London: John Wiley.

Spears, R., & Lea, M. (1994). Panacea or panopticon? The hidden power in computer-mediated communication. *Communication Research, 21,* 427-459.

Sproull, L., & Kiesler, S. (1991). *Connections: New ways of working in the networked organization.* Cambridge: MIT Press.

Steinfield, C. W. (1986). Computer-mediated communication in an organizational setting: Explaining task-related and socioemotional uses. In M. L. McLaughlin (Ed.), *Communication yearbook 9* (pp. 777-804). Beverly Hills, CA: Sage.

Steinfield, C. W., & Fulk, J. (1990). The theory imperative. In J. Fulk & C. W. Steinfield (Eds.), *Organizations and communication technologies* (pp. 13-25). Newbury Park, CA: Sage.

Thompson, J. D. (1967). *Organizations in action.* New York: McGraw-Hill.

Trevino, L. K., Daft, R. L., & Lengel, R. H. (1990). Understanding managers' media choices: A symbolic interactionist perspective. In J. Fulk & C. W. Steinfield (Eds.), *Organizations and communication technologies* (pp. 71-94). Newbury Park, CA: Sage.

Turkle, S. (1984). *The second self: Computers and the human spirit.* New York: Simon & Schuster.

Turner, J. A. (1987). Understanding the elements of system design. In R. J. Boland & R. A. Hirschheim (Eds.), *Critical issues in information systems resources* (pp. 97-112). Chichester: John Wiley.

Valacich, J. S., Paranka, D., George, J. F., & Nunamaker, J. F., Jr. (1993). Communication concurrency and the new media: A new dimension for media richness. *Communication Research, 20,* 249-276.

Vergragt, P. J. (1988). The social shaping of industrial innovations. *Social Studies of Science, 18,* 483-513.

Walther, J. B. (1992). Interpersonal effects in computer-mediated interaction: A relational perspective. *Communication Research, 19,* 52-90.

Walther, J. B., Anderson, J. F., & Park, D. W. (1994). Interpersonal effects in computer-mediated interaction: A meta-analysis of social and antisocial communication. *Human Communication Research, 21,* 460-487.

Walther, J. B., & Burgoon, J. K. (1992). Relational communication in computer-mediated interaction. *Human Communication Research, 19,* 50-88.

Weizenbaum, J. (1976). *Computer power and human reason: From judgment to calculation.* New York: W. H. Freeman.

Williams, E. (1977). Experimental comparisons of face-to-face and mediated communication: A review. *Psychological Bulletin, 84,* 963-976.

Williams, F., Rice, R. E., & Dordick, H. S. (1985). Behavioral impacts in the information age. *Information and Behavior, 1,* 161-182.

Winner, L. (1977). *Autonomous technology: Technics-out-of-control as a theme in political thought.* Cambridge: MIT Press.

Winner, L. (1986). *The whale and the reactor: A search for limits in an age of high technology.* Chicago: University of Chicago Press.

Zmud, R. W. (1990). Opportunities for strategic information manipulation through new information technology. In J. Fulk & C. W. Steinfield (Eds.), *Organizations and communication technologies* (pp. 95-116). Newbury Park, CA: Sage.

Zuboff, S. (1988). *In the age of the smart machine: The future of work and power.* New York: Basic Books.

CHAPTER CONTENTS

7 Communication Aspects of Dyadic Social Influence in Organizations: A Review and Integration of Conceptual and Empirical Developments

BRUCE BARRY
MARY R. WATSON
Vanderbilt University

This chapter presents a review and synthesis of research on dyadic social influence in organizations, defined as the communication processes through which an individual participant within a complex organization elicits cognitive, emotional, and behavioral change from another individual in the pursuit of social objectives. Distinct streams of dyadic influence research have developed in various literatures and rely on divergent methods; this analysis crosses disciplinary boundaries to include work in communication theory, social and industrial/organizational psychology, and sociology, among others. The review considers (a) conceptual models of the process of dyadic influence, (b) efforts to identify and catalog influence-seeking methods, and (c) empirical studies of the antecedents, correlates, and consequences of influence method selection. Within each section, research issues, trends, and limitations that are specifically relevant to understanding influence in organizations are discussed. The authors introduce a framework of dyadic social influence that integrates and extends the various approaches and perspectives examined in the review.

INTRODUCTION

The study of communication aspects of social influence, broadly conceived, is the study of how individuals and social units use verbal and

AUTHORS' NOTE: An earlier and abbreviated version of this chapter was presented at the 1994 annual meeting of the Academy of Management in Dallas, Texas.

Correspondence and requests for reprints: Bruce Barry, Owen Graduate School of Management, Vanderbilt University, 401 21st Avenue South, Nashville, TN 37203.

Communication Yearbook 19, pp. 269-317

nonverbal strategies to modify the cognitions, beliefs, attitudes, values, and behaviors of others. In this chapter we consider the case of interpersonal, or dyadic, social influence in complex organizations: the communication processes and situational contexts through which an individual organization member (an influence "agent") elicits emotional, cognitive, and/or behavioral change from another individual organization member (an influence "target") in the pursuit of social objectives. Commonly regarded as a basic and ubiquitous social phenomenon (e.g., Barry & Bateman, 1992; Cobb, 1984; Dillard, Segrin, & Harden, 1989; Kipnis, 1984; Marwell & Schmitt, 1967a), interpersonal influence has attracted substantial research attention from a number of perspectives and disciplines (for recent reviews, see Boster, 1990; O'Keefe, 1990; Seibold, Cantrill, & Meyers, 1985, 1994; Wheeless, Barraclough, & Stewart, 1983). An inspection of the literature reveals, however, that conceptual and operational variety across disciplines continues to hinder theoretical and practical integration (Nemeth & Staw, 1989; Raven, 1992).

In organizational life, influence as goal-driven interpersonal behavior is central to the attainment of organizational objectives. At a macro level, political processes, including the exercise of influence, are mechanisms by which organizations resolve conflicts among competing interests (Salancik & Pfeffer, 1977). At a micro level, individual actors seek to manage the opinions and activities of others in the pursuit of both individual and organizational goals. Social influence in organizations is often associated with the exercise of leadership grounded in formal authority (Porter, Allen, & Angle, 1981). However, given the widely accepted proposition that the ability to exert influence in organizations is not exclusively a function of position power (Mechanic, 1962), the study of social influence is essential to an understanding of behavior in organizations that goes well beyond the application of formally vested power and authority (Mowday, 1978). Research indicates that managers spend as much as three-fourths of their time engaged in verbal communication activities (Mintzberg, 1973), which form the primary vehicle for the transmission of influence attempts. Indeed, it has been argued that the postindustrial trend toward flatter, more decentralized authority structures in work organizations compels organizational participants to depend less on exercising power and more on gaining and exerting social influence if they are to be effective (Kanter, 1984; Sashkin & Burke, 1987).

The purpose of this chapter is to review and integrate research on dyadic influence in an effort to (a) take stock of what we know about dyadic influence that is relevant for organizational contexts, and (b) use this integration to extend our conceptualization of the dyadic social influence process. Given the breadth and diversity that characterize work on social influence, we begin by specifying a working definition of *dyadic social influence* and by defining the scope of this review. We next review existing literature, bringing together research from communication theory, social and industrial-organizational psychology, interpersonal sociology, and related areas. This review has three parts: (a) a discussion of theoretical formulations that model the process of dyadic influence seeking, (b) a synthesis of attempts by researchers to develop inventories of the tactical options available to influence seekers, and (c) an analysis of empirical explorations of the antecedents, correlates, and consequences of tactical choice. Not intended as an exhaustive chronicle, this review instead focuses on identifying trends and pointing out limitations of the research to date. In the final section, we present an integrative framework of organizationally based dyadic influence that synthesizes and extends the extant literature. The framework is transactional in nature, treating the influence attempt as a reciprocal exchange that transpires within an evolving social context (Miller, Boster, Roloff, & Seibold, 1987; Perloff, 1993).

Definitions

Intuitively, dyadic influence can be thought of as the exercise of social control. Kipnis, Schmidt, and Wilkinson (1980) captured this idea in subtitling their inductive study of organizational influence behavior "Explorations in Getting One's Way." Working toward a more precise definition, however, raises questions about the basic phenomenon under study. Is what we label influence the *ability* of an agent of influence to exert social control? Or is it the actual, identifiable *actions* the agent undertakes? Is it the changes in cognition and/or behavior that we observe in an influence target? Or is it the intrapsychic processes that mediate? Are we concerned only with intentional behavior, or does influence also describe subconscious or even accidental processes and outcomes?

Following Lewin (1951), French and Raven (1959) conceptualized influence in terms of the effects of countervailing psychological processes involved when an agent of influence exerts forces for change and a target of influence projects forces that may resist change. Change, ultimately, results from the combination of all forces operating in a given situation. In his theory of social influence situations, Kelman (1974; Kelman & Hamilton, 1989) adds the requirement that the target's behavior following the influence attempt differs from what it would have been in the absence of the influence attempt. This implies a measure of resistance to induction on the part of the influence target. The behavioral change need not necessarily take the form intended by the agent of influence; the only requirement is that behavior changes—in whatever direction—as a consequence of induction by an influence agent. Thus, it is reasonable to assume that the induction of influence reflects a mixture of deliberate and unintentional elements flowing from social agent to target in the context within which induction occurs. Investigations of the *methods* of influence, however, tend to focus on situations where influence goals are explicit and known to the influence agent, and to examine intentional, deliberate actions taken by agents in the pursuit of those goals (Cody, Canary, & Smith, 1994). As with the Seibold et al. (1985, 1994) reviews, our focus is primarily on research examining contexts where influence agents consciously pursue courses of action designed to facilitate instrumental goal attainment.

In light of these issues, and seeking to draw a workable boundary around the disparate body of research to be reviewed in the pages that follow, we define dyadic social influence as *the process through which an individual (agent) deliberately selects and presents verbal and/or symbolic actions directed at another individual (target) with the expectation that those actions will bring about a desired change in the cognitions and/or behaviors of the target that would not have otherwise occurred.* An influence *episode* encompasses the cycle of interpersonal activity (perceptions, behaviors, contextual elements) between agent and target given and pertaining to a specific compliance-gaining objective held by the agent. Influence *tactics* are specific communication behaviors and categories of behaviors employed by an agent within an episode in the pursuit of that objective.

Distinguishing influence from power. Although some writers have elected to use the terms power and influence more or less interchangeably (e.g., Salancik & Pfeffer, 1977), others see power and influence as distinct elements of the same process. Many conceptual approaches to power in organizations are grounded in one way or another in the notion of dependency (Emerson, 1962): One party is said to have power over the actions of another in situations where the latter's dependence on the former (e.g., for resources) exceeds the former's dependence on the latter. Thus, in the dependency formulation, power is not something an individual *has* or *does*; it is an emergent property of social relations. Theories of power (e.g., Pfeffer, 1981) identify the types of activities and relations between individuals and social units that enhance or attenuate dependency. Thus, power is an antecedent relational state regarding dependencies; social influence is the application of those dependencies in the pursuit of behavioral change. In French and Raven's (1959) words, "Influence is kinetic power, just as power is potential influence" (p. 152).[1]

Distinguishing influence from persuasion. It is also useful to be clear from the outset about how dyadic influence is distinguished from traditional research by communication scholars and social psychologists on interpersonal persuasion. Where the latter emphasizes message and source characteristics as predictors of individual attitude formation, dyadic influence research also considers the social context within which attitude change processes occur (Eagly & Chaiken, 1993). Hence, influence encompasses a broader range of social strategies for eliciting behavioral outcomes (Perloff, 1993). In this sense, dyadic influence is a superset of interpersonal persuasion, because message-centered argument directed at attitude change is but one of many possible strategies available to the influence agent (e.g., Kipnis et al., 1980; Wiseman & Schenck-Hamlin, 1981; Yukl & Falbe, 1990).

Scope of the Review

The conceptual focus of this chapter is on influence in organizations, which may be defined broadly as influence involving participants within deliberately structured social systems that are goal directed and identifiably bounded (e.g., Daft, 1995). Work organizations are the most common (and commonly investigated) example, although other collective forms that meet these criteria are within the purview of our analysis. Notwithstanding the sizable body of extant research that theorizes about or examines influence behavior exclusively within organizational contexts, our approach to the literature is broader. In addition to studies specifically addressing organizational issues, this review will cross disciplinary boundaries to include nonorganizational research that carries implications for understanding influence in the organizational sphere. Put another way, the boundaries of our review are defined not by the organizational context itself, but rather by the research issues, questions, and investigations that have the potential to inform that context. This opens the door for us to include a large volume of work produced by communication scholars and social psychologists that is generally free of contextual emphasis. On the other hand, we do exclude from the review streams of influence literature within specialized social contexts that are at best marginally relevant for a general understanding of influence in organizations; examples include compliance gaining in classroom interaction (e.g., Richmond & McCroskey, 1992), parent-child interaction (e.g., Oldershaw, Walters, & Hall, 1986), and physician-patient communication (e.g., Burgoon, Birk, & Hall, 1991).[2]

PROCESS MODELS OF DYADIC INFLUENCE

In this section, we review contributions made by nine conceptual frameworks and models that theorize about the process through which dyadic influence episodes develop and evolve. We organize this section by discussing, first, models that take the perspective of the agent; we then move to those that consider the target more central, and finally discuss those that allow significant attention to both agent and target. Although three of the nine frameworks explicitly model organizationally based processes, they all incorporate process features that are relevant to interpersonal influence involving organizational actors. A summary of the key characteristics of each model appears in Table 7.1.

The Perspective of the Agent

Marwell and Schmitt's model of compliance-gaining behavior. Building on theories of social exchange from sociology and social psychology (e.g., Blau,

TABLE 7.1
Conceptual Models of the Dyadic Influence Process

Study	Dyadic Emphasis	Context	Role of Cognitions	Noteworthy Contributions
Cobb, 1984	target	organization	moderate	complex array of antecedents; focus on target arousal; iterative process for agent
Dillard, 1990a	agent and target	unspecified	moderate	goal/plan/action sequence; dual path—planning may precede or follow decision to engage
Kelman, 1974; Kelman & Hamilton, 1989	target	unspecified	moderate	significant role for goals; effect of tactics on target perceptions; multiple conformity processes
Kipnis, 1974, 1976	agent	unspecified (but implies downward when context is organization)	minimal	resources overcome resistance; role of irrationality; norms (region of inhibition); recursive processes; metamorphic effects of power
Marwell & Schmitt, 1967a	agent	unspecified (applied to adolescent behavior)	moderate	complex array of antecedents; resources, including repertoire; criticality of learning/norms; target perceptions follow from tactical choices made by agent
Porter, Allen, & Angle, 1981	agent	organization (exclusively upward)	moderate	includes steps leading up to the influence attempt; complex array of antecedents; individual difference variables specified; recursion—perceived outcome modifies agent belief system
Raven, 1992	agent and target	unspecified (applied to organizations and political/ historical contexts)	minimal	differentiates power bases from preparatory devices; rationality—power efficacy assessed as costs/benefits; conceptualizes effects of outcomes on subsequent perceptions
Schein, 1977	agent	organization (downward; managers)	minimal	resources central, in terms of how they are perceived; congruence of individual and organizational goals drives choice of tactics
Tedeschi, Bonoma, & Schlenker, 1972; Tedeschi, Schlenker, & Lindskold, 1972	agent and target	unspecified	prominent	role of rationality—expected utility drives tactical choices made by agent; targets weigh expected value of compliance based on perceptions of agent and message characteristics

1964; Homans, 1961; Thibaut & Kelley, 1959), Marwell and Schmitt's model treats agents as social actors who make deliberate, goal-directed actions ("compliance-gaining behaviors" in the model's parlance) that are accessible to them (in the agent's "behavioral repertoire"), available at the lowest cost, and anticipated to be effective. A central emphasis is "previous learning," which results from antecedent characteristics of the "background" of the influence episode—personal resources of the target, previous experience of the agent in the current situation, agent social variables, and previous interaction with target. Influence-seeking behaviors that have not been practiced (i.e., are not learned elements of the actor's repertoire) and that are not perceived to be effective (based on previous learning) will not be selected. Social norms are also a point of emphasis in the model: Behaviors viewed as normatively appropriate to the target of influence may be inappropriate to the agent, and vice versa. When normative judgments of the agent and target are not congruent, this incongruence may result in the agent's being ineffective in influencing the target.

Kipnis's theory of power acts. Drawing on Cartwright (1965), Kipnis (1974, 1976) presented a process model that describes the sequence of events that precedes a power holder's decision to invoke resources in the pursuit of influence, as well as the stages of an influence-seeking encounter that ensue from such a decision. An important contribution of the Kipnis model is its analysis of the likelihood of recursion in the event of noncompliance, suggesting that the power holder might modify original needs, abandon the attempt, or invoke a different means (Kipnis, 1974). In the event a different means is invoked, Kipnis argued, it is likely that the tactics subsequently selected will be more extreme and may occur in either a positive or a negative direction. A second contribution lies in Kipnis's (1974) conceptualization of the "metamorphic effects of power" (p. 109), which suggests that access to and use of institutionally based resources over time alter an agent's self-concept and perceptions of the target individual. This perspective—casting agent perceptions of self and other as mediating the linkage between target responses and subsequent agent behavior—is prominent within the transactional framework we introduce later in this chapter.

Schein's model of individual power and political behavior in organizations. Noting the lack of research attention regarding political behavior in organizations, Schein (1977) developed a model of influence in which bases of power (French & Raven, 1959; Hickson, Hinings, Lee, Schneck, & Pennings, 1971) play a key role. Among the first to conceptualize influence behavior within the specific context of work organizations, Schein argued that an organizational actor's tactical choices will follow from the actor's situational perceptions regarding resources available and desired, as well as regarding the target's available resources. A key contribution of the model is found in its focus on organizational and individual goals. Given congruent goals, the agent will likely use *overt* influence methods that are a function of a legitimate power base. Where the goals are incongruent, however, the agent is likely to express overt intents and means that are congruent with organizational goals while actually using *covert* means to enact personal goals.

The Porter, Allen, and Angle model of upward influence in organizations. Drawing on the work of Mayes and Allen (1977), among others, the Porter et al. (1981) model treats organizational political behaviors as social influence attempts that are discretionary, that are designed to promote or protect actors' self-interests, and that threaten the self-interests of others (pp. 111-112). The Porter et al. model addresses only *upward* political influence (i.e., influence directed toward higher levels of the organization's formal hierarchy), and a basic distinction is drawn between overt and covert influence-seeking behaviors. One distinguishing characteristic of Porter et al.'s episodic influence model is its emphasis on features of the influence process that precede the actual application of an influence technique, including, for example, the recognition of opportunities, decision to engage in influence, and the selection of an influence target. Most other process frameworks of dyadic influence take the desire to influence and the establishment of an influence target as given. With its numerous propositions and directional hypotheses addressing the effects of relevant personal and situational factors on specific cognitions and decisions, the Porter et al. model depicts the influence process with a higher degree of specificity than other models discussed here. In addition, with its broad treatment of stages ranging from pre- to post-influence behavior, Porter et al.'s framework is explicit in its representation of feedback mechanisms that suggest the induction of influence is a sequential, iterative process.

The Perspective of the Target

Kelman's model of influence situation structure. The conceptual origins of Kelman's (1974; Kelman & Hamilton, 1989) model lie in large measure in Kelman's theory of attitude change processes (e.g., Kelman, 1958), which include compliance, identification, and internalization. His model treats influence attempts as events where the agent communicates to a target that adoption of a new behavior will have implications for the target's goals. The model's focus is on perceptual processes that mediate the linkage between agent behavior and target response. Successful influence follows from target perceptions that the situation has motivational *significance,* that the agent is *instrumental* to target goals, and that the induced behavior is *relevant* and desirable. Kelman's work also highlights qualitative differences in the types of conformity achieved in different influence situations. Although the model as given is generic to cases of positive influence, Kelman discussed modifications that distinguish influence resulting in compliance from identification and internalization. The probability that one of these processes in particular will occur is a function of how the model's situational determinants (significance, instrumentality, relevance) are evoked.

Cobb's episodic model of power. In Cobb's (1984) model, approaches to the study of influence in organizations (referred to as "power in action") are structured into phases of the influence process. One unique feature of the model is extensive consideration of antecedent conditions pertaining to the agent (psychological orientation, political skills, and personal power base), target (readiness and ability to act), and situation (formal, informal, congruence, and cross-level factors). Cobb's model makes two important contributions. First, it provides an extended treatment of arousal, which is regarded as more than a simple trigger for the formation of behavioral intentions; different arousal stimuli can evoke different kinds of responses from the target. Second, Cobb theorized about how target responses create cycles of behavior through which agents iterate the influence attempt. The model makes predictions regarding agent handling of target behavioral blocks (e.g., situational constraints, inability, or misinformation), target performance without congruent intentions, and target noncompliance.

The Perspective of Both the Agent and the Target

Tedeschi's subjective expected utility model. Tedeschi and his associates have applied a single underlying framework—subjective expected utility (SEU) theory in decision making—to the behavior of influence agents, or sources (Tedeschi, Schlenker, & Lindskold, 1972), and to the reactions of influence targets (Tedeschi, Bonoma, & Schlenker, 1972). The Tedeschi approach assumes that agents and targets are rational actors who act in accord with judgments of expected value. Influence agents weigh the probabilities of obtaining particular influence outcomes and the worth of these outcomes in deciding whom to influence, how to influence, and, indeed, whether even to attempt influence. Influence targets evaluate the expected value, or believability, of compliance requests that determine eventual compliance or noncompliance. Perceptions by parties to the influence attempt occupy a central role: The model provides causal linkages describing how agent and message characteristics shape key target perceptions; different agent and message characteristics are hypothesized to predict differentially these target perceptions. Empirically, Tedeschi and his colleagues noted that support for this general framework is more pronounced on the negative side (for threats and warnings) than with respect to positive contingencies (promises and commendations) (Tedeschi, Bonoma, & Schlenker, 1972).

Dillard's goal-driven model of influence. Building on a long research tradition examining goals and human behavior (e.g., Miller, Galanter, & Pribram, 1960), Dillard (1990a) introduced a model that views dyadic influence through the lens of goal-planning-action sequences. Influence attempts are presumed to be goal driven, both for agents, who must decide whether and how to influence, and for targets, who must decide whether and how to resist. A contribution of the model is its contingency prediction regarding whether influence agents, given a salient goal, will make the decision to engage the target *before* or *after* generating a tactical plan. Dillard argued that approach/avoidance dynamics constitute the contingency factor: When approach forces predominate, the decision to influence will come first. On the other hand, when the target is not convinced that an influence attempt must be made, the agent may defer a decision to proceed until a satisfactory plan has been conceived. Given target resistance, the model cycles through an iterative process of goal reevaluation and tactic implementation until the agent either gains compliance or reverses the decision to engage.

Raven's power/interaction model. Raven (1992) incorporated the French and Raven (1959) bases of power as the central focus of a comprehensive two-part conceptual model of the influence process—one part focusing on the agent and the other on the influence target. The model treats situational factors as "preparatory devices" that serve the purpose of making various bases of power operative for the agent. The Raven model does not, however, fully develop the conceptual process through which an agent chooses among available power bases and enacts the influence attempt. Rather, tactical behavior remains a "black box," with the remainder of the model simply a feedback mechanism that informs both future motivations to influence and future assessments of available power bases. A key contribution of Raven's (1992) approach is the attention given to subsequent effects on agent-target relations: "The influence attempt, successful or unsuccessful, has very likely changed both the influencing agent and the target, changed their perceptions of themselves, changed their perceptions of the other" (p. 234). Although several of the process models discussed here hint at linkages between influence outcomes and situational perceptions, Raven's treatment is the most expansive to date.

Analysis of Process Models

The models discussed above represent a useful cross-section of approaches that have been taken to describing the mechanism of influence induction. They vary, for example, from an emphasis on the agent of influence (Kipnis, Marwell & Schmitt, Porter et al., Schein) to the target (Cobb, Kelman) to both (Dillard, Raven, Tedeschi et al.). Some focus specifically on influence seeking in organizational settings (Cobb, Porter et al., Schein), and although others address dyadic behavior within no particular, specified social context, they remain relevant for understanding influence processes in organizations. The models range from a general depiction of the influence act (Kipnis, Schein) to a highly specific set of propositions about individual and situational predictors (Porter et al.). Some are more cognitive in their explanations (Kelman, Cobb, Marwell & Schmitt, Tedeschi et al.) than others (Kipnis, Porter et al., Raven, Schein). We raise three integrative issues below.

First, existing models have yet to integrate fully the roles of both agent and target into a common framework. Two approaches explicitly address dyadic influence from both agent and target perspectives, but via separate, parallel models, with intersections that are implied at best (Raven, 1992; Tedeschi, Bonoma, & Schlenker, 1972). Others incorporate the dyad member who is not the primary focus of the model, but elaborate that side of the process only superficially (e.g., Cobb, 1984; Dillard, 1990a; Kelman & Hamilton, 1989; Kipnis, 1974; Marwell & Schmitt, 1967a). The development of a conceptual treatment of dyadic influence as interactive and reciprocal requires a more genuine integration of agent and target perspectives than has been produced to date.

Second, we note in existing models widely varying degrees of precision with respect to the specification of antecedent conditions, characteristics, and processes that drive the influence-seeking process. The Porter et al. (1981) upward influence model is highly explicit in delineating situational and individual difference factors thought to affect stages of the influence process. Cobb (1984) and Marwell and Schmitt (1967a) also posited a wide array of antecedents, but relied more on the specification of categories of factors than on an extensive inventory of individual variables.

Beyond differences in the extensiveness of lists of antecedent factors, there are divergent approaches to the nature of those factors. For example, elements of the influence situation are variously specified as *objective* conditions or "resources" available to agents (Cobb, 1984; Kipnis, 1974; Marwell & Schmitt, 1967a; Porter et al., 1981; Schein, 1977) and as *perceptions* of situational factors (Porter et al., 1981; Raven, 1992; Tedeschi, Bonoma, & Schlenker, 1972). Some approaches incorporate goals (Dillard, 1990a; Kelman, 1974; Raven, 1992; Schein, 1977), social norms (Kipnis, 1974; Marwell & Schmitt, 1967a; Porter et al., 1981; Raven, 1992), and prior learning (Marwell & Schmitt, 1967a), whereas others do not. As suggested earlier, in no model we know of are antecedent conditions differentially relevant for agent and target described in a common framework.

Third, existing models may oversimplify the role of rationality for the agent and target. Most models implicitly assume rational behavior (e.g., Cobb, 1984; Dillard, 1990a); others explicitly state this assumption (Marwell & Schmitt, 1967a; Raven, 1992; Tedeschi, Bonoma, & Schlenker, 1972; Tedeschi, Schlenker, & Lindskold, 1972). An exception is the Kipnis (1974, 1976) model, which explicitly proposes that agents may act irrationally—that is, that agents may gain satisfaction simply by altering the target's outcomes. Theorists have generally overlooked the prospect that both agents and targets may act irrationally, using decision rules not calculable by rational measures. A supposedly rational behavioral choice by either party may actually seem "irrational" from the perspective of the other party. Further, "rational" decisions may be based on inaccurate perceptions of factors, and thus may be irrational in an objective sense.

THE TACTICAL CONTENT OF INFLUENCE ATTEMPTS

Where process theories of influence explore the cognitive and behavioral mechanisms through which an influence attempt unfolds and evolves, content-based approaches analyze the specific compliance-seeking substance of influence attempts—the tactical behaviors enacted by the agent of influence in an attempt to gain compliance from an influence target. In this section, we give an overview of various attempts that researchers have made to identify and inventory these methods. The section that follows contains a more detailed review of empirical investigations of the antecedents and consequences of tactical choice.

Identifying and Classifying Influence Tactics

A sizable body of research has focused on the identification and classification of specific influence-seeking behaviors; these have been reviewed at length elsewhere (Kellermann & Cole, 1994; Seibold et al., 1985, 1994), and an extensive treatment is beyond the scope of this chapter. In Table 7.2, we highlight selected studies that have incorporated the development of taxonomies of dyadic influence tactics in ways that inform an organizational perspective on influence seeking. Intended to be illustrative rather than comprehensive, the table includes studies for which (a) the development of a broad-based taxonomy of influence-seeking tactics was a primary research objective, or (b) the taxonomy used to address broader research questions represented a substantive extension or departure from earlier classification schemes. Excluded are studies that adapted existing inventories with minor modifications, as well as studies that addressed a limited subset of influence-seeking behaviors.[3] We offer three observations that will help synthesize tactics identification and classification research.

A first observation concerns basic methodology that separates studies of influence behaviors into two camps. Some researchers have employed what are labeled *deductive* methods, wherein theoretical approaches to and intuitive readings of social power and social relations are marshaled in an attempt to derive conceptually a list or taxonomy of strategic behaviors. Included in the deductive approach are early taxonomies grounded in theory (e.g., Etzioni, 1961; Parsons, 1963) as well as schemes that reflect a synthesis and reconceptualization of prior taxonomies (e.g., Mowday, 1978, 1979; Vecchio & Sussmann, 1989). Critics have argued that deductive approaches amount to little more than "armchair speculation" (Kipnis & Schmidt, 1983, pp. 304-305), and have questioned whether such inventories account for the full range of tactics employed by influence seekers (Cody, McLaughlin, & Jordan, 1980). Consequently, a number of researchers (e.g., Falbo, 1977; Fitzpatrick & Winke, 1979; Kipnis et al., 1980; Wiseman & Schenck-Hamlin, 1981) have argued that better and more complete taxonomies emerge from *inductive* strategies whereby messages constructed by research subjects in response to real or hypothetical situations are examined to induce a set of influence methods. Although inductively drawn taxonomies have been prevalent in organizational research on influence since the early 1980s, questions have been raised about their value (e.g., Miller et al., 1987), and new appeals for the development of conceptually grounded (or "feature-based") schemes for classifying tactics have surfaced (e.g., Barry, 1992; Kellermann & Cole, 1994; O'Keefe, 1994).

As a second observation, we note significant variety in the quantity of influence tactics identified by different researchers, as well as in the complexity with which those tactics have been classified hierarchically. Taxonomic approaches to clustering and nesting tactical behaviors range from simple, one-level distinctions (e.g., Deutsch & Gerard, 1955) to multilevel hierarchical classification schemes (Hirokawa & Miyahara, 1986) to more complex tree diagrams of properties (Schenck-Hamlin, Wiseman, & Georgacarakos, 1982). An assortment of strategies have been employed to develop these taxonomic structures: Some were developed by the researchers intuitively (e.g., Clark, 1979) or conceptually (e.g., Tedeschi, Bonoma, & Schlenker, 1972), whereas others used statistical methods, such as factor analysis (Ansari, 1989; Buss, Gomes, Higgins, & Lauterbach, 1987; Fitzpatrick & Winke, 1979; Kipnis, Castell, Gergen, & Mauch, 1976; Marwell & Schmitt, 1967b) and multidimensional scaling (Falbo, 1977).

For consistency, in the third column of Table 7.2 we use the terms *behavior,* *category,* and *dimension* to label levels of abstraction with respect to the tactics contained within taxonomies.[4] *Behaviors* refers to elemental tactics, which exist as individual messages or (in the case of nonverbal tactics) individual actions. The number of individual influence-seeking behaviors identified in studies in the table range from none (Parsons, 1963, who conceptualized only aggregate categories) to as many as 58 (Kipnis et al., 1980). To provide information about nested taxonomy structures, we use the terms *categories* and *dimensions* in Table 7.2 to denote aggregations of behaviors. *Categories* are groupings of similar behaviors (e.g., actions grouped by Kipnis et al., 1976, into a class of "accommodative" tactics, or actions grouped by Yukl & Tracey, 1992, into a class of "pressure" tactics). Across studies, categories range in number from as few as 2 (Deutsch & Gerard, 1955) to as many as 10 (Vecchio & Sussmann, 1989). *Dimensions* take tactical clusters to an additional level of aggregation. For some taxonomies (e.g., Clark, 1979; Hirokawa & Miyahara, 1986; Newton & Burgoon, 1990), dimensions are essentially second-order categories that aggregate first-order categories at a further level of abstraction. For others, dimensions describe underlying properties that define tactical types (e.g., the 2×2 typologies proposed by Parsons, 1963; or Tedeschi, Bonoma, & Schlenker, 1972).

The range of taxonomic structures found in the literature raises questions about whether and how appropriate categories or dimensions of influence can

TABLE 7.2

Selected Taxonomies of Dyadic Influence Tactics

Study	Label	Taxonomy Size and Structure[a]	Source/Method[b]	Context	Literature
Ansari, 1989	influence strategies/tactics	49 behaviors (5 categories)	synthesized (factor analysis)	organizational (downward) (India)	psychology
Buss, Gomes, Higgins, & Lauterbach, 1987	tactics of manipulation	35 behaviors (6 categories)	inductive (factor analysis)	close relationships	psychology
Clark, 1979	communicative strategies	41 behaviors (7 categories; 3 dimensions)	conceptualized	unspecified	communication
Cody et al., 1986	compliance-gaining strategies	(7 categories)	synthesized and conceptualized	unspecified	communication
Deutsch & Gerard, 1955	normative and informational social influence	(2 dimensions)	conceptualized	unspecified	psychology
DuBrin, 1989, 1991	influence tactics	16 behaviors (3 dimensions)	synthesized	organizational	psychology
Etzioni, 1961	types of power		conceptualized	unspecified	sociology
Falbo, 1977	power strategies	16 behaviors (4 categories; 2 × 2 dimensions)	inductive (multidimensional scaling)	unspecified	psychology
Fitzpatrick & Winke, 1979	interpersonal conflict strategies	44 behaviors (5 categories)	inductive (factor analysis)	friendship relationships	communication
Hirokawa & Miyahara, 1986	influence strategies	19 behaviors (10 categories; 4 categories; 2 dimensions)	synthesized and conceptualized	organizational (downward)	communication
Kipnis, Castell, Gergen, & Mauch, 1976	means of influence	17 behaviors (5 categories)	synthesized and conceptualized (factor analysis)	close relationships	psychology

Source	Term	Behaviors/Categories	Method	Context	Discipline
Kipnis, Schmidt, & Wilkerson, 1980	influence tactics	58 behaviors (8 categories)	inductive	organizational	psychology
Marwell & Schmitt, 1967a	compliance-gaining strategies	30 behaviors (6 categories)	synthesized	unspecified	sociology
Marwell & Schmitt, 1967b	compliance-gaining techniques	16 behaviors (5 categories)	synthesized (factor analysis)	unspecified	sociology
Mowday, 1978, 1979	influence methods	(5 categories)	synthesized	organizational	organizational behavior
Newton & Burgoon, 1990	interpersonal influence strategies/tactics	36 behaviors (6 categories; 3 dimensions)	synthesized and conceptualized	close relationships	communication
Parsons, 1963	modes of influence	4 categories (2 × 2 dimensions)	conceptualized	unspecified	sociology
Porter, Allen, & Angle, 1981	influence methods	5 categories (2 dimensions)	synthesized	organizational (upward)	organizational behavior
Schenck-Hamlin, Wiseman, & Georgacarakos, 1982	compliance-gaining strategies	14 behaviors (4 categories)	inductive	unspecified	communication
Schilit & Locke, 1982	methods of influence (event factors)	19 behaviors	inductive	organizational (upward)	organizational behavior
Tedeschi, Schlenker, & Lindskold, 1972	modes of influence	(4 categories; 2 × 2 dimensions)	conceptualized	unspecified	psychology
Vecchio & Sussmann, 1989	forms of influence	(10 categories)	synthesized	organizational (downward)	organizational behavior
Wheeless, Barraclough, & Stewart, 1983	compliance-gaining techniques	(3 dimensions)	synthesized and conceptualized	unspecified	communication
Yukl & Falbe, 1990; Yukl & Tracey, 1992	influence tactics	(9 categories)	synthesized and conceptualized	organizational	psychology

a. *Behaviors* refers to individual messages or actions. Nested hierarchies of tactics are shown in parentheses where researchers have grouped behaviors for classification purposes. Where listed, *categories* are groupings of similar behaviors, and *dimensions* are underlying structural properties of influence-seeking behaviors.

b. Indicates whether a deductive (synthesized from previous work or newly conceptualized by current researchers) or inductive approach was used to glean an inventory of tactics. Where applicable, statistical methods used to group behaviors into categories are shown in parentheses.

be identified. O'Keefe (1990) suggests that the number of eligible dimensions or classification schemes that can be devised to study compliance gaining may be limitless. Noting that many taxonomies amount to "an unprincipled crazy quilt of categories, with little conceptual coherence" (p. 208), O'Keefe proposes that researchers eschew the quilt and focus instead on formulating research questions that identify well-defined message features (e.g., prosocial versus antisocial behaviors). As long as some clearly defined message dimension drives a particular investigation, it becomes less important that any number of other dimensions are fathomable.

A third observation concerns the variety of social contexts within which taxonomy-development research has taken place. A few researchers have focused on the development of tactical inventories that are specifically appropriate to the context of formal organizations (DuBrin, 1989, 1991; Kipnis et al., 1980; Mowday, 1978, 1979; Yukl & Falbe, 1990). Among these studies, there is variety with respect to the direction of influence under investigation: Some refer specifically to upward (Porter et al., 1981; Schilit & Locke, 1982) or downward (Ansari, 1989; Hirokawa & Miyahara, 1986; Vecchio & Sussmann, 1989) influence attempts, whereas others are not direction specific (e.g., Kipnis et al., 1980). Most of the work identified in Table 7.2, and indeed most taxonomic research on influence (see Kellermann & Cole, 1994), is essentially context-free, addressing interpersonal influence activities without regard for the social settings within which they occur (e.g., Marwell & Schmitt, 1967b; Schenck-Hamlin et al., 1982). Because behavior in organizations reflects both formal and informal ties among organizational participants, we also include in Table 7.2 a few studies that address the particular nonorganizational social context of close or friendship relationships (Buss et al., 1987; Fitzpatrick & Winke, 1979; Kipnis et al., 1976; Newton & Burgoon, 1990). Finally, it is interesting to note that there is almost no variety in the *cultural* context of tactics identification research: With one exception (Ansari, 1989), all of the studies included here were conducted using American subjects.

Evaluation of Taxonomy Research

It is evident from the information displayed in Table 7.2 that consensus on the range and structure of available influence tactics is elusive, to say the least. In a comprehensive review published more than a decade ago, Wheeless et al. (1983) criticized the taxonomic products of both deductive and inductive approaches as lacking "coherence and comparability among studies" (p. 106). More recently, Kellermann and Cole (1994) analyzed at length the disorder and confusion created by efforts to classify compliance-gaining messages, concluding that "current typologies do not provide clear, specific, distinct, and delimiting definitions that are based on theoretically important features" (p. 49). Yet more than 30 years following the earliest attempts to catalog such behaviors, researchers continue to embark on new efforts to develop tactical inventories. We believe that the seemingly persistent dissatisfaction of influence researchers with extant inventories and taxonomies—and their consequent motivation to reinvent this wheel repeatedly—can be explained in both conceptual and empirical terms.

Conceptually, we construe the surfeit of taxonomies as a reflection of how difficult it is to characterize the subtle properties of many influence-seeking behaviors. Interpersonal communication often involves the transmission of verbal and nonverbal messages that may be intended—and received—in multiple ways, depending on how a message is framed (Norton, 1983; Pinkley, 1990) and transmitted (Daft & Lengel, 1984). Viewing social influence in these terms, it is fair to ask whether this level of behavioral complexity can be analyzed without explicit attention to the relational and perceptual processes that underlie the selection and deployment of influence tactics. Although some studies included in Table 7.2 assumed particular social contexts (e.g., formal organizations, close relationships), the structural dimensions or categories of taxonomies are not generally linked to features of the underlying social-cognitive context within which influence occurs. For example, tactical behaviors as defined in existing taxonomies could be thought of (and classified) in terms of characteristics of ongoing agent-target relationships, interpersonal goals, social expectancies, and other processes of social perception within the dyad. Presumably, these sorts of social-cognitive processes drive a target's interpretation of the influence seeker's intentions (e.g., Roloff, 1994). As such, they offer avenues for the development of conceptually grounded classification schemes describing tactical behavior. In the absence of a theoretical integration of social perception and behavior, we fear that influence researchers will continue to strive for—and perhaps continue to be dissatisfied with—additional taxonomies of influence-seeking behavior that fail to capture critical contextual elements.

Empirically, the body of research exploring antecedents and consequences of influence tactic selection also explains in part the abundance of tactical classification schemes. Findings from this literature (reviewed next) revealing the determinants of tactical choice are disjointed and isolated, rather than incremental and integrative. Levels of measurement reliability associated with inventories of tactical behavior are frequently marginal (e.g., Benson & Hornsby, 1988; Cheng, 1983; Deluga, 1988; Erez, Rim, & Keider, 1986; Kipnis & Schmidt, 1988; Schmidt & Kipnis, 1984; Yukl & Falbe, 1990), and efforts to refine the psychometric quality of these instruments (e.g., Littlepage, Van Hein, Cohen, & Janiec, 1993; Schriesheim & Hinkin, 1990; Yukl, Lepsinger, & Lucia, 1992) are rare. There continue to be "troublesome gaps" in the lists of tactics that constitute influence instruments (Miller et al., 1987, p. 98). Empirical findings often run counter to expectations, and effect sizes are usually modest. This adds up to a tenuous empirical foundation for understanding dyadic influence, which encourages researchers to continue to refine and even overhaul taxonomies of tactical behavior.

ANTECEDENTS AND CONSEQUENCES
OF TACTICAL CHOICE

The value of knowing the range of influence behaviors agents select and use is bounded by our ability to determine (a) the situational conditions under which agents will act in particular ways, (b) the impact of individual differences on influence behavior, and (c) the consequences of influence tactics choices. A substantial volume of research in these areas has been undertaken outside of organizational contexts, but much of it is nevertheless valuable for enhancing our understanding of organization-based influence. In this section, we consider research conducted in each of these three domains that speaks to organizational contexts.

Situational Effects

The study of dyadic influence presupposes that characteristics of particular influence situations affect strategy selection and influence outcomes (Cody & McLaughlin, 1980). Situational aspects of dyadic influence have received much greater research attention from communication scholars than from organizational scientists, and our review is focused accordingly. Beginning with Miller, Boster, Roloff, and Seibold (1977), researchers have pursued two primary objectives with respect to situational factors: (a) identifying the dimensions of compliance-gaining situations, and (b) examining the ability of situational variables to predict influence method choice.

With respect to the identification of situational dimensions, Cody and his associates (Cody et al., 1986; Cody & McLaughlin, 1980; Cody, Woelfel, & Jordan, 1983) and Hertzog and Bradac (1984) developed similar comprehensive typologies (see Cody & McLaughlin, 1985, for a review). Working inductively and employing multidimensional scaling, cluster analysis, and confirmatory factor analysis, Cody and McLaughlin (1980) identified seven situational dimensions: intimacy, rights to persuade, dominance, resistance, personal benefits, relational consequences, and situation apprehension. Each dimension is a perception on the part of the agent held in advance of the choice and application of an influence method. Hertzog and Bradac (1984), using a larger number of situations and more sensitive forms of analysis, extended the Cody and McLaughlin (1980) typology. Three of their five situational dimensions overlap the Cody and McLaughlin dimensions of resistance, dominance, and relational consequences. To these, Hertzog and Bradac added agent/target shared values/rules and gender relevance. However, it is conceivable that values and gender relevance are not situational dimensions at all, but rather manifestations of individual differences of the influence agent and target.

With respect to research exploring the predictive power of situational variables on influence tactic choice, we organize our analysis into four categories: (a) studies investigating the *nature of the relationship* between the agent and target, which includes both general approaches to relational closeness and organization-specific roles and styles; (b) research considering the role of *organizational characteristics*; (c) studies examining influence *goals* as determinants of tactical behavior; and (d) investigations that consider *multiple situational antecedents* within a single study.

Nature of the Relationship

Intimacy. Intimacy is generally the closeness of the personal relationship between agent and target (e.g., Cody & McLaughlin, 1980). In general, increased levels of intimacy between the agent and target are associated with use of positive strategies (e.g., make the other person feel good, encourage positive affect, offer rewards, justification), whereas lower levels of intimacy are associated with use of negative strategies (e.g., manipulation, punishment) (Cody, McLaughlin, & Schneider, 1981; deTurck, 1985; Fitzpatrick & Winke, 1979; Miller et al., 1977; O'Hair, Cody, & O'Hair, 1991).

The results of several studies suggest that intimacy may affect an individual's choice of tactics because agents consider the level of intimacy when evaluating the potential effectiveness of influence attempts. In intimate relationships, where the response of the target can be better anticipated and where aspects of the relationship between agent and target are potentially significant, agents are more likely to use threats of personal rejection (Cody et al., 1981; Fitzpatrick & Winke, 1979) and emotional appeals (Fitzpatrick & Winke, 1979). Where the probability of relationship termination is judged to be high, agents are more likely to use coercion and debasement (Buss et al., 1987). Beyond the use of specific tactics, there is some evidence to suggest that influence agents feel comfortable with a wider range of strategies within relationally close dyads, possibly because the bonds of intimacy permit more spontaneous and less conventional behavior (Sillars, 1980).

Superior/subordinate power. In organizations, leader power typically has been conceptualized as precipitating the use of either directive (Kipnis, 1976) or collaborative (Kanter, 1977) tactics, or both (Tjosvold, Andrews, & Struthers, 1992). Findings reported by Tjosvold et al. (1992) suggest that relative *subordinate* power is the determining factor: Managers tend to use directive influence when the power balance favors the agent, but are more likely to use collaborative tactics when both agent and target are powerful. Relative power between agent and target is implied when organizational psychologists investigate influence "direction"—the relative agent-target position within an organizational hierarchy (upward, downward, or lateral). There is mixed evidence regarding linkages between direction and tactical choice. The results of some studies suggest that *upward* influence attempts are more likely to involve techniques of rational persuasion, with subordinates more likely to use logical presentations (Schilit & Locke, 1982) and reason (Chacko, 1990) than other types of tactics. Other findings, however, suggest that influence direction may not be relevant in tactics choice. Barry and Bateman (1992) and Yukl and Falbe (1990), using self-report measures of strategy selection, found rational persuasion to be among the tactics used most frequently, regardless of influence direction. Even when tactical differences based on influence direction do surface, the differences are generally small, suggesting that the direction of influence is not a key determinant of tactic selection (Yukl, Falbe, & Youn, 1993; Yukl & Tracey, 1992).

Leadership style. Participative leadership has been shown to be positively associated with both the frequency (Cobb, 1986) and directness (Krone, 1992) of subordinate upward influence attempts. Cobb (1986) found an increase in both upward and lateral influence attempts in environments of participation. Krone (1992) found that subordinates who participate in organizational decision making and who perceive themselves as having in-group relationships with their supervisors use more direct, rational, and overt influence methods. Similarly, Ansari and Kapoor (1987), in a lab study with Indian subjects, found that upward influencers were more likely to use rational strategies when the target's leadership style was participative rather than authoritarian. Less participatory styles tend to increase political influence attempts (Krone, 1992) and to be related to the use of more negative (assertive and threatening) upward influence strategies.

Regarding leadership effectiveness, there is evidence that poor leadership may increase the use of negative upward influence tactics by subordinates. Chacko (1990) found that higher education administrators who perceived their supervisors as exhibiting few leadership behaviors (low in initiating structure and consideration) tended to use more assertive tactics and to be more likely to circumvent authority. Consistent with this conclusion, Deluga (1991) found hard upward influence approaches (appeal to higher authority, coalition building, and assertiveness) to be inversely correlated with supervisor effectiveness and satisfaction with the supervisor. Although these findings can be interpreted to suggest that leader behavior affects subordinate upward influence, it is important to note that causality in these cross-sectional studies cannot be determined.

Subordinate performance. There is limited empirical support for a relationship between evaluated performance and a supervisor's choice of influence methods. Ansari (1989) found agents more likely to use positive influence methods (e.g., reward and exchange) with subordinate targets who were good performers and more likely to use negative influence methods (e.g., assertion and negative sanction) with poor performers. A bit further afield from traditional settings for research on workplace psychology, Kipnis et al. (1976), in a study of housewives who employed maids, found a negative relationship between use of direct influence attempts and evaluations of the maids. In each of these studies, although researchers can hypothesize causality, causal inferences are once again tenuous.

Subordinate communication style. Distinguishing attractive (attentive, friendly, relaxed) from unattractive (inattentive, unfriendly, unrelaxed) subordinate communication styles, Garko (1992) found managers more likely to use assertive strategies, coalition-building strategies, appeals to higher authority, and threats of sanctions with unattractive communicators, more likely to use friendliness with attractive communicators, and equally likely to use reason with both types of communicators.

Target resistance. In a novel experiment, Wilson, Cruz, Marshall, and Rao (1993) used an attribution theory framework to examine how influence tactics vary depending on the excuses for noncompliance offered by the target. Subjects (agents) tried to convince influence targets to honor a commitment to participate in a research project; targets were trained confederates who resisted in predetermined ways that reflected manipulations of the locus (internal versus external cause of the event providing the excuse), stability (consistency of the event), and controllability (by the target) of excuses for noncompliance. Wilson et al. found that agents (a) showed greater persistence when target excuses were controllable and unstable, (b) used tactics addressing obstacles to compliance more often when excuses were controllable and unstable, and (c) used antisocial tactics (such as warnings) when excuses were controllable. This study is unique for its theoretical focus on attribution as the basis for tactic selection, as well as for its method involving a "real" influence attempt within an experimental design.

Organizational Characteristics

A small number of studies have considered organization-level attributes in connection with influence method selection, including ownership (public versus private) (Schilit & Locke, 1982), organization size (Schilit & Locke, 1982), professional norms (Erez & Rim, 1982), climate (political versus rational) (Cheng, 1983), type of organization (Aguinis, Nesler, Hosoda, & Tedeschi, 1994; Schilit & Locke, 1982), and unionization (Kipnis et al., 1980). For the most part, macro-level variables have not been a central research focus in these studies. An exception is a study in which Krone (1992) found that influence agents in decentralized authority structures relied more on open and direct methods of influence than did agents in more centralized organizations. In general, however, the organization-level findings that emerge from these studies are fragmented and inconsistent. Beyond empirical uncertainties, there is little in the way of credible theory to suggest that variance in interpersonal influence processes can be reliably explained by organization-level constructs. It is important to note, however, that failure to control for structural variables may confound the results of influence research undertaken in organizational settings (Schilit & Locke, 1982). For example, Schilit and Locke (1982) found that informal methods of influence were more common in small or private organizations than in large or public organizations, and

Krone's (1992) study reported differences based simply on the organizations to which influence seekers belonged.

Goals of the Agent

Compliance-gaining situations may also be examined in terms of the agent's influence goals and subgoals, considering how the goals of the influence-seeker drive strategy choice (e.g., Dillard et al., 1989). To the extent that goals exist at the locus of a constellation of perceived situational factors, goals are potentially important as markers for complex situational information.[5] Dillard's (1990b) review of efforts by psychologists and communication scholars to create taxonomies of influence goals presents data indicating that goals affect the influencer's motivation and tactical choices. For example, perceived importance of the influence objective was associated with agents' use of tactics involving reason and evidence, whereas goals pertaining to the quality of interaction and of the relationship were linked to the use of tactics that highlight the consequences of (non)compliance. More recently, Cody et al. (1994) proposed a typology of 11 compliance-gaining goals and have charted a research agenda that considers how goals combine with personality factors and social-cognitive processes to predict influence-seeking behavior.

Goals have been examined within the specific context of workplace influence, with some consistency in results. Studies by Kipnis et al. (1980) and Schmidt and Kipnis (1984) found greater use of reason-based and coalition-building strategies when actors are trying to initiate change or promote new ideas, and greater emphasis on assertiveness and ingratiation tactics when they are trying simply to manipulate job behavior (e.g., receive assistance, assign work, improve performance). In the Kipnis et al. findings, there were also minor differences in goal-tactic associations depending on the direction of influence (up, down, lateral). Howell and Higgins (1990) studied idea champions, defined as those with a goal to promote organization innovation. Consistent with the work of Kipnis and colleagues, Howell and Higgins found that champions used coalition and reason more than did nonchampions; moreover, champions relied more than nonchampions on assertive tactics and appeals to higher authority.

At least two studies have explicitly compared tactical choices given the pursuit of individual versus organizational goals. Ansari and Kapoor (1987), in a scenario-based experiment with a sample of undergraduates at a university in India, found that subjects striving to achieve personal goals relied most heavily on ingratiation tactics, whereas subjects pursuing organizational goals employed a combination of methods that included the use of rational persuasion, upward appeal, and blocking tactics. Schmidt and Kipnis (1984), with a managerial sample from the United States and a correlational design, found a variety of associations between goals and tactics that only partially overlap Ansari and Kapoor's results. Because of methodological and cultural differences, it is difficult to move beyond the broad observation that tactics vary with organization-based influence goals.

Multiple Situational Antecedents to Influence

Perhaps the greatest weakness of empirical investigations of the predictive power of situational variables is that, despite the complexity of real situations, individual studies have generally examined no more than one or two situational factors at a time. Two exceptions that examined a larger set of situational factors deserve mention. Cody et al. (1986) explored the effects of all seven situational dimensions in the Cody and McLaughlin (1980) typology on influence strategy selection. Although a number of predictors were identified, the overall goodness-of-fit chi-square was nonsignificant (indicating a good model fit) for only one of the seven logistic regression models, leading Cody et al. to conclude that "[situational] perceptions do not, in concert, predict selection of strategies" (p. 416).

Dillard and Burgoon (1985), who also investigated all seven Cody and McLaughlin (1980) situational dimensions simultaneously, concluded that "across the two studies the effects attributable to the situations were relatively few in number and small in size" (p. 301). However, Dillard and Burgoon declined to infer that situational factors lack predictive power, arguing instead for the need to consider other situational variables, as well as how situational dimensions might interact with one another and with individual difference variables.

These and other published studies (e.g., Aguinis et al., 1994; Burleson et al., 1988; Hunter & Boster, 1987; Jackson & Backus, 1982) call into question the importance of situational variance for the prediction of influence method choice. Still, most writers have been reluctant to dismiss the role of situation, and have looked elsewhere for explanations. Some have suggested that the problem lies in the definition of situational dimensions (e.g., Cody et al., 1986). Others struggling to explain the limited amounts of variance explained by situational dimensions point to methodological issues (e.g., Burleson et al., 1988; Jackson & Backus, 1982). Still others cite confounding of situational variables and message content (Jackson & Backus, 1982). Rarely (Dillard, 1988, and O'Keefe, 1990, are exceptions), however, do researchers revisit the dependent variable side of the equation and question the appropriateness of the most widely used lists and typologies of influence-seeking behaviors.

Individual Difference Antecedents

Stable individual attributes are widely regarded as important determinants of individual and group behavior in organizations (e.g., Davis-Blake & Pfeffer, 1989). With respect to social influence, the proposition that choices about tactics vary in meaningful ways with individual differences has received substantial attention from influence researchers. For the most part, this line of investigation has focused on variables that describe the *agent,* with relatively scant attention to how target characteristics affect tactical selection. We focus our analysis on individual difference variables having clear potential relevance for behavior in organizations, and structure the discussion around three themes: demography, personality, and tactical profiles.

Demography

Culture. Studies of cultural differences in dyadic influence have been undertaken primarily in managerial contexts. A recurring finding is the frequency of use of reason-oriented strategies by managerial agents, which appears to be common across a number of cultures. Sullivan and Taylor (1991) found that Japanese managers, like American, British, and Australian managers (Kipnis & Schmidt, 1983), used reasoning most frequently with their subordinates.

There is evidence that cross-cultural differences in influence styles may be related in part to cultural norms concerning the nature of the influence request. Hirokawa and Miyahara (1986), in a comparative study of American and Japanese managers, found that Americans preferred punishment strategies when the requested behavior was obligatory (e.g., arrive to work on time), but anticipated using rationale or reward strategies to elicit nonobligatory behaviors (e.g., put in extra work). Japanese managers, however, preferred altruism or rationale in obligatory situations, and altruism in nonobligatory situations. In a similar vein, Kim and Wilson (1994) found that American and Korean evaluations of influence tactics and their effectiveness varied based on social appropriateness. Finally, in a synthesis of nine previous influence studies and a comparison of Americans and Colombians, Fitch (1994) found that the use of directive tactics was consistent with cultural values.

Other studies lend credence to an interaction between culture and gender, albeit in inconclusive ways. Consistent with a body of previous research using American subjects, Ansari (1989) found that Indian male subjects were more likely than females to use direct influence behaviors. However, he failed to find that Indian females use indirect behaviors more than their male counterparts. Although Ansari cited changing sex roles as an explanation, an alternative rationale might be that cultural differences in India preclude direct comparisons to studies conducted using American subjects. In a study using both Anglo and Chicano subjects, sex differences in managerial behaviors were found only in the Anglo portion of the subject pool (Ayers-Nachamkin, Cann, Reed, & Horne, 1982). Chicano women, on the other hand, tended to exhibit managerial behavior that was more similar to that of the male subjects.

Sex. Sex has been examined in a plethora of studies of influence methods, but the findings from these studies are mixed. The primary focus of most of these studies has been the sex of the agent, although some have also investigated the sex of the target. Perhaps the most consistent finding regarding sex differences has been that men use influence tactics that are more direct, reward based, and even coercive, whereas women use more indirect and collaborative methods (e.g., Broverman, Vogel, Broverman, Clarkson, & Rosenkrantz, 1972; Falbo & Peplau, 1980; Gruber & White, 1986; Offermann & Schrier, 1985). Other findings suggest that male managers rely more on punishment-oriented strategies, whereas female managers prefer rational and altruistic approaches (Harper & Hirokawa, 1988). In a unique study involving a "real" compliance-gaining task in the laboratory (as opposed to a scenario-based task), White (1988) found that the agent's motive (self-interest versus altruism) and the target's reaction (insulting versus not) combined to affect differentially when male and female influencers would exhibit reward-based versus coercive behaviors. Fitzpatrick and Winke (1979) explored paired sex effects in the agent-target dyad. Comparing same-sex with opposite-sex pairs, they found that males in same-sex friendships tended to use nonnegotiation tactics, whereas females in same-sex friendships used emotional appeals, empathic understanding, and personal rejection. Further, they found that both sexes were more likely to use emotional appeals with opposite-sex others than with same-sex others.

However, a number of studies have found no sex differences or differences that were small or inconsistent (Buss et al., 1987; Dreher, Dougherty, & Whitely, 1989; DuBrin, 1989; Kipnis et al., 1980; Schlueter, Barge, & Blankenship, 1990; Steil & Weltman, 1992; Vecchio & Sussmann, 1991; Yukl & Falbe, 1990), raising questions about the theoretical or practical significance of sex differences in dyadic influence (but see Eagly, 1995, for a provocative discussion of the scientific and political implications of psychological studies of sex differences). With respect to dyadic influence, we side with researchers who argue that observed sex differences in behavior can be attributed to other situational and individual difference factors (Hirokawa, Mickey, & Miura, 1991), among which are position of relative strength or weakness (Howard, Blumstein, & Schwartz, 1986), power of the job (Mainiero, 1986), personal power of the individual (Hirokawa, Kodama, & Harper, 1990), and legitimacy of the request (Hirokawa et al., 1991).

Personality

Machiavellianism. The Machiavellian personality construct (Christie & Geis, 1970) is relevant to organizational contexts as an indicator of an individual's orientation to the use of power or influence, including his or her view of the appropriateness of deceptive and manipulative influence techniques. Machiavellianism has been the subject of several studies of interpersonal influence and communication, with inconsistent results. Researchers have found that individuals scoring high on the Machiavellian trait tend to prefer prosocial influence methods in low intimacy situations (Roloff & Barnicott, 1978), use nonrational and indirect influence tactics (Falbo, 1977), employ blocking tactics (Vecchio & Sussmann, 1991), and are more flexible than others in their influence attempts (Grams & Rogers, 1990). At a more basic interactional level, there is evidence that Machiavellians are more likely than other influence seekers to attempt to interact with the target. They avoid asocial tactics such as evasion (which preclude or limit interaction with targets; Grams & Rogers, 1990) and are more likely to seek out opportunities to praise the target and to express values similar to the target's (Pandey & Rostogi, 1979). A problem with Machiavellianism as a predictor of influence seeking and other interpersonal behaviors is that the construct—as measured by the Likert-style Mach IV instrument—may not be unidimensional (Hunter, Gerbing, & Boster, 1982; O'Hair & Cody, 1987).

Dogmatism. Dogmatism (Rokeach, 1960) is an indicator of the rigidity of beliefs held by the individual. With respect to the agent, the emphasis has been less on specific strategies predicted by the dogmatism trait than on the extent of the variety of strategies selected by high versus low dogmatics. Although effect sizes vary, studies have generally found that as dogmatism increases, an agent's use of (or willingness to use) multiple influence techniques increases (Boster & Stiff, 1984; Dillard & Burgoon, 1985; Hunter & Boster, 1987; Roloff & Barnicott, 1979). On the target side, there is evidence from persuasion research that dogmatism is related to influence efficacy, because of differences in argument processing (DeBono & Klein, 1993). Specifically, high-dogmatic targets tend to be persuaded by experts regardless of argument strength, whereas low-dogmatic targets evaluate the strength of the message regardless of the expertise of the agent.

Need for achievement and need for power. Influence methods choice has been linked to personality characteristics that reflect the motivational implications of human needs (McClelland, 1985), including "need for achievement" (the desire to succeed at challenging tasks) and "need for power" (the desire to have influence over others). Two organizational studies by Mowday (1978, 1979) have shown that individuals high in need for power tend to be rated by their subordinates as exercising influence attempts more frequently, tend to use fewer appeals to policy and more manipulation tactics, and tend to use more persuasive arguments. Chacko (1990) surmised that high need-for-achievement administrators tend to use more reason and coalition-building tactics because they like the difficulty of these tactics. Need for achievement and power have also been shown to be positively related to influence effectiveness. Schilit (1986) found that middle-level managers who were high in need for achievement or need for power were more successful in upward influence attempts.

Locus of control. Locus of control (Rotter, 1966) captures the extent to which individuals view events as under their own control (labeled "internals") versus determined by outside or uncontrollable forces ("externals"). Wheeless et al. (1983) argued that locus of control—of both agent and target—deserves to be considered in connection with investigations of influence tactics and outcomes. On the agent side, they argued that internals not only are more likely than externals to exert influence effectively, but are more likely to select different influence methods. On the target side, Wheeless et al. suggested that externals, with their greater need for belonging and esteem, are more responsive to influence strategies that invoke the target's relationship with the agent than are internals. Empirical work has focused solely on agents, with mixed support for these predictions. In a study using student subjects reacting to hypothetical situations, Canary, Cody, and Marston (1986) found that internals preferred methods that capitalized on rationality, the manipulation of positive feelings, and relational ties between agent and target. In an organizational study of actual behavior over time, Farmer, Fedor, Goodman, and Maslyn (1993) reported that externals were more likely to use soft strategies and to avoid rational persuasion.

Self-monitoring. There is evidence that the self-monitoring trait (Snyder, 1974), defined as the individual tendency to regulate behavior to match situational constraints for the sake of public appearances, is related to tactical behavior. In a series of studies, Smith, Cody, Lovette, and Canary (1990) found that high self-monitors are more expressive when tactical appeals focus on emotional and relational issues. Sex emerged as a moderating variable, with tactics used by males more likely than those of females to vary based on self-monitoring scores: High-self-monitoring males exhibited greater use of certain strategies (compromise, emotional appeals, coercion, referent influence) than did low-self-monitoring males. Farmer et al. (1993) found a positive association between self-monitoring and the use of ingratiation tactics, but failed to find a predicted negative relationship with "hard" tactics such as assertiveness and upward appeal.

Verbal aggressiveness. Several recent studies have investigated the relationship between verbal aggressiveness, defined as the tendency to communicate in a way that attacks the self-concept of others, and influence behavior (Boster, Levine, & Kazoleas, 1993; Infante, Anderson, Martin, Herington, & Kim, 1993; Infante, Riddle, Horvath, & Tumlin, 1992). In a study designed to tease out the behavioral proclivities of those who score high on the Verbal Aggressiveness Scale (Infante & Wigley, 1986), Infante et al. (1992) found that high verbal aggressives used more teasing, swearing, attacks on target competence, and nonverbal influence behaviors than did low verbal aggressives. In addition, high verbal aggressives perceived verbally aggressive behaviors to be less hurtful that did low verbal aggressives. These authors suggest that awareness training might decrease the use of verbal aggression behaviors, suggesting that the verbal aggressiveness trait might be at least partly situation specific. Lim's (1990) study of response to resistance found that agents who received unfriendly (based on disagreement) resistance from targets responded with more verbal aggressiveness more quickly than did recipients of friendly resistance. Because Lim's study looked at verbal behavior over five sequential periods, causal conclusions are more appropriate here than in the vast majority of influence studies, which have used cross-sectional data. Finally, there is limited evidence to suggest that communication styles may interact with one another. For example, Boster et al. (1993) found an interaction between verbal aggressiveness and argumentativeness when they examined agent persistence on a negotiation task.

Other personality measures. Isolated studies have linked other personality measures with influence tactics choice. Lamude and Scudder (1993) found that both blue- and white-collar managers who scored high on Type A behavior (Bortner, 1969) were more likely to be perceived by subordinates as using antisocial (punishment-oriented) influence methods. Savard and Rogers (1992) found that individuals high in self-efficacy (Bandura, 1977) persisted longer in successive influence attempts than did those with low self-efficacy. Buss et al. (1987) reported that subjects who scored high on the Neuroticism scale (Eysenck & Eysenck, 1975) used more silent treatment and regression manipulation tactics. They also found the use of coercive tactics to be correlated with the arrogance and quarrelsome subscales of the Interpersonal Adjective Scale (Wiggins, 1979), and the use of debasement tactics to be correlated with laziness. Finally, Applegate (1982) found that individuals with higher levels of cognitive complexity tend to use a greater number of strategies and to use strategies that are more adapted to the influence target than do individuals with lower levels of cognitive complexity.

Tactical Profiles

Up to this point, the emphasis with respect to individual differences has been on demographic and dispositional characteristics that predict the selection and use of influence tactics. In a small number of studies of organizational participants, however, researchers have used clustering techniques to define individual differences by the profiles of tactics individuals display in their influence-seeking behavior. Perreault and Miles (1978) explored how characteristics of the influence target and of the agent-target relationship are associated with the selection and combination of influence strategies by organizational members. Drawing on theories of social power (French & Raven, 1959) and impression management (Tedeschi, Schlenker, & Bonoma, 1971), Perreault and Miles used multiple discriminant analysis to identify five higher-order influence strategy "mixes" or profiles: "noninfluencers" (who rarely use any of the strategies), "expert influencers," "referent influencers," "position powerwielders," and "multiple strategy influencers." These researchers reported an array of associations among these mixes and agent perceptions of the target and of the dyadic relationship; for example, expert influencers (using expertise a great deal) tend to be in positions of authority relative to, and to have low-intimacy relationships with, the target.

Kipnis and Schmidt (1988), using cluster analysis, classified influence agents into one of four influence styles: "shotgun influencers," who report high amounts of usage of all influence methods; "ingratiators," who exhibit dominant use of ingratiation and friendliness strategies; "tactician influencers," who exhibit dominant use of rational persuasion strategies; and "bystanders," who report low amounts of usage of all methods.

Consequences of Influence Methods

Despite the obvious importance of understanding the consequences of strategic choices made by influence seekers, relatively few researchers have studied the outcome side of the dyadic influence process. The handful of (predominantly organizational) studies that have addressed consequences of tactical choice have examined (a) social-cognitive outcomes related to perceptions of the tactics used within influence attempts, (b) perceived or actual effectiveness of the influence attempt, (c) job-related outcomes, and (d) tactical combinations.

Social-Cognitive Outcomes of Tactical Choice

In exploring how agents and targets of influence differ in their perceptions of the methods used in influence attempts, Erez et al. (1986) found that influence agents more frequently report that they use "strong" tactics (e.g., assertiveness, rationality, sanctions), whereas targets emphasize the presence of "weak" tactics (e.g., exchange, manipulation) in their perceptions of the influence methods directed at them. Beyond their interesting attribution theory implications, the Erez et al. findings call into question the validity of instruments designed to measure strategic influence that rely exclusively on agent self-reports of generalized influence behavior.

Target perceptions of agent behavior are important because there is consistent evidence that these perceptions predict dyad-relevant attitudes. In a study of downward influence in a work setting, Vecchio and Sussmann (1989) found that discrepancies between the influence behaviors subordinates *prefer* their supervisors use and the behaviors supervisors *actually* use were negatively related to subordinate satisfaction with supervision and to the quality of the leader-subordinate relationship. In addition, there is evidence that tactical choices made by agents elevate target perceptions of job satisfaction (Roach, 1991), feelings of satisfaction with supervision (Richmond, McCroskey, & Davis, 1986), attributions of agent power (Hinkin & Schriesheim, 1990), and assessments of the agent's communication competence (Johnson, 1992). However, the connection between tactics and perceptions may run in the other direction—affecting how *agents* perceive their targets. O'Neal, Kipnis, and Craig (1994) found that agents who used coercive techniques were more likely to evaluate targets negatively than were agents who used rational techniques. O'Neal et al. interpreted this finding as an indication that influence agents devalue those they can control, with coercive tactics more likely to result in the relinquishing of more control to the agent.

In summary, there is ample evidence that the choices agents make about influence methods have the potential to elicit a variety of social-cognitive outcomes that are relevant for achievement and success in organizational contexts. The research that informs this conclusion, however, lacks integration or conceptual coherence. The effects of tactical behavior on social-cognitive processes is a research area that is ripe for theory building.

Influence Effectiveness

Surprisingly, research on the effectiveness of compliance-gaining tactics and strategies is recent and relatively scant. In work settings, there is mixed evidence that tactical effectiveness varies by the organizational direction of an influence attempt. Yukl and Tracey (1992) found that tactics of ingratiation and exchange were effective in lateral and downward influence situations, but ineffective in upward influence attempts. Other tactics (consultation, inspirational appeals, and rational persuasion) were effective regardless of influence direction. Falbe and Yukl (1992), with similar results, draw the conclusion that soft tactics are generally more effective than hard tactics. Barry and Bateman (1992), on the other hand, found rationality tactics effective only for lateral dyads (where neither agent nor target occupies a hierarchically superior position), and found that tactics of persistence (influence through repetition or exaggeration) are negatively associated with influence success (as perceived by the agent) for all directional agent-target relationships.

Barry and Shapiro (1992) used a laboratory role-play scenario to investigate the effects of tactical combinations on likely compliance. Some subjects were enticed with an offered exchange of benefits in return for compliance, others were not. Results indicated that the use of soft tactics (friendliness and flattery) elevated compliance in the absence of an offered exchange, but had no effect when an exchange was offered. These researchers framed their findings in terms of the elaboration likelihood model of persuasion (Petty & Cacioppo, 1986), arguing that an offered exchange may motivate targets to evaluate the influence request attentively, thus mitigating the heuristic impact of soft tactics.

Influence effectiveness as a dependent variable is valuable on its face, but has yet to attract much research attention. Part of the problem is methodological: The reliance by many researchers on measures that assess influence-seeking behavior across individual episodes (e.g., Kipnis et al., 1980) or in response to hypothetical episodes (e.g., Cody et al., 1986) precludes attention to effectiveness outcomes. Effectiveness research not only requires that actual incidents be sampled, but also benefits from the collection of data from both sides of the influence dyad—which is rare and often costly. Fortunately, there appears to be an upswing in interest in the designing of studies of effectiveness, as well as in the methodologies needed to undertake those studies.

Job Outcomes

In their study of managerial influence styles, Kipnis and Schmidt (1988) examined how four styles (shotgun, ingratiator, tactician, bystander) are related to performance evaluations, salaries, and stress. Their results indicate that male subordinates who exhibit a shotgun influence style (high usage of all influence methods) are evaluated less favorably by superiors and have lower incomes, more job tension, and greater levels of stress than do subordinates who exhibit a tactician style (dominant use of rational persuasion). In a somewhat divergent finding, Dreher et al. (1989), using data on salaries of M.B.A. graduates, reported a relationship between increased use of upward influence strategies—which may be construed as a shotgun approach in the Kipnis and Schmidt argot—and higher salary attainment.

In a study relating intrinsic (job and life satisfaction) and extrinsic (pay, promotions, and job level) career success to the use of influence tactics, Judge and Bretz (1994) found tactics aimed at increasing supervisor affect to be positively related to both extrinsic and intrinsic career success. In contrast, influence tactics aimed at increasing perceptions of competence on the job were negatively correlated with both measures of career success. This finding suggests that influence-seeking styles may have *long-term* consequences for organizational actors (e.g., see Ferris & Judge, 1991, for a review of human resource management issues from a social influence perspective).

Tactical Combinations

Recent research by Yukl et al. (1993) has examined how tactics are combined and sequenced within particular influence-seeking encounters. We treat this research as an outcome study because of its focus on the likelihood that certain tactics will be used as initial versus follow-up gambits. In this sense, a choice of a tactic by an agent may be an "outcome" of an earlier choice. Yukl et al. found that inspirational appeals, consultation, ingratiation, and legitimating tactics are more likely to be used in combination with one another, whereas rational persuasion is the tactic used most often both alone and in combination with other tactics. Maslyn, Fedor, and Farmer (1994) took the investigation of tactical sequences one step further: In addition to assessing tactics choices after a failed attempt, they found that both personal and situational characteristics differentially predicted choice of tactics within initial and follow-up influence attempts. Research on combinations is not well developed to this point, lacking both empirical sophistication and any explicit theoretical underpinnings. Nevertheless, it is encouraging that researchers are heeding the frequently heard call for studies that move beyond first-strike compliance gaining to examine influence as a dynamic, multistage process.

Evaluation of Antecedents and Consequences Research

Despite the rich variety of situational factors and individual differences that have been examined in connection with tactical choice in dyadic influence, important methodological issues temper our ability to synthesize empirical findings into a coherent conceptual framework. One major issue concerns the very basic question of level of analysis in dyadic influence research. Some researchers adopt the individual compliance-gaining episode as the object of investigation. In these studies, subjects may be asked to *react* to hypothetical influence attempts that encompass situational manipulations (e.g., Barry & Shapiro, 1992; deTurck, 1985), or they may be asked to *recall* and describe actual influence attempts they have experienced in their own recent pasts (e.g., Cody et al., 1986; Falbe & Yukl, 1992; Maslyn et al., 1994). Other researchers (including many in the organizational sciences) elicit from subjects self-reports of influence-seeking behavior in the aggregate—perhaps with reference to a particular target, but over time and across influence encounters, without reference to any one particular episode (e.g. Kipnis et al., 1980; Perreault & Miles, 1978; Yukl & Falbe, 1990). The implications of choices of method among these options are far from trivial, as situational effects (in the form of contextual antecedents) may be episode specific. The trend in recent dyadic influence research seems to be toward a greater emphasis on tactical combinations and effectiveness metrics (e.g., Falbe & Yukl, 1992), which suggests to us a need for greater focus on the study of influence at the level of the individual episode.

A related methodological concern is the measurement issue that pertains to recording tactical behavior within specific episodes. In some research, structured questionnaire responses measure the likelihood of use of individual strategies (the "selection" method); in other cases (especially with recalled critical incidents), subjects provide open-ended descriptions of influence attempts (the "construction" method). In a seven-part comparison study, Burleson et al. (1988) concluded that selection methods are highly sensitive to social desirability bias, whereas construction methods are more likely to capture the effects of situations and individual differences. (The Burleson et al. study and its conclusions have been fervently challenged by Boster, 1988; Hunter, 1988; and Seibold, 1988.) In response to methodological concerns, some have advocated greater reliance on observational methods to record compliance-gaining behavior as it occurs, the associated costs and difficulties notwithstanding (Dillard, 1988; Yukl & Falbe, 1990). One attempt to do this in the laboratory, with subjects manipulated into initiating influence attempts with an experimental confederate, was disappointing in its inability to find variance in influence method selection (Boster & Stiff, 1984).

A further limitation is the preponderance of cross-sectional data in research examining situational antecedents and consequences of dyadic influence-seeking behavior. Although researchers can infer associations among situational factors, tactical choices, and influence outcomes, they cannot tease out the causal nature of these relationships (Barry & Bateman, 1992), including the extent to which situation perception may follow from ongoing dyadic influence behavior. In this sense, cross-sectional research fails to capture the iterative and reciprocal aspects of dyadic influence episodes.

AN INTEGRATIVE FRAMEWORK
OF DYADIC INFLUENCE

Scholars have noted that research on dyadic influence is empirically substantial but theoretically underdeveloped (e.g., Miller et al., 1987). As a step toward conceptual integration, we bring together extant theoretical perspectives and empirical findings within a framework capturing the contextual elements of an organization-based dyadic influence attempt. Figure 7.1 depicts an influence episode as a reciprocal transaction between agent and target. Consistent with process theorists (e.g., Cobb, 1984; Dillard, 1990a; Porter et al., 1981; Raven, 1992; Tedeschi, Bonoma, & Schlenker, 1972), the sequence of events constituting an episode is conceptualized as an ordered series of cognitive and behavioral stages. With balanced attention to the dynamic perceptual variables that drive both agent and target behavior within a reciprocal framework, we seek to capture, at least in rudimentary form, what Miller et al. (1987) call the "interactional, multifunctional, adaptive character of communicative influence" (p. 110).

For both agent and target, the many variables and constructs that make up the context of an influence episode are grouped as characteristics, resources, and situation perceptions. *Characteristics* include measurable individual demographic and personality attributes, as well as organization-level indicators of structure and culture, that are relevant to the process of initiating (for the agent) or responding to (for the target) a compliance-gaining episode. *Resources* encompass skills, abilities, experiences, objective constraints (e.g., time pressures), and ephemeral mood states that are operative and available for each member of the dyad at the time the influence episode takes place. Situational context is conceptualized as an array of *perceptions* regarding self, other, and the dyadic relationship (Jones, 1990), and regarding the influence-seeking episode (e.g., Cody et al., 1986; Cody & McLaughlin, 1980; Jackson & Backus, 1982). In the model, the constellations of relevant resources and perceptions for each dyad member are characterized as *resource fields* and *perceptual fields,* respectively. Individual variables subsumed under these fields in the figure and in the discussion below are drawn from (a) empirical research findings that are supportive of the variable's role, (b) research streams that argue convincingly for the variable's role but have yet to be supported empirically, or (c) theoretical perspectives that are plausible but as yet untested.

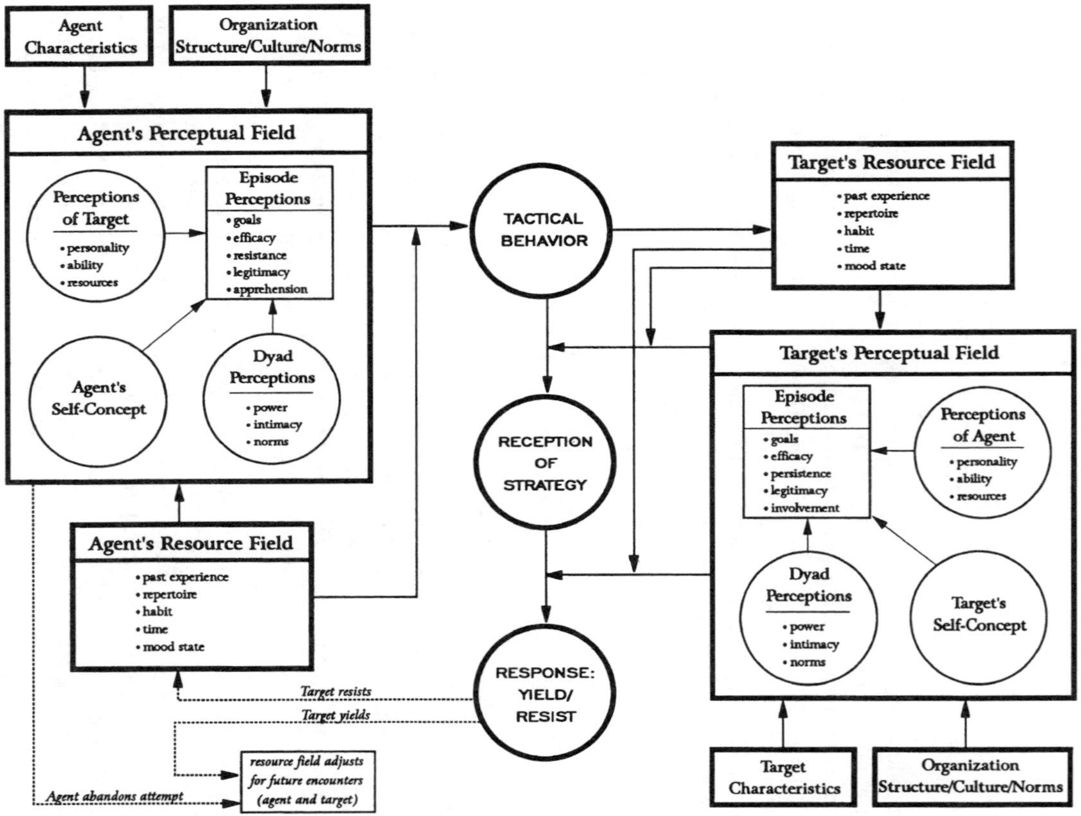

Figure 7.1. Transactional Framework of a Dyadic Social Influence Episode

The framework's basic assumption is that actors' perceptual fields are embedded within the sequence of social interaction that constitutes an influence attempt (Darley & Fazio, 1980). For both agent and target, perceptions are a joint function of individual characteristics, organizational properties, and episode-relevant resources. (Personal characteristics, organizational characteristics, and resources of agent and of target may be construed as entry points to the model in the sense that they are exogenously determined, although resources may also be modified dynamically within the influence episode.) Perceptions held by the *agent* drive tactical choices. Perceptions held by the *target* play a role in both the target's comprehension of the strategy selected by the agent and the formulation of a response. A target's response entails either yielding or resistance (which can take the form of explicit refusal, questioning, debate, nonresponse, or the like). When resistance occurs, agent resources and perceptions, adjusted in light of target behavior, will predict subsequent actions by the agent. Fundamentally, the agent encountering resistance chooses either to persist in or to abandon the influence attempt (Dillard, 1990a). The episode ends when either the target yields to the agent's (intact or modified) request or the agent abandons the influence attempt.

The Influence Agent's Perceptual Field

At the core of the social psychological process through which one adopts a strategy for achieving influence is the array of perceptions held by the influence agent (e.g., Cody & McLaughlin, 1985). Our depiction of the perceptual field in Figure 7.1 incorporates three sets of situational perceptions that drive compliance-gaining strategies. First, agents bring to the influence episode a set of prior perceptions regarding the disposition, personal abilities, and relevant resources of the target. Second, agents initiate the episode with self-perceptions that define the personal identity they hope to project in social interaction (Jones, 1990). Third, beyond self-concept and other-evaluation, the unfolding influence episode activates a subjective assessment of the nature of the agent-target relationship (grouped in Figure 7.1 under the rubric of *dyad perceptions*), including perceptions of relative power within the dyad and judgments about the closeness or "intimacy" of the relationship (Cody & McLaughlin, 1980, 1985; deTurck, 1985; Fitzpatrick & Winke, 1979; Miller et al., 1977). Dyad perceptions also reflect relevant social norms governing interaction between agent and target (Ajzen & Fishbein, 1980; Cialdini, 1993; Zimbardo & Leippe, 1991).

In light of perceptions regarding self, the influence target, and emergent characteristics of the agent-target dyad, agents enact an assessment (episode perceptions) of the opportunities and constraints involved in the specific influence request at hand. As shown in the figure, these include assessments of compliance-gaining goals that are operative in the situation (Ansari & Kapoor, 1987; Dillard, 1990a, 1990b; Schmidt & Kipnis, 1984), of self-efficacy regarding the attainability of successful influence (Savard & Rogers, 1992), of the level and form of resistance expected from the target (O'Hair et al., 1991; Wilson et al., 1993), of the extent to which the request is one the agent has the legitimate right to make of the target (Cody & McLaughlin, 1980, 1985), and of the degree of anxiety or apprehension the agent expects to encounter in carrying out this influence attempt (Greene & Sparks, 1983). Episode perceptions are treated within the model as causal products of the agent's constellation of judgments regarding self, other, and dyad.

Agent and Organization Characteristics

Empirical studies of influence examining individual differences have typically investigated the impact of demographic (e.g., Falbo & Peplau, 1980; Farmer et al., 1993) or dispositional (Boster & Stiff, 1984; O'Hair & Cody, 1987; Roloff & Barnicott, 1978) variables on tactical choice. Although research findings regarding the direct effects of individual differences have been elusive and inconsistent, we suggest an important role for agent characteristics in shaping the perceptions that guide agent influence-seeking behavior. Machiavellianism (Christie & Geis, 1970), for example, as a trait that speaks to how individuals regard others' motives, may be expected to influence the agent's assessment of the target's personal qualities and interactional goals. Dispositional variables that pertain to an individual's self-presentation and sense of control, such as locus of control (Rotter, 1966), self-monitoring (Snyder, 1974), and self-esteem (Bandura, 1977), may well affect dyadic-level perceptions of relative power and relational intimacy. In general, the findings of empirical studies of individual differences in dyadic influence argue for the proposition that individual differences are more likely to shape the array of perceptions that drive tactical choice, rather than directly predict such choices.

As discussed earlier in this review, organizational characteristics have been investigated as determinants of influence behavior, but not extensively. Although research hints at the relevance of organization-level variables (e.g., Cheng, 1983; Krone, 1992; Schilit & Locke, 1982), we adopt the position that, as with individual characteristics, organizational attributes drive tactical choices indirectly to the extent that they influence the perceptions of actors regarding norms of behavior and other situational factors. Hence, in Figure 7.1, organizational characteristics that define structure, culture, and macro-level norms are included as exogenous determinants of participants' perceptual fields.

The Influence Agent's Resource Field

Although individual differences and situational perceptions have captured most of the attention of researchers exploring antecedents of tactical selection, there are other relevant antecedents that fit neither category. In Figure 7.1, we group these additional contextual elements under the rubric of *agent resources.* These include objective situational constraints on the influence agent's actions, such as time limits or pressures; the agent's behavioral habits and tendencies that tend to recur; relevant past experiences, either with the same or similar target individual or with a similar influence objective; and the agent's transitory emotional or mood state, which has been shown to affect the construction of persuasive messages (Bohner & Schwarz, 1993) and other interpersonal dynamics (Isen & Baron, 1991). The notion of "resources" as an exogenous determinant of influence-seeking behavior has found expression in conceptual frameworks of dyadic influence (e.g., Kipnis, 1974; Schein, 1977), but is underexplored empirically. In the model presented here as Figure 7.1, resource field variables are cast as direct antecedents of perceptual judgments that, in turn, predict tactical behavior. We further hypothesize that certain resources, such as habits and time pressures, moderate associations between perceptions and tactical selection.

The Influence Target's Perspective

Working from a presumption that social influence is essentially a process of "reciprocal sense making" (Ginzel, Kramer, & Sutton, 1992), we depict the perceptual and dispositional antecedents of the influence target's actions in Figure 7.1 as structurally similar to those of the agent, with minor modifications. Targets, like agents, bring relevant perceptions, individual difference characteristics, and personal resources to the influence episode. The tactical behaviors chosen and enacted by the influence seeker are presumed to affect target perceptions through mediating resource variables (see Rhodes & Wood, 1992). Target perceptions are also held to be a function (like agent perceptions) of exogenous target characteristics—both demographic and dispositional (e.g., Haugtvedt & Petty, 1992)—as well as of organizational attributes. Within the target's perceptual field, we postulate a similar set of causal linkages among different types of perceptions as we did for agents: Perceptions regarding the specific influence situation at hand follow from judgments about the other person, about self, and about the relational qualities and normative features of the agent-target dyad.

We construe the set of episode-relevant perceptions that are salient for the influence target as somewhat different from those salient for the agent. The agent's *efficacy* judgment refers to an assessment of the likelihood that successful influence will obtain; the target's efficacy judgment addresses the likelihood that he or she can successfully resist. The agent perceives some level of likely *resistance* on the part of the target, whereas the target assesses the *persistence* he or she expects the agent to exhibit in pressing the influence request. The agent enacts tactical behavior with varying levels of anticipated anxiety, or situation *apprehension,* whereas the target experiences varying levels of *involvement,* defined as the personal importance of the influence request (Petty & Cacioppo, 1979).

The overall relationship between target perceptions and target responses to the influence request are treated in the model as multifaceted. Following McGuire's (1985) two-stage framework of attitude change, we draw a distinction between (a) the target's *reception* of tactical behavior (i.e., target's ability to comprehend, recall, and retain the substance of the influence attempt), and (b) the target's formulation of a behavioral *response*. In Figure 7.1, target perceptions are postulated as relevant at both stages. Essentially, our approach construes perceptual adjustment as the cognitive "filter" (Reis & Shaver, 1988) through which the influence target interprets the agent's actions. We do not argue, however, that resource changes and perceptual adjustments fully mediate the effects of tactical choices on target interpretations and responses; thus, direct (vertical) linkages appear in the center of Figure 7.1 connecting tactical behavior, strategy reception, and responses. Our intention is to suggest that under some circumstances, such as when a target is unable or unwilling to process influence-seeking messages actively, cognitive elaboration (which in the present model takes the form of perceptual adjustment) may be circumvented (Petty & Cacioppo, 1986).

At a basic conceptual level, the target's response behavior may be characterized as a dichotomous choice between yielding to the influence request and resisting it. In reality, resistance can take many forms (Ashforth & Lee, 1990) and can be communicated interpersonally through a variety of strategies (Burroughs, Kearney, & Plax, 1989; McLaughlin, Cody, & Robey, 1980; Metts, Cupach, & Imahori, 1992; O'Hair et al., 1991). Drawing on conceptualizations of the effects of influence outcomes on subsequent perceptions (Kipnis, 1974; Marwell & Schmitt, 1967a; Raven, 1992), we propose in the model that target resistance affects aspects of the agent's perceptual field through the mediating process of resource adjustment. For example, initial resistance may heighten the salience of time pressures, alter an agent's affective mood state, or in any case provide a novel bit of experiential information about the target or the issue. Working from a newly revised field of perceptions (Cobb, 1984; Dillard, 1990a; Raven, 1992), the agent may elect to persist with new or reinforced tactical behavior, or may abandon the influence attempt. Regardless of how the episode ends, the resource fields that both dyad members take from the exchange—and bring to future interpersonal encounters—are (potentially) altered by the fact that this episode occurred.

CONCLUSION

This review suggests that research on dyadic influence, although abundant in scope and volume, lacks the kind of cumulative coherence that would facilitate an efficient inventory and synthesis of empirical findings. One unfortunate problem is that interesting theoretical perspectives remain essentially untested. Empirical researchers draw on this body of conceptual work very infrequently, and efforts to revisit theory in light of empirical findings are rare. Another difficulty is that the studies constituting the ample body of empirical work have followed disciplinary and methodological paths sufficiently diverse as to resist inductive theory building. Put simply, dyadic influence is a topic that attracts the attention of researchers who study essentially the same constructs and phenomena from a variety of academic perspectives and who publish their work in disparate literatures.

The framework in Figure 7.1 reflects an effort to overcome boundaries of discipline, argot, and methodology in order to integrate and extend previous work, both conceptual and empirical, on dyadic influence. The range of constructs and variables that influence researchers have considered is sizable, both in numbers and types. Although intended as a synthesis and distillation, this model is not a simple reduction to a parsimonious set of predictors; indeed, its complexity reflects the difficulty involved in trying to account for all factors that affect a particular class of social interaction. The temptation of normal science is to explain as much outcome variance as possible with as few predictors as possible. The reality of dyadic influence is a constellation of individual factors, social constructs, and cognitive processes that combine in myriad ways to produce countless, and frequently subtle, variations in behavior.

We conclude by sketching key implications of this analysis for future research. First, notwithstanding the many previous attempts to identify and classify tactical behaviors, consensus on a taxonomy that is both conceptually sound and empirically valid—within organizations or other contexts—remains elusive. Equally elusive is consensus on whether it is even worthwhile to work toward a single "best" typology. We agree with arguments (e.g., Kellermann & Cole, 1994; O'Keefe, 1990) that influence tactics research should focus less on creating inclusive inventories and more on differentiating tactics conceptually in ways that comport with particular research questions and contexts. The implication is that influence researchers should identify in conceptual terms the dimensions of behavior that are relevant to a specific research context or question, and then formulate or adopt a taxonomy that reflects those dimensions. A programmatic approach that combines deductive and inductive methods is ideally suited to enhancing the validity of typologies: Working initially from theory, researchers could evaluate and reformulate a conceptual typology in light of qualitative data of the kinds that have been gathered and used to construct inductive typologies.

Second, the foregoing discussion suggests that interaction effects among the individual and situational factors that constitute an influence episode may be paramount, and need greater research attention. The empirical record raises doubts about the ability of single individual and situational characteristics to predict influence behaviors and outcomes. Our model argues for a more expansive perspective on the structure of influence *situation,* with a wider variety of contextual elements under investigation. We further advocate greater attention to causal connections among antecedents, not just between antecedents and compliance-gaining behaviors, as a way to shed light on the dynamics of interpersonal perception that guide influence behavior.

Third, we discern the need for a greater focus on both sides of the dyad—on agent *and* target. Investigations that look only at an influence agent's perceptions and likely actions, although commonplace perhaps because of the methodological complications of group-level research, cannot account for situational variance that has meaning only in the context of a dyadic relationship. This becomes particularly important in the conceptualization of social influence as iterative and reciprocal, rather than as a one-shot, one-way flow of interaction. Although our framework is intended to advance this viewpoint, an observation made 6 years ago by Cody and McLaughlin (1990) still rings true: An interactional view of the compliance-gaining process is "not fully apparent in the social influence literature" (p. 3).

Fourth, and in a related vein, we urge researchers to move away from the use of methods that contrive hypothetical scenarios or elicit generalized self-report assessments of influence-seeking behavior over time, without reference to particular, actual influence episodes. Beyond the obvious psychometric concerns about recall accuracy and social desirability, reliance on cross-episodic measures inherently obfuscates the predictive power of dyadic and contextual forces that are situation specific. Obviously, the study of social interaction sequences in vivo is both difficult and costly. The study by Wilson et al. (1993) on attribution processes in compliance-gaining interactions demonstrates that clever research designs can overcome some of these obstacles.

Finally, and to return to a recurrent theme, the need for cross-disciplinary fertilization is compelling. The ubiquitousness of dyadic social influence as a basic aspect of interpersonal behavior—both in and out of organizations—is something with which scholars in various disciplines are in consistent agreement. Yet, as we have seen, the study of dyadic influence has been undertaken within distinct but parallel investigative spheres. Greater attention to integration holds the promise that incrementally meaningful research advancements will supplant isolated and duplicated efforts.

NOTES

1. Some psychologists have cultivated an alternative, dual-process approach that treats power and influence as distinct ways to change behavior: The use of power coerces compliance, whereas the use of influence engenders noncoerced acceptance (Moscovici, 1976; Turner, 1991). Although such a distinction is certainly relevant conceptually to an understanding of strategies for influence, it obfuscates the role of relational power as part of the social backdrop for dyadic influence-seeking behavior. Accordingly, we adopt the perspective taken by several of the process models reviewed in the next section, that power is more appropriately cast as an antecedent, emergent property of the social relationship between parties to an influence episode.

2. We also exclude the literature on "mutual influence" (Cappella, 1985, 1987), which focuses on the microstructure of conversational interaction, not on goal-directed activity that seeks to elicit attitudinal or behavior change from others.

3. For example, efforts to identify and classify impression management tactics (e.g., Gardner & Martinko, 1988; Kumar & Beyerlein, 1991; Tedeschi & Melburg, 1984) are narrowly focused on a subset of influence-seeking behaviors, and hence are not represented in Table 7.2. Also notable by its the absence is the French and Raven (1959) model of power bases. Although some researchers (e.g., Mowday, 1978, 1979) propose tactics taxonomies that resemble the French and Raven inventory, we treat the power bases themselves as antecedent conditions that set the stage for tactical selection.

4. These labels for levels of abstraction are arbitrary, as is the number of levels one might choose to label. Less arbitrary is our decision to avoid the use of the term *tactic* to label any one particular level. Because *tactic* appears in the literature as a generic term for constructs at various levels that define influence-seeking activity, we choose not to encumber it with a precise level-of-analysis meaning that would contradict, or at least confuse, common usage.

5. We thank an anonymous *Communication Yearbook* referee for suggesting this interpretation.

REFERENCES

Aguinis, H., Nesler, M. S., Hosoda, M., & Tedeschi, J. T. (1994). The use of influence tactics in persuasion. *Journal of Social Psychology, 134,* 429-438.

Ajzen, I., & Fishbein, M. (1980). *Understanding attitudes and predicting social behavior.* Englewood Cliffs, NJ: Prentice Hall.

Ansari, M. A. (1989). Effects of leader sex, subordinate sex, and subordinate performance on the use of influence strategies. *Sex Roles, 20,* 283-293.

Ansari, M. A., & Kapoor, A. (1987). Organizational context and upward influence tactics. *Organizational Behavior and Human Decision Processes, 40,* 39-49.

Applegate, J. L. (1982). The impact of construct system development on communication and impression formation in persuasive contexts. *Communication Monographs, 49,* 277-289.

Ashforth, B. E., & Lee, R. T. (1990). Defensive behavior in organizations. *Human Relations, 43,* 621-648.

Ayers-Nachamkin, B., Cann, C. H., Reed, R., & Horne, A. (1982). Sex and ethnic differences in the use of power. *Journal of Applied Psychology, 67,* 464-471.

Bandura, A. (1977). Self-efficacy: Toward a unifying theory of behavioral change. *Psychological Review, 84,* 191-215.

Barry, B. (1992). *A model of dyadic social influence in organizations.* Paper presented at the 52nd Annual Meeting of the Academy of Management, Las Vegas.

Barry, B., & Bateman, T. S. (1992). Perceptions of influence in managerial dyads: The role of hierarchy, media, and tactics. *Human Relations, 65,* 555-574.

Barry, B., & Shapiro, D. L. (1992). Influence tactics in combinations: The interactive effects of soft versus hard tactics and rational exchange. *Journal of Applied Social Psychology, 22,* 1429-1441.

Benson, P. G., & Hornsby, J. S. (1988). The politics of pay: The use of influence tactics in job evaluation committees. *Group and Organization Studies, 13,* 208-224.

Blau, P. M. (1964). *Exchange and power in social life.* New York: John Wiley.

Bohner, G., & Schwarz, N. (1993). Mood states influence the production of persuasive arguments. *Communication Research, 20,* 696-722.

Bortner, R. W. (1969). A short rating scale as a potential measure of pattern A behavior. *Journal of Chronic Disease, 22,* 87-91.

Boster, F. J. (1988). Comments on the utility of compliance-gaining message selection tasks. *Human Communication Research, 15,* 169-177.

Boster, F. J. (1990). An examination of the state of compliance-gaining message behavior research. In J. P. Dillard (Ed.), *Seeking compliance: The production of interpersonal influence messages* (pp. 7-17). Scottsdale, AZ: Gorsuch Scarisbrick.

Boster, F. J., Levine, T., & Kazoleas, D. (1993). The impact of argumentativeness and verbal aggressiveness on strategic diversity and persistence in compliance-gaining behavior. *Communication Quarterly, 41,* 405-414.

Boster, F. J., & Stiff, J. B. (1984). Compliance-gaining message selection behavior. *Human Communication Research, 10,* 539-556.

Broverman, I. K., Vogel, S. R., Broverman, D. M., Clarkson, F. E., & Rosenkrantz, P. S. (1972). Sex-role stereotypes: A new appraisal. *Journal of Social Issues, 28*(2), 59-78.

Burgoon, M., Birk, T. S., & Hall, J. R. (1991). Compliance and satisfaction with physician-patient communication: An expectancy theory interpretation of gender differences. *Human Communication Research, 18,* 177-208.

Burleson, B. R., Wilson, S. R., Waltman, M. S., Goering, E. M., Ely, T. K., & Whaley, B. B. (1988). Item desirability effects in compliance-gaining research: Seven studies documenting artifacts in the strategy selection procedure. *Human Communication Research, 14,* 429-486.

Burroughs, N. F., Kearney, P., & Plax, T. G. (1989). Compliance-resisting in the college classroom. *Communication Education, 38,* 214-229.

Buss, D. M., Gomes, M., Higgins, D. S., & Lauterbach, K. (1987). Tactics of manipulation. *Journal of Personality and Social Psychology, 52,* 1219-1229.

Canary, D. J., Cody, M. J., & Marston, P. J. (1986). Goal types, compliance-gaining, and locus of control. *Journal of Language and Social Psychology, 5,* 249-269.

Cappella, J. N. (1985). The management of conversation. In M. L. Knapp & G. R. Miller (Eds.), *Handbook of interpersonal communication* (pp. 393-438). Beverly Hills, CA: Sage.

Cappella, J. N. (1987). Interpersonal communication: Definitions and fundamental questions. In C. R. Berger & S. H. Chaffee (Eds.), *Handbook of communication science* (pp. 184-238). Newbury Park, CA: Sage.

Cartwright, D. (1965). Influence, leadership, and control. In J. G. March (Ed.), *Handbook of organizations* (pp. 1-47). Chicago: Rand McNally.

Chacko, H. E. (1990). Methods of upward influence, motivational needs, and administrators' perceptions of their supervisors' leadership styles. *Group and Organization Studies, 15,* 253-265.

Cheng, J. L. C. (1983). Organizational context and upward influence: An experimental study of the use of power tactics. *Group and Organization Studies, 8,* 337-355.

Christie, R., & Geis, F. L. (1970). *Studies in Machiavellianism.* New York: Academic Press.

Cialdini, R. B. (1993). *Influence: Science and practice* (3rd ed.). New York: HarperCollins.

Clark, R. A. (1979). The impact of self interest and desire for liking on the selection of communicative strategies. *Communication Monographs, 46,* 257-273.

Cobb, A. T. (1984). An episodic model of power: Toward an integration of theory and research. *Academy of Management Review, 9,* 382-393.

Cobb, A. T. (1986). Informal influence in the formal organization: Psychological and situational correlates. *Group and Organization Studies, 11,* 229-253.

Cody, M. J., Canary, D. J., & Smith, S. W. (1994). Compliance-gaining goals: An inductive analysis of actors' goal types, strategies, and successes. In J. A. Daly & J. M. Weimann (Eds.), *Strategic interpersonal communication* (pp. 33-90). Hillsdale, NJ: Lawrence Erlbaum.

Cody, M. J., Greene, J. O., Marston, P. J., O'Hair, H. D., Baaske, K. T., & Schneider, M. J. (1986). Situation perception and message strategy selection. In M. L. McLaughlin (Ed.), *Communication yearbook 9* (pp. 390-420). Beverly Hills, CA: Sage.

Cody, M. J., & McLaughlin, M. L. (1980). Perceptions of compliance-gaining situations: A dimensional analysis. *Communication Monographs, 47,* 132-148.

Cody, M. J., & McLaughlin, M. L. (1985). The situation as a construct in interpersonal communication research. In M. L. Knapp & G. R. Miller (Eds.), *Handbook of interpersonal communication* (pp. 263-312). Beverly Hills, CA: Sage.

Cody, M. J., & McLaughlin, M. L. (1990). Introduction. In M. J. Cody & M. L. McLaughlin (Eds.), *The psychology of tactical communication* (pp. 1-29). Clevedon, England: Multilingual Matters.

Cody, M. J., McLaughlin, M. L., & Jordan, W. J. (1980). A multidimensional scaling of three sets of compliance-gaining strategies. *Communication Quarterly, 28,* 34-46.

Cody, M. J., McLaughlin, M. L., & Schneider, M. J. (1981). The impact of relational consequences and intimacy on the selection of interpersonal persuasion tactics: A reanalysis. *Communication Quarterly, 29,* 91-106.

Cody, M. J., Woelfel, M. L., & Jordan, W. J. (1983). Dimensions of compliance-gaining situations. *Human Communication Research, 9,* 99-113.

Daft, R. L. (1995). *Organization theory and design* (5th ed.). St. Paul, MN: West.

Daft, R. L., & Lengel, R. H. (1984). Information richness: A new approach to managerial behavior and organizational design. In L. L. Cummings & B. M. Staw (Eds.), *Research in organizational behavior* (pp. 191-233). Greenwich, CT: JAI.

Darley, J. M., & Fazio, R. H. (1980). Expectancy confirmation processes arising in the social interaction sequence. *American Psychologist, 35,* 867-881.

Davis-Blake, A., & Pfeffer, J. (1989). Just a mirage: The search for dispositional effects in organizational research. *Academy of Management Review, 14,* 385-400.

DeBono, K. G., & Klein, C. (1993). Source expertise and persuasion: The moderating role of recipient dogmatism. *Personality and Social Psychology Bulletin, 19,* 167-173.

Deluga, R. J. (1988). Relationship of transformational and transactional leadership with employee influencing strategies. *Group and Organization Studies, 13,* 456-467.

Deluga, R. J. (1991). The relationship of subordinate upward-influencing behavior, health care manager interpersonal stress, and performance. *Journal of Applied Social Psychology, 21,* 78-88.

deTurck, M. A. (1985). A transactional analysis of compliance-gaining behavior: Effects of noncompliance, relational contexts, and actors' gender. *Human Communication Research, 12,* 54-78.

Deutsch, M., & Gerard, H. (1955). A study of normative and informational social influences on individual judgment. *Journal of Abnormal and Social Psychology, 51,* 629-636.

Dillard, J. P. (1988). Compliance-gaining message-selection: What is our dependent variable? *Communication Monographs, 55,* 162-183.

Dillard, J. P. (1990a). A goal-driven model of interpersonal influence. In J. P. Dillard (Ed.), *Seeking compliance: The production of interpersonal influence messages* (pp. 41-56). Scottsdale, AZ: Gorsuch Scarisbrick.

Dillard, J. P. (1990b). The nature and substance of goals in tactical communication. In M. J. Cody & M. L. McLaughlin (Eds.), *The psychology of tactical communication* (pp. 70-90). Clevedon, England: Multilingual Matters.

Dillard, J. P., & Burgoon, M. (1985). Situational influences on the selection of compliance-gaining messages: Two tests of the predictive utility of the Cody-McLaughlin typology. *Communication Monographs, 52,* 289-304.

Dillard, J. P., Segrin, C., & Harden, J. M. (1989). Primary and secondary goals in the production of interpersonal influence messages. *Communication Monographs, 56,* 19-38.

Dreher, G. F., Dougherty, T. W., & Whitely, W. (1989). Influence tactics and salary attainment: A gender-specific analysis. *Sex Roles, 20,* 535-550.

DuBrin, A. J. (1989). Sex differences in endorsement of influence tactics and political behavior tendencies. *Journal of Business and Psychology, 4,* 3-14.

DuBrin, A. J. (1991). Sex and gender differences in tactics of influence. *Psychological Reports, 68,* 635-646.

Eagly, A. H. (1995). The science and politics of comparing women and men. *American Psychologist, 50,* 145-158.

Eagly, A. H., & Chaiken, S. (1993). *The psychology of attitudes.* Fort Worth, TX: Harcourt Brace Jovanovich.

Emerson, R. M. (1962). Power-dependence relations. *American Sociological Review, 27,* 31-41.

Erez, M., & Rim, Y. (1982). The relationships between goals, influence tactics, and personal and organizational variables. *Human Relations, 35,* 871-878.

Erez, M., Rim, Y., & Keider, I. (1986). The two sides of the tactics of influence: Agent vs. target. *Journal of Occupational Psychology, 59,* 25-39.

Etzioni, A. (1961). *A comparative analysis of complex organizations.* New York: Macmillan.

Eysenck, H. J., & Eysenck, S. B. (1975). *Eysenck Personality Questionnaire manual.* San Diego, CA: Educational Testing Service.

Falbe, T., & Yukl, G. (1992). Consequences for managers of using single influence tactics and combinations of tactics. *Academy of Management Journal, 35,* 638-652.

Falbo, T. (1977). Multidimensional scaling of power strategies. *Journal of Personality and Social Psychology, 35,* 537-547.

Falbo, T., & Peplau, L. A. (1980). Power strategies in intimate relationships. *Journal of Personality and Social Psychology, 38,* 618-628.

Farmer, S. M., Fedor, D. B., Goodman, J. S., & Maslyn, J. M. (1993). *Factors affecting the use of upward influence strategies.* Paper presented at the 53rd Annual Meeting of the Academy of Management, Atlanta, GA.

Ferris, G. R., & Judge, T. A. (1991). Personnel/human resources management: A political influence perspective. *Journal of Management, 17,* 447-488.

Fitch, K. L. (1994). A cross-cultural study of directive sequences and some implications for compliance-gaining research. *Communication Monographs, 61,* 185-209.

Fitzpatrick, M. A., & Winke, J. (1979). You always hurt the one you love: Strategies and tactics in interpersonal conflict. *Communication Quarterly, 27,* 3-11.

French, J., & Raven, B. H. (1959). The bases of social power. In D. Cartwright (Ed.), *Studies in social power* (pp. 150-167). Ann Arbor, MI: Institute for Social Research.

Gardner, W. L., & Martinko, M. J. (1988). Impression management: An observational study linking audience characteristics with verbal self-presentations. *Academy of Management Journal, 31,* 212-219.

Garko, M. G. (1992). Persuading subordinates who communicate in attractive and unattractive styles. *Management Communication Quarterly, 5,* 289-315.

Ginzel, L. E., Kramer, R. M., & Sutton, R. I. (1992). Organizational impression management as a reciprocal influence process: The neglected role of the organizational audience. In B. M. Staw & L. L. Cummings (Eds.), *Research in organizational behavior* (Vol. 14, pp. 227-266). Greenwich, CT: JAI.

Grams, W. C., & Rogers, R. W. (1990). Power and personality: Effects of Machiavellianism, need for approval, and motivation on use of influence tactics. *Journal of General Psychology, 117,* 71-82.

Greene, J. O., & Sparks, G. G. (1983). The role of outcome expectations in the experience of a state of communication apprehension. *Communication Quarterly, 31,* 212-219.

Gruber, K. J., & White, J. W. (1986). Gender differences in the perceptions of self's and others' use of power strategies. *Sex Roles, 15,* 109-118.

Harper, N. L., & Hirokawa, R. Y. (1988). A comparison of persuasive strategies used by female and male managers I: An examination of downward influence. *Communication Quarterly, 36,* 157-168.

Haugtvedt, C. P., & Petty, R. E. (1992). Personality and persuasion: Need for cognition moderates the persistence and resistance of attitude changes. *Journal of Personality and Social Psychology, 63,* 308-319.

Hertzog, R. L., & Bradac, J. J. (1984). Perceptions of compliance-gaining situations. *Communication Research, 11,* 363-391.

Hickson, D. J., Hinings, C. R., Lee, C. A., Schneck, R. E., & Pennings, J. M. (1971). A strategic contingencies theory of intraorganizational power. *Administrative Science Quarterly, 16,* 216-229.

Hinkin, T. R., & Schriesheim, C. A. (1990). Relationships between subordinate perceptions of supervisor influence tactics and attributed bases of supervisory power. *Human Relations, 43,* 221-237.

Hirokawa, R. Y., Kodama, R. A., & Harper, N. L. (1990). Impact of managerial power on persuasive strategy selection by female and male managers. *Management Communication Quarterly, 4,* 30-50.

Hirokawa, R. Y., Mickey, J., & Miura, S. (1991). Effects of request legitimacy on the compliance-gaining tactics of male and female managers. *Communication Monographs, 58,* 421-436.

Hirokawa, R. Y., & Miyahara, A. (1986). A comparison of influence strategies utilized by managers in American and Japanese organizations. *Communication Quarterly, 34,* 250-265.

Homans, G. C. (1961). *Social behavior: Its elementary forms.* New York: Harcourt, Brace & World.

Howard, J. A., Blumstein, P., & Schwartz, P. (1986). Sex, power, and influence tactics in intimate relationships. *Journal of Personality and Social Psychology, 51,* 102-109.

Howell, J. M., & Higgins, C. A. (1990). Leadership behaviors, influence tactics, and career experiences of champions of technological innovation. *Leadership Quarterly, 1,* 249-264.

Hunter, J. E. (1988). Failure of the social desirability response set hypothesis. *Human Communication Research, 15,* 162-168.

Hunter, J. E., & Boster, F. J. (1987). A model of compliance-gaining message selection. *Communication Monographs, 54,* 63-84.

Hunter, J. E., Gerbing, D. W., & Boster, F. J. (1982). Machiavellian beliefs and personality: Construct invalidity of the Machiavellianism dimension. *Journal of Personality and Social Psychology, 43,* 1293-1305.

Infante, D. A., Anderson, C. M., Martin, M. M., Herington, A. D., & Kim, J. (1993). Subordinates' satisfaction and perceptions of superiors' compliance-gaining tactics, argumentativeness, verbal aggressiveness, and style. *Management Communication Quarterly, 6,* 307-326.

Infante, D. A., Riddle, B. L., Horvath, C. L., & Tumlin, S. A. (1992). Verbal aggressiveness: Messages and reasons. *Communication Quarterly, 40,* 116-126.

Infante, D. A., & Wigley, C. J. (1986). Verbal aggressiveness: An interpersonal model and measure. *Communication Monographs, 53,* 61-69.

Isen, A. M., & Baron, R. A. (1991). Positive affect as a factor in organizational behavior. In L. L. Cummings & B. M. Staw (Eds.), *Research in organizational behavior* (Vol. 13, pp. 1-53). Greenwich, CT: JAI.

Jackson, S., & Backus, D. (1982). Are compliance-gaining strategies dependent on situational variables? *Central States Speech Journal, 33,* 469-479.

Johnson, G. M. (1992). Subordinate perceptions of superior's communication competence and task attraction related to superior's use of compliance-gaining tactics. *Western Journal of Communication, 56,* 54-67.

Jones, E. E. (1990). *Interpersonal perception.* New York: W. H. Freeman.

Judge, T. A., & Bretz, R. D. (1994). Political influence behavior and career success. *Journal of Management, 20,* 43-65.

Kanter, R. M. (1977). *Men and women of the corporation.* New York: Basic Books.

Kanter, R. M. (1984). *The change masters: Innovation for productivity in the 1980s.* New York: Simon & Schuster.

Kellermann, K., & Cole, T. (1994). Classifying compliance-gaining messages: Taxonomic disorder and strategic confusion. *Communication Theory, 4,* 3-60.

Kelman, H. C. (1958). Compliance, identification, and internalization: Three processes of attitude change. *Journal of Conflict Resolution, 2,* 51-60.

Kelman, H. C. (1974). Further thoughts on the processes of compliance, identification, and internalization. In J. T. Tedeschi (Ed.), *Perspectives on social power* (pp. 125-171). Chicago: Aldine.

Kelman, H. C., & Hamilton, V. L. (1989). *Crimes of obedience: Toward a social psychology of authority and responsibility.* New Haven, CT: Yale University Press.

Kim, M., & Wilson, S. R. (1994). A cross-cultural comparison of implicit theories of requesting. *Communication Monographs, 61,* 210-235.

Kipnis, D. (1974). The powerholder. In J. T. Tedeschi (Ed.), *Perspectives on social power* (pp. 82-122). Chicago: Aldine.

Kipnis, D. (1976). *The powerholders.* Chicago: University of Chicago Press.

Kipnis, D. (1984). The use of power in organizations and in interpersonal settings. In S. Oskamp (Ed.), *Applied social psychology annual 5* (pp. 179-210). Beverly Hills, CA: Sage.

Kipnis, D., Castell, P. J., Gergen, M., & Mauch, D. (1976). Metamorphic effects of power. *Journal of Applied Psychology, 61,* 127-135.

Kipnis, D., & Schmidt, S. M. (1983). An influence perspective on bargaining within organizations. In M. H. Bazerman & R. J. Lewicki (Eds.), *Negotiating in organizations* (pp. 303-319). Beverly Hills, CA: Sage.

Kipnis, D., & Schmidt, S. M. (1988). Upward-influence styles: Relationship with performance evaluations, salary, and stress. *Administrative Science Quarterly, 33,* 528-542.

Kipnis, D., Schmidt, S. M., & Wilkinson, I. (1980). Intraorganizational influence tactics: Explorations in getting one's way. *Journal of Applied Psychology, 65,* 440-452.

Krone, K. J. (1992). A comparison of organizational, structural, and relationship effects on subordinates' upward influence choices. *Communication Quarterly, 40,* 1-15.

Kumar, K., & Beyerlein, M. (1991). Construction and validation of an instrument for measuring ingratiatory behaviors in organizational settings. *Journal of Applied Psychology, 76,* 619-627.

Lamude, K. G., & Scudder, J. (1993). Compliance-gaining techniques of type-A managers. *Journal of Business Communication, 30,* 63-79.

Lewin, K. (1951). *Field theory in social science.* New York: Harper.

Lim, T. (1990). The influences of receivers' resistance on persuaders' verbal aggressiveness. *Communication Quarterly, 38,* 170-188.

Littlepage, G. E., Van Hein, J. L., Cohen, L. M., & Janiec, L. L. (1993). Evaluation and comparison of three instruments designed to measure organizational power and influence tactics. *Journal of Applied Social Psychology, 23,* 107-125.

Mainiero, L. (1986). Coping with powerlessness: The relationship of gender and job dependency to empowerment-strategy usage. *Administrative Science Quarterly, 31,* 633-653.

Marwell, G., & Schmitt, D. R. (1967a). Compliance-gaining behavior: A synthesis and model. *Sociological Quarterly, 8,* 317-328.

Marwell, G., & Schmitt, D. R. (1967b). Dimensions of compliance-gaining behaviors. *Sociometry, 30,* 350-364.

Maslyn, J. M., Fedor, D. B., & Farmer, S. M. (1994). *Predicting influence tactics: The dynamic nature of antecedents.* Paper presented at the 54th Annual Meeting of the Academy of Management, Dallas.

Mayes, B. T., & Allen, R. W. (1977). Toward a definition of organizational politics. *Academy of Management Review, 2,* 672-678.

McClelland, D. C. (1985). *Human motivation.* Glenview, IL: Scott, Foresman.

McGuire, W. J. (1985). Attitudes and attitude change. In G. Lindzey & E. Aronson (Eds.), *Handbook of social psychology* (3rd ed., Vol. 2, pp. 233-346). New York: Random House.

McLaughlin, M. L., Cody, M. J., & Robey, C. S. (1980). Situational influences on the selection of strategies to resist compliance-gaining attempts. *Human Communication Research, 7,* 14-36.

Mechanic, D. (1962). Sources of power of lower participants in complex organizations. *Administrative Science Quarterly, 7,* 349-364.

Metts, S., Cupach, W. R., & Imahori, T. T. (1992). Perceptions of sexual compliance-resisting messages in three types of cross-sex relationships. *Western Journal of Communication, 56,* 1-17.

Miller, G. A., Galanter, E., & Pribram, K. H. (1960). *Plans and the structure of behavior.* New York: Holt, Rinehart & Winston.

Miller, G., Boster, F., Roloff, M., & Seibold, D. (1977). Compliance-gaining message strategies: A typology and some findings concerning effects of situational differences. *Communication Monographs, 44,* 37-51.

Miller, G. R., Boster, F. J., Roloff, M. E., & Seibold, D. R. (1987). MBRS rekindled: Some thoughts on compliance gaining in interpersonal settings. In M. E. Roloff & G. R. Miller (Eds.), *Interpersonal processes: New directions in communication research* (pp. 89-116). Newbury Park, CA: Sage.

Mintzberg, H. (1973). *The nature of managerial work.* New York: Harper & Row.

Moscovici, S. (1976). *Social influence and social change.* London: Academic Press.

Mowday, R. T. (1978). The exercise of upward influence in organizations. *Administrative Science Quarterly, 23,* 137-156.

Mowday, R. T. (1979). Leader characteristics, self-confidence, and methods of upward influence in organizational decision situations. *Academy of Management Journal, 22,* 709-725.

Nemeth, C. J., & Staw, B. M. (1989). The tradeoffs of social control and innovation in groups and organizations. In L. Berkowitz (Ed.), *Advances in experimental social psychology* (pp. 175-210). San Diego, CA: Academic Press.

Newton, D. A., & Burgoon, J. K. (1990). The use and consequences of verbal influence strategies during interpersonal disagreements. *Human Communication Research, 4,* 477-518.

Norton, R. (1983). *Communicator style: Theory, application, and measures.* Beverly Hills, CA: Sage.

Offermann, L. R., & Schrier, P. E. (1985). Social influence strategies: The impact of sex, role, and attitudes toward power. *Personality and Social Psychology Bulletin, 11,* 286-300.

O'Hair, D., & Cody, M. J. (1987). Machiavellian beliefs and social influence. *Western Journal of Speech Communication, 51,* 279-303.

O'Hair, M. J., Cody, M. J., & O'Hair, D. (1991). The impact of situational dimensions on compliance-resistance strategies: A comparison of methods. *Communication Quarterly, 39,* 226-240.

O'Keefe, D. J. (1990). *Persuasion: Theory and research.* Newbury Park, CA: Sage.

O'Keefe, D. J. (1994). Compliance gaining: From strategy-based to feature-based analyses of compliance gaining message classification and production. *Communication Theory, 4,* 61-68.

Oldershaw, L., Walters, G. C., & Hall, D. K. (1986). Control strategies and noncompliance in abusive mother-child dyads: An observational study. *Child Development, 57,* 722-732.

O'Neal, E. C., Kipnis, D., & Craig, K. M. (1994). Effects on the persuader of employing a coercive influence technique. *Basic and Applied Social Psychology, 15,* 225-238.

Pandy, J., & Rastogi, R. (1979). Machiavellianism and ingratiation. *Journal of Social Psychology, 108,* 221-225.

Parsons, T. (1963). On the concept of influence. *Public Opinion Quarterly, 27,* 37-62.

Perloff, R. M. (1993). *The dynamics of persuasion.* Hillsdale, NJ: Lawrence Erlbaum.

Perreault, W. D., & Miles, R. H. (1978). Influence strategy mixes in complex organizations. *Behavioral Science, 23,* 86-98.

Petty, R. E., & Cacioppo, J. T. (1979). Issue involvement can increase or decrease persuasion by enhancing message-relevant cognitive responses. *Journal of Personality and Social Psychology, 37,* 1915-1926.

Petty, R. E., & Cacioppo, J. T. (1986). The elaboration likelihood model of persuasion. In L. Berkowitz (Ed.), *Advances in experimental social psychology* (Vol. 19, pp. 123-205). New York: Academic Press.

Pfeffer, J. (1981). *Power in organizations.* Marshfield, MA: Pitman.

Pinkley, R. L. (1990). Dimensions of conflict frame: Disputant interpretations of conflict. *Journal of Applied Psychology, 75,* 117-126.

Porter, L. W., Allen, R. W., & Angle, H. L. (1981). The politics of upward influence in organizations. In B. M. Staw & L. L. Cummings (Eds.), *Research in organizational behavior* (pp. 109-149). Greenwich, CT: JAI.

Raven, B. H. (1992). A power/interaction model of interpersonal influence: French and Raven thirty years later. *Journal of Social Behavior and Personality, 7,* 217-244.

Reis, H. T., & Shaver, P. (1988). Intimacy as an interpersonal process. In S. W. Duck (Ed.), *Handbook of personal relationships* (pp. 367-389). New York: John Wiley.

Rhodes, N., & Wood, W. (1992). Self-esteem and intelligence affect influenceability: The mediating role of message reception. *Psychological Bulletin, 111*, 156-171.

Richmond, V. P., & McCroskey, J. C. (1992). *Power in the classroom: Communication, control, and concern*. Hillsdale, NJ: Lawrence Erlbaum.

Richmond, V. P., McCroskey, J. C., & Davis, L. M. (1986). The relationship of supervisor use of power and affinity-seeking strategies with subordinate satisfaction. *Communication Quarterly, 34*, 178-193.

Roach, K. D. (1991). University department chairs' use of compliance-gaining strategies. *Communication Quarterly, 39*, 75-90.

Rokeach, M. (1960). *The open and closed mind*. New York: Basic Books.

Roloff, M. E. (1994). Validity assessments of compliance gaining exemplars. *Communication Theory, 4*, 69-81.

Roloff, M. E., & Barnicott, E. F. (1978). The situational use of pro- and anti-social compliance-gaining strategies by high and low Machiavellians. In B. D. Ruben (Ed.), *Communication yearbook 2* (pp. 193-205). New Brunswick, NJ: Transaction.

Roloff, M. E., & Barnicott, E. F. (1979). The influence of dogmatism on the situational use of pro- and anti-social compliance-gaining strategies. *Southern Speech Communication Journal, 45*, 37-54.

Rotter, J. B. (1966). Generalized expectancies for internal versus external control of reinforcement. *Psychological Monographs, 80*(1, Whole No. 609).

Salancik, G. R., & Pfeffer, J. (1977). Who gets power—and how they hold on to it. *Organizational Dynamics, 5*, 3-21.

Sashkin, M., & Burke, W. W. (1987). Organization development for the 1980s. *Journal of Management, 13*, 393-417.

Savard, C. J., & Rogers, R. W. (1992). A self-efficacy and subjective expected utility theory analysis of the selection and use of influence strategies. *Journal of Social Behavior and Personality, 7*, 273-292.

Schein, V. (1977). Individual power and political behaviors in organizations: An inadequately explored reality. *Academy of Management Review, 2*, 64-72.

Schenck-Hamlin, W. J., Wiseman, R. L., & Georgacarakos, G. N. (1982). A model of properties of compliance-gaining strategies. *Communication Quarterly, 30*, 92-100.

Schilit, W. K. (1986). An examination of individual differences as moderators of upward influence activity in strategic decisions. *Human Relations, 39*, 933-953.

Schilit, W. K., & Locke, E. A. (1982). A study of upward influence in organizations. *Administrative Science Quarterly, 27*, 304-316.

Schlueter, D. W., Barge, J. K., & Blankenship, D. (1990). A comparative analysis of influence strategies used by upper- and lower-level male and female managers. *Western Journal of Speech Communication, 54*, 42-65.

Schmidt, S. M., & Kipnis, D. (1984). Managers' pursuit of individual and organizational goals. *Human Relations, 37*, 781-794.

Schriesheim, C. A., & Hinkin, T. R. (1990). Influence tactics used by subordinates: A theoretical and empirical analysis and refinement of the Kipnis, Schmidt, and Wilkinson subscales. *Journal of Applied Psychology, 75*, 246-257.

Seibold, D. R. (1988). A response to "Item desirability in compliance-gaining research." *Human Communication Research, 15*, 152-161.

Seibold, D. R., Cantrill, J. G., & Meyers, R. A. (1985). Communication and interpersonal influence. In M. L. Knapp & G. R. Miller (Eds.), *Handbook of interpersonal communication* (pp. 551-611). Beverly Hills, CA: Sage.

Seibold, D. R., Cantrill, J. G., & Meyers, R. A. (1994). Communication and interpersonal influence. In M. L. Knapp & G. R. Miller (Eds.), *Handbook of interpersonal communication* (2nd ed., pp. 542-588). Thousand Oaks, CA: Sage.

Sillars, A. L. (1980). The stranger and the spouse as target persons for compliance-gaining strategies: A subjective expected utility model. *Human Communication Research, 6,* 265-279.

Smith, S. W., Cody, M. J., Lovette, S., & Canary, D. J. (1990). Self-monitoring, gender and compliance-gaining goals. In M. J. Cody & M. L. McLaughlin (Eds.), *The psychology of tactical communication* (pp. 91-134). Clevedon, England: Multilingual Matters.

Snyder, M. (1974). Self-monitoring of expressive behavior. *Journal of Personality and Social Psychology, 30,* 526-537.

Steil, J. M., & Weltman, K. (1992). Influence strategies at home and work: A study of sixty dual career couples. *Journal of Social and Personal Relationships, 9,* 65-88.

Sullivan, J., & Taylor, S. (1991). A cross-cultural test of compliance-gaining theory. *Management Communication Quarterly, 5,* 220-239.

Tedeschi, J. T., Bonoma, T. V., & Schlenker, B. R. (1972). Influence, decision, and compliance. In J. T. Tedeschi (Ed.), *The social influence processes* (pp. 346-418). Chicago: Aldine.

Tedeschi, J. T., & Melburg, V. (1984). Impression management and influence in the organization. In S. B. Bacharach & E. J. Lawler (Eds.), *Research in the sociology of organizations* (pp. 31-58). Greenwich, CT: JAI.

Tedeschi, J. T., Schlenker, B. R., & Bonoma, T. V. (1971). Cognitive dissonance: Private ratiocination or public spectacle? *American Psychologist, 26,* 685-695.

Tedeschi, J. T., Schlenker, B. R., & Lindskold, S. (1972). The exercise of power and influence: The source of influence. In J. T. Tedeschi (Ed.), *The social influence processes* (pp. 287-345). Chicago: Aldine.

Thibaut, J. W., & Kelley, H. H. (1959). *The social psychology of groups.* New York: John Wiley.

Tjosvold, D., Andrews, I. R., & Struthers, J. T. (1992). Leadership influence: Goal interdependence and power. *Journal of Social Psychology, 132,* 39-50.

Turner, J. C. (1991). *Social influence.* Pacific Grove, CA: Brooks/Cole.

Vecchio, R. P., & Sussmann, M. (1989). Preferences for forms of supervisory social influence. *Journal of Organizational Behavior, 10,* 135-143.

Vecchio, R. P., & Sussmann, M. (1991). Choice of influence tactics: Individual and organizational determinants. *Journal of Organizational Behavior, 12,* 73-80.

Wheeless, L. R., Barraclough, R., & Stewart, R. (1983). Compliance-gaining and power in persuasion. In R. N. Bostrom (Ed.), *Communication yearbook 7* (pp. 105-145). Beverly Hills, CA: Sage.

White, J. W. (1988). Influence tactics as a function of gender, insult, and goal. *Sex Roles, 18,* 433-448.

Wiggins, J. S. (1979). A psychological taxonomy of interpersonal behavior. *Journal of Personality and Social Psychology, 37,* 395-412.

Wilson, S. R., Cruz, M. G., Marshall, L. J., & Rao, N. (1993). An attributional analysis of compliance-gaining interactions. *Communication Monographs, 60,* 352-372.

Wiseman, R. L., & Schenck-Hamlin, W. (1981). A multidimensional scaling validation of an inductively-derived set of compliance gaining strategies. *Communication Monographs, 48,* 251-270.

Yukl, G., & Falbe, C. M. (1990). Influence tactics and objectives in upward, downward, and lateral influence attempts. *Journal of Applied Psychology, 75,* 132-140.

Yukl, G., Falbe, C. M., & Youn, J. Y. (1993). Patterns of influence behavior for managers. *Group and Organization Studies, 18,* 5-28.

Yukl, G., Lepsinger, R., & Lucia, T. (1992). Preliminary report on development and validation of the influence behavior questionnaire. In K. Clark, M. Clark, & D. P. Campbell (Eds.), *The impact of leadership* (pp. 417-427). Greensboro, NC: Center for Creative Leadership.

Yukl, G., & Tracey, J. B. (1992). Consequences of influence tactics used with subordinates, peers, and the boss. *Journal of Applied Psychology, 77,* 525-535.

Zimbardo, P. G., & Leippe, M. R. (1991). *The psychology of attitude change and social influence.* Philadelphia: Temple University Press.

CHAPTER CONTENTS

8 Argumentativeness and Verbal Aggressiveness: A Review of Recent Theory and Research

DOMINIC A. INFANTE
Kent State University

ANDREW S. RANCER
University of Akron

A good deal of research on argumentativeness and verbal aggressiveness has been conducted in the communication discipline in this and the previous decade. The research has been based on a personality trait model that was used to conceptualize a very basic idea—that some aggressive behaviors are constructive and others are destructive. The present chapter reviews this research. The conceptualization and measurement of argumentativeness and verbal aggressiveness are reviewed first. Then, conclusions from the research are stated and the research relevant to the conclusions is cited. Major results are presented, along with implications. The chapter emphasizes the importance of argumentative communication. A central contention is that argumentativeness has been an approach to conceptualizing concerns of the communication discipline since antiquity, and study should continue along these lines because results suggest the impact of the communication curriculum.

E ARLY Sophists roamed ancient Greece fulfilling a great need in the city-states and fledgling democracies—they taught citizens how to argue effectively. Arguing was an essential skill for success, because, for instance, Athenians represented themselves in judicial and legislative situations. The Sophists' teachings, it might be contended, represent the beginnings of what is now known as the communication discipline.

The principles of argumentation taught by early Sophists such as Lysias, Hippias, and Protagoras were developed further and refined by a considerable number of rhetoricians, including some of the great thinkers of the time,

Correspondence and requests for reprints: Dominic A. Infante, School of Communication Studies, Kent State University, Kent, OH 44242.

Communication Yearbook 19, pp. 319-351

especially Plato and Aristotle. Although there have been disputes, such as whether invention belongs to philosophy or to rhetoric, the principles of argumentation have traveled through the centuries as a cohesive body of knowledge and today represent a framework of principles termed *argumentation theory*.

The central purpose of argumentation theory, we believe, is to enable people to argue constructively and effectively. Although the communication discipline has diversified greatly in the twentieth century, learning how to argue constructively and effectively remains a major reason students take courses in communication. This will not change soon, nor should it, as argumentative communication is crucial in a democracy. It is essential to the judicial and legislative institutions of the United States, and also to the countless private and public discussions that support, inform, and influence those institutions.

Thus, we believe there is good reason for the communication discipline's continuing interest in and emphasis on argumentative communication. We will not attempt in this chapter to identify the many areas of research and pedagogy in the field that are concerned, directly or indirectly, with argument. Instead, we will focus on one particular area, a relatively recent line of research that represents a distinctive approach to argument while having its roots clearly in the Ancients' concern for constructive and effective argumentation.

PURPOSE

In this chapter we will review theory and research that have taken a personality approach to the study of argumentative communication. This approach involves investigation of the traits of argumentativeness and verbal aggressiveness. Locus of attack distinguishes the two: Argumentativeness involves attacking the positions that others take on given issues; verbal aggressiveness involves attacking the self-concepts of those others, rather than their positions. We consider both traits because, although they are statistically independent, they "go together" in several ways: One is sometimes confused with the other; one can influence the other; both are aggressive forms of communication; they represent opposite poles on a constructive-destructive communication outcomes continuum; and it is probably difficult to understand one adequately without understanding the other.

There are several reasons for this review. First, the personality approach to the study of argumentativeness and verbal aggressiveness has been utilized for almost 15 years, and has resulted in numerous studies across nearly all of the areas of traditional communication research, reported in a variety of outlets. The broad application of the argumentativeness and verbal aggressiveness models is a fairly distinctive feature of this line of research. The many findings represent a body of knowledge that, as of yet, is unspecified because the results have not been summarized. We hope to improve the state of current knowledge by piecing together the diversity of results, thus providing a more focused and refined understanding of the traits of argumentativeness and verbal aggressiveness.

Our second reason for undertaking this review is to clarify what has been learned from past studies in order to illuminate directions for future research. Argumentativeness and verbal aggressiveness research has not stagnated in the sense that there appears to be nowhere for it to proceed, but the research seems to have settled into a pattern, the value of which has not been questioned.

Third, we believe that an understanding of what it means to be argumentative will clarify at least some of the *raison d'être* of the communication discipline. As pointed out above, the discipline began with activities aimed at making people more argumentative, the assumption being that this would benefit individuals. The teaching of skills for advocacy and for the defense of positions and for the refutation of the positions other people take remains a valued and fundamental objective of the communication curriculum. If research has found argumentative behavior to be constructive and valuable, these findings should be disseminated, because this not only supports an ancient assumption of the discipline but also provides a rationale for continued practice and study. Such evidence can contribute to the discipline's identity by establishing more precisely where our teachings lead.

Our final reason for taking on this review is that there is a need for a more complete understanding of verbal aggression. Verbal aggression can be a very destructive form of communication, and communication scholars should study it extensively in order to develop methods for controlling it. This also is consistent with a purpose of the discipline since the times of ancient Greece: to reduce the use of irrational and destructive discourse. For instance, early theorists identified the *ad hominem* fallacy and other forms of faulty reasoning, including excessive use of emotional appeals. The communication discipline has championed rational discourse since Plato and Aristotle, most notably, and that mission will be furthered by an investigation of verbal aggression aimed at the control of its occurrence.

We will first explain the theoretical structure and supporting research that have guided argumentativeness and verbal aggressiveness research. We will provide an examination of a model of aggressive communication in order to position the two traits with respect to other kinds of aggression. Next, we will discuss the measurement of argumentativeness and verbal aggressiveness, especially in terms of reliability and validity. We will then review the research on these two traits according to themes that have emerged, and state conclusions that seem justified in view of the research.

We limit this review mainly to published research. More than 100 convention papers and numerous dissertations and theses have been based on the argumentativeness and verbal aggressiveness models, but we cite here only a few of those to illustrate particular points. We focus this review on an examination of research on the two traits of interest, and not on situational research in which, for instance, verbal aggression has been manipulated (e.g., Greenberg, 1976).

AGGRESSIVE COMMUNICATION

Argumentativeness and verbal aggressiveness are both aggressive forms of communication. A communicative behavior is "aggressive if it applies force . . . symbolically in order, minimally, to dominate and perhaps damage, or maximally, to defeat and perhaps destroy the locus of the attack" (Infante, 1987a, p. 158). Many behaviors besides arguing and verbal aggression are aggressive in nature. Moreover, some of these behaviors are bad and others are good. A model of aggressive communication clarifies this and provides a framework for the research examined in this chapter.

The model posits that aggressive communication is controlled mainly by a cluster of four communication traits that interact with factors in the environment to energize message behavior (Infante, 1987a). The factors in the environment that interact with these traits are aggression inhibitors (e.g., penalties for certain aggressive behaviors) and disinhibitors (e.g., alcohol consumption). Two of the traits are basically constructive and two are destructive; thus, aggression can be good or bad, or both good and bad.

Assertiveness and argumentativeness are the constructive traits. Assertiveness is the more global of the two, and includes the characteristics of personal ascendance, dominance, and forcefulness, and use of assertive behavior to achieve personal goals while creating positive affect in receivers. According to Costa and McCrae's (1980) three-factor model of personality, assertiveness is a facet of the "extroversion dimension" of personality.

The trait of argumentativeness includes the characteristics of advocacy for and defense of positions on issues simultaneous with the refutation of the positions that other people take (Infante & Rancer, 1982). Argumentativeness is a subset of assertiveness because all argument is assertive, but not all assertiveness involves argument (e.g., a request). The model of argumentativeness posits that the trait is a result of competing approach-avoidance motivations that are activated because arguing inherently involves evaluation. A high argumentative is a person who is high on approach motivation and low on avoidance. A low argumentative is low approach-high avoidance. There are at least two types of moderates. "Conflict-feelings" moderates are high on approach and high on avoidance; they argue mainly when the probability of success is high and the importance of failure is low because they wish to avoid the anxiety typically stimulated by the possibility of losing an important argument. "Apathetic" moderates are low approach and low avoidance and argue generally when the incentive of success is high, as they neither like nor dislike arguing and engage in it mainly for utilitarian reasons.

The argumentativeness model includes factors of the situation—the probability and importance of success and failure—that interact with approachavoidance motivation to produce argumentative behavior in the particular situation. This constitutes an interactionist approach to personality (e.g., Epstein, 1979; Magnusson & Endler, 1977). Two studies support the model's central contention that including the situational probability and importance perceptions along with trait argumentativeness improves predictions for the situation based on the trait alone (Infante, 1987b; Infante & Rancer, 1982).

The two destructive traits in the model of aggressive communication are hostility and verbal aggressiveness. Hostility is the more global and includes the characteristic of using messages to express irritability, negativity, resentment, and suspicion (this description is based in part on the model developed by Buss & Durkee, 1957). Hostility is a facet of the neuroticism dimension of personality (Costa & McCrae, 1980).

The trait of verbal aggression involves attacking the self-concepts of others in order to inflict psychological pain, such as humiliation, embarrassment, depression, and other negative feelings about self (Infante & Wigley, 1986). The model of verbal aggressiveness specifies that there are several types of verbally aggressive messages: character, competence, background, and physical appearance attacks, ridicule, threats, profanity, maledictions, teasing, and nonverbal emblems. A recent study by Kinney (1994) suggests there are three broad domains of self-concept attack: group membership, personal failings, and relational failings. Four causes of verbal aggression are posited: psychopathology, disdain, social learning, and argumentative skill deficiencies. A recent study found that high verbal aggressives are distinguished from other people in their more frequent use of competence, background, and physical appearance attacks, and also the use of teasing, ridicule, profanity, and emblems (Infante, Riddle, Horvath, & Tumlin, 1992). Moreover, high verbal aggressives seem desensitized to the hurt caused by verbal aggression, because they do not view verbally aggressive messages as hurtful, unlike other people. The main reasons high verbal aggressives have given for their use of verbal aggression include having disdain for the target, wanting to be mean to the target, trying to appear "tough," and being in discussions that degenerate into verbal fights.

As with argumentativeness, verbal aggressiveness is viewed as a subset of a more global trait, in this case, hostility. That is, all verbal aggression is hostile, but not all hostility involves verbal aggression. Because argumentativeness and verbal aggressiveness are situated in different, independent dimensions of personality (extroversion and neuroticism, respectively), it is expected that the two traits are not related. Thus, high, moderate, and low argumentatives are equally likely to be high verbal aggressives. This assumption has been supported in several studies (e.g., Infante & Rancer, 1982; Infante & Wigley, 1986). This is important because the model of aggressive communication contends that because argumentativeness is a constructive trait it should not share variability with a set of negative behaviors.

MEASUREMENT

Considerable attention has been devoted to measuring aggressive forms of communication, especially from a trait perspective. Because this review does not include assertiveness and hostility research, we will not discuss measures of these traits (for a brief review of research and measures, see Infante, 1987a). Only the scales that have been used in the research reviewed in this chapter will be discussed at this time.

Argumentativeness has been measured using the Argumentativeness Scale (Infante & Rancer, 1982), a 20-item scale with 10 items for measuring motivation to approach argumentative situations and 10 items for measuring avoidance. The difference between approach and avoidance is the computed trait argumentativeness score. A good deal of evidence is available concerning the reliability of the scale. Reliabilities reported in the studies reviewed here have typically been in the .80-.90 range. Moreover, the measure appears stable across time ($r = .91$ in a 1-week, test-retest study; Infante & Rancer, 1982) and across cultures (the intercultural studies reviewed below observed reliabilities typically around .84).

Dowling and Flint (1990) claim that because all of the Argumentativeness Scale items do not specify "argument over controversial issues," respondents may interpret some of the items as pertaining to arguments over relational issues, which may include quarrels, fights, bickering, and the like. However, instructions accompanying the scale state: "This questionnaire contains statements about arguing controversial issues" (Infante & Rancer, 1982, p. 76). Dowling and Flint (1990) recommend including the phrase "argument over controversial issues" in each of the 20 scale items. An alternative, because the 20 items can appear very repetitious with the same phrase in each item, would be simply to underline or boldface the instructions to the scale to emphasize the idea of "arguing controversial issues."

Considerable evidence supports the validity of the scale. The original article describing the scale's development reported four separate validity studies (for a discussion of the validation of the Argumentativeness Scale, see DeWine, Nicotera, & Parry, 1991). Much of the research covered in this chapter is relevant to the construct validity of the scale because hypotheses were derived from a theoretical framework that was tested using the scale. If the scale behaves as theory says it should, this is interpreted to mean the operationalization of the construct is valid.

The Verbal Aggressiveness Scale has been used to measure trait verbal aggressiveness (Infante & Wigley, 1986). This scale contains 20 items with a 5-point linear rating format. Techniques for measuring socially undesirable behavior employed by Buss and Durkee (1957) in their Hostility-Guilt Inventory were utilized; for example, assume the existence of the behavior and ask where, when, and so on, it is elicited. Reliabilities reported for the scale typically are in the low to mid .80s. The Verbal Aggressiveness Scale also appears stable across time: An $r = .82$ for a 4-week, test-retest study was reported (Infante & Wigley, 1986).

Reliability across cultures has been observed (reliabilities of around .81 were calculated in the intercultural studies reported below). A good deal of validity evidence, besides that reported in the article on the scale's development, suggests that the scale measures what it is intended to measure (for a discussion of the validity of the Verbal Aggressiveness Scale, see DeWine et al., 1991). Probably the strongest evidence pertains to construct validity. Several organizational communication and family communication studies have observed levels of verbal aggressiveness, as measured by the scale, that were predicted by the theoretical framework for the study. For instance, a study of interspousal violence found that husbands and wives in violent marriages were more verbally aggressive than spouses in nonviolent marriages (Infante, Chandler, & Rudd, 1989).

Factor analysis of the Verbal Aggressiveness Scale (Infante & Wigley, 1986) revealed two factors. However, the scale was interpreted as unidimensional because the factors seemed to be due only to item wording. All of the positively worded items loaded on one factor and all of the negatively worded items loaded on the other factor. On the other hand, the Argumentativeness Scale was designed to measure two dimensions of argumentative motivation, approach and avoidance, and was constructed to determine whether positive-negative item wording or approach-avoidance item content explained the hypothesized multidimensionality. This was done by wording some approach items negatively and some avoidance items positively. The results of factor analyses support the view that the scale has two dimensions, one measuring approach and one measuring avoidance (Infante & Rancer, 1982). That is, the positively worded approach items and those worded negatively all loaded on the same factor, whereas the negatively worded avoidance items, along with those worded positively, all loaded on the other factor.

Trait argumentativeness is computed by subtracting the sum of the 10 avoidance items from the sum of the 10 approach items. Researchers should consider the two types of motivation separately when identifying the different types of moderates (e.g., the "apathetic moderate" who is low on both approach and avoidance), when combining trait and state factors in predicting behavior in a particular situation (see Infante & Rancer, 1982, for the algebraic expression of this), and when there is a particular interest in each (e.g., whether two cultures differ in approach motivation). In cases where the interest is in the general trait score, one can simply reverse the scoring for the avoidance items and then sum the approach and avoidance items.

Despite the apparent reliability and validity of the two scales, alternative measurement techniques should be developed so that knowledge is not bound by peculiarities or as-yet-undiscovered measurement errors in the current scales. It would be prudent to measure the argumentativeness and verbal aggressiveness constructs in various ways.

A possible alternative measure of argumentativeness might be developed from a procedure used in a recent study (Infante & Rancer, 1993) in which participants were asked the number of times during the past week they had advocated a position or attempted to refute another person's position on 11 different types of controversial issues. Similarly for verbal aggressiveness, participants in a study (Infante, Riddle, et al., 1992) were asked the number of times they used 10 different types of verbally aggressive messages during the past 4 weeks. These techniques have considerable face validity because participants are asked directly for the frequency of the very thing being measured. However, because social desirability factors sometimes influence the reporting of aggressive communication, the development of indirect methods of measurement, such as a TAT, should be explored.

Some research has explored whether argumentativeness has a social desirability component. Nicotera (1994), for example, has explored the relationship between argumentativeness and social desirability. It was thought that some individuals who believe arguing is negative and socially undesirable may be responding to the judged social desirability of the scale rather than to an actual behavioral tendency. Any potential relationship between social desirability and argumentativeness may be especially important in research testing for sex differences in argumentative behavior. In a test of this relationship, Nicotera (1994) found argumentativeness to be positively, but weakly, related to social desirability. In the study, social desirability explained less than 6% of the variance in argumentativeness scores. The results also indicated that males perceived argumentativeness to be more socially desirable than did females. In a related investigation, Chen (1994) found that *regardless of sex,* individuals scoring high on a social desirability measure were lower in argumentativeness.

In assessing the relationship between these factors, it is important to recognize that these findings may underscore inherent differences between individuals in U.S. culture, rather than point to any potential problems with the Argumentativeness Scale. That is, for low argumentatives (and females), arguing may not be a socially desirable behavior. Nicotera (1994) proposes that both argumentativeness and social desirability are influenced by another factor—beliefs about arguing. Responses to both scales (social desirability and argumentativeness) may be influenced by underlying beliefs about arguing. Research in this area (e.g., Rancer & Baukus, 1987; Rancer, Baukus, & Infante, 1985; Rancer, Kosberg, & Baukus, 1992) strongly suggests that underlying belief structures about arguing differentiate high and low argumentatives and males and females. We will review this research later in the chapter.

CONCLUSIONS ABOUT ARGUMENTATIVENESS
AND VERBAL AGGRESSIVENESS

The research on argumentativeness and verbal aggressiveness has tended to focus on certain themes or issues, and the results allow several conclusions to be drawn. We will review the literature that appears to support more than a dozen conclusions. Other claims could be made, but we limit the conclusions presented here to those substantiated by several studies.

Argumentativeness is constructive,
whereas verbal aggressiveness is destructive.

Perhaps the most striking feature of the body of research based on the argumentativeness and verbal aggressiveness frameworks is that the outcomes of argumentativeness are positive and all of the outcomes of verbal aggression are negative. This supports the model of aggressive communication, which contends that argumentativeness is a constructive trait and verbal aggressiveness is a destructive one. This also supports an ethical position taken recently—that the destructiveness of verbal aggression warrants the communication discipline giving considerable attention to developing methods of controlling such aggression (Infante, 1995). Further, this conclusion is directly relevant to one of the purposes of this review of literature—to determine whether knowledge of what it means to make people more argumentative supports assumptions that have been part of the communication discipline since antiquity. Teaching students to argue effectively and constructively has been a central part of the communication discipline for more than 2,000 years. The rather massive and unequivocal finding that argumentativeness is constructive upholds this tradition.

Many of the studies in this literature review are relevant to the conclusion that a constructive-destructive distinction between the traits is justified, but we will mention only a few here. Argumentatives have been found to be perceived as higher in credibility than low argumentatives (Infante, 1981, 1985; Onyekwere, Rubin, & Infante, 1991), and verbal aggression produces lower credibility scores (Infante, Hartley, et al., 1992). Spouses who are more argumentative, as opposed to verbally aggressive, are higher in marital satisfaction (Sabourin, Infante, & Rudd, 1993), and violence in a marriage is more probable when spouses are high verbal aggressives (Infante et al., 1989). Argumentatives are more likely than low argumentatives to be seen as leaders in group problem-solving discussions (Schultz, 1982). Verbal aggression stimulates reciprocity that can disrupt influence situations (Infante, 1989). Argumentative supervisors are perceived favorably by their subordinates (Gorden, Infante, & Graham, 1988), whereas verbally aggressive superiors are particularly disliked (Infante & Gorden, 1991).

The constructive-destructive conclusion is not limited to a particular context. Argumentativeness and verbal aggressiveness have been investigated in interpersonal, small group, organizational, family, pedagogical, intercultural, and political contexts. In view of the cross-contextual consistency of the findings, the conclusion that argumentativeness is constructive and verbal aggressiveness is destructive may be considered very robust.

Argumentativeness and verbal aggressiveness are related to other communication predispositions.

Communication has been viewed from a trait perspective. Traits, or predispositions toward certain kinds of communication, have been a central focus of theory-building efforts in communication for almost three decades. The importance of studying communication from this perspective is understandable, given that communication traits and predispositions have been found to account for significant variance in both observed communication behavior and communication-based perceptions (Infante, 1987a; McCroskey & Daly, 1987). A major premise of this predispositional perspective argues that an individual's behavior exhibits a great degree of cross-situational consistency.

Given that argumentativeness and verbal aggressiveness are predispositions toward communication, it is reasoned that they should be slightly or moderately related to other communication predispositions and traits. Hence, a number of studies have investigated the relationship of other traits to the aggressive predispositions of argumentativeness and verbal aggressiveness. In a seminal study, we correlated the two dimensions of argumentativeness (approach and avoid) with several communication predispositions (Infante & Rancer, 1982). Tendency to approach arguments was correlated significantly and negatively with communication apprehension (McCroskey, 1970), unwillingness to communicate, and approach-avoidance (Burgoon, 1976), and positively correlated with predispositions toward verbal behavior (Mortensen, Arnston, & Lustig, 1977). Tendency to avoid arguments was significantly and positively related to communication apprehension, unwillingness to communicate, and approach-avoidance, and negatively with predispositions toward verbal behavior. Recall that Chen (1994), treating social desirability as a personality trait, found that individuals high in social desirability orientation are higher in communication apprehension and lower in argumentativeness.

Richmond, McCroskey, and McCroskey (1989) examined the relationship of argumentativeness and self-perceived communication competence. Argumentativeness was significantly related to a total self-perceived competence score, as well as to scores on competence in public speaking; speaking in groups, dyads, and meetings; and communication with strangers, acquaintances, and friends. Well-managed conflict depends, in part, on increasing the potential number of viable solutions to the conflict. Locus of control is one predisposition that has been found to influence behaviors associated with successful interaction behavior. Canary, Cunningham, and Cody (1988) discovered that the *effort* and *ability* dimensions of the Conflict Locus of Control Scale (indicative of an internal control orientation) correlated significantly and positively with the approach dimension of the Argumentativeness Scale. The dimensions of powerlessness, chance, and situational contingencies (indicative of an external control orientation) correlated significantly and positively with the argumentative avoidance dimension. Thus, argumentativeness appears to be related to an internal locus of control orientation toward conflict. Internal locus of control orientation has been associated with less coercion, greater rationality, and greater positive feelings of the target (Canary et al., 1988). Mongeau (1989) tested the relationship between argumentativeness and need for cognition, reasoning that in addition to a strong behavioral component, argumentativeness involves a predisposition to process information rigorously and cognitively (i.e., need for cognition). Need for cognition and argumentativeness were found to be moderately correlated. Thus, although both traits involve a predisposition to argue cognitively and to counterargue, they do not measure the same construct. Mongeau suggests that argumentativeness influences message processing in a fashion similar to need for cognition, and is an important factor in persuasion.

Receiver apprehension, an individual's level of anxiety in processing messages (Wheeless, 1975), was thought to be negatively related to argumentativeness. Wigley (1987) reasoned that because individuals motivated and skilled in arguing are more adept at message processing and data assimilation, the two traits should be negatively correlated; the results of Wigley's study support this speculation and suggest that training in argumentativeness may also reduce levels of receiver apprehension. Wigley, Pohl, and Watt (1989) explored the relations among conversational sensitivity, laudativeness (predisposition to praise verbally), and verbal aggressiveness. A significant negative relationship was observed between verbal aggressiveness and laudativeness, and the correlation between conversational sensitivity and verbal aggressiveness was not significant. This finding led Wigley et al. to speculate that individuals low in conversational sensitivity may use verbal aggressiveness to avoid conversations, whereas those high in conversational sensitivity may use verbal aggressiveness as a tool of persuasion. Nicotera, Smilowitz, and Pearson (1990) found argumentativeness to be related to innovativeness, ambiguity tolerance, and a solution-oriented conflict style. Finally, Rancer, Kosberg, and Silvestri (1992) investigated the relationship between the dimensions of self-esteem and aggressive communication. For argumentativeness, the personal power dimension of self-esteem emerged as the strongest predictor. This dimension encompasses feelings of power, success at leadership, being assertive, and having a strong impact on others. Defensive self-enhancement emerged as a powerful predictor of verbal aggressiveness (Rancer, Kosberg, & Silvestri, 1992). Individuals high in verbal aggressiveness are less open, more defensive, less modest, and tend not to acknowledge mistakes. Moral self-approval and personal power dimensions of self-esteem have also been found to be significantly predictive of verbal aggressiveness.

Individuals differ in belief structures about arguing and verbal aggression.

One line of inquiry in research on aggressive communication predispositions has explored belief structures of individuals who vary in argumentativeness and verbal aggressiveness in order to understand why individuals differ on these traits. To that end, Fishbein and Ajzen's (1975) theory of reasoned action has been applied as a framework for extending knowledge about aggressive communication predispositions. According to the theory of reasoned action, behavior is linked to attitudes and beliefs, and predispositions are controlled by the set of beliefs an individual learns to associate with the object of the predisposition. Thus, one way to understand aggressive communication is to explore the belief structures people have about arguing and employing verbal aggression.

Several studies have utilized this framework. Rancer et al. (1985) label the belief structures people have about arguing as "hostility," "activity/process," "control/dominance," "conflict/dissonance," "self-image," "learning," and "skill." They found that these belief structures also distinguish individuals who vary in the trait. Rancer et al. found that a greater proportion of high argumentatives than low argumentatives in their study had positive beliefs about activity/process, control/dominance, conflict/dissonance, self-image, learning, and skill. The proportion of low argumentatives was highest in terms of negative beliefs about hostility, control/dominance, and conflict/dissonance. High, moderate, and low argumentatives were found to differ on two functions of arguing: cultivation and antagonism. Argumentatives view arguing as a source of information; low argumentatives do not. Low argumentatives view arguing as a behavior that reveals their lack of argumentative and rhetorical competence. High argumentatives perceive arguing as a means of reducing conflict, whereas low argumentatives view arguments as unfavorable and hostile acts that should be avoided at all costs.

In an extension of this research, Rancer, Kosberg, and Baukus (1992) determined which beliefs best predict argumentativeness and which beliefs best discriminate high and low argumentatives. They found that argumentatives held beliefs that suggested arguing has enjoyable, functional, and pragmatic outcomes, as well as positive impacts on their self-concepts. Low argumentatives' beliefs about arguing were in the opposite direction. Rancer and Baukus (1987), utilizing the beliefs framework, concluded that males and females differ in belief structures about arguing, with females holding more negative beliefs about arguing than do males. Some research has also investigated beliefs about engaging in verbal aggression. Infante, Riddle, et al. (1992) found differences in beliefs about verbal aggression between those who vary in the trait. High verbal aggressives believed competence attacks, physical appearance attacks, and threats to be less hurtful to others than did individuals low in verbal aggressiveness.

Aggressive communication behavior is a
joint product of predispositional and situational factors.

Argumentativeness and verbal aggressiveness are "interactional" approaches to personality. Basically, this means that behavior in a situation is understood to be a joint product of situational factors and the characteristics of the individual; traits "interact" with the situation (Andersen, 1987; Epstein, 1979; Magnusson & Endler, 1977). Moreover, an interactional approach to personality contends that both the situational and trait approaches are deficient because each does not account for the variability in behavior explained by the other; however, the interactional approach considers both sources of behavioral variability.

Several studies have identified situation factors that modify the predictions that would be made from trait argumentativeness alone. Two studies tested the algebraic interactional model, which posits that perceptions of the probability and importance of success (situational factors) combine with trait argumentative approach motivation, whereas the probability and importance of failure interact with avoidance motivation to affect motivation to argue in a particular situation (Infante, 1987b; Infante & Rancer, 1982). Both studies supported the model. Onyekwere et al. (1991) found ego involvement in the topic of an argument affected behavior of high and low argumentatives in that ego-involving issues stimulated greater motivation to argue and enhanced argumentative behavior. A recent study suggests that high argumentatives, when compared with moderate and low argumentativeness, argue more on certain topics (social, political, personal behavior, others' behavior, and moral-ethical issues), whereas other topics (sports, entertainment, religious issues) are argued as much by low as by high and moderate argumentatives (Infante & Rancer, 1993). Stewart and Roach (1993) investigated how the topic of argument and religious orientation influence argument. They found that although trait argumentativeness explained most of the variance in willingness to argue, extrinsically religious persons were more willing to argue than were either intrinsically religious or proreligious persons. Nonreligious persons were more willing to argue than were proreligious persons. Overall, participants indicated more satisfaction in arguing the religious than the nonreligious issue. In one study we conducted, we found that the argumentativeness of an individual and that of his or her adversary interacted to determine motivation for arguing in a specific situation (Rancer & Infante, 1985). Waggenspack and Hensley (1989) examined how interpersonal situation (social or conflict) and gender influence preference for having a partner who is argumentative. Finally, a series of studies found that the success of being argumentative in an organizational communication context depended upon also being low in verbal aggressiveness and having an affirming communicator style—that is, relaxed, friendly, and attentive (Gorden, Infante, & Izzo, 1988; Infante & Gorden, 1985b, 1987, 1989, 1991).

Studies also indicate that verbal aggressiveness is influenced by the situation. Verbal aggression varies as a function of whether a conflict is violent or not (Infante, Chandler Sabourin, Rudd, & Shannon, 1990). Lim (1990) found that verbal aggressiveness in a persuasion situation is influenced by the friendliness of persuasion resistance. Along this line, Infante, Trebing, Shepherd, and Seeds (1984) found verbal aggressiveness to depend upon the individual's argumentativeness and the obstinacy of his or her opponent. A study conducted from the perspective of the receiver found that whether more argumentative people received verbal aggression depended upon the gender of the message source (Infante, Wall, Leap, & Danielson, 1984). A related study found that when an individual is argumentative, his or her receiving verbal aggression depends upon not only the gender of the opponent, but also the message strategy and aggressive response to the opponent (Infante, 1989).

In sum, numerous situational factors influence aggressive forms of communication. Situational variables and traits should be considered together in attempts to explain behavior. This conclusion supports Andersen's (1987) position on adoption of an interactional approach to studying communication.

Males are higher than females in both aggressive traits.

The question of whether sex differences exist in aggressive communication has implications for communication behavior and issues of self-esteem, and potentially for outcomes of conflict episodes. Motivation and skill in argument have been suggested as components essential in the management and resolution of social and personal conflict (Rancer, Kosberg, & Baukus, 1992) and have been related to self-esteem (Rancer, Kosberg, & Silvestri, 1992). Sex differences in argumentativeness and verbal aggressiveness may adversely influence positive outcomes associated with productive conflict management and may negatively influence self-esteem. Sex differences in aggressive communication are also important because expectancy violations play a critical role in communication outcomes (Burgoon, 1978, 1983). Perceived sex differences (i.e., perceptions of generalized males and females) can create generalized expectancies or stereotypes that may influence communication. Expectations for others' behavior are more readily violated when those expectations are based on inaccurate stereotypes. Finally, if there are sex differences in aggressive communication, one group may enjoy less of what has been found to be constructive about argumentativeness, and the other may be burdened by the destructive outcomes associated with verbal aggressiveness.

Available evidence does suggest the existence of sex and gender differences in argumentativeness and verbal aggressiveness. Males score higher than females in both argumentativeness (Infante, 1982, 1985; Nicotera & Rancer, 1994; Schultz & Anderson, 1984) and verbal aggressiveness (Infante, Wall, et al., 1984; Infante & Wigley, 1986; Nicotera & Rancer, 1994). Darus (1994) found that men scored higher than women on both trait and work-related argumentativeness. Interestingly, women were higher on work-related than trait argumentativeness; this may mean women avoid arguing less on the job than they do in other communication contexts. Rancer and Dierks-Stewart (1985) explored both biological and psychological differences in argumentativeness; they observed no differences according to biological sex, but found significant differences in argumentativeness when individuals were classified according to psychological gender orientation. Individuals classified as instrumental (masculine) were higher in argumentativeness than those identified as expressive (feminine), androgynous, or undifferentiated. Rancer and Baukus (1987) assert that males and females differ in their beliefs about arguing. In their study, females, to a greater degree than males, held beliefs that arguing is a hostile and combative communication behavior used for dominating and controlling others. Infante (1989) explored whether males and females respond differently to highly argumentative adversaries; he found that when an adversary used verbal aggression, males were provoked to become more verbally aggressive, whereas females became more argumentative.

Nicotera and Rancer (1994) observed significant differences between the sexes on both self-reported and stereotyped perceptions of argumentativeness and verbal aggressiveness. Males self-reported higher on both traits than females, but several sex-based aggressive communication stereotypes emerged. Males perceived "generalized" females' traits to be related: The higher they perceived females to be on argumentativeness, the higher they perceived them to be on verbal aggressiveness. The same relationship emerged for females' perceptions of "generalized" males. This tendency to see highly argumentative individuals of the opposite sex as also highly verbally aggressive may produce dysfunctional consequences during social conflict episodes. These documented sex differences in both self-reports and stereotyped perceptions of aggressive communication behavior underscore the need for training to help sensitize individuals to sex stereotyping in aggressive communication, as well as to enhance motivation and skill in argument and decrease verbal aggressiveness. Sex differences in argumentativeness may begin to diminish as the importance and desirability of argumentative behavior becomes more recognized and normative across U.S. society.

Cultures vary in their predispositions for aggressive communication.

Interest in communication between cultures has been stimulated by increased attention to cultural diversity, increased international business, greater cooperation among nations, growth in international travel, and increased numbers of multinational organizations. In intercultural communication, conflict can result from the differing contextual and interactional norms of the parties to the communication. Thus, interpersonal conflict may be more difficult to manage in such contexts because of the focus on both real and perceived differences between interactants. Differences in predispositions for aggressive communication may contribute to perceived or actual cross-cultural conflict.

Argumentativeness and verbal aggressiveness have been examined within the context of intercultural and cross-cultural communication. Explorations of the two traits across various cultures have identified and clarified differences in conflict styles across and between cultures. Prunty, Klopf, and Ishii (1990a, 1990b) examined differences in argumentativeness between Japanese and American college students. The researchers observed differences between the two groups on the general tendency to approach arguments and on the overall general motivational trait, and Americans reported significantly higher levels. Harman, Klopf, and Ishii (1990) compared Japanese and Americans on verbal aggressiveness. No differences were observed between the two groups, between Japanese women and American women, or between Japanese men and American men on verbal aggressiveness. For both cultures, however, males were observed to be higher than females in verbal aggressiveness. In one study, Americans were found to be higher in argumentativeness than Koreans, but no significant differences were observed between Korean and American males (Jenkins, Klopf, & Park, 1991). The difference between Koreans and Americans apparently is that American women are more argumentative than Korean women.

Because both scales have been used with diverse cultures, particularly Asian cultures, Suzuki and Rancer (1994) tested the scales for conceptual and measure equivalence across cultures. They also assessed the construct validity of each scale in a different cultural context. This research found that the two-factor solution for the Argumentativeness Scale developed in the United States is generalizable to Japanese culture. A two-factor solution (reflecting positive and negative item wording) was also found for the Verbal Aggressiveness Scale when applied to the Japanese culture. That the two constructs are independent held true equally for the United States, a low-context culture, and Japan, a high-context culture. The construct validity of both scales was also established for the cross-cultural sample. This research underscores the importance of testing the conceptual equivalence of an instrument developed in one culture and used in different cultures.

Cross-cultural differences in aggressive communication in and between low-context cultures have also been observed. For example, both Finnish and Norwegian cultures have been found to be higher than U.S. culture in argumentativeness (Klopf, Thompson, & Sallinen-Kuparinen, 1991; Rahoi, Svenkerud, & Love, 1994). These results suggest that even low-context cultures differ on aggressive communication predispositions. Some research has examined aggressive communication predispositions among ethnic and racial groups within a given macroculture. Sanders, Gass, Wiseman, and Bruschke (1992) examined the relationship between individuals' ethnicity and argumentativeness and verbal aggressiveness. Whereas they observed no significant differences among Asian Americans, European Americans, and Hispanics on argumentativeness (all participants in the study were born in the United States), they found Asian Americans to be significantly higher than European Americans and Hispanics on verbal aggressiveness. Nicotera, Rancer, and Sullivan (1991) found that African Americans and European Americans did not differ in argumentativeness, but that African Americans reported higher levels of verbal aggressiveness. This finding supports some qualitative research that suggests that in conflict episodes, African Americans may fail to separate the issue from the person (Kochman, 1981).

Regional differences and regional identification have also been investigated pursuant to aggressive communication. Andersen, Lustig, and Andersen (1987) suggest that regional culture can explain variance in patterns of communication behavior and communication predispositions. Geddes (1990) sought to investigate potential regional variations in aggressive communication in the United States. Although the results of this study revealed no significant differences between American northerners and southerners on either trait, Geddes speculates that the study sample of young, relatively affluent, well-educated, and relatively mobile college students may be less affected by regional influences than the members of the general population of a given region. However, when Geddes (1992) used an alternative taxonomy to classify regional variations, northerners were found to be higher on verbal aggressiveness than midwesterners and southerners. A difference approaching significance ($p = .057$) was observed for argumentativeness, with northerners reporting higher levels than southerners.

Argumentativeness leads to greater relational satisfaction,
whereas verbal aggressiveness leads to decreased satisfaction.

According to the conceptualization of both predispositions, one would expect that argumentativeness would lead to greater relational satisfaction and verbal aggressiveness would lead to decreases in satisfaction. Several studies have explored this speculation. Infante (1982) investigated whether being high in argumentativeness is related to perceived difficulty in interpersonal relations. His results indicated that satisfaction with interpersonal relations and ability to relate to peers did not significantly discriminate high, moderate, and low argumentatives. Thus, at least from the perspective of the argumentative, relational satisfaction is not negatively influenced by the trait.

Relational satisfaction is also related to patterns of communication *within* relationships. Millar and Rogers (1987) found that husbands who achieved dominance and relational control were higher in satisfaction than were husbands whose wives were domineering. Domineering wives provided fewer support messages to their spouses, and wives' domineeringness was negatively related to their own marital satisfaction and to both spouses' communication satisfaction. Sabourin et al. (1993), as part of a comprehensive investigation on verbal aggression in marriage, studied marital satisfaction among violent couples, nonviolent but "distressed" couples (couples in therapy), and nondistressed couples. Nondistressed couples indicated more marital satisfaction than did either the violent or the distressed but nonviolent couples. This finding is consistent with the assumptions of the model of aggressive communication. Husbands from violent relationships reported greater satisfaction than their wives (Sabourin et al., 1993). This finding is consistent with Millar and Rogers's (1987) research findings and underscores the relationships among satisfaction, dominance, and relational control. Studies have explored whether couples similar in aggressive communication and/or higher in their levels of satisfaction exhibit behaviors different from couples who are dissimilar and/or less satisfied. Rancer, Baukus, and Amato (1986) found that husbands and wives who were dissimilar on argumentativeness reported more overall marital satisfaction than couples classified as similar. Because most of the couples in the dissimilar group had husbands higher than wives in argumentativeness, Rancer et al. (1986) speculate that a "traditionalism" factor may operate to influence satisfaction. That is, for a traditional couple, a more argumentative husband may be acceptable according to conventional sex role norms. Segrin and Fitzpatrick (1992) found that depression and verbal aggressiveness were lowest in marriages classified as "traditional." Payne and Sabourin (1990) found that husbands were more satisfied with their marriages when their wives were high argumentatives. Whether this finding contradicts the results of the Rancer et al. (1986) study is not clear, because Payne and Sabourin did not classify couples as to whether the husband and wife were at the same or different levels of argumentativeness. Payne and Sabourin also observed that marital satisfaction was higher when perceived verbal aggressiveness in the marriage was lower. Segrin and Fitzpatrick discovered that husbands and wives who were more depressed were also more verbally aggressive in their message behavior. The more wives were verbally aggressive, the greater the level of depression reported by the husband; however, wives' depression was not related to their husbands' verbal aggressiveness. Finally, Nicotera and DeWine (1991) studied the accuracy of perceptions of levels of aggressiveness and found that a person's spouse was more accurate in assessing his or her level of argumentativeness than was the person's coworker.

Verbal aggressiveness is a catalyst to physical violence,
whereas argumentativeness may prevent it.

Relatively recent research suggests that both argumentativeness and verbal aggressiveness are related to physical violence, with the former as a preventive and the latter as a catalyst. Although violence is pervasive in U.S. society, this line of research to date has mainly focused on family violence, specifically abusive husbands and abused wives. There are indications, however, that the research is beginning to explore other areas, such as date rape and the corporal punishment of children.

The basic thinking for the research on family violence is that verbal aggression in a marriage is a catalyst to violence under certain conditions: when one or both spouses have a latent hostile disposition because of undissipated anger from societal, personal, and situational sources, and the spouses are unskilled argumentatively. In such circumstances family conflict over a relatively innocuous issue can result in violence because argumentative skill deficiencies lead to verbal attacks being misdirected to the other person's self-concept instead of his or her position on the issue. The anger stimulated by the verbal aggression can act as a catalyst in that it triggers a realization of undissipated anger. This excitation transfer can intensify easily, especially in a cycle of verbal aggression reciprocity, and mount to a level where it manifests symbolically as physical violence. Being skilled argumentatively reduces the likelihood of a person's being caught up in this sequence of events because skill in attacking and defending positions on issues involves differentiating the locus of attack (issues versus self-concept). Although a skilled arguer might decide to shift the attack from the issue to the person, perhaps due to a factor such as disdain, this personal attack would not be due to the person's inability to continue the discussion of the issue, as is the case with the unskilled arguer who resorts to attacking the most available target (i.e., one's opponent) once he or she is unable to attack the opponent's position.

Infante et al. (1989) term this conceptual framework an argumentative skill deficiency model of interspousal violence. These researchers tested the model in a study that posited physically abusive marriages would be higher in verbal aggressiveness but lower in argumentativeness (a counterintuitive prediction) when compared with nonabusive spouses, and the model was supported. This study took a monadic approach—that is, the researchers studied the reports of one spouse from each couple. Sabourin et al. (1993) undertook a recent dyadic examination of the model, studying the reports of both the husbands and wives in the couples in their sample. This study replicated Infante et al.'s (1989) earlier findings and extended understanding by investigating the role of verbal aggression reciprocity. Sabourin et al. also refined the existing knowledge by including a comparison group (distressed but nonviolent couples) in addition to the usual control group (nondistressed, nonviolent couples). A study by Infante et al. (1990) determined that character attacks and to some extent competence attacks best differentiated violent marital disputes from the disputes of nonviolent husbands and wives. Rudd, Burant, and Beatty (1994) found that abused women reported using indirect compliance-gaining strategies during violent disputes—aversive stimulation and ingratiation.

This line of communication research on interspousal violence may be expanding to other interpersonal relationships. Andonian and Droge (1992) have speculated that aggressive forms of communication may explain other forms of aggressive interpersonal behavior, such as date rape. Their thinking, which their study supports, is that acceptance of date rape myths is related positively to verbal aggressiveness and negatively to argumentativeness. A second area for this line of research concerns corporal punishment of children. A communication model of corporal punishment (Infante, in press) posits that corporal punishment is communicative behavior employed by parents who are less competent communicators, who also are low argumentatives and high verbal aggressives.

Argumentativeness enhances organizational life,
whereas verbal aggressiveness damages it.

A good deal of the argumentativeness and verbal aggressiveness research has investigated the organizational communication context. Much of this research has been based on the independent-mindedness theory of organizational communication. A basic tenet of the theory suggests that employees want the values held by society to be reflected and affirmed in the workplace (Gorden & Infante, 1987; Infante & Gorden, 1987). Thus, "American" corporations should encourage freedom of speech and promote individualism and independent-mindedness. When organizations affirm important values, along with employees' self-concepts, strong organizational commitment develops (Gorden & Infante, 1991). Among other things, this suggests that methods of management based on orientations not espoused by American society, such as autocracy or collectivistic values, will not work well in American organizations. American individualism mandates particular organizational communicative behaviors.

The basic idea, then, in light of this framework, is that argumentativeness and verbal aggressiveness are very relevant organizational communication behaviors. A communication climate that sanctions argumentativeness reinforces the value of free speech. Organizations that urge employees to argue corporate issues to enhance management's decision making on those issues are very American in that they eschew autocracy and believe that participative decisions are more acceptable. According to this view, supervisors should encourage subordinates to argue corporate issues, and subordinates, in turn, should believe that workplace argumentativeness is an act of corporate loyalty, because management's decision making is improved by the input. Argumentativeness in the workplace is a way of conceptualizing "employee voice" (Gorden, 1988; Gorden, Infante, & Graham, 1988; Gorden, Infante, & Izzo, 1988).

The importance of verbal aggressiveness in the workplace is apparent in that individuals want their self-concepts affirmed by their employing organizations (Gorden & Infante, 1987). Supervisors are valued when they show sensitivity to subordinates' self-concepts. Employees develop loyalty and commitment to organizations that inspire the employees to feel good about themselves. This means subordinates want superiors to be low in verbal aggressiveness. In fact, verbal aggressiveness may be more important than many other factors in superior-subordinate communication (Infante & Gorden, 1991). Low verbal aggressiveness by supervisors affirms the subordinate's self-concept. Research also suggests that relaxed, friendly, and attentive behaviors along with low verbal aggressiveness constitute an "affirming style" (Gorden, Infante, & Izzo, 1988; Infante & Gorden, 1987, 1989, 1991). An affirming style is essential for argumentativeness to be perceived as constructive organizational behavior. One important implication of these findings is that superiors and subordinates should be taught the skills of argumentation theory and how to practice those behaviors while affirming the self-concepts of other people.

Several studies have investigated various parts of this framework. Infante and Gorden (1985b) examined how subordinates' perceptions of their superiors' argumentativeness and verbal aggressiveness relate to several important outcomes derived from corporatist theory. In another study, these researchers also examined favorable organizational outcomes, especially in terms of argumentativeness and gender (Infante & Gorden, 1985b). Three studies emphasize that outcomes are favorable when supervisors and subordinates communicate in the workplace in a style that is argumentative and affirming (Infante & Gorden, 1987, 1989, 1991). Gorden, Infante, and Graham (1988) found that subordinates preferred supervisors who encouraged argument even when subordinates were low argumentatives; that is, subordinates like to feel free to argue even though they may not actually like arguing. Nicotera and DeWine (1991) found that employees who are more nonconfrontational and avoidant in their conflict management styles are less willing to discuss controversial issues. Darus (1994) observed that persons' trait argumentativeness is a strong predictor of argument in the workplace and also found evidence for the cross-situational consistency of argumentative behavior. Finally, Infante, Myers, and Burkel (1994) examined 74 specific organizational disagreements and found that disagreements with constructive outcomes were characterized by argumentativeness, whereas destructive disagreements were distinguished by verbal aggressiveness.

Communication between parent and child is enhanced
when parents are argumentative, affirming in communicator style,
and low in verbal aggressiveness.

Research has explored how communication between parents and children is influenced by argumentativeness and verbal aggressiveness. Studies in the organizational context reviewed above reveal the benefits of a highly argumentative style that is affirming and low in verbal aggressiveness for both superiors and subordinates. This type of style should generalize to the parent-child dyad because it constitutes another type of superior-subordinate relationship.

To that end, studies have applied this framework to the investigation of correlates of parenting behavior that may be predictive of parenting styles and orientations. Bayer and Cegala (1992) investigated the styles of parents of 5- to 12-year-old children. Parents with an "authoritative" style (e.g., used reason with children, encouraged give-and-take) were found to be lower in verbal aggressiveness and higher in argumentativeness. Conversely, parents with an "authoritarian" style (e.g., used unilateral control messages, were low in affect display, discouraged verbal responses from children) were higher in verbal aggressiveness and lower in argumentativeness. This finding is especially important because the development of positive self-concepts in children has been negatively related to their receiving authoritarian-style parenting (Bayer & Cegala, 1992). In a study that focused exclusively on the father-son dyad, Beatty, Zelley, Dobos, and Rudd (1994) examined the relationships between fathers' verbal aggressiveness and argumentativeness and sons' reports of fathers' sarcasm, criticism, and verbal aggressiveness. The results indicate a strong relationship between sons' perception of their fathers' communication and their fathers' self-reported argumentativeness and verbal aggressiveness, with fathers' verbal aggressiveness contributing most of the variance (Beatty et al., 1994). Thus, men's perceptions of their fathers' verbal aggressiveness, sarcasm, and criticism are "significantly based in their fathers' verbal aggressiveness" (Beatty et al., 1994, p. 413). This study underscores the influence of fathers' communicative behavior on their sons' development and strengthens the relationship between verbal aggressiveness and authoritarian parenting style identified by Bayer and Cegala (1992). Perceptions of fathers' verbal aggressiveness appear to constitute an important factor in men's social development.

Bayer and Cegala (1992) report that verbal aggressiveness directed at children from parents is now being viewed as a form of child abuse. Infante (in press) offers an aggressive communication theory-based perspective on another parental behavior that can be perceived as child abuse or that may lead to abuse—corporal punishment. Infante conceptualizes corporal punishment as one of the messages (i.e., a tactilic message) in a sequence of failed communication attempts to influence a child's behavior. Because corporal punishment is conceptualized as a type of message, its effectiveness as a message can be evaluated. Infante contends that corporal punishment becomes more likely when parents suffer from an argumentative skill deficiency (i.e., a lack of skill in generating arguments designed to influence a child's behavior to comply with the wishes of the parent). Parents with high motivation and skill in argumentative communication, and who are also affirming and low in verbal aggression, tend to be more successful in achieving compliance gaining from their children. These communicatively competent parents tend not to blame the receiver (the child) for unsuccessful persuasive attempts, and resort less to corporal punishment based on the perceived "stubbornness" of the message receiver (the child). The most constructive form of parent-child communication, then, is affirming and low in verbal aggressiveness. Because a child learns much from the behavior modeled by parents, the optimum case suggests that the child will reciprocate this constructive form of communication during interpersonal conflict episodes. Thus, both parents and children need to know how to argue constructively (Infante, in press).

Argumentativeness results in enhanced credibility perceptions, whereas verbal aggressiveness reduces credibility.

Some of the research on argumentativeness and verbal aggressiveness has investigated how these traits affect source credibility. Because one study manipulated argumentativeness (Infante, 1985) and another manipulated verbal aggressiveness (Infante, Hartley, et al., 1992), the relationships discussed in this section are assumed to be causal. The fundamental finding is that argumentativeness enhances a person's credibility, whereas verbal aggressiveness reduces it.

Argumentativeness and credibility were examined because of the assumption that higher levels of argumentativeness indicate more skill in arguing. Two studies suggest that this idea is valid (Infante, 1981; Onyekwere et al., 1991). More skillful advocacy, refutation, and rebuttal behaviors in communication situations may indicate that the argumentative is a more competent communicator. Two types of evidence support this speculation. In one study, individuals' self-perceptions of their communication competence were related to argumentativeness (Richmond et al., 1989). In another study, observers' ratings of individuals' communication competence were predicted by argumentativeness (Onyekwere et al., 1991).

If argumentatives are more competent communicators in situations that involve controversial issues, a relationship of argumentativeness with credibility could be anticipated. Although argumentatives being expected to score higher on the competence dimension of credibility is obvious, differences also were expected for trustworthiness and dynamism dimensions. Argumentatives may be seen as more trustworthy because it may be believed that information from them is dependable, that they are sincere and can be relied upon. Greater dynamism may be evident because more approach and less avoidance motivation for situations involving controversy may create more of a sense of enjoyment and enthusiasm in a person's behavior, resulting in an impression of activity or animation. Three studies have supported these ideas (Infante, 1981, 1985; Onyekwere et al., 1991). A further implication of this thinking is that if argumentatives are more competent and credible communicators in situations where the topic of communication is a controversial issue, then it could be expected in group decision-making situations that leadership will tend to be exercised by argumentatives. Schultz (1982) found that group members who were more argumentative were seen by other members as leaders in a decision-making process.

Whereas a positive relationship between argumentativeness and credibility is evident, a negative relationship appears to be the case for verbal aggressiveness and credibility. The thinking here is that verbal aggression is destructive communication in that it attacks a person's self-concept in order to hurt the person psychologically. This type of message behavior is concerned with the person rather than with the issue supposedly being discussed. Observers should perceive such lack of issue-related communication unfavorably in terms of the competence dimension of credibility. Moreover, attacking people in order to hurt them should have a negative effect on the trustworthiness dimension of credibility, as such behavior may be viewed as an indication of undesirable character traits. Infante, Hartley, et al. (1992) found considerable support for these ideas in the case of a person initiating verbal aggression in an argument. However, when an individual who is the target of verbal aggression reciprocates the attack, observers are more forgiving in terms of the target's credibility, as long as the target does not use a high level of verbal aggression in reciprocating. A political communication study has revealed findings consistent with these ideas. Downs, Kaid, and Ragan (1990) investigated television viewers' perceptions of a spirited televised exchange in 1988 between then Vice President George Bush and CBS anchorman Dan Rather. Bush, who was seen as initiating verbal aggression, had his credibility derogated by viewers, but Rather, who reciprocated verbal aggression, did not suffer such a reduction in credibility.

High motivation and skill in argumentative
communication enhance persuasive outcomes.

Some of the research in argumentativeness and verbal aggressiveness has examined how the persuasion process is influenced. This research has studied both the source and the receiver. Because argument is inherent in the process of persuasion, researchers thought that an individual difference regarding argumentative behavior should prove illuminating. For instance, argumentatives discover more arguments (Kazoleas, 1993; Rancer & Infante, 1985) that, moreover, are of higher quality (Infante, 1981; Onyekwere et al., 1991) in persuasion situations. Hample and Dallinger (1987) examined this argumentative activity in terms of how arguments are edited cognitively. They discovered that high and low argumentatives use different criteria in deciding which arguments to use and which to suppress in an influence situation.

The research that has inquired about the argumentativeness of the persuasion source has yielded a number of findings. For example, high, compared with low, argumentatives are perceived as more credible persuaders (Infante, 1981, 1985; Onyekwere et al., 1991); use a greater diversity of influence strategies and sometimes are more persistent (Boster & Levine, 1988; Boster, Levine, & Kazoleas, 1993); are less willing to use compliance-gaining strategies that create negative feelings in receivers (Infante, Anderson, Martin, Herington, & Kim, 1993); are more reluctant to use their power (e.g., legitimate power) to force compliance (Roach, 1992, 1995); encourage other people to express their views on controversial issues (Gorden, Infante, & Graham, 1988); are more effective in upward influence situations (Infante & Gorden, 1985b, 1987); are judged by their superiors as having more constructive persuasion styles (Gorden, Infante, & Izzo, 1988); are not easily provoked by obstinate opponents into using verbal aggression (Infante, Trebing, et al., 1984); are judged as more competent persuaders (Onyekwere et al., 1991); and are seen as leaders in group influence situations (Schultz, 1982). There also are several findings concerning persuasion situations in which the argumentative person is the receiver. When compared with other people in this situation, argumentatives are more inflexible on their position when others try to persuade them (Infante, 1981); generate more counterarguments when considering persuasive messages, and thereby are persuaded less (Kazoleas, 1993); may generate more ideas that are favorable to a persuader when they initially agree with the source's position (Levine & Badger, 1993); perhaps due to their inflexibility, attract more verbal aggression (Infante, Wall, et al., 1984); are the targets of verbal aggression more by male than by female sources (Infante, 1989); display more attitude-behavioral intention consistency in response to persuasive messages (Mongeau, 1989); and appear to receive less verbal aggression and physical violence in marital disagreements (Sabourin et al., 1993).

*Motivation to argue can be increased and
verbal aggressiveness decreased through training.*

That argumentativeness is constructive and verbal aggressiveness destructive appears to be supported by the corpus of research reviewed in this chapter. Numerous positive outcomes associated with being argumentative have been identified, including less egocentric thinking, greater social perspective taking, more creativity, better problem solving (Johnson & Johnson, 1979), greater communicative competence (Onyekwere et al., 1991), increased credibility (Infante, 1981, 1985), more favorable organizational communication outcomes (Infante & Gorden, 1985a, 1985b, 1987, 1989, 1991), higher levels of self-esteem (Rancer, Kosberg, & Silvestri, 1992), and greater leadership skills (Schultz, 1982). Concomitantly, research has revealed a number of negative outcomes associated with being verbally aggressive: lower credibility (Downs et al., 1990; Infante, Hartley, et al., 1992), more unfavorable organizational outcomes (Infante & Gorden, 1985a, 1985b, 1987, 1989, 1991), less relational satisfaction (Payne & Sabourin, 1990; Rancer et al., 1986; Segrin & Fitzpatrick, 1992), and a greater tendency toward physical aggression and violence (Infante et al., 1989). This body of research supports the assumptions of the theory of aggressive communication (Infante, 1987a); highlights one of the missions of the communication discipline, which is to counteract irrational discourse; and underscores the need for training efforts regarding aggressive communication.

The concern then becomes how we might modify personality traits and communication predispositions. In order to influence or affect some traits (e.g., self-esteem), traditional therapeutic avenues (e.g., counseling) may be necessary. However, some communication predispositions, such as communication apprehension, have been found to respond favorably to programs that focus on cognitive orientations and skill development.

Since antiquity, the communication discipline has advanced the notion that individuals can become better at arguing. To that end, several recent programs have been offered that have aimed to change motivation to argue. Kosberg and Rancer (1991) reviewed several pedagogical methods for increasing motivation and skill in argument: Infante's (1988) Inventional System, Wilson and Arnold's (1983) Topical System of Invention, and Cognitive Training in Interpersonal Conflict (Anderson, Schultz, & Courtney Staley, 1987). Anderson et al. (1987) have demonstrated that cognitive training in argument and conflict management can positively influence individuals to enhance their motivation to argue. Infante (1985) used a "cued-argument" procedure to induce low argumentative women to argue, and those who employed the cuing procedure were viewed as more credible than were those who were not trained. Nelson (1970) and Infante (1971) have demonstrated that topical systems can enhance the ability to generate arguments.

Rancer, Kosberg, and Baukus (1992) recommend that a major component of argumentation, interpersonal, and communication conflict courses should focus on the articulation of positive beliefs associated with arguing. Rather than focusing initially or exclusively on skills development, instructors should focus their early pedagogical efforts on the relationship between argumentative skill and self-concept, pragmatic outcomes associated with arguing constructively, and motivation to argue. Research has also explored the relationship of skills training in argumentation and argumentative motivation. Infante (1982) found that the amount of high school training in argumentation was the best discriminator of high and low argumentatives. In recent research, Colbert (1993) found that students with experience in competitive debate (value and/or policy) were significantly lower in verbal aggressiveness and higher in argumentativeness than were students without debate training or experience. Specific methods of debate training may be differentially effective in enhancing argumentativeness and reducing verbal aggression. Policy debate training may enhance argumentative motivation without affecting verbal aggressiveness, whereas value debate training may lower verbal aggressiveness without influencing argumentativeness (Colbert, 1993). Sanders, Wiseman, and Gass (1994) found that training in argumentation enhanced students' critical thinking abilities, especially their ability to discern weak arguments, improved self-reported effectiveness in arguing, and decreased verbal aggressiveness. The training did not, however, affect argumentativeness. Sanders et al. (1994) speculate on the stability of the argumentativeness trait, and they suggest further that longer exposure to training and more skills-based training may be necessary to influence this predisposition.

Infante (1995) offers several recommendations designed to help individuals understand and control verbal aggressiveness. He advances a programmatic plan with the goals of having students understand and develop strategies for controlling verbal aggressiveness, and provides pedagogical activities designed to stimulate internalization of these strategies and knowledge. He also includes numerous approaches to preventing the occurrence and/or escalation of verbal aggressiveness.

CONCLUSION

We mentioned earlier that there are four reasons we undertook this review of research based on the argumentativeness and verbal aggressiveness models. First, the body of knowledge on the two traits is not clear, because extensive results have not been summarized. This review has been designed to improve clarity by identifying conclusions substantiated usually by several studies. In that regard we have specified 13 conclusions, each of which we have supported with a diversity of specific research findings, that represent the parameters of knowledge about the two traits. Of course, many of the studies we have mentioned produced results aside from those mentioned here. We have attempted to abstract what we believe are the main themes in the rather extensive research on the two traits. Our distillation of the research findings into a relatively small number of conclusions is intended to make it easier for readers to conceptualize the meanings of argumentativeness and verbal aggressiveness.

Our second reason for undertaking this review has been to clarify the findings of past research in order to illuminate directions for future research. In that regard, we suggest the need for several types of research. First, the rather unequivocal conclusion that the effects of argumentativeness are constructive and those of verbal aggressiveness are destructive supports the ethical position taken recently by Infante (1995) and indicates a need for research on how to foster the former trait and control the latter. Second, research on these traits has been almost exclusively from a psychological perspective, which means an emphasis on the individual, especially in terms of self-perceptions and how one person is perceived by another. This also means that very little is known in terms of how the discourse of argumentatives differs from that of other people. A recent study by Kazoleas (1994) points in that direction by analyzing the verbal behavior of argumentatives in group deliberations. Another point that is now obvious is that much of the knowledge presented in this review is based on research that has utilized the Argumentativeness Scale and the Verbal Aggressiveness Scale. Although a considerable amount of research (reviewed above) suggests that these scales are reliable and valid, it would be prudent to develop other ways of measuring these two traits, so that our knowledge is not so dependent upon a particular conceptualization.

A third reason we have taken on this review is that we believe that knowledge of what it means to be argumentative clarifies part of the *raison d'être* of the communication discipline. Sophists such as Lysias, Hippias, and Tisias made their livings in ancient Greece by teaching people how to be more argumentative. More than 2,500 years later, many of us in the communication discipline ply essentially the same trade. If these teachings result in desirable outcomes, a declaration of such should be useful in helping the discipline understand better where its teachings lead. In that regard several of the conclusions offered in this review are relevant.

Our fourth reason for producing this review is our awareness that, because of its destructiveness, we need to understand verbal aggressiveness in order to learn how to control it. Along this line, Infante (1995) recently has derived several methods of controlling verbal aggression from the literature; he recommends that these should be taught in communication classrooms. Further research should provide additional implications for the control of verbal aggression. The communication discipline is in a unique position to display leadership in this area because of communication scholars' expertise in message behavior and experience in the study of verbal aggression.

REFERENCES

Andersen, P. A. (1987). The trait debate: A critical examination of the individual differences paradigm in interpersonal communication. In B. Dervin & M. J. Voigt (Eds.), *Progress in communication sciences* (Vol. 7, pp. 47-52). Norwood, NJ: Ablex.

Andersen, P. A., Lustig, M., & Andersen, J. (1987). Regional patterns of communication in the United States: A theoretical perspective. *Communication Monographs, 54,* 128-144.

Anderson, J., Schultz, B., & Courtney Staley, C. (1987). Training in argumentativeness: New hope for nonassertive women. *Women's Studies in Communication, 10,* 58-66.

Andonian, K. K., & Droge, D. (1992, October). *Verbal aggressiveness and sexual violence in dating relationships: An exploratory study of antecedents of date rape.* Paper presented at the annual meeting of the Speech Communication Association, Chicago.

Bayer, C. L., & Cegala, D. J. (1992). Trait verbal aggressiveness and argumentativeness: Relations with parenting style. *Western Journal of Communication, 56,* 301-310.

Beatty, M. J., Zelley, J. R., Dobos, J. A., & Rudd, J. E. (1994). Fathers' trait verbal aggressiveness and argumentativeness as predictors of adult sons' perceptions of fathers' sarcasm, criticism, and verbal aggressiveness. *Communication Quarterly, 42,* 407-415.

Boster, F. J., & Levine, T. (1988). Individual differences and compliance-gaining message selection: The effects of verbal aggressiveness, argumentativeness, dogmatism, and negativism. *Communication Research Reports, 5,* 114-119.

Boster, F. J., Levine, T., & Kazoleas, D. (1993). The impact of argumentativeness and verbal aggressiveness on strategic diversity and persistence in compliance-gaining behavior. *Communication Quarterly, 41,* 405-414.

Burgoon, J. K. (1976). The unwillingness-to-communicate scale: Development and validation. *Communication Monographs, 43,* 60-69.

Burgoon, J. K. (1978). A communication model of personal space violations: Explication and an initial test. *Human Communication Research, 4,* 129-142.

Burgoon, J. K. (1983). Nonverbal violations of expectations. In J. M. Wiemann & R. P. Harrison (Eds.), *Nonverbal interaction* (pp. 77-111). Beverly Hills, CA: Sage.

Buss, A. H., & Durkee, A. (1957). An inventory for assessing different kinds of hostility. *Journal of Consulting Psychology, 21,* 343-349.

Canary, D. J., Cunningham, E. M., & Cody, M. J. (1988). Goal types, gender, and locus of control in managing interpersonal conflict. *Communication Research, 15,* 426-446.

Chen, G.-M. (1994). Social desirability as a predictor of argumentativeness and communication apprehension. *Journal of Psychology, 128,* 433-438.

Colbert, K. R. (1993). The effects of debate participation on argumentativeness and verbal aggression. *Communication Education, 42,* 206-214.

Costa, P. T., & McCrae, R. R. (1980). Still stable after all these years: Personality as a key to some issues in adulthood and old age. In P. B. Baltes & O. G. Brim (Eds.), *Life-span development and behavior* (Vol. 3, pp. 65-102). New York: Academic Press.

Darus, H. J. (1994). Argumentativeness in the workplace: A trait by situation study. *Communication Research Reports, 11,* 99-106.

DeWine, S., Nicotera, A. M., & Parry, D. (1991). Argumentativeness and aggressiveness: The flip side of gentle persuasion. *Management Communication Quarterly, 4,* 386-411.

Dowling, R. E., & Flint, L. J. (1990). The Argumentativeness Scale: Problems and promise. *Communication Studies, 41,* 183-198.

Downs, V. C., Kaid, L. L., & Ragan, S. (1990). The impact of argumentativeness and verbal aggression on communicator image: The exchange between George Bush and Dan Rather. *Western Journal of Speech Communication, 54,* 99-112.

Epstein, S. (1979). The stability of behavior: 1. On predicting most of the people much of the time. *Journal of Personality and Social Psychology, 37,* 1097-1126.

Fishbein, M., & Ajzen, I. (1975). *Belief, attitude, intention, and behavior: An introduction to theory and research.* Reading, MA: Addison-Wesley.

Geddes, D. S. (1990). Verbal aggression and argumentativeness: Regional differences. *Carolinas Speech Communication Annual, 6,* 44-56.

Geddes, D. S. (1992). Comparison of regional interpersonal communication predispositions. *Pennsylvania Speech Communication Annual, 48,* 67-93.

Gorden, W. I. (1988). Range of employee voice. *Employee Responsibilities and Rights Journal, 1,* 283-299.

Gorden, W. I., & Infante, D. A. (1987). Employee rights: Context, argumentativeness, verbal aggressiveness, and career satisfaction. In C. A. B. Osigweh (Ed.), *Communicating employee responsibilities and rights* (pp. 149-163). Westport, CT: Quorum.

Gorden, W. I., & Infante, D. A. (1991). Test of a communication model of organizational commitment. *Communication Quarterly, 39,* 144-155.

Gorden, W. I., Infante, D. A., & Graham, E. E. (1988). Corporate conditions conducive to employee voice: A subordinate perspective. *Employee Responsibilities and Rights Journal, 1,* 101-111.

Gorden, W. I., Infante, D. A., & Izzo, J. (1988). Variations in voice pertaining to dissatisfaction/satisfaction with subordinates. *Management Communication Quarterly, 2,* 6-22.

Greenberg, B. S. (1976). The effects of language intensity modification on perceived verbal aggressiveness. *Communication Monographs, 43,* 130-139.

Hample, D., & Dallinger, J. M. (1987). Individual differences in cognitive editing standards. *Human Communication Research, 14,* 123-144.

Harman, C. M., Klopf, D. W., & Ishii, S. (1990). Verbal aggression among Japanese and American students. *Perceptual and Motor Skills, 70,* 1130.

Infante, D. A. (1971). The influence of a topic system on the discovery of arguments. *Speech Monographs, 38,* 125-128.

Infante, D. A. (1981). Trait argumentativeness as a predictor of communicative behavior in situations requiring argument. *Central States Speech Journal, 32,* 265-272.

Infante, D. A. (1982). The argumentative student in the speech communication classroom: An investigation and implications. *Communication Education, 31,* 141-148.

Infante, D. A. (1985). Inducing women to be more argumentative: Source credibility effects. *Journal of Applied Communication Research, 13,* 33-44.

Infante, D. A. (1987a). Aggressiveness. In J. C. McCroskey & J. A. Daly (Eds.), *Personality and interpersonal communication* (pp. 157-192). Newbury Park, CA: Sage.

Infante, D. A. (1987b). Enhancing the prediction of response to a communication situation from communication traits. *Communication Quarterly, 35,* 308-316.

Infante, D. A. (1988). *Arguing constructively.* Prospect Heights, IL: Waveland.

Infante, D. A. (1989). Response to high argumentatives: Message and sex differences. *Southern Communication Journal, 54,* 159-170.

Infante, D. A. (1995). Teaching students to understand and control verbal aggression. *Communication Education, 44,* 51-63.

Infante, D. A. (in press). Corporal punishment of children: A communication theory perspective. In M. A. Straus & M. Donnelly (Eds.), *Corporal punishment of children in theoretical perspective.* New Haven, CT: Yale University Press.

Infante, D. A., Anderson, C. M., Martin, M. M., Herington, A. D., & Kim, J. (1993). Subordinates' satisfaction and perceptions of superiors' compliance-gaining tactics, argumentativeness, verbal aggressiveness, and style. *Management Communication Quarterly, 6,* 307-326.

Infante, D. A., Chandler, T. A., & Rudd, J. E. (1989). Test of an argumentative skill deficiency model of interspousal violence. *Communication Monographs, 56,* 163-177.

Infante, D. A., Chandler Sabourin, T., Rudd, J. E., & Shannon, E. A. (1990). Verbal aggression in violent and nonviolent marital disputes. *Communication Quarterly, 38,* 361-371.

Infante, D. A., & Gorden, W. I. (1985a). Benefits versus bias: An investigation of argumentativeness, gender, and organizational communication outcomes. *Communication Research Reports, 2,* 196-201.

Infante, D. A., & Gorden, W. I. (1985b). Superiors' argumentativeness and verbal aggressiveness as predictors of subordinates' satisfaction. *Human Communication Research, 12,* 117-125.

Infante, D. A., & Gorden, W. I. (1987). Superior and subordinate communication profiles: Implications for independent-mindedness and upward effectiveness. *Central States Speech Journal, 38,* 73-80.

Infante, D. A., & Gorden, W. I. (1989). Argumentativeness and affirming communicator style as predictors of satisfaction/dissatisfaction with subordinates. *Communication Quarterly, 37,* 81-90.

Infante, D. A., & Gorden, W. I. (1991). How employees see the boss: Test of an argumentative and affirming model of superiors' communicative behavior. *Western Journal of Speech Communication, 55,* 294-304.

Infante, D. A., Hartley, K. C., Martin, M. M., Higgins, M. A., Bruning, S. D., & Hur, G. (1992). Initiating and reciprocating verbal aggression: Effects on credibility and credited valid arguments. *Communication Studies, 43,* 182-190.

Infante, D. A., Myers, S. A., & Burkel, R. A. (1994). Argument and verbal aggression in constructive and destructive family and organizational disagreements. *Western Journal of Communication, 58,* 73-84.

Infante, D. A., & Rancer, A. S. (1982). A conceptualization and measure of argumentativeness. *Journal of Personality Assessment, 46,* 72-80.

Infante, D. A., & Rancer, A. S. (1993). Relations between argumentative motivation, and advocacy and refutation on controversial issues. *Communication Quarterly, 41,* 415-426.

Infante, D. A., Riddle, B. L., Horvath, C. L., & Tumlin, S. A. (1992). Verbal aggressiveness: Messages and reasons. *Communication Quarterly, 40,* 116-126.

Infante, D. A., Trebing, J. D., Shepherd, P. E., & Seeds, D. E. (1984). The relationship of argumentativeness to verbal aggression. *Southern Speech Communication Journal, 50,* 67-77.

Infante, D. A., Wall, C. H., Leap, C. J., & Danielson, K. (1984). Verbal aggression as a function of the receiver's argumentativeness. *Communication Research Reports, 1,* 33-37.

Infante, D. A., & Wigley, C. J. (1986). Verbal aggressiveness: An interpersonal model and measure. *Communication Monographs, 53,* 61-69.

Jenkins, G. D., Klopf, D. W., & Park, M. S. (1991, July). *Argumentativeness in Korean and American college students: A comparison.* Paper presented at the annual meeting of the World Communication Association, Jyvaskyla, Finland.

Johnson, D. W., & Johnson, R. T. (1979). Conflict in the classroom: Controversy and learning. *Review of Educational Research, 49,* 51-70.

Kazoleas, D. (1993). The impact of argumentativeness on resistance to persuasion. *Human Communication Research, 20,* 118-137.

Kazoleas, D. (1994, November). *Are argumentatives really more argumentative? The behavior of argumentatives in group deliberations over controversial issues.* Paper presented at the annual meeting of the Speech Communication Association, New Orleans.

Kinney, T. A. (1994). An inductively derived typology of verbal aggression and its association to distress. *Human Communication Research, 21,* 183-222.

Klopf, D. W., Thompson, C. A., & Sallinen-Kuparinen, S. (1991). Argumentativeness among selected Finnish and American college students. *Psychological Reports, 68,* 161-162.

Kochman, T. (1981). *Black and white styles in conflict.* Chicago: University of Chicago Press.

Kosberg, R. L., & Rancer, A. S. (1991). Training in argumentativeness. *Speech Communication Annual, 5,* 97-107.

Levine, T. R., & Badger, E. E. (1993). Argumentativeness and resistance to persuasion. *Communication Reports, 6,* 71-78.

Lim, T. S. (1990). The influence of receivers' resistance on persuaders' verbal aggressiveness. *Communication Quarterly, 38,* 170-188.

Magnusson, D., & Endler, N. S. (1977). Interactional psychology: Present status and future prospects. In D. Magnusson & N. S. Endler (Eds.), *Personality at the crossroads: Current issues in interactional psychology* (pp. 3-35). Hillsdale, NJ: Lawrence Erlbaum.

McCroskey, J. C. (1970). Measures of communication-bound anxiety. *Speech Monographs, 37,* 269-277.

McCroskey, J. C., & Daly, J. A. (Eds.). (1987). *Personality and interpersonal communication.* Newbury Park, CA: Sage.

Millar, F. E., & Rogers, L. E. (1987). Relational dimensions of interpersonal dynamics. In M. E. Roloff & G. Miller (Eds.), *Interpersonal processes* (pp. 117-139). Newbury Park, CA: Sage.

Mongeau, P. A. (1989). Individual differences as moderators of persuasive message processing and attitude-behavior relations. *Communication Research Reports, 6,* 1-6.

Mortensen, C. D., Arnston, P. H., & Lustig, M. (1977). The measurement of verbal predispositions. *Human Communication Research, 3,* 146-158.

Nelson, W. F. (1970). Topoi: Functional in human recall. *Speech Monographs, 37,* 121-126.

Nicotera, A. M. (1994). *An assessment of the Argumentativeness Scale for social desirability bias.* Unpublished manuscript, Howard University.

Nicotera, A. M., & DeWine, S. (1991). Understanding entry into controversy at work and at home. *Communication Research Reports, 8,* 89-99.

Nicotera, A. M., & Rancer, A. S. (1994). The influence of sex on self-perceptions and social stereotyping of aggressive communication predispositions. *Western Journal of Communication, 58,* 283-307.

Nicotera, A. M., Rancer, A. S., & Sullivan, R. G. (1991, November). *Race as a factor in argumentativeness, verbal aggressiveness, and beliefs about arguing.* Paper presented at the annual meeting of the Speech Communication Association, Atlanta, GA.

Nicotera, A. M., Smilowitz, M., & Pearson, J. C. (1990). Ambiguity tolerance, conflict management style and argumentativeness as predictors of innovativeness. *Communication Research Reports, 7,* 125-131.

Onyekwere, E. O., Rubin, R. B., & Infante, D. A. (1991). Interpersonal perception and communication satisfaction as a function of argumentativeness and ego-involvement. *Communication Quarterly, 39,* 35-47.

Payne, M. J., & Sabourin, T. C. (1990). Argumentative skill deficiency and its relationship to quality of marriage. *Communication Research Reports, 7,* 121-124.

Prunty, A. M., Klopf, D. W., & Ishii, S. (1990a). Argumentativeness: Japanese and American tendencies to approach and avoid conflict. *Communication Research Reports, 7,* 75-79.

Prunty, A. M., Klopf, D. W., & Ishii, S. (1990b). Japanese and American tendencies to argue. *Psychological Reports, 66,* 802.

Rahoi, R., Svenkerud, P., & Love, D. (1994). *Searching for subtlety: Investigating argumentativeness across low-context cultural boundaries.* Unpublished manuscript, Ohio University.

Rancer, A. S., & Baukus, R. A. (1987). Discriminating males and females on belief structures about arguing. In L. B. Nadler, M. K. Nadler, & W. R. Todd-Mancillas (Eds.), *Advances in gender and communication research* (pp. 155-173). Lanham, MD: University Press of America.

Rancer, A. S., Baukus, R. A., & Amato, P. P. (1986). Argumentativeness, verbal aggressiveness, and marital satisfaction. *Communication Research Reports, 3,* 28-32.

Rancer, A. S., Baukus, R. A., & Infante, D. A. (1985). Relations between argumentativeness and belief structures about arguing. *Communication Education, 34,* 37-47.

Rancer, A. S., & Dierks-Stewart, K. J. (1985). The influence of sex and sex-role orientation on trait argumentativeness. *Journal of Personality Assessment, 49,* 69-70.

Rancer, A. S., & Infante, D. A. (1985). Relations between motivation to argue and the argumentativeness of adversaries. *Communication Quarterly, 33,* 209-218.

Rancer, A. S., Kosberg, R. L., & Baukus, R. A. (1992). Beliefs about arguing as predictors of trait argumentativeness: Implications for training in argument and conflict management. *Communication Education, 41,* 375-387.

Rancer, A. S., Kosberg, R. L., & Silvestri, V. N. (1992). The relationship between self-esteem and aggressive communication predispositions. *Communication Research Reports, 9,* 23-32.

Richmond, V. P., McCroskey, J. C., & McCroskey, L. L. (1989). An investigation of self-perceived communication competence and personality orientations. *Communication Research Reports, 6,* 28-36.

Roach, K. D. (1992). Teacher demographic characteristics and level of teacher argumentativeness. *Communication Research Reports, 9,* 65-71.

Roach, K. D. (1995). Teaching assistant argumentativeness: Effects on affective learning and student perceptions of power use. *Communication Education, 44,* 15-29.

Rudd, J. E., Burant, P. A., & Beatty, M. J. (1994). Battered women's compliance-gaining strategies as a function of argumentativeness and verbal aggression. *Communication Research Reports, 11,* 13-22.

Sabourin, T. C., Infante, D. A., & Rudd, J. E. (1993). Verbal aggression in marriages: A comparison of violent, distressed but nonviolent, and nondistressed couples. *Human Communication Research, 20,* 245-267.

Sanders, J. A., Gass, R. H., Wiseman, R. L., & Bruschke, J. C. (1992). Ethnic comparison and measurement of argumentativeness, verbal aggressiveness, and need for cognition. *Communication Reports, 5,* 50-56.

Sanders, J. A., Wiseman, R. L., & Gass, R. H. (1994). Does teaching argumentation facilitate critical thinking? *Communication Reports, 7,* 27-35.

Schultz, B. (1982). Argumentativeness: Its effect in group decision-making and its role in leadership perception. *Communication Quarterly, 30,* 368-375.

Schultz, B., & Anderson, J. (1984). Training in the management of conflict: A communication theory perspective. *Small Group Behavior, 15,* 333-348.

Segrin, C., & Fitzpatrick, M. A. (1992). Depression and verbal aggressiveness in different marital couple types. *Communication Monographs, 43,* 79-91.

Stewart, R. A., & Roach, K. D. (1993). Argumentativeness, religious orientation, and reactions to argument situations involving religious versus nonreligious issues. *Communication Quarterly, 41,* 26-39.

Suzuki, S., & Rancer, A. S. (1994). Argumentativeness and verbal aggressiveness: Testing for conceptual and measure equivalence across cultures. *Communication Monographs, 61,* 256-279.

Waggenspack, B. M., & Hensley, W. E. (1989). Perception of the argumentativeness trait in interpersonal relationship situations. *Social Behavior and Personality, 17,* 111-120.

Wheeless, L. R. (1975). An investigation of receiver apprehension and social context dimensions of communication apprehension. *Speech Teacher, 24,* 261-268.

Wigley, C. J. (1987). Student receiver apprehension as a correlate of trait argumentativeness. *Communication Research Reports, 4,* 51-53.

Wigley, C. J., Pohl, G. H., & Watt, M. G. S. (1989). Conversational sensitivity as a correlate of trait verbal aggressiveness and the predisposition to verbally praise others. *Communication Reports, 2,* 92-95.

Wilson, J. F., & Arnold, C. C. (1983). *Public speaking as a liberal art* (5th ed.). Boston: Allyn & Bacon.

CHAPTER CONTENTS

9   Intercultural Communication
Competence: A Synthesis

GUO-MING CHEN
University of Rhode Island

WILLIAM J. STAROSTA
Howard University

As we encounter ever greater cultural and co-cultural diversity, the careful study of intercultural communication competence becomes increasingly important. Only through competent intercultural communication can persons from different cultures communicate effectively and appropriately in the upcoming global society. Following a recounting of themes of research on intercultural communication, this chapter presents arguments concerning individuals' need to negotiate multiple identities in terms of culture, race, ethnicity, gender, and religion in the interdependent and interconnected network of global society. This requires a functional and theoretical transformation of the study of intercultural communication competence.

A S we grow increasingly aware of the global interdependence of people and cultures, we confront ever shifting cultural, ecological, economic, and technological realities that define the shrinking world of the twenty-first century. The development of new ways of living in the world together is pivotal to further human progress; we must learn how to see things through the eyes of others and add their knowledge to our personal repertoires. Such a global mind-set can result only from competent communication among peoples form diverse cultures.

INTERCULTURAL COMMUNICATION COMPETENCE: WHY?

The citizens of the twenty-first century must learn to see through the eyes, hearts, and minds of people from cultures other than their own. Several important trends of the late twentieth century have transformed the world into

Correspondence and requests for reprints: Guo-Ming Chen, Communication Studies, University of Rhode Island, 106 Independence Hall, Kingston, RI 02881-0812.

Communication Yearbook 19, pp. 353-383

a global village: technology development, globalization of the economy, widespread population migrations, the development of multiculturalism, and the demise of the nation-state in favor of sub- and supranational identifications. In order to live meaningfully and productively in this world, individuals must develop their intercultural communication competence.

Technology Development

The development of communication and transportation technology linking every part of the world has served to interconnect almost every aspect of life at the onset of the twenty-first century (Frederick, 1993; Porter & Samovar, 1994). Today the flow of ideas and information increasingly transcends national boundaries. People can also travel to anywhere in the world much more quickly than ever before. The faster travel speeds wrought by transportation technology have introduced increasing face-to-face communication among people from different cultures.

Globalization of the Economy

The progress of communication and transportation technology has rendered global markets more accessible and the business world more interrelated and international than in the past. Regional trade alliances have become the "new world order." The trend toward a global economy is bringing people from different cultures together. It requires representatives from multinational corporations to communicate with those in other parts of the world to retain a competitive space in the global economic arena. The interdependence among international economies reflects the important role that intercultural communication plays now and will play increasingly in the next century. The development of greater intercultural understanding has become an essential element of global business (Adler, 1991; Mead, 1990).

Widespread Population Migrations

As cultural interconnectedness has increased as a result of technology development, we have also witnessed remarkable population migrations across national borders. The United States especially has felt the impacts of this trend. In 1990, the U.S. Census revealed that the first-generation foreign-born population in the United States had reached almost 20 million. About 8.7 million immigrants entered the United States between 1980 and 1990. At least 32 million persons residing in the United States speak a first language other than English, and 14 million of these do not speak English fluently. These figures indicate that the increasing numbers of immigrants have restructured the fabric of American society. The United States has become much more culturally diverse than it has been in the past.

This multiethnic structure makes intercultural contact among co-cultures inevitable. Members of the various co-cultures and ethnic groups residing in the United States must learn to adjust to one another's identities. This trend demands that individuals learn to communicate in ways that are effective in such a diversifying society (Nieto, 1992).

The Development of Multiculturalism

The changing demographics described above stand to affect every aspect of life in the United States. Johnston and Packer (1987), for example, predict that the increasing diversity of workforce and social life in the United States will dramatically affect organizational life in the twenty-first century. The new workforce will comprise persons who are diverse in race, culture, age, gender, and language. Cultural diversity, or multiculturalism, will become the norm rather than the exception in American life. Thus, intercultural communication scholars need to address those issues that will help people learn to work and live together without being deterred by the differences they may bring to their encounters. The development of greater intercultural understanding and intercultural communication competence is an essential part of human life in the contemporary age.

De-Emphasis on the Nation-State

As new immigrants arrive and co-cultures make headway in achieving fuller participation in U.S. society, the very idea of national identity will surely change. Increasingly, the United States is pulled into regional alliances, such as NATO or NAFTA, that are larger than the nation. In addition, we see the reassertion of ethnic and gender differences within the nation; for instance, women have begun to talk as women, African Americans as African Americans, and Native Americans as Native Americans. The ability to negotiate the meanings and priorities of diverse identities has become a prerequisite of attaining interpersonal competence in modern society (Collier & Thomas, 1988).

The five trends described above combine to provide a foundation for the indispensability of intercultural communication competence in our increasingly global society. The world has become more interdependent and interconnected, and the nation-state has become more culturally heterogeneous. These developments foster within individuals multiple, simultaneous identities in terms of culture, ethnicity, race, religion, nationality, and gender (Belay, 1993). Intercultural communication competence therefore functions to nourish a human personality in which people are aware of their multiple identities and are able to maintain a multicultural coexistence in order to develop a "global civic culture" (Boulding, 1988). In other words, intercultural communication competence transforms a monocultural person into a multicultural person. This transformation is achieved through symmetrical interdependence that enables persons to demonstrate "tolerance for differences and mutual respect among cultures as a mark of enlightened national and global citizenship" in individual, social, business, and political institutions levels (Belay, 1993).

Based on this theoretical foundation, the following discussion of intercultural communication competence is divided into five sections. These address, in turn, the nature of communication competence, approaches to the study of intercultural communication competence, a model of intercultural communication competence, a critique and directions for future research, and a summary and conclusion.

THE NATURE OF COMMUNICATION COMPETENCE

Although 50 years of conceptualizing have provided a theoretical and practical foundation for intercultural communication, it remains a fresh field. The study of intercultural communication dates back to the works of political scientists and anthropologists in the 1940s and 1950s. Whereas linguist Edward Sapir wrote about this topic in the 1920s, it took Benjamin Whorf to frame his work more fully as a communication question. As sociologists, linguists, and communication scholars have developed an interest in intercultural communication, two separate schools of thought—cultural dialogue and cultural criticism—now inform research in intercultural communication (Asante, Newmark, & Blake, 1979). Both schools have spawned significant research in intercultural communication. One of the main topics studied by the two groups is intercultural communication competence, or the effective means whereby individuals can understand cultural commonalities and move beyond cultural differences in order to reach the ideal goals advocated by cultural dialogists and cultural critics. But, we ask, What is communication competence?

Definition of Communication Competence

Two concepts have long been applied in discussions of communication competence: effectiveness and appropriateness. *Effectiveness* refers to an individual's ability to produce intended effects through interaction with the environment. This ability is treated either as a basic human skill that is obtained through learning and socialization processes (Weinstein, 1969; White, 1959) or as an acquired ability that is related neither to personal intellect nor to education (Foote & Cottrell, 1955; Holland & Baird, 1968). In either case, the ability is understood to increase as the individual's awareness of relevant factors increases (Argyris, 1965a, 1965b). In addition, ideally, competent communicators should be able to control and manipulate their environments to attain personal goals. In order to maximize such goals, individuals must be able to identify them, get relevant information about them, accurately predict others' responses, select communication strategies, implement these communication strategies, and accurately assess the interaction results (Parks, 1985, 1994).

A more systematic view of effectiveness in communication relates the concept to both interactants. To be competent in communication, a person must not only feel competent, but his or her ability should be observed and confirmed by the people with whom he or she interacts. Thus, communication competence should be judged based on individuals' abilities to formulate and achieve objectives, to collaborate effectively with others, and to adapt to situational variations (Bochner & Kelly, 1974). Rubin (1983) has further considered communication competence to be a kind of impression based on the individual's perception, an impression the individual forms of both his or her own and others' behaviors. Through this impression, a person makes guesses about the internal states of those with whom he or she is interacting.

Finally, Wiemann (1977) synthesizes the concept of communication competence from the perspective of effectiveness. He conceptualizes communicative competence as "the ability of an interactant to choose among available communicative behaviors in order that he may successfully accomplish his own interpersonal goals during an encounter while maintaining the face and line of his fellow interactants within the constraints of the situation" (p. 198). This definition argues simultaneously that competent communication is other oriented and that communicators have to accomplish their own goals.

Whereas some scholars conceive of communication competence as a function of perceived effectiveness, others look at it from the viewpoint of appropriateness. Wiemann and Backlund (1980) explain appropriateness in the communication process as follows:

Appropriateness generally refers to the ability of an interactant to meet the basic contextual requirements of the situation—to be effective in a general sense. . . . These contextual requirements include: (1) The verbal context, that is, making sense in terms of wording, of statements, and of topic; (2) the relationship context, that is, the structuring, type and style of messages so that they are consonant with the particular relationship at hand; and (3) the environmental context, that is, the consideration of constraints imposed on message making by the symbolic and physical environments. (p. 191)

The "appropriateness of behavior" thus implicates three kinds of ability. First is the ability to recognize how context constrains communication, so that one acts and speaks appropriately by combining capabilities and social knowledge to recognize that different situations give rise to different sets of rules (Lee, 1979; Trenholm & Rose, 1981). Second is the ability to avoid inappropriate responses. An inappropriate response is defined as "one which is unnecessarily abrasive, intense, or bizarre. It is also likely to result in negative consequences that could have been averted, without sacrifice of the goal, by more appropriate actions" (Getter & Nowinski, 1981, p. 303). Third is the ability to fulfill appropriately such communication functions as controlling, sharing feelings, informing, ritualizing, and imagining (Allen & Wood, 1978). We extend Grice's (1975) recommendations concerning appropriateness in interaction to include the following:

1. Say just enough—not too little or too much.
2. Do not say something that is false—or speak about something for which you lack evidence.
3. Relate your contribution to the topic and situation.
4. Be clear about what you are saying, and say it with dispatch.

These guidelines specify the four elements of appropriate communication: quantity, quality, relevance, and manner of message sending.

To summarize, communication competence requires appropriateness, and "the fundamental criteria of appropriateness are that the interactants perceive that they understand the content of the encounter and have not had their norms and rules violated too extensively" (Spitzberg & Cupach, 1984, p. 101).

Definition of Intercultural Communication Competence

The literature treats intercultural communication competence in much the same way as it does communication competence in general (Hammer, 1988; Lustig & Koester, 1993; Martin, 1989; Ruben, 1989; Spitzberg, 1988, 1989; Wiseman & Koester, 1993). The only difference is, in addition to looking at communication competence as effective and appropriate interaction, intercultural communication scholars place more emphasis on contextual factors. They conceive of communication competence not only as effective and appropriate interaction between people, but as effective and appropriate interaction between people who identify with particular physical and symbolic environments. This orientation resembles that of communication scholars who emphasize competence as a context-specific behavior (Spitzberg & Cupach, 1984).

Although researchers conceive of communication competence as the ability to interact effectively and appropriately with others, their definitions betray greater or lesser degrees of ambiguity, confusion, and imprecision. For example, from Wiemann's (1977) synthesized definition, the question arises, What constitute "available communicative behaviors" and "constraints of the situation"? These concepts are not clear, and require definition. To alleviate the problem in defining communication competence and to apply the concept to intercultural settings, intercultural communication competence can be conceived of as the ability to negotiate cultural meanings and to execute appropriately effective communication behaviors that recognize the interactants' multiple identities in a specific environment. This definition emphasizes that competent persons must know not only how to interact effectively and appropriately with people and environment, but also how to fulfill their own communication goals by respecting and affirming the multilevel cultural identities of those with whom they interact.

Types of Competence

How do individuals interact across multiple cultural identities? Spitzberg and Cupach (1984) propose seven generic types of competence: fundamental competence, social competence, social skills, interpersonal competence, linguistic competence, communicative competence, and relational competence. *Fundamental competence* involves the general ability to adapt effectively to a new environment in order to achieve goals. In this sense, fundamental competence comprises the cognitive capacities that individual communicators need to be effective cross-situationally. *Social competence* involves specific, rather than general, abilities. Spitzberg and Cupach include within social competence the skills of empathy, role taking, cognitive complexity, and interaction management. *Interpersonal competence* is the ability to accomplish tasks and achieve goals through successful communication. Even though interpersonal competence is part of both fundamental competence and social competence, it is especially related to how individuals execute certain skills to control their environments in order to achieve goals in particular communication situations. Linguistic competence and communicative competence both relate to language and messages in the interaction process. *Linguistic competence* (a concept that stems from the work of Chomsky, 1965) is specifically the ability to use language properly. *Communicative competence* entails not only the knowledge of how to use language, but also knowledge about how to execute one's language knowledge appropriately. To be communicatively competent, a person must be able to convey messages appropriately in a given context of interaction. Finally, *relational competence* comprises many of the other six kinds of competence, but independent and reciprocal processes of interactions are among its most important aspects. An individual must establish certain degrees of relationships with others before he or she can interact effectively with them and achieve his or her goals. Such relationships cross multiple dimensions of language, profession, ethnicity, and nation.

Spitzberg and Cupach's view of competence suggests that individuals have unitary and unchanging cultural identities. By contrast, we view culture as a set of preferences and possibilities that inform, rather than determine, given interactions. Communicators both shape and are shaped by these familiar meanings. Especially as individuals draw from multiple identities, interactions may not perfectly resemble any one cultural expectation.

APPROACHES TO THE STUDY OF
INTERCULTURAL COMMUNICATION COMPETENCE

To understand the mutual negotiation of cultural meanings in intercultural communication, Dinges (1983) and Collier (1989) have classified the study of intercultural communication competence into different approaches. Dinges (1983) identifies six approaches to the study of intercultural communication competence: "overseasmanship," subjective culture, multicultural person, social behaviorism, topology, and intercultural communicator. The overseasmanship approach, first presented by Cleveland, Mangone, and Adams (1960), identifies common factors in effective performances among sojourners, or individuals on extended, nonpermanent stays in cultures other than their own. To be considered competent according to this approach, a sojourner must show the ability to convert lessons from a variety of foreign experiences into effective job-related skills.

The subjective culture (isomorphic attribution) approach requires individuals to have the ability to understand the causes of interactants' behaviors and reward them appropriately, and to modify their own behaviors suitably according to the demands of the setting (Triandis, 1976, 1977). This ability to understand the reasons that members of other cultures give for their behaviors must be based on accurate cognition of the differences in cognitive structure between cultures.

The multicultural person approach emphasizes that a competent person must be able to adapt to exceedingly difficult circumstances by transcending his or her usual adaptive limits (Adler, 1975, 1982). The individual must learn to move in and out of different contexts, to maintain coherence in different situations, and to be dynamic.

The social behaviorism (culture learning) approach emphasizes that successful intercultural coping strategies depend more on the individual's predeparture experiences, such as training and sojourning in another country, than on inherent characteristics or personality (Guthrie, 1975). That is, to be competent in intercultural interaction, a person must learn discriminative stimuli to obtain social rewards and to avoid punishments that will create hardship (David, 1972).

The typology approach develops different models of intercultural communication competence. Most of the models place sojourners' behavioral styles on a continuum from most to least effective. For example, Brislin (1981) proposes that a successful intercultural interaction must be based on the sojourner's attitudes, traits, and social skills. He asserts that nonethnocentrism and nonprejudicial judgments are the most valuable attitudes for effective intercultural interaction. Ethnocentrism is the judgment of an unfamiliar practice by the standards and norms familiar to one's own group or culture. The major adaptive personal traits Brislin mentions include personality strength, intelligence, tolerance, social relations skills, recognition of the potential for benefit, and task orientation. Finally, important social skills are knowledge of subject and language, positive orientation to opportunities, effective communication skills, and the ability to use personal traits to complete tasks.

Finally, the intercultural communicator approach emphasizes that successful intercultural interaction centers on communication processes among people from different cultures. In other words, to be interculturally competent, an individual must be able to establish interpersonal relationships by understanding others through the effective exchange of verbal and nonverbal behaviors (Hall, 1959, 1966, 1976).

Collier (1989) identifies four categories of approaches to intercultural communication competence: ethnography of speaking, cross-cultural attitude, behavioral skills, and cultural identity. The ethnography of speaking approach assumes that meaning, conduct, and cultural membership are interdependent, thus, competence must be contextually defined (Geertz, 1973; Hymes, 1971, 1972). In order to achieve communication goals, an individual must correctly perceive, select, and interpret the specific features of the code in interaction and integrate these with other cultural knowledge and communication skills (Saville-Troike, 1982). The cross-cultural attitude approach assumes that understanding the culture of those with whom one is communicating and developing a positive attitude toward that culture are the keys to attaining communication competence across cultures. Studies by Chen (1989), Abe and Wiseman (1983), Gudykunst, Wiseman, and Hammer (1977), and Wiseman and Abe (1984) have examined the concept from this perspective. The behavioral skills approach assumes that "humans are goal directed and choice making beings, and that humans can distinguish between skills which will be effective and skills which will not be effective" in interaction (Collier, 1989, p. 294). Thus, competent persons are able to identify and adopt those effective skills in intercultural interaction (Chen, 1992; Hammer, 1989; Ruben, 1976, 1977; Ruben & Kealey, 1979). Finally, the cultural identity approach assumes that communication competence is a dynamic and emergent process in which interactants are able to improve the quality of their experience by recognizing the existence of each other's cultural identities (Collier, 1989, 1994; Cupach & Imahori, 1993). Thus, interculturally competent persons must know how to negotiate and respect meanings of cultural symbols and norms that are changing during their interactions (Collier & Thomas, 1988; Y. Y. Kim, 1994a). In addition, Ward and Searle (1991) have found that cultural identity significantly affects adaptation to a new culture.

Although the approaches described above provide useful perspectives from which to study intercultural communication competence, they fail to give a holistic picture that can reflect the global civic culture in which people can mutually negotiate their multiple identities. In the following section we attempt to synthesize these approaches into a model of intercultural communication competence.

A MODEL OF
INTERCULTURAL COMMUNICATION COMPETENCE

After scrutinizing the existing approaches to the study of intercultural communication competence, we can synthesize them into a model of "interactive-multiculture building" (Belay, 1993). The model aims at promoting interactants' abilities to acknowledge, respect, tolerate, and integrate cultural differences, so that they can qualify for enlightened global citizenship. The model represents a transformational process of symmetrical interdependence that can be explained from three perspectives: (a) affective, or intercultural sensitivity; (b) cognitive, or intercultural awareness; and (c) behavioral, or intercultural adroitness.

The Affective Process: Intercultural Sensitivity

The affective perspective of intercultural communication competence focuses on personal emotions or the changes in feelings that are caused by particular situations, people, and environments (Triandis, 1977). The affective process especially carries a notion that interculturally competent persons are able to project and receive positive emotional responses before, during, and after intercultural interactions. These positive emotional responses will in turn lead to acknowledgment of and respect for cultural differences. This process is the development of intercultural sensitivity (Bennett, 1986; Bhawuk & Brislin, 1992; Chen & Tan, 1995; Gudykunst, Ting-Toomey, & Wiseman, 1991).

Four personal attributes form the foundation of the affective perspective on intercultural communication competence: self-concept, open-mindedness, nonjudgmental attitudes, and social relaxation. *Self-concept* refers to the way in which a person sees him- or herself. An individual's self-concept not only serves as his or her key to communication, but it mediates how the person relates to the world. One of the most important elements of self-concept is self-esteem. Adler and Towne (1993) have summarized research in this area, and they note that the communication behaviors of high self-esteem individuals and low self-esteem individuals differ significantly. Persons with high self-esteem, compared with persons with low self-esteem, are more likely to think well of others, are more accepted by others, perform well when being watched, feel more comfortable when working with superiors, and can defend themselves against the negative comments of others. Persons with high self-esteem also tend to feel more positively toward out-group members. In intercultural encounters, which often involve psychological stresses associated with the need to complete a task and establish relationships with others, self-esteem helps individuals to calculate whether or not they can fulfill particular needs (Brislin, 1981; Ehrlich, 1973; Ting-Toomey, 1993). Other aspects of self-concept can also affect intercultural communication. For instance, an interculturally competent person must have a good, optimistic outlook that inspires confidence in his or her interactions with others (Foote & Cottrell, 1955; Hawes & Kealey, 1979, 1981); must show a stable and extroverted personality (Gardner, 1962); and must show self-reliance, perseverance, and reliability (Harris, 1973; Smith, 1966). All these personality traits combine to cultivate a positive self-concept that can lead to intercultural communication competence (Chen, 1995b; Scollon & Scollon, 1995).

Open-mindedness refers to individuals' willingness to express themselves openly when it is appropriate and to accept others' explanations. This positive trait is parallel to one of the characteristics of a multicultural person, who is willing to accept different patterns of life and to accept, psychologically and socially, a multiplicity of realities (Adler, 1977). In other words, open-minded persons possess an internalized broadened concept of the world that enables them to understand that an idea can be rendered in many different ways (Bennett, 1986; Hart & Burks, 1972). Open-mindedness entails a willingness to recognize, appreciate, and accept different views and ideas in intercultural interaction. It allows people to understand and acknowledge other people's needs and, further, can transform such understanding to actions (Smith, 1966; Yum, 1989). It is a process of mutual validation and confirmation of cultural identities that fosters a favorable impression in intercultural communication (Ting-Toomey, 1989).

Being *nonjudgmental* means holding no prejudices that will prevent one from listening sincerely to others during intercultural communication. At the same time, being nonjudgmental allows others to be psychologically satisfied and happy that they have been listened to actively. Mutual satisfaction of interactants is a measure of intercultural communication competence (Hammer, 1989; Ruben, 1988).

Nonjudgmental and open-minded attitudes nurture a feeling of enjoyment of cultural differences in intercultural interactions. Interculturally competent persons not only need to acknowledge and accept cultural differences, but should establish a sentiment of enjoyment, which usually leads to a satisfactory feeling toward intercultural encounters (Chen & Tan, 1995). Researchers have identified three kinds of enjoyment in intercultural interactions that are necessary for intercultural communication competence: (a) the enjoyment of interacting with people from different cultures (Randolph, Landis, & Tzeng, 1977), (b) the enjoyment of improving working relations with others from different cultures (Fiedler, Mitchell, & Triandis, 1971), and (c) the enjoyment of carrying out one's own duties in another culture (Gudykunst, Hammer, & Wiseman, 1977).

Finally, *social relaxation* refers to the ability to reveal little anxious emotion in intercultural communication. It is assumed that a series of crises usually occur in the initial experiences of sojourners, and feelings of anxiety usually originate from the psychological lack of security that individuals feel when entering new situations (Gudykunst & Hammer, 1988; Herman & Schield, 1961; Sanders & Wiseman, 1993; Stephan & Stephan, 1992). The symptoms of social anxiety include excessive perspiration, rocking movements, rigidity of posture, speech disturbances, hesitations, and lowered response tendencies (Spitzberg & Cupach, 1984; Wiemann, 1977). To be competent in intercultural communication, an individual must overcome such stumbling blocks, which can include feelings of anxiety when communicating with those from different cultures (Barna, 1994).

The four personal attributes described above form the affective basis of intercultural communication competence. They enable an individual to be sensitive enough during intercultural interactions to acknowledge and respect cultural differences. They increase the level of a person's compatibility with a new cultural environment, and thus help alleviate the impact of culture shock (Kim, 1988, 1991; Kim & Gudykunst, 1988; Oberg, 1960; Smalley, 1963). In other words, they expedite the process of psychological adaptation by increasing a person's general psychological well-being, self-satisfaction, and contentment within a new environment.

In general, psychological adaptation in intercultural interaction is associated with the ability to cope in situations where social difficulties cause frustration, stress, and alienation due to cultural differences (Furnham & Bochner, 1982; Rogers & Ward, 1993). A great deal of research based on the affective perspective of intercultural communication competence has addressed individuals' abilities to handle psychological stress in new environments (Hammer, 1987; Hammer, Gudykunst, & Wiseman, 1978; Searle & Ward, 1990; Ward & Searle, 1991; Wiseman & Abe, 1984). However, this line of research needs to be extended to examine how people can identify their own multiple identities in the process of psychological adaptation during intercultural encounters.

To summarize, affectively, intercultural communication competence demands positive emotion that enables individuals to be sensitive enough to acknowledge and respect cultural differences. The affective process of intercultural communication is built on four personal attributes: self-concept, open-mindedness, nonjudgmental attitudes, and social relaxation.

The Cognitive Process: Intercultural Awareness

The cognitive perspective of intercultural communication competence emphasizes the changing of personal thinking about the environment through the understanding of the distinct characteristics of one's own and others' cultures (Triandis, 1977). It is the process of reducing the level of situational ambiguity and uncertainty in intercultural interactions. With little visible discomfort, confusion, or nervousness, an individual can adapt to situational demands in a new environment with no noticeable personal, interpersonal, or group consequences, and can cope with the changing environment rapidly and comfortably (Ruben, 1976; Ruben & Kealey, 1979).

The cognitive process of intercultural communication competence, then, provides an opportunity for the individual to develop an awareness of cultural dynamics and to discern multiple identities in order to maintain a state of multicultural coexistence. This is the ability of intercultural awareness, which comprises two aspects of understanding: self-awareness and cultural awareness (Brislin, Landis, & Brandt, 1983; Gudykunst et al., 1991; Pruegger & Rogers, 1993).

The implementation of conversationally competent behaviors in interaction requires self-awareness, the individual's ability to monitor or to be aware of him- or herself (Spitzberg & Cupach, 1984). Self-awareness facilitates competent intercultural communication and helps a person to adjust to cultures other than his or her own (Brislin, 1981; Gudykunst, 1993; Triandis, 1977). A person who is high in self-awareness or self-monitoring is likely to be sensitive to the expressions and self-presentation of his or her counterparts in intercultural communication, and knows how to use these behavioral cues to guide his or her own self-presentation (Berger & Douglas, 1982; Chen, 1995b; Gudykunst, Yang, & Nishida, 1987; Hammer, 1989).

The factors that account for self-awareness or self-monitoring include (a) concern with the social appropriateness of one's self-presentation, (b) attention to social comparison information as cues to situationally appropriate expressive self-presentation, (c) the ability to control and modify one's self-presentation, (d) the use of this ability in particular situations, and (e) the modification of one's expressive behavior to meet the requirements of particular situations (Snyder, 1974, 1979, 1987). These factors play important roles in the process of intercultural communication (Gudykunst & Ting-Toomey, 1988; Trubisky, Ting-Toomey, & Lin, 1991).

Cultural awareness refers to an understanding of the conventions of one's own and others' cultures that affect how people think and behave. This includes understanding the commonalities of human behavior and differences in cultural patterns. Based on some of the universal commonalities of human behavior, such as eye contact, turn taking, gesturing, and the use of politeness norms, an individual can begin to understand how people from diverse cultures adapt such universal behaviors to the unique expectations of intercultural communication settings (Bond, 1988; Brown, 1991; Fiske, 1992; John, 1990; Kiesler, 1983; Schwartz, 1990; Schwartz & Bilsky, 1987; Schwartz & Sagiv, 1995; Strack & Lorr, 1990; White, 1980). The process of becoming culturally aware promotes not only the understanding of cultural variability but also positive feelings toward the search for a common ground of multicultural coexistence. Cross-cultural understanding alerts individuals as to those points where differences come into play.

Thus, understanding the dimensions of cultural variability provides ways of identifying how communication differs across cultures. In important studies on the dimensions of cultural variability, Parsons (1981) has identified five pattern variables, Kluckhohn and Strodtbeck (1960) have identified five cultural value orientations, Hall (1976) has labeled cultures as high-context or low-context, and Hofstede (1980) has named four dimensions of cultural variability.

Because all cultures tend to favor particular ways of processing the data around us, misunderstandings concerning these differing thought patterns often lead to problems in intercultural communication. Therefore, to be effective in intercultural interaction, an individual must first learn how arguments are supported and knowledge is determined in the culture in which he or she will be interacting (Glenn & Glenn, 1981; Harris & Moran, 1987; Oliver, 1962). In other words, before a person can modify his or her communication patterns to be congruent with the cues given by unfamiliar interactants, he or she must understand any cultural differences that exist (Hall, 1959; Hall & Whyte, 1963). If interactants change their behaviors to be congruent with those of their culturally different counterparts, they may improve their chances of reaching mutual understanding and of maintaining a fruitful multicultural coexistence. Many studies have tried to identify the myriad ways in which cultures differ (Althen, 1992; Barnlund & Yoshioka, 1990; Chang & Holt, 1991; Chen & Chung, 1994; L. Chen, 1993; Cocroft & Ting-Toomey, 1994; Fitch, 1994; Goldman, 1994; Hecht, Sedano, & Ribeau, 1993; Ishii, 1992; Ishii & Bruneau, 1994; Kim & Wilson, 1994; Klopf, 1992; H. Ma, 1990; R. Ma, 1992; Marriott, 1993; Martin, Hecht, & Larkey, 1994; Stewart & Bennett, 1991; Suzuki & Rancer, 1994; Ting-Toomey, 1991; White & Barnet, 1995).

The development of cultural awareness resembles the idea of making a "cultural map" or "cultural theme"; the emphasis is on the importance of cultural knowledge for competent intercultural communication. Kluckhohn (1948) asserts that cultural awareness requires an understanding of a "cultural map": "If a map is accurate, and you can read it, you won't get lost; if you know a culture, you'll know your way around in the life of a society" (p. 28). Turner (1968) indicates that to be aware of a culture means that one understands the "cultural theme"—the thread that goes through a culture and organizes it as a recognizable system. The theme acts as a guide for people's thinking and behavior, and appears repeatedly in daily life.

The key components of a cultural map or theme that affect intercultural communication competence include social values, social customs, social norms, and social systems. Studies by Abe and Wiseman (1983), Chen (1989), Hammer et al. (1978), Jain and Kussman (1994), Lustig and Koester (1993), Martin (1987, 1989), and Yum (1988) have shown that intercultural communication competence requires an understanding of these cultural components. As more than one cultural identity comes into play, maps are overlaid on other maps, and themes upon themes.

To summarize, individuals tend to be more competent in intercultural communication as they acquire greater degrees of cultural awareness and self-awareness. Self-awareness involves knowledge of one's own personal identity; cultural awareness involves understanding how cultures vary. Both combine to provide a framework for communication competence in a global society (Barnlund, 1994).

The Behavioral Process: Intercultural Adroitness

The behavioral perspective of intercultural communication competence stresses how to act effectively in intercultural interactions. Intercultural adroitness, the ability to get the job done and attain communication goals in intercultural interactions, comes into play. Intercultural adroitness corresponds to communication skills. It consists of those verbal and nonverbal behaviors that enable us to be effective in interactions. Such behaviors in intercultural communication include message skills, appropriate self-disclosure, behavioral flexibility, interaction management, and social skills.

Message skills, in the context of intercultural communication, refers to the ability to use the language of a culture other than one's own. Intercultural communication competence begins with message skills, which include the following: linguistic competence, or the knowledge of the rules underlying the use of language (Chomsky, 1965); the ability to code skillfully and to create recognizable messages in the process of communication (M. Kim, 1994; Y. Y. Kim, 1994b; Milhouse, 1993; Parks, 1976; Weber, 1994); the ability to understand one's counterpart's language; and the ability to recognize the meanings of nonverbal behaviors (Anderson, 1994; Barna, 1994; Dolphin, 1994). Many studies have shown that fluency in the other culture's language is the key element in effective intercultural interaction (Deutsch & Won, 1963; Giles, 1977; Martin & Hammer, 1989; Morris, 1960; Selltiz, Christ, Havel, & Cook, 1963; Sewell & Davidsen, 1956; Ting-Toomey & Korzenny, 1989).

Besides language itself, message skills include the ability to use descriptive and supportive messages in the process of interaction. The use of descriptive messages entails the use of concrete and specific feedback as opposed to judgment of another's behaviors. Nonjudgmental attitudes help interactants to avoid defensive reactions from their counterparts (Bochner & Kelly, 1974; Gibb, 1961; Hammer, 1989). Supportiveness is the sine qua non for effective communication. It is important for communicators to know how to support others effectively and to reward them in communication with cues such as head nods, eye contact, facial expressions, and physical proximity (Olebe & Koester, 1989; Parks, 1985, 1994; Ruben, 1976, 1977, 1988; Spitzberg, 1991; Wiemann, 1977).

Message skills are tempered by self-disclosure, or the willingness to reveal information about oneself openly and appropriately to one's counterparts during intercultural interactions. What is considered appropriate self-disclosure varies among cultures, as do appropriate topics of conversation and appropriate forms of address for persons at varying levels of intimacy and at given levels of social hierarchy (Chen, 1995a; Nakanishi, 1987; Nakanishi & Johnson, 1993). In addition, to be classified as self-disclosure, messages must be intentional and the information revealed to others must be significant and previously unknown to them (Adler & Towne, 1993). Appropriate self-disclosure is one of the main elements of individual competence in communication, and can lead to achievement of personal communication goals (Bochner & Kelly, 1974; Spitzberg, 1991).

The contextual ambiguity common in interactions between people from different cultures produces a predictably high level of uncertainty (Gudykunst, 1985). Reduction of this uncertainty level can often be achieved through mutual self-disclosure. Studies have demonstrated appropriate self-disclosure to be one of the components of intercultural communication competence, especially regarding depth and breadth of self-disclosure (Chen, 1989, 1990, 1993b). This finding helps to illustrate the social penetration model, wherein relationships develop from superficial to more personal levels through the depth and breadth of information individuals disclose (Altman & Taylor, 1973; Gudykunst & Nishida, 1983, 1986; Knapp, 1978).

Behavioral flexibility is the ability to select appropriate behaviors in different contexts and situations (Bochner & Kelly, 1974). This concept makes up the creativity or flexibility dimension of intercultural communication competence. Behaviorally flexible persons are accurate and adaptable when attending to information, and are able to perform different behavioral strategies in order to achieve communication goals (Parks, 1985). Behavioral flexibility is considered a dimension of intercultural communication competence (Chen, 1992; Imahori & Lanigan, 1989; Martin, 1987; Martin & Hammer, 1989; Ruben, 1977; Spitzberg, 1994; Wiemann, 1977). It is expressed through verbal immediacy cues; behaviorally flexible individuals know how to use different kinds of intimate verbal behaviors to establish interpersonal relationships. Moreover, behaviorally flexible persons must be good at "the alternation and co-occurrence of specific speech choices which mark the status and affiliative relationships of interactants" (Wiemann, 1977, p. 199).

Interaction management is the ability to speak in turn in conversation and to initiate and terminate conversation appropriately. This encompasses also the ability to structure and maintain the procedure of a conversation (Spitzberg & Cupach, 1984), or the ability to develop a topic smoothly in interaction. Individuals with good interaction management skills allow all participants in a discussion the chance to contribute. Interaction management is one of the major dimensions of intercultural communication competence (Chen, 1989; Olebe & Koester, 1989; Ruben & Kealey, 1979; Spitzberg, 1994). Guidelines for effective management of interactions in U.S. culture include the following, summarized by Wiemann (1977): (a) Interruptions are not permitted, (b) only one person may talk at a time, (c) speakers' turns should be appropriately interchanged, and (d) speakers should pay full attention to their counterparts. These standards do not apply to all cultures, clearly; for instance, African and African American interaction rules allow two speakers to talk at one time, at least briefly, during shifts between speakers (Sanders, 1995). Moreover, the African American tradition of "call and response" may be falsely interpreted by European Americans as "interruption"; rather, it represents the cocreation of messages.

Communication skills also include such social skills as empathy and identity maintenance. Empathy, or the ability to feel the same emotions as another person (Adler & Towne, 1993), has been long recognized as a central element of effective interpersonal communication. This ability has also been called "affective sensitivity" (Campbell, Kagan, & Krathwohl, 1971), "telepathic or intuition sensitivity" (Gardner, 1962), and "perspective taking" (Parks, 1976). Empathic persons are able to judge accurately their communication counterparts' behavior or internal states (Parks, 1994). Empathic individuals are usually able to respond accurately to the feelings and thoughts of those with whom they are interacting, and so this trait is highly valuable in intercultural communication (Chen, 1992; Chen & Tan, 1995; Ruben, 1976, 1977). In interaction, empathic persons generally demonstrate reciprocity of affect displays, verbal responses that show understanding, and active listening. Empathy is viewed as one of the elements of intercultural communication competence (Bennett, 1979, 1986; Gudykunst, 1993; Hwang, Chase, & Kelly, 1980; Yum, 1988).

Identity maintenance refers to the ability to maintain one's counterpart's identity in interaction. Because the need to learn who we are is one of the reasons we communicate with others, communicatively competent persons not only understand themselves in interaction but also inform their counterparts about who they are. Thus, in order to achieve smooth interaction, a communicatively competent person maintains his or her counterpart's identity. The skill of identity maintenance is learned through experience, and the use of identity maintenance skills varies with different situations and different personal goals (Collier, 1989; Parks, 1976; Ting-Toomey, 1989, 1993) and with movement from one salient identity to another.

To summarize, individuals become more competent in intercultural communication as they improve their degree of intercultural adroitness, which involves message skills, knowledge regarding appropriate self-disclosure, behavioral flexibility, interaction management, and social skills. The behavioral perspective of intercultural communication competence emphasizes the ability to act effectively to achieve the goal of multicultural interdependence and interconnectedness in the global village.

The three perspectives of the intercultural communication competence model described above form the three sides of an equilateral triangle. All are equally important, and all are inseparable, forming a holistic picture of intercultural communication competence. The model integrates different approaches to the study of intercultural communication competence specified by scholars (Collier, 1989; Dinges, 1983). It provides a guideline for future research in this area.

CRITIQUE AND
DIRECTIONS FOR FUTURE RESEARCH

Since the germination of the field of intercultural communication in the early 1950s, communication scholars have continued to search for better models to explain the concept of intercultural communication competence. After more than four decades, communication scholars have produced an abundance of literature in this line of research. Unfortunately, however, this literature is fragmentary and lacks a holistic view. Conceptually, scholars in the area of intercultural communication competence have been unable to provide a consistent framework for an understanding of the notion of inter-dependence and interconnectedness of the complex multicultural dynamics in the contemporary age. Operationally, they have failed to provide a clear direction for the development of a valid and reliable intercultural communi-cation competence instrument that is appropriate to our current global society.

The problem originates in the lack of a proper interpretation of global interaction processes. The trends of technology development, globalization of the economy, widespread population migrations, development of multicul-turalism, and the demise of the nation-state in favor of sub- and supranational identifications have shrunk and multiculturalized the world, and traditional perceptions of *self* and *other* must be redefined. The global context of human communication and the need to pursue a state of multicultural coexistence require that we abolish the boundaries separating *me* and *you, us* and *them,* and develop a theory of communication competence that takes into account individuals' multiple identities. Although a few researchers have shown interest in this line of research (Casmir, 1993; Collier, 1989; Collier & Thomas, 1988; Hecht & Ribeau, 1991; Starosta & Olorunnisola, 1995), the study of intercultural communication must take it one step further.

In addition to this philosophical issue, the study of intercultural communi-cation competence has other problems. We describe below some of the specific areas scholars should address in future research.

At the conceptual level, intercultural communication competence scholars face five challenges. First, as the concept of intercultural communication competence grows more sophisticated, it becomes confused with the defini-tion of the term *competence*. Argument continues as to whether competence is an inherent ability (trait) or a learned ability (state). Although we under-stand *competence* to refer to personal attributes and to communication skills, future research needs to figure out whether trait competence and state com-petence can be treated separately or must be considered together.

The second challenge for the study of communication competence centers on whether *competence* refers to knowledge or performance. Chomsky (1965) considers competence to be simply the knowledge of the speaker-hearer's language, and Phillips (1983) considers Chomsky's competence to be merely the first step toward communication competence. He conceives of compe-tence as the understanding of a new situation and its requirements. Chomsky and Phillips treat competence as an individual's knowledge. Although McCroskey (1982) and Spitzberg (1983) further identify distinctions among motivation, knowledge, and skills for the conceptualization of communication competence, the existing definitions suffer from a degree of incompleteness, especially when we apply the concept to intercultural settings, in which we have to consider that the process of communication demands not only situational knowledge but behavioral skills as well. Future research ought to include both knowledge and performance as elements of intercultural communication competence.

Third, the confusion between the terms *effectiveness* and *competence* must be resolved if we are to arrive at a clear conception of communication competence. Many scholars use the word *effectiveness* instead of *competence* (e.g., Hammer et al., 1978; Ruben, 1988). Others use *effectiveness* and *competence* interchangeably (e.g., Ruben, 1976, 1977; Ruben & Kealey, 1979). Usage of these terms should be standardized in future studies. We believe that *competence* is the preferable word, especially in intercultural communication settings. As we have indicated, effectiveness is only one of two elements in a conceptualization of competence. The second, appropriateness, plays a role of equal significance. In other words, to be competent in intercultural interaction, individuals must communicate both effectively and appropriately.

Fourth, culture-general versus culture-specific approaches to the study of intercultural communication competence continue to be a problem. Most of the existing research on intercultural communication competence has taken a culture-general approach. The current trend in this line of research strongly demands balance between the two approaches. Recent studies, for instance, have begun to examine communication competence from Chinese, Indian, Japanese, and Korean perspectives (Chen, 1993a; Hegde, 1993; Miyahara, 1993; Yum, 1993). A coherent theme around which these researchers conceptualize communication competence is "harmony," which appears to be an element of most Asian cultures. Studying intercultural communication competence from a culture-specific perspective in order to find common themes within cultures may shed new light on the field.

Finally, the application of studies in intercultural communication competence has been confined mainly to the intercultural adaptation process of sojourning in a new culture. We suggest that the scope of intercultural communication cannot be divorced from the full scope of the communication environment of the global civic culture, which can be conceptualized as having interpersonal, group, organizational, national, and supranational levels.

On the operational level, we face three challenges. First, we have to clarify where intercultural communication competence resides. Ruben (1989) proposes three alternatives:

1. The message sender alternative claims that competence is what an individual displays or possesses.
2. The message receiver alternative claims that competence is based on the evaluation of the message receiver, no matter what the sender possesses.

3. The dyadic, systemic, or culture-based alternative claims that competence is based on relational, social, or cultural rules instead of on an individual such as the sender or the receiver.

The Western cultural orientation to the study of intercultural communication competence tends to focus on the first two of these alternatives. Other cultures, such as Asian cultures, seem to focus more on the third alternative. For instance, the measurement of communication competence from the Japanese cultural perspective seems to focus on the concept of "group" as a unit of analysis (Miyahara, 1994); from the Korean cultural perspective, communication competence tends to be observed from an interpersonal rather than an individual point of view (Yum, 1994).

Second, we must decide how intercultural communication competence should be assessed. Use of self-report scales, other-report scales, or the two together remains possible. If intercultural communication competence is a product of personal attributes and behavioral skills, then both self- and other-report methods should be used. Yet, although the use of both methods in combination assures the external validity of the data, it becomes difficult to bridge any discrepancy between the self- and other-report measures unless a more acceptable scale is created. This problem becomes critical in an intercultural communication setting. For example, people from different cultures may have different perceptions of or attitudes toward the processes and instruments used in the study, including scale items and how to use particular scales (Campbell, 1969; Klopf & Cambra, 1983; Martin, 1993).

Third, and finally, how should we measure intercultural communication competence? Although we have proposed three perspectives from which to view the measurement of intercultural communication competence, we can clearly see that the existing literature in this area strongly reflects a Eurocentric point of view. This Western bias has caused a reliance on the positivism tradition, which in turn identifies a set of Western-oriented elements as the components of intercultural communication competence. We urge future researchers to try to discover more and different elements to account for intercultural communication competence from non-Western cultural perspectives. For instance, instead of following the above components of intercultural communication competence, Chen (1994) notes that the four elements of communication competence from the Chinese cultural perspective are the ability to control emotion, the ability to express feelings indirectly, the ability to save another's face, and the ability to recognize distinctions in relations with in-group members versus relations with out-group members. Similarly, Yum (1994) identifies five elements that can be used to measure communication competence from the Korean cultural perspective: empathy, sensitivity, indirectness, being reserved, and transcendentality. Thus, an instrument that is sufficient for the measurement of intercultural communication competence may have to account for multiple voices, multiple competencies, and multiple identities.

SUMMARY AND CONCLUSION

As we encounter ever greater cultural and co-cultural diversity, the careful study of intercultural communication competence becomes increasingly important. Only through competent intercultural communication can persons from different cultures understand each other. Sitaram and Cogdell (1976) proclaim, "All people of the world should study intercultural communication." This broad dictum emphasizes the necessity for all of us to learn more about ourselves and members of cultures other than our own.

Communication competence has been studied for many years, but its application to intercultural interaction continues to evolve. In this chapter we have extracted three perspectives on intercultural communication competence from the existing literature. We have considered how the *competence* relates to the intercultural setting. The six types of competence discussed in this chapter—fundamental, social, interpersonal, linguistic, communicative, and relational—can be treated as interdependent dimensions of communication competence. We have also argued that culture and communication competence are inseparable.

The approaches to the study of intercultural communication competence discussed above lead to a three-perspective model: (a) The *affective* perspective represents intercultural sensitivity, promoted through positive self-concept, open-mindedness, nonjudgmental attitudes, and social relaxation; (b) the *cognitive* perspective represents cultural awareness, which includes self-awareness and the understanding of one's own and others' cultures; and (c) the *behavioral* perspective represents intercultural adroitness based on message skills, appropriate self-disclosure, behavioral flexibility, interaction management, and social skills. We have proposed directions for future research along these lines, focusing on the conceptual and operational problems that scholars face.

The indispensability of intercultural communication competence in our increasingly global society demands that communication scholars enhance the functions of the concept and expand the scope of research in this area. The study of intercultural communication competence should be extended to include research concerning the multiple identities that individuals maintain in our interdependent and interconnected global society. The scope of intercultural communication competence should penetrate different levels of intercultural communication to ensure the integration of various communication demands in terms of culture, ethnicity, race, gender, and religion. These processes will require a functional and theoretical reorientation for the study of intercultural communication competence (Taylor, 1994).

REFERENCES

Abe, H., & Wiseman, R. L. (1983). A cross-cultural confirmation of the dimensions of intercultural effectiveness. *International Journal of Intercultural Relations, 7,* 53-67.

Adler, N. J. (1991). *International dimensions of organizational behavior.* Belmont, CA: Wadsworth.

Adler, P. (1975). The transnational experience: An alternative view of culture shock. *Journal of Humanistic Psychology, 15,* 13-23.

Adler, P. (1977). Beyond cultural identity: Reflections upon cultural and multicultural man. In R. Brislin (Ed.), *Culture learning: Concepts, applications, and research.* Honolulu: University of Hawaii Press.

Adler, P. (1982). Beyond cultural identity: Reflections on cultural and multicultural man. In L. A. Samovar & R. E. Porter (Eds.), *Intercultural communication: A reader* (pp. 389-405). Belmont, CA: Wadsworth.

Adler, R. B., & Towne, N. (1993). *Looking out/looking in.* New York: Harcourt Brace Jovanovich.

Allen, R. R., & Wood, B. S. (1978). Beyond reading and writing to communication competence. *Communication Education, 27,* 286-292.

Althen, G. (1992). The Americans have to say everything. *Communication Quarterly, 40,* 413-421.

Altman, I., & Taylor, D. (1973). *Social penetration: The development of interpersonal relationships.* New York: Holt, Rinehart & Winston.

Anderson, J. W. (1994). A comparison of Arab and American conceptions of "effective" persuasion. In L. A. Samovar & R. E. Porter (Eds.), *Intercultural communication: A reader* (pp. 104-113). Belmont, CA: Wadsworth.

Argyris, C. (1965a). Explorations in interpersonal competence, I. *Journal of Applied Behavioral Science, 1,* 58-83.

Argyris, C. (1965b). Explorations in interpersonal competence, II. *Journal of Applied Behavioral Science, 1,* 255-269.

Asante, M. K., Newmark, E., & Blake, C. A. (1979). *Handbook of intercultural communication.* Beverly Hills, CA: Sage.

Barna, L. M. (1994). Intercultural communication stumbling blocks. In L. A. Samovar & R. E. Porter (Eds.), *Intercultural communication: A reader* (pp. 337-346). Belmont, CA: Wadsworth.

Barnlund, D. C. (1994). Communication in a global village. In L. A. Samovar & R. E. Porter (Eds.), *Intercultural communication: A reader* (pp. 95-103). Belmont, CA: Wadsworth.

Barnlund, D. C., & Yoshioka, M. (1990). Apologies: Japanese and American styles. *International Journal of Intercultural Relations, 14,* 193-206.

Belay, G. (1993). Toward a paradigm shift for intercultural and international communication: New research directions. In S. A. Deetz (Ed.), *Communication yearbook 16* (pp. 437-457). Newbury Park, CA: Sage.

Bennett, M. J. (1979). Overcoming the golden rule: Sympathy and empathy. In D. Nimmo (Ed.), *Communication yearbook 3* (pp. 407-433). New Brunswick, NJ: Transaction.

Bennett, M. J. (1986). A developmental approach to training for intercultural sensitivity. *International Journal of Intercultural Relations, 10,* 179-196.

Berger, C. R., & Douglas, W. (1982). Thought and talk: Excuse me, "but have I been talking to myself?" In F. E. X. Dance (Ed.), *Human communication theory: Comparative essays* (pp. 42-60). New York: Harper & Row.

Bhawuk, D. P. S., & Brislin, R. (1992). The measurement of intercultural sensitivity using the concepts of individualism and collectivism. *International Journal of Intercultural Relations, 16,* 413-436.

Bochner, A. P., & Kelly, C. W. (1974). Interpersonal competence: Rationale, philosophy, and implementation of a conceptual framework. *Speech Teacher, 23,* 279-301.

Bond, M. H. (1988). Finding universal dimensions of individual variation in multicultural studies of values: The Rokeach and Chinese value surveys. *Journal of Personality and Social Psychology, 55,* 1009-1015.

Boulding, E. (1988). *Building a global civic culture: Education for an interdependent world.* New York: Columbia University Press.

Brislin, R. W. (1981). *Cross-cultural encounters: Face-to-face interaction.* Elmsford, NY: Pergamon.

Brislin, R. W., Landis, D., & Brandt, M. E. (1983). Conceptualizations of intercultural behavior and training. In D. Landis & R. W. Brislin (Eds.), *Handbook of intercultural training: Vol. 1. Issues in theory and design* (pp. 1-35). Elmsford, NY: Pergamon.

Brown, D. E. (1991). *Human universals.* Philadelphia: Temple University Press.

Campbell, D. T. (1969). Reforms as experiments. *American Psychologist, 24,* 409-429.

Campbell, R. J., Kagan, N., & Krathwohl, D. R. (1971). The development and validation of a scale to measure affective sensitivity (empathy). *Journal of Counseling Psychology, 18,* 407-412.

Casmir, F. L. (1993). Third-culture building: A paradigm shift for international and intercultural communication. In S. A. Deetz (Ed.), *Communication yearbook 16* (pp. 407-428). Newbury Park, CA: Sage.

Chang, H. C., & Holt, G. R. (1991). More than relationship: Chinese interaction and the principle of Kuan-Hsi. *Communication Quarterly, 39,* 251-271.

Chen, G.-M. (1989). Relationships of the dimensions of intercultural communication competence. *Communication Quarterly, 37,* 118-133.

Chen, G.-M. (1990). Intercultural communication competence: Some perspectives of research. *Howard Journal of Communications, 2,* 243-261.

Chen, G.-M. (1992). A test of intercultural communication competence. *Intercultural Communication Studies, 2,* 63-82.

Chen, G.-M. (1993a, November). *Communication competence: A Chinese perspective.* Paper presented at the annual meeting of the Speech Communication Association, Miami, FL.

Chen, G.-M. (1993b). Self-disclosure and Asian students' abilities to cope with social difficulties in the United States. *Journal of Psychology, 127,* 603-610.

Chen, G.-M. (1994, November). *A conceptualization and measurement of communication competence: A Chinese perspective.* Paper presented at the annual meeting of the Speech Communication Association, New Orleans.

Chen, G.-M. (1995a). Differences in self-disclosure patterns among Americans versus Chinese: A comparative study. *Journal of Cross-Cultural Psychology, 26,* 84-91.

Chen, G.-M. (1995b). A model of intercultural communication competence. *Mass Communication Research, 50,* 81-95.

Chen, G.-M., & Chung, J. (1994). The impact of Confucianism on organizational communication. *Communication Quarterly, 42,* 93-105.

Chen, G.-M., & Tan, L. (1995, April). *A theory of intercultural sensitivity.* Paper presented at the annual meeting of the Eastern Communication Association, Pittsburgh, PA.

Chen, L. (1993). Chinese and North Americans: An epistemological exploration of intercultural communication. *Howard Journal of Communications, 4,* 342-357.

Chomsky, N. (1965). *Aspects of the theory of syntax.* Cambridge: MIT Press.

Cleveland, H., Mangone, G. J., & Adams, J. C. (1960). *The overseas Americans.* New York: McGraw-Hill.

Cocroft, B. K., & Ting-Toomey, S. (1994). Facework in Japan and the United States. *International Journal of Intercultural Relations, 18,* 469-506.

Collier, M. J. (1989). Cultural and intercultural communication competence: Current approaches and directions for future research. *International Journal of Intercultural Relations, 13,* 287-302.

Collier, M. J. (1994). Cultural identity and intercultural communication. In L. A. Samovar & R. E. Porter (Eds.), *Intercultural communication: A reader* (pp. 36-44). Belmont, CA: Wadsworth.

Collier, M. J., & Thomas, M. (1988). Cultural identity: An interpretive perspectives. In Y. Y. Kim & W. B. Gudykunst (Eds.), *Theories in intercultural communication* (pp. 99-120). Newbury Park, CA: Sage.

Cupach, W. R., & Imahori, T. T. (1993). Identity management theory: Communication competence in intercultural episodes and relationships. In R. L. Wiseman & J. Koester (Eds.), *Intercultural communication competence* (pp. 112-131). Newbury Park, CA: Sage.

David, K. (1972). Intercultural adjustment and applications of reinforcement theory to problems of culture shock. *Trends, 4,* 1-64.

Deutsch, S. E., & Won, G. Y. M. (1963). Some factors in the adjustment of foreign nationals in the United States. *Journal of Social Issues, 19,* 115-122.

Dinges, N. (1983). Intercultural competence. In D. Landis & R. W. Brislin (Eds.), *Handbook of intercultural training: Vol. 1. Issues in theory and design* (pp. 176-202). Elmsford, NY: Pergamon.

Dolphin, C. Z. (1994). Variables in the use of personal space in intercultural transactions. In L. A. Samovar & R. E. Porter (Eds.), *Intercultural communication: A reader* (pp. 252-263). Belmont, CA: Wadsworth.

Ehrlich, H. (1973). *The social psychology of prejudice.* New York: John Wiley.

Fiedler, F., Mitchell, T., & Triandis, H. (1971). The culture assimilator: An approach to cross-cultural training. *Journal of Applied Psychology, 55,* 95-102.

Fiske, A. P. (1992). The four elementary forms of sociality: Framework for a unified theory of social relations. *Psychological Review, 99,* 689-723.

Fitch, K. L. (1994). A cross-cultural study of directive sequences and some implications for compliance-gaining research. *Communication Monographs, 61,* 185-210.

Foote, N. N., & Cottrell, L. S. (1955). *Identity and interpersonal competence.* Chicago: University of Chicago Press.

Frederick, H. H. (1993). *Global communication and international relations.* Belmont, CA: Wadsworth.

Furnham, A., & Bochner, S. (1982). Social difficulty in foreign cultures: An empirical analysis of culture shock. In S. Bochner (Ed.), *Cultures in contact: Studies in cross-cultural interaction.* Elmsford, NY: Pergamon.

Gardner, G. H. (1962). Cross-cultural communication. *Journal of Social Psychology, 58,* 241-256.

Geertz, C. (1973). *The interpretation of cultures: Selected essays.* New York: Basic Books.

Getter, H., & Nowinski, J. K. (1981). A free response test of interpersonal effectiveness. *Journal of Personality Assessment, 45,* 301-308.

Gibb, J. (1961). Defensive communication. *Journal of Communication, 11,* 141-148.

Giles, H. (Ed.). (1977). *Language, ethnicity, and intergroup.* London: Academic Press.

Glenn, E. S., & Glenn, C. G. (1981). *Man and mankind: Conflict and communication between cultures.* Norwood, NJ: Ablex.

Goldman, A. (1994). The centrality of "ningensei" to Japanese negotiating and interpersonal relationships: Implications for U.S.-Japanese communication. *International Journal of Intercultural Relations, 18,* 29-54.

Grice, H. P. (1975). Logic and conversation. In P. Cole & J. Morgan (Eds.), *Syntax and semantics 3: Speech acts* (pp. 107-142). New York: Academic Press.

Gudykunst, W. B. (1985). A model of uncertainty reduction in intercultural encounters. *Journal of Language and Social Psychology, 4,* 79-98.

Gudykunst, W. B. (1993). Toward a theory of effective interpersonal and intergroup communication: An anxiety/uncertainty management (AUM) perspective. In R. L. Wiseman & J. Koester (Eds.), *Intercultural communication competence* (pp. 33-71). Newbury Park, CA: Sage.

Gudykunst, W. B., & Hammer, M. R. (1988). Strangers and hosts: An uncertainty reduction based theory of intercultural adaptation. In Y. Y. Kim & W. B. Gudykunst (Eds.), *Cross-cultural adaptation: Current approaches* (pp. 106-139). Newbury Park, CA: Sage.

Gudykunst, W. B., Hammer, M. R., & Wiseman, R. (1977). An analysis of an integrated approach to cross-cultural training. *International Journal of Intercultural Relations, 2,* 99-110.

Gudykunst, W. B., & Nishida, T. (1983). Social penetration in Japanese and American close friendships. In R. Bostrom (Ed.), *Communication yearbook 7* (pp. 592-610). Beverly Hills, CA: Sage.

Gudykunst, W. B., & Nishida, T. (1986). The influence of cultural variability on perceptions of communication behavior associated with relationship terms. *Human Communication Research, 13,* 147-166.

Gudykunst, W. B., & Ting-Toomey, S. (1988). Affective communication across cultures. *American Behavioral Scientist, 31,* 384-400.

Gudykunst, W. B., Ting-Toomey, S., & Wiseman, R. (1991). Taming the beast: Designing a course in intercultural communication. *Communication Quarterly, 40,* 272-286.

Gudykunst, W. B., Wiseman, R., & Hammer, M. R. (1977). Determinants of a sojourner's attitudinal satisfaction: A path model. In B. D. Ruben (Ed.), *Communication yearbook 1* (pp. 415-425). New Brunswick, NJ: Transaction.

Gudykunst, W. B., Yang, S. M., & Nishida, T. (1987). Cultural differences in self-consciousness and unself-consciousness. *Communication Research, 14,* 7-36.

Guthrie, G. (1975), A behavioral analysis of culture learning. In R. W. Brislin, S. Bochner, & W. J. Lonner (Eds.), *Cross-cultural perspectives on learning.* New York: John Wiley.

Hall, E. T. (1959). *The silent language.* Garden City, NY: Doubleday.

Hall, E. T. (1966). *The hidden dimension.* Garden City, NY: Anchor.

Hall, E. T. (1976). *Beyond culture.* Garden City, NY: Anchor.

Hall, E. T., & Whyte, W. F. (1963). Intercultural communication: A guide to men of action. *Practical Anthropology, 9,* 83-108.

Hammer, M. R. (1987). Behavioral dimensions of intercultural effectiveness: A replication and extension. *International Journal of Intercultural Relations, 11,* 65-88.

Hammer, M. R. (1988, November). *Communication skills and intercultural communication competence: A review and research agenda.* Paper presented at the annual meeting of the Speech Communication Association, New Orleans.

Hammer, M. R. (1989). Intercultural communication competence. In M. K. Asante & W. B. Gudykunst (Eds.), *Handbook of international and intercultural communication* (pp. 247-260). Newbury Park, CA: Sage.

Hammer, M. R., Gudykunst, W., & Wiseman, R. (1978). Dimensions of intercultural effectiveness. *International Journal of Intercultural Relations, 2,* 382-393.

Harris, J. G. (1973). A science of the South Pacific: An analysis of the character structure of the Peace Corp volunteer. *American Psychologist, 28,* 232-247.

Harris, P. R., & Moran, R. T. (1987). *Managing cultural differences.* Houston: Gulf.

Hart, R. P., & Burks, D. M. (1972). Rhetorical sensitivity and social interaction. *Speech Monographs, 39,* 75-91.

Hawes, F., & Kealey, D. J. (1979). *Canadians in development: An empirical study of adaptation and effectiveness on overseas assignment* (Technical report). Ottawa: Canadian International Development Agency.

Hawes, F., & Kealey, D. J. (1981). An empirical study of Canadian technical assistance. *International Journal of Intercultural Relations, 5,* 239-258.

Hecht, M. L., & Ribeau, S. (1991). Sociocultural roots of ethnic identity: A look at black America. *Journal of Black Studies, 21,* 501-513.

Hecht, M. L., Sedano, M. V., & Ribeau, S. R. (1993). Understanding culture, communication, and research: Applications to Chicanos and Mexican Americans. *International Journal of Intercultural Relations, 17,* 157-166.

Hegde, R. (1993, November). *Communication competence: An Indian perspective.* Paper presented at the annual meeting of the Speech Communication Association, Miami, FL.

Herman, S., & Schield, E. (1961). The stranger group in cross-cultural situations. *Sociometry, 24,* 165-176.

Hofstede, G. (1980). *Culture's consequences: International differences in work-related values.* Beverly Hills, CA: Sage.

Holland, J. L., & Baird, L. L. (1968). An interpersonal competence scale. *Educational and Psychological Measurement, 28,* 503-510.

Hwang, J. C., Chase, L. J., & Kelly, C. W. (1980). An intercultural examination of communication competence. *Communication, 9,* 70-79.

Hymes, D. (1971). Competence and performance in linguistic theory. In R. Huxley & E. Ingram (Eds.), *Language acquisition: Models and methods* (pp. 3-26). New York: Academic Press.

Hymes, D. (1972). Models of the interaction of language and social life. In J. Gumperz & D. Hymes (Eds.), *Directions in sociolinguistics: The ethnography of communication* (pp. 1-71). New York: Holt, Rinehart & Winston.

Imahori, T. T., & Lanigan, M. L. (1989). Relational model of intercultural communication competence. *International Journal of Intercultural Relations, 13,* 269-286.

Ishii, S. (1992). Buddhist preaching: The persistent main undercurrent of Japanese traditional rhetorical communication. *Communication Quarterly, 40,* 391-397.

Ishii, S., & Bruneau, T. (1994). Silence and silences in cross-cultural perspective: Japan and the United States. In L. A. Samovar & R. E. Porter (Eds.), *Intercultural communication: A reader* (246-251). Belmont, CA: Wadsworth.

Jain, N. C., & Kussman, E. D. (1994). Dominant cultural patterns of Hindus in India. In L. A. Samovar & R. E. Porter (Eds.), *Intercultural communication: A reader* (pp. 95-103). Belmont, CA: Wadsworth.

John, O. P. (1990). The "big five" factor taxonomy: Dimensions of personality in the natural language and in questionnaires. In L. A. Pervin (Ed.), *Handbook of personality: Theory and research* (pp. 66-100). New York: Guilford.

Johnston, W. B., & Packer, A. H. (1987). *Workforce 2000: Work and workers for the 21st century.* Indianapolis: Hudson Institute.

Kiesler, D. J. (1983). The 1982 interpersonal circle: A taxonomy for complementarity in human transactions. *Psychological Review, 90,* 185-214.

Kim, M. (1994). Cross-cultural comparisons of the perceived importance of conversational constraints. *Human Communication Research, 21,* 128-151.

Kim, M., & Wilson, S. R. (1994). A cross-cultural comparison of implicit theories of requesting. *Communication Monographs, 61,* 210-235.

Kim, Y. Y. (1988). *Communication and cross-cultural adaptation.* Clevedon, England: Multilingual Matters.

Kim, Y. Y. (1991). Communication and cross-cultural adaptation. In L. A. Samovar & R. E. Porter (Eds.), *Intercultural communication: A reader* (pp. 383-391). Belmont, CA: Wadsworth.

Kim, Y. Y. (1994a). Beyond cultural identity. *Intercultural Communication Studies, 4,* 1-24.

Kim, Y. Y. (1994b). Interethnic communication: The context and the behavior. In S. A. Deetz (Ed.), *Communication yearbook 17* (pp. 511-538). Thousand Oaks, CA: Sage.

Kim, Y. Y., & Gudykunst, W. B. (Eds.). (1988). *Cross-cultural adaptation: Current approaches.* Newbury Park, CA: Sage.

Klopf, D. W. (Ed.). (1992). Communication practices in the Pacific basin [Special section]. *Communication Quarterly, 40,* 368-428.

Klopf, D. W., & Cambra, R. E. (1983). Communication apprehension in foreign settings: The results of exploratory research. *Communication, 12,* 37-51.

Kluckhohn, C. (1948). *Mirror of man.* New York: McGraw-Hill.

Kluckhohn, C., & Strodtbeck, F. (1960). *Variations in value orientations.* New York: Row, Peterson.

Knapp, M. (1978). *Social intercourse: From greetings to goodbye.* Boston: Allyn & Bacon.

Lee, L. (1979). Is social competence independent of cultural context? *American Psychologist, 34,* 795-796.

Lustig, M. W., & Koester, J. (1993). *Intercultural competence: Interpersonal communication across cultures.* New York: HarperCollins.

Ma, H. K. (1990). The Chinese Taoistic perspective on human development. *International Journal of Intercultural Relations, 14,* 235-250.

Ma, R. (1992). The role of unofficial intermediaries in interpersonal conflicts in the Chinese culture. *Communication Quarterly, 40,* 269-278.

Marriott, H. (1993). Politeness phenomena in Japanese intercultural business communication. *Intercultural Communication Studies, 3,* 15-38.

Martin, J. N. (1987). The relationships between student sojourner perceptions of intercultural competencies and previous sojourn experience. *International Journal of Intercultural Relations, 11,* 337-355.

Martin, J. N. (Ed.). (1989). Intercultural communication competence [Special issue]. *International Journal of Intercultural Relations, 13*(3).

Martin, J. N. (1993). Intercultural communication competence: A review. In R. L. Wiseman & J. Koester (Eds.), *Intercultural communication competence* (pp. 16-32). Newbury Park, CA: Sage.

Martin, J. N., & Hammer, M. R. (1989). Behavioral categories of intercultural communication competence: Everyday communicators' perceptions. *International Journal of Intercultural Relations, 13,* 303-332.

Martin, J. N., Hecht, M. L., & Larkey, L. K. (1994). Conversational improvement strategies for interethnic communication: African American and European American perspectives. *Communication.Monographs, 61,* 236-255.

McCroskey, J. C. (1982). Communication competence and performance: A research and pedagogical perspective. *Communication Education, 31,* 1-7.

Mead, R. (1990). *Cross-cultural management communication.* New York: John Wiley.

Milhouse, V. H. (1993). The applicability of interpersonal communication competence to the intercultural communication context. In R. L. Wiseman & J. Koester (Eds.), *Intercultural communication competence* (pp. 184-203). Newbury Park, CA: Sage.

Miyahara, A. (1993, November). *Communication competence: A Japanese perspective.* Paper presented at the annual meeting of the Speech Communication Association, Miami, FL.

Miyahara, A. (1994, November). *A conceptualization and measurement of communication competence: A Japanese perspective.* Paper presented at the annual meeting of the Speech Communication Association, New Orleans.

Morris, R. T. (1960). *The two-way mirror: National status of foreign students' adjustment.* Minneapolis: University of Minnesota Press.

Nakanishi, M. (1987). Perceptions of self-disclosure in initial interaction: A Japanese sample. *Human Communication Research, 13,* 167-190.

Nakanishi, M., & Johnson, K. M. (1993). Implications of self-disclosure on conversational logics, perceived communication competence, and social attraction. In R. L. Wiseman & J. Koester (Eds.), *Intercultural communication competence* (pp. 168-183). Newbury Park, CA: Sage.

Nieto, S. (1992). *Affirming diversity.* New York: Longman.

Oberg, K. (1960). Culture shock: Adjustment to new cultural environments. *Practical Anthropology, 7,* 177-182.

Olebe, M., & Koester, J. (1989). Exploring the cross-cultural equivalence of the Behavioral Assessment Scale for intercultural communication. *International Journal of Intercultural Relations, 13,* 333-347.

Oliver, R. T. (1962). *Culture and communication: The problem of penetrating national and cultural boundaries.* Springfield, IL: Charles C Thomas.

Parks, M. R. (1976, December). *Communication competence.* Paper presented at the annual meeting of the Speech Communication Association, San Francisco.

Parks, M. R. (1985). Interpersonal communication and the quest for personal competence. In M. L. Knapp & G. R. Miller (Eds.), *Handbook of interpersonal communication* (pp. 171-201). Beverly Hills, CA: Sage.

Parks, M. R. (1994). Communication competence and interpersonal control. In M. L. Knapp & G. R. Miller (Eds.), *Handbook of interpersonal communication* (2nd ed., pp. 589-618). Thousand Oaks, CA: Sage.

Parsons, T. (1951). *The social system.* Glencoe, IL: Free Press.

Phillips, G. M. (1983). A competent view of "competence." *Communication Education, 33,* 25-36.

Porter, R. E., & Samovar, L. A. (1994). An introduction to intercultural communication. In L. A. Samovar & R. E. Porter (Eds.), *Intercultural communication: A reader* (pp. 4-25). Belmont, CA: Wadsworth.

Pruegger, V. J., & Rogers, T. B. (1993). Development of a scale to measure cross-cultural sensitivity in the Canadian context. *Canadian Journal of Behavioural Science, 25,* 615-621.

Randolph, G., Landis, D., & Tzeng, O. (1977). The effects of time and practice upon culture assimilator training. *International Journal of Intercultural Relations, 1,* 105-119.

Rogers, J., & Ward, C. (1993). Expectation-experience discrepancies and psychological adjustment during cross-cultural reentry. *International Journal of Intercultural Relations, 17,* 185-196.

Ruben, B. D. (1976). Assessing communication competency for intercultural adaptation. *Group and Organization Studies, 1,* 334-354.

Ruben, B. D. (1977). Guidelines for cross-cultural communication effectiveness. *Group and Organization Studies, 2,* 470-479.

Ruben, B. D. (1988). Human communication and cross-cultural effectiveness. In L. A. Samovar & R. E. Porter (Eds.), *Intercultural communication: A reader* (pp. 331-338). Belmont, CA: Wadsworth.

Ruben, B. D. (1989). The study of cross-cultural competence: Traditions and contemporary issues. *International Journal of Intercultural Relations, 13,* 229-240.

Ruben, B. D., & Kealey, D. J. (1979). Behavioral assessment of communication competency and the prediction of cross-cultural adaptation. *International Journal of intercultural Relations, 3,* 15-47.

Rubin, R. B. (1983, November). *Conceptualizing communication competence: Directions for research and instruction.* Paper presented at the annual meeting of the Speech Communication Association, Washington, DC.

Sanders, J. A., & Wiseman, R. L. (1993). Uncertainty reduction among ethnicities in the United States. *Intercultural Communication Studies, 3,* 1-14.

Sanders, O. (1995). *A multi-phase analysis of African American women's communication at a public transit setting.* Unpublished doctoral dissertation, Howard University.

Saville-Troike, M. (1982). *The ethnography of communication.* Baltimore: University Park Press.

Schwartz, S. (1990). Individualism-collectivism. *Journal of Cross-Cultural Psychology, 21,* 139-157.

Schwartz, S., & Bilsky, W. (1987). Toward a psychological structure of human values. *Journal of Personality and Social Psychology, 58,* 878-891.

Schwartz, S., & Sagiv, L. (1995). Identifying culture-specifics in the content and structure of values. *Journal of Cross-Cultural Psychology, 26,* 92-116.

Scollon, R., & Scollon, S. (1995). *Intercultural communication: A discourse approach.* Oxford: Basil Blackwell.

Searle, W., & Ward, C. (1990). The prediction of psychological and sociocultural adjustment during cross-cultural transitions. *International Journal of Intercultural Relations, 14,* 449-464.

Selltiz, C., Christ, J. R., Havel, J., & Cook, S. W. (1963). *Attitudes and social relations of foreign students in the United States.* Minneapolis: University of Minnesota Press.

Sewell, W. H., & Davidsen, O. M. (1956). The adjustment of Scandinavian students. *Journal of Social Issues, 12,* 9-19.

Sitaram, K. S., & Cogdell, R. T. (1976). *Foundations of intercultural communication.* Columbus, OH: Merrill.

Smalley, W. A. (1963). Culture shock, language shock, and the shock of self-discovery. *Practical Anthropology, 10,* 49-56.

Smith, M. B. (1966). Explorations in competence: A study of Peace Corps teachers in Ghana. *American Psychologist, 21,* 555-556.

Snyder, M. (1974). Self-monitoring of expressive behavior. *Journal of Personality and Social Psychology, 30,* 526-537.

Snyder, M. (1979). Cognitive, behavioral, and interpersonal consequences of self-monitoring. In P. Pliner, K. R. Blankenstein, I. M. Spigel, T. Alloway, & L. Krames (Eds.), *Advances in the study of communication and affect: Perception of emotion in self and others* (pp. 181-201). New York: Plenum.

Snyder, M. (1987). *Public appearances, private realities.* New York: Friedman.

Spitzberg, B. H. (1983). Communication competence as knowledge, skill, and impression. *Communication Education, 32,* 323-329.

Spitzberg, B. H. (1988, November). *Progress and pitfalls in conceptualizing and researching intercultural communication competence.* Paper presented at the annual meeting of the Speech Communication Association, New Orleans.

Spitzberg, B. H. (1989). Issues in the development of a theory of interpersonal competence in the intercultural context. *International Journal of Intercultural Relations, 13,* 241-268.

Spitzberg, B. H. (1991). Intercultural communication competence. In L. A. Samovar & R. E. Porter (Eds.), *Intercultural communication: A reader* (pp. 353-365). Belmont, CA: Wadsworth.

Spitzberg, B. H. (1994). A model of intercultural communication competence. In L. A. Samovar & R. E. Porter (Eds.), *Intercultural communication: A reader* (pp. 347-359). Belmont, CA: Wadsworth.

Spitzberg, B. H., & Cupach, W. R. (1984). *Interpersonal communication competence.* Beverly Hills, CA: Sage.

Starosta, W. J., & Olorunnisola, A. A. (1995, April). *A meta-model for third culture development.* Paper presented at the annual meeting of the Eastern Communication Association, Pittsburgh, PA.

Stephan, C. W., & Stephan, W. G. (1992). Reducing intercultural anxiety through intercultural contact. *International Journal of Intercultural Relations, 16,* 89-106.

Stewart, E. C., & Bennett, M. J. (1991). *American cultural patterns: A cross-cultural perspective.* Yarmouth, ME: Intercultural Press.

Strack, S., & Lorr, M. (1990). Three approaches to interpersonal behavior and their common factors. *Journal of Personality Assessment, 54,* 782-790.

Suzuki, S., & Rancer, A. S. (1994). Argumentativeness and verbal aggressiveness: Testing for conceptual and measurement equivalence across cultures. *Communication Monographs, 61,* 256-279.

Taylor, E. W. (1994). A learning model for becoming interculturally competent. *International Journal of Intercultural Relations, 18,* 389-408.

Ting-Toomey, S. (1989). Identity and interpersonal bond. In M. K. Asante & W. B. Gudykunst (Eds.), *Handbook of international and intercultural communication* (pp. 351-373). Newbury Park, CA: Sage.

Ting-Toomey, S. (1991). Intimacy expressions in three cultures: France, Japan, and the United States. *International Journal of Intercultural Relations, 15,* 29-46.

Ting-Toomey, S. (1993). Communication resourcefulness: An identity negotiation perspective. In R. L. Wiseman & J. Koester (Eds.), *Intercultural communication competence* (pp. 72-111). Newbury Park, CA: Sage.

Ting-Toomey, S., & Korzenny, F. (Eds.). (1989). *Language, communication, and culture: Current directions.* Newbury Park, CA: Sage.

Trenholm, S., & Rose, T. (1981). The compliant communicator: Teacher perceptions of classroom behavior. *Western Journal of Speech Communication, 45,* 13-26.

Triandis, H. C. (1976). *Interpersonal behavior.* Monterey, CA: Brooks/Cole.

Triandis, H. C. (1977). Subjective culture and interpersonal relations across cultures. In L. Loeb-Adler (Ed.), Issues in cross-cultural research [Special issue]. *Annals of the New York Academy of Sciences, 285,* 418-434.

Trubisky, P., Ting-Toomey, S., & Lin, S. (1991). The influence of individualism-collectivism and self-monitoring on conflict styles. *International Journal of Intercultural Relations, 15,* 65-84.

Turner, C. V. (1968). The Sinasina "big man" complex: A central culture theme. *Practical Anthropology, 15,* 16-23.

Ward, C., & Searle, W. (1991). The impact of value discrepancies and cultural identity on psychological and sociocultural adjustment of sojourners. *International Journal of Intercultural Relations, 15,* 209-226.

Weber, S. N. (1994). The need to be: The socio-cultural significance of black language. In L. A. Samovar & R. E. Porter (Eds.), *Intercultural communication: A reader* (pp. 221-226). Belmont, CA: Wadsworth.

Weinstein, E. A. (1969). The development of interpersonal competence. In D. A. Goslin (Ed.), *Handbook of socialization theory and research* (pp. 753-775). Chicago: Rand McNally.

White, G. M. (1980). Conceptual universals in interpersonal language. *American Anthropologist, 82,* 759-781.

White, M. I., & Barnet, S. (Eds.). (1995). *Comparing cultures: Readings on contemporary Japan for American writers.* Boston: Bedford.

White, R. W. (1959). Motivation reconsidered: The concept of competence. *Psychological Review, 66,* 297-333.

Wiemann, J. M. (1977). Explication and test of a model of communicative competence. *Human Communication Research, 3,* 195-213.

Wiemann, J. M., & Backlund, P. (1980). Current theory and research in communicative competence. *Review of Educational Research, 50,* 185-199.

Wiseman, R. L., & Abe, H. (1984). Finding and explaining differences: A reply to Gudykunst and Hammer. *International Journal of Intercultural Relations, 8,* 11-16.

Wiseman, R. L., & Koester, J. (Eds.). (1993). *Intercultural communication competence.* Newbury Park, CA: Sage.

Yum, J. O. (1988). The impact of Confucianism on interpersonal relationships and communication patterns in East Asia. *Communication Monographs, 55,* 374-388.

Yum, J. O. (1989, November). *Communication sensitivity and empathy in culturally diverse organizations.* Paper presented at the annual meeting of the Speech Communication Association, San Francisco.

Yum, J. O. (1993, November). *Communication competence: A Korean perspective.* Paper presented at the annual meeting of the Speech Communication Association, Miami, FL.

Yum, J. O. (1994, November). *A conceptualization and measurement of communication competence: A Korean perspective.* Paper presented at the annual meeting of the Speech Communication Association, New Orleans.

CHAPTER CONTENTS

10 Intercultural Communication Training: Review, Critique, and a New Theoretical Framework

AARON CASTELAN CARGILE
HOWARD GILES
University of California, Santa Barbara

This chapter offers a critical examination of the literature on intercultural communication training and a generalized model of the usually implicit process of training. Though limited, some research has tested various outcomes outlined by this model and has produced some supportive, although largely inconclusive, results. The authors argue that an array of important intergroup constituents of the training process remain obscured at best, and disregarded at worst. For instance, negative attitudes and stereotypes about the target host group can compromise attention toward, and acceptance of, much training material. Context, by means of its historical backdrop and the norms it provides, can also restrict training effectiveness. These and other intergroup dynamics can frustrate the training process and even work against the goals it seeks; indeed, boomerang effects have been documented. This chapter offers a new model of intercultural training that affords considerable theoretical status to intergroup processes.

TODAY, we live in a world where Marshall McLuhan's term "the global village" has rich significance for many people. Technology has already radically changed the shape of interaction on this planet. Every day, unprecedented numbers of people from different groups and cultures are drawn into contact, inviting promise (and also potential conflict) into our world. Such relationships can be particularly problematic if we consider their potential for *mis*communication. Having been socialized in different cultures, participants often bring to interactions radically diverse ways of communicating and understanding communication. Thus, because of both the promises

AUTHORS' NOTE: We gratefully acknowledge James J. Bradac and Diane Mackie for their constructive comments on an earlier draft. Additionally, our thanks to the editor, Brant Burleson, and three anonymous reviewers for their useful suggestions that improved this chapter.

Correspondence and requests for reprints: Aaron Castelan Cargile, Department of Communication, University of California, Santa Barbara, CA 93106-4020.

Communication Yearbook 19, pp. 385-423

and the difficulties involved in intercultural communication, scholars have taken a keen interest in the process and have developed numerous training techniques intended to help individuals interact effectively regardless of their differences. Indeed, intercultural training has long been advocated as a means of facilitating favorable and productive intercultural interactions (Brislin, 1981; Harris & Moran, 1979; Mendenhall & Oddou, 1986; Tung, 1981; Worchel & Mitchell, 1972). Those in nonacademic circles, too, have celebrated the presumed benefits (e.g., Caudron, 1991; Derderian, 1993) and have helped encourage the widespread use of training seen today.

However, as many authors point out, these techniques frequently lack theoretical grounding (Adler, 1983; Black & Mendenhall, 1990; Bochner, 1982; Brislin, 1981; Gudykunst & Hammer, 1983; Landis, Brislin, & Hulgus, 1985), and little empirical research has been conducted to determine their effectiveness (Albert, 1986; Harrison, 1992; Wexley, 1984). Nonetheless, intercultural training is being embraced by many; thus, in this chapter we take a critical look at it by reviewing the available methods and the extant empirical research on the effectiveness of these methods. Although there is a considerable literature, we shall argue that it is seriously restricted by its mere focus on culture per se. Researchers have spent their efforts trying to help trainees overcome cultural differences and have neglected the impact that fundamental *intergroup* dynamics can have on the process of cross-cultural training.[1]

A REVIEW OF TRAINING PROGRAMS

In the views of most communication scholars (e.g., Carbaugh, 1993; Condon & Yousef, 1985; Philipsen, 1989) and other researchers (e.g., Black & Mendenhall, 1990; Brislin, 1978; Triandis, 1976), intercultural interactions are more problematic than intracultural ones because the participants' behaviors are shaped by culture in ways usually not recognized. As Gudykunst and Hammer (1983) put it, the "pressures resulting from differing cultural values, communication styles, norms, and behaviors are acutely felt in the international arena of human interaction" (p. 120). In order to help people cope with these pressures and conduct intercultural interactions more effectively, programs of intercultural training have been developed. As Gudykunst and Hammer continue, "These difficulties and interpersonal conflicts that arise from the interaction of people with cultural differences occupy the central concern of intercultural training efforts" (p. 120).

By *intercultural training,* we mean, more specifically, training aimed at changing participant responses unidirectionally in order to accommodate culturally different others (see Giles, Coupland, & Coupland, 1991). In other words, intercultural training teaches people to think and behave as individuals from different cultural groups might think and behave. This includes primarily "predeparture" training for those planning to voyage abroad, but also relates importantly to many "diversity" training programs popular today (see Winterle, 1992). In both cases, awareness and understanding of cultural differences are paramount. However, diversity training usually does not emphasize unidirectional, behavioral accommodation. As Sims and Sims (1993) note, "The goal of [diversity] training is to acquaint employees with ways to increase individual, work group, and organizational effectiveness through a better appreciation and understanding of . . . diversity and difference" (p. 74). Diversity training is intended to help people understand cultural differences, but behavior is often expected to be *mutually,* not unidirectionally, accommodative. The appropriate metaphor is a team working better together, not a stranger in a strange land. Thus, in this review of intercultural training we do not expressly address the particular conditions and demands of diversity training. However, to the extent that diversity training requires participants to accommodate in their appreciation and understanding of culturally different others, many of the concerns raised here will also apply directly to aspects of diversity training.

For intercultural training as described above, then, the primary goal, broadly speaking, is to improve intercultural effectiveness (Brislin, 1989). Put another way, it is to help trainees avoid the difficulties and conflicts that can arise when individuals from different cultural groups interact. The concept of *effectiveness,* however, can be broken down to accommodate more concrete objectives. Effectiveness has been operationalized as adjustment, task effectiveness, and communication effectiveness (Blake & Heslin, 1983; Kealey & Ruben, 1983). Therefore, most intercultural training programs are designed to help trainees (a) achieve general satisfaction with their personal situations in their host countries (adjustment—as defined by Torbiörn, 1982), (b) perform better on tasks related to their occupations, and/or (c) communicate more effectively (i.e., in a way that "minimizes misunderstandings"; see Gudykunst & Kim, 1992). Of these three objectives, the goal of making communication more effective clearly assumes a position of primary importance. This is because effective communication will facilitate adjustment and task effectiveness, but adjustment and task effectiveness may not necessarily lead to effective communication. For this reason, it can be argued that the primary goal of training is to make people more effective by making their communication with hosts more effective—a goal that, of course, represents unidirectional accommodation, as discussed above.[2]

The number of ways developed to achieve these goals is large. As a result, it is practically impossible to address each technique independently, and so scholars in the past have usually relied on various classification schemes when writing about the field. For example, the first such scheme, formulated by Downs (1969), describes existing programs as fitting one of four different models: the intellectual model, the area simulation model, the self-awareness model, or the culture awareness model. Through the years, other typologies

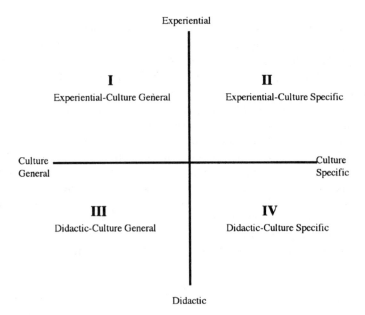

Figure 10.1. A Classification Scheme for Training Techniques
SOURCE: Gudykunst and Hammer (1983, p. 126). Copyright 1983 by W. B. Gudykunst. Reprinted by permission.

followed that added to Downs's framework (Bennett, 1986), developed new models (Bhawuk, 1990; Brislin, Landis, & Brandt, 1983; Brislin & Pedersen, 1976; Warren & Adler, 1977), or conceptualized programs according to which component of interaction (i.e., cognitive, behavioral, or affective) they focused upon (Brislin, 1989; Triandis, 1977). Hereafter, we discuss the intercultural training literature by relying on the most parsimonious typology to date—that of Gudykunst and Hammer (1983).

Gudykunst and Hammer (1983) differentiate training techniques along two major dimensions: didactic versus experiential and culture specific versus culture general. Didactic approaches (or the "university model"; Harrison & Hopkins, 1967) use a lecture format in an institutional setting for training, whereas experiential approaches attempt to involve the participant intellectually, emotionally, and behaviorally—most often in a simulated environment or role play. Culture-specific training provides information about a particular culture and guidelines for interacting with people from that culture. Culture-general techniques, on the other hand, rely on a "sample of experiences" (Triandis, 1977) that reflect worldwide variations in culture and aim at increasing the trainee's understanding of culture's global influence on human behavior. As Figure 10.1 illustrates, all major training methods can be located in one of four quadrants based on the combination of approaches they adopt.

In line with the foregoing, Quadrant I designates a number of training techniques that emphasize participation for learning about the general influence of culture. The most frequently used methods involve either simulations or structured discussions. Typically, simulations are designed to make trainees aware that not everyone in the world operates as they do; the most popular simulation is the game BAFA BAFA (Shirts, 1973). Briefly, in this game trainees are divided into two groups, the "Alphas" and the "Betas," and each group learns a different set of rules for behavior. Asked to follow these new rules, members from the two groups interact with one another and inevitably discover communication to be frustrating, confusing, and anxiety-provoking, because their behaviors are no longer coordinated. The new rules for behavior are a substitute for culture, and the exercise is meant to simulate the experience of cross-cultural interaction.

Quadrant II consists of approaches that are experiential-culture specific, such as role plays, area simulations, field trips, bicultural workshops, and behavior modeling. Of these, role plays and behavior modeling are the most widely used because they do not require the recruitment of host nationals (unlike bicultural workshops), nor do they demand the time and costs associated with field trips or elaborate area simulations. Role plays have been useful for allowing trainees to gain insight into the experiences of culturally different others. For example, a participant can be asked to play the role of a host national in a situation that is problematic for him or her because of cultural background (e.g., a Japanese business manager asked for a personal opinion on a project). By working through the situation and receiving feedback, trainees can develop the skills they need to communicate more effectively with members of particular cultural groups in the specific situations they have enacted.

Quadrant III consists of methods that are didactic-culture general, involving traditional academic approaches (i.e., lecture format) and other techniques that emphasize "learning how to learn" (see McCaffery, 1986). One of the more popular of these is the "culture-general assimilator" (Brislin, Cushner, Cherrie, & Yong, 1986; Cushner & Brislin, 1995), which is an outgrowth of the "culture (specific) assimilator" or the "intercultural sensitizer" developed by Fiedler, Mitchell, and Triandis (1971). Through the presentation of "critical incidents" (problematic scenarios of intercultural communication), the aim is to provide "attribution training" (Albert, 1986). Trainees read a critical incident and then select one of four interpretations that they think best fits the host culture's view of the situation. They then check their responses against a key that explains why each interpretation is correct or incorrect. If incorrect, they are asked to choose again until they select the correct response. The culture-general assimilator was developed with the assumption that there are certain experiences common to all intercultural interactions, regardless of the particular cultural group members involved (Cushner, 1989). Thus, it is intended not only to make trainees more aware of culture, but also to provide them with an understanding of the general interactional and attributional dynamics involved in cross-cultural communication (e.g., perceptions of time and space, the importance of roles, and differing rituals and superstitions).

Quadrant IV comprises those approaches that are both didactic and culture specific in nature. As a number of researchers have noted, these techniques have dominated the field and include elements such as university lectures, language learning, and the culture (specific) assimilators mentioned above (e.g., Bennett, 1986; Brislin, 1978; Harrison, 1992). The most frequently used method is the "area studies" program, which is essentially a presentation focused on a particular country and its inhabitants. Frequently, such programs include both environmental briefings (i.e., description of the locale, history, geography, politics, economics, and so on) and cultural orientations. These orientations, much like the briefings, consist largely of the presentation of "facts" about particular cultural groups and their behaviors. Usually, they take the form of lists of "dos and don'ts" readily available in popular books. For example, Goldman (1988) presents a list of 188 types of communicative behaviors typical of Japanese who engage in communication with Americans. Providing access to specific data and generalizations about a culture is believed to facilitate trainees' effectiveness in interactions with host nationals and to make them more comfortable about residing in a foreign land.

Understandably, this review has not been exhaustive (for book-length treatments, see Brislin & Pedersen, 1976; Landis & Brislin, 1983), but it is intended to be representative, to give the reader some appreciation of what is typically implied by the term *intercultural training*. With a view to explicating assumptions underlying the various training methods, we propose the generalized model of intercultural training depicted in Figure 10.2.

Description of the Model

Before detailing the specifics of the framework, we want to emphasize that this is a *generalized* model of training effects. We make no claim that this heuristic represents every training method, or all training goals and outcomes. In fact, actual outcomes are likely to be more complex than the model represents. However, this model traces the major routes charted toward intercultural effectiveness by focusing on the goals and outcomes most logically implied by each method.

Under the first column, headed "Training Techniques," are listed the four quadrants just discussed. To the right are the immediate outcomes that these techniques aim to produce (namely, awareness, behavioral skills, and knowledge). The connecting arrows between the first two columns are dashed because not all techniques included in a given category seek the same immediate outcomes. Gudykunst and Hammer (1983) group training methods together based on the means (experiential or didactic) and content (culture general or specific) of instruction, not by their goals or intended outcomes.

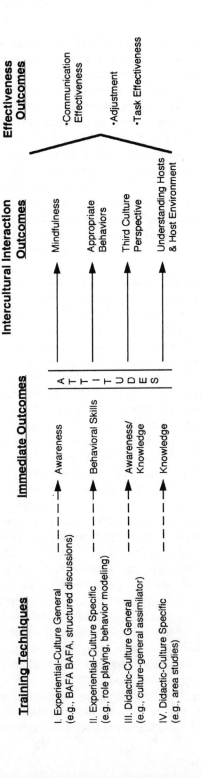

Figure 10.2. A Generalized Model of Intercultural Training as Currently Practiced

Thus, one technique that is experiential and culture specific aims to promote behavioral skills (e.g., behavior modeling), whereas another focuses on the development of awareness and knowledge (e.g., bicultural workshops). That said, this is an exception rather than the rule. In addition, and as is apparent in Figure 10.2, almost all intercultural training methods are based on expected concomitant changes in trainees' attitudes toward culturally different others. This is reflected by research on the techniques' effectiveness, which employs either generalized attitude measures, such as "world-mindedness," or measures of attitudes toward target host groups (e.g., Quadrant I methods—Bruschke, Gartner, & Seiter, 1993; Gudykunst, 1979; Quadrant II methods—Landis, Brislin, & Hulgus, 1985; Quadrant III methods—Lefley, 1985; Quadrant IV methods—Bird, Heinbuch, Dunbar, & McNulty, 1993; Crespo, 1982). Attitude measures are frequently suggested or undertaken, but the theoretical rationales for them are not explicated in any depth (e.g., Hughes-Wiener, 1986).

Following these proposed immediate outcomes, changes are presumed to take place in actual subsequent interactions. Some of the labels for the interactional outcomes are borrowed from other literatures, as the concepts seem to match well the anticipated changes. The first of these is "mindfulness," a term Gudykunst uses often in discussions of intercultural communication (e.g., Gudykunst & Kim, 1992; Gudykunst & Nishida, 1994). When people act unreflectively and according to behavioral scripts or habits, they are said to act "mindlessly" (Langer, 1978)—and this can pose great risk for intercultural communication. If people interact with culturally different others as though those others are culturally similar to themselves, or if they unreflectively judge strangers by their own norms and standards, miscommunication is almost inevitable. Thus, the purpose of training techniques that are both experiential and culture general is not only to raise awareness of culture, but, more important, to encourage the consideration of potential differences *during interaction*. In other words, training should encourage mindfulness. According to Langer (1989), there are three qualities of mindfulness: "creation of new categories," "openness to new information," and "awareness of more than one perspective" (p. 62). Thus, Quadrant I techniques, although not imparting any specific information, aim implicitly to develop the generalizable skill of mindfulness in trainees.

Quadrant II training techniques aim to develop specific behavioral skills. Such skills are taught quite simply because it is believed that they will lead trainees to behave appropriately during interaction with host nationals. The techniques in Quadrant III seek to bring about a mix of awareness and knowledge such that trainees may engage a "third culture perspective" during interaction (Casmir & Asuncione-Lande, 1988; Hammer, Gudykunst, & Wiseman, 1978). In essence, this refers to the psychological space resulting from the conjoining of two or more cultures and is similar to mindfulness in that it involves reflectiveness and liberation from a single point of view. However, it is slightly different because it requires an understanding of the culture or cultures with which one's native cultural view is conjoined. We opted for this dynamic outcome label because, in addition to raising awareness, Quadrant III techniques also provide information about the ways in which cultures vary. Such information thus moves the trainee from a general state of mindfulness to a third culture perspective that involves understanding something about another's cultural background.

Lastly, techniques that are both didactic and culture specific are those that provide information about particular host nations and their people with a view to developing knowledge that ideally would lead to an understanding of the hosts and their environment *during interaction*. As any technique succeeds in facilitating interaction that is mindful, informed, and appropriate, training should help trainees communicate, adjust, and work more effectively. Having described the training process, we will now address the question of whether or not these training techniques really produce the outcomes modeled here.

A REVIEW OF TRAINING EFFECTIVENESS

With the plethora of approaches to intercultural training available, one might expect that many systematic and objective evaluations of such programs would have been conducted. Does a technique accomplish all of its goals? What (other) impacts does it have, and under what conditions? And what are its limitations? Unfortunately, as mentioned above, issues of progress evaluation have generally been neglected (Albert, 1986; Harrison, 1992; Wexley, 1984). All too often, many of those who design and implement training programs have been impressed by the trainees' expressed reactions to them as well as by anecdotal evidence, and it is taken on faith that the interventions are effective. However, some empirical evidence does exist to help answer the above questions.

Beginning with the techniques we label experiential-culture general, there are a few studies that provide insight into their effectiveness. Of the several simulations, only one, BAFA BAFA, has received any attention from researchers. In testing whether or not the simulation makes trainees more sensitive to cultural differences, two studies have reported favorable trends (Dunn & Wozniak, 1976; Thomas, Moore, & Sams, 1980); however, these were limited in scope and inconclusive. More comprehensive studies have reported no differences between experimental and control groups (Jackson, 1979) or mixed results (Bredemeier, Bernstein, & Oxman, 1982). A relatively recent study, in fact, found some *negative* effects of the simulation (Bruschke et al., 1993). Although BAFA BAFA increased participants' motivation to do better in an intercultural communication course, it also increased scores on a scale measuring dogmatism/ethnocentrism.

Evaluation research on other experiential and culture-general techniques has been equally disappointing. Four studies examined changes in attitudes

resulting from intercultural contact and structured discussions and, in three
of these (Gudykunst, 1977, 1979; Kiyuna, 1977; Moran, 1974), outcomes did
not differ from those of a control group. One workshop experience did,
however, influence the formation of cross-cultural friendships, although this
difference was not maintained 6 months after participation (Gudykunst, 1977,
1979). The only supportive evidence comes from the fourth study, which
reported an increase in "world-mindedness" after a 10-week program of
planned intercultural experiences (Steinkalk & Taft, 1979).

   Research on techniques that are experiential-culture specific is also limited
and, generally, not encouraging. One study compared the effectiveness of
techniques used in a bicultural workshop (discussion and role playing with
target hosts) to other training methods (Landis, Brislin, & Hulgus, 1985).
Those participating in this "contact only" group were rated more favorably
(than a control) by target hosts on a behavioral task in which they played the
role of target hosts. However, and perhaps more important, participants in the
"contact only" group also developed more unfavorable attitudes toward the
target hosts than did control respondents. In a similar study, Harrison (1992)
compared the effectiveness of behavioral modeling techniques with other
methods. Although a combination of behavior modeling and cultural assimilator training was most effective, participants in conditions of behavior
modeling alone learned more material and performed a role play with target
hosts better than those receiving no training at all. No attitudinal measures
were included in this study. Unfortunately, this is the only empirical study
that has investigated the effectiveness of behavior modeling or role-playing
techniques in intercultural training (Harrison, 1992). Although research has
been almost universally supportive of these techniques' general effectiveness
in organizational training (e.g., Burke & Day, 1986; Decker, 1982; Latham &
Saari, 1979), their utility for intercultural training has not yet been adequately
demonstrated.

   More encouraging, but still entirely too limited, are two studies that
evaluated techniques that are didactic and culture general in the form of the
culture-general assimilator. Cushner (1989) prepared a group of adolescent
international exchange students to live in New Zealand by training them with
the culture-general assimilator over a 2-day period. Compared with students
trained with techniques typical to bicultural workshops (i.e., small group
discussions and role plays), culture-general assimilator trainees were better
able to analyze critical incidents similar to those in the assimilator and to
explain their own experiences of personal misunderstanding, and, subsequently,
reported greater adjustment to life in New Zealand. Similarly, a study by Ilola
(1989) found that participants with culture-general assimilator training developed their ability to solve difficult critical incidents.

   Up to this point, it is clear that research on intercultural training has
suffered simply because there has not been enough of it. This is not the case,
however, for at least one technique included in the last category of training

methods (i.e., didactic-culture specific). In fact, the majority of all intercultural training research efforts have been focused on this single technique—the culture assimilator (see, for example, Albert & Adamopoulos, 1980; Becker, 1982; Chemers, Fiedler, Lekhyananda, & Stolurow, 1966; Harrison, 1992; Landis, Brislin, Swanner, Tzeng, & Thomas, 1985; Mitchell, Dossett, Fiedler, & Triandis, 1972; O'Brien, Fiedler, & Hewett, 1971; O'Brien & Plooij, 1977; Yarbro, 1988). In the 20 or so studies that have been conducted, it has been quite clearly demonstrated that the culture assimilator is a useful tool for imparting cultural information. Participants have been consistently better able to make "isomorphic attributions" (i.e., to interpret critical incidents as do host nationals) than have untrained participants on tests similar to the assimilator itself (e.g., Chemers, 1969; Landis, Day, McGrew, Thomas, & Miller, 1976). Other findings have shown that trained participants also report better relations with host nationals (Fiedler et al., 1971; Worchel & Mitchell, 1972) and appear to resist stereotyping more than do their control counterparts (Landis, Tzeng, & Thomas, 1981; Weldon, Carlston, Rissman, Slobodin, & Triandis, 1975).

However, as Albert (1983) notes in a review of culture assimilator research, the effects of such training on attitudes and behaviors are mixed and inconclusive. In two studies, assimilator-trained individuals received more favorable ratings acting the role of target hosts in a role play than did untrained persons (Landis, Brislin, & Hulgus, 1985; Mitchell & Foa, 1969). Another study, however, reported no differences between groups on this measure (Hulgus & Landis, 1979), and when working with (confederate) target hosts on a task, assimilator trainees were actually rated *less* favorably by the hosts than were untrained others (Weldon et al., 1975; Randolph, Landis, & Tzeng, 1977). In an examination of attitudinal outcomes, Crespo (1982) found no difference between trained and untrained groups in attitudes toward target hosts, whereas two other studies found that assimilator training resulted in more *negative* attitudes (Landis, Brislin, & Hulgus, 1985; Randolph et al., 1977). Thus, cultural assimilator training clearly provides for a greater understanding of cultural information, but its other effects are equivocal at best, and can be deleterious at worst.

Another didactic and culture-specific technique that has been evaluated is area studies training. Despite claims that area studies are ineffective (Tung, 1981), Earley (1987) found that such training favorably influenced performance appraisals and self-assessments of adjustment. However, in another study, Bird et al. (1993) reported that although such training increased participants' knowledge about the target culture, it did not affect their behavioral intentions, and even contributed *negatively* to their attitudes about target hosts.

To date, mostly single techniques of intercultural training have been evaluated—and the results have not been favorable in terms of effective outcomes. Yet rarely do entire programs of training consist of a single technique, and most use a variety of approaches in order to prepare trainees as fully as possible for intercultural encounters. In recent years, consideration has been afforded the question of which techniques should be used in combination, and in what order (e.g., Brislin & Yoshida, 1994; Gudykunst & Hammer, 1983; Harrison, 1992). Generally, effectiveness research on programs using more than one technique has been more encouraging than the studies reviewed above would lead one to expect.

In an exploration of the effects of a training program using both didactic and experiential approaches, Hammer and Martin (1992) found that trainees were better able to reduce their uncertainties and, to a lesser extent, relieve their anxieties about interaction with host nationals than were individuals in a control group. However, because they found no significant differences with respect to a behavioral outcome measure, the researchers suggest that "more cognitively oriented objectives may be more easily attainable than affective or some behavioral goals" (p. 179). A second study, by Lefley (1985), also produced similarly positive results. Among mental health care professionals, a program of training using didactic and cultural immersion techniques increased perceptions of cultural differences among various population groups (i.e., raised awareness) in addition to improving the participants' therapeutic skills when working with a poor African American client in a role play.

Two other field studies examined real training outcomes. Among North Americans studying Spanish in Costa Rica, a treatment program that included traditional training methods along with psychotherapeutic techniques resulted in trainees' reporting fewer symptoms of psychological distress and thereby perhaps facilitating more adjustment than those in a control group (Befus, 1988). Training for counselors working with African American female clients also had a positive impact (Wade & Bernstein, 1991). Clients assigned to interculturally trained counselors rated their counselors higher on credibility and relationship measures, returned for more follow-up sessions, and expressed greater satisfaction with counseling than did those assigned to counselors who had no such training.

Although considerably less reliable, other real training outcomes have been indexed by surveys. Expatriate managers consistently demonstrate a need for intercultural training (see Mendenhall & Oddou, 1985), and several surveys have sought to chart the effectiveness of such training. Unfortunately, most have employed corporate officials (e.g., human resource managers) as respondents and not the expatriates themselves. For example, Tung (1981) surveyed a sample of corporate vice presidents and foreign operation directors about the selection and training of personnel for overseas assignments. She concludes that the relationship between training (nonspecific) and job failure is strong ($r = .63$). However, this correlation is based on only *eight* respondents who indicated that their firms both trained employees and evaluated their success in the posting. Perhaps more reliable results come from a study by Black and Gregersen (1991), who surveyed 220 expatriates about their experiences abroad. Surprisingly, programmatic training correlated negatively with all three indicators of the expatriates' adjustment. Apart from surveys, no other empirical studies have explored the effectiveness of expatriate training.

In addition to the single studies described above, two literature reviews also provide some insight into the effectiveness of training. Most recently, Deshpande and Viswesvaran (1992) employed Hunter and Schmidt's (1990) meta-analytic framework to evaluate the effectiveness of training reported in 21 studies (15 of which we have already described or referenced here). The entire sample used at least one of the following dependent measures: cross-cultural skills, adjustment, and performance. The skills hypothesized to result from training included three types: self skills (i.e., feelings of well-being and self-confidence), relationship skills (i.e., reports of favorable interactions with host nationals), and perception skills (i.e., identifying host national perspectives on interaction). Hence, there were five outcome variables in all. For two of the outcome measures, self skills and perception skills, the authors conclude that the effect of training is clearly consistent and positive. The chances are that training's relationship to the other three outcomes is also positive, but the connection is not nearly as robust. Thus, trainees generally feel good about training and learn to recognize different cultural perspectives, whereas reports of good relations, adjustment, and performance, though favorable, are less frequent.

Using the same dependent measures, Black and Mendenhall (1990) also reviewed the effectiveness of training as reported in 29 studies (17 of which we have already described or referenced here). Although they did not employ any statistical technique of meta-analysis, their review suggests that intercultural training generally has a positive impact on all of the above-mentioned outcome measures. However, these authors are clear about the *many* methodological difficulties present in the studies they reviewed, in that, for instance, most of the studies did not use control groups and relied on self-report data. As a result, they conclude that the empirical literature provides only guarded support for the proposition that intercultural training has a positive impact on cross-cultural effectiveness.

A Final Word on Effectiveness

What, then, does the total of all this research tell us about the training process? Referring back to the model (see Figure 10.2), there is some very limited evidence that training can influence favorably the three constituent parts of cross-cultural effectiveness. We have seen it in a few of the individual studies reviewed (e.g., communication effectiveness [Worchel & Mitchell, 1972], adjustment [Befus, 1988], and task effectiveness [Wade & Bernstein, 1991]), and also in the qualified conclusions of the meta-analyses (Black & Mendenhall, 1990; Deshpande & Viswesvaran, 1992). Thus, it is possible that training may help produce the long-term outcomes it intends, although this has not yet been clearly established. It is clearer that training can sometimes—albeit not always—produce most of the *immediate* outcomes described: It can develop awareness (e.g., Lefley, 1985), behavioral skills (e.g., Landis, Brislin, & Hulgus, 1985), and most surely knowledge (e.g., Bird et al., 1993). Training has not, however, usually shifted attitudes in the desired direction (e.g., Randolph et al., 1977).

When it comes to important questions about training's impact on intercultural *interaction,* little has been established. As the model illustrates, in order for a trainee's skills, knowledge, and awareness to pay effectiveness dividends, the trainee must call upon them while communicating with hosts. If a trainee is aware of cultural differences, has knowledge about those differences, and can perform behaviors perfectly coordinated with those of the host, yet is not mindful, fails to use his or her knowledge in making attributions, and behaves incongruously during interaction, training will never likely lead to intercultural effectiveness. Thus, before we can conclude that the immediate outcomes usually produced do in fact lead to the potential outcomes of cross-cultural effectiveness, we must first study interaction outcomes. Unfortunately, very few studies have attempted to do this (i.e., examined unscripted interaction between trainees and target hosts; Chemers, 1969; Chemers et al., 1966; Randolph et al., 1977; Weldon et al., 1975), and their results are, once again, mixed.

Overall, then, research on the effectiveness of intercultural training provides some indication of what happens to trainees, yet large and critical aspects of the process remain obscured. When alternative and, arguably, more incisive models of training's impact are considered, this lack of knowledge in the face of continued reliance on current training techniques should cause concern.

A CRITIQUE OF INTERCULTURAL TRAINING

As we have already noted, approaches to intercultural training have frequently been criticized for their lack of theoretical grounding (Adler, 1983; Black & Mendenhall, 1990; Bochner, 1982; Brislin, 1981; Gudykunst & Hammer, 1983; Landis, Brislin, & Hulgus, 1985). Surprisingly, training has most often been undertaken without thorough consideration of the assumptions that support it. Having presented these assumptions in the form of a generalized model (see Figure 10.2), we shall now consider alternative models of training's effects based largely on both theoretical and empirical work in the area of intergroup relations and communication (see Williams & Giles, 1992).

The term *intergroup* refers here to individuals' perception of people as members of distinct social categories rather than as those similar to or just like themselves. Individuals frequently construct this distinction between us (the in-group) and them (the out-group) and, in doing so, invite another dimension of perceptual and communicative dynamics to the relationship. Intergroup dynamics first impinge upon training while the training itself takes place. Consequently, they may help account for those findings that show that training does not consistently produce the immediate outcomes intended (e.g., Jackson, 1979; Weldon et al., 1975). We begin this critique with a discussion of these dynamics as well as the limitations that they present for training. We then will develop a theoretical nexus between immediate outcomes and the long-term outcomes of effectiveness by exploring some of the intergroup dynamics involved in intercultural interaction. Finally, we will consider several negative intergroup outcomes engendered by training.

Limits During Training

Becoming aware of, and learning about, other cultural groups is an undertaking much similar to, and in fact sometimes includes, learning a second language. Both tasks are intimately intertwined with the individual's feelings about the cultural group itself—so intertwined that it is difficult to separate one from the other. Learning Japanese is not an exercise in the abstract, but an experience that can pull the learner closer toward the Japanese people themselves (see Gardner, 1985). The same can be said for intercultural training. Learning about Japanese culture, society, and norms of behavior can draw an individual toward the Japanese and their way of life. For this reason, when considering whether or not students of a second language or of cultural training will succeed in learning the lessons with which they are presented, one must also consider students' attitudes toward, and beliefs about, the cultural group in question.

Fortunately, psychologists studying second-language acquisition realized this long ago (e.g., Jordan, 1941), and have studied the relationship between attitudes toward a cultural group and achievement in that group's language. The conclusion, after more than 50 years of research, is that the relationship is a strong one (Gardner & Clément, 1990). Positive attitudes toward a cultural group facilitate language learning, and negative attitudes retard it. For example, Gardner and Lambert (1959) found that the success of English-speaking Canadians in learning French depended in large part on their attitudes toward French Canadians. Similarly, in Louisiana, positive attitudes toward French Americans were associated with greater vocabulary in and better comprehension of French, whereas negative attitudes were tied to poor vocabulary and comprehension (Gardner & Lambert, 1972). The impact of negative attitudes was, in fact, so great throughout many such studies that Gardner and Lambert (1972) comment that "widely shared negative stereotypes of certain peoples [frequently] appeared to make the work of a language teacher *almost impossible*" (p. 144; emphasis added).

Given the influences that negative attitudes and stereotypes have on language learning, it is quite reasonable to expect that negative attitudes could have a similar impact on intercultural training. Yet, surprisingly, no research to date has reported on this possibility. Of course, as we have described, attitudes have been included in the training process—they are considered ultimately to influence trainee effectiveness. However, they have not been conceptualized as a potent variable influencing trainee learning. Not only do the second-language studies suggest that this will be the case, but other research on attitudes and stereotypes also points in this direction.

To begin with, both attitude theory and research on attitudes propose that attitudes guide attention. In the words of Allport (1935), "Attitudes determine for each individual what he will see and hear" (p. 806). The basic process, as articulated by cognitive dissonance theory (Festinger, 1957), is one of selective exposure. Quite simply, this theory predicts that individuals will seek out information consonant with their attitudes and avoid dissonant information. People enjoy receiving support for the attitudes they hold, but information that challenges their attitudes produces an uncomfortable state of cognitive dissonance. One way of avoiding such dissonance, then, is to avoid attending to dissonant information.

A number of studies have supported this prediction of selective exposure. Brock and Balloun (1967) found that when confronted with information that either upheld their views or challenged them, both committed churchgoers and smokers acted to expose themselves more only to information that supported their attitudes. In reviewing the research on selective exposure, Frey (1986) reported that "in some experiments in which subjects were asked which pieces of information they did not want to see, there was a significantly greater tendency to avoid dissonant as opposed to consonant information" (p. 69). This tendency has also been detailed outside laboratory settings. In survey research, Sweeney and Gruber (1984) found that Nixon supporters reported less interest in, and attention to, the Watergate hearings than did undecided citizens. Although not all empirical research has been supportive, the evidence is robust enough that selective exposure is currently regarded as a genuine phenomenon in research and theorizing (Eagly & Chaiken, 1993). For this reason, then, we should expect that trainees with negative attitudes about their target host communities may be avoiding information that does not support those negative attitudes. Unfortunately, this would mean that some people may not be attending to the content of much intercultural training.

In addition to attitudes, stereotypes may also be influencing attention. As Wilder (1993) states, "Evidence from social cognition research suggests that cognitive schemes (such as stereotypes) can channel a person's attention to notice and process more fully information that is consistent with those schemas" (p. 80). For example, Rothbart, Evans, and Fulero (1979) found that expectations given prior to behavioral information influenced respondents' recall of that information. These and other similar results (e.g., Berman, Read, & Kenny, 1983) imply that selective processing arises during the encoding of social information (i.e., attention). Thus, a trainee is likely to avoid or not process fully any information that contradicts his or her (negative) stereotypes about target host group members.

Finally, constraints on trainee attention are imposed not only by cognitive processes, but also by affective ones. Isen (1984) reports that affective states tend to impair the processing of affectively incompatible material, either at encoding or at retrieval. For example, a study by Mackie and Worth (1989) demonstrated that participant recall of group member descriptions was more stereotypical and less accurate when the recalled traits were inconsistent with participants' moods. Such research is relevant here because training, in some cases, can induce negative affective states among participants. If an individual dislikes members of culture X, constant discussion about culture X members is likely to make him or her feel uncomfortable. The individual would then be less likely to attend to and process any favorable information about them. Even if persons do not hold negative attitudes about a particular cultural group initially, some experiential training techniques (such as BAFA BAFA) aim to induce a negative affective state in trainees. Under such conditions, it should be expected that trainees' attention to or processing of favorable information will be compromised.

In light of these tendencies to avoid counterattitudinal, counterstereotypical, and counteraffective information, why has the most robust finding of intercultural training research been a positive relationship between training and the development of knowledge? This is reasonably accounted for by the demand characteristics of most studies. Participating in a "study" and anticipating some sort of evaluation, volunteers (doubtless positively inclined anyway) are extremely likely to attend to and process presented information, regardless of its nature. However, in real-life training situations, such demand characteristics are diminished greatly, if not absent. Thus, despite evidence to the contrary, training may not in fact fully develop knowledge about target host group members in all trainees because of individuals' tendency to avoid attending to and processing information dissonant with their own attitudes, stereotypes, and feelings. Of course, this dynamic is not the only one operating during training. For example, there is a tendency to seek useful information regardless of its nature (Eagly & Chaiken, 1993). Thus, a negative disposition toward host group members will not always predict inattention to positive information about the group. Even so, this represents an important dynamic of the intercultural training process that has heretofore been largely ignored.

A second limitation that occurs during the training itself relates to people's acceptance of information. For any technique to be effective, trainees must not only attend to the information and points of view presented, but also accept them. Knowledge does not imply acceptance, and this is an important distinction neglected by the training literature. In her discussion of stereotypes, Devine (1989) clarifies that "although one may have knowledge of a stereotype, his or her personal beliefs may or may not be congruent with the stereotype" (p. 5). Although this is in reference to negative stereotypes, the same must also be true for the positive stereotypes and/or other information presented during training. Exercises in a cultural assimilator may tell us that lying on the part of a Japanese woman is not attributable to her being "sneaky" or "duplicitous" but, rather, to her desire to save another's "face." However, we may come to "know" this information without having to accept, really believe, endorse, or even fully understand it.

In fact, there is evidence to suggest that this not only can happen, but most likely will happen if a trainee holds negative attitudes about the target host group. Turning again to cognitive dissonance theory, Festinger (1957) has emphasized that "forced exposure to attitudinally uncongenial information would be characterized by biased perception and evaluation of the information" (cited in Eagly & Chaiken, 1993, p. 596). Indeed, a number of studies have shown that counterattitudinal information is evaluated negatively. For example, Cacioppo and Petty (1979; Petty & Cacioppo, 1979) have demonstrated twice that people list more counterarguments for counterattitudinal than for proattitudinal messages. Similarly, Lord, Ross, and Lepper (1979) found that both proponents and opponents of capital punishment rated briefings that confirmed their own views as more convincing and better conducted than briefings that disconfirmed their views. Working from a different theoretical model (Fazio, 1986), Houston and Fazio (1989) also found that individuals with more accessible attitudes about the death penalty (either pro or con) evaluated purported social scientific research on the subject in a manner biased toward their own preexisting views. Thus, it should be expected that trainees presented with counterattitudinal information will be not only less likely to attend to that information, but also less likely to evaluate it positively and accept it.

Closely related to the above is a third limitation dealing with attitude and stereotype change. Specifically, because the aim of training is not only to have trainees understand and accept new information but also to have them integrate such information so that it will serve as the basis of new, more positive attitudes and stereotypes, several social and psychological dynamics that are ready to frustrate these efforts must be considered.

As Eagly and Chaiken (1993) claim, "The idea that people ordinarily would be willing to change their attitudes is not plausible when analyzed with care" (p. 559). Indeed, it seems naive to expect trainees to change any negative attitudes they have toward target host groups just for the asking when one realizes that those attitudes fill several important functions for the trainees. In Katz's (1960) description, an attitude may serve one or more of four personality functions: Attitudes can (a) be instrumental in helping a person achieve rewards and avoid punishments (utilitarian function), (b) help organize and simplify the world (knowledge function), (c) be a means for expressing personal values and aspects of a person's self-concept (value-expressive function), and (d) bolster a person's self-esteem when they downgrade others (ego-defensive function).

Although Katz does not discuss it, another social function that attitudes may serve is similar to the ego-defensive function he describes. Not only individuals, but also entire groups can develop and nurture negative attitudes about out-groups that help improve the collective in-group identity. Thus, "skinheads" improve their own group identity by maintaining negative attitudes about other ethnic groups and social classes. More and more, scholars are changing their conceptions of attitudes to accommodate this very real, functional intergroup perspective (see Giles, 1992). For example, Billig (1987) suggests that attitudes are not simply enduring evaluations about stimulus objects. Instead, he sees them in a wider historical and rhetorical context as positions in an argument and embedded within particular social controversies fashioned at any one time. Therefore, because of the functions that attitudes serve, attempts to change them are likely to be resisted unless the underlying motivational bases, both psychological and social, are also addressed.

Attitude resistance to change may stem not only from motivational concerns, but also from cognitive ones. Many theorists believe that attitudes are embedded in larger cognitive networks. This makes the process of change difficult, because a shift in attitudes would reverberate throughout the entire molar structure (e.g., Scott, 1968; Sherif, Sherif, & Nebergall, 1965). Such interconnectedness means that the whole network ends up providing resistance to change in a single attitude. Indeed, research tends to confirm this view (e.g., Ball-Rokeach, Rokeach, & Grube, 1984; Hendrick & Seyfried, 1974), thus suggesting further difficulties associated with changing trainee attitudes.

Perhaps more critical to the success of training than changing trainees' attitudes is changing their beliefs or stereotypes about the target host group. However, much in the same way people's attitudes resist change, so too do their stereotypes. Like attitudes, stereotypes have a number of similar motivational bases (see Tajfel, 1981) that, unless otherwise addressed, will inhibit change. Additionally, several research reviews have indicated that cognitive processes and cognitive biases will also ensure the persistence of stereotypes and their resistance to change (see Hamilton & Trolier, 1986; Stephan, 1989). For example, ambiguous information is often interpreted in ways that make it fit relevant stereotypes (Razran, 1950; Sagar & Schofield, 1980), and disconfirming evidence can be organized in ways that leave original stereotypes unaltered (Wilder, 1984). For these reasons, the designers of cross-cultural training programs should not anticipate that the simple provision of new information will be sufficient to change old stereotypes.

Returning to the model of intercultural training (Figure 10.2), it can now be seen that the move from training technique to immediate outcome is not a necessary one. Any reasonably strong attitude or stereotype, when negative, is likely to complicate the move greatly, if not prevent it altogether. Yet even if a trainee is attentive and accepting, and begins to change his or her attitudes and stereotypes about the target host group, this will not ensure the long-range outcome of effectiveness. This is because effectiveness is mediated by *interaction,* and the lessons successfully learned during training must compete with other intergroup dynamics to shape intercultural interactions.

Intercultural Interaction Dynamics

As we have proposed, training is not the only force with the potential to shape intercultural interactions. There are many such forces, perhaps innumerable, that help determine how people communicate with one another. We wish now to identify a few and highlight the possibility that training, even when successful, may, on many occasions, be powerless to influence trainee behavior favorably.

The first dynamic of interaction relevant to training effects is context. Quite clearly, context is a fundamental component of interaction, and it impinges at two different "levels": the larger sociostructural context and the immediate social situation (see Giles & Coupland, 1992). In order to understand communication, it is necessary to account for the sociostructural context in which it occurs. Intercultural interactions always take place in a historical context of cultural group relations that has important impacts on people's behaviors. Consider, for example, that Americans and Italians relate to each other very differently now than they did 50 years ago (i.e., in Europe during World War II). The context changed, and so did the interactions. Political, historical, economic, and linguistic realities are elements that, together, constitute this sociostructural context. Depending on the nature of these elements, they can radically change communication behaviors—regardless of the amount, type, or success of training the interactants have received. For example, if political tensions are running high between two groups (e.g., North and South Koreans during arms negotiations), communication between members of those groups is likely to be more adversarial than otherwise. The context of interaction may thus overwhelm good intentions and relegate appropriate behaviors to a position of lowest priority. Yet even if a trainee manages to remain personally unaffected by the context and wants to apply all of his or her knowledge and experience to the facilitation of favorable interaction, it might be socially risky for him or her to do so (e.g., How would my peers react if they see me getting along with "these kinds of people"?). In this way, sociostructural contexts are an important influence on interaction and can limit the effects of training.

In addition to parameters of the sociostructural context, we must consider also that both the hearer's and the speaker's behaviors occur within the frame of some immediate social situation. They take place within the context of a job interview, a dinner among friends, a sporting event, or some other occasion, and people's behaviors are shaped and constrained by the roles played within that immediate social situation. Thus, a trainee may be unable to make full use of the skills developed in training because his or her role in a situation prevents it. For example, a business manager may not have the luxury to be mindful in reserving judgment of a host national employee's behavior until a culturally appropriate explanation can be found if the job requires a prompt evaluation of the person.

The immediate social situation is important not only for the roles that it features, but also because it affects the salience of the participants' identities. Identities are an important influence on interaction because, first, they situate interlocutors in the larger sociostructural context, and second, they alone can encourage prejudiced behavior. Furthermore, identities are context dependent to the extent that they sometimes are negotiated or created out of situated interactions (Clément & Giles, 1993).

As Tajfel and others have described (see Tajfel & Turner, 1986; Turner & Giles, 1981), all social behavior can be characterized by its position along a continuum with two extremes: interindividual versus intergroup behavior. At the former extreme, interlocutors respond to one another as unique human beings. Consequently, most of the interaction that takes place is "determined by the personal relationships between the individuals and by their respective individual characteristics" (Tajfel, 1978, p. 41). An example of an encounter displaying this type of behavior would be an intimate discussion between best friends. At the other end of the continuum lie "intergroup" behaviors. As Tajfel (1978) describes it, "The intergroup extreme is that in which all of behavior of two or more individuals toward each other is determined by their memberships in different social groups or categories" (p. 41). For example, two soldiers (who may previously have been close friends or family members) on a battlefield aim to kill simply because they identify each other as members of another (enemy) group. Understanding that social interaction can often be determined exclusively by people's social group memberships is critical for explaining the relevance of identities in cross-cultural encounters.

As Gudykunst (1995) points out, one of the major factors affecting communication is the self-concept or identity. Turner (1987) explains that an individual's self-concept consists of three general types of identity: human, social, and personal. A person's human identity refers to aspects of the self held in common with all other humans. The social identity is derived from group memberships (e.g., seeing oneself as a woman, a senior, an African American, a student, and/or an American). The personal identity is made up of the self-conceptions that distinguish the individual from other members of his or her social groups. Together, these three identities serve as the bases for social interaction. The identities are extremely fluid; take, for instance, the example of a discussion between friends. Initially, it may be the case that the two people see themselves simply as unique individuals and interact accordingly.

However, as they are talking, one of them notices the other is wearing a Star of David pendant and suddenly becomes aware of his own identity as a Palestinian. Accordingly, he starts to criticize his friend for Israel's recent retaliation against Palestine. Of course, the two friends "knew" about each other's social group memberships all along, but those identities did not affect their behaviors until they became salient. It is in this manner that identities influence communication.

To summarize briefly, people have multiple identities, the salience of which shifts interaction along an interindividual-intergroup continuum. The immediate social situation is important here because features of that situation direct the salience of various identities. Individuals thus slip in and out of particular group memberships as the situation demands (Collier & Thomas, 1988; Liebkind, 1989), and this fluidity determines which aspects of the sociostructural context are relevant. For example, it was only when the hypothetical friends mentioned above recognized each other as Palestinian and Jew that the political and historical aspects of context began to shape their interaction.

Identities are important for understanding behavior not only because they connect people to the larger context of group relations, but also because, even in the absence of context, as we shall see below, they can affect interaction in a direct and powerful manner. Researchers have found that when social identities are salient and encounters are defined in intergroup terms—as is frequently the case with intercultural interactions—barriers to effective communication are erected through discriminatory behaviors (Gudykunst, 1986).

To this point, most of this critique has been directed at training situations and interactions affected by negative group relations. When trainees arrive for training with negative attitudes and stereotypes, their training will be compromised. When they interact in tension-filled contexts, their behavior is not likely to be felicitous. However, poor group relations are not necessary in order for the effects of successful training to be limited. Social identity theory and numerous studies suggest that the *mere perception* of two distinct social groups, in the absence of any negative context, is sufficient to provoke responses that are competitive and discriminatory in nature.

In its essence, social identity theory (Tajfel & Turner, 1986) posits that a person's social identity (i.e., identity derived from group memberships) forms an important part of his or her self-concept, and that people try to achieve—by various comparatively differentiating means—a positive sense of social identity. In other words, people are inclined to promote any group with which they identify strongly and to devalue any group to which they do not belong, because these actions enhance their own sense of positive self-esteem. Proposed in these terms, the theory accounts for a large set of empirical findings described as the "minimal categorization effect" (e.g., Billig & Tajfel, 1973; Brewer, 1979; Turner, 1983). In these experiments, participants are divided into two groups ostensibly on some trivial basis (e.g., whether they like the abstract artist Klee or Kandinsky) and then are asked to allocate rewards for anonymous in-group and out-group members. Reliably, respondents discriminate competitively in favor of their own (largely mundane) group. More interestingly, respondents also tend to sacrifice the absolute gain of their group when it ensures an advantage relative to the other group. More than 20 such experiments in this paradigm suggest that people take advantage of any situation defined in intergroup terms to boost their own social identity and self-esteem through discrimination (see Taylor & Moghaddam, 1994).

In addition to instances of material partisanship, other forms of bias also have been observed in intergroup situations devoid of any significant sociostructural context. For example, many studies have found that simple group distinctions are sufficient cause for biased evaluations of out-group members (e.g., Doise et al., 1972; Rabbie & Wilkens, 1971) and their work (e.g., Ferguson & Kelley, 1964; Turner, 1978). Additionally, people are most likely to attribute negative acts to personal traits when an actor is identified as an out-group member, but to situational factors when the actor is determined to belong to the observers' own group (e.g., Pettigrew, 1979). Thus, prejudiced responses have been observed to take a variety of shapes. It is important to note that this prejudice is strongly associated with the increased salience of intergroup identities. In a number of studies, the more participants became aware of group distinctions, the more inclined they were to act in discriminatory ways (e.g., Dustin & Davis, 1970; Gerard & Hoyt, 1974). Given that in-group language and communicative characteristics are often valued highly by those who strongly identify with their national and cultural groups, it is, ironically, these very features (verbal, nonverbal, discursive) that trainees may often wish to differentiate on (see Cargile, Giles, & Clément, in press; Gallois, Giles, Jones, Cargile, & Ota, 1995; Giles & Viladot, 1994).

This general pattern of prejudiced responses deserves recognition in discussions of intercultural training, because it is likely to interfere with the application of knowledge and skills successfully developed in training. Intercultural interactions are frequently experienced in intergroup (rather than interpersonal) terms. Thus, helpful (positive) information and experiences provided by training may not be brought to bear due to the discriminatory tendencies provoked increasingly by group distinctions.

The need for positive social identity, however, is not the only reason favorable intercultural interactions may not follow directly from training. Features of cognitive processing may also complicate the application of training lessons learned. These features relate mainly to the distinction between automatic and controlled processing. In attempting to understand better how people respond to cues in their environments, theorists have distinguished between those responses that are spontaneous and unintentional because of some well-learned set of associations (i.e., automatic) and those that require the active attention of the individual (i.e., controlled; see Shiffrin & Schneider, 1977). When people enter a training situation, they most likely bring with them a number of well-learned responses to members of the target host group. The training experience must then compete to supplant these "old" responses in order to facilitate favorable future intercultural interactions. Even if, despite all of the previously discussed roadblocks, trainees successfully learn and accept "new" responses, they may not always exhibit these new responses because of the demands of controlled processing. Because old, stereotypical responses have a longer history of activation, they are easily accessible and automatically called upon in the presence of target group members (Smith & Branscombe, 1985). Responses learned in training, however, demand controlled processing because they are newer and less well established cognitive structures. This differential ease in processing, then, suggests that trainees are likely to exhibit old, stereotypical responses in interaction, despite training's development of any new personal beliefs (Devine, 1989).

As Higgins and King (1981) argue, nonprejudiced responses require both the inhibition of automatically activated stereotypes and the intentional activation of nonprejudiced beliefs. Although this is certainly possible (training can facilitate favorable intercultural interactions), understanding the cognitive processes involved can provide a trainee with a better appreciation of the limits imposed by interaction on training. Such limits can be imposed by anything that would compromise a trainee's ability or motivation to perform the above-described controlled processing.

Perhaps the most important limit to the type of processing needed in intercultural encounters is caused by anxiety. As Gudykunst and Shapiro (1994) have demonstrated, individuals' anxiety tends to be higher during initial interactions with members of other cultural groups than with people from their own cultures. Such anxiety then has the effect of encouraging reliance on well-learned stereotypes, because the active processing of information is "distracting," and can sap individuals' ability to interact appropriately (see Wilder, 1993). Other limits to controlled processing include time (Neely, 1977) and the perceived importance of or involvement in a situation (Showers & Cantor, 1985). Together, these factors represent dynamics of interaction that can limit the effectiveness of training.

One last, transactive feature of interaction that deserves consideration is host responsiveness (another factor prominent in the second-language acquisition literature; see Genesee, Rogers, & Holobrow, 1983). Intercultural communication is an interactive process; thus, hosts' reactions to trainees must be included in any conceptualization of the training process (see also Kim, 1988). It is surely the case that host nationals most often react favorably to trainees who display mindfulness and an accommodating knowledge of the host society and culture. However, host nationals are people too, with attitudes, beliefs, motives, and identities of their own. Thus, it is quite possible that they may feel threatened by competent performances. For example, the Japanese are said to be among the friendliest people in the world—until a foreigner develops behavioral competencies that are "too good." The Japanese are willing to accept the foreigner as long as he or she assumes the role of a foreigner. But when a nonnative tries to assume the role of a Japanese, he or she is often quickly isolated (Hildebrandt & Giles, 1983; Suzuki, 1975). Such behavior most closely resembles the concept of divergence, as developed by Giles and his colleagues (see Giles & Coupland, 1992).

Divergence is the term coined to describe the way in which speakers accentuate speech and nonverbal differences between themselves and others (Giles & Powesland, 1975). For example, when members of low socioeconomic status groups come to employ certain lexical markers that are traditionally the property of high socioeconomic status groups, members of the latter groups are frequently seen to drop those markers and develop new ones (Giles, 1978); such distancing would be considered "upward divergence." Because this phenomenon has been widely documented (e.g., Bourhis & Giles, 1977; Bourhis, Giles, Leyens, & Tajfel, 1979; Taylor & Royer, 1980), the real potential for divergence on the part of host nationals must be given consideration in discussions of intercultural training. Such divergence tends to confuse communication, so we must view not only trainees' behaviors as barriers to effective interaction, but also host responses.

Now that we have given fuller consideration to the dynamics of training and intercultural interaction, it should be obvious that training may not always (or even usually) promote intercultural effectiveness, unless, that is, such processes are acknowledged and contained (see also Fox & Giles, 1993; Hewstone & Brown, 1986).

Unanticipated Negative Outcomes

Although intercultural training has been undertaken as a sincere effort to facilitate intercultural interactions, it may be that, besides sometimes failing to produce positive outcomes, training encourages a few unwanted responses. Specifically, training can indeed increase the salience of intergroup distinctions, reinforce negative attitudes toward host nationals, and foster perceptions of host homogeneity.

As we have already described, interactions can be viewed along a continuum ranging from interindividual to intergroup in nature. Because of our need for positive self-esteem, those encounters seen in intergroup terms are opportunities for discrimination and improving our social identities. The more interaction is seen in intergroup terms, the greater the tendency for discrimination. Unfortunately, this dynamic of human communication is not favorable for intercultural interactions. With all of the overt physical and behavioral differences involved, intercultural communication tends naturally to be experienced in intergroup terms. Even so, people from different cultures can and frequently do interact on an interindividual basis. This ability to relate to others interpersonally (and, consequently, in a less prejudiced way), however, may be corrupted by intercultural training. The focus in training is on learning about other cultural *groups*. The group is the unit of discussion and analysis throughout, and this can sometimes adversely affect trainees' chances of relating to host nationals as unique individuals.

Another negative outcome of training is more than theoretical at this point. As previously discussed, there is disturbing evidence that training, instead of improving attitudes toward host nationals, sometimes actually erodes existing attitudes (e.g., Bird et al., 1993; Landis, Brislin, & Hulgus, 1985). Having reviewed the literature on the effects of negative attitudes on attention and information processing, it seems to us more likely the case that training may reinforce previously held negative attitudes rather than corrupt positive ones. Mildly negative attitudes can guide attention toward negative aspects of the host culture and encourage unfavorable processing of information provided during training. As a result, trainees may come away with stronger and more salient negative views of host nationals. In this manner, in some cases, training may serve only as a stone on which to sharpen damaging attitudes and may function to inhibit outcomes of effectiveness.

A final unanticipated and negative outcome of training stems, like the first one discussed, from an exclusive focus on the cultural group. By providing trainees with information about the target host culture group, training encourages an undifferentiated view of host nationals (McCaffrey, 1986). Every host is seen in the same light and understood in the same terms. Although a few researchers suggest that trainers should warn trainees against this habit (Brislin & Yoshida, 1994), a simple warning will not sufficiently counteract the effects of hours, even days, of learning to treat (all) hosts similarly. The inevitable tendency to view little variability within other cultural groups that trainees will develop is important because it has several negative consequences. First, and most important, trainees are likely to be less flexible than necessary in their dealings with hosts, even when situations demand flexibility. The truth is that cultural heuristics will not apply to all hosts, yet trainees are not adequately prepared to deal with individual differences. Second, although perceptions of homogeneity will make trainees more likely to apply the useful or "correct" information provided in training, it will also encourage them to make other, perhaps damaging, generalizations. As a study by Krueger and Rothbart (1988) has demonstrated, stereotypical judgments are more often made of an individual if that person is a member of a group perceived to be more, rather than less, homogeneous. Finally, perceptions of homogeneity encourage hypothesis-confirming strategies of information gathering. Thus, trainees may ignore new, potentially important information in interactions when they have inadvertently learned to perceive all host culture members as similar. Although these negative outcomes certainly will not affect all trainees at all times, it is important at least to be aware of them so that we may weigh the opportunity of benefit against the risks of potential harm when undertaking intercultural training.

TOWARD A NEW MODEL OF TRAINING EFFECTS

As this critique has demonstrated, the literature on intercultural training presents a naive and limited view of training effects. Training is discussed and practiced as if it leads reliably and directly to beneficial immediate interaction and long-term effectiveness outcomes (see Figure 10.2). Unfortunately, however, this cannot be the case when numerous intergroup and other related processes exist. Such features must surely complicate training; therefore, we have developed a new, more realistic model of training effects that incorporates the points discussed above (see Figure 10.3).

Before detailing the features of the model, we must point out that, although this model represents an improvement over previous models, it focuses exclusively on the effects of intergroup factors as developed in this critique. It assumes that any given training technique has been properly administered, under optimal conditions. Of course, this assumption may be too generous provided the important pragmatic constraints that may be operating. For example, the amount of time available for training may be too short and thereby may compromise the effectiveness of a technique. Similarly, as Paige (1986) has discussed, the trainers themselves may not be trained properly to administer training. These and other elements may violate the assumption made by this model and would thus provide alternative explanations for failure not explicitly incorporated here.

Having noted the above assumption, we begin our description of the model on the far left, with the introduction of some training technique (e.g., BAFA BAFA, role playing, or culture assimilator). Attention processes, directed by the trainee's attitudes and stereotypes, then mediate the development of awareness, knowledge, and/or skills. Unlike in the previous model, however, these immediate outcomes do not guarantee successful interaction. A trainee must first evaluate fairly and accept the offered awareness, knowledge, and skills (i.e., believe them to be true and socially appropriate) before he or she will act based upon them. Again, the trainee's attitudes and stereotypes will influence whether he or she evaluates the learned information in a fair or biased manner. If the trainee accepts the information, it can help change his or her preexisting attitudes and stereotypes. However, this is not likely to happen because of human beings' functional, motivational, and cognitive resistance to change.

Once training has taken place, the trainee moves on to interact with culturally different hosts. As the model underscores, a number of different factors will influence the trainee's behavior in this situation. First, if the trainee has accepted the information and experiences developed during training, he or she will formulate new, enlightened responses that influence behavior. These new responses may be learned behavioral skills, spontaneous reactions grounded in a knowledge of culture, or simply reactions that promote the intention to act mindfully. These new responses will be further bolstered—and their chances of actually occurring greater—when a trainee's

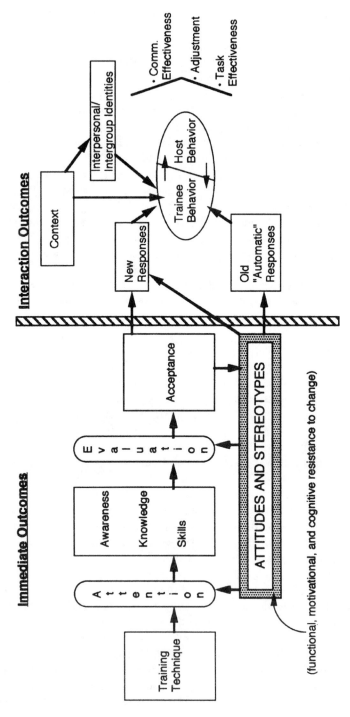

Figure 10.3. A General Model of Cross-Cultural Training Effects

attitudes and stereotypes have been successfully changed by the training experience. However, it is possible that even if a trainee accepts the training and intends to use new responses, he or she may fall back on old, "automatic" responses based on old, unchanged attitudes and stereotypes. Additionally, the context of interaction (both sociostructural and immediate) may shape a trainee's behavior directly through norms or indirectly by contributing to the salience of interpersonal and intergroup identities. Finally, trainee behavior is situated in interaction with the host, whose own behavior affects the trainee. The outcomes of this interaction and countless others like it then lead, over time, to the long-term outcomes of communication effectiveness, adjustment, and task effectiveness. In sum, this revised model constitutes a more socially sensitive general model of intercultural training effects than that depicted in Figure 10.2.

SUMMARY AND CONCLUSION

We began this chapter with a review of the techniques that constitute the current state of intercultural training. Through an examination of discussions of the techniques and the techniques themselves, we developed a generalized model of the usually implicit process of training. Though limited, some research has tested various outcomes outlined by the model and has produced supportive though largely inconclusive results. However, critical aspects of the process remain obscured, and this prompted a reevaluation of the model. Before pursuing further needed empirical examinations, should we really trust an atheoretical model that has been more frequently assumed than considered?

Under scrutiny, we believe that the model proves inadequate. Through a critique of intercultural training, we have pointed out a number of previously disregarded intergroup dynamics that greatly complicate the training process. For example, trainees' negative attitudes and stereotypes about the target host group (which are quite likely to exist, depending upon the groups involved) will compromise their attention toward and acceptance of much training material. These same attitudes and stereotypes will also effectively resist the present untutored attempts to change them. Context, through aspects of the intergroup relations that it embodies and the norms that it provides, will limit the extent of training's touch. Intergroup identities, regardless of the groups involved, will encourage discrimination that interferes with the application of those lessons successfully learned in training. Other aspects of interaction, such as anxiety, time, and level of involvement, will make worse an already developed cognitive predisposition to act mindlessly and to rely on old stereotypes when communicating with hosts. And finally, the responses of hosts themselves may ruin what chances there are for favorable interactions. Clearly, then, training must compete with a variety of potent dynamics in order to produce the outcomes that it intends. These dynamics may not only frustrate training efforts, but may turn them to work against the goals they seek. Training may lead to trainees' holding stronger and more salient negative attitudes, consistent intergroup perceptions, and greater estimations of homogeneity among hosts. Recognizing that the training process is much more complicated than previously described, we have developed a new model that incorporates the above dynamics as a step toward a better understanding of training effectiveness.

What now should be done to continue improving our understanding and practice of intercultural training? Most important, researchers need to undertake studies that will investigate features of the new model. Are the processes implicated by intergroup and attitudinal research and theory really functioning as predicted in the context of intercultural training? Lacking such evidence, however, a few general suggestions can nonetheless be made about improving the practice of training based on the information already available. First, trainers should be aware of the attitudes, stereotypes, and social representations held by trainees about others. These can be surveyed as part of the much-neglected step of "needs assessment" (see Brislin & Yoshida, 1994). As Nwosu and Mabra-Holmes (1994) argue, training programs that are adapted to the particular needs of the trainees and their organizational environments are better able to produce effectiveness outcomes. For example, if it is found that most trainees have intense negative feelings about the target host group, those feelings should be addressed and not glossed over. Perhaps some motivational basis for the attitudes can be discerned and targeted, or perhaps the feelings relate to misperceptions in the nature and history of the intergroup relationship, misperceptions that can be clarified. Whatever the case, we cannot expect to "remedy" all or even some negative attitudes, but being aware of them is crucial step toward dealing with them more effectively than at present. Second, training should be informed by the current psychological literature regarding stereotype change. For example, a study by Kreuger and Rothbart (1988) suggests that temporal stability is an important quality of information that can change a stereotype. Perhaps by emphasizing the consistency of a given behavior across time, training can be more effective in shaping individuals' beliefs about cultural groups. Third, those trainees who come to know and accept the information and experiences developed in training can be taught techniques to help ensure that they call upon that information when interacting with host nationals. Research by Devine and Monteith (Devine, 1989; Devine & Monteith, 1993; Monteith, 1993) suggests that individuals can come to control automatic stereotype activation through a learned process of heightening self-focus after a prejudice discrepancy experience. Unfortunately, good answers have not been found for every problem raised by this discussion, but at least there are places to begin improving training.

As this critique has demonstrated, the conceptualization and practice of intercultural training has neglected important constraints imposed by both attitudes and stereotypes in addition to the intergroup features of real intercultural communication. As a result, good-faith efforts to prepare individuals to interact with host nationals may often be useless and, at worst, they may be harmful. Our aim here has been, primarily, to describe these lacunae, although we have considered briefly a few ways in which the process can be improved based on this discussion. Doubtless, many more suggestions can be made and more elaborate theoretical models developed as concerns raised by this and subsequent critiques are addressed in a systematic manner. Global health, safety, and economic development depend on effective intercultural communication. Let us not be discouraged by criticism; rather, let us use what is seen to be of value in it constructively and productively to serve these goals better.

NOTES

1. Although we have made every effort to present a review and critique that is as current as possible, we have not included an important new second edition of the *Handbook of Intercultural Training,* edited by Landis and Bhagat, because it was in preparation at the time this chapter was written.
2. As used throughout this chapter, the terms *hosts* and *host nationals* refer to members of the cultural group with whom the trainee is planning to interact. They may be actual hosts if the trainee travels abroad to their country, but when interaction occurs in the trainee's country (where the trainee may be said to be technically the host), the terms still refer to members of groups that are culturally distinct vis-à-vis the trainee.

REFERENCES

Adler, N. (1983). Cross-cultural management research: The ostrich and the trend. *Academy of Management Review, 8,* 226-232.

Albert, R. D. (1983). The intercultural sensitizer or culture assimilator: A cognitive approach. In D. Landis & R. W. Brislin (Eds.), *Handbook of intercultural training: Vol. 1. Issues in theory and design* (pp. 186-217). Elmsford, NY: Pergamon.

Albert, R. D. (1986). Conceptual framework for the development and evaluation of cross-cultural orientation programs. *International Journal of Intercultural Relations, 10,* 197-213.

Albert, R. D., & Adamopoulos, J. (1980). An attributional approach to culture learning: The culture assimilator. In M. Hamnett & R. W. Brislin (Eds.), *Research in culture learning: Language and conceptual studies* (pp. 53-60). Honolulu: University of Hawaii Press.

Allport, G. W. (1935). Attitudes. In C. Murchison (Ed.), *Handbook of social psychology* (pp. 798-844). Worcester, MA: Clark University Press.

Ball-Rokeach, S. J., Rokeach, M., & Grube, J. W. (1984). *The great America Values Test: Influencing behavior and belief through television.* New York: Free Press.

Becker, L. L. (1982). *The cultural assimilator in education settings: A comparison of cross-cultural training techniques.* Unpublished doctoral dissertation, University of Nebraska, Lincoln.

Befus, C. P. (1988). A multilevel treatment approach for culture shock experienced by sojourners. *International Journal of Intercultural Relations, 12,* 381-400.

Bennett, J. (1986). Modes of cross-cultural training: Conceptualizing cross-cultural training as education. *International Journal of Intercultural Relations, 10,* 117-134.

Berman, J. S., Read, S. J., & Kenny, D. A. (1983). Processing inconsistent social information. *Journal of Personality and Social Psychology, 45,* 1211-1224.

Bhawuk, D. P. S. (1990). Cross-cultural orientation programs. In R. W. Brislin (Ed.), *Applied cross-cultural psychology* (pp. 325-346). Newbury Park, CA: Sage.

Billig, M. (1987). *Arguing and thinking: A rhetorical approach to social psychology.* Cambridge: Cambridge University Press.

Billig, M., & Tajfel, H. (1973). Social categorization and similarity in intergroup behavior. *European Journal of Social Psychology, 3,* 7-52.

Bird, A., Heinbuch, S., Dunbar, R., & McNulty, M. (1993). A conceptual model of the effects of area studies training programs and a preliminary investigation of the model's hypothesized relationships. *International Journal of Intercultural Relations, 17,* 415-435.

Black, J. S., & Gregersen, H. B. (1991). Antecedents to cross-cultural adjustment for expatriates in Pacific Rim assignments. *Human Relations, 44,* 497-515.

Black, J. S., & Mendenhall, M. (1990). Cross-cultural training effectiveness: A review and a theoretical framework for future research. *Academy of Management Review, 15,* 113-136.

Blake, B. F., & Heslin, R. (1983). Evaluating cross-cultural training. In D. Landis & R. W. Brislin (Eds.), *Handbook of intercultural training: Vol. 1. Issues in theory and design* (pp. 203-223). Elmsford, NY: Pergamon.

Bochner, S. (1982). *Cultures in contact: Studies in cross-cultural interaction.* Elmsford, NY: Pergamon.

Bourhis, R. Y., & Giles, H. (1977). The language of intergroup distinctiveness. In H. Giles (Ed.), *Language, ethnicity and intergroup relations* (pp. 119-135). London: Academic Press.

Bourhis, R. Y., Giles, H., Leyens, J. P., & Tajfel, H. (1979). Psycholinguistic distinctiveness: Language divergence in Belgium. In H. Giles & R. St. Clair (Eds.), *Language and social psychology* (pp. 158-185). Oxford: Basil Blackwell.

Bredemeier, M. E., Bernstein, G., & Oxman, W. (1982). BAFA BAFA and dogmatism/ethnocentrism: A study of attitude change through simulation gaming. *Simulation & Games, 13,* 413-436.

Brewer, M. B. (1979). Ingroup bias in the minimal intergroup situation: A cognitive-motivational analysis. *Journal of Personality and Social Psychology, 86,* 307-324.

Brislin, R. W. (1978). Structured approaches to dealing with prejudice and intercultural misunderstanding. *International Journal of Group Tensions, 8,* 33-48.

Brislin, R. W. (1981). *Cross-cultural encounters: Face-to-face interaction.* Elmsford, NY: Pergamon.

Brislin, R. W. (1989). Intercultural communication training. In M. K. Asante & W. B. Gudykunst (Eds.), *Handbook of international and intercultural communication* (pp. 441-457). Newbury Park, CA: Sage.

Brislin, R. W., Cushner, K., Cherrie, C., & Yong, M. (1986). *Intercultural interactions: A practical guide.* Beverly Hills, CA: Sage.

Brislin, R. W., Landis, D., & Brandt, M. E. (1983). Conceptualizations of intercultural behavior and training. In D. Landis & R. W. Brislin (Eds.), *Handbook of intercultural training: Vol. 1. Issues in theory and design* (pp. 118-154). Elmsford, NY: Pergamon.

Brislin, R. W., & Pedersen, P. (1976). *Cross-cultural orientation programs.* New York: Gardner.

Brislin, R. W., & Yoshida, T. (1994). *Intercultural communication training: An introduction.* Thousand Oaks, CA: Sage.

Brock, T. C., & Balloun, J. C. (1967). Behavioral receptivity to dissonant information. *Journal of Personality and Social Psychology, 6,* 413-428.

Bruschke, J. C., Gartner, C., & Seiter, J. S. (1993). Student ethnocentrism, dogmatism, and motivation: A study of BAFA BAFA. *Simulation & Gaming, 24,* 9-20.

Burke, M. J., & Day, R. R. (1986). A cumulative study of the effectiveness of management training. *Journal of Applied Psychology, 71,* 232-245.

Cacioppo, J. T., & Petty, R. E. (1979). Effects of message repetition and position on cognitive response, recall, and persuasion. *Journal of Personality and Social Psychology, 37,* 97-107.

Carbaugh, D. (1993). Competence as cultural pragmatics: Reflections on some Soviet and American encounters. In R. Wiseman & J. Koester (Eds.), *Intercultural communication competence* (pp. 168-183). Newbury Park, CA: Sage.

Cargile, A. C., Giles, H., & Clément, R. (in press). The role of language in interethnic conflict. In J. Gittler (Ed.), *Racial and ethnic conflict: Perspectives for the social disciplines.* Greenwich, CT: JAI.

Casmir, F. L., & Asuncione-Lande, N. C. (1988). Intercultural communication revisited: Conceptualization, paradigm building, and methodological approaches. In J. A. Anderson (Ed.), *Communication yearbook 12* (pp. 278-309). Newbury Park, CA: Sage.

Caudron, S. (1991, December). Training ensures success overseas. *Personnel Journal,* pp. 27-30.

Chemers, M. M. (1969). Cross-cultural training as a means of improving situational favorableness. *Human Relations, 22,* 531-546.

Chemers, M. M., Fiedler, F. E., Lekhyananda, D., & Stolurow, L. (1966). Some effects of cultural training on leadership in heterocultural task groups. *International Journal of Psychology, 1,* 301-314.

Clément, R., & Giles, H. (1993). Deconstructing the "big picture": Perspectives and layers of interethnic communication. In S. A. Deetz (Ed.), *Communication yearbook 17* (pp. 539-550). Newbury Park, CA: Sage.

Collier, M. J., & Thomas, M. (1988). Cultural identity: An interpretive perspective. In Y. Y. Kim & W. B. Gudykunst (Eds.), *Theories in intercultural communication* (pp. 99-120). Newbury Park, CA: Sage.

Condon, J. C., & Yousef, F. (1985). *An introduction to intercultural communication.* New York: Macmillan.

Crespo, O. I. (1982). *Effects of cross-cultural training on the attributions and attitudes of students in a teacher-training program.* Unpublished doctoral dissertation, University of Illinois.

Cushner, K. (1989). Assessing the impact of a culture-general assimilator. *International Journal of Intercultural Relations, 13,* 125-146.

Cushner, K., & Brislin, R. W. (1995). *Intercultural interactions: A practical guide* (2nd ed.). Thousand Oaks, CA: Sage.

Decker, P. J. (1982). The enhancement of behavior modeling training of supervisory skills by the inclusion of retention processes. *Personnel Psychology, 35,* 323-332.

Derderian, S. (1993, April). International success lies in cross-cultural training. *HR Focus,* p. 9.

Deshpande, S. P., & Viswesvaran, C. (1992). Is cross-cultural training of expatriate managers effective? A meta-analysis. *International Journal of Intercultural Relations, 16,* 295-310.

Devine, P. G. (1989). Stereotypes and prejudice: Their automatic and controlled components. *Journal of Personality and Social Psychology, 56,* 5-18.

Devine, P. G., & Monteith, M. J. (1993). The role of discrepancy-associated affect in prejudice reduction. In D. M. Mackie & D. L. Hamilton (Eds.), *Affect, cognition, and stereotyping: Interactive processes in group perception* (pp. 317-344). San Diego, CA: Academic Press.

Doise, W., Csepeli, G., Dann, H. D., Gouge, C., Larsen, K., & Ostell, A. (1972). An experimental investigation into the formation of intergroup representations. *European Journal of Social Psychology, 2,* 202-204.

Downs, J. F. (1969). Fables, fancies, and failures in cross-cultural training. *Trends, 2*(3). (ERIC Document Reproduction Service No. ED 034 953)

Dunn, T. P., & Wozniak, P. R. (1976). Simulation review. *Simulation & Games, 7,* 471-475.

Dustin, D. A., & Davis, H. P. (1970). Evaluative bias in group and individual competition. *Journal of Social Psychology, 80,* 103-108.

Eagly, A. H., & Chaiken, S. (1993). *The psychology of attitudes.* Fort Worth, TX: Harcourt Brace Jovanovich.

Earley, P. C. (1987). Intercultural training for managers: A comparison of documentary and interpersonal methods. *Academy of Management Journal, 30,* 685-698.

Fazio, R. H. (1986). How do attitudes guide behavior? In R. M. Sorrentino & E. T. Higgins (Eds.), *The handbook of motivation and cognition: Foundations of social behavior* (pp. 204-243). New York: Guilford.

Ferguson, C. K., & Kelley, H. H. (1964). Significant factors in overevaluation of own-group's product. *Journal of Abnormal and Social Psychology, 69,* 223-228.

Festinger, L. (1957). *A theory of cognitive dissonance.* Evanston, IL: Row, Peterson.

Fiedler, F. E., Mitchell, T., & Triandis, H. C. (1971). The culture assimilator: An approach to cross-cultural training. *Journal of Applied Psychology, 55,* 95-102.

Fox, S., & Giles, H. (1993). Accommodating intergenerational contact: A critique and theoretical model. *Journal of Aging Studies, 7,* 423-451.

Frey, D. (1986). Recent research on selective exposure to information. *Advances in Experimental Social Psychology, 19,* 41-80.

Gallois, C., Giles, H., Jones, C., Cargile, A., & Ota, H. (1995). Accommodating intercultural encounters: Elaborations and extensions. In R. Wiseman (Ed.), *Intercultural communication theory* (pp. 115-147). Thousand Oaks, CA: Sage.

Gardner, R. C. (1985). *The social psychology of second language learning.* London: Edward Arnold.

Gardner, R. C., & Clément, R. (1990). Social psychological perspectives on second language acquisition. In H. Giles & W. P. Robinson (Eds.), *Handbook of language and social psychology* (pp. 495-517). New York: John Wiley.

Gardner, R. C., & Lambert, W. E. (1959). Motivational variables in second language acquisition. *Canadian Journal of Psychology, 13,* 266-272.

Gardner, R. C., & Lambert, W. E. (1972). *Attitudes and motivation in second language learning.* Rowley, MA: Newbury House.

Genesee, F., Rogers, P., & Holobrow, N. E. (1983). The social psychology of second language learning: Another point of view. *Language Learning, 33,* 209-224.

Gerard, H. B., & Hoyt, M. F. (1974). Distinctiveness of social categorization and attitude toward ingroup members. *Journal of Personality and Social Psychology, 29,* 836-842.

Giles, H. (1978). Linguistic differentiation between ethnic groups. In H. Tajfel (Ed.), *Differentiation between social groups: Studies in the social psychology of intergroup relations* (pp. 361-393). New York: Academic Press.

Giles, H. (1992). Current and future directions in sociolinguistics: A social psychological contribution. In K. Bolton & H. Kwok (Eds.), *Sociolinguistics today: International perspectives* (pp. 361-367). London: Routledge.

Giles, H., & Coupland, N. (1992). *Language: Contexts and consequences.* Pacific Grove, CA: Brooks/Cole.

Giles, H., Coupland, N., & Coupland, J. (Eds.). (1991). *Contexts of accommodation.* New York: Cambridge University Press.

Giles, H., & Powesland, P. F. (1975). *Speech style and social evaluation.* London: Academic Press.

Giles, H., & Viladot, A. (1994). Ethnolinguistic identity in Catalonia. *Multilingua: Journal of Cross-Cultural and Interlanguage Communication, 13,* 301-312.

Goldman, A. (1988). *For Japanese only: Intercultural communication with Americans.* Tokyo: Japan Times.

Gudykunst, W. B. (1977). Intercultural contact and attitude change: A review of literature and suggestions for future research. In N. Jain (Ed.), *International and intercultural communication annual* (Vol. 4, pp. 1-16). Annandale, VA: Speech Communication Association.

Gudykunst, W. B. (1979). The effects of an intercultural communication workshop on cross-cultural attitudes and interaction. *Communication Education, 28,* 179-187.

Gudykunst, W. B. (Ed.). (1986). *Intergroup communication.* London: Edward Arnold.

Gudykunst, W. B. (1995). Anxiety/uncertainty management (AUM) theory: Current status. In R. Wiseman (Ed.), *Intercultural communication theory* (pp. 8-58). Thousand Oaks, CA: Sage.

Gudykunst, W. B., & Hammer, M. R. (1983). Basic training design: Approaches to intercultural training. In D. Landis & R. W. Brislin (Eds.), *Handbook of intercultural training: Vol. 1. Issues in theory and design* (pp. 118-154). Elmsford, NY: Pergamon.

Gudykunst, W. B., & Kim, Y. Y. (1992). *Communicating with strangers: An approach to intercultural communication.* New York: McGraw-Hill.

Gudykunst, W. B., & Nishida, T. (1994). *Bridging Japanese/North American differences.* Thousand Oaks, CA: Sage.

Gudykunst, W. B., & Shapiro, R. (1994, November). *Communication in everyday interpersonal and intergroup encounters.* Paper presented at the 80th Annual Meeting of the Speech Communication Association, New Orleans.

Hamilton, D. L., & Trolier, T. (1986). Stereotypes and stereotyping: An overview of the cognitive approach. In J. F. Dovidio & S. L. Gaertner (Eds.), *Prejudice, discrimination, and racism* (pp. 127-163). New York: Academic Press.

Hammer, M. R., Gudykunst, W. B., & Wiseman, R. L. (1978). Dimensions of intercultural effectiveness: An exploratory study. *International Journal of Intercultural Relations, 2,* 382-393.

Hammer, M. R., & Martin, J. N. (1992). The effects of cross-cultural training on American managers in a Japanese-American joint venture. *Journal of Applied Communication Research, 20,* 162-183.

Harris, P., & Moran, R. T. (1979). *Managing cultural differences.* Houston: Gulf.

Harrison, J. K. (1992). Individual and combined effects of behavior modeling and the cultural assimilator in cross-cultural management training. *Journal of Applied Psychology, 77,* 952-962.

Harrison, R., & Hopkins, R. (1967). The design of cross-cultural training. *Journal of Applied Behavioral Science, 3,* 431-460.

Hendrick, C., & Seyfried, B. A. (1974). Assessing the validity of laboratory-produced attitude change. *Journal of Personality and Social Psychology, 29,* 865-870.

Hewstone, M., & Brown, R. (1986). Contact is not enough: An intergroup perspective on the "contact hypothesis." In M. Hewstone & R. Brown (Eds.), *Contact and conflict in intergroup encounters* (pp. 1-44). Oxford: Basil Blackwell.

Higgins, E. T., & King, G. (1981). Accessibility of social constructs: Information-processing consequences of individual and contextual variability. In N. Cantor & J. F. Kihlstrom (Eds.), *Personality and social interaction* (pp. 69-121). Hillsdale, NJ: Lawrence Erlbaum.

Hildebrandt, N., & Giles, H. (1983). The Japanese as subordinate group: Ethnolinguistic identity theory in a foreign language context. *Anthropological Linguistics, 25,* 436-466.

Houston, D. A., & Fazio, R. H. (1989). Biased processing as a function of attitude accessibility: Making objective judgments subjectively. *Social Cognition, 7,* 51-66.

Hughes-Wiener, G. (1986). The "learning how to learn" approach to cross-cultural orientation. *International Journal of Intercultural Relations, 10,* 485-505.

Hulgus, J. F., & Landis, D. (1979). *The interaction of two types of acculturative training: A laboratory study.* Unpublished manuscript, Indiana University/Purdue University.

Hunter, J. E., & Schmidt, F. L. (1990). *Methods of meta-analysis: Correcting for error and bias in research findings.* Newbury Park, CA: Sage.

Ilola, L. (1989). *Intercultural interaction training for preservice teachers using the culture-general assimilator with a peer interactive approach.* Unpublished doctoral dissertation, University of Hawaii.

Isen, A. (1984). Toward understanding the role of affect in cognition. In R. Wyer & T. Srull (Eds.), *Handbook of social cognition* (Vol. 3, pp. 179-236). Hillsdale, NJ: Lawrence Erlbaum.

Jackson, M. W. (1979). An antipodean evaluation of simulation in teaching. *Simulation & Games, 10,* 99-138.

Jordan, D. (1941). The attitudes of central school pupils to certain school subjects and the correlation between attitude and attainment. *British Journal of Educational Psychology, 11,* 28-44.

Katz, D. (1960). The functional approach to the study of attitudes. *Public Opinion Quarterly, 24,* 163-204.

Kealey, D. J., & Ruben, B. D. (1983). Cross-cultural personnel selection criteria, issues, and methods. In D. Landis & R. W. Brislin (Eds.), *Handbook of intercultural training: Vol. 1. Issues in theory and design* (pp. 155-175). Elmsford, NY: Pergamon.

Kim, Y. Y. (1988). *Communication and cross-cultural adaptation.* Clevedon, England: Multilingual Matters.

Kiyuna, K. (1977). Building closer relations between Asians and American university students. *Communication, 6,* 51-55.

Krueger, J., & Rothbart, M. (1988). The use of categorical and individuating information in making inferences about personality. *Journal of Personality and Social Psychology, 55,* 187-195.

Landis, D., & Bhagat, R. (Eds.). (in press). *Handbook of intercultural training* (2nd ed.). Thousand Oaks, CA: Sage.

Landis, D., & Brislin, R. W. (Eds.). (1983). *Handbook of intercultural training* (Vols. 1-3). Elmsford, NY: Pergamon.

Landis, D., Brislin, R. W., & Hulgus, J. F. (1985). Attributional training versus contact in acculturative learning: A laboratory study. *Journal of Applied Social Psychology, 15,* 466-482.

Landis, D., Brislin, R., Swanner, G., Tzeng, O., & Thomas, J. (1985). Some effects of acculturative training: A field evaluation. *International Journal of Group Tensions, 15,* 68-91.

Landis, D., Day, H. R., McGrew, P. L., Thomas, J. A., & Miller, A. B. (1976). Can a black "culture assimilator" increase racial understanding? *Journal of Social Issues, 32,* 169-183.

Landis, D., Tzeng, O., & Thomas, J. A., (1981). *Some effects of acculturative training: A field evaluation.* Indianapolis: Center for Applied Research and Evaluation.

Langer, E. (1978). Rethinking the role of thought in social interaction. In J. Harvey, W. Ickes, & R. Kidd (Eds.), *New directions in attribution research* (Vol. 2, pp. 35-58). Hillsdale, NJ: Lawrence Erlbaum.

Langer, E. (1989). *Mindfulness.* Reading, MA: Addison-Wesley.

Latham, F. P., & Saari, L. M. (1979). The application of social learning theory to training supervisors through behavior modeling. *Journal of Applied Psychology, 64,* 239-246.

Lefley, H. P. (1985). Impact of cross-cultural training on black and white mental health care professionals. *International Journal of Intercultural Relations, 9,* 305-318.

Liebkind, K. (1989). Conceptual approaches to ethnic identity. In K. Liebkind (Ed.), *New identities in Europe* (pp. 25-40). Hants, England: Gower.

Lord, C. G., Ross, L., & Lepper, M. R. (1979). Biased assimilation and attitude polarization: The effects of prior theories on subsequently considered evidence. *Journal of Personality and Social Psychology, 37,* 2098-2109.

McCaffery, J. A. (1986). Independent effectiveness: A reconsideration of cross-cultural orientation and training. *International Journal of Intercultural Relations, 10,* 159-178.

Mackie, D. M., & Worth, L. T. (1989). Processing deficits and the mediation of positive affect in persuasion. *Journal of Personality and Social Psychology, 57,* 27-40.

Mendenhall, M., & Oddou, G. (1985). The dimensions of expatriate acculturation: A review. *Academy of Management Review, 10*(1), 39-47.

Mendenhall, M., & Oddou, G. (1986). Acculturation profiles of expatriate managers: Implications for cross-cultural training programs. *Columbia Journal of World Business, 21*(4), 73-79.

Mitchell, T. R., Dossett, D. L., Fiedler, F. E., & Triandis, H. C. (1972). Culture training: Validation evidence for the culture assimilator. *International Journal of Psychology, 7,* 97-104.

Mitchell, T. R., & Foa, U. G. (1969). Diffusion of the effect of cultural training of the leader in the structure of heterocultural task groups. *Australian Journal of Psychology, 1,* 31-43.

Monteith, M. J. (1993). Self-regulation of prejudiced responses: Implications for progress in prejudice-reduction efforts. *Journal of Personality and Social Psychology, 65,* 469-485.

Moran, R. (1974). *Personality correlates and changes in worldmindedness after an intercultural group experience.* Unpublished doctoral thesis, University of Minnesota.

Neely, J. H. (1977). Semantic priming and retrieval from lexical memory: Roles of inhibitionless spreading activation and limited-capacity attention. *Journal of Experimental Psychology, 106,* 226-254.

Nwosu, P. O., & Mabra-Holmes, E. (1994, November). *The centrality of organizational culture audits in multicultural diversity training.* Paper presented at the 80th Annual Meeting of the Speech Communication Association, New Orleans.

O'Brien, G. E., Fiedler, F. E., & Hewitt, T. (1971). The effects of programmed culture training upon the performance of volunteer medical teams in Central America. *Human Relations, 24,* 304-315.

O'Brien, G. E., & Plooij, D. (1977). Comparison of programmed and prose culture training upon attitudes and knowledge. *Journal of Applied Psychology, 4,* 499-505.

Paige, R. M. (1986). Trainer competencies: The missing conceptual link in orientation. *International Journal of Intercultural Relations, 10,* 135-158.

Pettigrew, T. F. (1979). The ultimate attribution error: Extending Allport's cognitive analysis of prejudice. *Personality and Social Psychology Bulletin, 5,* 461-476.

Petty, R. E., & Cacioppo, J. T. (1979). Issue involvement can increase or decrease persuasion by enhancing message-relevant cognitive responses. *Journal of Personality and Social Psychology, 37,* 1915-1926.

Philipsen, G. (1989). Speech and the communal function in four cultures. In S. Ting-Toomey & F. Korzenny (Eds.), *Language, communication, and culture: Current directions* (pp. 79-92). Newbury Park, CA: Sage.

Rabbie, J. M., & Wilkens, G. (1971). Intergroup competition and its effect on intragroup and intergroup relations. *European Journal of Social Psychology, 31,* 302-310.

Randolph, G., Landis, D., & Tzeng, O. C. S. (1977). The effects of time and practice upon culture assimilator training. *International Journal of Intercultural Relations, 1,* 105-119.

Razran, G. (1950). Ethnic dislikes and stereotypes: A laboratory study. *Journal of Abnormal and Social Psychology, 45,* 7-27.

Rothbart, M., Evans, M., & Fulero, S. (1979). Recall for confirming events: Memory processes and the maintenance of social stereotypes. *Journal of Experimental Social Psychology, 15,* 343-355.

Sagar, H. A., & Schofield, J. W. (1980). Racial and behavioral cues in black and white children's perception of ambiguously aggressive acts. *Journal of Personality and Social Psychology, 39,* 1590-1598.

Scott, W. A. (1968). Attitude measurement. In G. Lindzey & E. Aronson (Eds.), *Handbook of social psychology* (2nd ed., Vol. 2, pp. 204-273). Reading, MA: Addison-Wesley.

Sherif, C. W., Sherif, M., & Nebergall, R. E. (1965). *Attitude and attitude change: The social judgement-involvement approach.* Philadelphia: W. B. Saunders.

Shiffrin, R. M., & Schneider, W. (1977). Controlled and automatic human information processing: II. Perceptual learning, automatic attending, and a general theory. *Psychological Review,*
84, 127-190.

Shirts, G. (1973). *BAFA BAFA: A cross-cultural simulation.* La Jolla, CA: Simile II.

Showers, C., & Cantor, N. (1985). Social cognition: A look at motivated strategies. *Annual*
Review of Psychology, 36, 275-305.

Sims, S. J., & Sims, R. R. (1993). Diversity and difference training in the United States. In R.
R. Sims & R. F. Dennehy (Eds.), *Diversity and differences in organizations: An agenda for*
answers and questions (pp. 73-92). Westport, CT: Quorum.

Smith, E. R., & Branscombe, N. R. (1985). *Stereotype traits can be processed automatically.*
Unpublished manuscript, Purdue University.

Steinkalk, E., & Taft, R. (1979). The effect of a planned intercultural experience on the attitudes
and behaviors of the participants. *International Journal of Intercultural Relations, 3,* 187-197.

Stephan, W. G. (1989). A cognitive approach to stereotyping. In D. Bar-Tal, C. F. Gaumann, A.
W. Kruglanski, & W. Stroebe (Eds.), *Stereotyping and prejudice: Changing conceptions*
(pp. 37-57). New York: Springer-Verlag.

Suzuki, T. (1975). *Tozaserta Gengo: Nihongo no Sekai.* Tokyo: Shinchosha.

Sweeney, P. D., & Gruber, K. L. (1984). Selective exposure: Voter information preferences and
the Watergate affair. *Journal of Personality and Social Psychology, 46,* 1208-1221.

Tajfel, H. (1978). Introduction. In H. Tajfel (Ed.), *Differentiation between social groups: Studies*
in the social psychology of intergroup relations. New York: Academic Press.

Tajfel, H. (1981). Social stereotypes and social groups. In J. C. Turner & H. Giles (Eds.),
Intergroup behavior (pp. 144-165). Chicago: University of Chicago Press.

Tajfel, H., & Turner, J. C. (1986). The social identity theory of intergroup behavior. In S. Worchel
& W. G. Austin (Eds.), *Psychology of intergroup relations* (pp. 7-24). Chicago: Nelson-Hall.

Taylor, D. M., & Moghaddam, F. M. (1994). *Theories of intergroup relations: International*
social psychological perspectives (2nd ed.). Westport, CT: Praeger.

Taylor, D. M., & Royer, E. (1980). Group processes affecting anticipated language choice in
intergroup relations. In H. Giles, W. P. Robinson, & P. M. Smith (Eds.), *Language: Social*
psychological perspectives (pp. 185-192). Oxford: Pergamon.

Thomas, M. B., Moore, H. B., & Sams, C. (1980). Counsellor renewal workshop in sex equality.
Counsellor Education and Supervision, 20, 56-61.

Torbiörn, I. (1982). *Living abroad.* New York: John Wiley.

Triandis, H. C. (1976). *Variations in black and white perceptions of the social environment.*
Urbana: University of Illinois Press.

Triandis, H. C. (1977). Theoretical framework for evaluation of cross-cultural training effectiveness. *International Journal of Intercultural Relations, 1,* 19-46.

Tung, R. (1981). Selecting and training of personnel for overseas assignments. *Columbia Journal*
of World Business, 16(1), 68-78.

Turner, J. C. (1978). Social categorization and social discrimination in the minimal group
paradigm. In H. Tajfel (Ed.), *Differentiation between social groups: Studies in the social*
psychology of intergroup relations (pp. 101-140). New York: Academic Press.

Turner, J. C. (1983). Some comments on "The measurement of social orientations in the minimal
group paradigm." *European Journal of Social Psychology, 13,* 351-367.

Turner, J. C. (1987). *Rediscovering the social group.* Oxford: Basil Blackwell.

Turner, J. C., & Giles, H. (Eds.). (1981). *Intergroup behavior.* Chicago: University of Chicago
Press.

Wade, P., & Bernstein, B. L. (1991). Culture sensitivity training and counselor's race: Effects on
black female clients' perceptions and attrition. *Journal of Counseling Psychology, 38*(1), 9-15.

Warren, D., & Adler, P. (1977). An experiential approach to instruction in intercultural communication. *Communication Education, 26,* 128-134.

Weldon, D. E., Carlston, A., Rissman, A. K., Slobodin, L., & Triandis, H. C. (1975). A laboratory test of effects of culture assimilator training. *Journal of Personality and Social Psychology, 32*, 300-310.

Wexley, K. N. (1984). Personnel training. *Annual Review of Psychology, 35*, 519-552.

Wilder, D. A. (1984). Intergroup contact: The typical member and the exception to the rule. *Journal of Experimental Social Psychology, 20*, 177-194.

Wilder, D. A. (1993). The role of anxiety in facilitating stereotypic judgment of outgroup behavior. In D. M. Mackie & D. L. Hamilton (Eds.), *Affect, cognition, and stereotyping: Interactive processes in group perception* (pp. 87-106). San Diego, CA: Academic Press.

Williams, A., & Giles, H. (1992). Prejudice-reduction simulations: Social cognition, intergroup theory, and ethics. *Simulation & Gaming, 23*, 472-484.

Winterle, M. (1992). *Workforce diversity: Corporate challenges, corporate responses.* New York: Conference Board.

Worchel, S., & Mitchell, T. R. (1972). An evaluation of the effectiveness of the culture assimilator in Thailand and Greece. *Journal of Applied Psychology, 56*, 472-479.

Yarbro, C. L. M. (1988). *An assessment of the ability of the culture-general assimilator to create sensitivity to multiculturalism in an educational setting.* Unpublished doctoral dissertation, University of Houston.

AUTHOR INDEX

SUBJECT INDEX

Adaptive structuration theory (AST), 251-253
Adult child-elderly parent relationship, 28-29
Affective states and intercultural communication, 362-364, 401
African Americans, 192, 334-5, 368
Agents and influence tactics, 273-278, 287-291
See also Dyadic social influence in organizations
Aggressive communication. *See* Argumentativeness and verbal aggressiveness
Aging process, xv, 1-3
cognitive system, 4-16
future research directions, 37-39
language, 16-23
relationships, 24-37
AIDS (acquired immune deficiency syndrome), 74-8
Alaska, community ties and knowledge gaps in, 197
Alzheimer's disease, 27
American Association of Retired Persons, 2
Analysis:
antecedents and consequences research, 300-301
content, 169-173
electronic messages, 231
experimental, 174-176
message, 16, 58-59
meta-, 166-171
nonexperimental, 173-174
process models, 278-279
regression, 4
statistical, 170-171
See also Knowledge gap hypothesis
Annual overviews, x
Annual Review of Psychology, xiii
Anxiety and intercultural communication training, 408
Appropriate communication, 356-358
Areas studies training, 395
Argumentativeness and verbal aggressiveness, xvii, 319-322
aggressive communication, 322-323
belief structures, individual, 329-330
constructiveness and destructiveness, 327
credibility perceptions, 341-342
culture influencing, 333-335

gender, 326, 332-333
as a joint product of predispositional and situational factors, 330-332
measuring, 324-326
modifying, 343-345
organizational life, 338-339
parent-child relationship, 339-340
persuasion process, 342-343
relational satisfaction, 335-336
relationship to other communication predispositions, 328-329
violence, physical, 336-337
Artifact, technology as the material, 230-235, 254-259
See also Computer-based communication technologies (CBCTs)
Asian cultures, 334, 371
Assertiveness, 134, 322
Attachment, life-span, 28-29
Attitude theory, 8-13, 399-404
Automatic processing and intercultural communication training, 407-408

Behavioral perspective of intercultural communication competence, 367-369
Behavior modeling and intercultural communication training, 389, 394
Beliefs and communication competence with older adults, 8-13
Belief structures and argumentativeness/verbal aggressiveness, 329-330
Biden, Joseph, 139
Bundy v. Jackson (sexual harassment), 121

Canalization and mass media, 208
Caregiving function of the adult child, 29
Case studies, 231
Causal agency, 250
Ceiling effects and knowledge gap hypothesis, 210-211
Change agent perspective, 243-246
Characteristics and influence methods, organizational/individual, 289-290, 301-306
Characteristics/structures associated with sexual harassment, 122-126

ABOUT THE EDITOR

BRANT R. BURLESON (Ph.D., University of Illinois at Urbana-Champaign, 1982) is Professor in the Department of Communication at Purdue University, where he teaches courses in communication theory, interpersonal communication, and the philosophy of the social sciences. His research interests center on communication skills acquisition and development, social-cognitive foundations of strategic communication, effects of communication skills on relationship formation and development, and supportive forms of communication, such as comforting. His research has appeared in several edited volumes and journals, including the *American Journal of Family Therapy, Child Development, Communication Monographs, Communication Research, Family Relations, Human Communication Research, Journal of Language and Social Psychology,* and *Quarterly Journal of Speech.* He has held several offices in both the International Communication Association and the Speech Communication Association and has served on the editorial boards of more than a dozen major journals. Recently, he coedited (with Terrance Albrecht and Irwin Sarason) *Communication of Social Support: Messages, Interactions, Relationships, and Community* (1994).

ABOUT THE AUTHORS

MIKE ALLEN (Ph.D., Michigan State University, 1987) is Associate Professor of Communication at the University of Wisconsin—Milwaukee. His primary research focus is on the use of meta-analysis to summarize existing bodies of research and the application of such methodologies and findings for use in curriculum development and public policy. His summaries have included comparing methods of reducing communication apprehension, choices among persuasive message designs, comparisons of heterosexual and homosexual parenting, the relationship between faculty research productivity and teaching evaluations, and the effects of pornography. His recent publications include articles in the *Journal of Communication, Mediation Quarterly, Communication Theory, Western Journal of Communication, Journal of Applied Communication, Psychological Bulletin, Argumentation and Advocacy,* and *Communication Education.* He is coeditor (with R. Preiss) of *Prospects and Precautions in the Use of Meta-Analysis* (1994).

BRUCE BARRY (Ph.D., University of North Carolina, Chapel Hill, 1991) is Assistant Professor in the organization studies area at the Owen Graduate School of Management at Vanderbilt University. His research focuses primarily on the social psychology of dyadic processes in organizations, with attention to interpersonal social influence, conflict and negotiation, relationship dynamics, applications of social trap theory, and perceptions of procedural justice. His recent work has appeared in *Organizational Behavior and Human Decision Processes, Journal of Applied Social Psychology, Human Relations,* and the *International Journal of Organizational Analysis.*

AARON CASTELAN CARGILE (M.A., Purdue University, 1992) is a doctoral candidate in the Department of Communication at the University of California, Santa Barbara. In addition to intercultural communication training, his current research interests focus on the role of emotions in language attitude processes and the development of a lay theory of intergroup conflict. His work has appeared in *Language and Communication, Intercultural Communication Theory,* and *Racial and Ethnic Conflict: Perspectives for the Social Disciplines.*

GUO-MING CHEN (Ph.D., Kent State University, 1987) is Associate Professor of Communication at the University of Rhode Island. He is the recipient of the 1987 Outstanding Dissertation Award presented by the SCA International and Intercultural Division. He is the founding president of the Association for Chinese Communication Studies, and currently serves as chair of the ECA Intercultural Communication Interest Group and at-large member of the SCA Legislative Council. He also serves on the editorial board of the

Howard Journal of Communications. His primary research interests are in the areas of intercultural communication competence, intercultural conflict management and negotiations, cultural values and language, and intercultural communication education. His articles have appeared in the *Journal of Cross-Cultural Psychology, Communication Quarterly, Journal of Psychology,* and other communication journals.

JOHN R. FINNEGAN, Jr. (Ph.D., University of Minnesota, 1985) is Associate Professor of Epidemiology at the University of Minnesota School of Public Health. His research interests include community-based public health campaigns and the role of mass media as a social institution. His recent published work has appeared in the *Journalism Quarterly, Gazette, American Journal of Public Health,* and the *American Journal of Health Promotion.*

HOWARD GILES (Ph.D., University of Bristol, England, 1971) is Chair of Communication at the University of California, Santa Barbara, and Affiliate Professor of Linguistics and Psychology there, as well as Honorary Professor of Psychology and Communication at the University of Wales, Cardiff. Previously, he served as Head of the Department of Psychology at the University of Bristol. He is founding coeditor of both the *Journal of Language and Social Psychology* and the *Journal of Asian Pacific Communication,* general editor of the Sage Publications book series Language and Language Behaviors, and coeditor of the Blackwell book series Social Psychology and Society. He has published widely in the areas of language attitudes, intercultural communication and relations, and intergenerational communication, and is a Fellow of the British Psychological Society, the International Communication Association, and the Gerontological Association of America.

JAKE HARWOOD (Ph.D., University of California, Santa Barbara, 1994) is Assistant Professor of Communication Studies at the University of Kansas. His research focuses on communication with, by, and about the elderly, and how that relates to cognitive (e.g., stereotypes) and societal (e.g., mass media) representations of particular age groups. His research draws on theories of social identity, intergroup behavior, and communication accommodation. As such, the research on aging extends and applies to research in intercultural domains. His recent publications have appeared in the *International Journal of the Sociology of Language, Journal of Applied Communication Research,* and *Discourse and Society,* and he has most recently coauthored (with Howard Giles and Ellen Ryan) a chapter in the *Handbook of Communication and Aging Research.*

JENNIFER HERRETT-SKJELLUM (M.A., University of Wisconsin—Milwaukee, 1993) is an Instructor at East Mississippi Community College. Her primary area of research involves the representation of women in the mass media as well as how women create images for the media. Her work has examined how women create explicit sexual images for consumption by other women and issues concerning the use of mediated communication. She has presented numerous papers at national conventions.

MARY LEE HUMMERT (Ph.D., University of Kansas, 1987) is Associate Professor in the Communication Studies Department at the University of Kansas, a Research Associate in the university's Gerontology Center, and recipient of a 5-year research grant from the National Institute on Aging. Her research focuses on the relationship between stereotypes of the elderly and communication. Her work has appeared in such journals as *Psychology and Aging, Communication Research, Journal of Personality and Social Psychology, International Journal of Aging and Human Development,* and the *Journal of Gerontology: Psychological Sciences.* She is coeditor (with John Wiemann and Jon Nussbaum) of *Interpersonal Communication in Older Adulthood: Interdisciplinary Theory and Research* (1994).

DOMINIC A. INFANTE (Ph.D., Kent State University, 1971) is Professor Emeritus of Communication Studies at Kent State University. He taught at the State University of New York, Albany, the University of South Florida, and Queens College of the City University of New York before returning in 1976 to teach at Kent State. He is the author of *Arguing Constructively* and coauthor of *Building Communication Theory.* He has also written several chapters for edited books and has published numerous articles in communication, psychology, and business journals. His research has focused on argumentativeness and verbal aggressiveness, and he has applied the models he has developed of these two constructs to understanding aggressive communication in interpersonal, family, and organizational contexts. His most recent research, concerning communication and the corporal punishment of children, will soon be published as a chapter in a book featuring sociological studies of corporal punishment.

MICHELE H. JACKSON (Ph.D., University of Minnesota, 1994) is Assistant Professor of Communication at the Florida State University. Her research interests include the integration of communication technology and group interaction, strategies of on-line communication, and decision-making processes in groups. She is currently investigating the relationships between technology design and use.

JOANN KEYTON (Ph.D., Ohio State University, 1987) is Associate Professor of Communication at the University of Memphis. Prior to her academic career, she worked as an analyst at the Federal Reserve Bank of Kansas City. Her current research interests include sexual harassment, especially as it relates to organizational culture, organizational work groups, and children's task groups. Her research on these topics has been published in the *Journal of Business Ethics, Management Communication Quarterly, Small Group Research,* and in several edited collections. She serves on the editorial boards of *Communication Monographs, Communication Studies,* and *Small Group Research.* In addition to her teaching and research responsibilities, she is a consultant and speaker on sexual harassment.

SANDRA METTS (Ph.D., University of Iowa, 1983) is a Professor in the Department of Communication at Illinois State University, where she teaches courses in interpersonal communication, intercultural communication, language, and research methods. Her research interests focus on the management of problematic social and relational episodes, including embarrassment, relationship disengagement, deception, relational transgressions, and sexual communication. Her recent books include *Self-Disclosure* (with Val Derlega, Sandra Petronio, and Stephen Margulis) and *Facework* (with William Cupach). Her work has also appeared in a variety of journals, including *Communication Monographs, Human Communication Research,* and *Journal of Social and Personal Relationships,* as well as in edited volumes such as the *Handbook of Interpersonal Communication, Communication Yearbook 13, Studying Interpersonal Interaction, Human Sexuality: The Societal and Interpersonal Contexts, Theoretical Perspectives on Relationship Loss,* and *AIDS: A Communication Perspective.*

JON F. NUSSBAUM (Ph.D., Purdue University) is Professor of Communication at the University of Oklahoma and a Senior Fellow at the Oklahoma Center on Aging, University of Oklahoma Health Sciences Center. He is coauthor of *Communication and Aging* (with T. Thompson and J. Robinson), editor of *Life-Span Communication: Normative Processes,* and coeditor of *Interpersonal Communication in Older Adulthood: Interdisciplinary Theory and Research* (with M. L. Hummert and J. M. Wiemann) and *Discourse and Lifespan Identity* (with N. Coupland). He has published more than 50 journal articles and book chapters, including recent articles in *Ageing and Society, International Journal of Aging and Human Development, Communication Quarterly,* and *Communication Education.* He was named a Fulbright Research Scholar (United Kingdom) for the 1991-1992 academic year, and was appointed Visiting Professor at the University of Wales College of Cardiff to study interpersonal communication and successful adaptation to the aging process. His current research interests include the study of friendship across the life span and intergenerational relationships.

ANDREW S. RANCER (Ph.D., Kent State University, 1979) is Associate Professor of Communication in the School of Communication at the University of Akron. His research interests are in the areas of interpersonal communication and communication theory and focus on how the predispositions of argumentativeness and verbal aggressiveness influence human communication behavior. He is currently studying aggressive communication predispositions among radio talk show hosts and callers. He has written several chapters for edited books, and his work on aggressive communication has appeared in *Communication Monographs, Communication Education, Communication Quarterly,* and other journals. His recent paper written with S. Suzuki, "Argumentativeness and Verbal Aggressiveness: Testing for Conceptual and Measurement Equivalence Across Cultures," was published in *Communication Monographs* (Vol. 61, 1994). He is also coauthor of *Building Communication Theory.*

BRIAN H. SPITZBERG (Ph.D., University of Southern California, 1981) is Professor of Communication at San Diego State University. He has coauthored two scholarly books on interpersonal competence and is coeditor of *The Dark Side of Interpersonal Communication.* His recent publications include articles on jealousy, conflict management, and the assessment of interpersonal skills. He is currently working on several projects, including research into anger and conflict, research on sexual coercion, and a second volume of chapters on the dark side of interpersonal relationships.

WILLIAM J. STAROSTA (Ph.D., Indiana University, 1973) is Graduate Professor of Rhetoric and Intercultural Communication at Howard University. He is founding editor of the *Howard Journal of Communications.* He currently serves as Chair of the SCA International and Intercultural Communication Division, and of the ECA Voices of Diversity Interest Group. He has conducted sponsored research in India, Canada, and Sri Lanka. His most recent research concerns Gandhian Satyagraha, coverage of interethnic conflict, emic rhetorical criticism, and third culture building. His work has appeared in the *International Philosophical Quarterly, Political Communication and Persuasion, International and Intercultural Communication Annual, World Communication, International Journal of Intercultural Relations, Journal of Black Studies, Educational Communication and Technology Journal, Quarterly Journal of Speech,* and other speech communication journals.

K. VISWANATH (Ph.D., University of Minnesota, 1990) is a faculty member in the School of Journalism and a Center Scholar with the Center for Health Policy Studies at the Ohio State University. He is interested in using macrosocial approaches to the study of mass communication. His most recent research has focused on mass communication and social change and health communication in both national and international contexts. He has been involved in guided social change projects in India and the United States, and has published in a variety of journals, including *Gazette, Media, Culture & Society, Health Communication, Journalism Quarterly, Communication Research, American Behavioral Scientist,* and *Health Education Research.*

MARY R. WATSON is a doctoral candidate in organization studies at the Owen Graduate School of Management at Vanderbilt University. Her research focuses on the changing nature of the employment relationship, with particular interest in the performance implications of contemporary human resource management practices. Her dissertation examines the impact of downsizing messages on organization constituents. She is coauthor (with Thomas A. Mahoney) of a chapter on the evolution of modes of workforce governance in *Employee Representation: Alternatives and Future Directions* (edited by B. Kaufman and M. Kleiner, 1993).

ANGIE WILLIAMS (Ph.D., University of California, Santa Barbara) is Assistant Professor of Communication at the University of Oklahoma. She was previously Research Fellow in Sociolinguistics at the University of Wales College of Cardiff. She has recently contributed articles to the *International Journal of Aging and Human Development, Journal of Applied Communication Research,* and *Language and Communication.* Her research focuses on intergroup accommodation, especially as it applies to intergenerational communication.